DEAD OF NIGHT

An Illustrated Compendium of True Life Ghost Stories, Urban Legends and Unexplained Phenomena from the Haunted Heart of Merseyside

LEE WALKER

Edited by Jonathan & Corinna Downes
Original Artwork by Grant Walker & Paul White
Photographs by Steve Humphries, Lee Walker and Stevie Gee
Cover by Shaun Histed-Todd
Typeset by Jonathan Downes
Cover and Internal Layout by Jon Downes for CFZ Communications
Using Microsoft Word 2000, Microsoft , Publisher 2000, Adobe Photoshop.

First edition published 2011 by CFZ Publications

CFZ PRESS
Myrtle Cottage
Woolfardisworthy
Bideford
North Devon
EX39 5QR

© CFZ MMXI

All rights reserved. Without limiting the rights under copyright reserved above, no part of this publication may be reproduced, stored in or introduced into a retrieval system, or transmitted, in any form of by any means (electronic, mechanical, photocopying, recording or otherwise), without the prior written permission of both the copyright owners and the publishers of this book.

ISBN: 978-1-905723-76-8

For My Angel, Angie
'The Joy At The End Of Heart's Longing'

GLOSSARY

A Brief Guide to Some of the 'Scouse-ism's & Other Forms Of Colloquial Language Contained Within This Book

NESH: Someone who professes to be freezing cold when the average temperature drops a mere degree or two below the sub-tropical

GAB: To chatter incessantly with all the vocal dexterity of a particularly mealy-mouthed politician, carnival huckster or market-stall trader (who are of course, when you get right down to it, essentially one and the same thing)

BOSS: Someone or something that is way, way beyond the merely, 'sound' or 'pretty good.' ie: 'That trip to Istanbul in 2005, or that Bunnymen reformation gig at the Academy, or that comedy slot by John Bishop, or "the way I spat that chewie out into the air and caught it smack on the volley with the toes of me trainees," was **boss**!'

SNIDEY-ARSE: Someone who is irredeemably mean, whether it's where money is concerned (ie: 'get the ale in will yer, lid. It's your round, yer snidey-arse!), or else have a propensity to criticise/pick on someone far less fortunate than themselves, (a little like The West's current foreign policy towards nations that can't fight back too much; Libya, Iraq, Afghanistan, etc), or else would happily sell out their best friend for a four pack of extra strong lager, a joint and a bag of greasy chips for the inevitable, subsequent munchies.

And who but a total Snidey Arse would do that?

KECKS: Merseyside term for trousers, be they combats, jeans, work pants, or those ripped at the knees affairs that make you look like you've been slashed by a dwarf with a plainly evident grudge against kecks (of any variety)....

ARL BIDDY: Any female person considered to be impossibly ancient, by the percipient. For The New Ferry Horror Society, whose average age was eleven at the time the events in half of this book take place, 'impossibly ancient' qualified as anyone a day over the age of 19!

ARL ARSE: Male equivalent of the above, or alternatively, someone who is tighter with money than a boil-washed pair of skinny-fit jeans, or else severely lacking in any degree of empathy for their fellow human beings (see also Snidey Arse, and in a wider context, members of the Tory Party, world dictators, and Simon Cowell)

WORRA TIT: Simply put, someone who has consistently displayed all the warmth and wit of William Hague at his most constipated

HE'S TOTALLY OFF HIS CAKE!: Someone who has decided it might be a boss idea to create a Hadron Collider, a machine that will likely achieve absolutely sod-all for the advancement of science or the good of mankind, but might well succeed in opening up an inter-dimensional gateway to admit hordes of Lovecraft-ian, Cthullu-type creatures, the numberless, nameless Lurkers On The Threshold, that are intent on eradicating humanity, to enter our world and er.... eradicate humanity!

Or else someone who believes that Blue ever really stood a decent chance of winning the Eurovision Song Contest.

GAZANGAS: The female gender's 'little puddings of delight,' or biologically functional female organs: mammary glands, that produce milk to feed young offspring (delete where your PC-sexist/Roy Chubby Brown tolerance level dictates).

SLAP-HEAD: `slappy` = bald

SMACK-HEADS: Heroin addicts who talk in voices that sound like an automaton slowly winding down, and who all-too frequently wind up chasing their personal Dragon all the way to Hell.

ALKIES: Poor lost individuals who eschew the escapism afforded by drug-induced transcendental mind-trips for the senses-numbing submersion in the 'blessed waters of oblivion.'

SPIT-WADS: Clumps of chewed up paper, transformed by mischievous pupils into gluey, saliva-soaked balls and fired from the ends of plastic rulers, to land with a hugely satisfying sccchhhlllopp sound as they struck their target – the blackboard, the ceiling, or for extra thrills (and unlimited kudos for the courageous launcher), the back of a teacher's head....

GYPOS: *Daily Mail*-endorsed slang for 'travelling people,' who, The Guardians of Middle-Class Sensibilities are quick to point out are likely made up of the aforementioned Alkies, and Smackheads, and are also sure to include amongst their unwashed number: thieves, murderers, rapists and curly, long-haired layabouts who were very likely the "scum-bags" responsible for having the temerity to push Charles and Camilla's swanky car a little bit during the Tuition Fees Riot, and attempt to bring down 'Western Civilisation' in the process....

TOTALLY SPANGLES: An old-fashioned reference to people whose sexual preferences were open to question, 'inspired' by the ahem 'fruity' funky sweets of the 1970s.

KIDDER: A form of greeting to male friends passing by on the street (or encountered in the pub or at the match or some similar social occasion), along the lines of 'Hail-fellow-well-met.'

Usually, though not always, this salutation, ie: "S'appenin,,kidder!,' is muttered from the twisted corner of the mouth, with scarcely a glance in their friend's direction, as though imparting some secret code. **(See also, La, Lad, and, latterly, an amalgamation of La and Kidder; Lid)**

SCALLYS: Ragamuffins, Urchins, street-wise duckers and divers....

GLIMPSES IN THE TWILIGHT
Introduction

Ok, I know from bitter experience that this is normally the part of a book most readers either skip over in a two-thirds disinterested manner, or choose to ignore completely, but I really want to make a few things clear before we get started in earnest.

I'd like to begin, if I may, with explaining exactly why I felt the need to write this semi-autobiographical Fortean treatise/mundane compilation of pompously overwritten mumbo jumbo *(delete where your personal views deem to be applicable),* in the first place.

And no. It most certainly wasn't inspired, if that's quite the right word, by the twin motivations of financial gain or some over-blown notion of my own self-importance, though I'm sure the vast serried ranks of cynics that seem, sadly, to make up a sizeable minority of the planet's population will sneer dismissively or roll their eyeballs heavenwards at any claims to the contrary.

Can I honestly blame them?

I mean, I have to readily concede that I'm hardly going to turn my nose up at the prospect of earning myself a few 'extra bob,' and I can't deny that it's one of *The Great Intractable Truisms* that those who 'work' within the hallowed halls of paranormal academia, have egos so inflated they could cross the Atlantic on their own hot air (doubtless sparking a sensational, news headline-making UFO wave in the process).

I've sometimes thought, in my more uncharitable moments, that it must be a prerequisite for anyone seeking to gain some form of paid employment in the sometimes lucrative field of supernatural phenomena, be it writing, investigating, or lecturing about the subject, that they must first adopt a haughtily superior attitude both towards each other and all those poor unfortunates forced to eke out a living performing some comparatively dreary, nine to five, dead-end job.

God knows, I've been around long enough to see more than enough first-hand examples of this conceited arrogance, having spent a large chunk of my life editing a moderately successful small press publication called *Dead Of Night* (and yes, film trivia fans, the name of the magazine was indeed intended as an homage to the 1945 Ealing Studios classic horror movie), and thereby unwittingly entered the tragi-comedy played out in a madhouse that is the black and shuttered domain of the paranormal investigator. I've seen alleged mystics and psychics, dowsers and mediums, monster-hunters and Satanists, exorcists and Ufologists, wannabe warlocks and Lord have mercy, even high-falutin', thick-spectacled former Ministry Of Defence officials with Catholic-sounding surnames, all of whom virtually jump up and down yelling; *'Look at me, look at me, look at MEEEEEEE!'* on occasion, like kids at a spoiled brats convention, not out of any sense of real or imagined achievement, but for the simple fact that they want their Warholian fifteen minutes, and you better believe they're gonna make damn sure they get it!

So I guess I can forgive you if you choose to turn a deaf ear to my protestations, but the fact remains, the real motivation for my putting pen to paper is, I would like to think, a tad more noble, inspired as it was by, of all things, an alcohol-fuelled remark at the fag-end of our firm's annual Christmas party, a couple of years back.....

> "I'm not being funny, Lee, but I don't know why you feel compelled to write about this type of crappy, made-up weird stuff, when there's more than enough real-life horror to be going on with right now..."

I remember I was confronted by the shape of that brusque statement, uttered in the world-weary tones of the eternally scornful on a bleak and sleety afternoon in mid-December. It was one of those eye-watering, bone-chilling kind of days, the sort that makes you heartily glad you're snug indoors and not out walking the city streets with your head bowed and your shoulders hunched in a vain attempt to escape the raw, biting wind whipping in from the Mersey.

I was stood in the bar, in the company of Mikey Jopson, long-time friend, business associate, and, as it turned out, occasional purveyor of personal criticism. He was also a litigation solicitor who worked in a nice plush office with a breathtaking view of the city of Liverpool waterfront, and the fact that he made a living making dodgy whiplash claims on behalf of clients who'd been involved in the most minor of car accidents didn't seem to trouble his conscience a great deal. But I digress. I'd just shouted in the umpteenth round of drinks at *The Station Restaurant & Bar*, a trendy, and therefore obscenely expensive watering hole situated at the far end of Hamilton Square, in the midst of a wholly agreeable beer buzz and a setting that was as seasonally idyllic as a scene from that wonderful old Frank Capra movie. The gaily-decorated dining area was bathed in the flickering glow of candlelight, a real log fire was blazing away merrily in the centre of the room and a selection of carols was drifting from a series of tactfully hidden speakers.

And then suddenly, and quite without preamble, Mikey had leaned towards me, and with booze-tainted breath, issued his "don't know why you write this kind of stuff," pronouncement, all the while shaking his head as though he were regarding a particularly unpleasant lower form of life, a bloated, bloodsucking leech say, or "a slug in the afterbirth," to quote the Tooth Fairy in Thomas Harris's excellent novel, *Red Dragon*), shattering my little yuletide reverie. Okay, I have to admit it was hardly the most disparaging aside I've had to deal with over the years. In my day job as a criminal law defence clerk, I have to be incredibly thick-skinned, dealing as I do with the daily verbal abuse spouted by veritable legions of hyper-manic smackheads, coke-heads, and *Skol Super* slurpers (and that's just one's work colleagues, as the old joke goes). Certainly, Mikey's drink-slurred observation didn't provoke the sort of wild-eyed, foaming at the mouth response he'd doubtless been hoping for. You might think me a tad overly sentimental, but I've always loved this time of year, and it was going to take more than a throwaway comment, no matter how disputable, to darken my festive mood any.

And anyway, I knew from past experience, this comment was merely the prelude to embarking on another of those endless debates concerning that hoary old chestnut: the reality or otherwise of what, for want of a better term, we call 'otherworldly phenomena.' (Although to be honest, Mikey had long ago christened such things with a slightly less dignified title, namely; '*a great big steaming pile of Ghost chasing, Nessie-hunting spoon-bending, alien-believing, crackpot conspiracy-flying HORSESHIT!,*' which may not be quite as trip-off-the-tongue-catchy, granted, but has an undeniably good beat!)

As bones of contention go the subject is right up there with the rights and wrongs of capital punishment, the proposed ban on fox hunting and who really should have won the most recent edition of *The X-Factor*, and I guess most people have at least fleetingly discussed this fascinating topic at some time in their lives.

It might sound a little immodest, but I like to think I've managed to glean some degree of knowledge over the years about a field, (in my mind's eye; a wind-blasted meadow, bathed in the eldritch glow of permanent twilight), where there really are very few, if any, 'experts.' Enough to hold my own in an essentially meaningless barroom *tête à tête*, anyway.

Which, given the circumstances, was just as well.

Mikey, to use the colloquial phrase, was totally 'on one,' and all the signs were it was going to take more than a few tired old standard replies to rein him in a tad.

> "I mean just look at the shit that's been flying around these last few years...Just fuckin' LOOK AT IT!"

...he yelled, waving his hands in barely concealed frustration.

> "God almighty, we've had September 11th, the Bali Bomb, mass starvation in Darfur, endless war in Palestine and Afghanistan, and don't even get me *started* on Iraq..."

I sighed, handing him a fresh pint of *Carlsberg* before he had a chance to crank up the gears and do just that. I disagreed with that mad, imperialistic crusade every bit as much as he did, but his 'illegal invasion' diatribes had been known to last for several *hours* and I could think of better ways of spending the remainder of our Yuletide shindig than having my ears bent by a constant stream of righteous anger. No matter how justified that anger might be.

> "Alright, Mikey,"

I said, taking a sip of my ice-cold lager.

> "I take your point. But don't think I haven't had me fair share of sleepless nights questioning the morals and ethics of indulging in my 'all-consuming-obsession,' as you call it. Please don't *ever* think that."

Mikey didn't say anything. He simply smirked and although I don't pretend there was nothing remotely supernatural about it, I was suddenly filled with a prescient certainty that I was going to be in for a long, hard night.

I raised my glass to my lips once more and took a couple of hefty swigs before sighing loud enough to alert the world to the birth of a new martyr.

> "Honestly mate, there have been times, usually just before I unleash another hopelessly overdue edition of my mag on the country's newsstands, I've lain awake till the early hours with nothing for company but a splitting headache and a maddeningly nagging conscience.
>
> But I suppose, when you get right down to it, I find I can justify my publishing this type of stuff in two ways."

> "Yeah right,"

Mikey snickered.

> "And what might those be? No wait, don't tell me. Let me guess. A noble intent to educate the ignorant masses? A one-man mission to solve mysteries, the answers to which have eluded the greatest minds in academia? Or is it simply down to making a few extra bob by exploiting the beliefs of the eternally gullible?"

"I'm not even gonna dignify those remarks with a response,"

I replied through gritted teeth, knowing full well I was about to respond big time. I glanced around the packed dining area and spotted a couple of miraculously spare seats.

"Come on, maybe you'll find it easier to understand what I'm on about if I tell you about an incident I heard about from an impeccable source a few months back. It might take a while. Why don't we go and grab a seat over there by the fire?"

Mikey nodded, although he looked about as sceptical as someone who's just received notification that he was a lucky, lucky, winner in a *Reader's Digest'* prize draw.

The moment we sat down with our drinks the front door suddenly burst open admitting an icy blast of frigid December air along with a couple of girls in their early twenties giggling unselfconsciously as they walked arm in arm over to the bar. I noticed their thick winter coats were speckled with already-melting flakes of snow; a presage of the full-blown blizzard that would sweep across the county well before closing time. The door had only been open for a second or two before it slammed back on its hinges, but that was all the time it took for a needle-sharp chill to stab deep into my bones and I shivered uncontrollably as I edged still closer to the roaring fire.

"Not getting nesh in your old age are yer, Lee?"

Mikey grinned over the rim of his pint.

"If you move any closer to those flickering flames, you're gonna wind up sitting in 'em. You don't wanna end up like Eddy Woodward in *The Wicker Man*, do yer?"

"Oh, heeelarious,"

I replied, desperately trying to keep my teeth from chattering like a pair of castanets. "And I suppose those globulous layers of fat engulfing your body help to insulate you against the freezing cold, do they?"

Mikey, who had always been as skinny as the proverbial rake, didn't respond to that one. He just kept right on grinning that annoying, self-satisfied grin, and it took a gargantuan effort on my part to suppress a keening desire to leap up and wipe that smile right off his face.

Instead, I glanced over my shoulder at the rows of our firm's staff, most of whom had pushed themselves away from the empty-plate laden banquet table with a stifled, though none the less contented burp, with a cheap paper party hat perched precariously on their heads, and a glass of complimentary wine close to hand. Some were half-heartedly picking at their desserts, stomachs not yet quite stuffed to capacity, whilst others were busily engaged in those grand old time-honoured traditions of sharing the latest gossip, drawing up surreptitious lists of their personal *'Top Ten Fittest & Ugliest Members Of The Opposite Sex In The Office,'* laughing too loudly at a string of bawdy jokes, or else bursting into a hopelessly out-of-tune rendition of some endlessly sprawling prog-rock 'classic' (and really struggling with the incredibly complicated three-part harmonies in the middle eight).

Still others were making loud-mouthed pronouncements and displaying the kind of wisdom that only seems to surface when you've been drinking for several hours straight, were shamelessly flirting with the person they've secretly fancied for ages, or were embarking on a series of increasingly pathetic attempts to chat up the stunningly attractive barmaids and waitresses and were rewarded with the sort of withering put down that's apt to slice through your Christmas cheer like a blade-sharp winter icicle piercing your gonads.

And over in the far corner, a girl whose name I couldn't for the life of me recall, was sobbing quietly, unnoticed or ignored by everyone but me, a spill of red wine that in the iridescent half-light looked too much like blood, pooled across that supposedly closely-guarded *Top Ten Ugliest Person List* that had with capricious inevitability, managed to wind up in the hands of the one individual who was never meant to see its contents: Someone who had recently been dumped by a long-term lover, or who had had their face erupt in a veritable bean feast of yellow-headed acne overnight, or had found themselves stuck in a relationship that was slowly developing into a kind of drifting, eternal grief, the sort that makes you despondent and jaded and old before your time.

For the briefest moment, I actually considered going over to speak to the girl, but Mikey, as persistent as ever, stopped me dead in my tracks. In truth, this was probably just as well. After all, what words of comfort could I have offered her other than a series of inane banalities that would, in all likelihood, have only made matters worse?

"Are you gonna sit there staring into space all night?"

...he said.

"Or are you gonna spill this great big revelation of yours and have me eating humble pie till it comes out me ears?"

I shook my head and turned back to face my nemesis and I remember thinking; *Me old Mate Mikey, is going to take some major convincing here. Do I really want to spend the remainder of this evening chasing a hopelessly lost cause when there is still so much of Christmas still to celebrate?'*

The answer to that was a big fat no, and I opened my mouth to say as much. But before I could do so, I found myself being struck momentarily dumb by the dawning of an immutable truth, the impact of which couldn't have been much greater if it had chosen to manifest itself in the form of a Dickensian spirit, all rattling chains and relentlessly grim demeanour, as it held open an impossibly large, leather-bound volume filled with a yellowed-with-age parchment that closely resembled human skin.

And the plain, black, foot-high lettering inscribed there would spell out a stark and simple message.....

**'Sometimes the Story Simply DEMANDS To Be Told,
And Never Mind The Consequences!'**

And hot on the heels of that little epiphany, came another, equally powerful; 'Wouldn't I feel like a first class fool (or kingsize balloonhead, as we Merseysiders tend to refer to people who's collection of marbles is a trifle on the thin side), if I were to simply clam up, hand Mikey his victory, and by implication vindicate all those who believe authors who write about the paranormal crawled from the same gene pool as the Saddam Husseins and Osama bin Ladens of this world.

If I missed this opportunity to punch a few holes in that particular dark veil of ignorance, I'd wind up kicking myself all the way home, and never mind the rapidly thickening snow flurries clearly visible beyond the tinsel-lined windows.

With a mental sigh and fortifying myself with a confidence-boosting gulp of ale, I finally began speaking of the events that had all but overtaken John Weate, the head of the firm's criminal department, and someone who also happened to be a very good friend of mine, during the late spring, early summer of 2002......

TOUCHED FROM A DISTANCE

And this is what, in essence, John told me, one rainy November afternoon, when work, for once, was a little on the slow side, and there was nothing in our agendas that was so urgent it couldn't wait till the following day........

No matter how worldly wise you may think you are, perhaps as an unhappy consequence of the ordeals that life can heartlessly throw your way, there may come a point when the force field of assumed emotional invincibility you were sure you'd built around yourself can, in the end, prove to be about as effective as the walls of Jericho, torn asunder by one almighty bugle blast.

A word or two of reassurance, if I may. I want you to know that I could never be described as being what you would term an overly gullible man. I am, I like to think, justifiably renowned for my ability to evaluate the merits or otherwise of any given criminal case by employing the cold, analytical manner of a laboratory scientist or a forensic expert.

There are at least two very good reasons for this excessive diligence. Firstly, to ensure I make as few mistakes as possible when dealing with matters that could have a devastating effect upon the lives of both the client and their family and friends. And secondly, when poring over the bloodied shards of our client's lives on a daily basis, it's often very easy to become emotionally involved in a case, and that in turn can lead to an endless succession of dark nights of the soul as you lie awake pondering the terrible things that you sooner or later come to find exist beneath the tissue thin fabric of what passes for everyday normality. And these grinning, capering horrors don't exclusively dwell amongst the ghettos and seldom-trodden backstreets of any given city, as you might suppose. They can nestle and thrive every bit as comfortably behind the white-laced curtains of leafy green suburbia.

'Portentous meditations of life's veil of tears,' my wife Val, likes to call them, and whilst I have to admit that is sweetly poetic and strangely comforting, I find I prefer to call them what they truly are; 'Sleep depriving guilt trips,' of the sort I imagine are suffered by just about everyone involved n the legal profession at some point in their careers, irrespective of whether they care to admit it or not. Your involvement, however fleeting, in a client's wrongful conviction or assisting in the acquittal of someone whom you know in your heart of hearts to be guilty of some terrible crime, can weigh heavily upon one's mind in the wee small hours.

Not that I've ever yearned for my full quota of restful sleep. From a very early age, my dear Dad instilled in me a strong work ethic and an outlook on life that had effectively taught me to live each and every day as though time were running out and damned fast. I've never felt any qualms whatsoever about being up and about the very moment the first grey finger of dawn poked a hole in the bedroom's stygian darkness, *(and now who's being flowery and poetic?)*

Even as a child, and then during my teenage years at university, I refused to conform to the rites of the habitual slug-a-bed student, the type that gradually emerge from beneath the covers like some bleary-eyed hibernating animal stirred by the onset of spring.

It'll come as little surprise then, that on the day we're concerned about here, I was sat at my paper-cluttered desk in our firm's main office situated in the centre of downtown Birkenhead, beavering away long before any other member of staff had clocked in. I was engrossed in my workload, oblivious to the world beyond the tiny, stuffy box room that served as the Senior Partners private quarters. Never a particularly cheery place at the best of times, on this unseasonably damp mid-July morning, it felt as cold and funereal as a snow-covered Soviet war grave. The only window, dusty and speckled with bird droppings, looked out upon a plain brick wall that stretched upwards for as far as the eye could see, preventing all but the merest hint of daylight from penetrating the oppressive gloom. I was surrounded by shelves that quite literally groaned beneath the combined weight of stacks of yellow box files and countless plastic buckets brimming with pink-ribboned sets of legal documents. The uniform monotony was relieved only by an old lithograph of Liverpool's Anglican Cathedral, a diploma from Manchester University, and a plain, wooden-framed practising certificate. Oh, and above the door there was a joke sign that read *'NO SOLICITORS'* which doubtless provided hours of constant hilarity to the easily amused.

Despite the dismal surroundings, or maybe in some crazy way because of them, I worked non-stop that day, not even pausing for a dinner break, or a single cup of lukewarm coffee, and it wasn't until my stomach began growling like the death groan of a terminally depressed moose that I finally pushed back my seat and rose wearily from the still paper-strewn desktop. I stifled a yawn, massaged my aching neck and decided what work I had left to do, I could just as easily get stuck into at home. I set about heaving three large baskets filled to overflowing with a collection of yet more files, towards the office entrance just as the Birkenhead Town Hall clock chimed 6:15pm, and paused for a second after I'd stepped through the revolving door. I was a little amazed to see Hamilton Square bathed in painfully sweet summer light, the aftermath of the day's downpour still apparent, but receding in the sultry heat. The pavements were glistening and thin tendrils of steam were rising from the roofs of the black Hackney cabs lined up opposite *The Station Restaurant & Bar.*

The heady scent of late blooming flowers wafted across the acre or so of parkland vying for prominence with the salty tang of the nearby river, and I was struck by a sudden, powerful wave of nostalgia as I watched a group of kids heading for one of the fields in the centre of the Square, some kicking a football, others screeching with high-pitched laughter as they took turns dodging the rainbowed arc of a lawn sprinkler's misty spray.

I sighed wistfully as I turned and headed for the car park, trying hard to ignore the pain as the handles of those incredibly heavy plastic buckets dug in to the palms of my hand *(and something about the way my fingers looked right then, gnarled and bloodless, and vaguely inhuman, dredged up a memory, the precise nature of which remained tantalisingly out of reach until later that evening).* It was a blessed relief to finally reach my car, and I all but slung the files into the boot before collapsing into the driver's seat, catching my reflection in the rear-view mirror as I did so. I did a little double-take at the face staring back at me. It was wearing the dopey, aw shucks smile of a love-sick teenager, and I remember thinking to myself, 'God, it really doesn't take much to make a person moderately cheerful, does it?'

I shrugged my shoulders and could almost physically see the remnants of my bad mood slowly melt away like a morning fog burnt off by the heat of a high noon sun.

I put the key in the ignition, and drove home with the window wound all the way down and *Summer Breeze*, by the *Isley Brothers* drifting from the car stereo....

When I knocked at the front door of our modest, three up, two down council house on the outskirts of Upton Village, and no one answered, I didn't worry unduly. At least not at first. My two sons, Mark and Roger, were seldom in and displayed an uncanny talent for disappearing from the face of the Earth whenever they heard me struggling with my key with a couple of bundles of 'homework' under my arms.

Sweating profusely, and displaying all the suppleness of a fully-fledged contortionist, I somehow managed to haul the infernal baskets from the boot, get the key in the lock., turn it, push the door open, and stagger across the threshold into the hallway. I shouted for Val to come and give me a hand, and mumbled an obscenity under my breath when no one replied. I called her name again as I dropped the files in an untidy heap on the living room floor, and when still she never answered, I wondered whether she'd maybe slipped out to one of the local late shops for a bottle of wine to go with our tea. I made my way to the kitchen to see if she'd left a 'post it' note on the fridge door, as she usually does when she's had to run on an errand, but the only things attached to the uniform white surface were a couple of holiday postcards, a faded England World Cup squad sticker, and an invitation to a friend's 50th birthday party. 'Ah, well,' I thought. 'Val probably assumed she'd be back long before I got home. Maybe she bumped into one of her friends on the way back from the shops. My wife can certainly gab. She talks that much I'm often reminded of that old Robin Williams joke... 'You could hook her mouth up to a generator and she could supply enough power to light the whole of Liverpool for a month!'

Yeah, that made sense. It made perfect sense. So why did I feel just the faintest stirrings of unease as I grabbed a cool drink from the fridge? Normally I would have settled for a can of Pepsi, but almost without thinking, I pulled out a bottle of lager and after pressing it against my forehead for a few blessed moments, I chugged down its contents in several large gulps. The resultant ice-cold beer buzz served to calm me a little and I was just reaching for another when I suddenly remembered that of course, Val was looking after our two and a half year old grandson, Dominic, today, and that she'd arranged to take him back to our daughter, Sally's, in the early evening. That was why the house was empty. I couldn't believe I'd forgotten and it crossed my mind that the pressures of my job must be really getting to me if such an important event could slip from my mind with the ease of a dentist's appointment. I'd loved Dominic dearly from the very moment I'd first set eyes on him, one cold February morning, a tiny bundle wrapped in a knitted cardigan and a woolly hat, both three sizes too big for him, and I lived for the occasions when my daughter brought him round, or asked Val and I to baby-sit for her while she was at work or wanted a night out with friends.

I kicked myself for not having left work a little earlier, and in a bid to halt the tide of bitter disappointment that threatened to engulf me, I sought solace by doing what I usually do when plagued by such gnawing pangs of conscience; I decided I might as well set about clearing as much work as possible, before my wife returned alone....

Don't worry. The deliciously cruel irony of the situation was not lost upon me. But that terrible knowledge didn't prevent me from returning to the living room which sometimes doubled as my study, though, and the moment I sat down and began to organise the files into a tidy pile, my mind was once more fully focused upon the task in hand. I have no way of knowing for sure, of course, but I'm pretty certain that as I began ploughing my way through the stack of work what Val likes to call my *'Perry Mason On Da Case'* expression. She'd once secretly snapped a picture of me whilst I'd been poring over a mound of committal papers, and I'd been shocked, and not a little amused when she handed me the photograph a few weeks later over dinner at our favourite restaurant. I'd barely recognised the fiercely intense-looking man hunched over his desk, jaw firmly set, his lips twisted into a grimace of feverish determination, and I recall being struck by a powerful image from a book I'd once had to study during my schooldays, many years earlier. It was the story of Faust, the man who had foolishly sold his soul to the Devil in exchange for a lifetime's worth of earthly pleasures, and it had featured a detailed illustration of him seated at his desk, trying desperately to figure out a way out of his damnable pact as the clock ticked inexorably towards midnight and the payment of that awful debt.

I'd passed the photo back to Val with a nervous chuckle and found myself making a spontaneous promise that I'd try from that moment on to take it a little easier and not devote so much precious time to pursuing my career, and she'd smiled, her face radiant in the soft red glow of the table lamp and we'd raised our glasses and drank a toast to a more relaxed and carefree future.

And we'd both known in our hearts that, with the best will in the world, there was more chance of Satan being forced to shell out for a shiny new pair of rollerskates than there was of me ever being true to such a promise.

You perhaps won't find it quite so unbelievable then, that when my wife strode purposefully into the room an hour or so after I'd arrived home, I barely afforded her a second glance. In fact, it was only when she stood before me, placed her hands on the table and spoke in a husky whisper I would have regarded as being enormously sexy in any other circumstances, that I fully acknowledged her presence

        'John,'

…she said.

        'I need to talk to you for a minute.'

My heart sank as I fully expected to be subjected to the third degree for my not being home from the office in time to see my grandson.

Knowing full well I was in the wrong, and being keen to avoid an argument I was inevitably going to lose, I sought to postpone the confrontation in the vain hope that she might forget about it later.

        'Not now, Val,'

I sighed with an air of exaggerated weariness.

        'Can't you see I'm busy?'

Normally, this arrogant dismissal would have been more than enough to cause my wife to spin round on her high heels and march out of the room without another word, granting me a temporary stay of execution, but, as I was about to find out, there was nothing remotely normal about this set of circumstances.

        'Please John,'

…she persisted.

        'Just hear me out, will you. This might be really important.'

The concern in her voice served to grab my attention, and when I looked up from my papers, I was shocked to see there was a strange expression on her face and her eyes were glistening with what appeared to be unshed tears. I immediately switched off my dictating machine, got to my feet, and walked quickly around the desk.

> 'What's wrong?'

I asked, trying to ignore the viper's nest of half-formed fears that were slowly uncurling in the pit of my stomach. She didn't answer straight away. Instead she smiled an unbearably sad smile, and a thousand questions arose in my mind. But before I could give voice to any of them, she asked me one of her own;

> 'Have you ever spoken to Dominic about your father?'

Now it was my turn to be rendered momentarily speechless. That particular question had not featured anywhere amongst The Unspoken Thousand.

> 'Have you?'

…she repeated, peering at me intently.

> 'Even in the most offhand of ways? Perhaps when you've taken Dominic out for a walk in the park. Or when it's been your turn to put him to bed? I know how much you love to talk to him, John. Is it possible you mentioned your Dad, at any point? Please try and remember.'

I didn't answer straight away. I had to think long and hard. I was pretty sure I hadn't made reference to Tom, my father, who had died when I was a teenager thirty years earlier, within earshot of the baby. But I wasn't absolutely positive that was the case. I think it's entirely possible that I may have made some whispered, half-to-myself reference to him while I was tucking Dominic into the spare bed on the occasions Sally requested he stay with us overnight.... Perhaps something along the lines of how I wished my Dad had lived long enough for him to see that I'd managed to realise all of the hopes and aspirations he'd ever held for me, that he'd been granted the opportunity to hold his grandkids in his arms or sit them down on his knee and tell them one of his many incredible stories, or even that he'd had the chance to invite me along to his local for a single Sunday afternoon pint.....

My dad had spent all his working life toiling in a chemical factory on the smog-choked outskirts of Widness, and I never saw anywhere near as much of him as I would have liked. The truth is, he was so dog-tired when he came home after slogging his way through another impossibly-long shift, his hands and face smeared with a thick, oily grime that no amount of bathing could ever completely remove, he would invariably fall fast asleep in his favourite armchair before the roaring coal fire not long after he first set foot through the door.

I truly loved him, though, and the memories of the rare occasions we got to spend some quality time together are something I treasure above all my worldly possessions.

I've always tried to be completely honest with my wife. It's one of the things that have served to ensure our marriage has stood the test of time, whilst the foundations of so many of our friend's have been swept away by a tidal wave of white lies, half-truths and outright deceit. And so I told her that I couldn't be one hundred per cent certain of the answer to her question, either way.

> 'Okay, fair enough,'

…she nodded, satisfied that I wasn't being deliberately evasive.

> 'And I suppose you *would* know if you'd ever shown Dominic a photo of your father?'
> 'Now, that's something that I *can* be sure of,'

I replied without a moment's hesitation. There were no framed photographs of my Dad lining the shelves or hanging on the walls of our house. I'd long ago placed the two hundred or so pictures I had of him in a series of albums which I kept in a large wooden trunk in a dusty corner of the attic, a lovingly compiled memorial to infinite kinds of loss.

'If, for some reason, I wanted to show Dominic a photo of me Dad,'

I said,

'I know for a fact I'd remember having to rummage around in that box-full of memorabilia to find something suitable. I can't recall the last time I even went up in the attic, but I'm sure it was before Dominic was even born.'

'I was sure you'd say that,'

Val said, before surprising me still further by suddenly hugging me fiercely, her voice a soft and urgent whisper in my ear.

'I want you to come upstairs with me for a minute.'

I was going to make a predictable crack about her developing a highly original seduction technique, but it died on my lips when she solemnly took me by the hand and began leading me towards the staircase. There was an undeniable tension in the air, but it certainly wasn't anything remotely sexual about it. We stopped directly outside my youngest son, Roger's bedroom, and despite the summer warmth that permeated the house, Val shivered and I noticed goosebumps had risen on her arms. The bedroom door was standing slightly ajar, and without a word, she pushed it all the way open. I'm not at all sure what I expected. The room was in its usual state of wild, teenage-resident disarray, but I couldn't help but be struck by how quiet and still the room seemed in my son's absence. It seemed almost irreverent to break that cathedral-like silence, and I had time to marvel at the way the sounds from beyond our son's bedroom travelled on the evening air, as a diagonal shaft of sunset speared through a gap in the curtains and dust motes danced lazily in sympathy for the dying day: The canned laughter of a TV sit-com. A neighbour's dog howling mournfully in the backyard. A mother calling for her children to come in, supper was ready. The discordant chimes of a passing ice cream van….

They were the sounds of the familiar made strange, and I felt overcome with a vague melancholy, though I couldn't for the life of me have said why.

'Well?'

I asked finally.

'What is it you wanted to show me?'

For a single, endless moment I didn't think she was going to answer.

And then, like a car engine hot-wired by one of our more resourceful clients, she was off and running….

'I'm going to have to ask you to do two things, before I tell you what happened this afternoon, John. Firstly, I need you to promise me you won't, at any stage start giggling like a loon whilst making twirly finger motions in the general direction of your temporal lobe. And secondly, I need you to place your natural scepticism on hold for at least as long as it takes for me to get the story out.

You're nodding your head. That's as good a promise as I'm gonna get?

Okay, I guess that'll have to do.

Let me begin by telling you the day had started out perfectly normally. After you'd left for the office, I got stuck into some washing and ironing before Sally came around with the baby about 11-ish. We had a cup of coffee before she had to head off to work, and I gave Dominic his dinner just after mid-day. He had a little nap after that while I half-watched a couple of crappy soaps with cardboard sets and wooden actors and plot-holes the size of John Kerry's massive big Billy-bouffant head.

And then, having just about retained the will to live, I decided to embark on yet another epic attempt at smartening up our Roger's room so that it didn't resemble the chaotic aftermath of a cluster bomb explosion.

I took Dominic upstairs with me, and decided to start upon this heroic endeavour by tidying Roger's bed. I'd just scooped up the tangled mass of blankets that were lying in their customary heap on the floor, when I heard Dominic chunnering merrily away to someone and I glanced across the room and saw that there was absolutely no one there.

And had I *really* expected anyone to have tip-toed silently into the house for some crazy reason without me being aware of it? Cold hard logic suggested our grandson was merely talking to an imaginary playmate of the sort I used to have when I was his age. Simple as that.

The thing is though, I couldn't help noticing Dominic seemed to be staring at the far wall, the one plastered with the Everton FC and *Libertines* tour posters, with an intensity that was more than a little frightening.

Not that Dominic seemed to be scared in any way. Just the opposite, in fact. His eyes were wide open in an owlish double O of wonder, as though he were watching one of those gobsmacking firework displays, like the ones we used to take the kids to in Arrowe Park, every Bonnie Night. And as he gawped, he continued to jabber away like one of those grinning black peddlers, desperately trying to sell their tacky wares to gullible tourists on cheap package holidays.

And, almost despite myself, I found I was trying to make sense of what Dominic was saying, Although to be honest, it was pretty much the usual mixture of half-recognisable words and unintelligible baby-talk.

And yet, as undeniably soft as it sounds, my curiosity was so aroused that I went right out and asked him who he thought he was talking to.

'Hey, Dominic,' I said, hating the patronising tone that crept into my voice – the sort we reserve for very young children and the mentally retarded. 'Who are you talking to? Your special friend?'

'No' Dominic immediately replied, keeping his gaze fixed firmly on the far wall. And then he suddenly raised his hand, pointed straight ahead and whispered in a voice filled with an almost adult-certainty; 'Grandad!'

I smiled at that *(and was there just the tiniest bit of relief in that smile? I think maybe there was)*. I assumed he was talking about you, John.

'No, hon,' I said Grandad's at work right now. You'll see him later on today, though."

'Grandad,' Dominic repeated, more forcefully this time, still pointing at the poster-strewn wall. 'Grandad. Grandad. *GRANDAD!*'

He was yelling now, and on impulse, I walked over to the wall and peered closely at the pictures, sure I would see someone closely resembling you, John, or maybe his other Grandad, the one he hasn't seen since last Christmas 'cos he lives in Coventry, and never bothers his arse to stay in touch. Oh, there *were* a couple of baldy-headed Everton players who looked like a pair of identical twins stood in the middle of the back row of the team poster. But I honestly couldn't see anyone that looked *especially* like you.

But still, Dominic continued to virtually chant; *'Grandad, Grandad, Grandad….'* Over and over like a terminally scratched CD, and it crossed my mind to tell him gently but firmly, to please quit it before he drove me totally round the bend, when he suddenly paused in mid-rant, cocked his head to one side as if he were being told something of great interest, and then instantly froze the blood in my veins by quietly announcing; 'Grandad's *dead!*'

That he said this so matter-of-factly only served to make his statement all the more chilling. My head spun like I'd knocked back one too many double-whisky and cokes, and I think if I hadn't leaned back against the wall for support, I might have had real trouble staying on my feet. When I finally managed to regain some degree of composure, I ran over to Dominic, and placed my arms on his shoulders, just about resisting the temptation to physically shake him from his trance-like state.

'Your Grandad's *not* dead,' I all but shouted at him. I told you, he's at work. He'll be home in a few hours.'

I may as well have been talking to my *own* imaginary friend for all the good it did, though. He just continued to stand there with his head to one side, like a cute puppy that's been promised a treat and I was struck again by how natural, how regular, how *real* the one-way conversation had seemed.

And then I was struck by something else: The air in the room had turned a shade colder. It was a subtle change, nothing dramatic, like. But it definitely seemed to have cooled by a couple of degrees, as though a cloud had briefly obscured the sun, and I remembered having read somewhere that such sudden drops in temperature are supposed to be a sign that you're in the presence of some otherworldly entity; the invisible spirit of a dead person, for example.

Real fear slithered into my skin, then, and instinctively I swept Dominic up in my arms and dashed out of the room on to the landing. He didn't protest at all, but he kept glancing back over his shoulder as though he still had unfinished business to discuss and it took all of my willpower not to break into a run and hurtle headlong down the stairs, a recipe for disaster if ever there was one.

As it was, I managed to methodically plod all the way down to the ground floor, as if I didn't have a single care in the world, though I breathed a sigh of relief when I finally reached the bottom stair.

I set Dominic down and knelt before him worried that I may have spooked him by my actions. He seemed fine, if a touch puzzled, and I offered up a silent prayer to whatever god looks out for very young children, for granting me that small mercy.

'Sorry about that, Dominic,' I said hurriedly. 'I think we'll leave tidying the bedroom's for now. There's a nasty draught up there, and we wouldn't want you to catch a cold now, would we?'

I coughed when he didn't reply, and then tried a grin on for size. It was so forced it felt like my face was going to split, but I wore it for Dom's sake, just the same.

'Tell you what, why don't I fix us both a nice cool glass of orange juice,' I suggested, though in truth I could have done with something a good deal stronger, right then. I glanced across the hallway and saw bars of cheery, afternoon sunlight slanting through the windows, and heard the banal tones of a DJ waffling on about some no mark celebrity or other on the radio in the kitchen, an air of welcome normality descended so quickly I was soon berating myself for acting like a frightened schoolgirl. The kind that had been mortally afraid that the coats hanging on the back of their bedroom door were transformed into a child-eating bogeyman in the dead hours of the night, or that the Pierrot character cavorting across their wallpaper could, after dark, take the form of a hideously made-up clown intent upon sneaking up on their intended victim the second they closed their eyes.

I took Dominic by the hand to lead him towards the kitchen, and was startled when he suddenly began dragging his feet and craning his neck, determined to see something only he could see, right at the top of the stairs. That was bad enough. When he started holding that eerie, one-way conversation again, it was all I could do to stifle a scream.

Once more, he was nodding and shaking his head and mumbling half-coherently, and when I tried to pull him away, her resisted with a fierce determination.

And then he looked back at me, looked back up at the landing, and for all the world as though he were imparting information to me from that invisible source, said, 'Yes,... Yes...Grandad *IS* dead!'

And that was quite enough for me. I'm not ashamed to say I panicked, and swept Dominic into my arms for a record-breaking third time in the space of that single afternoon. I ran along the hallway and strapped him into his pushchair as fast as I could with shaking hands like I had a bad case of the DTs.

I raced us both out of the house, then, with no clear idea of where we were headed. I almost ran along the streets into Upton Village, ignoring the puzzled expressions on the faces of passers-by, and didn't pause for breath until I reached the centre of Arrowe Park. I leaned against the green-painted metal fence that encloses the children's play area, and simply stared into space, seeing but not seeing the groups of excited kids being watched over by their doting mothers as they took turns on the see-saws, slid down slides or pushed each other on the swings.

I must have looked a right state, as visibly shaken as I undoubtedly was, but if one of those parents had wandered over to ask me what was wrong, could I honestly have told them?

Probably not.

I certainly don't think I would have voiced the quite terrifying possibility that had begun to form in my mind during the mad dash from our house, anyway, the true shape of which I hadn't been able to fully see until that moment: What if Dominic, my daughter's son, whom I love every bit as much as I love my own two boys....What if he hadn't been talking to an imaginary friend, after all, but actually has some kind of a psychic gift, the ability to see dead people, like that kid in *The Sixth Sense?*'

What if the "Grandad" he'd been referring to had actually been his *Great* Grandad, Tom?'

And, oh God, John. What if Dominic has been holding a conversation with your father, who passed away twenty five years or so ago?'

And that was it.

Val simply couldn't say anything else, and perhaps she didn't need to.

She choked back a sob and covered her face with her hands like she was desperately trying to render herself invisible.

I tried to console her. Though if I'm honest, my words sounded feeble when pitched against her undoubted sincerity.

Despite my having very little interest in the subject, I was aware of the supposed ability of very young children to see apparitions that we adults are unable to perceive as we have that "magical gift" educated right out of us from the moment we hit our teens.

For herself, Val, never renowned for her gullibility, remained convinced that Dominic had seen something, even if she never sought to press the case that Dom had spoken top my father, and I loved her all the more for that. Perhaps, we would, in time, have forgotten all about the incident, or at best relegated it to the status of fireside ghost story to be told and re-told each succeeding year.

But then, just one week later, two things happened in quick succession that caused even a dyed-in-the-wool sceptic like me to wonder….

Firstly, on one of the all-too rare occasions that I had five minutes to spare in the office, I was sat at my desk with a plastic cup of lukewarm tea and the morning newspapers. I couldn't face the heavy moralising tone of the broadsheets, so I headed straight for the sports pages of *The Liverpool Daily Post*, checked the TV listings to see if there was anything remotely interesting on the box that evening, and then turned to the local news section on the off-chance some of our client's cases had been deemed worthy of making it into print. I cursorily glanced at the assembled articles; a piece on the latest Mersey Rail strike, a review of *The Zutons* gig at The Academy, and another (very likely doomed) attempt to resurrect *Cammell Laird's* Shipyard….. **

And then my eyes very nearly popped out on their stalks when I saw a sepia-toned photograph of a crowd of cloth-capped workmen trudging across a railway footbridge back in 1957. Despite the grey, industrial backdrop, the sludgy river flowing through a stretch of deserted dockland, the iron suspension bridge, a church spire as black as a witches' Halloween hat, the men looked as proud as old soldiers marching to the Cenotaph on Remembrance Sunday.

And there, right at the front of the picture, was my Dad, frozen in time, looking a little weary alongside his smiling friend, but striding purposefully to accomplish whatever task it was he had set out to do with steely determination.

** 'CAMMELL LAIRD SHIPYARD': Founded in 1828, this Birkenhead-based company rose from humble beginnings on the banks of the River Mersey, to become one of the most famous names in the history of British shipbuilding, and was responsible for creating and launching such famous vessels as the HMS *Ark Royal*, the second *Mauretania*, in 1939 and the *Ma Roberts*, (built for Dr Livingstone's Zambezi expedition in 1858) Sadly, although still very much in business, Cammel Laird's glory days are nothing but an increasingly distant memory, due to the nationwide decline in maritime-related industry, but the County's citizens can still derive a great source of pride from the shipyard's illustrious past.

I sat there for what seemed like the longest time, gazing at the photo trying to decided how I felt and whether its appearance now - exactly seven days after my Grandson's "experience" - actually *meant* anything or not.

The cold, analytical part of me was quick to dismiss the whole thing as nothing more than mere coincidence. A somewhat spooky set of chance circumstance, to be sure, but nonetheless entirely explicable in purely rational terms.

The second thing that happened on the following Sunday afternoon however, forced even a hard-nosed sceptic like yours truly to at least contemplate something I had previously considered to be impossible.....

Val and I had invited the family, including our Sally, (who remained blissfully ignorant of what had transpired a week or so earlier), and Dominic, round for a traditional roast dinner. Afterwards, as we were sat in the living room having a few drinks and half-watching some footy game featuring a couple of Premiership also-rans, an idea suddenly occurred to me.

The copy of the *Daily Post* featuring the photograph of my Dad from the impossibly distant-seeming year of 1957 had been placed at the front of the newspaper rack at the side of my favourite armchair. I picked it out, placed it on the dining table, and turned directly to the relevant page.

I then nonchalantly called Dominic over to come and take a look at the picture, without giving him the slightest hint of what it showed.

The rest of the family hastily gathered around, keen to see his reaction, and I think the scene that unfolded will be forever etched in my memory; the caught-breath silence that descended in the wake of my request. The way my Grandson looked positively angelic, his face bathed in a ray of soft, buttery sunlight as he studied the picture intently. The lace curtains blowing gently in the early evening breeze. The dust motes that danced like gleaming nuggets of truth within the bric-a-brac that passes for our daily lives.

I can't ever claim to be remotely prescient, but I think I'd known from the moment that I'd first reached for the newspaper, that although my Grandson had never before seen a portrait of my father, he would nevertheless recognise him immediately.

And so it proved.

    'Grandad!'

...he stated, pointing authoritatively and without hesitation at the glasses-wearing, black-coated figure crossing that long-ago footbridge.

    'There's Grandad!'

I didn't sleep very well that night.

I was kept awake by both recent events and the constant replaying in my mind of one of the most abiding memories I have of my father. Its focus was a two week summer holiday I'd spent on a caravan site near the Welsh town of Prestatyn, when I was about 11 years old, and about to start secondary school.

'One beautifully clear morning, my Dad had hired a boat and taken me on a fishing trip. To this day, I remember the warmth of the wet sand oozing between my toes as we dragged the old rowing boat from its beachside moorings. I recall too the achingly lonesome cry of the seagulls swooping gracefully in the cloudless blue skies. The white-sailed yachts slowly circling the bay. The lonely-looking lighthouse. A tanker bound for some exotic clime.

'When we were about a mile or so offshore, my Dad picked up his fishing rod, wrapped his gnarled hands around mine and we cast the line together. And we waited while the sun beat down on our backs and caused dazzlingly bright hypnotic sparkles of light to flash across the huge expanse of water.

'We only caught a couple of non-descript tiddlers, and we threw them back almost immediately, but that didn't matter. We had a fantastic time, anyway, engaging in carefree conversation, sharing jokes and him telling me stories, some funny, some sad, just a boy and his father, Kings Of The Seven Seas and all they surveyed.

'And then, with the sun finally dipping slowly towards the horizon, he'd said we'd best be heading back, that Mum would be getting worried. But before he began pulling on the oars, he said he had something he needed to ask of me first, and he begged me to listen closely to what he had to say. He raised his hands and gazed at them with barely concealed disgust, as though he had never truly seen them prior to that moment.

''You know what, son.' He began, his voice almost cracking with emotion. 'I've spent my whole working life using these hands, and now they're so wracked with arthritis they're pretty much next to useless.'

'He lowered them, wincing as he did so, and I noticed it took a real effort for him to speak again.

'When he did, however, his voice was strong and clear. 'Promise me you'll try your very best at school to get the necessary qualifications to get you to college or university. Promise me you'll study hard so you'll never have to stagger home with your back bent and your muscles aching and your face etched with the irremovable filth that leaves these deep sets of lines that make you look far older than your years and you're not so knackered when you get home you can't spend enough meaningful time with your family, the way I've been forced to do. Please promise me you'll try your very best."

'I didn't hesitate for a second. I didn't even pause to consider the implications of precisely what it was he wanted me to achieve. I only know that if he had ordered me to single-handedly sail our tiny boat around the globe and back right then, I'd have grabbed the oars and rowed till my arms dropped off. If my Dad believed I could do it, if he had the requisite faith in me, I was convinced there was nothing I couldn't accomplish.

"I promise," I said and licked the tip of my little finger before crossing my heart the way all the kids I hung around with did back then, and my father smiled at me, and I smiled right back, and then he hugged me so fiercely I felt nothing could ever harm us or come between us and the future seemed to stretch ahead into a land of fabulously bright dreams……'

"Well, Mikey."

I said with a sigh, leaning back in my chair, just about all-talked out and not a little exhausted.

"I would humbly contend stories like that give *all* of us a reason to hope. To dare to believe that there might, to paraphrase Shakespeare, be 'more things in heaven and earth than are dreamt in your philosophy,' that maybe science doesn't have all the answers."

I drained the lukewarm dregs of my pint, and grimaced at the bitter aftertaste. "At the very least, they provide me with the inspiration to write about this type of stuff. I mean, if only *one* of the countless thousands of accounts of supernatural phenomena I've dutifully recounted over the years prove to be true, then…."

I didn't finish the sentence. I simply left its import hanging in the beery air like the swirling blue smoke of an after-dinner cigar.

Mikey didn't respond. He just stared off into the middle distance, apparently lost in deep thought. He was either considering the head-spinning implications of the tale I'd related or had been so mind-numbingly bored by the whole thing that he was simply wondering what to have for tea when he got home. I like to *think* it was the former.

And I'd really like to think that the eternal sceptic, someone who's trained to deal with cold hard facts and verifiable truths, had been forced to ask himself a series of extremely difficult questions: Was it at all possible that spirits of the dead can on occasion call in lonesome voices from some otherworldly realm?

Could he afford to give the slightest degree of credence to the notion that restless apparitions sometimes walk the desolate night time landscapes and dustless highways?

And was it at all feasible that the shades of the departed can sometimes be compelled to let their loved ones know they continue to watch over us, to make us aware that they share the joy of unrealised ambition and of seeing the hopes they had for us fulfilled?

Personally, I'd love to believe that all of the above is true, and I told my friend as much on that snowy December evening at *The Station Restaurant & Bar,* as the blazing log fire was reduced to a few glowing embers and people were beginning to button up their coats and drift reluctantly towards the exits.

As motivations for writing this book go, I would argue there are few so worthy.

So, this one's not for ego.

This one's not for monetary gain.

This one's for the sceptics who still have somewhere within them the capacity to dream....

Lee Walker
Moreton, Merseyside
April, 2011

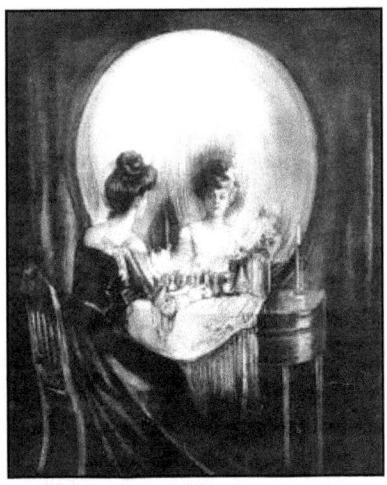

BOOK ONE

WHERE THE GHOSTS OF MEMORIES GATHER

'My Merseyside!* What airy hosts
Turn still thy gilded vanes.
What winds of Elf that with grey ghost,
People thine ancient lanes?'

(With apologies to H.P.Lovecraft, May, 1927)

Every town in every county of the British Isles, it seems, has within its environs, both natural and artificial, a whole host of what, for want of a better term we call *'Haunted Places'*.

It's like a national law or something, and although it's a safe bet you'll never find reference to this in any of the perennially dusty, leather-bound volumes that line the legal statutes section of your local library, that doesn't make it any less 'legally-binding' than say, the laws which dictate the highway speed limit or the age of sexual consent.

Put simply, it's much the same kind of indisputable edict that decrees every town in every county *must* have its fair share of places where, whatever the season, the air is frequently filled with gusts of laughter, a joyful, carefree sound that stirs the emotions like a spiritual drifting across a cotton field in the American 'Deep South'. Places where groups of hooded ASBO-dodging youths gather to sit and swap the latest gossip whilst taking turns to chug on a lukewarm plastic bottle of *White Lightning*. Places where slightly older lads awkwardly fumble to be men with *faux*-reticent girls, mechanically playing their roles in the meat-market version of teenage romance. Places where the middle-aged are struck with a giddying sense of bittersweet nostalgia by something as seemingly innocuous as a set of initials carved into the weathered arm of a park bench, or the faintest whiff of the salty smell of the ocean carried on a summer breeze. Places where smart-suited town elders, their faces etched with the cruel lines of endless mourning gather to remember the fallen of two World Wars….

Places infused with an indefinable, though none the less potent magic.

Places of sanctuary.

Places serene.

That these type of locations exist is irrefutable. And so, by the same token, are there places where it is popularly considered unwise to walk alone in the twilight, 'amidst the gloaming' when the sun has been squeezed to a thin orange line on the horizon.

You usually find them, (and perhaps on occasion, *they* find *you*), situated at the furthest, least populated outskirts of the city, the seedy, ramshackle depths of the ghetto, or the long-neglected corner of some farmer's field.

But sometimes, these places are so disconcertingly close to home, that though you may not be outwardly aware of anything remotely sinister about your surroundings, still you can somehow *feel* their presence like the frigid breath of a January wind, raising your hairs on the back of your neck and raising gooseflesh on your arms.

These places to hastily ride by on the way to somewhere bright…

Godforsaken Places.

Haunted Places.

> *'We all of us start out knowing magic….*
> *But then we get that magic educated right out of our souls'*
>
> Robert R McCammon – *'Boy's Life'*

The fair county of Merseyside, where I was born and raised, although justifiably more famous for its picturesque riverfront, its two successful football teams, and the time-enduring tunes of *'Four Lads Who Shook The World,'* has as rich a vein of 'ghostly lore' as anywhere else within these 'Enchanted Isles'. The briefest of glances through the pages of any work dealing with local folk-tales, urban legends and wild rumour, will reveal literally hundreds of stories concerning what, for want of a better term, we call 'paranormal phenomena'.

I recall during the now sadly distant days of childhood, greedily devouring such stories (along with *'Movie Monsters'* *''World Of Horror,'* and *'House Of Hammer'* magazines), at such a prodigious rate, it sometimes seemed my head would burst wide open with what *HAL*, the super-computer from Kubrick's *2001*, would doubtless define as 'Total Sensory Overload'), I was entirely captivated, not to say, deliciously frightened, by virtually every aspect of the subject from a very early age, and in truth, there were many things that served to instigate this obsession with the weird and macabre. One particular 'inspiration' that I can recall, with near-prefect clarity however, was the treasured reward I received for achieving top marks in my Reading Class, during my fourth year at Church Drive Primary School. I would have been about eight at the time and can remember I was barely able to contain my excitement when I was told I could have any book I wanted from the extensive library in the Main Assembly Hall, and I spent my entire dinner hour that day methodically wading through the hundreds of titles that lined the shelves. In the process, and without the assistance of any teacher, I learned a very valuable lesson: Choosing a book, when you can only pick the *one* is a very serious business, worthy of much deliberation.

By the time the bell rang for the start of the next period, I was still undecided between Thor Heyerdhal's *Kon Tiki Expedition*, a book on the lost tribes of the Amazon rainforest and a somewhat battered copy of a book called *Lancashire's Folklore, Ghosts and Legends*.

I finally plumped for the latter when Miss Chandler, the trendy young tutor, leaned over my shoulder, pointed a perfectly manicured, bright-red nail-varnished finger at the cover and said

> 'Oh, you'll *love* this, Lee. It's full of stories about Witches and Warlocks and Faeries and Goblins and people who reckon they can foresee the future! I have an idea someone with an imagination as vivid as yours will find this type of stuff absolutely fascinating!'

She smiled and I caught a faint whiff of her expensive perfume and felt the warmth of her breath on the nape of my neck and I experienced a funny sensation, like a horde of insects far too crawly to be mere butterflies, had suddenly hatched deep in the pit of my stomach.

> 'Honestly,'

…she insisted.

> 'You should give it a try'

I may only have been a boy of tender years whose only experience of 'the fairer sex' was that they were pretty adept in the art of trading ever-more disgusting insults in the school playground, but for the space of that single, endless moment, I had a inkling of how a knight in shining armour must feel when confronted with the sight of a swoon-some damsel in distress…I was so enchanted by Miss Chandler's unadulterated prettiness, I think I would have readily agreed if she'd have recommended *A Pictorial History of Hydraulic Actuators & Exhaust Valve-Timing Control For Internal Combustion Engines, Vol 93*, as being a rollicking rollercoaster of a good read.

It turned out she was right, of course. I was hooked from the first introductory page featuring Demons, Banshees, Faeries and Boggarts, and it proved to be the catalyst for everything that's followed ever since.

Not long after losing myself in the pages of this book, I started asking for horror novels and non-fictional works dealing with the occult and the supernatural for Christmas and birthday presents (along with the classic *Aurora Monster* model kits and cheap rubber Werewolf and Vampire masks).

Of course, not everyone approved of my all-consuming interest in the subject. It seemed I was constantly butting heads (in both a literal and figurative sense) with anyone who represented cold, hard reality, including the local hard-knocks who would laugh at anyone who wasn't interested in manly things like football and war films.

Many adults, too, including various teachers, friends and family members, warned against what they termed my *'unhealthy obsession.'* There were genuine concerns about my mental state, and I was forced to endure much shaking of heads and whispers that I might be a serial-killer in the making.

And something which occurred during the autumn of my penultimate year at Church Drive Junior School, a few months shy of my 11th birthday, will very probably provide irrefutable evidence that they were entirely right to worry about the influence of horror films and the occult upon my young, susceptible mind. I remember I was seated behind the graffiti-splattered desk top in Mrs Williams' Math Class, the day I first became acquainted with Forrest J Ackerman's seminal *Famous Monsters of Filmland* magazine.

It had been one of those eye-wateringly bright, windless afternoons; the sort that leave you feeling strangely restless, desperate for adventure, and escape from routine.

Trapped within the stuffy confines of the classroom however, the hours had dragged interminably, and the ringing of the Hometime Bell had seemed about a billion light years distant. As I recall, we pupils were supposed to be studying the myriad joys of long division and the twelve-times-table, but looking around, most of my fellow classmates had been either staring blankly into space or else were busy passing 'secret messages' to one another concerning the latest, hottest topical issues; the proposed government ban on 'Clackers,' the martial arts weapon of choice for the under-11, early 1970's generation, whether or not Karen Leathley really did have a virulent infestation of head lice (or *biddy's* as we used to call them back then), and the latest update on the progress of Jackie Morley's rapidly developing breasts were all making the major headlines back then, if my memory serves me correctly.

At the time however, I was more concerned with trying to ensure that old eagle-eyed Mrs Williams didn't catch on to the fact that I'd hidden the magazine I'd swapped with Ian Crossley for a *Wagon Wheel*, a packet of sweet-smelling *Parma Violets* and half a *Freddo Bar*, beneath a pile of tatty, dog-eared textbooks. Every time she turned her back to write another sum up on the blackboard, I would try to speed-read as much as I could without arousing her suspicion. *Famous Monsters of Filmland,* was one of those all-too rare publications that managed to fill the imaginative reader with a sense of wide-eyed wonder. Its pages were packed with crystal-clear stills and movie poster reproductions, fascinating facts and thought-provoking articles, all mixed together in an incredible, semi-organised mish-mash, not a little unlike the humble publication you hold in your hands, right now, dear reader.

Peering surreptitiously at its pages, the harsh fact of the mundanity of school-life, the sometimes soul-destroying passage of time between nine and three forty-five, was thrown into even sharper relief than was ordinarily the case, and my pulse raced with excitement as I stared wonderingly at the vast, dizzying array of words and images. You could call it a type of epiphany I suppose, but back then I knew only one thing for certain:

In the space of that single October afternoon, that craving for adventure had reached near insatiable levels.

But oh, like the respectable, mild-mannered Doctor Henry Jekyll after downing one of those smoky, bubbling, green-coloured potions, I soon discovered that there were to be some intriguing, not to say startling side-effects to be endured as a result.

And without wishing to come on like a latter-day Edward Van Sloan, stepping out from behind a set of velvet curtains to announce; in suitably sonorous tones;

'Mr Walker feels it would be a little unkind to present the following without just a word of friendly warning...'

I do feel duty-bound to state that having read what I'm about to relate, you may very well find yourself agreeing whole-heartedly with my former headmaster, the normally unflappable Mr Woodside, in calling for the Men-in-White-Coats to lock me in a padded cell with a packet of coloured crayons and an easy-to-read instruction pamphlet on Do-it-yourself basket-weaving.....

BY THE RED-GOLD GLOW OF OCTOBER

The Church Drive School Sports Day was held exceptionally late that year.

The summer of 1975 had been wet, windy and downright miserable (*some things, it seems, never change – dismal, crappy British summers are one of them*).

I remember it seemed I spent the entire six week's vacation gazing forlornly out of my bedroom window as torrents of rainwater went babbling along the gutters of Bolton Road East, and the net result of this constant downpour was that just about every field in the county was saturated to the point where they resembled the muddy hell of the pictures I'd seen of the Western Front back in 1916.

All official outdoor activities were subject to frequent delays and interruptions; The Port Sunlight Village Fete was postponed a grand total of nine times before the organisers finally conceded defeat and called it off altogether, and the New Ferry Fun Fair had to be cancelled in the interests of public health and safety, much to the dismay of both children and adults alike.

The rain didn't let up until September rolled around, but even then, it took the passing of several more weeks for the fields to drain sufficiently enough for the School Board to even consider the possibility of breaking with age-old tradition and hold the School Sports Day in the autumn. For the best part of a fortnight, the rumour mill went into overdrive, as pupils, teachers and local residents alike debated the prospects of the event taking place.

As it turned out, the Board gave the go-ahead and they were finally fixed for the second Friday in October, the eve of the half-term break.

The notoriously changeable weather permitting, of course

I guess most people were thrilled by this decision. Certainly, there was an almost Christmas-like atmosphere pervasive throughout the entire school that seemed to intensify as the event drew ever nearer. This high level of excitement might seem more than a little over-the-top to non-locals. I mean, it is true that The Port Sunlight School Sports Day wasn't ever going to rival The Olympics or the Commonwealth Games in terms of national importance or prestige.

To be perfectly honest, it wasn't even on a par with the Invalid Grandmother's *Stanna Chairlift* Finals.

It merely consisted of a series of contests most of which involved running with some sort of handicap, with (allegedly) hilarious results, ie; *'The Egg and Spoon Race,' 'The Sack Race,' 'The Three-Legged-Race'* and *The* er, *Running Quite Normally With No Real Hindrance Aside From Your Distinct Lack Of Fitness Race*, to name but a few.

Pool Bank, the largest field in Port Sunlight Village, was the favourite venue for this 'veritable feast of athletic prowess. The straight-(ish) lanes of the racetrack were marked out with white paint. There'd be a large marquee erected at one end from where you could purchase various refreshments; tea, orange juice and the like; several stalls selling everything from signed original artwork and hand-crafted pottery, to massive jars of home-made jam and marmalade. There was also a Winner's Podium; in reality, three wooden boxes covered with a slightly tattered Union Jack, which looked uncomfortably similar to the flag-draped coffins of fallen British soldiers.

The assembled crowds, mostly made up of the children's parents and other family members, would be herded behind a barrier of rope that stretched around the entire field, and from this vantage point they'd lustily cheer on their 'little darlings' (and on occasion, scream horrendous, foul-mouthed abuse at their kid's rivals) whilst some luckless soul who'd been 'volunteered' for the job of selling the photo-copied entertainment programmes, would move amongst them rattling a pink, plastic bucket.

The proceeds of these charitable donations would either go towards the United Reform Church Restoration Fund or the Teacher's Annual Christmas Piss-Up, depending on your level of cynicism.

Despite all this though, or maybe in some crazy way because of it, I'd still been looking forward to taking part in the event for which my best friend, Stevie Gee, and I had been selected: *'The Wheelbarrow Race.'*

Or at least I had been until two things happened in quick succession.

Firstly, the night before 'The Games', my mum and dad - who were always very liberal-minded where my watching horror films was concerned - allowed me stay up late to see the *Hammer* classic, *The Curse Of The Werewolf* (1961), starring the late, great, Oliver Reed (and not forgetting Michael Ripper, the wonderful, character actor, of course).

To say this movie had a profound effect upon me, would be like saying John Lennon had just the teensiest weensiest influence on the song-writing skills of Noel Gallagher.

I was transfixed from start to finish. The scene where the Werewolf (one of the most convincing lycanthropic creations ever thanks to the excellent make-up of Phil Leakey), breaks out its cell by tearing the door from its hinges and smashing it over the jailer's head, and then subsequently dashing across the village rooftops, raging at the assembled mob below, haunted my dreams later that night. Don't get me wrong. The movie didn't scare me much. On the contrary, I found myself actively rooting for the Werewolf, not least because here was a basically humble man, working in a local bakery, a slave to a meagre wage and the stifling constraints of 'civilised society', who defies the system by transforming himself (albeit involuntarily) into a wild animal – the primal, untamed beast within.

And having slipped the bonds of servility, this tragic/heroic figure is able to give free rein to the pent-up frustrations, the white-hot anger that burns within many of us who are doomed to eke out an existence on the very edge of the (excuse the pun) breadline.

I might not have truly understood these (admittedly) dime-store psychological insights back in my Junior School days, but I do remember thinking how truly wonderful it would be to have the means to rebel against our so-called 'betters', to stick two fingers up at authority figures, to embark upon a big, mad rampage along the 'corridors of power,' ripping to shreds the dusty piles of volumes containing the endless lists of rules and regulations mad by fat old men and women, keen to ensure the 'unwashed masses' are kept firmly in their place.

And as I lay awake on the wrong side of midnight, the only sounds the ticking of my Mickey Mouse alarm clock, and the gentle snoring of my brother in the bunk below me, I found myself more than simply *wondering* what it would be like to be afflicted with lycanthropy, but actually trying to dream up ways that I could become a real, living, breathing Werewolf.

I knew from some of the books I'd read, and films I'd seen, that there apparently were certain paths you could tread in order to achieve this admittedly unrealistic aim. (Hey, I *was* only ten years old!)

But some had the *'Sorry, Road Closed'* signs posted directly at their head.

For a start, my birthday is at the tail end of February, completely ruling out any church font-boiling, 'affront to God'-type scenario and the ensuing man-into-wolf curse that comes with being born on Christmas Day.

I could similarly dismiss the likelihood of my being bitten by another full-blown lycanthrope, seeing as how I couldn't claim to actually know of anyone who might have a propensity to undergo a lupine transformation every full moon (although I did have my suspicions regarding Mr Ambrose, our remarkably hairy supply teacher, who sometimes stood in when Mrs Williams was off ill. Certainly, the way his bushy black eyebrows knitted together above the bridge of his nose like a gigantic dead hairy caterpillar, could have been considered by some to be a dead giveaway).

And the thought of hanging around some desolate, mist-shrouded moor or sitting upon a fallen bough deep in the midnight woods, waiting patiently for a one hundred per cent genuine Werewolf to amble by, held no appeal whatsoever.

What was even more frustrating was that despite poring over countless *Plant Life of Britain* books, I'd failed to track down the likely location of any amount of flowering Wolfsbane[**]

That left only two other slightly less remote possibilities; The seeking of out of a Witch with a good working knowledge of Black Magic (even if he or she professed long and loud to only ever dabbling in *white*). For an unspecified price, she might be persuaded to cast a spell that would bring about the fulfilment of my dark desires.

Or, alternatively, I could simply don a fur cloak, parade around on all fours, and sample the blood of a freshly-killed animal – a squirrel, say, or a rabbit – and courtesy of the kind of sympathetic magic I'd read about in Sabine Baring-Gould's imaginatively titled *Book Of Werewolves,* quite literally *will* the transformation to take place.

That didn't really leave a whole pile of choice.

I finally drifted off to sleep that night dreaming of torch-wielding gangs, the terrified shriek of captured prey, and of a little boy straining at the bars that line his window, eyes bulging, teeth bared in feral fury as he snarls at a blood-red full moon....

****

The last Friday of the mid-Autumn term dawned clear and bright, instantly dispelling any remaining fears that the Sports Day would have to be cancelled yet again. Nearly everybody walked to school with a spring in their step that morning, even though the event itself didn't officially start until 1pm, and lessons were scheduled to carry on as normal right up until dinnertime.

I can't be sure, but I think we had double English first thing, and all I can clearly recall was that there was an air of barely repressed excitement and much wistful glancing at the clock on the far wall. I was excited, too, but for a far different reason. It was during the fifteen minute break that the second thing that I referred to earlier took place.

[**] According to ancient folklore, imbibing a potion made up of various parts of this wild plant, otherwise known as aconitum or Devil's Helmet, and which grows on mountainsides and high-altitude swathes of remote meadowland across Northern Europe, could induce lycanthropy.

It began with my announcing to a group of my best friends that I wouldn't be taking part in *The Wheelbarrow Race,* or in any other race for that matter, because I wanted to 'rebel against authority by going on 'a big mad one like Oliver Reed in that boss Werewolf film, last night.'

They didn't believe me, of course.

Why would they?

It was school policy that absolutely everybody had to play some part in 'The Games'. It was compulsory. No arguments. No dissent. You did as you were told and ran, skipped or hopped, you sold programmes or helped out with the chairs for the spectators who wanted to sit during the festivities….

You took part or you risked incurring the wrath of Mr 'Slappy' Harries, the Deputy Head, and the most feared teacher at Church Drive.

Oh, he might not have looked particularly menacing, at first glance. In fact, you could quite easily be forgiven for thinking he was one of those immensely kind-hearted, grandfatherly types, what with his bushy grey hair, tweed three-piece suit, and National Health glasses. Not to mention the Sherlock Holmes-type pipe that forever dangled from the corner of his mouth, its pleasingly woody fragrance hanging about him in swirly clouds.

But if ever there was a living, shining example of that hoary old cliché; 'appearances can be deceptive,' then Mr Slappy H provided it in spades.

As quick to anger as an especially irate buffalo afflicted with piles. As stern as the expressions on any of the US President's heads carved into the rock of Mount Rushmore. More mean-spirited than a snidey-arse combination of The Sheriff of Nottingham, Cruella De Ville deprived of her 101 Dalmatian-skinned coats, and Ebenezer Scrooge prior to his Christmas Eve 'conversion.'

The tales of those who had foolishly crossed the Deputy Head in some way had passed into the realms of school folklore. I don't propose to relate a whole bunch of incidents here, but I guess I'll make do with telling you that he'd been christened with the nickname 'Slappy' not just because he was as bald as the proverbial coot, but it was also due to the fact that he kept an old battered training shoe, a good size twelve or so, in the locked drawer of his desk. Its tread had been long since worn baby-cheek smooth by the frequent visits it had paid to the smarting backsides of those who had somehow transgressed THE LAW ACCORDING TO MR SLAPPY-BY-GOD-HARRIES, (and I often imagined a whole series of tenets, each of them engrave upon a chunky tablet of stone, and these Commandments would be stacked at the very back of the store cupboard in Mr Harries's classroom, and would feature everything from;

- Thou shalt never deface the cover of one's precious exercise book, and
- Thou shalt refrain from walking faster than a snail with a buggered hamstring along the corridors, to
- Thou shalt never raise one's voice above the merest fragment of a whisper when class is in session, and
- Thou shalt never utter words of cheek and damned impertinence when ordered to play rugby in ones underpants and a three-sizes-too-small, Billy-No-Make footy shirt from Lost Property, in the gonad-chilling depths of mid-winter, just because one's forgot one's sport shorts).

No wonder then that even the most aggressive of the school hard-cases strove to keep a low-profile when in his presence.

And yet, here I was, confidently assuring my friends, that I was intending to actively *seek* a confrontation with 'Slappy', by simply refusing point blank to participate in one of the most important dates in the school calendar.

Little wonder then that when I revealed my plans to each and everyone of my circle of friends, they regarded me with a mixture of outright scepticism and dark foreboding. Mikey Cartwright had given voice to the general consensus of opinion when he'd loudly exclaimed,

> "God, Slappy's gonna end up shooting you with that bleedin' starting pistol of his!"

The words had hung in the still October air, and I remember my friends had suddenly bowed their heads sorrowfully, as though they were standing gathered at the graveside of an old and trusted companion, which come to think of it, in their mind's eye at least, they kind of *were*.

I'd be lying if I said that I wasn't scared at this point. Nevertheless, I was determined to prove to everybody that I was not going to back down, that I had succeeded in adopting, the bestial, untamed attitude of a modern-day Werewolf. But still, the nagging question remained; How would I go about going the whole hog and taking on the appearance of a transformed lycanthrope?

An answer, of sorts, presented itself just as the chimes of the school bell signalled the end of first break. We began shuffling unenthusiastically toward the slope that led up to the row of classrooms, and it was as we were passing the grassy bank that formed three sides of the sunken playground, that I caught sight of the body of a dead pigeon lying amidst a pile of soggy autumn leaves.

Acting on some sudden, crazy impulse, I turned and scrambled half-way up the bank, the smell of wet earth and mouldy leaves filling my nostrils. I only paused momentarily to glance over my shoulder, when I'd reached the bird's carcass, and smiled to myself at the sight of the shocked faces of my friends, who'd stood frozen, their mouths open in a series of comical O's.

I bent down to study the dead pigeon more closely, and could see straight away that it had been killed fairly recently. It was stone cold to the touch, but it didn't smell too bad, and judging from the fact that there was a great gaping hole in its side, through which I glimpsed a set of glistening red innards and tiny slivers of bone, it was clear that the bird had met its end at the hands, or rather claws, of a predator, most likely a cat.

To this day, I have no firm idea of the motivation behind what I did next. The only half-arsed explanation that I've ever been able to come with is that I was 'inspired' by the vague recollection of a publicity still from *Curse Of The Werewolf*. It featured the lycanthrope as a slightly less-than-innocent child, a dead squirrel in his hands, droplets of blood dripping from his pointed, too-sharp teeth.

Did I, by some perverse sense of logic, imagine that I could transform myself into a Werewolf simply by chowing down on an already half-eaten pigeon? Yes, I think I truly did.

And so, as loony toons as it undoubtedly sounds, and with roughly half my class now stood watching in barely repressed horror from the top of the slope, I picked up the weightless bundle of feathers raised them to my mouth, and without even a moment's hesitation, bit deeply into the already gaping wound.

How I kept from immediately vomiting all over my school kecks will always remain a complete mystery to me. Even though this incident took place thirty-odd years ago (and two whole decades before I became a pretty strict vegetarian), I can still remember how indescribably awful those slimy, jelly-cold pigeon guts tasted on my tongue.

How they crunched between my teeth as I unthinkingly chewed.

How they slithered down my throat in one congealed lump, like a nest of dead entangled worms.....

I don't mind admitting I only took the one bite before raising the carcass above my head in a gesture of triumph and offering up what I hoped would pass for a dead-bird's- bowel's-simply-melt-in-my-mouth grin.

The expressions of surprise on the watching crowd had instantly turned to uniform disgust, and the air was rent with a chorus of 'Oh, *eeeeeewwwwghh's*' that were only silenced when Mrs Pierce, the English Language teacher, appeared at the school entrance and ordered everyone to head for their respective lessons, immediately.

> "And will Lee Walker, kindly put down that pigeon, get off the bank, and go and wash his hands thoroughly before he dares set foot in *my* class!"

…she shouted in a voice that brooked no argument.

I made a great show of reluctantly placing the bird back amongst its makeshift grave of fallen sycamore leaves, although in truth, I don't think I've ever been more relieved to see an authority figure arrive to take charge of a situation. As my fellow pupils began to drift away, some of them shaking their heads in disbelief, others making loud barfing noises, only a few of which actually sounded forced, I slowly made my way down the bank, and sauntered across to the boy's toilets, all the while whistling like I didn't have a care in the world. I'm not at all sure quite how I made it to the sanctuary of the loo without puking *en route*, but I'd barely locked the cubicle door behind me before I heaved into the lavatory bowl, the flood of steaming bile gushing with such force, I'd thought my neck would explode.

I was doubled over like that, spewing until there was positively nothing left to sick up, my stomach aching (like the time Mr Harris had 'accidentally' dropped a medicine ball on my belly when we doing sit-up exercises in the school gym), for what seemed like an impossibly long time.

When at last I managed to stagger from the toilet, sucking furiously on a couple of aniseed-flavoured Gob-stoppers I'd found at the bottom of my Liverpool FC satchel, I felt so light-headed I'd seen hundreds of tiny spots dancing like black dust motes before my eyes.

No one said anything when I set foot in the classroom. Not even Mrs Pierce. She merely glanced at me disdainfully from over the top of her horn-rimmed glasses, sniffed loudly, and with a sharp nod of her head indicated that I should sit down and get on with my work.

I was only too happy to at least pretend to comply. As I took my seat next to Ian Crossley, who didn't even look up from the essay he was preparing on Melville's classic *Moby Dick*. I was filled with the sure and certain knowledge that I had somehow succeeded in making a point: That I would openly defy the accepted order of things. That I would openly rebel against the norm. Even if that meant the inevitable, direct confrontation with Mr Harries; *The Demon Arse-Slapper Of Church Drive*….

****

The minute our class filed onto the sports field that chilly, sunbright afternoon, it was clear we'd have a record attendance for the games, that year.

> "Bloody hell, it looks like half the county's turned up"

Ian Crossley muttered under his breath, and even the normally impassive Dale Scott, (a tall, rangy lad, who during a school trip had famously dismissed the ancient Roman remains at Chester, as being nothing more than 'a crumbling pile of owld bricks') gave a low whistle of incredulity.

Ordinarily, you could expect, at best, a hundred 'supporters' to be stood behind the lines of rope that bordered the racetrack, and indeed, there had been occasions when the number of competitors far outweighed the amount of spectators. Not this time, however. There were groups of 'fans' standing in rows twenty or so deep, all around the field, so even by the most conservative of estimates, there must have been somewhere in the region of 500 people present at Pool Bank, that day.

Later, teachers and pupils alike would speculate on the reasons for this uncommonly large turn-out, and most would conclude that it was due to the combination of fine weather and the fact that so many other planned local events had been cancelled during the summer-that-never was.

There was perhaps, one other factor, too.

Something I neglected to mention earlier: All of those taking part, myself included, were not just competing for themselves. They were supposed to be representing four separate teams or 'Houses', namely; Eaton, Lever, Walker (nothing to do with yours truly) and Nairn.

At each of the previous four Sports Days, Eaton, the House to which I belonged, had emerged victorious, and as never before in the school's history had any team succeeded in winning 'The Title' five years on the trot, so the level of interest in the 1975 Games had been greatly increased.

For once, the assembled adults had not simply gathered to support their own prepubescent sons and daughters in some ultimately meaningless race. Instead, as former pupils of the school, they'd come to cheer or hurl insults (depending on their allegiance), at the members of the Eaton team, collectively itching, though they'd never admit as much to an outsider, to see if the record would remain intact or be well and truly broken.

We each had to report to the large tent that dominated the field to pick up our house bibs (Eaton's were coloured a decidedly sickly shade of yellow), along with our timetable of events.

The Wheelbarrow Race wasn't scheduled to start until round about 3:30pm, so there was nothing for it but to hang around and pretend to take an interest in 'The Games'. I went and stood with my friends near to the finishing line, and watched as Eaton made a more than promising start. They won *The Egg & Spoon Race, The Sack Race,* and the *Running Really Quite Fast Race*, with some ease, and came a creditable second in *The Three-Legged Event*. The excitement was building with each positive result for Eaton, and by the time *The Crab Football Tournament* was about to get underway, it was clear that only a calamitous loss of form in the last three events could conspire to rob our House of total victory.

And so it was that I found myself lustily screaming my encouragement during the games immediately prior to my planned non-appearance in that blasted *Wheelbarrow Race*. The thought of my being solely responsible for the team's failure to retain the title and achieve the record, was not a pleasant one.

When our closest rivals, Lever, almost drew level by winning the next couple of events, I have to admit I began to harbour serious misgivings concerning my refusal to take part.

Especially, seeing as how, amidst the uproar that greeted the Lever team's most recent successes, I'd caught sight of my Mum engaged in animated conversation with Stevie Gee's parents near the front of the crowd.

Yeah, looking back now, I honestly think things would have turned out a whole pile differently if it hadn't have been for a chance snidey remark courtesy of Wayne Williams, the obligatory class creep.

> "Well, there you go,"

…he grinned, the slimy grin of a politician out canvassing for votes.

> "I told yer Lee was gonna shit out when it came right down to it, didn't I?"

There was a general murmur of agreement from amongst those standing within earshot, and even Stevie Gee began to look hopeful that I had undergone a change of heart, as we were ushered towards the starting line by Mr Evans, the PE teacher.

> "Come along now, boys,"

…he ordered the competitors.

> "Time to show this crowd what you can do!"

> "Yeah, go for it, Lee!"

Wayne 'Creepozoid' Williams sniggered, tipping me a wink as I passed him by.

> "Hope scoffing that dead pigeon doesn't slow you down too much!"

And that was all it had taken to strengthen my rapidly weakening resolve.

My body had shuddered with a spasm of near uncontrollable anger, the world had swayed slightly out of focus, and from that moment on, an air of unreality had washed over me. Everything seemed to occur in a series of vivid, dream-like sequences, the memory of which has remained imprinted on my mind ever since:

> *The eight competitors traipse up to the Starting Blocks, their tense expressions eerily reminiscent of the ranks of American soldiers in the jungles of Vietnam, I'd once seen in a newspaper photograph, their faces etched with grim determination, as they marched stoically towards some unseen enemy…*

When they reach their allotted 100 metre lanes, Mr Harries, imposing even dressed in a tweed cap and skin-tight Adidas track suit, relates the rules and orders everyone to get into position. The excited babble of the spectators increases in intensity. I catch sight of my mum again and she waves enthusiastically, and offers a thumb's-up for good luck. I favour her with a half-hearted smile in response. The respective teams adopt their 'wheelbarrow' stance and Stevie Gee drops to the ground, the fingers of his hands splayed on the soft, green earth. He cocks one leg, like a dog about do its business, and glances over his shoulder to see why it is I haven't grabbed hold of the proffered 'handle'.

He opens his mouth to speak, but at that moment Mr Harries raises his air pistol, points it skywards and shouts:

> "On your marks! Get set! Wait for it! Wait for it! GO!"

The curiously flat-sounding gunshot is all but lost amid the wild cheering of the crowd as the three other teams go hurtling down the track in a mad dash for the Finish Line.

But I only stand there, rooted to the spot. As stubbornly immobile as the metal climbing frame in the school playground. The race reaches its conclusion, and the winners are mobbed by delighted supporters, but after a minute or so of celebration, the cheering becomes more sporadic, then gradually fades to a stunned silence. And for a while everything seems to stand still. No one says or does anything and I swear it's so quiet, I can hear the fallen leaves blowing along Pool Bank Road, their dry crackling, the sound of a dead and mirthless laughter.

I find myself staring into the middle distance, curiously detached from 'The Main Event.'

A plane drones drowsily overhead. A solitary magpie struts arrogantly along the path that leads to the entrance gate. And in one of the allotments at the edge of the field, a middle-aged man in a white baseball cap stands lighting a bonfire, the thin wisps of wood smoke spiralling into an autumn sky so cloudless, it's a convincing deception of June's soft blue.

Predictably, it's Mr Harries who shatters the silence. He bellows with rage as he stomps towards me.

> "What the hell do you think you're playing at, boy?"

…he screams into my face: a hurricane-force gale whooshing through a half-open window.

But incredibly, I am entirely unfazed by his anger. Unafraid of retribution. For once, his words carry all the weight of the ash-flakes drifting across from Mr Baseball Cap's bonfire, and the teacher's expression of bewildered disbelief at my refusal to begin quaking in my trainers, is something that will live with me if I live to be a hundred.

And when I curl my lip and actually snarl at him (a not half-bad attempt at a Lon Chaney Jr./Oliver Reed Werewolf impression), the bowel-looseningly terrifying Mr Harries backs away from me. The movement is so brief it's likely few if any of the onlookers even notice, but the fact remains, I see it. And in the space of the two or three seconds it takes for the teacher to regain his composure, I see something else.

I see him as he really is.

A lonely, embittered old man in a cloth cap and a faded blue tracksuit, who has maybe another couple of years tops, before he has to take involuntary retirement, the prospect of which fills him with the deepest, darkest dread.

I know, even as a child, I know nothing that Mr Harries can do or say, now or in the future can ever serve to terrify me the way it had during my previous three years at Church Drive. His power over me had always been due to the fact that he had always appeared to be some sort of inhuman, indestructible monster, as all-seeing, and as all-knowing as The Wicked Witch of the West or The Dark Lord in Tolkien's *Lord of the Rings*.

To suddenly learn that he was every bit as insecure, fallible and yes, downright scared as the rest of the us, was a shock that was right up there with finding out that Santa Claus didn't exist or hearing that Bill Shankly[**] had decided to call it a day as manager of Liverpool FC, but it certainly doesn't take me long to exploit the discovery.

I snarl loudly once more, then turn and run away from the race-tracks, away from the crowds, away from Mr Harries, not because I am afraid, but because I'm filled with a wild exultation, the giddying excitement that comes from openly defying convention and the accepted order of things. I run to the outer limits of the sports field, leap over the entrance gate, almost sending a couple of programme sellers flying as I do so, and scramble up one of the ancient, venerable-looking oak trees that line Pool Bank.

Once I've secured a decent vantage point, roughly three-quarters of the way from the uppermost branch, I turn to look back at the scene below me. Virtually everyone is standing around in obvious confusion. But several people, my school friends amongst, them, begin walking over towards me, some of them laughing, others, including Stevie Gee, more than a little angry, (it turned out that Eaton had managed to retain the trophy, but only because the result of the Wheelbarrow Race, won by Lever, was declared to be invalid due to my lycanthropic shenanigans).

Some of my friends try to encourage me climb down and 'face the music,' but I refuse to budge, even when my Mum comes across and tries to order me out of the tree, warning of dire consequences if I refused to do so.

And I stay put, snarling and growling at a school prefect who attempts to climb the oak so that he backs off, shaking his head and muttering,

"Oh, friggin' hell, just leave him up there. Worra tit. He's totally off his cake!"

Neither Mr Harries, nor any of the other teachers come near me, but a bunch of giggling girls saunter by, Jackie Morley, she of The Incredibly Expanding Gazangas fame, amongst them. She stares up at me, her eyes filled with a sense of pre-teenage wonder at my 'heroics'. And when she suddenly cracks a smile for my benefit, it's like seeing the sunrise after a cold, dark stormy night. The brilliance of it warms me, long after the crowds have drifted away, and the chill of autumn twilight finds me alone, teetering on the brink of a perverse sense of 'greatness.'

[**] William "Bill" Shankly, OBE (2 September 1913 – 29 September 1981) was a Scottish football player and manager, most noted for managing Liverpool between 1959 and 1974. One of Britain's most successful and respected football managers, Shankly was also a fine player whose career was interrupted by the Second World War. He played nearly 300 times in The Football League for Preston North End and represented Scotland seven times, as well as playing for Partick Thistle and Carlisle United.

Oh, of course, I am more than aware that I will soon be forced along the winding path to Inevitable Retribution and Punishment, and that when I eventually reach that destination, I'll very likely be chewed up and spat out like a stick of gum that's long since lost its flavour.

But for the briefest of moments, I know something of how it feels to be a true anti-hero; Robin Hood, Zorro, Count Dracula, The Incredible Hulk, The Frankenstein Monster, *THE WEREWOLF*.

And I find that I don't regret a single action, even at the dog-end of this seemingly endless day.

By the time I finally climb down from my perch, and begin the long walk home, the sun has already slipped around the tops of the trees, scattering claw-like shadows across the pavement.

And it seems as though the whole world is bathed in the red-gold glow of October....

THE SHARDS OF A BROKEN SPELL

*'Where the hills are fog, and the rivers are mist,
and the people passing at night on the empty walks sound like rain'*

Ray Bradbury

The October Country

ONE

Predictably, there were some pretty severe consequences to be faced in the wake of this incident.

My Dad, when he heard about it, confiscated every single one of my paperback horror novels, monster models and well-thumbed magazines. He even took away my *Brook Bond PG Tips* Prehistoric Animals album and my collection of cardboard *Dr Who* characters, the ones that came free with special boxes of *Weetabix*.

He also asked me to go down to the bottom of the garden to fetch a 'Whipping Stick.'

"And son,"

…he said, looking me squarely in the eye,

"I'm telling yer now, before you go, if you don't come back with one I think is big and sturdy enough, I'll go and get one!"

You know, looking back now, it seems I spent an unreasonably large portion of my childhood howling in squinty-eyed agony as penance for some minor (and okay, not so *minor*) misdemeanour or other.

But as painful as the punishment was, it couldn't hope to dissuade me from continuing to pursue my all-consuming obsession with monsters, ghosts and all manner of things macabre for long. Nor would it prevent me from constantly getting into various forms of trouble as a consequence, either, although it's safe to say I at least managed to keep my 'werewolf tendencies' firmly in check for the remainder of my school-days and beyond, even on the occasions I'd awoken to find myself bathed in the silvery slabs of a full moon.

The prospect of traipsing slowly down to my father's woodpile to select another 'whipping stick' with all the grim finality of a Death Row prisoner on a one-way trip to the electric chair, served to cure me of that affliction...

Students of Lycanthropy please take note: Here was one 'werewolf' who hadn't needed to rely on the services of an impossibly ancient gypsy crone and the casting of a complicated spell to lift the curse or be fortunate enough to win the pure, unconditional love of a fully-fledged virgin to quell the raging beast within.

A simple, sturdy common or garden stick had proven more than sufficient.

TWO

I think it was the following spring, mid-way through the Easter School Holidays, that my brother Grant and I got together with a bunch of like-minded friends to form a club we christened, with a quite magnificent display of originality:

'The New Ferry Horror Club'

The word 'club' however, was very quickly substituted for the far more estimable-sounding **Society,** the high falu-tin' ideals of youth decreeing if we really wanted to be taken seriously, we had to have a name that people, even supposedly know-it-all-adults, would consider at least half-way reputable. The kind of moniker that anyone who had the misfortune to suddenly find themselves being plagued by a hyperactive poltergeist, haunted by a demonic spirit from the *Ninth Circle Of Dante's Inferno*, or been abducted by sinister bug-eyed aliens for some nefarious purpose on a nightly basis, would confidently contact us for assistance, aware that our no nonsense attitude would burn through the labyrinth chicanery of other group's paranormal politics like a cigarette through a screen of silk....

..and in my mind's eye, I remember I always imagined a middle-aged couple, man and wife most likely, sat facing each other across the kitchen table in the harsh, unforgiving glare of a naked light bulb. Clearly they are at their wits end; The man struggling vainly to retain some modicum of composure, whilst his good lady sat, visibly shaking and on the verge of outright hysteria.

'What can we do?' she wails between sobs, wringing her hands in utter desperation. 'What can we do? Dear God, won't somebody help us, pleeeese?'

The husband, scruffily bearded and with greasy strands of greying hair dangling above a pair of eyes that haven't known restful sleep for weeks on end, sighs wearily and reaches into his trouser pocket to pull out his battered leather wallet. He withdraws a business card, stares intently at the address and phone number printed on it for a few silent seconds, and then, his mind made up, he pushes his chair back and gets quickly to his feet. He goes over to his wife, places his hand on her trembling shoulder and whispers reassuringly; 'Don't worry, love. I'm going to get us some help!'

She looks up at him expectantly, and dares to hope, but before she can say anything, the husband makes for the hallway and the old-fashioned, pinned-to-the-wall telephone, an Edwardian replica his granddaughter had bought him last Christmas, when all the world had seemed bathed in the rosy glow of bright expectation and the terror that had somehow crept into their lives had lain hidden, dormant, unimagined and undreamed of even in their darkest nightmares...

He lifts the receiver and prepares to dial...

The membership of our venerable organisation constantly chopped and changed with all the regularity of a political party's series of pre-election pledges, although the 'hardcore', which included my brother, Grant, and my two best friends at the time, Steve Gee, and resident sceptic, Philly Bennett, remained pretty much constant across the span of years that marked the transition from the comparatively carefree days of primary school, to the worry-fraught, angst-ridden lot of 'The Teenager'. It was heartening in the extreme to be able to form relationships with people who shared an obsession that we had initially believed to be mutually exclusive

Our Dad allowed us to convert the wood shed he'd built a few years earlier at the bottom of our garden into our Club-house, and it wasn't long before we'd plastered the walls with horror movie posters, stacked comics and magazines in haphazard piles for reading on rainy days, and installed our very own *Supernatural Library,* which initially consisted of four or five books, but which rapidly grew in size over the years until the cold winter of 1981, when I awoke early one morning to find our Grant burning the vast majority of them on a paraffin-soaked bonfire in the centre of my Dad's redundant vegetable plot directly opposite the club-house (*the reasons behind this dramatic method of disposal will become apparent in due course, Dear Reader*).

With the typically chauvinistic mindset of boys who had yet to discover the wonderfully pleasurable aspects of female company and therefore still believed them to be a complete and utter bothersome nuisance to be avoided at all costs, we adopted a strictly *No Girls Allowed* policy.

This exclusion especially extended to my then seven-year-old sister, Kearry, and whoever her 'bestest girl friend' happened to be at the time, (this nearly always seemed to be Adele Harrison, a near-neighbour who in her teenage years would blossom into a curvaceous beauty, with a penchant for wearing revealing halter tops and strapless bras and having her bare shoulders tickled with the feathery fronds of a woodland fern – but that's another story for another time!) They were constantly refused membership, despite their increasingly strident demands they be granted admission (which usually involved them banging on the door of the club-house, repeatedly stamping their feet and bawling like a couple of hideously off-kilter air raid sirens, all to no avail).

Not even the eventual intervention of my Dad, who, as the handing out of 'The Old 'Go And Gerra Stick Method Of Punishment' proved, could be very persuasive when he wanted to be, could force our hands concerning the No Female policy, as the following proves...

"Excuse me, lads,"

...he'd once shouted to us from the half-open extension window after our Kearry had gone running to him in floods of tears, one typically showery late-April morning.

"Would you care to join me inside for a few moments for a brief discussion?"

We'd each of us known, immediately, that this was by no means a casual invitation for a good old cheery chin-wag. His tone of voice may have been genial enough, but in reality this was a fully-fledged *order* that we didn't dare disobey, and the 'NFHS' members present that day, Grant, Philly, Stevie Gee and myself had dutifully gathered in line in the middle of my parents' living room like soldiers on parade.

My Dad was sat with his arms folded, perched on the arm of the large leather sofa that dominated that room, and it's strange the seemingly inconsequential things you remember on such ominous occasions, but I can still see in my mind's eye, as clearly as though it were yesterday, the way the early spring sunlight spilled through the white-laced curtains and glistened on the rain-soaked bunch of freshly-cut flowers my mum had picked earlier that day.

"Right, okay, are we all here?"

...he'd asked, miming a quick head count, as if he needed to mentally check whether an errant member of our Society had somehow gotten himself lost en route to the meeting.

"I've called you all here to announce that your sister and her friend have made me aware of your arguments regarding your club's current membership rules."

He paused, for what he no doubt intended to be dramatic effect, before adding;

> "I've decided to be fair and democratic in respect of this issue and give you boys a choice: And it's simply this: Either you let your sister and her mate join, or I'll knock down yer club-house by using yer heads as a set of wrecking balls!"

He'd smiled a smile that never touched his eyes, and then said pleasantly enough

> "Now boys, how does that sound?"

Philly had seemed anxious to point out that my Dad hadn't quite seemed to have grasped the concept of what constituted true 'democracy' in this country, but I nudged him in the ribs in mid-flow, sure that a heated debate concerning the differences between democracy and dictatorship at that point was likely to result in the **'Site Closed For Immediate Demolition'** signs going up on the door and shuttered windows of our HQ.

Instead, I'd quickly piped up with a suggestion that we could maybe compromise by allowing the girls to join our Society if they could prove themselves worthy by answering just a few simple questions on famous horror movies, or, in the unlikely event that they failed the quiz, they could take an undemanding and entirely painless physical 'Horror Test' of the sort anyone with the remotest interest in the subject would accept with a smile and a dismissive shrug of the shoulders.

> "All the boys who've joined our Society have had to pass *both* tests, but we'll only expect the girls to pass *one* of them,"

I said in my most reasonable voice.

> "Is that okay with you, Dad?"

My Father, keen to be seen as an even-handed arbiter, readily agreed that this was indeed fair and square, and we all shook hands with him to seal the agreement like real men, and filed slowly out of the living room without another word.

When we stepped back out into the garden, the rain clouds had all but vanished completely and the sun was beating down from a sky so impossibly blue, it seemed ready to shatter into a million pieces. Kearry and Adele were standing over by the bird table in the centre of the sparkling lawn, looking insufferably smug and self-satisfied, the way only seven-year-old girls can. They nudged each other as we walked past, and one of them - Adele, I think it might have been - was unable to suppress a giggle that spoke of a great victory already achieved.

> "Well, ladies,"

I'd said in my best Peter Cushing playing Baron Frankenstein voice,

> "...if you really wish to join our esteemed Society, please follow me."

Linking arms, as though they were marching gloriously towards some long-denied entitlement, (which I suppose, in their seven-year-old minds, they kind of *were*), they followed us to our headquarters.

THREE
THE CREEPING, CRAWLING TERRORS OF THE SPIDER ROOM

The Spider Room was a 'chamber of unspeakable horrors' that consisted of several planks of wood and some rusty sheets of corrugated iron we'd scavenged from the tip at the far end of our road being nailed together to corner-off a section of our club-house. There was a single thick wooden board that served as a door that could be secured with a padlock that looped through a rather clumsily attached bracket, (both of which we'd nicked without permission from my Dad's wood shed), and the only other entry to the 'room' was via a trap door up on the flat, plastic-sheeted roof. There was a set of step-ladders permanently leaned up against the side of our den which we used on the rare occasions we needed to use this method of entry.

The room had been built, unbeknownst to my Dad, with one purpose in mind: To ascertain the suitability of a prospective new member: If a candidate gave the correct answers to the aforementioned oral exam they had to spend a full five minutes trapped in *The Spider Room* whilst they were showered, via the trap door, with all manner of creepy-crawlies, not just spiders, or even insects (although there *were* plenty of them, to be sure), but earthworms, slugs, snails, even the occasional frog or toad, if we could get our hands on them), without begging for release. If they failed either test, and so far no one had, they were immediately back-heeled on the grounds that they were either sorely lacking in the requisite knowledge of all things horrific or worse, were so scared of a few relatively tiny insects they couldn't possibly be trusted to take part on our planned expedition to the Matto Grosso in the depths of the Amazonian rainforest to search for surviving dinosaurs. (We'd all read about or seen on TV natural history programmes the huge bird-eating spiders, giant, poisonous millipedes and endless, unstoppable armies of soldier ants that thrived amidst the countless miles of thick, steaming jungle, so there was definitely no place for the kind of coward who would squeal like a baby if a tiny weevil happened to run over their shoe).

Prior to these initiation ceremonies taking place, the NFHS founder members would spend an hour or so looking under rocks and stones for earwigs and centipedes, raid the rotten, crumbling posts of next door's garden fence for woodlice and pluck the fattest, hairiest spiders direct from the centre of their intricately-woven webs. Once we'd collected enough (and 'enough' could be anything from a couple of squirmy handfuls to Biblical-Plague-size-portions, depending on how heartlessly cruel we were feeling towards the candidate at the time), we'd place them in empty tins of my dad's discarded *Castella* cigar containers, and drill holes in the lids to allow the assorted insects to be able to breathe. It was important for us to ensure they remained alive and wriggling for the duration of the ordeal, you see. We knew from past experience that showering someone with the dried-out husks of dead beetles and curled-up arachnids didn't have anywhere near the same scream-inducing effect as lively, constantly squirming ones. Especially in the near-total darkness of *The Spider Room.* They got under your hair and skittered across your scalp, driving you, if you'll pardon the pun, bug-crazy trying to scratch them out, or else they raced across your cheek and down the back of your neck or even horror of horrors, crawled between your lips as you opened your mouth to scream....

Of course, I could only *imagine* how any of that must have felt, because the privileges of being a founder member of the Society meant that I never had to actually undergo the ordeal myself.

Unlike the two unfortunate young ladies who had all-too willingly marched towards their date with destiny on that rain-washed, April morning.

*****

At first, of course, Kearry and Adele must have been so supremely confident they'd already as good as joined. They were very probably picturing the glorious moment when they would be sitting alongside us in the club-house, taking great delight in watching us fume with righteous indignation as they made typically 'girly' suggestions for improving the décor of our HQ, which doubtless involved the inclusion of sweet-smelling flowers, *'Tiny Tears' Dolls* and huge posters of *Jimmy Osmond, David Cassidy* and *The Bay City Rollers.*

As they stood at the entrance to the club-house, still linking arms, and with big happy smiles beaming on their lightly freckled faces, I almost felt a twinge of sympathy and prescient regret for them.

Almost

But then Adele suddenly opened her mouth, popped in a bright pink *Anglo* penny bubbly, and began chewing with all the charm and sophistication of a manically masticating cow.

"So,"

...she said, blowing a large bubble to such extremes, it burst with a sound like a firecracker,

"What do you we have to do to join, then?"

"Yeah, we haven't got all day you know",

...my sister chimed in.

"And we can't wait to show you the ideas we've got for making the den so much, much nicer inside!"

That's all it had taken for any last remnants of pity and second thoughts to go wheeling away like a helium balloon torn from a child's grasp by a sudden gust of wind.

"You know what, you're right,"

I said, raising my hands like a carnival showman.

"Let's get this show on the road".

"Yes, let's!"

...the girls chorused

I quickly explained to them what everyone - my Dad included - had agreed at the meeting: they would have to pass one of two tests in order for them to ever set foot in the club-house, but that I had every confidence they'd easily sail through the first of these; the Horror Quiz, a mere three questions after all, 'El-lickety splitto, 'cos honest to God, the answers are so easy peasy, lemon-squeezy!

"Okay-so-fire-away,"

Adele piped up in a scornful, sing-song voice.

"Right you are",

I replied.

"Here's question number one:

What was the name of the famous Vampire played in the movies by both Bela Lugosi and Christopher Lee, and who once lived in a place called Transylvania?"

"Drack-leah!"

...they both answered without a moment's hesitation.

"*Slight* mis-pronunciation, there,"

I said,

> "...but yes, I think we can accept that as a being the right answer, can't we boys?"

I turned to my friends, who each nodded their confirmation.

> "Okay, that's a total thumbs up. An excellent start there, girls. Now, are you ready for question number two? It is a little bit harder?"

> "We're ready!"

> "Nice one. What's the name of the giant, green-skinned, fire-breathing lizard that enjoys stomping on various Japanese cities, usually Tokyo?"

> "Godzilla!"

Kearry yelled with the confidence of a gambler who is on a lucky roll, brimming with the certainty that they are just one short step away from winning the golden jackpot.

> "One hundred per cent correct!"

I announced.

> "Wow, you're doing really well, girls. You're almost there. How does it feel to be so very, very *close*?"

> "It feels great,"

Adele responded with something that sounded pretty close to genuine enthusiasm, and again my conscience was pricked for a second or two. Then she promptly blew another of those unfeasibly gigantic chewing gum bubbles, popped it even louder than before, and drawled:

> "So what's the question?"

> "Oh, I'm so glad you asked,"

I replied, struggling to keep the irritation out of my voice.

> "But please remember girls, I can only accept the first answer you give, so make sure you think long and hard before either of you shout out."

I paused, and then added:

> "Are you *sure* you're both ready?"

> "Yes,"

Kearry said puffing out her cheeks and swallowing a click in her throat, whilst Adele just rolled her eyes and mumbled something under her breath.

> "Alright. And don't forget, if you get this right, you're a fully-fledged member of The New Ferry Horror Society. But if you get this wrong, you'll have to take the second test: A stint in *The Spider Room* for the both of you!"

I paused dramatically for an imaginary drum roll to echo across the stillness as the late morning slid towards early afternoon..

And posed the final question....

> "Who were the joint executive producers of the original, 1933 version of King Kong?"

There was a moment of stunned silence, as their jaws worked in a vain attempt to articulate an answer they could never, in a million years, hope to even guess at, and then their faces suddenly crumpled, and on the verge of tears they found their voices to ask:

> "How the heck are we supposed to know *that?*"

> "Oh, come on, everyone who knows anything about horror, knows it's Merian C. Cooper and Ernest B Schoedsack!"

I said, as though I'd just asked them both to name the name of the horse in *Champion-The Wonder Horse.'*

> "But don't worry, ladies",

I continued.

> "You're not beaten yet....Please step this way."

I beckoned them across the threshold of the club-house for what would prove to be the first and only time.

*****

Several things changed forever in the space of the few short moments it took for us to tell my sister and her friend the rules of the test and for them to willingly step into *The Spider Room:* I can still see the mad sequence of events clearly in my mind, like a series of stills collected in an old photo album: The musty-smelling darkness into which Kearry and Adele entered. The door being firmly locked behind them with an audible click, a noise that sounded so *final,* before they could even hope to have second thoughts. The trapdoor in the roof being opened by Philly. Our Grant and I emptying four or five, jam-packed *'Castella'* tins worth of insects into the void. The ensuing fifteen seconds or so of pregnant silence.

And then the *screaming.*

A series of high, keening wails, that had us virtually tearing the padlock off and allowing the girls to career hysterically in a mad, blind panic along the garden path, leaving a trail of scuttling, wriggling, creatures in their wake...

How *many* were the ways in which things were truly and irrevocably altered from that moment on?

Let us *count* the ways....

> First off, we completely demolished *The Spider Room* in a frenzied attack, using a combination of lump hammers, monkey wrenches and crowbars, long before my Dad had a chance to make good on his threat to reduce it to splinters by introducing our fragile skulls to several thick planks of sturdy timber.

And once it was reduced to a pile of chopped and splintered wood, it never once crossed our minds to ever even think of rebuilding it.

Secondly, we immediately abandoned our NFHS *'Males Only Policy'* by unanimous, silent consent: The guilt and remorse reflected in the eyes of my brother and my assembled friends spoke a thousand times louder than any amount of raised *'Er, what the hell just happened there?'* chorus of voices/could ever hope to do.

Thirdly, and most importantly, a great and immutable truth was revealed to me that day: When we hurt the ones we love, there is always an unconscionable price to pay for our thoughtless actions.

Kearry (and for all I know, Adele), have since fallen victim to a fairly serious bout of Arachnophobia, an affliction that persists to this very day, and although my little sister is now all-grown up, happily married, and the proud mother of twin seven-year-old boys who are so life-affirmingly perfect they could stir the time-frozen pulse of a fossilised reptile, still, there are those times, whenever I'm lucky enough to be in her company that I can't help but notice the way her smile suddenly drops from her face like a camera shutter at the mere sight of a crane fly batting its wings and multi-jointed-wiry legs against the kitchen window pane in a futile bid for freedom or throw her hands over her mouth when confronted with the sight of a tiny money spider spinning its diaphanous web across the thorn-strewn stems of a rose bush...

There were other things, too.

We're not finished yet.

Not by a long chalk.

But we'll get to them in due course...

First though, let me tell you about The Murphy House....

NIGHTMARES AND DAYDREAMS

'Kaleidoscope of memories spin,
Like motes of time on faded film,
That plays on mind's eye silver screen,
An endless sequence of dark dreams...'

The Lids, *'In Dark Dreams'*

It would prove to be one of the biggest regrets of my formative years that we never actually got around to visiting many of the places featured in the seemingly never-ending catalogues of local 'Haunted Places' we had compiled after trawling through countless library books and listening with pinned-back lugholes to the stories spun by our fellow Merseysider's.

I want you to understand though, that was never due to any lack of enthusiasm on our part. Nor were we ever lacking the necessary courage to make any of these pilgrimages. When you get right down to it, I guess the truth of the matter was that back then, we simply believed every dilapidated, lonely-looking building we set eyes upon was very likely crawling with all kinds of hideously grinning spectres or forlorn, eternally wandering spirits. So really, what was the point in traipsing up and down the county, when there were at least two suitably eerie candidates right on our doorstep, so to speak. One stood at the bottom end of Woodhead Road, and came replete with a set of cracked, grime-covered windows, through which you could sometimes catch a blurry glimpse of a toothless old crone forever gazing out at the world, from the dubious comfort of a rickety rocking chair.

The other, just around the corner from my house, was in an even worse state of disrepair. Every square inch of it appeared to have decayed, gone bad from within, like an apple that's rotten to the core, and it was easy to believe no one had set foot in the place for decades.

My family and I knew differently however. Only a few months prior to the house falling into its state of terminal decline, it had been home to an elderly couple by the name of Murphy.

Mr John Murphy, a carpenter by trade, was held in high regard by just about every kid in the district, mostly because he simply loved making hand-crafted toys which he then gave away to all and sundry, usually at Christmas or upon the occasion of some kid's birthday, though he'd be just as likely to hand them out for the simple reward of seeing a child's face flushed with pure delight.

And he was always immaculately dressed. That was one of the things you immediately noticed about him. He always wore a spotless, perfectly-ironed shirt and tie and he had trouser creases so sharp you could chop old carrots with them.

Early one September morning, when I was just ten-years-old, Mr Murphy's wife, Doris, who he worshipped with a reverence that bordered on the evangelical, passed away whilst undergoing treatment for cancer at Clatterbridge Hospital, and almost overnight, his whole personality underwent the most dramatic of changes. He became something of a recluse, and on the rare instances he did venture outside, he looked dog-tired and his once-spotless clothes were badly crumpled as though they had frequently been slept in.

But most crucially as far as we kids were concerned, Mr Murphy stopped making toys.

I recall, (being too young then to truly understand or appreciate the profound sense of loss and unbearable despair that follows in the wake of the death of a loved one), asking my dad why kind old Mr Murphy hadn't returned my cheery wave whilst I was walking home from school one afternoon. My dad had smiled sadly, took me to one side and said in an uncharacteristically soft voice,

> "I don't think he meant anything by it, son. The truth is, he most probably didn't even see you."
>
> "What do you mean,"

I enquired, honestly perplexed.

> "Is he going blind, or something?"
>
> "In a way,"

...he said, and was silent for a long moment, before finally adding,

> "It's kind of hard to put into words, but I'm guessing that the day his wife passed away....Well, it's like the light went out in his eyes. And he doesn't see much past his precious memories anymore."

If I remained a little mystified by my Dad's somewhat cryptic (for a 10-year-old) explanation for Mr Murphy's strange behaviour, I had no trouble at all making sense of the contents of an overheard conversation between my parents, a few months later.

I remember I'd awoken in the middle of the night filled with a desperate need to go to the toilet. I'd glanced across at the luminous Mickey Mouse alarm clock that stood atop a pile of comic books and saw it was a little after one-thirty. I'd wondered if anyone else in the house was awake and strained my ears for the muted drone of the downstairs TV, but the only sound was the light snoring of my brother in the bunk directly below mine. I'd always considered it to be bordering on a form of parental abuse that the only loo was situated downstairs, necessitating a seemingly endless hike across the bedroom floor in a desperate search for the light switch.

(And how often did I imagine that as I reached my hand into the pitch black darkness, my fingers would encounter a row of incisor-like teeth, all slick and greasy as if fixed in a triumphantly leering grin? Or that as my bare feet trudged gingerly across the cold linoleum, I'd feel something skitter across my toes, a scurrying rat, a snake, or the hairy caress of a fat, bloated spider?)

I'd struggled manfully therefore to ignore the patently un-ignorable, but in the end I'd inevitably been faced with the stark choice that comes to all who awake with a full-to-bursting bladder in the dead of night; either tie a knot in it, soil one's bedclothes, or run the gamut of the gibbering horrors that lurk in the darkness.

And really, when you get right down to it, there's no actual choice at all.

I stumbled sleepily from my bed, ignored the light switch (just in case), tip-toed quietly onto the landing, and paused half way down the stairs when I realised I could hear the sound of my Mum and Dad talking in the front room, their voices hushed, but still clearly discernible.

And when I was able to catch a few words, enough anyway to make sense of what they were discussing, I suddenly forgot I needed the toilet.

I can't remember the precise details of the conversation, but the gist of it was this:

Old Mr Murphy, apparently overcome with grief, had locked his front door and bolted his windows firmly shut. He'd then opened a bottle of sherry and placed a photograph of his dear departed Doris, in the centre of his dining room table. God alone knows how long he'd sat there, nursing his drink and gazing longingly at the picture of his wife, but at some point, when the bottle was roughly three quarters empty, he'd climbed onto one of his intricately carved, hand-made chairs, tied a length of good strong rope into a noose, slipped it around his frail neck and kicked the chair out from under him.

The body wasn't found for the best part of a fortnight. That may seem a little hard to believe in this day and age, but his long period of self-imposed seclusion meant that no one really had any cause to miss him, and it was only when his next door neighbours became aware of an awful stench, 'like rotting fish mixed with week-old cat shit', emanating from The Murphy House, that people grew concerned....

This was a truly earth-shattering revelation, indeed.

With my hand clapped over my mouth, I waited for a few minutes before opening the living room door, so that my parents wouldn't suspect that I'd been secretly eavesdropping on them, and with a mumbled apology made my way to the loo.

It sounds awfully callous looking back now, but I have to say I could hardly wait to tell my friends this earth-shaking news the next day at school. You have to understand that I was just a kid who's number one ambition in life (alongside playing centre forward for Liverpool FC, and maybe succeeding in stealing a kiss off Jackie Moorely, upon whom I had a king-size crush at the time), was to come face to face with a real, honest-to-God ghost. I was convinced that according to the rules of 'supernatural logic', seeing as how Mr Murphy had committed the cardinal sin of taking his own life in such a melodramatic fashion, there was a better than even chance the premises would now be home to his unquiet spirit.

Here was something worthy of studying right on my proverbial doorstep.

Yes, indeed. No doubt about it. As far as The New Ferry Horror Club, were concerned, this was a red-hot, major news headline, and following its initial broadcast, for the next three weekends, we assembled at our headquarters, and whiled away countless hours drawing up various plans of action as to how we should set about investigating the case. The best, and it seemed, most sensible of these strategies; namely, camping out in the back garden of the house to conduct an all-night stake-out, was ultimately rejected as being unworkable, not least because no one we knew actually had a tent.

In the end, having exhausted all other possibilities, we were left facing an awkward but unavoidable truth; the only way we could satisfy ourselves that the house was truly haunted was to actually enter the now-empty (aside from any resident apparitions, of course) Murphy residence.

And so it was, at first light on an unseasonably cold Saturday morning, a week before school broke up for the Easter Holidays, the five founder members of our little group, my brother Grant and I, Steve Gee, Philly Bennett and Jason Barnes, gathered outside the disappointingly ordinary-looking house situated near the bottom end of Bolton Road East, and stood there for a good half hour, daring each other to open the front gate, and be the first to 'step across the threshold.'

It's fair to say that talking about making decisions and then actually getting round to acting on them, was one of our club's greatest failings, though it was true we'd spent the days leading up to this moment arming ourselves with all the necessary 'Ghost-hunting Caboodle'. This amounted to a set of white dinner candles my mother had bought at the height of the energy crisis of 1973, when electricity blackouts had become as common as 'Space Hoppers,' a silver-plated crucifix Philly had 'borrowed' from his sister's dressing table, a packet of salt (which my Famous Monsters Exorcist Special assured me was a hugely efficacious protection against the powers of evil), and a cassette recorder to capture on tape, should the opportunity arise, a message 'from the other side.'

We stood there for the best part of half an hour glancing nervously over our shoulders as the pale sun crept slowly over the far horizon. I knew each of us were silently praying that no one should happen to wander along and ask us what the hell we were up to, and it took the sound of the milkman's van slowly making its way down the next street for us to summon up the courage to push open the wrought-iron gate. I can't speak for the others, but I found it helped to kid myself that I was a latter-day Professor Van Helsing, as we made our way in single file around the rear of the building.

The garden was wildly overgrown with high, rank-smelling weeds, even this early in the season, and they all but obscured any obvious sign of a convenient point of entry. It was only when we carefully pushed a thick clump of mottled ivy aside that we eventually managed to locate a ground-floor window that was slightly ajar. Forcing it all the way open didn't prove too difficult, and we formed a queue to heave ourselves through into The Murphy House proper.

It seems more than a little ridiculous looking back now, but so wrapped up were we in accomplishing our Great Mission, the notion that there was anything remotely illegal about breaking into the premises in this way, never once crossed my mind. It was only later that evening, tucking into a bar of chocolate as I watched one of my favourite TV programmes, Starsky & Hutch, the two cooler than the Fonz cops hot on the trail of the bad guys, that I'd felt a sudden lurching in the pit of my stomach and nearly choked on my Curly Wurly. The realisation had belatedly dawned that if we'd been caught in The Murphy House, we would likely have been arrested, charged with burglary, and left facing a less-than delightful trip to the magistrates court. Worse, I'd found myself struck by the mental image of us being locked up in a row of cold, wet, solitary confinement cells, miles from home, for years without end, like Stewart Granger in The Prisoner Of Zenda.

Come to think of it, the bathroom into which my friends and I had climbed that chilly morning, when winter seemed reluctant to loosen its icy grip, in many ways resembled my childhood's conception of what a prison cell might look like. The floors were caked in filth and the air hung heavy with a vast array of nose-wrinkling odours, the most readily identifiable of which were mildew, dry-rot, and age-old sweat. A pile of dead leaves that looked as though they'd been there since the previous autumn, were piled beneath the chipped and cracked porcelain sink, the stained bath was crawling with insects and fat, hairy spiders, and adjacent to the toilet bowl, a cloud of bluebottles swarmed busily over the mutilated corpse of some small furry mammal, most likely a rat, though none of us were keen to investigate further.

Having quickly ascertained that there wasn't anything worth seeing here, we quickly wrenched at the door that opened onto the tiny porch and the empty kitchen beyond. We had no business with these rooms, and we scarcely afforded them a second glance. The oppressive silence of the house was broken only by the sound of our footsteps echoing hollowly on the uncarpeted wooden floorboards as we strode purposefully towards the lounge; the room where John Murphy had killed himself barely three weeks earlier.

The door to our objective was standing open just the tiniest crack, emitting a thin sliver of pale morning light, and Philly was the first to reach it. He paid no heed to my brother's pleas that maybe this whole thing wasn't such a great idea after all, and instead favoured us with what he liked to call his 'Philly-sophical Smile,' and raised his hands to push it all the way open...

I recall feeling a perverse stab of disappointment when the door failed to creak like a death groan on its rusted hinges the way they always do in those countless House On Haunted Hill-type horror movies my parents sometimes allowed me to stay up and watch, usually depending on whether or not I had school the next day, and this sense of anti-climax grew the second we stepped into the room.

I'm not all sure what we expected to find, exactly.

But it turned out that we certainly didn't need to bother with any of the 'Ghost-Hunting Caboodle' we'd brought with us.

The lounge had been stripped bare of everything, almost as though no one had lived here for decades. All of the furniture, including the 'intricately-carved hand-made chair', which Mr Murphy had used to launch himself, spinning and kicking, into the next life, had gone.

There was nothing to see....and still less to feel.

There was no inexplicable 'cold spot.'

No pervasive atmosphere of regret and sorrow.

No whispering suggestion of a ghostly presence.

Nothing.

Except...

Except for the dusty collection of crumpled papers stacked haphazardly upon the front windowsill.

Upon closer inspection, they turned out to be letters, all of them devoid of envelopes. All of them written in the same delicate, sloping hand. And all of them addressed to the same person; the late Mrs Doris Murphy.

In ordinary circumstances, the inane contents of an old man's scribblings to his beloved wouldn't have interested me in the slightest, but partly out of frustration at having had our hopes of acquiring any evidence whatsoever of the paranormal utterly dashed, and partly out of a morbid kind of curiosity, I grabbed a fistful and began to read the first few lines.

Typically, it was the ever-observant Stevie Gee who first perceived the significance of the dates at the head of each letter. I'd naturally assumed Mr Murphy had written to his wife while she was terminally ill in hospital, and had then, for some reason decided against sending them or handing them to her in person.

But what Steve had noticed almost immediately was that the earliest of the notes was dated October 12th 1974, and they went right on through to early March of this year, 1975.

Which was more than a little strange, because, of course, his wife had passed away the previous September!

> "Friggin' hell, he must have been totally off his 'ead,"

Steve had muttered, shaking his head in bewilderment.

> "He was still writin' letters to his missus, six months after she'd popped her clogs!"

These words had barely fallen from his lips before we all of us heard the thud of what sounded like a heavy object striking the ceiling directly above our heads.

It could have been anything. A precariously-placed bedside lamp, that had been teetering on the brink for God knew how long. A picture frame that hadn't been affixed to the bedroom wall properly. A shelf over laden with thick, hard-backed novels that had finally collapsed beneath their combined weight.

Anything.

But the fact remains, the twin concepts of the sane and the logical are notoriously difficult to grasp a hold of when irrational fear slithers into your skin and a whole host of terrifying images go skittering through your mind. Hard-headed realists will delight in telling you that being scared of the dark, the shadows that gather in the far corner of a sunlit room, the crooked lane that leads through the wildwood, is childishly immature. Something we should consign to the talcum-scented realm of the nursery. But I've often found myself nodding in agreement with the actress Peggy Cummins, who wisely stated in Night of the Demon, one of my favourite ever movies;

> 'You could learn a lot from children. They believe in things that exist in the dark, until we tell them it isn't so. Maybe we've been fooling them.'

Besides, whatever the reality or otherwise of supernatural phenomena, I did honestly believe, (and still do), that certain houses can somehow retain within the bricks and mortar, the pain and misery of the people who lived out their lives there. And at that precise moment in time, it's my opinion, you'd have been hard pressed to find anywhere this side of Castle Dracula, where the mood was more suited to the complete abandonment of 'the logical and sane,' in favour of boarding the good ship, 'Total And Utter Panic!'

We dropped the letters on the floor, then turned as one and raced for the exit, and it seemed no matter how fast we tried to run we moved in dream-time slow-motion, just the same. An eternity passed before we finally reached the bathroom window, and could set about making our escape. I somehow wound up being the last in line, and that's not an experience I want to repeat any time soon. I was literally jumping up and down in frustration, watching my friends take their turn to hurl themselves out into the weed-infested, litter-strewn garden, and at one point I had to grit my teeth to keep from losing control completely and shoving them head first through the window onto the tangled mass of knee-high grass that passed for a lawn.

It was just as I was preparing to clamber onto the edge of the none-too-safe-looking sink that I heard strange sounds coming from somewhere behind me.

I hesitated for a second, curiosity once more overcoming my fear, and struggled to try and identify its source. It wasn't anything like the almighty crash of a few moments earlier. It was more a warm, lullaby sound. A gentle creaking that brought to mind images of a grandmother's favourite rocking chair, or a wooden rowing boat adrift on calm waters.

Or a length of 'good strong rope,' hung from a rafter, suspending a literal dead weight....

This last thought, coupled with the fact that the noises appeared to be emanating from the direction of the living room got me moving faster than a squirrel with a firework tied to its tail, and I all but dived through the bathroom window, hit the lawn running and didn't slow down until I'd reached the blessed sanctuary of The Horror Club HQ, at the bottom of our own wonderfully familiar garden.

I was soon joined by my fellow members, all of whom were quite naturally anxious to learn what had happened to make me race down the street like the hounds of Hell were at my heels. The strange thing is, I really wanted to share with them what I thought I'd heard back there in that run-down, all-but derelict house, but something prevented me from doing so. Perhaps my reluctance was born of uncertainty at what, if anything, I had heard.

The day had started out grey and miserable, but the afternoon turned out blue-skied and clear, and there is no greater dispeller of your darkest fears than glorious sunshine and a few hours spent in the company of friends. I was suddenly sure I must have imagined those sounds. Either that, or given the admittedly eerie circumstances, I'd mistaken the entirely ordinary for the supernatural.

Those prosaic explanations had certainly made perfect sense when reviewed in the fresh green light of early April, when all seemed right with the world and everything was in its place. So I told my companions that I'd just been a trifle spooked at having been the last man out, so to speak, and that was all there was to it.

I'm not sure whether they completely believed me or not, but no one spoke up to say they never did, and I left it at that. Thinking about it now, though, I'm not so certain Stevie Gee was taken in. As I mentioned earlier, he saw a lot of things other people didn't seem to pick up on, armed with a pair of extra-powerful field glasses. He had uncanny intuition. He could see right through people like Ray Milland in The Man with X-Ray Eyes and he could suss out a bull-shitter within seconds of them uttering their first sentence.

He could also see that I was still clutching a couple of letters that I'd been sure I'd discarded back in the Murphy's lounge...The ones the grief-stricken old man had composed to his dead wife.

> "You'd better take them back,"

Grant said, his face clouded with a kind of superstitious dread.

> "I'm scared what might happen if you don't."

He didn't need to elaborate any further.

I knew only too well what had crossed his mind.

It was one of those peculiar beliefs exclusive to the lore of children; like sniffing dandelions makes you wet the bed, tread on an ant and it's sure to rain, stare into a mirror and say the Lord's Prayer backwards and the Devil will appear over your left shoulder.

Or, steal the property of the dead and get visited in the dead of night by the vengefully irate spirit you've offended.

So, yes, I knew the risk I was taking by keeping hold of the letters, but there was no way I was returning to that damned house, short of being dragged there, kicking and screaming all the way.

> "Thanks for the warning, like, but I think I'll take me chances."

I muttered quietly, trying desperately to avoid doubtful stares of my companions.

> "At least until tomorrow, anyhow."

> "Well, it's your funeral,"

Philly replied, shaking his head. And that was the last word on the subject.

We whiled away the remainder of the afternoon engaged in the more regular type of pursuits enjoyed by most kids our age, and ghosts and otherworldly phenomena were banished to furthest corners of our minds.

That evening though, as I was saying goodbye to my friends at the front gate, I called Philly to one side and asked him if he could maybe borrow me his sister's silver crucifix, 'just in case, like…'

He readily agreed and when I hit the sack that night I carefully placed the cross beneath my pillow and whispered a prayer for Angelic protection, a powerful combination that seemed to work, because contrary to my expectations, I slept like the proverbial log.

Until the wee small silent hours, that is…

It was then that I experienced what I can only describe as a 'waking dream' (though maybe 'waking nightmare' would be more accurate). It began with a white-sailed clipper ship pulling into some tropical harbour, and a sailor with a grizzled, weather-beaten face smoking a pipe as he rocked slowly back and forth on a deckchair at the edge of the quayside. The scene was the epitome of serene peacefulness. The sun was high in a sky so blue it looked about ready to shatter into a million pieces. It seemed I could almost smell the salty tang of the ocean and feel the warm sirocco breeze caressing my face….

And then the scene slowly dissolved, and I was gradually transported back to the mundane surroundings of my bedroom, and I quickly became aware that the air was filled with the sleepy/dreaded sound of a soft and gentle creaking…

I had my face to the wall and refused at first to turn around and see what I instinctively knew to be awaiting. But even as I strove to ignore the source of that now familiar sound, I found myself craning my neck to gaze upon it anyway.

And sure enough, hanging from a thick length of twisted rope was the body of John Murphy, his head down as though he were staring intently at the non-descript bedroom carpet. I had time to study the way the silver moonlight reflected upon his balding pate, illuminating it like one of my Aurora Glow-In-The-Dark Monster model kits, before he suddenly raised his face to mine, grinned mirthlessly, and then he opened his eyes.

His features were hideously bloated. There were flecks of white foam on his wormy lips, and live things crawled in the wispy remnants of his hair. As I watched in horrid fascination, a maggot the size of a mouse slowly emerged from his right nostril and fell to the floor with an audible plop.

And then he spoke, as I'd known he must eventually, and it was a voice that put me in mind of the noise those dead autumn leaves piled beneath the cracked sink in Mr Murphy's bathroom would make if they were free to blow across an empty school playground.

He pointed a bony finger in my direction and croaked menacingly;

    'Give me back what's mine! Give me back what's mine!'

…over and over, gradually slowing down like one of those old gramophone records…Until it stopped completely and his tongue lolled out, impossibly long and covered with sores. He ran it over his stubbly chin, dropped a lewd wink and somehow, began to move towards me…

I woke up for real, then, though I was still convinced beyond doubting that there was an unearthly presence in the room, regarding me with evil intent, and nothing, not the gentle snoring of my brother, the ticking of the alarm clock, or the knowledge that I was protected by the silver crucifix, could dilute the paralysing terror that held me in an immobile, vice-like grip. I was simply unable to move, my body slimy with cold beads of perspiration, hardly daring to breathe or swallow the click in my throat. I felt, in short, like I'd been drugged, unable to move or cry out, or indeed do much of anything other than lie there and wait for that unforgiving spirit to descend upon me, its horribly grinning face looming out of the darkness, its breath the smell of dead flowers rotting in a charnel house….

The horror only dissipated with the blessed coming of the dawn.

To this day, I can't say with any degree of certainty whether or not I dreamed the whole thing, or if I was truly visited by the ghost of Mr Murphy, but you can be sure I didn't waste any time in getting around to returning those letters early that very morning. I warily made my way to the bathroom window sill, still half-open, and threw the pages, which I'd tied together with a piece of red ribbon, inside without ever once looking back to see where they'd landed.

And I never set foot on the property ever again....

******

In the days and weeks that followed, my friends noticed a profound change in my attitude towards the ghostly aspects of paranormal phenomena. For a while, I wasn't able to view the subject with quite the same degree of... well, innocence is - I guess - the word I'm looking for. I still retained an interest. But it's true to say I confined my 'investigations' to simply reading about phantoms and such in books and magazine articles. I never told any of the members of The New Ferry Horror Club that I'd been so badly frightened by the dream (if such it was), of John Murphy's restless shade that I couldn't face setting foot in any other potentially 'haunted house.'

I didn't even tell them that I'd had the dream...it was something I'd kept locked away like a dirty secret hidden in the darkest depths of a wine cellar.

Until now.

And why now, you may well ask?

The reasons are as many as they are varied, but I think I'll settle for the one that is perhaps the most simple and readily explainable. Although that doesn't make it any less relevant, to my mind.

It's namely this: to all intents and purposes, 'The New Ferry Horror Club' largely disbanded within a fortnight of its founder members leaving Church Drive Junior and moving on to different secondary and grammar schools. Despite heartfelt pledges of undying allegiance and promises to stay in touch, we predictably wound up going our separate ways. Further evidence, if it were needed, that all too often, even the very best of childhood friends can lose touch and forget the magic times they spent together, until such things become nothing more than an attic memory.

Perhaps the drifting apart was a direct result of my apparent loss of enthusiasm and refusal to become involved in 'investigative field trips,' and if that is indeed so, then I can't help but feel a stab of aching sadness and regret that I idly sat by and allowed such a thing to happen.

The irony is, over the space of the next decade or so, long after the memory of that terrifying nightmare had faded to the point of forgetfulness, my interest (some would say obsession) with ghostly phenomena was rekindled anew, and has, if anything grown stronger than ever before. I have since spent a good deal of my spare time in the Civic Centre Library, studying and making copious notes on all manner of local weirdness. I discovered a whole stack of dusty literary works containing reams of largely forgotten folklore, read through piles of pamphlets and magazines and searched through reels of old newspaper clippings preserved on microfilm until my eyes felt like they were stalks.

At times, it appeared almost as though I were doing a penance. Trying in vain to make up for the wrongs committed in a time to which I could never hope to return. It seems to me now, that the very least I can do is attempt to chronicle the information I gleaned during those endless days as I made the typically awkward journey from boyhood to adulthood.

The following then, is - I would hope - a fitting tribute to the erstwhile members of The New Ferry Horror Society.

Wherever they may be....

THE GAP AND PROMENADE, NEW FERRY — No. KNF4.

BEACH AND RIVER, NEW FERRY — No. KNF1.

THE NEW FERRY HORROR SOCIETY'S FAVOURITE FRIGHTENERS
(Or 'Things That Would Scare The Halo Off An Angel')

'History without myth is a wasteland'
Greil Marcus

THE HORROR OF THE MERSEY MUD-FLATS

On the other side of the large disused oil storage depot, known since the 1940s, as 'The Big Hill' (a place you'll be hearing a great deal more about later in this book), is a thin strip of filthy, polluted sand, christened with the somewhat fanciful name of 'New Ferry Shore'.

Running from the permanently stinking entrance of a rat-infested sewer tunnel at one end, to the dilapidated pier near to *Camell Laird Shipyard*, that juts out into the Mersey like a skeletal finger, 'The Shore' also contained a stretch of mud-flats that should have provided a rich haven for many forms of wildlife, but which always seemed to be deserted, save for a lonely seagull or two and bunches of wispy, colourless reeds that looked as if they were in the process of permanently dying. The mud was a horrible, diseased-looking grey colour, and at the height of summer, during one those all-too rare dry spells, the surface of the sludge would grow hard and cracked like leprous skin.

'The Shore' hadn't always been this way, though. I'd seen many sepia-toned photographs in local history books that depicted a series of idyllic scenes from Edwardian times. Snapshots of smartly-dressed couples strolling along the esplanade, the women twirling their parasols, the men laden with overflowing picnic baskets. Of children emerging from the magnificent Olympian gardens that surrounded *The Royal Rock Hotel*, heading for the two or three miles of clean golden sand that shimmered in an eternal heat haze. And of out-of-town holidaymakers, walking the shoreline in search for a good spot to spread their tablecloths and beach towels to while away the sun-baked afternoon.

There'd been sideshow stalls and annual fairs, and every weekend from May through to September, a huge, white-tented marquee would be erected where bands would play, and music hall comedians and top class magicians would perform, transporting the audience for a few hours or so from the humdrum of the daily grind.

How things had dramatically changed by the middle of the century.

As recently as the 1960s, *The Royal Rock's* famously sprawling gardens had been heedlessly dug up and cemented over, and a series of roads had been built to criss-cross the lawns. Smoke-belching factories and foul-smelling chemical plants had sprung up like festering boils as a consequence of Liverpool suddenly becoming the busiest, and most financially lucrative port in the whole of England.

A heavy price to pay for surrendering the joys of scenic splendour to the iron-grey hand of industrial progress.

And another, was the vomited birth of the evilly treacherous Mud-Flats.

This stretch of sickly-coloured, pock-marked landscape resembled the lifeless, poisoned earth of Tolkien's Mordor, and was shunned by even the most determined of beachcombers.

And with good reason.

Local legend has it that more than one poor soul had been dragged into the *Invaders from Mars*-like Sucking Pit when the spring rains had turned the polluted earth into a deadly quicksand.

My dad used to delight in telling us that he knew of someone who survived spending three days and three nights stuck up to his neck in the mud following the flash floods in the spring of 1963. Fortunately, he was eventually rescued by a group of volunteers who were out searching for him. When he was pulled to safety, however, it was discovered that the only reason he hadn't submerged completely was the fact that he'd been standing atop a long-dead victim's head, who was stood atop another, who was stood atop another, who was....

Well, you get the general idea.

As urban legends go, it was right up there with the story doing the rounds when I was a kid, that *Space Dust*, an unaccountably hugely popular confectionery during the mid-1970s, consisting of a pile of tiny chewy spheres that you placed on your tongue where, after a few seconds they would make a highly audible popping noise before detonating like minuscule balls of dynamite. I guess it was *supposed* to be a pleasurable sensation, but they were certainly something of an acquired taste, and their appeal was dealt something of a death blow after it was rumoured that some unfortunate school kid had decided to empty several packets of the stuff straight down his throat on a dare, whereupon he duly exploded from the inside out; his stomach and intestines splattering across the classroom walls.

Coincidentally(?) these sweets disappeared from the shelves not long after this story became common knowledge.

(Above): The New Ferry Shoreline at high tide, with just a small portion of the treacherous mud-flats visible in mid-frame. At low tide, the Mersey recedes to a point in line with the finger-like promontory of highly-polluted filth – a potential death-trap that lies, at the moment this picture was taken, just beneath the seemingly placid surface....

But putting aside for a moment, the dubious nature of urban legend, and returning, as we must, to the mud-flats, I can remember when I was about twelve years old, waking in the early hours to the sound of my mum and dad arguing loudly in their bedroom.

Filled with a sense of dread, but unable to resist the voice that sought to reassure me that the best thing I could do to defuse the situation would be to make them aware I had awoken and, (hopefully), shame them into coming to their senses, I pushed open their bedroom door and stumbled, bleary-eyed, into their room.

I wasn't quite sure what to expect, but I certainly wasn't prepared for the sight of my semi-naked father bathed in the soft glare of the bedside table lamp, frantically ransacking his side of the wardrobe and throwing various items of clothing into one of the large bright red suitcases we normally used for our family holidays back then, all the while shouting at the top of his voice;

"I didn't *mean* to let her die! I didn't *mean* to let her die!"

My mum, meanwhile, all wild-haired and plainly even more terrified and confused than I was, desperately clung on to him screaming;

> "For God's sake, stop it! Nobody's dead. You're just having a nightmare!"

I just stood there, stunned, unable to speak, and it seemed like this macabre little episode would go on forever, my dad shoving clothing into the case, my mum begging him to snap out of it, and yours truly rooted to the spot, struck dumb, and consequently of bugger all use to anyone….

Until mercifully, my dad happened to glance in my direction, and something approaching recognition dawned in his eyes, and he stopped chucking clothing into that damn case (he was probably down to the basics like hole-ridden socks and seldom-worn underwear by then, anyway), and with a wracking sob that spoke of pure, unadulterated relief, he opened his arms and beckoned me to go to him. He hugged me and mum so tight, I literally had to struggle for breath, it was a good while before he was able to recover sufficient composure for him to explain what his nightmare (for such he now accepted it must have been), had been about.

He'd dreamed that he'd gone for a romantic stroll with my mum along New Ferry Shore, on a perfect summer evening, when from out of nowhere a sudden torrential downpour had sent them both scrambling for shelter. As they were running my dad let go of her hand for a second, and my mum had stumbled, and somehow found herself buried waist high in the evil-smelling filth of the Mud-Flats.

He tried desperately to drag her out, but his own feet soon sank deep in the cloying, clinging mire,, and he was forced to watch in helpless horror as his wife slowly disappeared below the surface, the vile mixture of oil slicks, raw sewage and chemical effluent from the nearby factories pouring into her open mouth and drowning out her screams forever.

He was suddenly able to free himself then, and in a blind panic had raced all the way home, convinced by the skewed, off-kilter logic of dreams, that he had been responsible for me mum's 'death' and was left with no other option, than to pack his case and make a run for it, living the life of a fugitive rather than have to face telling his children that he'd 'murdered' their mother…

The vision of my dad carelessly stuffing his clothing into a holiday suitcase, with flacks of white foam pooling at the corners of his mouth, and a look of 'God-help-me' panic in his eyes, is an image that has haunted me ever since.

And here's something else that has since stayed with me like a persistently unwelcome house-guest.

Having left New Ferry six years ago, for the 'verdant green pastures' of Moreton, five miles or so along the M53, I very rarely have cause to walk along 'The Shore', and I have to be honest and say that I don't consider that to be any great loss. The admittedly picturesque view of the Liverpool city skyline, on the opposite side of the river was always somewhat tainted by the depressing vista of the piles of broken bricks, battered shopping trolleys and burned out shells of abandoned motor vehicles that littered the oil-streaked stretch of sand. Not long before I moved away from the area, the local council announced, with a typical headline-seeking flourish, that they were embarking upon a major clean-up operation of New Ferry Shore, and I honestly wish them well in their endeavours. I can't help being a tad cynical though, and surmising that I don't think it's going to be challenging any of the beaches of North Wales as a popular holiday destination any time soon.

The truth is, even before upping sticks, I used to purposely avoid having to walk along The Shore, unless it was absolutely necessary to do so.

It wasn't the dreadful, nose-wrinkling smells emanating from the nearby *Water Treatment Works*.

It wasn't the persistent rumours (doubtless spread by local, blue-rinse Conservative types who worship at the altar of *The Daily Mail)*, that vicious, ruthless gangs of 'smackheads, insanely-grinning alkies, and shifty-eyed gyppos' use "the beach" as a communal meeting place, where they pounce on unsuspecting passers-by, live a life of indescribable debauchery, and hatch their heinous plans for the downfall of Western civilisation.'

It wasn't even the way the raw winter wind whipped across the Mersey, stinging your eyes and slicing through the thickest layers of clothing like a thousand icy blades, or the sky-darkening swarms of horseflies and tiny biting midges that descend like a Biblical plague the moment late spring comes rolling around once more.

This may sound like the illogical, paranoid ramblings of a man who thinks he is awake but is simply caught in the grip of a startlingly vivid nightmare, but I honestly didn't like visiting New Ferry Shore because I knew I'd always catch a glimpse of that poisonous-looking expanse of earth known locally as The Mud-Flats: the place where my dad once dreamed he saw my mum being slowly engulfed by that ever-hungry Sucking Pit.

And having, (however reluctantly), clapped eyes on that awful place, I *knew* I'd hear a siren voice. The same sweetly plausible tones that are sometimes said to tempt perfectly sane people to leap from high buildings or the sheer edges of white-faced cliffs.

> *'Come and take a walk across the mud-flats,'*

…it croons.

> *'It's perfectly safe. See, the curlews and oystercatchers skate across the surface. See, no harm ever comes to them. You can walk right down to the river's edge and admire the wonderful views. You can easily make your way safely across the mud-flats sur-fassssssse!'*

I refuse to listen, of course. And I have the ever present flocks of scavenging seagulls to thank for that; Their lonely, haunting cries sound too much like the hopeless screams of a woman who's been abandoned to her fate, and is filled with the immutable knowledge that she can never be saved…..

THE DALEKS

I honestly don't know of anyone between the ages of ten and thirteen, not even Nicky Ashton, by far the toughest lad at our infamous school of hard knocks, who wasn't mortally terrified of these Cyclopean, sink-plunger-armed, barely mobile, pepper pots.

Never mind the paradoxical conundrum that undoubtedly exists here. Despite the all-too obvious physical limitations of a supposedly higher extraterrestrial life-form, (or maybe in some crazy way *because* of them), the Daleks still retained their sinister aura, and the ability to terrify an entire generation. Perhaps it was their grating, metallic voices, their deadly ray gun, or their cries of '*Exterminate!, Exterminate!*' at the slightest provocation, (Dr Who neglecting to share his packet of *Jelly Babies*, for example). But what gave me a good-sized dose of the creeps was their total refusal to listen to reasoned argument, no matter how logical or rational, once they'd arrived at a decision or decided on a particular course of action. Usually, this involved the mass invasion of some sovereign territory, the inhabitants of which are pretty much incapable of defending themselves, which, come to think of it, sounds uncannily similar to Tony Blair's recent 'military adventures' carried out in the name of *'The War Against Terror,'* an 'empire-building' misnomer, the first initials of which, appropriately enough, you might think, spell out the acronym: *TWAT!*

But I digress.

There was something else, as well, though. Another of those (I'd like to think) poignant childhood memories I'd like to share with you, if I may…

When we were kids, my parents would often treat us to a Sunday afternoon trip to the once hugely-popular seaside resort of New Brighton.

During the fairly long bus journey, my dad would delight in telling the family how incredible the place had been back in its heyday at the dawn of the 20th Century, and of his own childhood memories from the mid to late 1950s. He'd been a Teddy Boy[**], back then, and I didn't have to imagine how he'd have looked. I'd seen plenty of photographs of him and his mates, resplendent in their drainpipe trousers and blue-suede brothel creepers, and with the quiffs of their *Brylcreem*-slicked hair dangling over their foreheads, and he told us he'd loved nothing better than driving along the sea front, with the car windows wound all the way down and Little Richard and Bill Hayley blasting from the radios of his battered *Ford Cortina*. They'd make believe they were in sunny California, cruising the beach roads in a brand new 1958 Convertible, its polished chrome gleaming with the reflected promise of endless summer.

The resort was hugely popular with both locals and out-of-towners, and from the start of the Easter Bank Holidays through to late September, a continuous stream of ferry boats crossed the river back and forth, whilst fleets of coaches arrived from all over Britain. They came to dance in The Ballrooms which burned down in 1969, or to experience the many attractions contained within The Tower, built to rival the one in Blackpool.

The sound of big band music carried dreamily on the warm summer breeze from the various dancehalls and ballrooms and bowling alleys, and the air was filled with the mouth-watering aromas from the vendor's hot dog stands and the sea-front bar & grills.

Sadly, in the years that had slipped by since my Dad's adolescence, the grandeur of New Brighton's glory days had long since faded, like some glamorously dazzling show girl whose former beauty has been withered by the remorseless passing of time.

Now all that remained were a couple of run-down bars and hotels, with letters missing from their drunkenly swaying signs and boards advertising quiz nights, *'Funky Discos'* and pub bands no one had ever heard of or were, in truth, ever likely to, their windows smeared with beer-stains and heartfelt regret. There was also a decrepit-looking amusement arcade and mini-fairground, surrounded on one side by rows and rows of red-bricked council houses and blocks of identical high-rises, where seagulls screamed and swooped to feast from the rows of overflowing bins, and on the other by the permanently choppy waters of the Irish sea, stained a sullen brown even on the sunniest, blue-skied of days due to the combination of various pollutants, oil-spills and stinking human waste that had been dumped in its waters.

The vast, bustling crowds of yesteryear had now dwindled down to a couple of hundred people at most, the vast majority of whom seemed to be wandering around with fixed, cheesy grins on their faces, as though they were simply *pretending* to be having fun.

I remember, years later, watching George A. Romero's seminal classic, *Dawn Of The Dead,* on a grainy, pirated video tape, and the scene where the mindless zombies shamble aimlessly around the shopping mall and drunkenly reel around the mini-fountains whilst hideous piped muzak provided a suitably soulless soundtrack, and being instantly reminded of the scene that greeted us every time we stepped off the bus.

[**]For those unfamiliar with the term, the British Teddy Boy (also known as Ted) subculture is typified by young men wearing clothes that were partly inspired by the styles worn by dandies in the Edwardian period, styles which Savile Row tailors had attempted to re-introduce in Britain after World War II. The subculture started in London in the 1950s, and rapidly spread across the UK, soon becoming strongly associated with American rock and roll. Originally known as *Cosh Boys*, the name *Teddy Boy* was coined when a 1953 *Daily Express* newspaper headline shortened *Edward* to *Teddy*.

My Dad would often sigh wistfully, the moment we arrived at the resort, and remark that seeing New Brighton in its current state was a little like waking up in the morning after a particularly good dream.

But I remember we always enjoyed our days out there, just the same.

We'd play each other at table footy and air hockey, or go for stomach-churning rides on the (*do yer wanna go faster!)*' waltzers and risk serious injury by colliding with each in our fragile *Bumper Cars*. If the weather was good, we'd walk out to the old fort at Perch Rock, set up a game of rounders on the beach or dip our green plastic fishing nets into shallow rock pools, and empty the tiddlers** we caught into jam jars filled to the brim with salty sea-water.

And throughout the day, we'd get to stuff our faces with fish-n-chips, *'Fab'* and *'Zoom'* ice lollies and flimsy little cardboard cones crammed to the brim with vinegar-soaked cockles. Back then, any worries about the possibility of a rapidly expanding waistline were as vague a conception to me, as trying to imagine the vast gulf of star-filled space that existed between the Earth and the planet *Skaro,* home of the ruthlessly evil Daleks.

Which, coincidentally, brings me to the most abiding memory of those long-ago summer afternoons; the unnervingly realistic-looking *Dalek* that stood like a sentinel in a small litter-strewn enclosure at the front of the resort's amusement arcade.

It certainly *looked* menacing enough, a testament to an invasive, extraterrestrial evil, but in truth, it didn't actually do an awful lot.

You simply inserted a ten pence piece into the coin slot located just below the robot's death ray, the red lights flashed on and off on either side of its shiny dome-shaped head,, you could waggle the ray gun and the 'sink-plunger' a little and it moved slowly backwards and forwards and side to side in a jerky fashion, emitting a decidedly half-hearted cry of *Exterminate!'* every twenty seconds or so. After a disappointingly short while it juddered to a halt, and you climbed out feeling distinctly under-whelmed. As rivetingly exciting fairground entertainment goes, it surely wasn't going to give the owners of *Blackpool Pleasureland* any cause for sleepless nights.

My mum and dad made no secret of the fact they used to think I was 'going soft in the head' (a perception they have, in all likelihood, been somewhat reluctant to revise as their eldest son supposedly 'matured' into adulthood) but following my first encounter with the ride, I refused point blank to take a seat inside the hollow, metallic body and go for a sedate spin around the arcade forecourt in case I somehow became trapped within its 'alien' casing, assimilated somehow with the implacable, non-negotiable evil of the *Dalek* race.

Doubtless there are dozens of wannabe psychologists out there who will nod their heads sagely at this point and suggest that the Dalek's displays of stubborn inflexibility served as a fictional reminder of the pig-headed attitude exhibited by certain teachers during my four years as a pupil at New Chester Road Secondary School - a large, ominous, Victorian monstrosity that loomed above the nearby shops and houses and had long-ago been christened by the 'inmates' with the hugely appropriate nickname of *'Colditz'*.

One of the harsh lessons I'd learned very early on as a pupil at that *'august residence of scholarship'* was that, even when you hadn't done anything remotely wrong, 'resistance to the rule of school law was futile' and you had to take your punishment like a man and not as *'some snivelling, little snot-nosed toe-rag who went bawling to their mum just because they'd had their head shoved down the bog by the school bully.'*

Bearing in mind, we're talking here about the Dark Ages of Corporal Punishment, meted out by sadists who'd think nothing of employing such hellish instruments of swift retribution as *The Cane, The Sole of The Sportsmaster's Training Shoe,* or *The Big, Thick Block of Wood-Type Thingy,* this was far easier said than done. I'd seen muscle-bound, multi-scarred adolescents (who'd quite happily dance 'The Watusi' on your head whilst singing some contemporary Glam Rock classic - *'Blockbuster'* by *Sweet,* seemed to be a particular favourite - for the hei-

---

** Little fish of indeterminate species.

nous crime of not allowing them to copy off you during a maths exam), reduced to a blubbering wreck after receiving 'six of the best' from an irate teacher.

One of the best (or worst, depending on your point of view), examples of this unyielding narrow-mindedness occurred when I was accused, quite unfairly, of slicing up several hundred reams of expensive coloured card from the store cupboard of the 'Arts and Crafts Department'. The teacher, Mrs Harries, a petite, dark-haired woman in her early 30's, whose gorgeously lilting Welsh accent belied her mean-hearted vicious streak, chose the end of an afternoon lesson to drag me out in front of the whole of Form 3:1, like a sacrificial victim.

"Right, Walker!"

…she yelled just as my fellow pupils were preparing to pack up and head for exits.

"Come out here, this instant!"

An expectant hush fell over the class, and everyone, even my closest friends, leaned forward eagerly, filled with anticipation like the ancient Romans in the local amphitheatre awaiting the release of the Christian-chomping lions.

Rudely shaken from my pleasant little daydream of scoring a last minute thirty-yarder against the Mancs at the Kop[*] end at Anfield, I got to my feet and slowly made my way past the desks with all the enthusiasm of a horse on its way to a glue factory.

"Hurry up, Walker. We haven't got all day!"

Mrs Harries glowered, as I made a hurriedly, speed of light mental check of all the things I'd done wrong in the last couple of days; the stomach upset that had resulted in me blocking the boys' toilets with a mountainous stack of loo roll, ripping out the double-page dinosaur poster from the stack of *Look And Learn* magazines, in Miss Cells' English class, flicking a hairy snot gobbler into Wayne Williams' can of *Diet Pepsi* when he wasn't looking, during that morning's first break…..

The possibilities were endless, but none of them really mattered a jot, because before I knew it, I was standing directly in front of Mrs Harries, and instantly my mind went as blank as a blackboard when the school's supply of chalk has gone AWOL.

"Well, Walker,"

…she began pleasantly enough, though I saw all too well her eyes were aflame with Celtic fury.

"I think perhaps you've got some explaining to do, isn't that right, boy?"

My mouth went dry and I felt my senses start to swim as I realised I couldn't answer. At least not until I knew what I was being accused of. So instead, I stared at my feet as though something of immense scientific interest was busy crawling across the surface of my shoe.

As I expected, my silence didn't improve her mood any.

"Don't just stand there like a blithering imbecile, Walker! Explain yourself, or I promise you will suffer the consequences."

"I dunno what you mean, Miss,"

---

[*] The most famous terraced bank in world football, named after The Battle Of The Spion Kop, which took place on January 24th, 1900, in South Africa during the Boer War. Spion Kop is a steep hill in Northern Natal, where the British forces, including several Lancashire regiments, with a strong Liverpool contingent, suffered 1,500 casualties, 243 of whom were killed in what became known as 'The Murderous Acre.'

I managed to mumble, still staring intently at that imaginary zoological wonder and its apparent foot fetish.

> "Oh, I *seeeee*"

…she sighed.

> "In that case, your classmates can count themselves indeed fortunate. It seems we are graced by the presence of a real-life, bona fide miracle!"

Miss Harries spread her arms wide like a latter-day revivalist preacher.

> "You are all of you witness to an enigma that would perplex the finest minds in academia!"

I tried desperately to think of something half-way intelligent to say in response. But all I could do was repeat the hopelessly inadequate;

> "Er, I dunno what you mean, Miss."

> "Well perhaps I can cast some light through your dark veil of ignorance,"

…the teacher said, opening the top drawer of her desk and pulling out a thick sheaf of coloured card. Each piece had been slashed diagonally three quarters of the way across their surface with some razor-sharp instrument, in all likelihood the black-handled guillotine.

> "It appears I have been labouring under a misapprehension that a *human* agency was responsible for this wanton act of vandalism,"

…she said sneeringly,

> "And all the time, it was some otherworldly entity with a grudge against expensive Art Department property."

She puffed out her cheeks and shook her head wonderingly.

> "Truly, this is a case of Holmesian dimensions, wouldn't you agree, Walker?"

> "Er, yy-yes, I er, s-s-suppose s-s-so,"

I stammered. I didn't have the slightest idea what the hell she was babbling on about, but I thought it safest just to simply agree with her.

This proved to be a bad move.

> "What kind of idiot do you take me for, Walker?"

…she yelled, all pretence of composure suddenly scattered to the four winds.

> "I *know* it was you, lad. You were seen by Mr Viner, skulking around outside the front doors of the classroom twenty minutes after the home-time bell. He said you were acting suspiciously and he was about to ask you what you were doing, but he got distracted by a couple of lads fighting in the school car park. I think you'd been up to no good, Walker. I think you've been on a solitary highly-priced, multi-coloured card-destroying mission. I think you and Mr Guillotine, here got together for a spot of happy chopping. Now, what have you got to say about that?"

I'd had quite a bit to say, as it turned out, because for a single delirious moment, I'd thought I was clean off the hook, and I had to struggle to suppress a smile that may have been misinterpreted as a gloating grin of triumph.

> "But Miss, it *can't* have been me,"

I said, meeting her eyes, filled with the new-found confidence of the soon-to-be reprieved.

> "I was training for the school footy team straight after our last lesson. We've got a big match on Satdee, Miss, against Rocky High, and I didn't wanna be late so I legged it for the team coach to take us up to the Oval Sports Centre, it leaves at four o clock and I was in me seat by ten to, at the very latest."

I paused for breath, before delivering what I assumed would be the killer lines.

> "Honest, Miss, you can ask Mr Heckle, our manager. He was checking his watch when I got on board the coach, so he can confirm the exact time. *He'll* tell yer. It *couldn't* have been me."

Knowing Miss Harries, as I did, I certainly wasn't expecting even the most half-arsed of apologies. I thought she'd simply grimace in frustration and tell me to get the hell out of her sight.

She didn't do either, though. Instead, as crazily illogical as it sounds, she remained stubbornly convinced that I was responsible and dismissed my 'water-tight' explanation with an irritated wave of her hand as though she was swatting some peskily bothersome insect and continued right on with her ridiculous accusations.

> "I don't care a fig what you say, Walker!"

…she thundered in a voice that brooked no further argument.

> "I know you are as guilty as sin. You're not talking your way out of *this* one. Now, bend over and touch your toes!"

So saying, she reached for the dreaded *Big Block of Wood-Type Thingy*.

> "But Miss, I didn't….."

> "Bend over and touch your toes!"

…she repeated

> "But Miss, it's not fair…"

> "Bend over and touch your toes!"

> "But…"

> "BEND OVER AND TOUCH YOUR TOES…..NOW!"

I wound up getting *'Seven of the Best.'* Of course, ancient school tradition dictates that it should only have been six, but as Miss Harries delighted in informing me, seven was her new lucky number, since she'd won the jackpot rollover at the St John's Social Club Bingo, the previous weekend, and so it only seemed right to her that she dole out an extra whack in due deference to the kindly *Gods of Good Fortune*.

The pitifully thin material of my school trousers provided little in the way of protection, and you can bet I spent the next few evenings watching *Ace Of Wands, Thunderbirds* and *The Tomorrow People* sat on a large stack of comfy cushions with a pained expression on my face as though I was afflicted with an exceptionally agonising case of piles.

As terrible as that punishment undoubtedly was however, infinitely worse was the two weeks-worth of detention I received as an added bonus.

I would honestly rather have received 'Seven *hundred* of the best' than be made subject to this massive restriction on my liberty, especially seeing as how it was spring time, the clocks had gone back, and the promise of *The Light Nights* lay stretched out before me like a road leading into a realm of endless possibilities.

Being kept behind for a good hour after my classmates had embarked upon The Mad Dash Steeplechase for the barbed-wire-framed school gates, was akin to spending 60 minutes in Purgatory, especially considering Detention Class was taken by my form teacher, Mr Malcolm Ward.

You might think I'm guilty of exaggerating a little here, but of course, it's highly unlikely you ever had the dubious pleasure of ever meeting him, and even if you had, you'd probably assume Mr Ward was, at worst, an essentially emotionless individual, the sort who seldom lost his temper and who spoke in a monotonous drone similar to that perfected by lay preachers, grey-suited politicians and that faceless announcer who reads out the *Radio Four* shipping forecast.

But, as any of my classmates in Form 5:1 could readily attest, an internal maelstrom constantly raged beneath the teacher's glacial exterior, and he was every bit as stubbornly mulish as Mrs Harries, so I figured could realistically forget about making any pleas for clemency, here. Attempting to reason with him would be as pointless an exercise as climbing to the top of a Welsh mountain at sunset to rage at the dying of the light, but that didn't stop me trying.

"Please, Sir,"

I said in my most imploring voice as I stood before Mr Ward outside the Science Labs on the first of the week-long detention sessions.

"I'm being punished for something I honestly haven't done, and...."

"Get a rag, Walker!"

…he said, cutting me short, and pointing at a ragged strip of terry cloth draped on the edge of a bucket filled with soapy lukewarm water. "I want the whole of this floor scrubbed so clean I'll be able to see my face in it."

"But, Sir, if you'd just hear me out, I..."

"Get a rag!"

"But, Sir..."

"GET-A-RAG! GET- A-RAG! GET-A-RAG!"

…he repeated over and over in a high-pitched robotic drone and for a mad moment, I was struck by this vivid mental image of Mr Ward's internal circuits sparking and fizzing, like an alien android faced with the refusal of its conquered subjects to obey a simple order.

It was abundantly clear that 'Resistance was futile,' so after sighing loud enough to alert the world to the birth of a new martyr, I clamped my mouth shut, got on my hands and knees and began rinsing out the frayed piece of cloth into the metal bucket.

And that's how it was every evening for the next two weeks. The 3:45pm bell would chime. I'd rise slowly from my desk at the conclusion of the day's final lesson with a heavy heart. Then, casting rueful glances at my classmates, who'd shake their heads and lower their gaze as though I were a condemned man heading for an appointment with the black-hooded hangman, I'd take the stairs up to the Science Lab, and find Mr Ward waiting there, as stony –faced as the statues of The Gods of ancient Athens.

Or the unnervingly realistic Dalek I'd seen standing like a sentinel in the litter-strewn enclosure of an amusement arcade, one long-ago summer.....

DOLLS & MANNEQUINS

I guess I can only speak for myself (and the other members of our Society), here, but as with clowns and those white-faced performing mime artists, I've always considered there to be something deeply disturbing about children's dolls and shop window dummies.

Perhaps you can lay the blame squarely at our old friend *Dr Who's*, door, (the purveyor of many children's nightmares – and doubtless more than a few adults, too), certainly in the case of the plastic mannequins, sometimes bald-headed, more often not bewigged, that stand in the shop windows of department stores dressed in the latest fashions, staring sightlessly at the passers-by with knowing half-smiles on their otherwise emotionless faces.

Thanks to a couple of particularly frightening story-lines featuring attempted invasions of Earth by 'The Nestene Intelligence': aliens capable of animating anything made from plastic and using it as a weapon against mankind[*], including flowers, deceptively-comfy chairs, and yes, shop window dummies, I often found it all-too easy to imagine these synthetic caricatures coming to life in the centre of town, full of evil intent, probably when most people were asleep, during the dark watches of the night.

Also, not too many years ago, there used to be an old curiosity shop directly opposite Bebington railway station - on the very edge of New Ferry - that specialised in stocking various items from the Victorian-era. The vast assemblage of collectible bric-a-brac on display in the shop window was dominated by a veritable army of china dolls, all rouge cheeks, garishly-painted lips and blank, staring eyes. Dead eyes, that nonetheless seemed to gaze out from the other side of the grimy glass window with a dull, stupid malevolence.

As cowardly as it might sound, I used to avoid walking past the shop, unless it was absolutely necessary, not least because whenever I did so, I would find myself after being plagued by a terrible recurring dream: I'd hear the sound of something scratching at my bedroom window. I'd slowly raise my head from the pillow and immediately wish I hadn't. For there, illuminated by a slab of silvery moonlight, I'd see a crowd of pale-white porcelain faces, staring in at me, their bright-red lips parted in a mirthless grin. I'd then see the source of the incessant scratching; the lethal-looking blades they clutched in their hands.

---

[*] The Autons, for the uninitiated, were the first ever *Dr Who* monsters to be filmed in decidedly grainy-looking colour, back in 1970, when Jon Pertwee, who many consider, myself included, the all-time definitive, exiled Timelord, battled a series of alien and indigenous threats to our planet with the trusty help of the British military in the shape of UNIT (United Nations Intelligence Taskforce).

The Autons crashed to Earth, cocooned in, of all things, a swarm of plastic meteorites. The inaugural Pertwee adventure, 'Spearhead From Space', filmed on location for added realism, (no painfully-thin cardboard studio sets at risk of collapse every time a Daemon, Silurian or, indeed Auton, happened to shuffle by), had the alien threat crashing to Earth, cocooned in, of all things, a swarm of plastic, pulsing meteorites. The Autons, humanoid robots that were animated by the Nestene Consciousness, look identical to shop-window dummies, except for the fact that they move around in a jerky fashion, and have the disconcerting habit of shooting or vaporizing people with weapons they conceal in their hands. Their name originates from **Auto Plastics**, the alien-controlled company that manufactures the Autons in their Quatermass-style factories. They were eventually defeated by the Doctor and his UNIT buddies, but were back a year or so later in another Pertwee story; 'The Terror Of The Autons.'

From the early 1970s onwards, the marvellously-named Mr Herbert Van Thal edited *The Pan Books of Horror Stories*, a series of paperbacks that featured both classic and contemporary short stories, the content of which has since been described by some commentator or other as 'the literary equivalent of the early 1980s so-called "video nasties."' The books' covers were nearly as luridly troubling as the stories contained within, featuring human skull-faced snowmen; glowing, green mummy-like visages; a severed bearded head in a hatbox.

We unanimously considered the most frightening cover though to be that adorning the *Fourth Pan Book of Horror Stories*, which featured a colour photograph of a child's doll lying discarded in a clump of sickly-looking weeds, its left arm missing, a hairy brown tarantula crawling across its wide-eyed, multi-cracked face.

(Incidentally, these portmanteau books were required reading for the members of New Ferry Horror Society, of course, and we used to recount some of the more gory sections to gross out the universally squeamish girls in our class. One of the stories we loved quoting from most was a charmingly delightful saga entitled 'Pieces of Mary' written by an author named Robert Ashley.

It began with one of the most memorable opening lines of all the stories I've ever read, before or since; 'Mary was rather a nice little girl, really. That is until she got her head chopped off.'

Stark and chilling in its simplicity, this line had a profound effect upon my young, impressionable mind, but at the risk of disappointing the editorship of that sworn guardian of the easily-offended sensibilities of the middle-class, middle-aged inhabitants of er, Middle England, The Daily Mail, *I did not suddenly find myself struck with a sudden, overwhelming compulsion to root around my Dad's woodshed in search of an axe, a hacksaw and a selection of pickling jars to store the various dismembered body parts of my near-neighbour's five-year-old daughter.*

As the great horror and cult film director David Cronenberg was quoted as saying when quizzed about his views regarding violence in the movies: 'Censors tend to do what only psychotics do: they confuse reality with illusion.'

This tale may be about as subtle as holding the Pamplona Bull Chase in the crockery department of Homebase, but I would contend that it has a certain primal power, and there's no doubt it has stayed with me ever since).

The reason our Society 'favoured', (if that's the right word) the cover of the Fourth edition of Van Thal's wonderful series of books was perhaps 'inspired' (bit dubious about the appropriateness of that word, too), by the frequent recounting of the following...

THE PRENTON DOLL HOUSE

One of the most persistent legends that was recounted in hushed, almost reverential whispers amongst my friends when I was a child, concerned a large, unnervingly realistic haunted doll's house that, according to the stories, (and there were many, of wildly varying degrees of believability, as you will soon see) stood in the garden of an otherwise perfectly ordinary council house in Prenton, just a few short miles from New Ferry.

I remember the one recurring theme that linked these ghoulish tales like the black-toned moniker of a some seedy seaside resort running through a cheap stick of multi-coloured rock, was that the doll's house, an exact replica of the owner's three-bedroomed semi, had been erected as a sort of 'shrine' to their 10-year-old daughter, their only child, who had been tragically killed by a hit and run driver whilst playing in the road just outside her home at some unspecified point in the then recent past.

To our minds, back then, it was considered creepy enough that parents, no matter how devastated by loss, had been so unable to deal with their grief, they'd felt compelled to build what amounted to a full-blown memorial in their own backyard.

> "I can't understand why they couldn't just make do with visiting their daughter's grave in Landican Cemetery, or wherever, like most normal people?"

...was my response upon first being told the story, when my friends and I were gathered under the red-bricked shelters in Church Drive Junior School's playground, one rain-soaked lunch hour.

> "I mean, I helped me Dad bury our cat, Ginger, at the bottom of the garden last summer, and I loved that cat more than any pet we've ever had before or since, and I miss him loads, but I didn't ask me Dad afterwards to build a friggin' big grave-stone down by the old rhododendron bushes in the shape of Ginger's favourite comfy armchair, just so's I could still feel *close* to him!"

My companions had nodded in agreement at that, before suddenly, by unspoken consent, racing around the echoey vastness of the shelters screeching *'Looneee-Looneee-Looneee!'* at the tops of their voices, whilst making exaggerated twirly-twirly motions with their fingers in the general direction of their temporal lobes, a sight which caused a group of ten-year-old girls standing nearby to drop the *Jackie* magazine they'd been poring over intensely, cluck their tongues dryly, and shake their heads at the hopelessly immature behaviour of *boys*.

But if the thought of erecting elaborate monuments to the dear departed on one's own doorstep, so to speak, was incomprehensible enough, there was a subsequent revelation a few days later that the Doll's House actually contained a life-size mannequin of the dead little girl that was dressed in the very same clothes she'd been wearing when she was killed. And, even worse, according to one of the more gruesomely imaginative lads in our class, the distraught, mentally unbalanced parents had driven over to the local cemetery late one moon-lit night and dug up their daughter's broken remains before wrapping them in a colourless sack cloth. They'd then gently placed the body in the boot of their car and driven home, anxiously glancing in their rear view mirrors for the dreaded lights of a passing police car, before placing the body in the garage overnight.

The following morning they'd called upon the services of a good friend who just happened to be a highly talented (not to say impeccably discrete) sculptor who had, for an undisclosed sum of money, perfectly preserved their daughter's corpse in wax like the murderous genius Vincent Price in that classic 1950s, fog-drenched horror movie. The artist had even used a wig fashioned from the girl's real hair, long and blonde and tied in pigtails with bright pink bows, as well as inserting her glassy eyeballs in the doll's sockets and fitting its mouth with her own teeth, which subsequently grinned in an obscene parody of a smile at passers-by.

The effigy had then been placed in the front window of the Wendy House, as a permanent memorial. A ghastly and futile act of defiance in the face of the grim inevitability of death

With these type of macabre stories doing the rounds of course, kids of all ages would frequently dare each other to climb over the garden wall after dark, walk right up to window and tap on the glass....

Of course, some braver souls bragged that they had all too readily accepted the challenge and not only calmly sauntered up to the gaily-curtained glass panes, but had taken the time to drop their pants, turn their back on the doll and given her shiny plastic visage a face-full of pale-white, pimple-ridden backside.

Without anything remotely of note occurring.

By all accounts, the doll just went on gazing indifferently into the middle distance the way all dolls - mummified remains of dead children or otherwise - are *supposed* to do...

The town of Prenton is only a few short miles away from New Ferry, and you might be forgiven for thinking that my ghost-obsessed friends and I would have been instantly drawn to the location of the Doll's House faster than a pack of cheetahs with fireworks tied to their collective tails the minute we'd first heard of its (alleged) existence. And to be perfectly honest, looking back now, I have no clear idea why it was that we didn't immediately set out to investigate the place first-hand, if only to satisfy ourselves there was at least some degree of truth in the legend, or whether in fact it was nothing more than the kind of horrific urban myth that kids had dreamed up to scare each other senseless with at Halloween or when sat around the flickering wood-fire during a mid-summer camping trip. It seems that every time we made plans to embark on an intrepid expedition to the barren wilds of Prenton, - in actuality, a whopping big 30 pence bus ride! - something seemingly more important came along to alter our plans at the last minute.

And so, for one reason or another, it wasn't until I was in my late teenage years that I finally got to the see for myself the Wendy House and its creepy occupant on a dark, sleety afternoon, a few weeks after Christmas. And even then the encounter was quite by accident. I'd somehow managed to take a simple wrong turn after getting off the bus in the middle of the town, whilst on the way to play football with a group of friends. This isn't anywhere near as spookily dramatic as it sounds by the way, nor is it some cliché-ridden prelude to an all-too predictable B-movie. The simple fact was that I'd hardly ever been to the area before, and just to add to the fun; the directions to the footy playing fields had been inscribed on a dog-eared scrap of paper by one of the lads I then worked with, who - coincidentally, or not - just happened to be playing for the opposition and whose handwriting and map-drawing abilities left a great deal to be desired. The minute I alighted from the bus, clutching the most useless document since Neville Chamberlain stood on the tarmac at Heston Aerodrome optimistically waving a slip of wind-blown foolscap, and blathering on inanely about "peace in our time."

The roads and rows of three-bedroomed terraced houses they contained all looked pretty much identical, with nothing to distinguish between them whatsoever. It was really no surprise then that I quickly found myself walking along what was patently the wrong street although I continued to trudge onwards with stubborn determination until I was roughly three quarters of the way down what proved to be a cul-de-sac, and I realised I could go no further unless my sheer pig-headed obstinacy 'inspired' me to vault over a series of garden fences and six-foot tall brick walls, most probably lined with vandal grease, in a bid to locate the elusive football pitches.

Having eventually conceded defeat, I uttered a world-weary sigh and prepared to head back the way I'd come.

It was only then that I noticed the street was completely deserted. But that was hardly surprising, seeing as it was only a degree or two above freezing, and a sleety rain gleefully stung any exposed area of flesh like a merciless welter of ice-cold pin pricks. And although it was only two in the afternoon, it was so dismal and gloomy the majority of the street-lights had been switched on already. I couldn't blame anybody for remaining indoors in such miserable conditions and to be honest, I'd been secretly hoping since I'd climbed out of bed that morning that the match would be called off, but despite the pessimistic predictions of most of my team-mates who I was due to meet up with, (and who I imagined, were already likely checking their watches and laying bets on the likelihood that I wasn't going to show), the game had been given the go-ahead.

I pulled the fur-lined hood of my coat more firmly over my head in a futile attempt to ward off the worst of the elements and dolefully began tramping back towards the bus stop with all the enthusiasm of a horse trotting to a glue factory.

I did raise my weary head on enough occasions though to notice that whilst the curtains of the houses I passed were uniformly drawn, here and there I could see traces of warm orange glows and the familiar flicker of television screens seeping through the various gaps in the thick, dark-coloured drapes, comforting reminders of the normality of everyday family life continuing serenely within.

I realised too that, aside from the slushy sound of my reluctant footsteps, it was deathly quiet and although there was nothing noticeably out of the ordinary about this suburban street, still there remained an undeniable aura of brooding melancholy, and I'd suddenly felt uncomfortable, as though I were being watched. I glanced nervously over my shoulder, half-convinced that I would detect the movement of a curtain, as if someone had been furtively observing me stood in the middle of their road, freezing and bedraggled and very obviously lost. But either the watchers were quicker than me or it had only been my imagination because there was no tell-tale quivering at the edges of any of the drapes, no moon-face peering out curiously at the stranger in their midst.

Aside that is, from the single, pale, oval-shaped visage framed by rosy pink lamp-light, staring out at me from the window of a child's Wendy House.

*****

And so here I was at last....

Finally I was stood before the legendary Prenton Doll's House, (and yes Dear Readers, it was indeed complete with its creepy inhabitant), one of the few supposedly genuinely haunted locations on Merseyside I'd somehow managed to avoid for more than fifteen years.

I know the question you're asking. Did it live up to the high level of terrifying expectations raised by the constant telling and re-telling of a thousand school-yard horror stories?

I guess, as is the case with most things that you've only ever previously *heard* about and spent time picturing in your mind's eye - probably late at night or during a particularly boring school lesson or business conference - on a stormy autumn afternoon, with leaves and assorted detritus spinning in the air like dark confetti, the answer is both yes and no.

As I slowly walked across to the garden containing the Doll's House in a kind of trance, (and quite how I hadn't noticed the building's existence straight away is a mystery in itself – perhaps I'd been too busy staring down at the increasingly treacherous pavement, scared I was going to go flying flat on my arse, just to put the icing, as it were, on what had up until that point been a completely wasted journey). I felt a mixture of both high excitement and not a little fear. The Wendy House, which was indeed, a fairly close approximation of the semi-detached house which towered above it, though the latter was painted a decidedly surrealistic shade of royal blue, stood roughly half-way across a large, tree-lined lawn that was well-tended, although the bleakness of the season had rendered the short grass wiry and unhealthy looking. The only other items of note in the garden were a small wooden shed and an empty metal clotheshorse that stood forlornly over on the concrete patio.

The doll, ah yes, the infamous *doll*, roughly the size of a ten-year-old girl, was stood there alright, A silent sentinel gazing from the windows of the small, tastefully decorated living room, and as I approached the three-foot high brick wall surrounding the property, I could see its wide blue eyes staring out at me with alarming intensity and its ruby-red lips parted in what was doubtless intended to be a cute and innocent smile, but which in actuality, held all the warmth and charm of a great white shark, a corrupt politician or a sick, perverted child-molester grooming their intended prey.

No doubt then the doll was sinister, whether the effect was intentional or not, and just seeing it for the first time, I can't deny it was impossible to suppress a shudder. This was, after all, the stuff of childhood nightmares made real.

Having said that, several things were abundantly clear to me straight away: The doll's long, flowing, sun-bleached blonde locks of hair were unmistakably synthetic, the eyes - whilst unnervingly piercing and realistic-looking - were made of marble or some-such cold, obsidian material, and the twin sets of pearly-white teeth, were obviously every bit as false as those I knew my beloved Nana Smith kept in a tall water-filled glass by her bedside.

Far be it from me to discredit a long-established Urban Myth, but here was, when all was said done, not the preserved remains of a long-dead little girl, replete with genuine body parts, but a doll, created in her likeness, but - for all that - a plastic doll, pure and simple...

Okay, I readily admit, I didn't quite have to the courage to accept that age-old dare to climb over the wall, walk right up to the window of the Wendy House, and press my face up against the glass so that I was almost kissing the effigy, but to be honest that was more down the fact that I was afraid the dead girl's parents might catch me in the act and call the police for the crime of trespassing on their property. After all, given the eerie reputation of the address locally, the couple probably took it in turns to stand sentry duty on the constant look-out for intruders.

Certainly, I had no reason to fear the now thoroughly discredited Wendy House and its sadly poignant occupant. This was nothing other than what its creators intended it to be: a memorial to their dear departed daughter, taken from them at such a tragically tender age.

And as I turned my back on the doll and prepared to walk away, did I for a terrible moment imagine that I could hear something slowly stirring in that miniature household? Something like the rustle of well-worn items of clothing?

Could I honestly say I discerned a series of dry, long-dead tendons stretching and snapping as a pale pink hand with unnaturally long fingers scratched at the windows...?

And would I be resorting to outright fallacy to suggest that the chill afternoon air was suddenly rent with the sound of a door creaking slowly open as something shuffled purposefully and with dark intent across that wiry stretch of grass?

Well now, come on really, what do you think?

*****

The power of dolls to terrorise though, came back to haunt me a whole two decades down the line, (a period of time that seems to me now, has slipped by with frightening ease), when *Channel Four* screened a deeply disturbing programme called *'My Fake Baby.'* It told the story of a desperately sad group of women who are obsessed with collecting eerily-life-like dolls of newly-born toddlers, and dressing and feeding them and taking them out in their prams as though they were real flesh and blood babies. Looking like something from one of David Lynch's more screamingly surreal nightmares, these badly-dressed, garishly made-up individuals spend an exorbitant amount of money and an even more obscene amount of time on these dolls either because they are unable to produce biological children of their own, or due to their sheer selfishness ie; they are physically able to have a baby, they just don't care for the nappy-changing, breast-feeding 'baggage' that comes with it.

In truth, I could only bear to watch half of the programme. I may be a veteran of countless horror films, but the sight of a bunch of tragically deluded, middle-aged women, caked in thick, pancake make-up and with a dress-sense that would have made Baby Jane Hudson look like the epitome of female fashion, was more than even my nerves could stand.

Moving on swiftly from this gratuitously gruesome programme, in 2008, *The Tampa Tribune*, published an account that sounds like the script to the latest entry in the *Child's Play/Chucky* franchise. A family from Lithia, Florida, USA, informed the press and a local TV station that a supposedly cuddly, programmable *Elmo (*from *Sesame Street) Doll,* revealed its dark side after a set of fresh batteries were installed. Instead of cheerfully singing songs or reciting the favourite colour of its two-year-old owner, James Bowman, the doll starting issuing verbal death threats. A squeeze of its fuzzy, fur-covered stomach intoned, in a totally inappropriately bright and breezy-sing-song voice;

'Kill James, Kill James, Kill James!'

"It's not something that you really would think would come out of a toy,"

Melissa Bowman, James' mother, commented to the media – which as understatements go, you might think, is a little like saying that anyone admitting to liking the music of Peter Andre, is likely to have their quotient of cool go vanishing into the ether.

"But once I heard the doll speaking, I was just kind of distraught."

The sinisterly monikered *"Elmo Knows Your Name"* Doll, which connects to a computer to learn certain phrases and names, 'had recently ran out of battery power' Bowman stated. 'About an hour after I put in the new ones, I noticed exactly what it was saying. It was especially frightening because Elmo is James' favourite character, he even has Elmo slippers, but the malfunctioning, death-threat-spouting Elmo was subsequently, and a tad understandably, kept away from Mrs Bowman's remarkably unruffled son.

> "This remains his absolute favourite toy,"

…she said.

> "So we've been going through a lot of hassle because he's trying to climb up the counter and up the closets to get it."

Fisher Price, the toy company that manufactures the dolls, were quick to seek to appease the disgruntled parent, and in a quite stunning display of generosity, offered to issue the Bowman family with a voucher for a replacement doll. Hopefully, one assumes, a loveable, huggable one that has doesn't display a penchant for issuing blood-curdling, homicidal threats to its infant owner. **

THE CURSE OF THE ATTIC DOLL

And to conclude this round-up of terrifying dolls and mannequins, I learned of the following story when I was the editor of *Dead Of Night Magazine,* back in the autumn of 2001…..

Back in the early 1990s, a man from Norfolk, North Virginia, USA, who we know only by the Christian name of 'Bill,' told Peter Park, a correspondent for the consistently excellent publication, *The Anomalist*, how he believed the house where he'd lived for over fifteen years, and which he was then in the process of selling, was haunted by what he termed 'an intensely evil presence.'

Mr Park was himself a witness to the alleged 'paranormal phenomena,' when Bill, a relatively recent divorcee, was busy clearing out the attic at his former home, which had been built in 1899, one dreary afternoon in late-February, while the wind howled mournfully in the eaves and sleet pattered on the rooftop like a thousand jagged fingernails.

Whilst he was rummaging around amidst the cardboard boxes of Christmas decorations, piles of old novels, and a couple of oak-wood trunks filled with a carefully preserved collection of birds' eggs, he came across a jagged hole in the middle of the bare floorboards. On closer inspection Bill noticed that it appeared to be scorched around the edges, and it was obvious the cavity had been created by someone chipping at the wooden planks with a chisel or a knife.

For some indefinable reason, the sight of the hole unnerved him, and before investigating further, he called out to Peter and a couple of female cleaners he had recently hired to help with the renovations elsewhere in the house. They quickly climbed up the stepladder and hauled themselves into the attic, and Bill didn't mind admitting he was glad of their company up there in the shadow-filled loft, with that desolate-sounding wind.

Peter was a little reticent, but the cleaners, let's call them, 'Jan' and 'Mary,' were plainly itching to find out what, if anything, was secreted within the hole and immediately took to exploring the inky-black emptiness with a series of long poles with hooks attached to them. When this course of action yielded little in the way of results, they elected to ignore Bill's advice to err on the side of caution, and fearlessly decided to explore the hole using nought but their bare hands.

Approximately four feet to one side of the opening, they came across an object tucked away under the floorboards. Feverish with excitement, the cleaners dragged out what appeared, from the state of it, to be a very old doll wear-

---

** Source: *The Tampa Tribune* 21st February, 2008.

ing a filthy, rotting 19th Century dress and apron. They held it up to the beam of the flashlight and saw that the doll was a somewhat crude representation of an African-American girl.

Upon seeing the thing close up, Bill was immediately struck by a feeling of intense dread, although at that precise moment he was unable to explain what it was about the doll that was so unsettling.

They stood around for a while, looking at the doll, and suddenly Jan, for reasons best known to herself, decided to initiate a game of catch and threw the object towards Mary, who caught it easily enough, and then let out a scream of agony, a cry that was curiously muffled, as though someone had clapped an invisible hand over her open mouth, in the confined space of the attic.

> "The damn thing just gave me an electric shock!"

…she yelled, frantically rubbing her hand, and dropping the doll to the floor, where it lay, face up, one eye open, the other half-closed as though it mocking the three of them, and daring one of them, *any* of them, to pick it up.

Bill, who was still convinced the girls were playing a practical joke on him, reached down and grabbed hold of the doll with the intention of throwing it unceremoniously into a nearby chest, half-filled with old, moth-eaten blankets and items of clothing he'd been intending to dispose of later that day. As he was about to do so, however, he experienced a sudden change of heart, and instead carefully placed the doll in an upright sitting position atop the pile of discarded apparel.

And he left the lid of the trunk wide open as he turned to his companions and said with a laugh that was slightly forced,
> "Well, we wouldn't want the poor little thing to suffocate, now would we?"

Despite his refusal to afford any degree of credence to the notion that it could physically harm anyone, Bill couldn't deny the mere sight of the doll chilled him to the bone and, if the truth were told, he didn't care too much for the way it felt when he held it in his hands, either.

He later told his friend, Peter.

> "I was the one who found Spike's body lying in the gutter, when I was riding my bike home from soccer practice. It was my first encounter with the messy aftermath of death, and amidst my shock and grief, I remember thinking it was a little strange that there wasn't the slightest trace of blood anywhere in the vicinity. But when I gingerly picked him up I could immediately tell he was all broken inside, and although he was still fairly warm to the touch, his head lolled crazily this way and that like it was on ball bearings."

He was unable to suppress a shudder at this point.

> "I know it sounds crazy, Pete, but I'm telling you, holding that doll in my hands… It felt somehow like it had died a violent death…And a fairly *recent* death at that. I mean, you'd have thought it would have been stone-cold having been buried down inside that hole for God knows how long. But I could have sworn that doll was radiating a kind of slowly fading warmth … like there was still a faint flicker of life somewhere within its plastic form…"

After dismissing the cleaners for the day, Bill and Peter set about locking every door of his former residence, and hailed a taxi, ostensibly to take them home. As it turned out however, and by unspoken mutual consent, they asked the cabbie to stop the moment they sighted the *Coors* and *Budweiser* signs flickering in the windows of a downtown dive bar. They figured they could both use a drink or two. And they sat nursing their bourbon on the rocks, surrounded by the comforting, smoke-filled air of normality; the hub of conversation merging with a baseball game on the TV, and *The Eagles* blissful harmonies floating from the *Wurlitzer* jukebox...

And back in the attic, the doll continued to sit bolt upright, its bright marble eyes glinting in a slab of moonlight that filtered through the dusty windowpane, as though it were patiently waiting for someone in the dead silence of that empty house.

Early the next morning, just before eight, the two men, both nursing killer hangovers, met up with the cleaning girls, to continue their work at the house on behalf of the people who were due to move in a few weeks down the line.

> "Okay, everyone, before we get stuck into doing anything else, why don't we all go up to the attic together,"

Bill, suggested, smiling sheepishly.

> "I want to clear out the remainder of my stuff, and bin the rest, as quickly as possible. I don't know about you, guys, but I really don't want to have to set foot in that attic again after today, if I can help it."

They immediately agreed, although with some degree of trepidation, and dragged down the stepladder to ascend in single file.

It was Bill who first stepped into the loft.

The first thing he noticed was how deathly quiet it seemed up there. The howling wind of the previous day had died down considerably, although it was still bitterly cold, and heavy snow was forecast for later that afternoon. He was shocked to find he could clearly hear the sound of his heart thudding away merrily in his chest and his knee joints cracking like pistol shots, ('*Getting fat and outta shape,*' a sly, insidious voice delighted in informing him, as he stood in the centre of the roof space; '*Gonna have to start working out some, bud, or you'll have a heart attack before you're forty!...And seeing as how you're already knocking on the dreaded door marked thirty **nine**...!*')

He paused to catch his breath and couldn't bring himself to look in the direction of the doll. At least, not at first. He waited until Peter, Annie and Mary had joined him, but even then it was only with the utmost reluctance.

As it turned out, his wariness proved to be well-founded and he felt gooseflesh spread up his arms as he glanced at the trunk directly beneath the dust-smeared glass of the skylight, on the other side of which snowflakes fell in silent thuds – the advance guard of the predicted full-blown blizzard. The lid of the chest was still standing wide open. The pile of blankets and old clothes were clearly visible, just as before and there was no sign that anything had changed since they'd left the attic, the previous evening.

Except, that is, that the doll was no longer sitting not-so-prettily on top of the heap of moth-eaten material.

Instead it was hanging from the rafters with a thick piece of rope tied around its scrawny neck, and Bill felt a cold, slimy worm of fear wiggle the length of his spine, as he watched the doll swing slowly back and forth, the creaking of the twine impossibly loud in the weighty silence.

> "Who the hell put that there?"

Bill shouted, angrily, convinced that someone had been playing a sick joke at his expense.

No one answered, and really no one had to. Bill was more than aware that he was the only one with a key to the house and there was absolutely no sign of a break-in. Even if someone had succeeded in gaining entry without leaving any trace of a forced entry, a quick search of the premises revealed that there was nothing missing whatsoever. Which begged the obvious question; why on earth would anyone take the time and trouble to enter the attic just to hang an ancient-looking doll from one of the wooden cross beams?

*****

In the days and weeks that followed, Bill was far too preoccupied with the stress and strain of moving house to give much consideration to the mystery, and it wasn't until well into the spring following the discovery of the doll, when he was pottering about in his new garden, that he suddenly remembered that which he had truly never really forgotten.

When Bill and wife had still been married, they had learned from an old woman named Abigail Critchley, the sketchy details of a tragedy that had happened at their house, many years before. Ms Critchley, their nearest neighbour, stated that when she was very young, she used to take piano lessons at the house, and at some point, she found that the then occupants had given birth to a retarded daughter. This would have been sometime between 1910 and 1920. The heartless couple had been so embarrassed by their progeny, that they locked her away like a dirty secret in the attic, and overcome with shame, the little girl had hung herself from the very same rafters as that African-American doll.

Peter's friends had an associate who claimed to have psychic powers, and he apparently warned them that there was an entity in the house *'something very sorrowful and unfulfilled,'* and that he could feel its presence throughout the building, though it was at its strongest in the attic.

After finding the doll hanging that morning, it was taken to another local psychic, a female, and when she took it out of the bag in which it had been transported, she promptly screamed and threw it to the floor. She said that she wanted nothing to do with it, that it was evil beyond belief, and that she felt, when she laid her hands on it, as though she were being suffocated. There was also an intense pain in her neck, as though she were being choked or hanged.

She told Peter's friend that they should get rid of the doll as soon as possible, to burn it in fact. She believed that there was an incredibly unhappy spirit desperate for release contained within, and that this was the only way to set it free.

A second opinion was sought from yet another psychic.

This one was less fearful, but he too confirmed that he had detected there was a 'strong entity' associated with the doll.

He offered to take the doll and place it in his collection of other strange objects upon which he would perform psychometry, the claimed ability to be able to psychically read the past history of an item by merely making physical contact with it.

About a month or so down the line, this psychic was found dead in his apartment from an apparent heart attack. Somewhat chillingly, the neighbour who discovered his body said that the psychic had died clutching the doll to his chest like an abandoned lover clinging desperately to a memento of happier days.

Mr Park's friend has theorised that the story behind the doll has its origins in the supposition that the former master of his old house had impregnated a young, live-in black girl. She later died in childbirth, but though the baby girl survived, the issue from such a union proved to be so embarrassing to the family that she was locked away, out of sight in the attic. Several years later, bored to distraction one day, the young girl hid her only companion, a doll, in a hole that she had chiselled in the attic floorboards.

And then, having weighed up her options, decided she had none....

Not in *this* world, at least.

She hung herself, just the way the first of the psychics had stated.

But she had refused to rest easy. Somehow, her angry, vengeful spirit had attached itself to the doll, and proceeded to haunt the house from that day on. The removal of the doll appeared to successfully exorcise the premises, but the doll itself, imbued with some malignant trace of its former owner, brought bad luck to everyone who touched it.

> "Something decidedly inhuman (in the truest sense of the word), hung that doll from the rafters to clearly signal its presence. Of that, I have no doubt whatsoever,"

Bill told anyone willing to listen.

> "I tried burying my head in the proverbial sand, and telling myself that there was a perfectly logical explanation for what was happening, but I guess, when you get right down to it, there's just no denying the terror of the incontestably real."

His belief in the reality of the supernatural was further bolstered by his friend Peter, who later mentioned to Bill that he had experienced an encounter with 'the evil presence' which, for reasons best known to himself, he'd chosen not to relate to anyone before.

> "As I was climbing the stairs to the second floor, helping you clear the house of your belongings, I was suddenly struck with a startlingly vivid mental image of a young girl hanging from the ceiling with a thick coil of rope tied tightly around her neck. I swear, Bill, I did not know the story behind the doll at that time, and I thought maybe I was going a little crazy, so I didn't say anything about the vision until now. I kept my counsel. I'm sure you can appreciate why that was.
>
> A couple of days later, on another visit to the house, you told me what you'd had learned about the doll from the psychics, and I found I was faced with an unpalatable, but unavoidable truth. Either I had been mentally 'touched' by the spirit trapped inside that pig-ugly doll or else I somehow picked up the image from your mind."

Whatever the case, it was hard to shake from my mind something I remember reading during my university days. It was one of those H.P. Lovecraft paperbacks, published by Arkham House, and the lines the author had written had never seemed more appropriate than they did right then:

> "There truly does seem to be present in certain old, supposedly inanimate objects 'a trace of some dim essence; more than form or weight, of a tenuous aether, indeterminate"

OMINOUS QUATERMASS-STYLE FACTORIES

The *'Land and Marine'* factory directly opposite our house on Dock Road North was an enormous, thickly-walled complex that slashed through the leafy suburbs like an ugly, ash-coloured scar.

From my bedroom window, I could clearly see its vast, intricate network of spitefully hissing pipes and thrumming machinery, sending clouds of evil-smelling fumes high up into the air day and night, and as no one in my family or my circle of friends seemed to know of anyone who actually worked at the plant, the factory's official purpose remained shrouded in mystery. Although the installation's name seemed to indicate it churned out parts for ships, boats and amphibious craft as well as cranes, bulldozers and farmers' tractors, the truth is for a horror-obsessed 12 year-old boy at least, it was all-too easy to believe this was just a convenient cover story aimed at obscuring the truth about what really went on behind the miles of impenetrable concrete walls, barbed wire fences and double-padlocked gates....

A top secret, government-sponsored project to manufacture flying saucers using back-engineered alien technology. A cabal of escaped Nazi scientists, attempting to create some weird kind of super-race by transplanting the heads of various animals onto human torsos suspended in a flotation tank filled to the brim with some sort of greenish-coloured liquid. A blood farm for resourcefully inventive vampires, replete with thousands upon thousands of rows of people of all ages, hung upside down with plastic tubing attached to their veins to provide fast-food sustenance on tap for the eternally bloodthirsty.

Or, was it - as was the case in *Quatermass II - Enemy From Space,* (a movie I first caught as part of a Saturday night *BBC Frightmare* double-bill whilst on a caravan holiday in North Wales, one long-ago summer) – that the factory was being run by a race of gigantic, extraterrestrial blob-like creatures intent upon taking over the Earth by enslaving the local populace, and forcing them to produce gallons of ammonia in huge black domes – the creatures' sole food source on their impossibly distant home planet?

(Above): The Land & Marine Factory : The ominous-looking domes and acres of steaming pipes, a dead ringer for the alien breeding plant in *Quatermass II: Enemy From Space*.

The movie's effects may have dated a little in these days of (occasionally) jaw-dropping CGI, but the plot-line still resonates with a degree of contemporary relevance given its central theme of shadowy Government conspiracy, and the innate mistrust of authority figures, in these terror-haunted times. Then there is the omnipotent threat from 'alien forces' whose sole intent is the eradication of freedom and individuality and the destruction of our Western way of life.

The film opens with Brian Donlevy's short-tempered Professor Quatermass, nearly being run off the road by another car careering out of control along some dark, rural road. The head of the Rocket Group is confronted by a typically perplexing mystery after stumbling from his own vehicle, clearly primed to blow his top (and launch his trusty toupee into orbit, while he's at it). Instead, he finds that the driver of the car, that's since screeched to a halt in a lay-by, is a woman desperately trying to get her boyfriend to the nearest hospital. The man, virtually unconscious, has a strange, V-shaped burn on the side of his face. The source of the injury, it seems, is a 'meteor' which the Professor decides to take back with him to study at his group's HQ.

Before he arrives there, however, his colleagues at the Rocket Group are already tracking a veritable shower of equally enigmatic 'meteorites', that fall to Earth in an impossibly slow manner.

It turns out that both incidents seem to have occurred in the exact same location: the eerie, marshy vista of Winnerden Flats.

When they set out to investigate the area the following day, Quatermass is aghast to find the quiet little village that had stood there for years beyond counting, has been replaced by a huge installation that bears an uncanny resemblance to the Professor's own designs for a moon base. The plant, (in reality, the *Shell Haven Oil Refinery* in Essex), is a mixture of twisting pipes, rows of windowless buildings and several gigantic domes, surrounded by high wire-mesh fencing and squads of heavily-armed guards, so mean and moody they make *Securicor* look about as menacing as Ken Dodd's *Diddymen*.**

What follows is a typically mid-1950s exercise in 'you-can't-trust-anyone-in-authority' style paranoia.

This is perfectly illustrated by the scene where the initially sceptical Inspector Lomax is suddenly provided with incontrovertible proof that even the Head of Scotland Yard is involved in the conspiracy: he has the v-shaped imprint of alien control burned onto his wrist.

The Professor meanwhile, makes a disconcerting discovery of his own. The official Government line that the factory only manufactures synthetic food for the good of humanity, turns out to be not so much an outright lie, as a distortion of the truth. It *does* indeed produce food, but solely for *alien* consumption.

Two scenes in particular had a lasting effect on me: mid-way through the film, *Quatermass*, Inspector Lomax and a London journalist with a fondness for Scotch whisky (played by a wisecracking, pre-*Carry On* Sid James), pay a visit to the settlement that has been constructed to replace the village of Winnerden Flats. It brought to mind the creation of the faceless 'New Towns' that had sprung up all across the country in the mid 1950s, including Liverpool. And by the time I was a teenager, 25 years or so later, hideous blocks of high-rise flats and rows of identical houses situated on the far-flung outskirts of the City, such as Kirby and Speke, with no trace of individuality, were the norm rather than the exception. The British Government destroyed whole communities with this enforced exodus, all but destroying the unique sense of character that had made Liverpool famous during its heyday. To me, these 'New Towns' had something of an *Invasion of the Bodysnatchers/Stepford Wives* artificiality about them, and certainly this was the case in the movie, where the townspeople who have been unwittingly helping to build the plant, (designed to feed and acclimatise the aliens so that they can breathe our air), act like personality-devoid robots because they are afraid they'll lose their jobs if they talk to outsiders. This is a fact which more than one film critic has pointed out gives the film a kind of proto-Marxian twist.

The other scene involves a bluff, down-to-earth Government minister (such a creature apparently did exist back in the late 1950s), named Vinny Broadhead. During an officially sanctioned visit to Winnerden Flats, with the Professor and Lomax, he wanders away from the main party to carry out some snooping on his own, only to fall into one of the 'synthetic-food-filled' domes and shambles in indescribable agony down the metal steps, covered head to foot with some evil chemical substance. A foul mixture of black, corrosive slime and strips of smoking flesh drip from his jerking body as he emits a scream, so high-pitched it's almost feminine; 'Quatermass,' he shrieks, 'I had to look. I slipped and fell in. No, don't *touch* me! The food…*It burns!*'

This harrowing scene had an especially disturbing effect upon me as it brought to mind a series of nightmare images of the poor man who had suffered a similar fate after accidentally (?) falling into a huge drum filled with acid whilst working at the *British Leather Company's* tan-yard in Birkenhead, a year or so before I first saw the film (*see elsewhere in this book for the full story, and see why I've seen fit to include a question mark alongside that mischievously ambiguous word, 'accidentally'*).

** For those of you outside the UK, or even inside the UK and under the age of about 35, 'The Diddy Men' are a creation of the British comedian Ken Dodd.

When Ken Dodd began playing seaside resorts, he mythologised his home area of Knotty Ash in Liverpool and created a miniature race of people who inhabited it.

Diddy is northern slang for "little".

The film ends with Quatermass successfully convincing the townspeople that they are being used as unwitting slaves to assist the extraterrestrial blobs to conquer the Earth, and in a literally explosive climax, the aliens are destroyed and the planet is saved. That is, until the next threat arrives (which as far as Quatermass is concerned is an invasion by proxy courtesy of long-buried buried spaceship discovered during an archaeological excavation at Hobb's Lane underground station in London).

I never found out for sure what it was they did over at the *Land & Marine* plant, just over the road from where I lived, but there were many occasions when I would gaze at the factory's drably grey façade and its vast array of steam-belching machinery, and wonder....

THE LEGEND OF 'OWLD NELL'S'

There used to be an archetypal haunted-looking house, one that would grace the cover of any work dealing with the supernatural, and built, appropriately enough, alongside a reputedly-haunted graveyard, standing at the point where Ellen's Lane became The Wiend, in the heart of Bebington, a proverbial stone's throw from where NFHS member Stevie Gee, used to live at the time.

You can forget all about the Murphy House, featured at the beginning of this book, which was, when you got right down to it, (for all the undeniably dread-filled atmosphere contained within), a typically nondescript, semi-detached council house situated on an ordinary, unremarkable road.

This was the real deal. The town's equivalent of the curse-ridden Fengriffen residence located in the midst of the bleak, desolate, windswept moors, Norman Bates' off-her rocker 'mother's' domain, the spook-laden mansion at the top of Haunted Hill, or indeed Hugh Crane's *'born bad,'* toweringly menacing edifice.

The *true* history of the house, and those who had lived there during the years of its existence, (it was demolished sometime during the late 1970s), has been lost in the mists of time, deemed unworthy of remembrance even by the most diligent of contributors to the local, *'all our yesteryears',* websites.

But us kids, back then, we had a name for it.

A name that seemed to suit the crumbling, ivy-strewn mansion very well.

Very well, *indeed.*

We called it 'Owld Nell's.'

*****

I couldn't honestly tell you when the building first came to be christened with that less-than-flattering nickname, aside from the fact that it seemed curiously apt, and it stuck like a particularly sloppy spit-wad fired at the class-room ceiling during a boring science lesson.

Urban legend dictated that the house was latterly owned by an elderly lady named, Nell, or Nelly, or some other derivative thereof, and maybe it was; who, but the teller of tall tales and camp-fire ghost stories, can say for sure?

What is for certain, is that it must once have been an extremely grand house; the former residence of *exceedingly* well-off people. When I first encountered it, however, on the day the rains finally came at the end of the long, drought-ridden summer of '76, it had long since been unoccupied, and had started to fall into a sad state of terminal disrepair.

Which, of course, only added to its air of eerie mystique.

'Owld Nell`s' stood at the end of a winding, tree-lined driveway, and was therefore rendered invisible from the main road. You only became aware it even existed, when you turned the third or fourth bend in the path that wound its way through the garden's foliage - impenetrably thick, even in the dead heart of winter - and were suddenly confronted with the dirty grey, clematis-covered walls of every Haunted House you ever read about, viewed on a cinema screen, or dreamt about in a nightmare you'd sooner forget.

The first thing you noticed was the house was entirely shuttered by graffiti-strewn wooden boards, save for the large, ground floor bay window, the pane of which, somehow (and vaguely disturbingly), remained intact. It admitted no amount of light, however, even on the very brightest of days. No shaft of cheery sunlight could ever hope to pierce that Stygian gloom, and you were struck by the distinctly unsettling impression that beyond the set of dusty, velvet drape curtains, there was nothing but a black howling void, an infinity of nothingness, where a host of Lovecraftian horrors lay in wait for the foolishly brave or unwary.

The slate roof was lined with several elegant chimney stacks, but no birds chose to nest in any of them. The grass of the front lawn was a sickly, yellowy colour, and a stone faerie statue with both of its butterfly wings sheared off, peered out disconsolately from between the tangles of weeds and rank-smelling undergrowth.

It was altogether a grim and foreboding property.

The very last place you would want to be within a hundred miles of, given a choice.

The thick, oaken, front door stood ajar, though.

And oh, that was the *thing*....

*****

My schoolmates used to talk about 'Owld Nell's' in hushed, but excitable whispers at every opportunity, (whilst some would-be comedian loudly whistled the theme tune to *The Twilight Zone,* as a background musical accompaniment). Thus, I tried to mentally steel myself prior to embarking on the short trip to the infamous house from my address in New Ferry, on a cool and drizzly early September morning.

Arriving at the scene of so many half-way believable stories, my initial impressions of 'Owld Nell's' were curiously ambiguous:

Fear, a skin-crawling sensation, like a host of tiny insects scuttling up and down my spine and across the nape of my neck?

Yes, there was that, certainly. But there was something else, too. A melancholic sense of awe. Of history unwritten, but nonetheless resonant. Of lives lived and moments shared. Of long, idyllic summer nights, the sweet-smelling air filled with laughter and the excited chatter of children and the exquisite melody of a Steinway grand piano wafting through the open window. Of thick snowfall and muffled shouts and the smoke from log fires fading to a misted haze on the pink-tinged horizon....

It was that damned open door, you see.

It spoke not only of the obvious invitation to enter, to step inside and walk the building's labyrinthine, pitch black corridors, with God only knew who or what for company, (and it was easy to imagine something eagerly grabbing your hand with cold, clasping, wormy fingers the moment you stepped over the threshold), but also as a poignant reminder that this building was once, in every sense of the word, a home, just like the row of smart, though essentially characterless, terraced houses that now stand in 'Owld Nell's' place.

The house may not have had a verifiable history, something you could look up and check out for yourself in the Civic Centre Library or on the Internet, but as so often happens in the absence of hard facts, the vine-like tendrils of local folklore and superstition thrived in abundance.

One of the most oft-told tales that was doing the rounds at the time I first visited the place was a veritable *'Tales from the Crypt,'* and furthermore one that served to act as a powerful deterrent to anyone thinking of entering the house.

Like most urban legends, there were probably many variations on the theme, but the story, as I remember it, went something like this...

*****

The mansion had stood empty since the late 1940s, after the last occupants, Nell, and her unnamed husband, let's call him Lionel, had both died on the premises in decidedly nasty circumstances, and people simply refused to live in the place following their deaths, despite the chronic housing shortage of the times.

Perhaps that shouldn't be too surprising however, when you hear what is alleged to have taken place at that once magnificent residence. Nell, who had married late in life, was often, to use the popular euphemism, 'four sheets to the wind,' and was also possessively jealous to the point of insanity. Lionel, meanwhile, a good fifteen-years younger than Nell, was a successful taxidermist, who, in a moment of hubris, (or out-right big-headedness if you'd prefer), had shown his middle-aged wife the tricks of his trade one rainy Sunday afternoon, and Nell, for once at least partly sober, had taken to the stuffing of dead animals like a duck (albeit a dead, perfectly preserved one), to water.

Not long after this crash course in taxidermy, Nell discovered that Lionel was having an affair. The precise details of how she came by this information differ depending on the storyteller, some say she found a love letter in the inside pocket of his jacket, others that he joined her in finishing off a vintage bottle of wine, and got so drunk he accidentally called Nell by his lover's name at the most inappropriate time imaginable; during the height of sexual passion.

Either way, though, it had the same effect.

Something inside Nell snapped, like the cracking of a rotten twig on a dark forest floor, and although on the face of it she pretended to forgive her husband in the wake of his tearful confessions and pledges of undying love, from that moment, Lionel was doomed.

The problem for Nell though, was that even in her psychotic state, a part of her knew implicitly that she loved her husband still and couldn't imagine life without him. She knew too, that she could never trust him and that is was only a matter of time before he embarked on another affair. But then, if she simply killed him, she'd still wind up all alone with nothing but the cold consolation of memories for company for the rest of her sorry life.

So, how to resolve that particular conundrum?

The answer came to her one dark, stormy night, while Lionel was alone, busy putting together a large order of native British mammals for Liverpool Museum, down in the converted cellar he used as his workshop.

He was so engrossed in what he was doing; he didn't hear Nell sneaking up behind him in her stockinged feet and only became aware she was there when he felt the first blow of the lump hammer crack open his skull. By then of course it was far too late. By the second or third stroke, Lionel's philandering days were well and truly over, and by the fourth, so was his life...

Nell only stopped when she saw she'd succeeded in splattering his brains all over the cellar walls. She then took a much-needed shower, changed her blood-soaked clothes, and - pausing only to take occasional sips of her glass of Chablis - she set about removing all of her dead husband's vital organs. Then after dumping them in a bucket, she proceeded to stuff his empty body with various spices in a rough approximation of the technique used by the ancient Egyptians to preserve their noble dead.

Nell then dragged the husk upstairs and placed it, with a loving wife's tender care, beneath the soft, warm blankets of their double bed.

And there it remained for several weeks, and each and every night - after she'd changed into her nightdress, cleaned her teeth and brushed her hair - Nell would lie down beside her perfectly preserved husband, and place her loving arms around him, pulling him close to her. (And you can bet my imagination ran wild at this point of the story, when I considered the awful possibility that she had likely preserved his 'wedding tackle,' and if she had, what she might get up to with it on long lonely nights).

When Lionel's employers, associates, and eventually the police, made enquiries as to where he had disappeared to, Nell simply told them that he had left her for another woman, packing his suitcases overnight without even bothering to give her a forwarding address.

Never the most sociable of people to start with, Nell thereafter became even more of a recluse, and seldom were the occasions that she ventured outside her front door. She had no other family or friends, arranged to have her groceries and other essentials hand-delivered from a store in Bebington Village, and whilst the garden grew wild and overgrown, the house - from the outside at least - was extremely well-kept.

No-one had any cause to suspect that murder most foul had been committed, and things might have gone on that way for a very long time if fate hadn't intervened on the evening of what should have been their silver wedding anniversary.

Nell had brought Lionel's body downstairs to celebrate the occasion and sat him in his favourite chair at the head of the dining table upon which she'd prepared a sumptuous candlelit meal. Neither of them, it seemed, had much of an appetite for food, although Nell had proven herself a real trooper by downing two bottles of vintage wine, and still managing to stagger to her feet at the end of the evening's festivities to engage in a slow, romantic waltz with her husband to a crackly old 78rpm copy of Glenn Miller's *Moonlight Serenade*, the song they'd chosen for their first dance at their wedding, all those years before.

She'd managed to drag Lionel to his feet, his body as limp and lifeless as a scarecrow's, and as Nell dragged him round the living room floor in a grotesque parody of tripping the light fantastic, she must have somehow lost her balance and gone sprawling head over heels, cracking her skull on the edge of that Steinway grand piano. She was dead before she hit the polished wooden floor in a crumpled heap.

She lay there for the best part of a week, and may have lain there longer still if it hadn't have been for the delivery boy calling at the house with an armful of pre-ordered groceries. He had noticed the awful smell that emanated from the letter box after he pushed it open to shout Nell's name, when no one answered his increasingly frantic knocking at the front door.

The police duly found Nell lying beneath her dead husband's perfectly preserved corpse in the middle of the living room floor with a swarm of grotesquely bloated bluebottles hovering lazily above the pool of congealed blood that had spread like a corona around her ruined head.

In the long years that have since slipped by, Owld Nell's restless spirit has reputedly haunted the premises, described by those who have claimed to have seen her, as being a pitifully thin, emaciated spectre with black hollows for eyes, and thin wispy hair barely covering her mottled scalp.

She carries a blood-stained sickle in one hand.

A heavy mallet in the other.

And her thin lips are parted in a hideous rictus grin...

THE CYCLOPEAN STONES OF *ESCAPE INTO NIGHT*

Some of the most terrifying fictional entities I've ever 'encountered' in any form of media, were featured in, as was so often the case back in the 1970s, a children's tea-time TV series called *'Escape Into Night.'* First screened back in 1972, (I don't think it's ever been shown since, and perhaps with good reason - it would doubtless scare children witless, even in these cynical, seen-it-all-before times), and only recently released on DVD, the memories of this programme have remained startlingly vivid and at the same time disconcertingly vague, not unlike, appropriately enough, the jumbled recollections of a fevered dream upon waking.

The series was based on Catherine Storr's wonderfully evocative 1958 novel, called *Marianne Dreams* about a young girl, (the titular Marianne), who, when confined to bed after a serious horse-riding accident, discovers she has the magical ability to 'dream herself' into the illustrations she's drawn in her sketchbook. And these basic,

though nevertheless striking caricatures, rendered in a childish scrawl, gave ample credence to the contemporary *Radio Times* review of the series which accurately described it as being *'a haunting story full of vivid images,'*

Although my clear, concise recollections of *Escape Into Night* are a trifle sketchy, (the inexorable passage of time and all that), the things that I do remember are a gallery of nightmarish snapshots, like the jumbled-up recollections of a half-remembered dream upon waking: a misshapen house with barred windows and a boarded-up front door, standing in the middle of a grim and desolate vista. A single, wind-blasted tree. A giant, massively out-of-perspective transistor radio with huge tuning dials, permanently broadcasting the mystic nonsense that exists between stations. Marianne's imaginary friend, the lonely, pyjama-clad Mark, afflicted with some crippling disease. A lonely, beckoning lighthouse. And over-riding all, the circle of stones – boulders really - sit, squat and bloated-looking, in the centre of the fenced garden like disinterested sentinels, until Marianne, in a fit of juvenile anger at some perceived insult issued by her companion, draws into 'reality' a single, Cyclopean eye on each of 'The Watchers,' who then spring to malign life, intent upon slowly, oh, so *slowly,* entering the house and killing the entrapped children within.

There was one scene in particular that fills me still with sickening, goose-bump-raising fear: Mark turns to Marianne and states that they can't leave the 'Paper House' because they are being watched. When our heroine looks out the window to see what Mark is referring to, she exclaims, in hushed, awed tones,

>'There are people out there!'

>'Look again,'

Mark insists.

And when she does, we see a single eyelid open, from the point of view of one of the living boulders, glaring malevolently at Marianne's shocked, pale-white oval face, as she peers out of the curtain-less windows.

A short while later, the over-sized transistor radio crackles into life and the room is filled with a chorus of flat, yet undeniably menacing, robotic voices: the voices of The Stones With Eyes.

'We are coming! We are coming!' the rocks declare, and another terrified glance out of the window confirms that they are, almost imperceptibly, creeping ever closer...

DEAD OF NIGHT

Of course, there is something irrefutably ominous about standing stones, in fact as well as fiction. Be they erected at sites of ancient veneration, the entrance to Neolithic burial chambers, or a solitary megalith leaning drunkenly in the middle of a desolate, wind-blasted heath, they can inspire feelings of awe, wonder and not a little dread, and it's all too easy to give credence to the folkloric beliefs that these vaguely human-shaped slabs of rock can be imbued with life at a witch's command, or when bathed in the bone-white glare of an autumn moon.

*****

Just as a little aside, I remember once reading about an East African big game hunter named Eric Dauncey Tongue in *Alien Animals,* a book by the respected Fortean authors, Janet and Colin Bord.

The details were tantalisingly brief but it seems that the formerly fearless huntsman, who had doubtless encountered all manner of dangerous animals in his native country, described the most frightening thing he had ever seen as something he'd encountered whilst walking one night at Hangley Cleave Barrows in Somerset, back in 1908. In his own words, he stated that what he saw was a 'crouching form, like *a rock with* matted hair all over it, and pale, flat eyes.'

When he spoke of the experience 20 years on, Eric still emphasised its terrifying nature. He believed the entity to have been a 'Barrow Guardian.'

A COLLECTION OF HORRORS IN THE MIDST OF LIVERPOOL CITY CENTRE
'Master Butchers, African Fetish Dolls & the Mummy's Sarcophagus'
One of my earliest and most frightening memories is of the day I got lost in the middle of St John's Market in Liverpool City Centre, during a pre-Christmas shopping trip with my mum and dad, when I was about six years old.

I can clearly remember that one minute I was calmly walking alongside my parents through the hyper-actively bustling market, staring wide-eyed at the brightly decorated shop fronts' stalls filled with the promise of fabulous, gaily-wrapped treasures and the pine-scented magic of the festive season, (and not even the potentially dispiriting sight of multiple, patently fake Santas standing on every street corner could dampen my sense of wondrous excitement). The next I was being pushed and shoved by crowds of impatient adults, a heaving sea of greedy humanity that seemed to be hell-bent on a mission to separate me from my parents by any means possible. And in this they were brutally successful. These scowling, grim-faced giants seemed to be possessed by some avaricious, 'get-the-hell-outta-my-way' Demonic entity, the expressions on their faces uniformly manic as they desperately hunted for a bargain or rushed home to put their feet up, having spent countless hours traipsing around Liverpool in the midst of consumer-driven pandemonium, whilst still others reeked of alcohol and stale cigarette smoke, and regarded me with hostile glares or drunken leers.

With shocking suddenness, I found I was completely disoriented and totally lost, and what I'd dreamed as I'd set out with my parents earlier that morning would be a landscape filled with all kinds of delightful enchantments, had been instantly transformed into a scene from a waking nightmare. It was so upsetting, even the reassuringly familiar Christmas carols that were being piped through the market's speaker system sounded discordant and unbearably tinny, and things were hardly improved much by the sight of the life-size cartoon figure of *'The Master Butcher'* suspended above the market's main meat counter.

It was supposed to be an eye-catching advert for the huge cut-price turkeys on display: *('Sumptuously Succulent & Festively Fresh!')* and it certainly succeeded in grabbing your attention, but not, to my terrified six-year-old mind at least, for any commercial reasons. I was convinced the figure bore a disturbing resemblance to a criminally insane serial-killer, what with its hideously too-wide, toothy grin, blood-soaked apron and its head, complete with bright red, spiky haircut, eternally nodding from side to side in a hypnotic fashion, casting alternative glances at the two-pronged meat fork in the one hand, and a lethal-looking cleaver in the other.

It seemed to be silently mocking me as I cried out for my mum and dad, who were absolutely nowhere to be seen. And I am not at all sure quite how I didn't surrender to total panic and run blindly through the crowds to wind up getting even more lost than I was already (if that were at all possible).

I'm not sure how long it was before some kind, elderly couple saw me cowering in fear amongst a row of hangers containing jeans and women's skirts, and took pity on me. After quickly establishing what had happened, they took me by the hand to search for my parents. Mercifully, they soon led me away from the manic grin of *'The Master Butcher'* and after a few minutes I was reunited with my Mum and Dad, who had anxiously been waiting for me at one of the main entrances. I raced over to them with my arms outstretched and tears of relief welling in my eyes. And when I began babbling incessantly about 'angry-faced giants,' and 'killer-butchers,' they immediately sought to reassure me that there were nothing to be scared of, and that I'd just been spooked by getting lost in an unfamiliar place in the midst of countless strangers.

And of course, they were right.

But all the same, I couldn't resist casting a fearful glance back over my shoulder as we headed for the exits...and there, still clearly visible over the tops of the assorted stalls selling food, clothing, jewellery, books and various types of electrical goods, was the blood-red spiky hair, bulging eyes and toothsome grin of *'The Master Butcher'*. I grabbed hold of my father's hand a little tighter, and he smiled down at me, and I felt a little better. I knew, even at my tender age, that the knife and cleaver-wielding monstrosity was nothing more than a cheap, garishly-painted advertising prop, and that it could no more harm than the Daleks, The Wicked Witch of the West, or the Troll hiding under the bridge, or a thousand other mythical characters that fascinated me as a child (and still do!)

But another part of me knew, with equal certainty, that later that very night I'd be wake to hear a cold, maniacal chuckling in the far corner of the bedroom, and a metallic scraping, that could only be the sound of cutting instruments being sharpened.....

One depressingly, drizzly Saturday morning towards the end of the school summer-holidays, my friends and I were desperate to kill a couple of hours before going to see the matinee showing of Dino De Laurentiis' re-make of *King Kong*, at Liverpool's *Odeon* cinema on London Road, (obviously, we didn't know then that the film was nothing short of an insult to the classic Willis O' Brien original, with its much-vaunted special effects proving to be about as ground-breaking as a paraplegic mole!)

After being chased out of several clothes and music stores in town by irate security staff, who rightly suspected we had little money to spend, we sought shelter in the City's impressive museum. Once inside, we whiled away a couple of hours walking around the magnificent Neo-Classical building, taking in the Dinosaur Exhibition, The Natural History Department and The Planetarium, before heading for the World Culture Floor, which, from previous visits, had always been one of my favourite displays. It featured detailed paintings, full-scale models and genuine archaeological artefacts from various cultures, including those of the Mayans, the American Indians and the ancient civilisations of Greece and Rome.

It was the three or four large rooms dedicated to Egyptology that were of greatest interest to me, however. When my friends and I stepped into the softly-lit chambers, we immediately saw that there was no one else around. The place was entirely deserted, and this only added to the unmistakably eerie atmosphere that permeated the exhibition, which consisted of a large selection of Egyptian relics, including intricately designed earthenware, artwork and jewellery.

But it was the sight of the numerous, marvellously ornate caskets containing the remains of the formerly highly exalted that truly caught the eye.

It was always difficult to dispel the irrational fear, inspired by countless horror movies and the reading of weird tales reproduced again and again in the pages of long out of print paperbacks and 'penny dreadfuls', that the heavy lid of one of those assembled sarcophagi would slide slowly open with a loud creak. There would be the sound of a throat parched brittle dry by constant exposure to the merciless Saharan sun, and a withered, heavily-bandaged arm would reach out, grasping at the relatively fresh air for the first time in over 3,000 years. It would smell of incredible age and dust, and the traces of various exotic herbs and spices the embalmers of old used to replace the corpse's internal organs, and its face would resemble a dried apple core, shrivelled and shrunken by the incessant heat of a long-ago Cairo-summer, its tongue-less mouth hanging wide open to reveal two hideous rows of black and broken teeth....

And then it would slowly clamber out of the coffin and its eyes would glow bright red, like two burning embers...and as it held us, frozen in place with the power of its hypnotic glare, it would start to shamble slowly towards us with its arms outstretched, intent on smothering us with a spicy-smelling, dry-bandaged embrace....

******

But if that particular horror was purely imaginary, the Ishi Konda, a wooden, carved North African fetish doll that was stood menacingly amidst a crowd of beautifully-carved wooden sculptures, was all too real.

The two-foot-tall semi-naked figure, its face twisted into a fearsome expression of bestial rage and a pair of huge, white-painted eyes, that glared balefully from the confines of a glass-fronted cabinet, seemed to emit waves of pure, unadulterated evil.

This impression was further enhanced by the fact that virtually every inch of its burnished, ebony body was filled with literally hundreds of old, rusted nails and a selection of broken knife blades that had been hammered powerfully into the very core of the doll by a succession of people consumed by feelings of intense and bitter hatred, believing that by doing so, they could inflict serious harm or even death upon a person who had wronged them in some way or other.

The accompanying information plaque noted wryly that judging from the number of nails and blade parts that had been inserted into the doll's squat and intimidating form, it had obviously been a highly effective instrument of revenge and destruction.

Further proof was provided by the notice's reference to how the curses uttered by the native tribesmen, doubtless tired of the white-man's incessant interference in their affairs, had been responsible for the deaths of countless missionaries back in the 1850s.

So dreadfully awesome were its alleged powers, that it was eventually confiscated by the increasingly worried leaders of the foreign missionaries and packed off in a secure wooden crate to England, where, having been separated from those who possessed the requisite knowledge to impart a death-dealing curse, it finally came to its (current) final resting place at Liverpool Museum.

From where it can do no harm.

And the fact that there was a large, single silver nail, strangely rust-free, and of far more recent design than the rest of the rough and ready spike-like ingots that had been pounded into the body of the doll well over a hundred years earlier, was nothing more than a bizarre trick of the light, or someone's idea of a practical joke.

Wasn't it?

******

Whenever I had the opportunity of visiting the museum, to lose myself amidst its winding, wonder-laden floors, I always left the exhibit I loved most of all until the very last.

Although it may sound to some to be about as exciting a prospect as watching James Blunt doing a spot of shopping in his carpet slippers, there was just something indefinably magical about what I always referred to as *'The Dark Victorian Lane'*. This was, in reality, little more than a life-sized, wrap-around, sepia-toned photograph of a Liverpudlian back-street, as it had been during the mid-19th Century.

It featured headscarf-wearing housewives hanging out their washing in tiny backyards, or engaged in eternal conversations with their similarly-garbed neighbours, whilst hordes of filthy street urchins played happily at their feet. There were real cobbled streets underfoot, complete with authentic water hydrants, road signs and gaslights, whilst a Dickensian soundtrack played in the background - the discordant swirl of the hurdy-gurdy and the barrel organ, children's laughter and drunken shouts, the cries of market stall-holders and street hawkers merging with the ominous sound of fog-horns from the ships and boats out on the Mersey, and the barely comprehensible call of the old Rag and Bone Man[*], that had always conjured up in my mind's eye, images of the corpse-gatherers during the terrible time of The Black Death, slowly passing people's houses with their hastily daubed white crosses on the wooden doors yelling 'Bring Out Yer Dead!'

---

[*] For those of you who don't remember; the Rag and Bone Man was a grubby, shabbily-dressed individual who travelled the city streets with a horse-drawn cart. One of my earliest childhood memories is of a dishevelled old man in a cloth cap and multi-stained jacket who used to push a cart along the street laden with, it seemed, nothing but piles of dirty brown scraps of clothing. I didn't ever get too close to the man, not least because he always looked as though he stank to high heaven so I never got to see whether the cart contained any actual bones or not.

My typically ghoulish imagination conjured up images of heaps of freshly acquired skeletons, (including human ones), some with traces of fresh blood and pieces of gristly flesh still attached to various parts of them buried under the stacks of discarded clothing. According to that font of all knowledge, Wikipedia: 'In the past the rags would be used for converting into fabrics and paper, the bones for making glue.

'Today, Rag and Bone Men mostly operate in very poor areas, although they do still appear in many parts of the Black Country.'

Incidentally, I found this snippet at the conclusion of the Wikipedia entry more than a little disturbing, though I'm not precisely sure why....

'In the North East of England, the Rag and Bone Man's horse often had balloons fastened to it. If a child gave what the Rag and Bone Man considered a reasonable amount of rags for example, then they would be given a balloon as a reward, This was forbidden by the Public Health Act, 1925, due to fears that the practice contributed to the spread of disease.'

DEAD OF NIGHT

SHADOWS

'Our shadows moved forward at our side like grim giants and on the walls the fantastic images over which they slipped trembled and flickered.'

E.T.A. Hoffman – *'Das Majorat'*

Sometimes, it was the most innocuous-seeming of things that gave us the creeps.

Had we for some unfathomable reason decided to advertise the fact that we were, on occasion, frightened by the black outlines our bodies cast when illuminated by natural or artificial light, we'd have been thoroughly lambasted with the immortal phrase, "Christ on a bike, kidder, that lad's scared of his own friggin' *shadow!*"

So we wisely kept *that one* to ourselves. Although, with hindsight, perhaps being afraid of shadows isn't really the indicator of absolute cowardice most people have always assumed it to be.

Consider the following:

A genius film director by the name of Paul Leni, made an entire silent movie about them, called appropriately enough, *Warning Shadows,* way back in *1922*. It's now widely considered to be a classic of German expressionistic cinema by film aficionados, and is also one of the most disturbing films of the Teutonic silent era, right up there with the likes of *The Cabinet of Dr Caligari,* (1920) and *Nosferatu,* (1922), (the latter featuring the particularly frightening sequence pictured above, where Count Orlok, (the most physically repulsive Vampire in the entire history of celluloid), slowly ascends the stairs of another potential female victim. We see only his looming silhouette on the white walls, all bent and hideously crooked, with impossibly-long, claw-like fingers, hooked nose and ears as pointed as a sewer rat's, a foul inhabitant of what one modern-day critic dubbed the *'Kingdom Of Shadows',* 'a netherworld of uncertain light and bottomless darkness.' And it wasn't only between-the-wars Germany that utilised shadows to such chilling effect. Val Lewton, the much-lauded naturalised American producer of such subtly atmospheric horror movies as *Cat People,* (1942) and *Isle of the Dead* (1945), once issued the memorable dictum; 'Audiences will people any patch of prepared darkness with more horror, suspense and frightfulness than the most imaginative writer could ever dream up.'

Then there was Tolkien's blasted land of Mordor, 'Where the shadows lie,' the menacing figure of the running crook in the *'Watch Out There's a Thief About'* posters that were popular back in the 1970s. There was the dark, towering form that dwarfed the puny humans in *The Land of the Giants* TV programme poster artwork, the terrifying shadow-person that entered a room, stood for few seconds as if contemplating its next move, before sitting itself down on a comfortable-looking white seat, splaying its fingers on the armrest as the camera rushes forward for an extreme close-up of its featureless head, during the opening titles of *Armchair Thriller,* to name but a few examples.

And then there was the folklore and legends concerning shadows to consider...

The idea that a shadow is actually a part of a person, has persisted in many parts of the globe and among hugely different and varied cultures. Many people once believed, and very likely still do, that it is considered to be extremely unlucky to walk on another person's silhouette. To do so is to cause great harm to that unfortunate person. This is because the shadow is seen as a manifestation of their soul, (or, at the very least, an essential part of the said person).

In certain of the Earth's more mountainous regions, it is said to be an omen of death if stones or pebbles happen to fall on a person's shadow, whilst in Wales (itself fairly well-endowed in the mountains department), if anyone sitting around the fireplace on Christmas Day casts a shadow that is minus its head, it is said they will die within the coming year.

Meanwhile, over in the United States, it's believed by some that if - for some hard-to-imagine reason - you are ever forced to walk through a bunch of holly bushes, it's possible that your shadow might wind up being left there forever, caught flapping on a prickly holly sprig for all eternity.

As one of the contributors to the excellent *Man Myth and Magic* magazine of the 1970s, once memorably opined:

> 'Just as a reflection in a mirror or in water was often deemed to be the living soul of its original, so also, perhaps more generally, was the shadow, that strange and lively image which at certain times follows its owner everywhere and faithfully copies all its actions, and at other times is nowhere to be found. In both these forms, the soul was thought to be visible because at that moment, it was out of the body and at large.'

It was believed by primitive peoples that a man's soul could temporarily leave its body, although doing so allowed one's immortal soul to become dangerously exposed, giving any passing Demon the opportunity to whisk it away to Hell. Unfortunately, many Shamans and occultists have stipulated that in order to travel on the 'astral plane', it was first necessary to allow just such a separation to occur. And, so long as the 'owner' was sufficiently careful and vigilant, they stated reassuringly, the shadow/soul would return safely to the physical body, no matter how far afield it may have roamed, reeled in the way an experienced angler skilfully lands his prize catch.

But the deal was very similar to the fate suffered by the victims in Wes Craven's *Nightmare on Elm Street* movies: Whatever befell the 'soul' during its brief stay in the dream/astral plane, the same fate was also suffered by the physical body of anyone foolish enough to play around with their 'spiritual essence.' As inadvisable moves go then, this vacation of one's corporeal self for any given length of time is - I would contend - right up there with walking over to Joe Pesci in a bar, and telling him to go and fetch his shoe-shine box.

THE OLD 'TIME-OBSESSED WOMAN' & THE CHILD SNATCHER

At the top end of Bolton Road East, on the very edge of New Ferry proper, stands a typically nondescript council house where an incredibly old woman once lived all alone. I never learned her actual age until - ironically - the day she passed away, but to my friends and me in our pre-teenage years, she looked like she was about a thousand years old. In fact, the first time we encountered her, on our way back from *Ruth's Newsagent's,* sometime Society member, and permanent smart-arse, Wayne Williams, once quipped:

"God, she looks like a female version of Boris Karloff in *The Mummy!*"

She had a set of false teeth that were terribly stained and seemed to be far too big for her mouth and she wasn't too bothered about applying the denture gum, either, because they kept falling out *en masse* every time she opened her mouth to speak. Her skin was creased and wizened, like a dried prune that's been left out in mid-day sun, and her sparse, wispy white hair framed her mottled skull like the gossamer threads of ancient spider-webs hanging in the corners of long-unopened tombs.

Each and every time we passed she would lie in wait, hidden behind the wildly overgrown hedge, or else would stand framed in her doorway if the weather was bad and shout across at us in a voice that was so wheezy it put me in mind of an old-fashioned set of bellows fanning the flames of a dying fire.

"What time is it?"

…she'd ask, as though the answer to that question was the most important thing in the world right then.

"I'm asking yer! What time is it?"

Well, we'd check our watches and tell her it was ten thirty, or whatever, and go to move on, already dismissing her from our minds. We invariably had things to do and places to be: footy practice on one of the fields in Port Sunlight Village, pitching our tents for an all-night camping session atop The Big Hill, or heading down to The Docks to listen to one of our friends, a middle-aged arc welder named *'Panama Jack',* relate a couple of his truly wondrous stories.

We'd be constantly stopped in our tracks however, no matter how urgent our errand, by The Old Lady shouting after us again to ask the identical question.

"I'm asking yer! What *TIIIIIME* is it?"

And there'd be an unmistakable undercurrent of anger in her voice then, as though we hadn't responded to her initial inquiry and had blatantly ignored her instead.

Somewhat sheepishly, we'd make a big show of intensely studying our watches and state that it was now ten-thirty one (or whatever) and go to walk on. We wouldn't get more than a couple of feet before that springy, increasingly irritated voice called out again:

"I'm asking yer! *WHAT TIME IS IT?"*

She'd repeat this question over and over, and it didn't matter how many times we replied, standing huddled together like a collection of juvenile, flesh and blood 'speaking clocks', she just went right on asking, until - in the end - we'd have no option other than to walk away shaking our heads at the perceived senility of extreme old age, and wonder aloud why she hadn't been placed in a residential home to live out the remainder of her days with some degree of dignity.

This exact same ritual was played out virtually every time we had occasion to walk past The Old Lady's house, which was virtually every day, and I honestly can't claim that any of us felt the slightest bit frightened by her appearance, or by her endless enquiries as to what the precise time was. After all, of what was there to be afraid? It was abundantly clear to each of us, young as we were back then, that she was nothing more than an unbearably lonely individual who was so desperate for some form of companionship she felt compelled to try and engage passers-by in conversation, no matter how inane the subject matter.

Or maybe, we assumed, she was simply terrified by the relentless passing of time. Such a concept maybe doesn't mean much when you're a kid aside from the occasions when it dragged by interminably during a parent-imposed curfew, or the echoing spaces of our nine to three forty-five school-days. It was easy to believe back then that my friends and I were going to live forever, but even at the ripe old age of 12, I'd quickly learned that the older you get the more time seems to be running out disconcertingly fast.

Our sympathetic views changed drastically, however, during a single late summer afternoon, when the storm the weathermen had been warning about for the best part of week, finally loomed on the horizon, an ominous gathering of bruised-looking thunderheads that had bubbled up suddenly in the midst of skies so blue they'd looked ready to shatter into a million pieces.

It was the September of 1976, and we'd been returning from a trek to New Ferry Market to purchase some 'essential supplies' for our club house (candles, matches, a padlock to keep out nosey parker non-members), and were anxious to reach the safety of 'The Den' before the heavens opened and soaked us all to the skin.

I remember as we reached the top end of our road I was struck by the weird quality of pre-storm light, the yellowish tint that threw everything, the rows of houses and parked cars, concrete lamp posts and the just-turning leaves of poplar trees and sycamores, into ultra sharp relief. It was like I was viewing the scene before me through a pair of 3-D glasses, the type you sometimes found taped to the front of wildlife magazines whose red and green-tinted lenses caused the images of boxing hares or hunting foxes or birds taking flight to leap from the page with an unnerving degree of realism.

There was an eerie stillness, too. A pregnant pause before the first ear-splitting thunderclap or jagged streak of lightning slashed across the skies and rent the air with its wild primeval fury.

We were so anxious to get indoors that we all but ran down Bolton Road East, and to be honest, the old, time-obsessed woman was the furthest thing from our minds.

She plainly hadn't forgotten about *us* though, because she was standing at the front gate, or at least the small portion of it that was visible between the thick, over-grown hedges, and we nearly jumped out of our skins when she shouted into our faces that oh-so-familiar refrain:

"WHAT TIME IS IT?"

The shock was enough to freeze us all in our tracks, and I've got to say, seeing her up close like that sent a shiver of revulsion running up and down my spine. All the long-buried fears of old women, nurtured by the countless fairy-tales I'd read at primary school came scrabbling to the surface like some vile, underground monstrosity driven from its hidey-hole by an insatiable desire to feed.

Suddenly I didn't see a frail, impossibly ancient crone, whose entire body had been bent and stooped by the burden of a lifetime's struggling to make ends meet, standing before me.

Instead, I saw a child-eating witch – the kind who doled out poisoned apples or turned their enemies into tiny English speaking house-mice or spent weeks fattening up their captives for eventual immersion in their coal-black, bubbling cauldrons.

I saw spittle fly when she spoke. The remains of undigested food stuck between her dentures. The ugly wart on her chin and the two jet-black whiskers that protruded from its centre that looked uncomfortably like insect hairs. I felt a gorge rise in my throat and it was all I could do to keep from vomiting all over her tatty, threadbare carpet slippers. Actually, I might have been completely unable to prevent myself from throwing up if the old lady hadn't surprised us by saying something completely unexpected at that moment.

"I can't make out the time on one of me clocks!"

…she declared in that pleading, desperate voice.

"I'm asking yer….Can one of you check it for me?"

We'd all backed off a little at this. I've never considered myself to be much of a coward, but the thought of setting foot in that unkempt, jungle-like garden, never mind stepping across the threshold and entering the witch's house was something that filled me with a sense of unutterable dread.

I mean, God only knew what unspeakable horrors lay in wait, concealed behind those deceptively ordinary walls.

As luck would have it, however, a lad from our class by the name of Michael Thomas happened to be in our company that day. He never normally hung around with the regular members of our gang, and had no real interest in the supernatural or horror movies and in fact, I'm not even sure who invited him along on that particular occasion. Whatever the case though, young Michael volunteered his services without a moment's hesitation and I remember thinking, 'Hey, maybe he's been entranced by a powerful 'glamour spell,' blinding him to the Old Lady's true nature and intentions'.

I'm ashamed to say though that no-one in our group attempted to stop Michael as he followed 'The Witch' (as I'd now come to regard her) along the scarcely discernible garden path. Perhaps we were *all* victims of her sorcery, I thought, but didn't say out loud, forced to stand in dream-like silence as our friend slowly walked to his doom.

Michael glanced back at us quizzically, as though we'd lost our collective marbles, and I recall 'The Witch' grinning a hideously lop-sided grin as she bade him enter her enchanted lair.

The door closed softly behind them, although the faint snicking of the latch was clearly audible in the heavy, breathless air. For a few endless moments we stood there, stock-still, none of us speaking, none of us able to tear our eyes away from the sight of the firmly closed, green-painted door. The thought crossed my mind we might never see Michael alive again, and though that notion was plainly absurd, even to a highly imaginative kid who was still a good five months short of their 13th birthday, a quick glance at the expressions on my friends' faces convinced me they were all thinking the exact same thing.

As it turned out though, Mikey emerged on his own, not five minutes later looking a little ashen, but otherwise completely unharmed.

Somewhat frustratingly for us, he refused to answer any of our excited questions about what he'd experienced within The Witch's Dark Domain, until we arrived at my mum and dad's back garden and the small wooden shed that served as our club-house.

Once inside, we sat around Michael in a semi-circle eager for him to spill the beans as the first penny-sized raindrops began pattering on the roof and windows like countless fingers thrumming a maddeningly insistent beat.

*****

The first thing Michael did was to dispel any preconceived notions we may have had that he'd entered some dark and dingy chamber lit by black, scented candles, and with strange cabbalistic symbols, hand-drawn pentagrams, and representations of *The Goat of Mendes* and other Demonic entities, perched upon an altar almost obscured by a thick cloud of incense.

On the contrary, he described it as being pretty much what you'd expect an old age pensioner's residence to look like. The living room was tidy and orderly and contained sensible, if somewhat bland items of furniture, including a large sofa, an old-fashioned radiogram and a small TV set shoved in a dingy corner like an afterthought. Certainly there was nothing outwardly remarkable about it.

Except for the incredible number of clocks, that is.

According to Michael, almost every available inch of wall-space seemed to have been taken up with timepieces of every imaginable size, shape and design.

There were Swiss cuckoo clocks, carriage clocks, antique clocks, sun clocks, water clocks, quartz clocks, time zone clocks and over by the far wall stood a couple of highly-polished mahogany Grandfather clocks, their pendulums poised at an angle like some bizarre instrument of medieval torture.

That was undeniably strange. What was even stranger was that not a single one of them appeared to be working. The hands of each were fixed at entirely different times and this understandably didn't make any kind of sense to our friend, but before he could think to ask the Old Lady for a solution to the mystery, she raised a single bony finger and pointed at one particular clock above the mantelpiece which he noticed was still ticking, be it ever so faintly.

"*That's* the one I can't tell the time on,"

…she announced hoarsely.

"The hands are too small, me eyes are bad, and I can't see what it says."
She paused, and Michael said she looked inexpressibly sad at that moment, although he couldn't for the life of him have said precisely why.

"Please, I'm asking you…I *really* need you tell me. What time is it?"

"Alright, missus, no problem,"

Michael said as he walked briskly over to the mantelpiece, thinking that the task was hardly going to rival any of Hercules' Twelve Labours in the difficult-to-achieve stakes. He did find, though, that it was no great surprise she'd had trouble reading the cheap-looking, novelty timepiece. It had a date counter, which had pictures of ridiculously tiny, green-eyed cartoon cats as opposed to anything resembling actual numbers, and a thin set of white whiskers that doubled as second and minute hands, and only by squinting up so close he could see his reflection staring back at him from the glass covering, could he answer the Old Lady's query with any degree of certainty.

So intently was he focusing on getting the time right, that he only gradually became aware there was a white piece of card attached to the wooden casing directly below the clock-face.

There wasn't much to read. It was entirely blank save for the name, Edith Aitken.

On impulse, Michael glanced quickly at the other clocks adorning the walls and saw that each one had a series of neat, hand-written notices containing the names of a variety of people, all of whom had the surname Aitken or Reynolds, posted beneath them.

These cards though, had two other things printed on them.

The date of the person's death.

And, corresponding with the numerous pairs of frozen clock-hands, the precise time they had died.

Michael spun around, and another half-formed question died on his lips as he saw the Old Lady had crept up silently behind him and was stood only a foot or so away. From that short distance, he saw her eyes flash in a slab of sallow pre-storm-light that spilled through a gap in the curtains, and how tears had welled in the bloodshot rims, like rainwater pooling in a dried up culvert.

She smiled wistfully and her dentures clacked like a pair of castanets as she whispered,

"Please, tell me, what time is it"

"Well, according to *this* it's about a minute or so after 11 o'clock,"

Michael replied.

> "But that can't be right,"

…he added quickly, shaking his head.

> "I mean, I'm not wearing a watch or anything, but it's gotta be three in the afternoon at the earliest. This clock's obviously broken just like all the others."

As if to confirm this, Michael noticed the ticking was slowing down, becoming ever more erratic, even as he spoke, although it didn't stop altogether.

But the Old Lady didn't appear to have heard a word he'd said. Indeed, she touched him gently on the shoulder in a show of gratitude.

> "Thank you so very much, son,"

…she said before turning and walking over to a comfortable-looking armchair. She sat herself down and Michael thought he could hear her joints creaking like a clipper ship on the high seas, as she did so. She seemed sprightly enough though as she picked up a framed, sepia-toned photograph depicting a young man in a soldier's uniform that had been on display in the centre of the coffee table.

> "I will see you soon, Joe,"

…she murmured, and though she was crying so hard now the tears rolled freely down her cheeks in salty rivulets, it was clear to Michael that she was weeping with relief and joy, and feeling like he was intruding on a deeply private moment, he began backing away towards the front door.

The last her saw of her, the Old Lady was sat staring intently at the photograph and clutching its wooden borders as though she were afraid it would slip from her spindly, crooked hands.…

****

The following morning, a Sunday, I walked up to *Ruth's Newsagent's* to get a few odds and ends for my Mum and the paper and half an ounce of *Golden Virginia* for my Dad.

Michael may have reassured the others that the Old Lady was a harmless individual with an unhealthy interest in recording her family members' exact time of death, but I decided to take the alternative route of going up Woodhead Road, and round the back of *The Anzacs*, just the same. I really didn't fancy running the risk of having her suddenly leaping out at me like a grotesque Jack in the Box, or a mechanical demon on a ghost train ride whilst I was on my own.

I was passing the second block of allotments, the vegetable plots tended by some of the elder local residents, when I heard the sound of men's voices coming from behind a high row of runner beans. I couldn't see who it was, but in truth I didn't need to. From the way they spoke I could tell immediately it was Ged Appleby and his younger cousin Les Wilson. Actually, it was Ged who was doing most of the talking, and there was really no great shock there. Mr Appleby, ('Pips' to his friends), was well-renowned as being New Ferry's Resident Gossip. *'A font of all knowledge,'* according to his own, (exceedingly biased) estimation. *'A nosey, interfering, loud-mouthed get!'* to the rest of the local population, 'Pip' knew everybody's business and took great delight in spreading the latest breaking news, especially if the tidings were, as so often seemed to be the case, of the thoroughly miserable variety.

And true to form, on this chilly, grey-skied morning, as the hottest summer in living memory finally gave way to autumn, the old 'Pipster' couldn't wait to spill the beans concerning a story that would be the talk of the entire neighbourhood before mid-day.

> "I see that arl biddy Edith Aitken finally kicked the bucket last night,"

I heard him say in his usual off-handedly insensitive tones.

> "Really, that *is* sad,"

Les replied.

> "Still, she had a good innings. How old was she? Do you know?"

> "A hundred and six, if yer can believe that!"

Pip announced, incredulously.

> "Just shows yer, being single for most of yer life can work wonders for yer health. I mean, look at me, stuck with the trouble and strife for the best part of thirty years, and I've got a couple of bastard stomach ulcers, a dicky ticker and bladder so packed full of gallstones I swear I can hear them rolling around inside me like a bleedin' big bag of marbles. Christ, Les, I'll be lucky to see seventy."

> "Oh, I'm sure you'll be around for many years to come,"

Les chuckled.

> "I'm enough of a God-fearing individual to believe we're all here for a specific purpose, and you provide an invaluable service to the good people of this town. I'm sure The Almighty isn't gonna be in any rush to deprive us lucky New Ferry-ites of their chief newscaster, anytime soon."

> "Knock off the bullshit, will yer,"

Pip responded.

> "...and let me finish me story."

> "Okey dokey, kidder, keep yer hair on! I take it Edith never married then?"

> "Well, yeah, she did. Ridiculously young, if yer ask me. She tied the knot when she was barely out of her friggin' teens to a serving soldier by the name of Joe Aitken."

'Pip' paused, for what he doubtless considered to be dramatic effect.

> "And wouldn't you just know it. Joe got blown to smithereens during the Battle of Ladysmith[*] at the height of the Boer War, barely three months after their wedding day. How's that for a big sloppy dollop of shitty luck?"

---

[*]The Battle of Ladysmith was one of the early engagements of the Second Boer War. A large British force, which had concentrated at the garrison town of Ladysmith launched a sortie on 30th October 1899, against Boer armies which were slowly surrounding the town. The result was a disaster for the British. The main body was driven back into the town, and an isolated detachment of 800 men was forced to surrender to Commandant De Wet. The Boers did not follow up their advantage by proceeding towards the strategically important port of Durban, and instead began a siege of Ladysmith, which was relieved after 118 days. As Boer General Piet Joubert foolishly said: "When God stretches out a finger, don't take the whole hand".

Les didn't reply, just whistled softly, and that was answer enough for 'Pip.'

"Anyhow," …he continued,

"Edith was so heart-broken, she never had eyes for anyone else, never- re-married or reverted back to her maiden name of Reynolds. There were no kids either, then or later in life. Even the comforting fact that she came from a large family and had many friends who used to visit her on a regular basis, eventually conspired to bite her on the arse. I suppose the one downside of living to such a ripe old age is that yer can wind up outliving yer nearest and dearest by a good twenty years or so. Certainly that's what happened with Edith Aitken. For the best part of two entire decades, she lived on her own with nuthin' but her memories to keep her company."

"God, that's awful,"

Les said solemnly.

"How come she was never placed in a residential home?"

"Cos she was a stubborn arl' bitch, who'd long since paid her mortgage off, had no outstanding debts and who valued her independence to the extent that nobody could have shifted her short of hiring the SAS to forcibly remove her at gunpoint to do the job, that's why!"

'Pip' replied with a snort of what might have been (for him) admiration.

"Her next door neighbours, Matty and his wife Edna, made it their business to constantly check on her welfare, did all her shopping, tidied around for her, checked the heating was on when the weather turned cold, and just, yer know, generally made sure she was alright.

They've been doing this for the past three years or so. Sounds like a real ball-acher of a responsibility if yer ask me, but I wouldn't mind betting they had an ulterior motive for performing this Good Samaritan double act. Maybe they thought old Miss Aitken had a fair wad of money stashed away somewhere, and with no close relatives around to leave it to in her will…"

"Or maybe they were simply doing it out of the goodness of their hearts",

Les interjected.

"I know we live in cynical times, Ged, but even you can't *entirely r*ule out the possibility they were just being neighbourly."

"Yeah, well, if yer believe that, yer'll believe Nixon's not a crook, Jeremy Thorpe's[*] not totally *Spangles,* and the Mars Viking Probe actually landed on Mars and not on some Hollywood stage set,"

Ged replied.

"But hey, think what yer want. It's a free country. Supposedly."

"Just get on with the story,"

---

[*] Jeremy Thorpe was a former Liberal Party Leader, who was forced to resign in May, 1976, when he was suspected of having a homosexual affair with a former male model by the name of Norman Scott.

Les sighed wearily.

"Will do, Mr Ghandi," **

Ged fired back, without missing a beat.

"I've nearly finished now, anyway.

I spoke to Edna myself about an hour or so ago, on me way back from the shops. She was sat on her front door step, in her dressing gown nursing a steaming mug of tea, and I thought that was a bit weird, that she'd probably had an argument with her fella or something. I wasn't being nosey or anything, but I had to ask her if she was okay, and I noticed then she was crying, so I walked up the garden path and plonked meself down beside her. It was hard work, but she finally managed to stop blubbing long enough to tell me that Matty was in the back kitchen cooking them both some brekkie, everythin was fine between them, but they'd both had a bit of a shock the night before.

I suggested that we both go inside, she'd catch her death sitting there in the freezin' cold, and it would be far more comfortable if she told me all about it over a nice bacon'n'brown sauce butty. Much to me empty stomach's relief she agreed.

We sat around the dining room table, and Matty appeared with three full English's, and a fresh pot of tea, and there was a roarin fire blazin in the grate, filled with real British coal, not one of them fancy imitation ones that give off the warmth but not the traditional smell of a proper open fire, and after we'd set about "filling our boots", (me and Matty did anyway. Edna just played around with hers, and I wound up finishing it off for her. Well, waste not want not), the couple took up the story between them.

It seems that Edna and her husband were watching the late film; *The Searchers*, with John Wayne obsessively hunting down the Injuns who'd kidnapped his niece, when she had a funny feeling "something was dreadfully wrong next door." She tried to ignore it at first, but like when yer wake up in the middle of the night and yer struck with the thought that yer haven't locked the front door properly, or yer've left one of the rings of the gas cooker glowin red, it was impossible to ignore. She tried to lose herself in the events on screen, but the sensation, vague as it was, nagged at her to the point where, long before the final credits, it had grown to a one hundred per cent certainty.

Edna and Matty have their own set of keys to Edith's house and after ten minutes or so of constantly badgering her husband, he finally agreed to go with her and check on their neighbour's well-being. The last time they'd seen the old lady had been first thing that morning, when Edna had brought in the milk from her doorstep for her, and she'd seemed "as right as rain", then.

The minute they stepped into the hallway of Miss Aitken's house though, Matty found himself sharing his wife's sense of unease. "It was deathly quiet," he told me. "And that deeply unsettlin' phrase, "as quiet as the grave," kept runnin round and round me head, and yer know what, it really wasn't that much of a surprise when we went

---

** The 'Mr Ghandi' reference was an ironic retort, probably totally lost on 'Pip.' Mahatma Ghandi, the great Indian political and ideological leader, who was famed for his preaching of civil rights, pacifism, equality and social justice,(not to mention vegetarianism),was the total antithesis of everything 'Pip,' a short-fused preacher of every man for himself, anti-immigration, anti-gay, borderline racism (not to mention a ravenous carnivore), stood for or believed in.

into the living room and found Miss Aitken's body slumped in her armchair with a photograph of her long-dead husband in her lap. If you didn't know better, you'd have thought she was merely havin a nap. I mean, her body was still warm to the touch, but she wasn't breathin'. She must have literally died just as we entered the house.

That was creepy as hell,"

…he added,

"But get this, Ged, what was even worse was the fact she was *smiling*.

And there was one more thing.

Yer know she's got about a hundred clocks scattered around the living room with the names and exact times of death of her deceased family members posted underneath 'em?

Right, well, there's this one clock on top of the mantelpiece. The only one in her whole collection that I've ever heard ticking. Something made me walk over to it, even as Edna clasped her hands to her mouth to stop herself from screaming at the sight of Edith's dead body.

I noticed the clock hands weren't moving. They were stuck at one minute past eleven.

I asked my wife "What time is it now?"

"11.02," she whimpered.

The ticking stopped completely, the room fell totally silent, and I saw the label that had been posted underneath the clock *"Edith Aitken"*, it said simply.

"Born 23rd June, 1872 - Died 5th September, 1976 - at 11.01pm"

*****

In a strange way, I came to miss the Old Lady in the days and weeks that followed the news of her death. Her passing seemed to me to be a kind of epitaph for the fast disappearing days of my childhood, if that doesn't sound a tad melodramatic. As the autumn finally lay claim to the golden, seemingly endless summer of 1976, and I stood on the very cusp of teenagerdom, I was faced with the daunting prospect of starting New Chester Road Secondary School, (and the horror stories I'd heard about *that* place were enough to give James Herbert the screamin meemies!), as well as potentially losing contact with some of the class-mates I'd grown up with; the ones who had been studious enough to pass for Wirral Grammar anyway.

I remember, on the last Sunday evening before the end of The Six Week's Holidays, gazing out of my bedroom window, feeling melancholy and not a little heart-sick as I experienced this thoroughly depressing epiphany, the sort that inspired a vivid cartoon light-bulb to suddenly ping into life above my head (although in this case, the bulb wasn't, by any stretch of the imagination, light, but jet-black and filled with some viscous substance, clotted and thick, like phlegm coughed up by a person riddled with terminal disease).

'Time Passes,' a mocking, school-masterly voice whispered in my ear, causing my insides to suddenly flop over the way they did when I was sat in the back seat of our car and my Dad drove at speed over a humped-back bridge or along a hilly stretch of road.

'Time Passes. Things Change.'

'And Not Always For The Better.'
'You Best Get That Clear As Crystal In Your Head, Right Now, Sonny-Jim!'
'It's Time To Put Away The Things Of Childhood.'
'You're A Young Man Now!'

*****

And if this message hadn't gotten through on that crisp, sun-bright September evening, as the mouth-watering smell of the last barbecue of the season merged with the familiar Sunday night odours of soap and freshly shampooed hair, it hit home big style a fortnight or so later when I was watching Nicholas Roeg's superb cinematic adaptation of Edgar Allan Poe's *Masque of The Red Death* …

In one particular scene, roughly mid-way through the movie, the cruel, Satan-worshipping Prince Prospero, who has invited the wealthy and privileged to seek sanctuary within the walls of his castle to escape the terrible plague that is decimating the local population, attempts to take his guests' minds off The Red Death, by holding a never-ending series of increasingly wild parties, culminating in the Grand Fancy Dress Ball (or Masque), of the story's title.

During one of these licentious shin-digs, Alfredo, a particularly lecherous middle-aged noble-man, places his arm around a voluptuous young lady, before guiding her over to a nearby couch.

> "Let me tell you about the anatomy of fear,"

…he states sitting beside her, his face mere inches from that of the obviously drunken maiden.

Overhearing this one-sided conversation, Prince Prospero, played by the ever-wonderful Vincent Price, sidles across to dismiss Alfredo's sermon before he can even begin.

> "What would you know of terror, Alfredo?"

Prospero enquires with a sneer.

> "Your senses are far too blunt!"

He then strides purposefully towards a huge clock that dominates the centre of the banqueting hall.

> "Listen!"

…he commands and the assembled throng give him their undivided attention, although whether this reverence is borne of fear of insulting their host, or because they are genuinely interested in what he has to say, is a matter for conjecture.

Either way, Prospero is playing to a (quite literal) captive audience.

> "What is terror?"

…he asks rhetorically.

> "Is it the ticking of a clock?
>
> Is it to awaken and hear the passing of time?
> Or is it the failing beat of your own heart?
> Or is it the footsteps of someone who, just a moment before, was in your room?"

He pauses for a second, to allow these disturbing images to settle in the minds of his assembled guests, and then, as if right on cue, the clock chimes the hour, its clanging, mournful tolls resounding around the cavernous hall, causing at least one woman in the crowd to flinch as though some ghostly unseen presence had suddenly caressed the nape of her neck.

Upon seeing the fear-filled expressions on the faces of his guests, the Prince laughs manically, and the sound of that sardonic cackling is every bit as merciless as the unrelenting march of time…

HORROR MAN: THE DOCK ROAD CHILD SNATCHER

One of the first and most forceful of commandments issued by my parents and teachers from a very early age was stark in its simplicity, but hugely effective in its deterrent capabilities....

'Never Speak To Strangers!'

Certainly, unlike so many other edicts issued by those I considered to belong to that semi-mystical cabal known collectively as *'Society's Authority Figures,'* it didn't simply go in one ear and out the other, or become subject to 'selective implementation' (or when I could be arsed taking heed, in plain simple English).

If anything, from the ages of five to fifteen, I probably took this warning far too literally and so much to heart that I constantly found myself on edge, my nerves tingling like Peter Parker's famous *'Spidey Sense,'* the moment I encountered anyone I considered to be old (which pretty much included anyone, man or woman, over the age of twenty-one) and who looked to me to be *remotely* strange. As to what actually defined *strange*, back then, well, that could be just about anything from an individual sporting a ridiculously bushy beard that all but obscured the person's face (especially if said person happened to be a *woman!*) or had a leering smile, a set of crooked teeth, long, straggly hair, or a pair of beetle-black eyebrows that met across the bridge of their nose (a tell-tale sign of Lycanthropy, according to the numerous books I'd read on the occult).

So, a goodly sized proportion of the adult population of Merseyside, at the time then, (especially seeing as how Birkenhead and its immediate environs, have long been known as the last refuge of the long-haired, patchouli-smelling, heavy metal-worshipping *'Sweat'* or *'Trog,'* and their female counterpart, the *'Sweat'* or er, *'Trogette'*).

There were, however, other far more traditionally sinister-looking individuals prowling the county's back roads and poorly-lit alleyways. These were more often than not, desperately lonely old men, homeless vagrants or down and out winos who were regarded with a mixture of contempt, suspicion and outright disgust by the 'fine, upstanding pillars of the community', and a fair degree of fear by kids such as yours truly, even if, in all actuality they were about as likely to harm a child as they were to win *The Lever Brother's Soap Factory Personal Hygiene Award.*

Unfortunately, human nature being what it is, people are, as a rule, quick to judge others by their appearance, and when you're dealing with society's terminal down and outs, it's all too easy to jump to the wrong conclusions.

As I've already stated, I could hardly claim to have ascended to the lofty peaks of the moral high ground when it came to making assumptions about so-called *'undesirables'*. And if there had been a local school-run competition for pupils to design a poster warning of the potential dangers of children talking to strangers, there's a strong likelihood the archetypal *'Bad Man,'* featured in the winning entry would closely resemble the middle-aged, simple-minded man who sometimes stood all alone beneath the flickering streetlight on the corner of Bolton Road East and Dock Road North, back in the mid-to-late 1970s.

I'm not precisely sure when the undoubtedly eccentric individual, who we christened *'Horror-Man,'* made his debut appearance in our home-town, although it must have been a little while after Old Mrs Aitken passed away, because I can't ever remember being forced to run the gauntlet of encountering *both* of these 'ead-da-balls' on the same day, located as they were, at opposite ends of the street. And praise the skies and pass the fizzy, *Alpine Lemonade* for that! The prospect would have had me begging on my hands and knees for my parents to up sticks for somewhere a good deal less stressful. Downtown Lebanon, for example. Or maybe Phnom Penh, Cambodia.

As it was, my friends and I had to risk endure *'Horror-Man's'* unwanted attentions on frequent occasions, just as we had that time-obsessed woman, almost as though the fingers of fate, the Lord God, or plain old coincidence had decreed it to be so, as some bizarre form of 'rite of passage.'

This particular 'weirdo' might have been completely harmless, but there was no denying that he looked the part, and it was easy to believe he was more than capable of preying on unwary children with promises of unlimited sweets or access to a litter of cute little puppies.

For a start, he was always dressed in one of two types of equally shabby clothing. In the summer, he sported a pair of flared, multi-stained trousers (and we didn't even want to imagine what the origins of what those various blemishes might have been), a dirty grey string vest though which poked wiry, chest hair, like dead winter grass thrusting through the cracks of a parched and blasted landscape, and a tweed jacket that was so full of holes it would have shamed a redundant scarecrow leaning drunkenly in an over-grown corner of a neglected farmer's field.

Alternatively, when the weather turned inclement, and a raw, biting wind howled in from the Mersey, he'd don a dirty brown, 'snorkel'-style coat* that was always buttoned right the way up to the chin, and with its fur-lined hood completely covering his head.

Not that *'Horror-Man's'* somewhat questionable fashion sense alone marked him out as being a potentially *bona fide* Child-Snatcher. It wasn't the fact that he was tall and gangly, and never uttered so much as a single word. Nor had it anything to do with his facial features, though it was fair to say he'd been whacked pretty soundly with Mother Nature's ugly stick. He could have been aged anywhere between fifty and sixty, had straggly hair that was receding rapidly at the front, and possessed pale, leathery skin, and a pair of squinting, piggy eyes, but if his less-than-handsome 'fizz-zog' turned your stomach a little, there certainly wasn't anything particularly frightening about his appearance.

What did mark him out as being a good deal more sinister than just your average lonely, unkempt vagrant, with a bizarre streetlight fixation, was the fact that every time me or any of my friends attempted to walk past this stony-faced sentinel, he waited until we were within touching distance before suddenly sticking out his left arm in a futile attempt to prevent us from turning the corner onto Dock Road North, whilst we kept our gaze firmly fixed on the concrete pavement. The reason his efforts were hopelessly half-hearted attempts to drag one of us kicking and screaming into a black, unmarked van, with a view to spiriting the victim away to some perverted nightmarish version of *Never Never Land*, was perfectly simple. This particular wannabe Child Snatcher had a fatal flaw in his strategy in that he only ever extended his arm at a height roughly two feet above our heads, the limb ramrod straight and immobile like one of those imposing statues of famous battlefield generals or ancient pagan gods, which meant he didn't actually make any physical contact with us whatsoever. We didn't even have to duck under his arm, although we did so, instinctively, just the same, almost as though we were passing beneath the suspended blade of a guillotine. But aside from being forced to endure the whiff of his body odour, (which smelled to me like a rancid combination of months-out-of-date sour milk, flea-bitten scally cat faeces and oozing pus from a deeply infected wound), no harm ever befell us, though that didn't make the experiences any less unsettling.

Fortunately, *'Horror-Man's'* appearances were somewhat sporadic, and it certainly wasn't like he was a permanent fixture, or anything. Over the period of a year or so, he haunted the periphery of our lives and we'd encounter him maybe a couple of times a month, usually at the point where we had begun to assume he'd either moved on to pastures (or street-lights) new, or been arrested or sectioned, or both, only for him to turn up in his usual position, standing motionless, as if he'd been patiently waiting for our arrival.

---

*Amazingly, these coats have since come back into fashion, although quite why this should be so is one of the great mysteries of our age – The garment may well be warm and snug and would doubtless be essential apparel if you were planning on ploughing a lonely furrow through the icy wastes of Antarctica, but it's got huge buttons the size of dinner plates that you have to try and insert into a tiny looped string fastener, and providing you have enough skin left on the tips of your fingers to actually do the coat up, you're left with what amounted to total tunnel vision. Trying to peer out at the world beyond the confines of the fur-lined hood is like looking through a submarine's periscope: the view dead ahead maybe entirely uncluttered, but you can't make out much of anything on either side. It must be responsible for causing more accidents on the roads than any amount of speeding drivers, or adverse weather conditions.

The only way we could get round him, if we wanted to go to my parents' house, was to take a lengthy detour, or risk walking in the middle of the road, which - seeing as how it was always extremely busy with lorries and trucks transporting heavy lifting equipment and machine components for the nearby *Land & Marine* factory - wasn't the most sensible of ideas. (I remember I once awoke screaming from a nightmare in which I'd seen one of my friends, I think it was the aforementioned Michael Thomas, mown down by one of these lumbering heavy goods vehicles. They were fairly slow moving, but had a disconcerting habit of sneaking up on you unawares, and I recall seeing the driver emerge shaking from his cab to stumble with a bucket and what looked to be a giant-size spatula over to where Mikey's body lay. I couldn't see clearly from where I was standing, but I was close enough to make out that he didn't so much pick Mikey's remains out from underneath the truck as scoop them up and slop them into the bucket like a mass of jellied eels soaked in gallons of tomato ketchup).

And so we'd run the gauntlet of *Horror-Man's* almost-assaults, and later, in the safety of the Clubhouse there'd be much nervous laughter at having survived another meeting with our would-be nemesis.

I'm not sure why none of us ever told our mums and dads, our teachers, or *even* the police, about *Horror Man*. Perhaps it was because he never actually did us any harm, or that we simply felt sorry for him. Looking back now, though, I think it might actually have been more to do with the fact that a good-sized part of us enjoyed being frightened by his presence, in the same way that we experienced a delicious thrill of fear every time we climbed aboard the Big Dipper at Blackpool Pleasure Beach, or sat perched on the edge of our sofas (and sometimes curled up in a ball behind them) whenever *Dr Who* was screened on a Saturday evening. It seems to me now that there existed a kind of unspoken agreement amongst us that decreed that if we blew up *Horror-Man* to the authorities, they'd likely see to it that he was immediately arrested and subsequently jailed or dragged off to Clatterbridge 'Funny Farm' by the Men in White Coats. And that would have been akin to having our favourite Time-Lord's scary as hell adventures banned by the *BBC,* or all of the stomach-churning roller-coaster rides at our local seaside resorts suddenly closed down by the council.

Does that type of reasoning sound a little crazy, not to say, wholly irresponsible?

Of course it does. But you have to remember we were applying the uncomplicatedly naïve form of logic exclusive to twelve-year-olds who are not yet grown up enough to appreciate that many things in life *aren't* just a simple matter of black and white, good and bad, or right and wrong.

God, those were the days.

*****

As it turned out, the unknown fate of *'Horror Man'*, for better or for worse, was sealed at some point during my second year at Bebington Secondary, when, without any active participation on our part, he finally vanished from the streets of New Ferry for good.

I remember that after he hadn't shown up in his usual position on the corner of Bolton Road East and Dock Road North, for more than a good few months, I more than half-expected to hear excited, whispered conversations in the school corridors between fellow pupils talking about 'the weirdo who had suddenly taken to hanging around the street-light' at the bottom of some urban road in nearby Bromborough or Spital or Eastham, frightening the local children as they tried to walk by, but I never did. And after a while, I began to forget all about him, having other, more pressing things to deal with, such as securing my place in the school footy team, dating girls, trying to save up for a home movie projector so we could shoot our very own blockbusting epic, organising raids on the Harvey Gang's territory and scrumping apples from Les and Pip's vegetable allotments, (although not necessarily in that order), and I'm sure that before too long, I'd have reached the point where my recollections of *Horror Man* became nothing more or less than a discarded attic memory.

But then, sometime during August 1980, three months after I'd left school for good and was about to start work on a YTS Electrical Engineering training scheme in Rock Ferry, *ITV* screened a particularly chilling episode of Roald Dahl's *Tales Of The Unexpected,* and the recollections of *Horror Man* came flooding back like the events of a forgotten dream sparked by some vaguely related occurrence in the midst of everyday routine.

DEAD OF NIGHT

Entitled '*The Fly Paper*', the plot ran roughly as follows:

As the programme opens, local police in some quiet suburban corner of England, find the body in a pond of a 12-year-old girl who has been reported missing for five days. A short while later, another young girl of roughly the same age, named Sylvia, is walking home from a piano lesson one evening, when she becomes convinced a strange man in shabby clothing, a potential child-molesting pervert, is following her. When she arrives safely at her home address without incident, she decides against contacting the police, and soon forgets all about this suspicious-looking character.

Subsequent events dictate that Sylvia really shouldn't have been so dismissively blasé about the incident, however, because the following day, she is returning home from school on the bus when she notices the same man sitting directly opposite her, and, much to her embarrassment, and not a little disquiet, he starts attempting to engage her in conversation. Nothing he says is particularly menacing or remotely sinister, but the very fact that he blatantly ignores Sylvia's obvious uneasiness with the situation, is more than a little unnerving.

Eventually, she decides she's had enough and gets off the bus within walking distance of her home, leaving the weird man waffling obliviously in mid-sentence. She races to the nearest public phone box (this being at the beginning of the 1980s, when mobile phones were still the sole province of fat cat businessmen and Wall Street traders and were the size of house-bricks), only to find it has been vandalised. Worse, the man has also gotten off the bus and walks over to Sylvia to carry on their one-sided conversation.

Before he can say anything, though, a benign-featured, middle-aged woman walks over and places a firm hand on the girl's shoulder.

> "Haven't you ever been told not to talk to strangers?"

…she asks Sylvia, pointedly, before glaring at the strange man and telling him that she knew exactly what he was up to and that he'd best make himself scarce.

> "Now come along, child,"

…she says in a brusque, but not unkind manner.

> "Just let this be a lesson to you. Which way are you going?"

Sylvia, hugely relieved, nods in the direction of her home.

The woman, who is carrying a shopping-basket full of sweet-smelling groceries, walks alongside Sylvia mumbling about how young girls really shouldn't talk to strangers not least because 'there are some funny people about these days.'

Sylvia looks over her shoulder and sees the man still standing there, staring after them. The woman catches her looking and suggests that it might be a good idea if they walked together in the direction of Sylvia's home, as she is sure they are being followed.

> "Oh, it's disgraceful,"

…she exclaims.

> "And with all the things you read in the papers. You can't be too careful, and you'll have to remember that in future. I really should ring the police."

As she says this, they turn a corner and are confronted with an idyllic cottage, which turns out to be the woman's home. She cheerily invites Sylvia inside for 'a nice cup of tea, to make sure you're all right,' and the girl, sweating in the humid summer heat, and her heart still fluttering after her encounter with '*The Bad Man*,' readily agrees.

She follows the woman along the overgrown garden path and steps into a clean, homely-looking kitchen. The woman places the kettle under the tap then hands the young girl a plate and a packet of biscuits and asks her to kindly arrange them on the chequered-cloth table.

Sylvia glances at the clock on the far wall, and realises she has to get going soon, or her parents will be worried. The woman reassures her that she really must finish her tea and biscuits first, and then they'll telephone the police and tell them about the 'strange man from the bus.'

She finds it difficult to disagree with the woman or refuse her invitation, even though she wrinkles her nose in disgust at the sight of a strip of flypaper hanging in the window. The surface of the foul, mucous-coloured material was covered with the bodies of dead flies, although several were still struggling weakly; their half-hearted buzzing confirmation of a fate that's long been sealed.

As she stares in horrified fascination at the insects' dying throes, she hears footsteps clomping along the garden path, although the woman appears not to have heard them approach, so intent is she in making up the pot of steaming tea.

But then she calls out, without looking round:

>"Just in time, Herbert,"

…and Sylvia spins towards the kitchen door as it slowly opens wide.

And the man from the bus strides purposefully into the room.

>"Well done, Mabel!"

…he says, closing the door behind him. He smiles knowingly, and smoothing his hands together adds,

>"Don't forget one for the pot!"

The last thing we see is Sylvia staring imploringly at the woman she'd assumed to be her benefactor, as she brings the teapot to the table, and the young girl notices for the first time that there are *three* cups and saucers laid there…..

A FOOTNOTE MASQUERADING AS AN AFTERTHOUGHT:

As I was putting this book together, I came across the following snippet printed in the March, 2009 issue of *Empire Magazine*, as part of an article previewing the re-make of the 1985 classic *'A Nightmare On Elm Street.'* Wes Craven, the writer/director of the first and best of the hugely popular Freddy Kruegar movies, told the author of the piece, how he first 'dreamed up' (if you'll pardon the pun), the idea for the razor-fingered child serial killer.

Apparently, when Wes was a young boy, he happened to look out of his bedroom window one night to be confronted with the sight of an old drunk wearing 'a battered, brown fedora,' standing on the opposite side of the road. Wes was unable to say precisely why, initially, but the sight of this man, swaying ever so slightly like a tall tree in a high wind, 'scared the crap out of me.'

'And then he happened to look directly into my eyes,' Craven recalled, causing him to leap back from the window to conceal himself in the darkness of his bedroom. 'I stood shaking in the shadows, and counted to a hundred or two hundred. I went back and he was still stood there with a big leer. That guy, whoever the hell he was, enjoyed scaring the shit out of a kid.'

I don't know about you, Dear Reader, but reading of Wes Craven's experience all those years ago, caused a question to come spiralling up from "The Well Of Great Unanswerables".

And it was namely this: 'Is it possible that there exists deep in the hearts of broken men ('those who've fallen from grace with God'), a desire to terrify the very young?

Or worse, is there a race of phantom bogeymen somewhere out there on the 'night side of nature,' an ancient species that thrives on feeding off the fears of children, the way a crawling parasite grows fat and bloated after sucking the blood of its unwitting host?

GHOSTLY NUNS

And here's a horror from our teenage years that, though it had its origins firmly based in fiction, would return to haunt us for *real*, twenty six years down the paths of our lives, and nearly 270 miles from home, in the midst of the Scottish Highlands.

But more about all that in just a little while.

First let me you about the roots of our fears of Ghostly Nuns.

As anyone who has ever seen the 1970-80's TV series *Armchair Thriller*, (either during the programme's heyday, or via the recently released DVD box-set), will likely confirm, the episode entitled *'Quiet As A Nun',* featured one of the most enduringly frightening images ever to be shown on the small screen. That of a faceless nun, silently sat in a rocking chair on the top floor of some seemingly-deserted church, waiting with inhuman patience for a young, candle-bearing woman to slowly make her way up the winding staircase.

The thing is though, the scene is so over-stuffed with tired old chiller genre clichés (that seemed as such, even as long ago as 1980), it really shouldn't work. There is the soundtrack, replete with ominous organ/ piano music mixed with the obligatory owl hooting unseen in the darkness and the wind whispering amongst the leaves of the midnight woods. Then the female victim-in-waiting, wandering alone in the dead hours, (as you do). And the cringe-inducing question, mouthed by a countless stream of hapless, witless victims, of both sexes, in equally innumerable horror films upon her entering this creepiest of premises: 'Is there anyone there?' A query that simultaneously announces her presence to the psychopathic killer/big hairy monster/ Demonic entity, or indeed, Ghostly Nun, lurking, maybe, up until that point, blissfully unaware of the intruder into their 'domain.'

Not any more, though.

The element of surprise, or the opportunity to slip away unnoticed has evaporated during the space of the few fleeting seconds it has taken for that hopelessly inane query to go echoing around the premises as effectively as if it had been yelled in a full, decibel-bothering voice, through a megaphone.

The hollow sound of the woman's high-heeled shoes as she takes her first tentative steps up the staircase.

The jump-shock of a startled pigeon flying just above her head, causing her to gasp in astonished surprise, and to drop and break her flash-light.

Her unlikely recovery of composure and stubborn refusal to simply call it a night and get the hell out of there in one piece, instead, lighting a single, flickering candle and continuing up the staircase whilst a gentle creaking sound emanates from somewhere directly above.

The age-old trick of the camera focusing first on the young woman's terrified expression (harking back at least as long ago as the famous shot of Maggie Philbin confronted by the horrific visage of Lon Chaney's remarkable make-up as Erik, in the 1923 version of *The Phantom Of The Opera*), as she finally lays her terrified eyes upon her nemesis, so that we have a few seconds to ponder the nature of the horrors that lie before her.

And then the camera reveals its pay-off shot, and all the clichés are rendered redundant at the sight of that Faceless Nun, reeking of Evil menace and intent as the woman screams in abject terror, and the figure rises slowly from its chair to strike her a single, silencing blow as the screen quickly dissolves prior to the end credits, leaving us shaken and left to imagine her fate in our darkest dreams...

Twenty-six years later, three of the founder members of the erstwhile *New Ferry Horror Society,* myself, Stevie Gee and my brother, Grant, made an expedition to Loch Ness, Scotland, in the summer of 1996....

IN THE SHADOW OF BOLESKINE

> *'If there's one thing I know, you can't control Evil. You can lock it up and burn it and bury it and pray that it dies, but it never will. It just rests awhile. You can lock your doors and say your prayers, but the Evil is out there, waiting.'*
>
> *'And maybe, just maybe, it's closer than you think'*
>
> **Tommy Doyle: Halloween – the curse of Michael Myers (1996)**

Is it possible for an entire area to be haunted by what, for want of a better word, we term Evil?

Haunted not just by a solitary headless horseman, or a single phantom monk doomed to walk an identical route on the anniversary of some dark and terrible deed?

Haunted the way other areas seem to be *blessed* with vistas of breath-taking natural beauty, a sense of inner peace or a deeply religious aura?

Can mere rock and shoreline, stream and greensward, meadow and valley somehow retain a vivid impression of horrors past and horrors yet to be?

Can a place simply be *'born'* bad?

Of course, there are those students of paranormal phenomena who wouldn't hesitate in telling you that it is indeed possible. And if you cared to politely enquire further, they'd doubtless delight in informing you (in that smug, patronising tone exclusive to certain schoolteachers, college lecturers and that maddeningly annoying smart-arse who knows the answers to every single one of the *Trivial Pursuit* questions), they've known about the existence of such places for years beyond counting.

Hell, they even have a name for them:

'Window Areas.'

Now, that's as good a name as any, I guess. And who am I to argue with what's long since become a universally accepted entry in *'The Paranormal Researcher's Bible'*, right alongside *'Close Encounters'*, *'Near Death Experiences'* and *'Spontaneous Human Combustion'*?

I make no apologies, however, for choosing to refer to these areas by another name. A name that from personal experience I consider to be far more appropriate:

'SHADOWLANDS'

A name for the type of place that seems to be permanently bathed in a scummy, yellowish wash of light, and where the air seems forever pregnant with heavy rain and thunder.

Where the moon rises like a spirit with a pale, humourless face amidst a sea of diamond-chip stars.

Where buildings stand at weird unnatural angles.

Where birdsong is muted.

The air is chilled.

And shadows lie eternal.

Shadowlands

If such places truly exist outside of the 'experts' wishful thinking, and this writer's somewhat fevered imagination, then the area around Boleskine House, overlooking the dark, brooding waters of Loch Ness, must surely stand as a shining (if that's *quite* the right word) example.

And yet, I'm sure a considerable proportion of the people reading this won't ever have even heard of the place. That's hardly surprising. You'll find little mention of it, even in Fortean circles, despite the fact that the infamous Satanist/occultist/drug-fiend/filthy pervert (delete where your personal opinion of the man decrees to be applicable), Aleister Crowley, once resided there. Not to mention Jimmy Page, the lead guitarist with the recently re-formed (albeit for one night only) *Led Zeppelin*.

Even books, DVD's and videos dealing specifically with the Loch and its legendary monster contain only the most cursory of references.

Illustrations and photographs of the locale are rarer still. There are several tourist, holiday-type snaps posted up on the Internet, but the sole examples I've come across featured in any paranormal publication were included in Simon Marsden's *Phantoms Of The Isles* (Guild Publishing 1990). That work includes a two-page, black and white spread of Boleskine burial ground looking suitably ominous. Interestingly, Marsden's attendant notes contain the following disturbing, and maybe starkly relevant lines:

> 'The whole enclosure (graveyard) had a particularly strange atmosphere, as if it were the centre of some powerful force.'

And later:
> 'Crowley may have unleashed Evil spirits that ran amok in the area.'

The validity of the latter we'll dwell upon in a little while.

Firstly, let me just confirm that Marsden's initial comment is bang on the mark. A personal trip to the area will be more than enough to convince anyone of that.

But therein lies an enigma.

It seems hard to believe, but even regular visitors to the Loch may remain blissfully ignorant of the existence of Boleskine, situated roughly half-way between the tiny, picturesque villages of Dores and Foyers. General Wade's Military Road, the endlessly winding B852, is comparatively shunned by the summer tourists in favour of the main A82 that runs directly along the opposite shoreline (and is therefore considered to be far more 'Nessie-spotting friendly').

My friends and I had been holidaying in the area since May, 1992, and we'd only come across the burial ground quite by accident during the early June of 1996. We'd been searching for the *Foyers Hotel* (from the grounds of which the first full-time monster-hunter, Tim Dinsdale filmed his now famously controversial footage that appears to show *something* traversing the surface of the Loch).

The memory of our 'discovery' remains startlingly vivid to this day, though to be honest, I often wish I could succeed in relegating its recollection to some forgotten corner of my mind, because all too frequently, the memory surfaces in my dreams, and on such occasions, I often find I scream myself awake into the rough, uncaring darkness…

****

I remember a miserable, rain-sodden afternoon, deep in the Scottish Highlands. The calendar insisted it was mid-August, but you would've been forgiven for thinking the cold, cheerless, grip of November still held sway. The sky was the colour of slate and a vicious wind swept up piles of crumpled leaves and spun them into mini-tornados.

We were driving, my fellow ex-*Society* members and I, (along with a couple of additional friends, Richie White and Simon Norris), along a narrow, winding road bordered on one side by steep, heavily-wooded slopes and on the other by a wild array of undergrowth so dense the vast expanse of water away to our left was only visible in brief, tantalising glimpses of foam-flecked grey.

Suddenly the road veered away from the Loch and the car, was all but engulfed in a thick canopy of trees. It was clear that even on the very brightest of days the enveloping foliage would admit no rich tapestry of sun and shade, only a vaguely depressing half-light, perfectly suited to the grimly forbidding vista that unexpectedly appeared over the next rise.

Richie, who was at the wheel, slowed the car down and brought it to a gradual halt. By unspoken consent we climbed out, and silently made our way across the road towards a walled graveyard situated smack in the middle of the proverbial nowhere.

There was no-one else around. The road was entirely devoid of traffic. I noticed there were no farms or houses in any the lush green fields either side of the ancient-looking enclosure. The only token signs of modern civilisation were the telegraph wires snaking their way through the roofs of the overhanging treetops.

It was an achingly lonely place, the atmosphere stiflingly oppressive. But we intrepid five were too consumed with burning curiosity to pay much heed. This unexpected discovery had filled us with barely suppressed excitement. We were eager to explore. And the rusted gate was standing open as if silently beckoning us to enter.

So enter we did…

A battered noticeboard was attached to the wall nearest to the entrance. Protected by a transparent plastic cover were a collection of children's notes and drawings. A placard informed the reader that the work was the product of the pupils of Foyers Primary School, and provided a brief but fascinating history of the burial ground. Reference was also made to the deliberate destruction of the attendant church, now little more than an empty, roofless shell, its crumbling walls all but hidden by thorny blackberry bushes and clumps of high stinging nettles.

There were details too, of how the cemetery had long been redundant, for the very good reason that by the middle of the 20th Century, there had simply ceased to be any room left for within the consecrated earth in which to bury the newly-dead.

> *'Things had become so bad,'*

…the childish scrawl, written entirely in block capitals, confided,

> *'...that the bones of the deceased were being buried in graves so shallow, packs of wild dogs had begun roaming the plot, digging up the remains almost the minute they were laid to rest.'*

Bodysnatching had apparently been rife around here, too, with doctors from nearby Inverness willing to pay a handsome price for any fresh cadavers upon which they could perform their medical experiments.

There was also mention of one particular headstone leaning drunkenly in the most neglected corner of graveyard riddled with what appear to be bullet holes. The story goes that during the Jacobite Rebellion in the 17th Century, a British patrol was passing the funeral of an insurgent who had been killed in action. On seeing present amongst the mourners those whom they suspected of being Jacobite sympathisers, they immediately opened fire hence the 'bullet holes' in the headstone.

It was not recorded whether anyone was actually killed or wounded in the attack.

We took our time looking around the enclosure and saw that it contained row after row of crumbling, moss-covered tombstones that proved upon closer inspection to be almost exclusively inscribed with the surname, Fraser.

The wind howled through the fissures in the ancient stone, like a lament for all that's dead or dying, and an even closer look at those crooked graves revealed that might be not so very far from the truth. The majority of the names engraved here are the final glorious epitaphs of those who have fallen on foreign battlefields in the service of their country, (Waterloo, South Africa, The Somme), or else were the equally tragic victims of inter-clan warfare.

Without warning, I was struck by the crystal-clear memory of my Grandmother's funeral that had taken place on a similarly dreary rain-swept afternoon, when I was just fourteen-years-old…

Then, as now, I am standing by a graveside, head bowed, shoulders hunched against the biting cold. My red-rimmed eyes fix upon the many wreaths and brightly-coloured bouquets. The simple, moving messages of condolence on the cards pinned to the flowers are quickly obscured by the incessant downpour. The words slide from the soggy attachments in thin rivers of ink like a woman's mascara pricked with salty tears.

The air hangs heavy with solemnity and grief. The only sounds are the muted sobbing of the assembled mourners and the vicar's sonorous tones as he utters banal words of cold comfort. From somewhere far off, barely within earshot, I hear the chimes of a travelling ice cream van, and the distance turns the child's nursery rhyme into a discordant melody of false good cheer, as though a demented circus clown, its face sweating greasepaint, had been let loose on an out of tune piano. I had an unwelcome image of it grinning insanely as it pummelled the keyboards with make-up stained gloved hands.

A chill that has nothing to do with the Godawful weather causes me to shudder uncontrollably, and as much as I loved my Nan, I think selfishly, "I wish they'd hurry up and get this over with. All this standing around and sobbing in the rain isn't gonna bring her back. Why can't anybody see that?"

And then I promptly burst into floods of tears of my own. The precious recollections of all the good times I spent in her company come flooding back in a deluge so powerful, I'm almost swept away by their sheer force. My mother puts her arm around me and I bury my face into the soft fabric of her coat silently cursing the God who could deign to take my Nan away, closing my ears to the murmured consolations that are now doing the rounds.

An eternity seems to pass.

No-one moves.

We're soaked to the skin and all cried out.
Time, it seems, has stood still.

Eventually though, as if on some unspoken cue, the congregation prepares to depart. And now, incredibly, I find I actually don't *want to leave. Walking away now, feels too much like desertion. Abandoning a much-loved family member just when they need you most. I'm all but dragged to the waiting hearse and its po-faced chauffeur. I reluctantly clamber aboard, slide into the back seat between my two brothers and glance back over my shoulder one more time.*

I see there's a blackbird perched atop my Nan's headstone. I can hear its plaintive song even through the thick, tinted glass, and it may sound crazy, but its sweetly, melodious 'voice' lightens my mood a little. I can't say precisely why, but for the first time on that terrible day, I feel a sense of inner calm begin to descend.

And then my heart skips a beat and I have to cover my mouth with my hand to stifle a cry of astonishment as single shaft of sunlight emerges from between a gap in the clouds. It spears down like a laser beam across the row of attendant headstones, their uniform whiteness turned blindingly bright. The blackbird, doubtlessly startled, suddenly takes to the air, and I watch it ascending to rejoin its flock, before flying towards the distant horizon, looking for all the world like a soul that had joyfully been set free....

*****

If the recalling of that cherished memory was meant to fortify me against my natural fear of death and the grave however, it proved to be hopelessly unsuccessful.

The Boleskine burial ground gives off a sickly ambience that's impossible to shake or ignore. No matter how nonsensical that may appear.

Here, it's easy to believe, the spirits of the dead remain chained to whatever is left of their physical remains for all eternity.

Worse, their understandable anger at being cut down in the prime of their lives has gleefully been harnessed by some powerful, inherently evil force that has existed here since the dawn of time. And over the passage of the centuries, all that resentment has been transformed into a bitter and twisted hatred, a poison that had turned the very earth sour.

Or at least, that was the overriding impression this terrible place etched upon me....

****

One thing the notice board fails to make mention of is the derelict-looking building standing roughly half-way along the opposite wall. This struck me as being more than a little odd, as although there is nothing outwardly remarkable about it, the fact remains that aside from the ruined church, it easily dominates the enclosure.

Intrigued, we walked in-between the tombstones, being careful not to tread on any of the actual graves lest we insult the fallen, towards the building's only entrance, a rotted oak door that, contrary to our expectations, was unlocked, and standing slightly ajar.

There was a brief argument that ensued as to who was going to be the first to enter. We stood motionless for a few long moments, as immobile as any of those grand sepulchres populating the graveyard. Not surprisingly, no-one seemed too keen to volunteer, but eventually, (and after a spot of mentally stealing ourselves), we all pushed the door fully open together and stepped across the threshold.

The tiny cottage, for that is what it must have been once, contained two levels.

The sole source of illumination is a small upstairs window, but even allowing for the time it took for our eyes to adjust to the pervasive gloom, it was quickly apparent that the ground floor, where the air is heavy with a dank, foetid aroma, was little more than an empty shell, not really worth exploring.

A set of wooden stairs, comparatively recently installed, led to the floor directly above. The original flight had, it seemed, long since been removed in its entirety. In total silence (a consensual quiet that would have appeared almost reverential any place save here), we ascended.

At first glance, this room too, seemed to be disappointingly empty.

The late afternoon light fell in grey slabs across the bare, wooden floor. Dust motes danced crazily like a swarm of maddened insects. There were no items of furniture, no outward trace of decoration. The place was as drab and colourless as the surface of some cold, dead alien planet. And the only sign that anybody had set foot within these walls in years, *decades* even, is some fresh kindling stacked in the grate of an old-fashioned fireplace.

Filled with a perverse sense of anti-climax,

> *(and what had we expected to find residing here, exactly? The angry ghost of some long-departed member of the Clan Fraser, berating us for having dared to disturb his centuries-old sleep? A bunch of black-cowled Satanists performing a secret and most likely obscene rite? A thickly-bearded, flesh and blood recluse, complete with kilt, lethal-looking Claymore and a near-pathological hatred of the English?),*

I glanced out of the single, grimy window, and noticed the wind had dropped dramatically, leaving in its wake a stillness that seemed unnatural and vaguely dream-like. Very little was moving in the landscape beyond the grubby glass panes save for a thin line of wood-smoke spiralling above the tree-laden hillside and a V-formation of Canadian geese, their song the soundtrack of incurable loneliness.

I was just about to suggest we should leave the building when Simon, suddenly exclaimed,

"Hang on a minute, lads. Have a look at this!"

I turned to see where he was pointing, and at first it was difficult to make out much of anything on the dust-covered floor. Gradually, however, I was able to discern a crudely-drawn circle containing a series of arcane symbols and what appeared to be a series of inscriptions written in some foreign language.

As someone who has more than a passing interest in occult matters, I thought perhaps I recognised some of the words as being some form of Latin or Hebraic, and like a birdwatcher who strongly suspects he has caught a glimpse of some rarely-seen species, I made a mental note to check up and confirm their identity and meaning when I got home.

There were more scribblings on the walls and all along the oak beams that criss-crossed the ceiling: a heady mixture of the esoteric and the entirely unintelligible.

And there…looking as out of place as a string of Christmas tinsel blowing across the sand dunes of some exotic sun-drenched beach, is a sentence in plain English:

'Do What Thou Wilt Shall Be the Whole of The Law'

Painted in a rusty shade of red, the colour of dried blood, there is something chilling about that seemingly innocuous phrase. Chilling, and at the same time, somehow familiar….

At the time, though, I couldn't quite recall where I'd heard it before. It lay on the brink of remembrance, like the memory of a dream upon waking.

I was still vainly racking my brains for an answer, when Grant and Stevie Gee announced a discovery of their own. They'd stumbled upon the charred remains of animal bones stacked in the darkest corner of the room. Resting on a shelf cluttered with discarded beer cans and several yellow-stained rags, is the clean-picked skull of some horned creature, a goat most likely. A used condom nestles beneath the jaw bone, and its depth-less, hollow eyes seem to regard me with the type of black, empty madness one presumes exists beyond the rim of the universe.

The sight of this, more than anything, was enough to cause a sensation of prickling horror to travel and down my spine.

A sense of Evil, intangible, yet nonetheless inarguably real, became so overpowering that we each of us turn and leave by the same unspoken consent with which we'd entered.

Though admittedly, a whole lot quicker!

It had been our intention to drive to Fort Augustus, and stock up with some provisions for the remainder of the holiday. We needed to get moving before the stores in the village closed for the day, and I'm sure we managed to convince ourselves that this was the sole reason for our obvious impatience to be away from this place.

We clambered back into the car, Simon gunned the engine, and prepared to steer the vehicle out of the lay-by in which we'd parked and back onto the road.

We breathed a collective sigh of relief and drove off to the sound of *The Clash* playing '*Gates Of The West*' blasting from the tape deck.

And then I suddenly remembered where I'd first seen those enigmatic words written in (*dried blood*) red paint on the walls of that godforsaken cottage.

'Do What Thou Wilt Shall Be the Whole of The Law'

I remember.

And in truth, had I ever *really* forgotten?

The Civic Centre Library, situated in the centre of the bustling village of Bebington, has always been one of my favourite places, and it often seems to me I spent half of my childhood and nearly all my teenage years with my head buried in a rollicking good novel, (I had a particular fondness for the works of J.R.R Tolkien, the wonderfully scary ghost stories of M.R. James and the crime/noir thrillers of Raymond Chandler, but the truth is I'd read just about anything if the story grabbed me), leafing through the piles of old magazines, or browsing amongst the reams of volumes that lined the shelves of the Adult and Junior sections; a vast collection of wondrous tales contained within their fabulously musty-smelling pages.

I loved the Reference Room the best.

It was like a tiny world of its own populated by a race that knew exactly what was expected of them and precisely what their place was in the grand scheme of things.

On any given day, (except on Wednesdays and public holidays when the building was closed), you could ascend the stairs, take a seat at one of the large, plastic-topped desks and pretend to read whilst really glancing surreptitiously about you at the timeworn rituals of the inhabitants.

Without fail, there'd be a group of college students or sixth-formers, their foreheads creased in concentration as they pored over massive tomes dealing with the Franco-Prussian War or Advanced Mathematics. The desk opposite would be occupied by several younger school kids, more often than not tittering over the pictures of human genitalia in the biology encyclopaedias or else trying to cough loudly to cover their tearing out of colour portraits of the latest rock singer or film star. There'd also be a cluster of old men constantly rustling their newspapers pointedly in gestures of mild annoyance, if anyone raised their voice above a whisper, courting couples who gazed lovingly into one another's eyes over the tops of a stack of *National Geographics*, and a young female librarian, her tight blouse and mini-skirt accentuating her hour-glass figure driving both the adolescents and the old men to distraction.

And presiding over all, was the dread-inducing form of the Head Librarian…An imposing, grim-faced woman with a spiteful kid-hating attitude that would put the wicked stepmother in *Hansel and Gretel* to shame. She would sit at the far end of the room, peering out at her domain with an expression on her face that simply *demands* that those assembled behave themselves.

At the front of her desk was a laminated placard inscribed with the words;

> This is the Public Library Reference Floor.
>
> People come here to study. All are welcome, but please remember to abide by these simple rules:
>
> 1: No books may be taken from this floor for ANY reason!
>
> 2: Anybody caught defacing or damaging books WILL be prosecuted!
>
> 3: In a library, silence is more than a virtue, it is an absolute NECESSITY!
>
> Thank you for your co-operation.
>
> 'HAVE A NICE DAY!'

Her name may or may not have been Mona. The kids, myself included, all called her that, (although never to her face, of course), and the way she always seemed to be constantly complaining, bitching, and well, moaning, no moniker was ever more appropriate. But woe betide the unfortunate person who was caught breaking any of the Three Commandments According To Mona. I've seen grown men cower in the face of her wrath. She handed out her reprimands with all the aplomb of a person who has spent much of their life joyfully inflicting misery on anyone who crosses their path, and forcing the weak to bend before her will.

But still, in spite of Mona, or perhaps in some perverse way because of her, I loved the library. Even if all of the memories of the place weren't exactly bathed in the warm glow of nostalgia.

For instance, I remember it was on a damp and misty afternoon in late November, 1980, when I first came across the words that would return to confront me 16 years or so later.

I can recall vividly the way the world beyond the circular windows, most of which were decorated with multi-coloured cardboard leaves, drawn and pasted on by children, looked grey and distant. The building was lit by soft, diffused lighting, and I was struck by the feeling that people passing by outside might well be glancing up at the library wearing the same expression as that of a weary traveller who, after spending countless hours aimlessly wandering lost on the moors, suddenly spies the welcoming light pouring from the windows of a remote farmhouse. And, perhaps thinking these thoughts, these passers-by might add an urgent spring to their step, anxious to get home that little bit faster.

I was idly leafing through a book on the history of witchcraft, the title of which now escapes me, when I came across a chapter dealing with modern-day Satanists and Black Magicians. In amongst the lurid pictures of Witch's

Sabbats and desecrated churches, was a black and white portrait of a striking-looking, bald-headed man with a pair of intense, almost hypnotic eyes. He seemed to be neither smiling nor frowning. The picture suggested here was a man possessed of great charisma. He was of indeterminate age, although the lines on his face seemed to indicate that too much emotional voltage had been running behind that inscrutable countenance for too long a time.

The caption beneath the photograph, had said simply;

> *'Aleister Crowley: The self-styled Great Beast 666. Raised by devoutly religious parents, he rebelled to become one of the most notorious Black Magicians of recent times.*
>
> *A former member of the infamous Golden Dawn, he was typically reviled by the popular press, who labelled him; "The Wickedest Man In The World."*
>
> *His most oft-quoted edict was:* **"Do What Thou Wilt Shall Be the Whole Of The Law"**

My interest aroused, I'd read the whole piece and spent the remainder of that day learning all I could about this mysterious figure, Aleister Crowley, though in truth, this didn't actually amount to a great deal. Just a tantalisingly brief synopsis of his life and times and some of the more sensational newsworthy events that had contributed to his notoriety.

There was something else, though…

Something that all but leaped off the page amidst the references to the Abbey at Thelema, the famous poem *'IO To Pan,'* and his many run-ins with McGregor Mathers (a fellow occultist and member of the Golden Dawn).

It was simply this:

> *'Aleister Crowley had once lived in a remote hideaway, deep in the Highlands of Scotland. He resided, for quite some time, in a secluded mansion screened from the roadside by a thick canopy of trees'*

The house where he lived, to paraphrase Shirley Jackson, has:

> '*…stood for a hundred years and may stand for a hundred more*'

It's a house that overlooks an ancient burial ground, the final resting place of many members of the Clan Fraser.

A place shunned by the locals, due to its evil repute, even to this day.

Boleskine burial ground on the banks of Loch Ness….

****

From the very moment that I remembered the origin of the jagged scribbling on the walls of that ramshackle cottage, and informed everyone else in the car pulling away from Boleskine, I just knew there was no away we would be able to simply drive off without affording ourselves a brief glimpse of Crowley's residence. The long journey back home to Merseyside would be even less bearable if we missed the opportunity to snap a few pictures of Boleskine House and scare ourselves silly during the dark nights leading up to Hallowe'en, passing the photographs around and swapping true-life horror stories at a beer-laden table in *The Bridge Inn*, while a bonfire blazed away merrily in the field outside and the rich, mouth-watering smell of baked potatoes and roasted chestnuts filled the late-October air.

Our curiosity quelled our fears, and by the time Simon began reversing the car back to the lay-by, being afraid was quite the furthest thing from my mind. Once more, we emerged from the car and began looking about us with renewed excitement.

It was clear from the beginning however, that the house was not going to be easy to locate. Even the most cursory of glances was enough to convince us all of that slightly dispiriting fact. There was only one building visible from the road, (aside from the cottage in the graveyard, of course), and though we raced towards it expectantly, we saw almost immediately that it was nothing other than a small lodge, inhabited, judging from the Mercedes parked in the driveway, by a fairly well-to-do family.

There was a child's tricycle lying on its side beneath the front window and a naked *Barbie* doll, propped up drunkenly against an apple tree. It was abundantly clear this was not the place we were looking for.

My brother, Grant, ever the practical one, suggested we knock and ask to see if they know the location of Boleskine House. If the occupants had lived there for any length of time, we surmised, they'd likely be able to tell us. We unlatched the gate, swung it open and were stopped in our tracks by the sound of a woman's voice calling to us from just down the road.

A middle-aged lady was walking towards us dressed in wellies and an all-weather anorak with the hood pulled up.

> "Excuse me,"

…she said in clipped tones, without a trace of a Scottish accent.

> "Do you mind telling me who that car belongs to, parked in that lay-by over there?"

She stood there with her hands on her hips, the gesture of someone who's just spoiling for an argument. I could only just about make out her face, obscured as it was by the anorak hood, but for one surreal moment I was convinced that standing there before me was Mona, the head librarian from the Civic Centre, come to decree a set of *new* Commandments:

> 1: Please do not park on the B-roads around Loch Ness.
>
> 2: Any trespassers found on the grounds of local residents will be immediately sacrificed to some obscure Demonic entity.
>
> 3: Around the former home of Mr Aleister Crowley Esq, silence is more than a virtue, it is a absolute necessity. If you speak too loudly, you'll likely wake the dead!
>
> Thank you for your co-operation
>
> HAVE A NICE DAY!

> "Will one of you kindly move the vehicle. It's causing an obstruction, and there's a Sunday School bus due this way, any moment, now!"

> "Alright, missus, keep yer hair on,"

Grant replied indignantly.

> "We won't be a minute."

Seeing she was somewhat placated, if not completely satisfied with this response, he seized the opportunity to add:

> "We heard a fella named Aleister Crowley used to live round here. I don't suppose you know whether the house is still standing, and if it is, *where* it is, by any chance?"

The second the words left his mouth the woman's expression of haughty intolerance changed to one of outright suspicion and hostility. And as people will do when they're caught momentarily off-guard, she answered the query with a couple of questions of her own.

> "Why do you want to know? We have more than enough strangers, worthless reprobates, the lot of them, hanging around here as it is. Why on earth should I seek to openly encourage others?"

> "What do you mean, 'strangers?'"

I jumped in.

> "You mean Satanists? Black Magicians? Devil Worshippers?"

> "I mean, 'strangers!'"

...she repeated, like a teacher explaining a simple math problem to a backward student.

> "I'm referring to people who come up here to the Highlands to plague us with their endless questions, their ceaseless trampling upon law-abiding residents' property, their constant vandalism of yonder Burial Ground and their quite honestly pathetic attempts at what they doubtless deem to be acts of homage to "The Dark Gods." For instance, dancing around stark naked in the fields at midnight, sacrificing a defenceless animal or two, or dressing up in a monk's cowl and sleeping off their drunken stupor on the very doorstep of Boleskine Hou..."

She caught herself, but too late. The confirmation that we sought, that Boleskine House did indeed still stand, had been unwittingly provided

'Mona' made a show of shrugging her shoulders resignedly.

> "Okay, so now you know. Mr Crowley's house is indeed around here, somewhere. But I'll be damned if I'm going to tell you the *precise* location. Now go and move your car like I told you. The school bus will be coming this way any moment, and your vehicle is causing an obstruction."

And with that, she stormed off, leaving the five of us standing in the middle of the road, rendered speechless by her departing glance of withering contempt.

Stevie Gee eventually broke the spell.

> "I suppose we'd better move the car, like she says. We know the house is somewhere on this stretch of road, probably overlooking the Burial Ground, if the books you read are right, Lee. But we could spend the rest of today traipsing up and down between here and Dores, and either break our necks in the woods, or get run-over by the Sunday School Bus..."

He paused momentarily, his brow furrowed in obvious puzzlement. And I think we all realised what he was going to say a nanosecond or so before he actually said it.

> "Hang on a minute. Today isn't Sunday. It's Monday. Bank Holiday Monday, to be exact. What the hell's that woman going on about?"

And he was right, of course. It was indeed a Monday. We'd been so concerned with our questions regarding the house, we'd completely forgotten what day it was. It's a common enough thing. When you're on vacation, the passage of the days, seemingly so important during the working week, becomes essentially meaningless, at least for as long as the fun and games can continue unabated.

But for a *local* to forget. Now that wasn't quite so likely, was it? Not if she was in possession of her full quota of marbles, anyway. No. It was my guess that she was smart enough to calculate that as dumb tourists, we'd have almost certainly lost track of the *time,* never mind the *days*. She'd just wanted to get rid of us 'strangers'' as quickly and as painlessly as possible.

We turned around, each of us intending to let her know in no uncertain terms, that she hadn't succeeded in fooling us, but when we turned to confront her, the road was empty for as far as the eye could see. There were only the trees, their overhanging branches forming a natural green canopy that stretched away into the distance like the arched cloisters of some mighty cathedral.

> "Where the hell did she go?"

I asked, my voice sounding tiny in the sudden quiet that had descended.

> "Maybe there's a farmhouse nearby, out of sight beyond those woods?"

Richie offered.

> "We just can't see it from here."

> "Yeah, that's likely it,"

…we muttered in unison.

> "There could be a whole bunch of crofts and cottages down the lane there, for all we know."

> "Oh aye. The owl biddy's probably watching us through her bedroom window, right now."

> "Probably laughin' her socks off."

> "What a conniving arl boot!"

And the fact is, looking at things from a cold, rational perspective that was very likely the truth of it. The woman had almost certainly put on a bit of speed the seconds are backs were turned, and had scurried home. She'd then charged upstairs and pressed her face against the window, anxious to keep an eye on us lest we set about disembowelling the local sheep with machetes so we could gorge ourselves on their blood…

That was certainly the logical explanation for where she'd disappeared to.

We'd been so concerned though with finding an answer to the question of where she'd gone, we'd completely ignored a query that was even more relevant. Bearing in mind that we'd just travelled up from the village of Dores, a good three miles distant, (and the direction from which the woman had first approached us), without seeing so much as a single habitation; where the hell had she come *from?*

That was one of the things that would later keep me awake at nights, afraid to sleep. Afraid to dream.

Another is something Steve said with typical black humour as we stood in the road, mentally debating our next move:

> "Hey, I know where that arl woman lives. I know where she'd be right at home. In the graveyard. In the graveyard with all the other dead things!"

****

I sincerely doubt we'd have ever found Boleskine House, that day at least, if it hadn't have been for the distant strains of Marvin Gaye floating in the Highland air, just then.

We'd been more than ready to abandon the search and continue with our interrupted journey to Fort Augustus. Hunting down the homes of the infamous could only hold your interest for so long.

It was Richie who heard the music first.

He was certainly the first to recognise the tune.

> "Hold on, there's music playing somewhere. Isn't that *I heard It Through The Grapevine?*"

And so it was. Marvin's voice drifted toward us sounding disembodied and somehow lost, like the helpless cry of a child that can't find its mother.

With the unspoken consent that had been a regularly recurring feature of this day, we walked towards the source of the music spread across the road, looking for all the world like the Wild Bunch all set for the final gunfight at the Battle of Bloody Porch.

We still had our hearts set on seeing that house and it was possible that whoever was playing that song might be able to help us with that quest.

It turned out we didn't have to walk very far. There was a small lodge a third of a mile or so from where we'd parked. When we'd passed it earlier, it had appeared to be nothing more than a derelict shell, and so we hadn't even slowed down to take a closer look. But now, as we approached the building, we could clearly see that there was a workman who appeared to be in his late thirties, painting the front entrance. He was atop a set of ladders, paintbrush in hand, whistling along to Mr Gaye's paean to the soon-to-be dumped, oblivious to us all.

Once again it was Grant who spoke up to grab the man's attention.

> "Excuse us, mate,"

…he said.

> "Have yer got any idea where Boleskine House is?"

The man turned to look at us, startled, and very nearly fell off his ladder. He took a good few seconds to regain his composure, and when he eventually found his voice, he said in mildly Scottish tones:

> "Well now, it could be that I do have a very good idea of where the house you are looking' for lies. But before I decide whether I should tell you or not, let me ask you a question. Why do you want tae know?"

I decided the best bet was to play the 'dumb tourist' role; we were simply intending to take a few holiday snaps of places of local interest (and when you got right down to it, was that really so far from the truth?). We must have come across as being fairly convincing because his face split into a grin as he said,

> "Och, why not? It cannae do any harm that I can see."

Then he slapped his thigh as though he were about to recite the world's funniest gag.

> "The thing is, fellas, you are gonna kick yerselves all the way back tae Liverpool, when I tell you. This building here, is Boleskine Lodge. I'm the head ground-keeper, the summer help and the caretaker all rolled in tae one.
>
> The path you see winding its merry way up the hill behind those gates over there… That driveway leads right up tae the house you's are lookin' for.' He paused, the amused grin slipped from his face momentarily.
>
> But you cannae go that way. The man who owns it is a wee bit paranoid about security. He's had more than his fair share of nutcases hangin' around his front door. He keeps guard dogs. Big mean, black hounds that'd tear a man's arm off without a second thought. And it's all alarmed with the very latest, high-tech surveillance equipment, too. So, I'm afraid youse have had a wasted journey. Tough luck, lads!"

Having imparted this information, he laughed so hard he very nearly fell off his ladder again, and he was still braying like a donkey as we walked dejectedly back the way we had come. And for all I know, he's still there at this moment, holding on to his not inconsiderable belly, hee-hawing fit to bust at the hopeless endeavours of a group of pig-ignorant Scousers.

****

Luckily for us, that cackling Scot's low opinion of us actually worked in our favour, and once were well out of sight, it was our turn to laugh, loud and long.

He obviously didn't know who he'd been dealing with. Three members of our group, Steve Gee, Grant and myself, were, as kids, original founder members of *The New Ferry Horror Society*, and as such were adept at gaining admittance into reputedly haunted houses.

In the summer of 1996, we were no longer children, secure in the naïve belief that latter-day Professor Van Helsings are not sent to prison for long periods of time if they're caught breaking into other people's property. But even if we couldn't actually get inside the place and take a look around, nothing short of a Demonic manifestation was going to stop us sneaking a glimpse and a couple of photographs of the *outside*….

We knew the location. Now all we had to do was find an alternative route to the driveway, and in the end the answer proved to be just as plain as day.

The house was obviously hidden from the road, just like the books had said, by a screen of gently rolling hills and thick clumps of fir trees. All we had to do was climb over a thin-wire fence that ringed the adjoining field, clamber up a steep embankment, and gaze down at the front of the house.

And with excitement and anticipation once more at a peak, we set out to do precisely that.

I suppose, after all we'd been through, the actual viewing of Boleskine House was always going to be something of an anti-climax.

Just as when we'd entered the top floor of that graveyard-keeper's cottage, in what by then seemed like an age ago, I'm not quite sure what I *expected* to see. But I couldn't help feeling an acute sense of disappointment wash over me like when you're burning up on some tropical beach and the large, white-capped wave heading your way that you hope will help cool you down, turns out to be horribly lukewarm.

The house was every bit as enormous as I'd anticipated it would be. And I guess, viewed from a different angle, after dark, bathed in moonlight, with a sickly glow pouring from its many windows, it might indeed appear suitably ominous.

But though we stood there, gathered together for what seemed like the longest time, it was impossible to shake the unpalatable truth that Boleskine House, the one-abode of The Great Beast, Aleister Crowley, looked so tediously *ordinary.*

I remember I looked back towards the burial ground, now several hundred feet below us, and then out across the surface of the Loch…And in the midst of that 'semi-permanent twilight,' with the dark clouds hanging so low they seemed set to swoop down and kissed the diseased earth, I found it easy to imagine how it might have been there in some dim and distant time before…Imagine and wonder if there had truly ever been a time when this place may have been 'spiritually-clean.' 'Elemental-free.' Held sacred.

And where the only shadows cast were the natural consequence of cheery summer sunlight….

BOLESKINE:
Before The Fall

The height of springtime.

A crisp, fresh Sunday morning.

The skies are clear and eye-wateringly bright, and sun-rays dart off the surface of the Loch, sparkling like a promise.

Paddle steamers cruise the shimmering waters and groups of well-to-do tourists sit on the grassy banks sipping their iced tea or tucking into picnic lunches.

Everything is right with the world.

God is over all.

And within the lovingly tended plot that marks the final resting place of members of the Clan Fraser, families file happily into the church. The tiny, rough-hewn building's stark simplicity makes it no less welcoming A minister with a kind, grandfatherly face stands at the lych gate, shaking hands with each and every one of his parishioners. Giggling young girls in pigtails and summer-white dresses. Sullen boys in stiffly starched shirts. The adults, conservative and God-fearing, who take their seats staring intently at the church's only decoration: the two rows of beautiful stained glass windows. Even the smallest child looks upon these colourful works of art with something approaching religious awe.

And perhaps, although they are very probably not even aware of it, something else, too. These intricate depictions of the Eternal Struggle Between The Forces Of

Good And Evil (The Temptation of St Anthony, The Revolt of the Fallen Angels, St Michael Defeating the Dragon), may have acted as a visual reminder of something they'd all rather forget.

A whispered hint of something that was given form in the dreams of even the most pious during the darkest hour of the night.

Confirmation of their ancestor's knowledge that there exists the very finest lines between a land that is blessed and a land that is cursed, and while it was likely certain places were simply born bad, perhaps, with the passing of time, they could be cleansed, reclaimed, Exorcised, if you will, by the thoughts and deeds of good men.

Perhaps Boleskine, once damned, was such a place.

And, if that were so, it followed that the faithful would do well to remain vigilant. Any lowering of their guard, one single failure to recognise Evil sneaking furtively into their midst, one careless acceptance of a seemingly well-intentioned stranger...Then the delicate balance could be tipped in favour of the Serpent Of Lies, and God, doubtless weeping, would turn His back upon the once-faithful. And The Dragon would emerge from the Pit, triumphant, the shadows it cast covering the land like a death shroud.

And yet, despite the oft-repeated warnings, it came to pass that those who had been appointed "Brotherhood of The Watch," proved fatally negligent in the task that had long ago been entrusted to them. And when the inevitable time of reckoning came around, and a smiling, bald-headed man had suddenly appeared amongst them, twirling a silver-tipped cane like a harmless, children's magician, they had forgotten the wisdom of their ancestors.

And if they hadn't exactly welcomed him with open arms, they had at least been far too willing to accept him at face value.

And the stranger, whose benign features were constantly lit by a grin that never touched his eyes, had been left to his own devices...Which was precisely what he'd wanted all along, of course.

Evil, the Elder had always taught, came in many guises, and more often than not, it is pleasant or at worst innocuous-seeming. It seeks a safe place, out of sight and out of mind, where it can take root. And once it obtains a foothold, it breeds like the most virulent strain of a killer disease, cancer, say, or bubonic plague. It has a voracious appetite, and it eats through everything, starting with all you've ever cherished or held dear to your heart, together with all the things you'd long since taken for granted. And it ends with the tragic, irreversible loss of innocence.

And the most terrible thing of all is that you don't even notice it is happening....Until it's far too late. The changes are as imperceptible as the movement of a clock hand, but every bit as inexorable as the passing of time.

Perhaps a few of the older generation, The Elders, would have perceived the differences. Fewer visitors to the area. A drop in the number of souvenir-hunting tourists with bulging purse-strings. A noticeable decrease in the number of residents at The Foyers Hotel.

And then, a gradual souring of the atmosphere. People finding excuses not to go to church. Doors once permanently open to friends and neighbours, now bolted firmly shut. Mistrust and suspicion beginning to tear long-standing friendships asunder. An increase in violent family feuds. Sudden and unexplained deaths amongst prominent local people.

And stories of the man who owned the house on the hill overlooking their church. Strange tales involving weird rituals and disappearing children, multi-coloured lights flashing in the Highland skies....

And of things seen on the road as day closed down.

Terrible things.

A coffin lying in the road, something grey and shapeless sitting hunched atop it.

A crawling eye that pulsates like a grotesque paper bag.

A nameless batrachian horror reportedly seen in the woods by a group of children bunking off Sunday School.

The church soon fell into state of disrepair, and the burial ground became disused.

The place became shunned.

The place became cursed.

The place became a Shadowland.

I shivered and decided there and then that my curiosity had been well and truly sated. It really was time to get moving. A shopping expedition had suddenly never seemed so enticing.

We clambered back down the hill, careful not to slip on the still-wet grass and vaulted over the barbed-wire fence. Our car was parked a little farther up the road and we tiredly began making our way towards it.

We hadn't walked more than a couple of yards when we noticed another car coming towards us. It gave us all a start because it had been the first vehicle we'd seen since arriving at Boleskine. We moved to the side of the road, almost having to lean on the wall of the burial ground in order to let the car pass, and as it did so, I felt a vague sense of unease. The driver was an ordinary-looking man staring straight ahead, as though concentrating fiercely on the road ahead of him. There was just the one female passenger, sat in front, and she appeared to be a nun. Certainly, she was wearing a wimple and I caught sight of her face as she turned towards us and smiled. The window on her side was half-open, and her outfit was blowing in the chilly breeze that had suddenly sprung up. I almost smiled back, but then the smile became a sickly, lopsided grin that I didn't care for one little bit...

I looked away quickly, glancing at the others to see if they'd seen, and judging by their expressions, it was clear that they had. There was something not quite *right* about the couple (just as there had been something indefinably odd about the middle-aged woman who had told us to move our car, earlier that day), but I was damned if I was going to stand there dwelling on just what it was that made them enigmatic in this, of all places.

The car slowly passed and we jogged the last few feet to the Rover, and not one of us said a word.

Simon gunned the engine.

We began to drive away in silence.

I looked back at the burial ground one final time. I couldn't resist. Despite the sick knot of fear that twisted away in the pit of my stomach.

And immediately wished I hadn't.

I saw, or thought I saw, a group of people standing in the middle of the graveyard.

Three people, to be precise.

A woman, whose features were obscured by the hood of her anorak.

An ordinary man who just stared sightlessly ahead.

And a nun, her habit billowing about her like a large black sail.

And all three of them were grinning.

I looked again, and saw only three, vaguely human-shaped gravestones.....

****

A few months after I wrote this piece, I was startled to come across an intriguing piece in Stuart Gordon's excellent *Book Of Curses* (Headline 1994).

Amidst the references to the Reverend Donald Omand, and his controversial contention that the Loch Ness Monster is not a real (in the accepted sense of the word), physical animal but a:

> '...malignant phantom from a prehistoric past, Evil and hateful, leaving witnesses paralysed with fear, or speaking of an abomination,'

...is the following tale.

The good Reverend had attempted to carry out an exorcism of the Loch, and together with his companion, the well-known paranormal researcher Ted Holiday, hired a boat in order to perform the ritual.

Three days later, at a place called Strone, the Loch-side house where they had been staying, there occurred what was described as an 'inexplicable manifestation.' At the time, Omand was warning Holiday not to approach an alleged UFO landing site near the village of Foyers, not far from Boleskine House. (Incidentally, Gordon alleges at this point that some time back in 1969, Boleskine burial ground had been visited by American tourists who had found, hidden under a grave slab, a tapestry embroidered with humped, worm-like creatures wrapped around a conch shell that made a braying sound when blown).

As Omand's hostess, a Mrs Cary, was also warning Holiday against heading for the UFO site, there was a sudden,

> '...tremendous rushing sound like a tornado outside the window,'

The garden was suddenly filled with 'indefinable frantic movement.' There were thuds, as if a bunch of heavy objects were striking the wall, and seen through the window was what looked like

> '...a pyramid-shaped column of blackish smoke revolving in a frenzy.'

Terrified out of her wits, Mrs Cary screamed, but apparently her husband, who was present throughout the incident, failed to see or hear anything out of the ordinary.

Eventually, the disturbance, whatever its true nature, ceased, and Mrs Carey then described seeing a:

> '...white circle of light on Ted Holiday's forehead...I thought the house had been struck by lightning with this light shooting across the room.'

Holiday was moved to comment that the beam of light, of which he'd remained blissfully unaware, had struck the exact same spot on his forehead as Reverend Ormand had earlier crossed with Holy Water.

The very next morning, over the road atop a slope leading down to Loch Ness, Holiday reportedly spotted a strange man, dressed entirely in black. His back was to the Loch, and he was glaring malevolently at Ted. He seemed to be wearing black leather or plastic gloves, a helmet, a mask and goggles *(which sounds unnervingly like a latter-day description of the infamous Spring-Heeled Jack)*. Displaying a remarkable degree of courage, Ted slowly approached the man, and as he drew close to him, he was disturbed to see that the figure appeared to have no eyes behind the lenses and that he could not discern any sound that the man was breathing. Holiday pretended to be gazing out across the Loch, then began to turn towards the mysterious entity. As he did so, he heard an odd whistling sound and swung right round to find the figure had disappeared seemingly without trace.

Understandably, Ted kept this experience to himself for a period of several months. Not even the good Reverend was aware of what had reportedly transpired. Ormand, not long after the attempted exorcism of the Loch, seemed more preoccupied with the fact that he believed there would be no more manifestations around the house, but that the Monster would continue to be seen by multiple witnesses.

> 'However,'

...he stated,

> 'long-standing astral forms are very difficult to dissolve. The original exorcism would therefore require to be reinforced on many further occasions in the future'.

A year later, Holiday returned to Loch Ness, only to be struck down by a heart attack on the very spot where he had encountered the enigmatic 'Man-In-Black.'

Five years later, a second heart attack killed him, aged 58.

****

Only a few short weeks after reading this article, I was pleased, and not a little surprised to receive the following press release courtesy of Rita Gould, author and former correspondent to *Dead Of Night Magazine*.

In the middle of February 1997, plans were well under way to begin the restoration of Boleskine House.

The clipping came in the form of a 'chilling warning given by Michael Dent, former buddy of millionaire pop star Jimmy Page, and custodian of the house for twenty years.'

On the 50th anniversary of Aleister Crowley's death, Malcolm was publicly urging Dingwall architect Sandy Gracie, who was set to restore the north wing of the 18th Century mansion to get the job done as quickly as possible, or face the dire consequences.

Dent was, according to the report, a 6ft 3in streetwise Londoner when he arrived in the sleepy hamlet of Foyers. Locals were, by this time, shunning Boleskine after dark, and although at first Dent was sceptical of the tales he caught around the corner of whispered conversations, he gradually came to believe there may be something to the stories after all….

> 'I have witnessed what can happen,'

…he was quoted as saying.

> 'My former wife and I got our eyes and ears opened over the time we spent at Boleskine. Most of the oddities occurred during upheavals in the house. I am not talking about wallpapering, but structural alterations. Any time there was anything major in hand, it was almost as if the house didn't like it. If we didn't get on with the job and get it finished, something would let us know about it. It was as though it was a reminder to get on with the job quickly and get it over with. Once the work was finished, the house would settle down.'

A further disturbance occurred when Malcolm, who took to making hand-crafted furniture, was getting ready to return to Boleskine back in 2001, and again, 'something' made itself known.

> 'There had been an upheaval getting the house ready for viewing, and I started moving some of my possessions. I was outside at the time when, without warning, and in what I can only describe as a great booming voice, something shouted *'WHAT ARE YOU DOING?'*
>
> When I got back inside the house, I was as white as a sheet. That little experience certainly scared me!'

Another more visual experience occurred when Malcolm and a group of his friends were discussing the occult over a few wee drams.

> 'We were discussing the house, Crowley, and what had happened at Boleskine, and had all initially expressed contrary views.
>
> As the evening wore on, we eventually found ourselves in agreement and there was a moment's eerie silence. At that point something happened that, looking back, was a very emphatic exclamation mark! A small porcelain figure of the Devil rose off the mantelpiece to the ceiling, then smashed into smithereens in the fireplace.'

The most overtly horrific experience of all was actually something Malcolm heard but was too terrified to open the door to….

> 'I was awakened in the wee small hours, and just knew something was wrong.
>
> I was quite literally terrified.
>
> Something was snorting, snuffling and banging. It sounded like some sort of huge beast.
>
> I had this clear picture in my mind of what the creature looked like, but there was no way I was gonna open that door to take a look. I had a knife on the bedside table and I opened the blade and just sat there. The blade was so small it wouldn't have done any good, but I was so frightened that I had to have something to hang on to.

The noise went on for some time, but even when it stopped, I still could not move. I sat on the bed for hours, and even when the daylight finally came it took lots of courage to open that door. Whatever was there, I have no doubt, was pure Evil.'

Malcolm added that he was glad that the old house had been taken on and was now being treated as a home.

'I had quite a few drawings of what Boleskine House looked like back in the 1920s.

If Sandy, the architect, wants any help, I will be only too happy to give it.'

But it seems Sandy, who had been working on the house for 20-odd years on and off, claims that he has never been worried about the house's reputation.

'The North Wing was destroyed by fire and we are rebuilding what was there so that the house will be as it was,' he told reporters at the time.

We are building up one room and doing re-roofing work. The latest work will go ahead as we get listed building planning consent. I have been working on an off since Jimmy Page had it 20 years ago. I can't say I have personally seen or heard anything strange over the years I have been involved with the house. '

I can't help wondering if Sandy would be quite so casually dismissive of the stories about the house if he ever had the misfortune to hear something on the other side of a blessedly closed door…A snorting, snuffling, banging something…Sounding for all the world like a huge beast trying to gain entry?

AMIDST THE DEPTHS OF THE WILD WOOD

*'Suddenly I stop,
But I know it's too late.
Lost in a forest
All alone. '*

The Cure -'A Forest'

I'm sure with hindsight, it would be all too-easy to drum up a smidgeon of cheap, (to use the Americanism) "dime-store" psychology, here. To state in a pseudo-Jungian style, that the source of our Society's fear of the Wild Wood, had it roots firmly entrenched in an inherited race memory handed down by our primitive ancestors. After all, in the distant past, the forest was home to all kinds of dangerous creatures, both real and imagined.

Either that, or it has its origins - like so many adult fears - based in the formative years of childhood; the still-powerful memory of countless fairy tales and the fireside ghost stories we recounted concerning the all-too real dark woods that marched along the borders of our home-town.

Or maybe it's a combination of the two.

It's a fact though, that the first true 'horror stories' I ever encountered had such a profound effect upon me that they went a long way towards providing the inspiration for my life-long interest in the supernatural.

I must have been about five years old, when I first heard the fables narrated during Reading Class by Miss Chandler, the attractive young woman I referred to earlier, with a then-fashionable Mia Farrow hair cut and a penchant for 'Mary Quant' mini-skirts and leather boots. I can still remember her perched on the edge of her desk, regaling the pupils with stories that would whisk us all away on a flight of pure imagination. I swear the circle of normally

fidgeting, inattentive kids sat in near total silence almost from the moment that Miss Chandler opened up the doorstep-thick collection of stories and began to read.

It seems to me now, that we were all of us quite simply enraptured; transported en masse from the familiar confines of the classroom to some mysterious, mythical realm that we believed in implicitly. And, for a little while at least, we were in thrall to the eternal fascination of the struggle between the twin forces of Good and Evil.

I sometimes think as we get older that we tend to quickly forget that the vast majority of these stories were populated with exactly the sort of fiendish cast you'd expect to find in an adult horror novel: Evil Dwarves, Human-Flesh-Eating Giants, Fire-Breathing Demons, Malevolent Faeries, Murderous Trolls, the list is as endless as the repertoire of tales that filled the pages of our teacher's magical book.

And the story that undoubtedly had the most profound effect upon me concerned a powerful combination of parental child abuse, a Cannibalistic Witch, and, overriding all, The Enchanted Forest; its densely-packed, black-green boughs identical to the Darkwoods of legend and folklore: from the Pine Barrens of New Jersey, to the Mirkwood of Middle Earth, from the tree-topped mound of Chanctonbury Ring in the South Downs of West Sussex, to the Black Hills of Burkitsville, Maryland.

The story of Hansel and Gretel, who lived at the forest's edge, together with their poor but essentially honest (if toadyingly spineless) father, and their cold-hearted, inherently wicked stepmother, filled me with a kind of spell-bound melancholy throughout my early school-days, and it's not too difficult to figure out why. For a start, there was the never far away fear exclusive to very young children born into a family constantly struggling to make ends meet, that one or both of their parents may not truly love them, or that even if they did, they might simply not be able to afford to look after them. The prospects, however unrealistic, of me being sent to some austere-looking boarding school a hundred miles from home, with claustrophobic high walls and prison-like regimentation, where the pupils are clannish and snobby and would rib you mercilessly for having a Scouse accent and a pudding basin haircut and a uniform three sizes too small and where the house-masters take turns to shove your head down the toilet bowl and made you drink the contents (and they were the ones that actually liked you) was something that filled me with stomach-churning dread, and was the cause of many sleepless nights.

Perhaps too, my obsession with the story had something to do with the (ultimately fruitless) ingenuity in the face of despair displayed by Hansel, the trail of white breadcrumbs he casts from his pockets as their father leads them into the very depths of the woods were he later plans to abandon them.

Perhaps it's the myriad eyes that peer curiously from the edge of the darkness, beyond the camp-fire's flickering glow.

Or then again, maybe it's the growing feeling of uneasiness the children experience when faced with the overnight disappearance of the trail home, (an unexpected feast for the woodland birds), and the gradual realisation that they are hopelessly lost in the middle of the forest.

Oh, and let's not forget Hansel and Gretel's stumbling upon the Gingerbread/Candy House, and the wizened Old Hag who beckons them in to help themselves to as much 'sweet stuff' as they can greedily cram into their hungry mouths.

The Witch, for such she is of course, (as well being one of the most oft-reported Night Terror Entities), who feeds on children and locks Hansel up in an iron cage with a view to fattening him up for a date with the oven, is suitably terrifying in appearance; with her wrinkled face, hooked-nose, snaggle-toothed grin and cackling laugh. Her only weakness is her short-sightedness, which proves in the end to be her undoing.

I'm sure there is likely to be plenty of people reading this who will doubtless be wearily shaking their heads at my ceaseless waffling about a child's fairy tale – something that should have long ago been consigned to the dustbin of childhood memories along with games of Conkers, *Whizzer And Chips* comics, 'Anglo Bubble Gum' and Scooby Doo cartoons. But I sincerely doubt that I'm the only one haunted by the memory of a story where people get lost out in the boondocks, maybe only a day or so's walk from the nearest town, but a million miles removed from what passes for civilisation (Daniel Myrick and Eduardo Sanchez's Blair Witch Project, anyone?)

So yes, I don't mind admitting that my friends and I were more than a little reluctant to enter the nearby woods of Storeton and Eastham, especially after sundown.

On the occasions that we did, we made sure we stuck close to the forest path, despite the fact that in reality it was little more than a dirt track, a winding sliver of mankind's creativity in the midst of the dark primeval...On either side of which all manner of things might lie in wait....

WHEN AUTUMN'S CRYSTAL EYE TURNS COLD

'When the air feels somehow brittle, like thin ice upon the ground,
When the cry of birds migrating is a lonely, haunting sound.
The world seems bathed in twilight through which lanes of memory pass,
And a veil of sad remembrance hangs like smoky, tinted glass.'

Lee Walker, March 2011

It must have been sometime in the early 1980s, that I first heard of the relatively little-known mystery of Clapham Wood.

I remember sitting in our Clubhouse one stormy September afternoon, with my head buried in my collection of an oft-reprinted periodical called *The Unexplained*, and there amongst the pages of issue 51, I came across an article co-authored by Toyne Newton and Hamish Howard, called 'Under The Greenwood Tree.'

The introduction had me hooked straight away. Described by the writer's as 'a doorway from the real world into the beyond,' Clapham Wood, situated not as you might reasonably expect smack in the centre of London, but rather nestling in the midst of England's South Downs, took on the semi-mythical status afforded to other areas associated with the paranormal; Loch Ness, Warminster, Pendle Hill, Heol Fenog, Chanctonbury Ring….

In the days that followed my reading the piece, and after telling my 'fellow members' all about it, we decided Clapham Wood was our number one, must-visit destination, and I spent many hours dreaming of embarking on an expedition to West Sussex, to investigate the place first-hand. The fact that I had just left school and was earning the princely sum of £20 per week on a YTS electrical engineering course, (half of which I had to pay to my parents for my keep), didn't serve to dampen my enthusiasm any.

I even went so far as to tell my then-girlfriend, Jane Neal, that my friends and I were planning to camp out in the woods the weekend before Hallowe'en, an alcohol-fuelled conversation at The Railway Inn, that went something like this….

The Gratifyingly Concerned, Miss Neal: God, it'll be freezing cold. Even with extra blankets. You said you've only got a summer-season sleeping bag. I went camping with some friends a couple of weeks ago, and it was bone-chillingly cold back then, in early-September, even with a couple of extra blankets and a duvet. I'm telling you, you'll wind up frozen solid, like mad Jack Torrance at the end of 'The Shining!'

The Foolishly Brave, Mr Walker: Oh, come on, Jane. We don't actually intend to camp out right in the middle of the woods. Only on the edge of them. We can always light a fire and...

The Gratifyingly Concerned, Miss Neal: Why don't you go to an organised site?

The Foolishly Brave, Mr Walker: Well, it's hardly gonna be warmer there, and besides there aren't any. I've checked.

The Gratifyingly Concerned, Miss Neal: It'd be a good deal safer, though. What if you're running through the woods in the middle of the night in the pitch black, and you end up tripping over a branch and whacking your head on a rock, or something?

The Foolishly Brave, Mr Walker: That's not gonna happen.

The Gratifyingly Concerned, Miss Neal: Well, it could. And what about wild animals?

The Foolishly Brave, Mr Walker: There aren't any wolves or bears in England any more, Jane. Not unless they've escaped from a zoo or a circus or something.

The Gratifyingly Concerned, Miss Neal: Well, that's a possibility, you must admit And anyway, don't forget, there were herds of red deer when we went camping that time in Devon.

The Foolishly Brave, Mr Walker: Er….

The Gratifyingly Concerned, Miss Neal: I know they're not as ferocious as bears or wolves, but they could easily like, trample on you or gore you with their horns.

The Foolishly Brave, Mr Walker: Maybe, if you were to inadvertently walk into their territory wearing a massive big pair of stag's antlers in the middle of rutting season!

The Gratifyingly Concerned, Miss Neal: Oh, whatever. Why the hell do you wanna go there, anyway?

The Foolishly Brave, Mr Walker: Well, there might be a coven of witches present, or it could be haunted by certain Demonic manifestations.

The Gratifyingly Concerned, Miss Neal: Oh, well that makes all the difference!

She promptly burst into tears, convinced we were heading straight into terrible, mortal danger, and of course I was to blame for feeding her fears, although the aforementioned writers, Toyne Newton and Hamish Howard, wherever they are these days, should at least be sharing some of the culpability.

According to their article, you see, incredibly weird things happened in Clapham Wood, which, to quote the authors,

> '…is an area of mystery and intrigue, where stunted trees twist and writhe as if in pain.'

They maintained that the district was rich in UFO sightings, Demonic manifestations, strange acoustic phenomena, and (here's the thing that frightened Jane the most), unexplained disappearances.

> "If any of you go there, none of you will ever come back!"

…she'd asserted in a voice that was tinged with such sincerity I didn't have the heart to shout her down.

I never went in the end.

None of us did.

And if we were to resurrect the idea of an expedition today, we'd likely be accused of ripping off the foolhardy exploits of Heather, Josh and Mikey and their one-way trip into the woods of Burkitsville, Maryland.

But I digress. To return to the article that had so enraptured me back then; our intrepid reporters, Newton and friend, inform us that

> '...on a hill above Clapham Village, as if protecting the parishioners from the dark woods beyond, stands the 13th century church of the Blessed Virgin Mary.'

The former rector of this quaint, Olde English chapel, the Reverend Neil Snelling, was one of those who were rumoured to have vanished in decidedly mysterious circumstances. Apparently, he'd last been seen shopping in the nearby town of Worthing, and had elected to walk back to his home in Steyning, a journey that would have taken him right through the heart of Clapham Wood. He was never seen again.

To add to the eeriness of the locale, there is a crater, believed to have been caused by a Second World War bomb, though others have since claimed that it was created by a meteorite that fell to Earth at some unspecified date. Whatever the truth, nothing is said to be able to grow within the confines of the barren hollow.

Even more disturbing are the reports that there are:

> '...mysterious little clearings containing ruins of old cottages'.

Who built them? And why were they abandoned?

These are just two of the questions that kept me awake on certain nights, when the wind whistled in the eaves and kicked at autumn's debris piling up in the gutter. Actually, writing this now, I'm struck by the uncanny certainty that Messrs Myrick and Sanchez, the co-directors of The Blair Witch Project, must at some time have also read this piece in The Unexplained. Either that, or else we've got ourselves a pretty strong case of life imitating 'art,' here. Not only do we have the perennially dark woods beset with rumours of strange phenomena dating back countless years, the small village/town living in the shadow of its baleful presence, and a spate of mysterious disappearances....

You can also include the abandoned house, hidden away in the middle of the woods owned by an old woman, living alone, who was reputed to be a witch.

She was, rather predictably, shunned by the local community and, though her being 'smitten by the palsy' was cited as the official reason for her becoming a pariah, it is considered to be far more likely, according to the authors, that:

> '...the old woman of the woods was the victim of one of the Witch hunts that were so prevalent at the time.'

Following a rather lengthy discourse concerning the many UFO sightings in the area, the investigators recount stories of how many animals, including dogs and horses have vanished without a trace whilst walking, often with their owners, in the woods.

There is a strangely haunting picture featured at this point. It is a photograph of a farmer standing smiling into the camera, his faithful Border collie at his side. He reminds me of my old Grandad, with his kind, careworn face and openly friendly demeanour. He is bathed in the noonlight of a clear, windless January day. The brown, sleeping fields of his farmland stretch away to the tree-lined horizon; the beginning of the woods, the bare branches clawing at the slate-grey sky....

The farmer's name is Mr John Cornford, and he reportedly lost one of his Border collies in mysterious circumstances in Clapham Wood, and I feel kind of sorry for him. But if I'm honest, there's a wistful kind of sadness reserved strictly for myself here, too. I miss my Grandad even though he died when I was very young. I can still recall how he used to push me in my pram around Sefton Park when I was a child, and the excitement-filled visits to each other's houses at Christmas and other special occasions.

It's hard to accept that all I have to remember him by is a faded colour snapshot that used to hang on our living room wall, and is now granted pride of place in my Dad's special photo album.

The picture is not all that dissimilar to the kind-faced farmer, and I often found myself wondering whether Mr Cornford has any grandchildren, and whether they help him out with the sowing of seeds in his fields at springtime, and help gather in the September harvest, or whether all these boys have to remember him by is a similar, frozen-in-time photograph, perhaps the very one that had inspired such feelings of melancholy in me the moment that I first saw it.

I'd always give pause for reflection at that point, before reluctantly turning the page, and moving on.

The Southern Paranormal Group, run by David Stringer, visited the woods in August 1977,

> '...with an open mind and a Geiger counter.'

Whilst exploring the area known locally as The Chestnuts, he glimpsed a dark, indeterminate shape, about 12 feet in height, which he later described, appropriately enough, as

> '...a black mass.'

He also encountered a large, white, flying disc that suddenly shot out from behind a group of nearby trees. At the same time, the dark form;

> '...the nameless dread of some Lovecraftian nightmare,'

…abruptly vanished.

When he dared at last to take a closer look at the area where he'd sighted the phenomena, Dave discovered a

> '...five-toed imprint, twice the width of a man's foot, but very narrow at the heel.'

He decided to make a rough sketch of the single footprint and later found, after indulging in a spot of research, that the imprint closely matched that of the Demon Amduscias, pictured in Colin de Plancy's classic work, Dictionnaire Infernal.

Finally, and perhaps most chilling of all, Dave and two of his student friends re-entered the woods a couple of years later, in 1979.

As they made their way along The Chestnuts route, they all felt an unnatural coldness seeping into their bones. This otherworldly icy breath ceased to trouble them the moment they left the area. Determined to track its source, they crossed the same vicinity a total of three times and on each occasion the temperature dropped dramatically.

Acting on impulse, one of the men - Paul Glover - aimed his camera at what he believed to be the epicentre of this phenomenon and clicked the shutter. None of the group actually saw anything at the time, but later, when the photographs were developed, a smoky image of what appears to be a goat's head, the traditional symbol of The Devil, took centre stage.

I used to gaze for what seemed like an eternity at this picture, feeling myself falling down the feathery slope of unreason as I did so.

And though I'd argue long and hard with myself as to the picture's authenticity, (the possibility that it was an out and out fake or a startlingly good example of coincidental simulacra – life imitating art, once again), I'd invariably find that these inner-disputes, in the end, carried all the weight of ash-flakes from a distant bonfire.

The second source of 'Wildwood-phobia' has its origins in a very nearly tragic event that occurred when I was just four months shy of my 11th birthday. Mid-way through our school's mid-autumn break, my Dad decided to get the kids from out from under my Mum's feet by taking myself, my brother, Grant, and my sister, Kearry, for a walk in Storeton Woods.

We set off on a still, overcast October morning, each of us weighed down with nothing more burdensome than a packed lunch and a couple of Ladybird Book guides to woodland plants and wildlife of Britain.

The journey from New Ferry to the sprawling green countryside of Storeton and the surrounding area required a good three-mile hike, but we all unanimously voted to make the trek on foot. Not for us the comforts afforded by a bus or train ride. We were intrepid explorers keen to enter a vast, untamed wilderness that, to a child's eyes, seemed to stretch away into infinity.

My father, a latter-day Professor Challenger, had led the way into the woods, taking great delight in showing us the Secret Places and Personal Landmarks that he recalled from when he was a teenager, as well as pointing out the various species of wildlife, so that we kids could make a note in our respective books.

I remember it was the type of day you hope will last forever, but which, all too soon draws to an end. And it seems no matter how much you manage to cram into those few sacred hours, still there remains so much that remains unseen, untouched and undone.

I'm sure that it was partly in an attempt to counter those feelings of imminent regret that, as the day wore on, Grant and I decided to climb one of the tallest trees in the whole of Storeton Woods – a giant sycamore, whose highest branches were almost lost to sight in the afternoon gloom.

> "God, imagine the view from up there,"

Dad had half-muttered to himself.

> "I bet you can see right across the Peninsula, all the way to the peaks of the Welsh mountains."

No sooner had the words fell from his lips than Grant had shot up the tree with all the natural agility of a gawky nine-year old, and the self-confident sure-footedness unique to spider monkeys and pre-teenagers who haven't yet been fully exposed to the fragility of life and limb.

I followed at a slower, more cautious rate after taking a sidelong glance at my Father's face, etched with the twin-born expressions of pride at my brother's display of fearlessness and a wistful sadness that he himself no longer possessed the physique to climb up there and see the view for himself.

Never having been blessed with much of a head for heights, I didn't dare look down until I reached a point where the sycamore's branches began to grow increasingly thin and, and I wasn't at all certain that they would support my body, skinny as it was in those days.

Leaning back against the reassuring solidity of the tree trunk, I lowered my gaze to peek between my battered, Billy-no-make trainers.

And almost immediately wished that I hadn't.

I'd assumed that I was at most, only half-way up the tree and had willed myself to fight the unsettling feelings that come with standing suspended on the delicate branches of a tree, high above the ground. But once I'd realised that I was in fact, only ten feet or so from the very top, I'd almost screamed aloud. The forest floor looked to be about a million miles below me and it was extremely hard to shake the notion that in my efforts to prove myself to my Father, I'd inadvertently climbed on to the very roof of the world. I'd felt too, a sudden stab of jealousy toward my Dad and my sister, safe on the leaf-strewn ground below me. Shrunk to the size of tiny Toy Town figures, they'd been scrabbling around looking for pine cones and conkers, and I found myself silently wishing with all my heart that I was down there with them.

Before I could even think about making the long journey back to terra firma however, a sudden shout from somewhere just above me served as a reminder that Grant had continued climbing even higher.

"Oh yeeeerrsss!"

He yelled breathlessly.

"You can see the mountains and everything from here! Come and have a look, Lee. You won't believe it, honest!"

The unrestrained excitement in his voice caused me to crane my neck to see just how far above me my daredevil of a brother actually was. And my heart stopped as I saw he was perched atop a branch that was so flimsy it barely looked capable of supporting someone half his size. As he stared out across a landscape that was invisible to me, I could see that the bough was bending crazily beneath him like a dowsing rod that's just detected an underground source of water.

I've heard it said that sometimes, in the wake of a major disaster, a 'gifted' person will come forward to claim they have had a premonition about the tragedy in the shape of a vision or a bad dream. I'm not sure whether or not I believe such things are truly possible, but what I do know for sure is that you didn't have to possess the 'gift' of second sight to predict what was going to happen in a matter of mere seconds to my brother, perched out on that treacherous branch.

It was plain to anyone born with eyes to see.

And hot on the heels of that disconcerting little fact, here came another, equally chilling. There was absolutely nothing anyone could do to prevent it.

That's not to say that I didn't at least try, of course.

In a voice choked with panic, I called out to Grant, warning him to climb down quickly. He either chose to ignore my advice, or else he didn't even hear me, his attention focused entirely on the wondrous view before him. I began shouting for my Dad, for what purpose, I can't precisely say, and it was then that I heard the sickening sound of wood snapping – a gut-wrenching noise that reverberated in the still forest air like a November firework.

After that, everything seemed to happen in slow motion.

I've always thought it strange the way your mind manages to record so much information in what amounts to no more than a few fleeting seconds. Storing it for future reference. Whether you choose to recall it or not.

I remember my brother fell past me without uttering a single cry. He simply dropped through the open space as silent as a show-room dummy, his face wearing the shocked/amused expression of someone who has just opened up a gaily-coloured package and been confronted by a springing, cackling Jack-in-the-box.

I remember too, his eyes were wide open, and his pupils were cartoonishly large.

I remember his arms flailing wildly, like a marionette at the mercy of a demented puppeteer.

I remember the way his blonde hair was swept back from his forehead, providing me with a vivid flash of how he would look in twenty or so years time, as an adult.

And most of all, I remember the brief disturbance of air, the tiniest breeze like the soft whisper of baby's breath, as Grant's body plummeted to the waiting earth below.

When he hit the floor, I felt sure that he must be dead.

My Dad's anguished cries as he kneeled over his son's lifeless form erased any lingering doubts. I couldn't move a muscle. I only looked on, like a spectator in the back row of the theatre, unable to tear my eyes from the heart-breaking calamity taking place on centre stage.

It was only when my Father screamed up at me to go and get help that I was able to snap out of it and get myself moving once more.

Although even as I scrambled back down the tree, I remained positive that Grant was entirely beyond saving, I was glad to have something with which to keep my mind occupied. I knew it was only a matter of time before the hot floods of tears came, and once they got started they would likely never stop. And so I raced headlong through the woods whilst my Dad carried Grant in his arms and Kearry ran bewildered in his wake. After an eternity, I finally reached the edge of the seemingly endless banks of trees, stumbled onto the main road and managed to flag down the first motorist that I saw.

Two nightmarish hours later, when I'd finally succumbed to the held-back outpourings of grief, an honest-to-God miracle occurred. Grant was sitting up in a hospital bed, grinning like he'd just been informed he'd won an all-expenses paid trip to 'Disney World.'

The doctors, who looked to be every bit as perplexed by his sudden recovery as ourselves stated that they believed Grant had been saved from serious injury or worse by the thick carpet of fallen leaves, pine cones and deadwood, spread around the base of the tree. He was kept in for overnight observation, but aside from a lump the size of a duck-egg on the right-hand side of his head, he was perfectly okay.

I couldn't believe it.

None of us could.

It seemed too good to be true, and I was almost afraid to give voice to my heartfelt relief lest it tempt fate and prove false. My brother was back home the following day, and before long the incident was consigned to the Big Book Of Walker Family Folklore, a tale to be recounted around the Christmas tree or upon the occasion of our Grant's birthday.

And not long after that, it was all but forgotten.

But not in my dreams….

In my dreams, the memory remains as startlingly vivid as ever. And worse, like a wound that's been left untreated, un-cleansed, it began to fester and turn bad…..

The dream when it came...

I'm climbing that damned tree in Storeton Woods, again. Grant is somewhere just above me. It's near dark and a howling wind dances among the few remaining leaves of the sycamore. It takes me all my strength just to cling on to the branches, and even as I struggle to do so, strips of brittle bark come away in my hand like the dried out skin of something long dead.

Someone calls my name.

I look down.

There's nobody there.

It's just me, Grant and The Dark Wood

And the whispering voices of people who are not really there.

So, I continue to climb. My brother tells me I simply won't believe the view from the top; A fairytale vista. The Welsh Mountains marching to the misted horizon. Rivers and streams, sunbright and sparkling. Farmer's fields ripe for the harvest.

'I hurry to join him on a branch that is impossibly thin and seems to be made of rubber. He smiles as I clamber up. Then he holds out his hands and points toward the valley below.

And finally, I see.

I see the Great And Wondrous View, revealed in all its glory.

The peaks of the mountains belching forth flame and thick, poisonous-looking clouds of smoke high into the air and turning the sky black and causing birds to fall dead in mid-flight.

The rivers and streams, blood-red waters, teeming with bloated mottled fish, floating belly-up.

The farmer's fields filled with rotted Jack o' Lanterns and thorny bushes, drooping under the weight of their fruit that throbs and pulsates like something awful inside is trying to get out. And in the centre of every pasture, a single scarecrow grins obscenely at the heaps of dead crows gathered at its feet.

Grant suddenly shrieks wildly and then leaps from the tree, and I try to grab him but I miss and he lands on the deadfall below with an audible thump.

I peer down into the semi-twilight, and at first I can't see anything. And then I spot his body lying with its limbs hideously askew, and I know that this time, my brother must be dead, there is no way anyone that irreparably broken could still be alive.

And then his eyes flicker open, pupil-less and as cold as marble, but glowing with a sickly luminescence. He smiles, revealing a set of jagged black teeth, and reaches out his twisted arms towards me, and although I'm 40-odd feet above him, I can somehow feel the heat of his foetid breath on my face as though he were stood right next to me.

I know then that it's not really my brother lying amidst the dirty-brown leaves and pine needles.

It's the Bogeyman. The Night Terror. The Thing That Gibbers And Capers In The Shadow-Filled Corners Of The Bedroom...

And having seen this dreadful realisation dawn on my face, It begins to giggle, a sound like foul water burbling over dangerous rocks.

'Don't you just love the view, Lee?' it croaks between the mirthless laughter. 'It makes you never want to leave this place. It really is a view to DIE for!'

And then suddenly I'm falling....

Falling towards that moon-white, up-turned face....

Falling....

Into the outstretched arms of the malevolent dead....

Falling.....

Falling.....

'MURDER-BALL' & THE RESIDENT SCHOOL BULLY

And here we have, for your delectation, a truly delightful Merseyside sporting pastime, that may or may not be unique to the county…

The rules were pretty simple. You'd be playing an ordinary game of football at break time when some lumbering dunderhead, with the obligatory ACAB (*'All Coppers Are Bastards'*) self-tattooed with the blue ink of a fountain pen on his knuckles, which he invariably dragged along the ground, grabbed the ball and ignoring the cries of those who simply wanted to continue playing their 30 odd-a-side school-yard match, would growl;

"Yer not playing football, yer little prick. Yer playing *Murder Ball!*"

Murder Ball was, as the name suggests, not a 'sport' for the remotely faint of heart or the type of weedy individual who went whingeing to the school playground monitor just because he had two of his front teeth knocked out and the words *'Wembley Trophy'* involuntarily etched on his forehead

The 'rules' were pretty simple, which was just as well seeing as how the main organisers just happened to be fully paid-up members of the New Ferry Union of School Bullies, whose combined IQ would have struggled to reach double figures.

'The game' basically involved everyone who *wasn't* a member of the NFUOSB, being chased around the playground by this gang of lunatics, who took turns kicking the pilfered ball against the fleeing, genuinely terrified victims. If you were unfortunate enough to have it hit you anywhere on your person, you were hastily frog-marched across to the walls of the bike shed, and thereafter subjected to your punishment for committing the heinous crime of not managing to successfully avoid the ball.

If you were lucky, 'The Murder-Ball' would be a bright orange-coloured, regulation weight, plastic monstrosity, which would undeniably sting like hell when it made contact with any exposed areas of flesh, especially on a freezing cold winter morning, but was infinitely preferable to being subjected to the alternative: The *Official* Murder Ball; a vaguely spherical, dubbing-soaked pudding of a 'casey,' that was kept in one of the heads of the NFUOSB'S personal lockers. This veritable instrument of torture was reserved for those 'snivelling wimps' who had either refused to play by the rules, tried to smart-mouth their way out of their predicament, or just happened to be cursed with possessing one of those 'make-yer-mad' faces, the kind that even the most mild-mannered of pupils at our school found it difficult to resist slapping every once in a while. Woe betide you if you fell into any of these categories: You would find yourself having to endure the ball being whacked at your puny body from point-blank range, leaving you covered in dark purple bruises, a burning set of cauliflower ears and a bloodied nose so bent out of shape it looked like Muhammed Ali had been using it as a training session punch-bag. One of the chief exponents of this laugh-a-minute 'game,' (hell, he might have even *invented* it) was one charming individual by the name of Reggie Robertson, our school's resident bully-in-chief and beater-up of anyone smaller than him. Which, seeing as how he was six-foot something, was just about everyone in the school.

Including me, of course.

During my time at Bebington Secondary, I somehow managed to avoid becoming yet another battered victim of Murder Ball. But I didn't escape the attentions of R. Robertson Esq.

No-one could be that doubly lucky, I guess.

*****

I had only just turned twelve-years-old the first time I ran foul of the type of heartless, sadistic, violence-obsessed bully that I had previously thought only ever existed in mid-19th Century novels like *Tom Brown's Schooldays*. Three whole decades have since elapsed, and yet, sometimes, when I close my eyes and choose to dwell upon it, I can still recall the sights, sounds, and (at the risk of sounding like Marti de Berg from the classic 'rockumentary' *This Is Spinal Tap*), smells of the occasion, as though it had occurred only yesterday. And with good reason.

It was May 26th, 1977.

The morning after Liverpool F.C. had gloriously won the European Cup for the very first time in Rome's Olympic Stadium, having beaten the German league champions, Borussia Moenchengladbach, 3:1.

I hadn't slept a wink since the Liverpool captain, Emlyn Hughes, had raised the giant trophy aloft - the Italian night sky lit up with the reflected glare of the floodlights and a thousand camera flashes - and I had gotten to school a full thirty minutes before the bell for registration. I was kicking a brand new black and white panelled casey around the all but deserted playground. The sky was a clear, dreamy blue. The air, still and breathless. But despite the fact that the temperature had already climbed into the high sixties, I refused to discard the thick, woollen scarf my Dad had given me after 'The Reds' quarter-final victory over Saint Etienne.

There was nothing particularly remarkable about it. Nothing to distinguish it from the countless number of similarly designed scarves, (two thin white lines, stretching horizontally along a sea of vibrant red), you could pick up outside Anfield on match days, or in the football souvenir-dominated market stalls that line the centre of Church Street, in Liverpool City Centre. And yet, it was one of my most treasured possessions, its acquisition seeming to magically coincide with my beloved team's march towards European glory, and as such it had assumed an almost talismanic quality.

Displaying the kind of irrational logic exclusive to obsessive gamblers, card sharks and football fanatics. I found I could never stand on The Kop, or listen to the match commentary on the radio, without first donning that particularly lucky scarf. Failure to do so would, I was certain, result in Liverpool stumbling to defeat. And so, there I was, on that impossibly bright, sunny morning, as late spring gave way to early summer, the scarf draped around my neck, the ball at my feet, re-enacting Liverpool's opening strike – complete with a Scouse-accented impression of Barry Davies' *'That's nice…That's McDermott…And that's a GOAL!'* commentary. I'd actually begun to wheel away in delight, ready to milk the acclaim of my imaginary team-mates, and 25,000 travelling Kopites, when I'd suddenly felt an almighty shove from behind that sent me sprawling in an undignified heap on the concrete floor of the playground.

I cracked my head a good one and I tasted a combination of grit and the flattened remains of a *Bazooka Joe*[*] Bubble Gum.

---

[*] Bazooka Joe is a comic strip character, featured on small comics included inside individually-wrapped pieces of Bazooka bubblegum. He wears a black eyepatch, lending him a distinctive appearance. He is one of the more recognizable American advertising characters of the 20th century, due to worldwide distribution, and one of the few identifiable ones associated with a confectionary.

My intended (oh-so-witty) response,

> "Who the do hell do yer think you are? Berti Vogts?" **

...died on my lips the second I'd dusted myself down and turned to confront my assailant.

I came face to face with (actually, face to *kneecap*, would have been more accurate) with Reggie Robertson... 'Reggie The Godfather', to his friends... 'Reggie The Neanderthal' to the other 99% of the pupils at my school.

It will surely come as little surprise to learn that the latter nickname was by far the more appropriate. Not that you would have ever gotten anyone (teachers included), to have chosen to voice that opinion within Reggie's earshot, Not unless for some bizarre reason, they fancied undergoing some free face reconstruction without the need for anaesthetic, taking a crash-course in bodily contortionism, or embarking upon a solo exploration of the dark, mysterious (not to say, smelly) depths of the boys' toilet bowel head-first, that is.

Reggie was a fifth-former at the time of this decidedly unwelcome encounter, two years older than me.

How best to describe him?

Let's see. You've seen Robert De Niro playing Max Cady in the 1991 remake of *Cape Fear*? Well, this was the 15-year-old version of that lunatic character. The only difference, good old Reggie didn't have to act crazy. He was the real deal. He was simply born that way.

> "I see the fuck-wits are out in force this mornin'"

...he said as he looked me up and down, an expression of disgust, as though he'd stumbled upon something unspeakably nasty that had crawled out from beneath a rock, clouding his features. Reggie was an Evertonian, albeit one that couldn't pick out the location of Goodison Park on an aerial shot of Liverpool, with a telescope the size of Jodrell Bank. That fact didn't make him any less bitter, however. Not one tiny iota.

> "Why are yer wearin' that piece of red an' white turd?"

...he snarled
> "Won a game 'ave yer?"

The tone of his voice, in fact his whole demeanour, told me I was in big trouble, and if my head hadn't have been spinning like an out of control roulette wheel, I would have legged it, right there and then.

As it was, I could only stand there, rocking slowly from side to side like a ship caught in the swell of turbulent seas. And you can be sure that this gormless, dumbstruck response didn't do anything to improve Reggie's temper.

> "I asked yer a question, yer little gobshite!"

...he shouted, thrusting his head towards mine so that I could see the stomach-churning combination of yellow-headed acne and adolescent bum-fluff running wild across his chin.

** Hans-Hubert "Berti" Vogts; born 30 December 1946 in Büttgen) is a retired German footballer and current manager of the Azerbaijan national team.

Vogts joined the boys' football team of local sports club VfR Büttgen in 1954 at the age of seven, staying with them until his 1965 transfer to Borussia Mönchengladbach. A right-side defender, his tenacity earned him the nickname "Der Terrier". He was one of the key figures during Borussia's golden years in the 1970s, when it won the Bundesliga five times, the German Cup once, and the UEFA Cup twice. Vogts also played in the 1977 European Cup Final defeat by Liverpool F.C.

I opened my mouth, frantically searching for a reply, but nothing came out, and I saw a sudden flash of malice spark deep within those sullen as old-quarry-water eyes. I instinctively moved to back away, but before I was even aware it was happening, he'd snatched the scarf from around my neck and whisked it away into the inside of his blazer pocket.

And then he grinned evilly as he spoke in a half-whisper;

> "I'm gonna fuckin' burn this piece of shite as soon as I get home tonight! What d'yer think about that, knobhead?"

Still grinning to himself as though he had cracked the world's funniest practical joke, he sauntered off towards the school-yard entrance where a group of his fellow cronies had begun congregating. Upon reaching them, he pointed back in my direction and half-withdrew the scarf. Their shared laughter carried on the move-less air, and with a heavy heart, I scooped up the football that Reggie had somehow overlooked, and trudged toward the main building. I was anxious about meeting up with my circle of friends. I craved their company, but not their inevitable questions as to the whereabouts of my 'lucky scarf,' on today of *all* days.

I paused momentarily upon reaching the entrance, glancing back over my shoulder at the gradually filling playground. I was struck by the impression that something had indefinably changed....

The sun still shone brightly in that flawless blue sky, but to me it seemed suddenly that a dark cloud had drifted across its face, obscuring the warmth of its rays....

****

The first lesson that morning was *Double History*, where we were supposed to be learning all about the colossal *USAF* bombers named after fit-sounding girls that pulverised the cities we learned about in *Geography*, later that afternoon, (to paraphrase the poet, Robert Jarrett).

To be perfectly honest, though, I didn't hear a word the teacher, Mr Tunley, a tall, gawky-looking individual, afflicted with terminal bad breath - which he insisted on exhaling into your face at every opportunity - had to say.

I was far too busy dealing with the overwhelming flood of emotions, raging away inside the pit of my stomach, though one particular feeling overrode all: a deep-rooted sense of shame. Part of it stemmed from my failure to even *attempt* to stand up to Reggie. My Dad had long-since instilled in me the strict admonishment that I should never, under any circumstances, allow myself to be browbeaten by anyone. He was, and always will be, a staunch supporter of that timeless classic:

> *'All bullies are essentially gutless cowards. If you simply refuse to be intimidated by their threats, they'll either back down, or at the very least, think twice before picking on you again!'*

I'd had this eulogy etched in the very core of my being ever since my first year at Primary School, and up until that fateful moment, I like to think I tried my level best to abide by this grand and noble principle.

Unfortunately, I knew from a wealth of bitter experience that sometimes, even the most well-intentioned slabs of fatherly advice, usually imparted during a family game of *Monopoly,* when you're seated by the fireside on a rain-swept Sunday afternoon, and all the world seems to be at peace, makes perfect sense. It's right up there with similar pearls of oft-repeated wisdom like; *'An apple a day keeps the doctor away,'* and *'Always clean behind yer lug-holes or yer'll find cabbages will start growin' there!'*

But that doesn't serve to make them any less mythological when bathed in the cold, unforgiving glare of reality.

I'd seen quite a few people brave enough to stand-up to 'Mr Evolutionary Throwback.' And never, in a single instance, did they remain standing for very long. One punch from either one of those large, calloused hands with the obligatory 'Love' and 'Hate' tattooed across the knuckles, was usually enough to ensure they took a first class, one-way ticket to Palookaville.

Nevertheless, the fact that I hadn't put up even a token gesture of defiance, left me feeling somewhat humiliated. What was even worse was knowing that I might as well bid a less-than-fond adieu to an item that had been given to me by my father. Something that I'd come to regard as a good luck charm, and that I'd intended wearing with pride at Liverpool's triumphant homecoming, later that evening.

I believe I stated at the outset that my recollections of this day remain vividly imprinted on my mind, and so they do, but I'm not at all sure if I can pinpoint the precise moment that my thoughts began to travel a less darker route. All I can say with any certainty is that sometime during those interminable ninety minutes, when Mr Tunley's voice had faded to an almost coma-inducing monotone, the twin-born feelings of loss and regret slowly began to fade, to be replaced by a cold, calculating anger. Almost before I was aware I was doing it, I'd set about figuring out a way I could somehow get even.

After all, I told myself, none of those eleven heroes (*'their raiment all red'*), from last night would have simply stood by and allowed such a terrible injustice to go unpunished.

That might sound corny as hell now, but you have to remember we're talking here about the days when greed and an-all-consuming obsession for success at any price hadn't yet conspired to devour the game of football completely, (although there were those who were plainly set about tearing down that road at a hell of a pace and never mind the speed limit).

To an impressionable twelve-year-old, on the brink of becoming a teenager, professional football players, especially those at my chosen club, were truly comic book super-heroes made flesh. (I simply couldn't imagine any of the Liverpool F.C. playing staff swearing, or smoking, or even doing anything as physically mundane as taking a crap or sticking their fingers up their nose in search of a great, big hairy 'snot-gobbler,' and once obtained - after a thorough and careful scientific inspection - flick it at the ceiling.

And whilst I struggled vainly for some half-workable plan, I was struck by the vivid mental image of my being chaired around the school-yard by my fellow pupils, milking the acclaim for having bettered the detestable bully.

Not that I ever truly believed for a second that I could ever hope to win in a one-to-one fight with Reggie. That was a path that led only to the emergency operation theatre at Walton Hospital, where, through a pair of pain-glazed eyes, I'd get to watch as a group of doctors and nurses stared right back at me, their faces as solemn as pall-bearers at a funeral, shaking their heads and mumbling between themselves;

> 'Oh dear God, this looks very bad!' How are we ever going to fix this one? It looks to me as though half his skull's been caved in! And how the hell are we going to sew his nose back on?'

Nope.

That was not a prospect that filled me with any degree of enthusiasm.

I had to try and think of something slightly more crafty…and, as is often the way with such dilemmas, it was just as my mind was beginning to aimlessly wander, that I found myself recalling, for no apparent reason, a wildlife programme I'd seen on BBC2, a few nights earlier. It was then that an idea came to me fully formed, in a sudden, flash of inspiration.

The documentary had been about fish. Archer fish, to be precise. A remarkable creature that caught its prey in a particularly unusual way…

For the first time since Reggie had sent me flying in the midst of a childishly innocent reverie, I afforded myself the tiniest genuine smile….

Five minutes before First Break, I put my hand up to be excused.

>'I need to go to the toilet, Sir. I think I'm gonna be sick!'

Placing my hand on my mouth, and heaving my shoulders for added authenticity, I raced for the door before Mr Tunley had even granted permission.

The boys' toilets were situated on the ground floor, near to the huge double doors that opened onto the playground. I had to run down several flights of stairs to be sure I'd be there in time for the ringing of the bell announcing the fifteen minute morning break. I'd be lying if I said I wasn't more than a little scared. Actually, I felt a lot like a lemming charging headlong towards the cliffs of endless oblivion. But I was also filled with wild sort of exhilaration, too. And because it's far easier to be braver when you're pretending to be someone else, I was at once Jason of the Argonauts prepared to battle the many-headed Hydra for possession of the Golden Fleece; Professor Van Helsing, hot on the trail of Count Dracula; Davey Crockett, prepared to defend the walls of the white adobe church in The Alamo; or King Kong, swatting at the bi-planes from the top of the Empire State Building….

And whilst part of me knew that Reggie was very likely to kick four shades of shite out of me, still, in a perverse sort of way, I was looking forward to the encounter, and the chance to strike a blow for the good guys….

Certainly, the omens appeared to be favourable, because when I pushed open the swing-back door and stepped into the toilets, I was amazed to find them deserted. Ordinarily, there would be at least four or five boys skulking in the darkest corner, indulging in a sly smoke or poring over a well-thumbed copy of *'Playboy'* or *'Mayfair,'*

The air was filled with a pungent combination of pine disinfectant, stale cigarette smoke and human sweat, but thankful that I was alone, I made my way over to the row of cracked porcelain sinks, and splashed cold water onto my face. I was pretty thirsty after legging it down the three flights from Mr Tunley's class, but I didn't quite dare swallow a gulp, though I was sorely tempted. My reluctance was based upon something a friend of mine, Ian Crossley, had once told me whilst sitting in his bedroom reading the latest *'Incredible Hulk'* comic, one sleety Sunday afternoon.

Apparently, his dad worked for the North West Water Company as a maintenance man, and his job frequently entailed his descending into the sewers to clear out the blocked drains or to repair a burst water pipe.

> "I asked me Dad one day, what was the worst thing he'd ever seen during his time down there, and he suddenly went dead quiet, which wasn't a bit like him at all. I badgered him for ages, but all he did was mumble something about how, on one occasion he'd had to investigate a blockage in one of the huge conduits that supplied the water to our school. As he'd approached the edge of this massive big pipe, he'd been shocked to see four pairs of brightly glowing eyes peering out at him. He'd thought at first they belonged to a pack of rats, "cos let's face it, son, there are absolutely millions of 'em down there!" But when he raised his torch and shone it in their direction, he caught a quick glimpse of a shiny black body supported by countless legs scuttling away into the deeper darkness. He wasn't sure what the hell it was, and he never reported what he'd seen to his superiors, or to anyone else for that matter. Not even when he stumbled upon the half-eaten remains of a fully-grown Alsatian, the cause of the blockage, near to the entrance of that same pipe…."

I'm not saying I believed Ian's Dads' story any more than I believed that Johnny Rotten was going to sing lead vocals on the next *Black Lace* single, but all the same, I wasn't too keen to take a chance, just in case.

Besides, no sooner was I busy wiping my face dry on a wad of paper towels, than the shrill ringing of the Break-time Bell had me pushing the door ajar wide enough so that I could see the writhing mass of whooping adolescence, as they stampeded for the exits like a herd of rampaging buffalo.

Amazingly, my luck continued to hold. Still, nobody attempted to enter the toilet area and, even better, when 'Troglodyte Reggie' and his band of not-so-merry men finally appeared, the crowd had thinned considerably. At least I didn't have to worry about fighting my way through a throng thereby losing the one advantage I had over my nemesis: the element of surprise.

I waited until Reggie was just a few short feet from the exit, mentally calculating the number of steps he would have to take before stepping over the threshold.

What happened next took place in a matter of seconds, but on the occasions I've since lain awake, re-enacting the incident over and over in my head, it seems to have occurred in one of those elegiac, slow motion replays beloved of the 'experts' on *Match Of The Day*.

I dodge back into the toilets, and thrust my head back under the cold water tap once more. I gulp a mouthful of (maybe) super-arachnid-contaminated water, and hold it in my puffed-out facial cheeks until it feels like they're about to burst. I catch a brief glimpse of my reflection in the mirror, and I look like I'm afflicted with a terminal case of mumps or else I'm auditioning for the part of Don Corleone in a re-make of *The Godfather*.

I step back through the door, and see Reggie standing framed in the exit, facing away from me, and a voice pipes up in my mind. **'Don't wait any longer! Let the Rumpus Begin!'**

I walk up behind him, my pace quickened partly by an eagerness to get this over with, and partly because I simply can't keep the water in my mouth much longer, and suddenly, I'm so close I can reach out and touch him…I can see the flakes of dandruff on the collar of his blazer. The greasy shine of the Brylcreem he uses to spike up his crew-cut. The jagged holes where he'd pierced his own ears with a safety pin.

And the Liverpool F.C. scarf stuffed carelessly into his right-hand pocket.

I can hardly dare believe my good fortune and I know that I'll never get a another chance like this…I tap him on the shoulder and he whirls round angrily to see who's disturbed him. Recognition dawns slowly and his lips curl with the beginnings of a cruel smile. He starts to speak, but:

"What the fuck do **you** want, yer little pri….?"

…is as far as he gets. I choose that precise moment to splat the palms of my hands across my full-to-bursting cheeks and squirt the water from my mouth, which shoots out in a veritable geyser smack into the middle of Reggie's astonished face.

The sheer power of its release fills me with a grim satisfaction, and I remember once more the archer fish, and how the TV programme had revealed its method of capturing the flying insects upon which it feeds: by spitting water at its prey.

Reggie's face turns livid with fury, his eyes bulge in a spit-and-water-flecked rage…But before he can react, quick as a flash, I whisk the scarf from his pocket, and filled with the clarity of absolute triumph, I turn and race back down the corridor toward the staff room, and blessed sanctuary.

And as I run, I hear my nemesis roar louder than an angry hippopotamus afflicted with piles, and though it may herald an ultimately inescapable disaster, at that moment, it sounds like the sweetest music to my ears.

I managed to avoid Reggie's clutches for the remainder of that day.

And as it turned out, for a good while after.

I knew he would get me in the end, though.

If this was a made-up story, the kind with an ending that belongs in a rightful, sane world, where all of the good guys win all of the time, I could tell you that the incident marked the beginning of the end of this particularly nasty bully's reign of terror. That I'd bested him in front of his cowardly cronies. Humbled him to the point where he could no longer command the same degree of fear and respect, even amongst his most loyal and trusted henchmen.

But of course, in *real* life, things very rarely work out so well. More's the bleedin' pity.

As it was, I was sent home early from school that Thursday mid-morning. I played up on the fact that I felt ill (and it certainly was true that my stomach was a little off – as though it were being squeezed by an immensely powerful hand). Mr Arden, the deputy headmaster, took one look at my too-pale complexion and had no hesitation in telling me to go home and go straight to bed, and although I spent the fifteen minute journey casting furtive glances over my shoulder, I didn't once catch sight of Reggie.

My mum was concerned that I really was sickening for something, but I assured her it was probably just an early summer cold, and that I'd been sent home merely as a precaution. Besides, there was no way on God's earth that I was going to miss seeing The Mighty Red's parade the European Cup around the City Centre later that evening.

It turned out to be a truly magical night, and it almost (only almost, like) made up for the disappointment of not being able to make it to Rome for the game itself.

The highlight for me?

Being able to wave that scarf, my heart nearly bursting with pride as the team passed by in an open-top, double-decker bus.

A thought leapt into my mind at that moment…Something I'd read somewhere, or heard spoken in a film;

> 'It's always possible to tell the true worth of a thing by the jealousy of its enemies.'

I think it's fair to say, I knew the true meaning of those words, that glorious evening in late-May…

In a city lost in celebration.

*****

I had originally intended to end this somewhat lengthy diatribe at around about this point, but I realise there are probably those of you out there who will doubtless fail to sleep easy in their beds if they don't find out how and when I received my comeuppance, courtesy of one Reggie Robertson.

Never wishing to be accused of being the root cause for mass bouts of insomnia, I will gladly oblige.

It didn't happen the next day.

I fully expected it to, of course. I'd tried to mentally prepare myself and take whatever was coming on the chin, so to speak (although, to be honest, I was rather less geared up to take it on any other, infinitely more sensitive part of my anatomy!).

But when I arrived back at school, I was greeted by Stevie Gee, fellow founder member of *The New Ferry Horror Society,* who told me the quite unbelievably good news that Reggie had been jumped by a gang of lads whilst stumbling through Mayer Park, 'bladdered out of his mind' on a six pack of *Carlsberg Special Brew*. He had wound up in Walton Hospital with fairly serious head injuries, although I didn't learn the precise details of the incident until a fortnight or so later, by which time he was off the critical list and was expected to make a full recovery, though it would be a long and painful process.

It turned out that Reggie had been rocking like a big ship near to the entrance to the park, accidentally, or deliberately, (it was kind of hard to tell where Mr Neanderthal was concerned), knocking into people as they walked by, muttering obscenities and generally making a nuisance of himself.

Sometime after nightfall, Ronnie had gotten into an argument with a bunch of Liverpool fans who had just returned from 'The Homecoming', 'over the water.' Exactly what had taken place wasn't clear, but it seems that there was a fight that ended with someone clobbering Reggie over the head with a snooker cue. The way I heard it, the sound of those cracks to the skull sounded like a hundred eggshells being trodden on by a twenty-stone man wearing reinforced diving boots.

He was left unconscious, lying face down in a pool of his own blood and vomit.

He never came back to darken the doors of our school ever again.

So it was that I didn't set eyes on Reggie until a year or so later, and when I did, I was forced to do a cartoonish double-take. He was barely recognisable. He appeared to have put on a couple of stone - had bloated, not to put too fine a point on it - and he had a deathly pale complexion and dark purple bangs under his eyes that made him look like a junkie who'd gone far too long without a fix.

I'd be lying if I said I felt any great degree of sympathy for him, but I suppose no-one deserves to turn out the way he had. Local folklore has it that Reggie had so many metal plates inserted in his skull to repair the damage, he was scared to venture outdoors without wearing a baseball cap in case it rained on his number one cut and he suffered a terminal attack of rust.

It was a further six months before he actually had the opportunity to actually confront me, however.

I'd been walking home from the local chippy one evening, carrying a fish supper for myself and a couple of portions of egg foo yung for my mum and dad. I also had a pocketful of loose change that jingled so loudly I may as well have been wearing a banner screaming *'Please Mug Me!'*

The quickest and easiest way to get to my home address was to take the short cut through the darkened, graffiti-strewn subway beneath the A41 Motorway. This was a prospect that always filled me with a sense of foreboding. This was partly due to the hard-to-shake feeling that something may be lying in wait in the midst of that pervasive gloom. Maybe something that had managed to crawl out of the underground water pipes and haul itself, wet and quivering, to the surface. Something consumed with a hunger that could no longer be satisfied by feeding merely on people's pets, canine or otherwise. Something equipped with *'four pairs of glowing eyes and a shiny black body supported by countless legs.'*

These fears were entirely imaginary, of course. Nothing was ever waiting. The subway was always empty.

Except for on this occasion.

An ebon silhouette suddenly pushed itself from the slick, tiled walls, and slowly made its way towards me. Only it hadn't been any imaginary, chitinous horror. It had been your friend and mine, Reggie Robertson. A fatter, feverish-looking version, granted, but still the same old, malicious bully when you got right down to it. This time he wanted my money (thankfully, I wasn't wearing that famous scarf - it had long since been awarded pride of place on my bedroom wall), but I was just as determined not to accede to his request.

"If yer don't hand it over right now, I'm just gonna have to take it off yer,"

Reggie said, his speech badly slurred, and it really wasn't hard to see why: the three-quarters empty bottle of *'Scrumpy Jack'* gripped firmly in his right hand was a dead give-away.

"Then yer'll just have to take it!"

I replied, hoping I sounded a good deal braver than I felt.

He pushed his face into mine, just as he'd done a year-and-a-half earlier.

"Giz yer money!"

...he repeated.

"No chance."

"Last warnin.' Giz it here, now!"

"No way."

His eyes flashed momentarily with the promise of immediate pain and violence. And then suddenly, it was gone, snuffed out of existence like a faulty light bulb. What replaced it was the mournful resignation of a man who's carried too great a burden all their lives. In Reggie's case, it was the weight of expectancy that comes with the reputation as being a 'hard-man.'

"I love a lad who stands up for himself!"

...he declared, and he leaned forward and actually planted a whiskery kiss on my cheek before shambling away, leaving me slack-jawed with amazement and hardly able to believe my luck. Especially seeing as how, at the time of writing, Reggie Robertson is serving a ten year stretch at *HMP Walton* for armed robbery after repeatedly whacking a security guard over the head with a baseball bat leaving said guard, who was married with three kids, permanently paralysed down one side and with a severe speech defect.

And there are those nights when I lie awake, to give thanks to whatever God it is that looks out for brave/suicidal teenagers (delete where your views deem to be applicable), that I caught Reggie in a relatively sanguine mood, or I might not be here now, to regale you with this 'era-defining epic.'

And what a sad loss to the world of literary genius that would have been...

THE TV TRAILER FOR *THE EXORCIST*

I was only nine years old when this infamous movie first hit the cinema screens around Merseyside, during the power-cut-ridden Winter of Discontent of 1973, but I can remember the near-hysterical furore that greeted its UK release like it was only yesterday.

At the time of the film's release, I was already a massive fan of the horror genre, but as *The Exorcist* had been awarded with an X-certificate[**], I had to make do with eagerly devouring the various newspaper clippings and reviews of the film (and the resultant hysteria surrounding it), as well as the regularly screened TV trailer, all of which of course, only served to whet my frustrated appetite still further.

It seems hard to believe that over a quarter of a century has passed since I sat before a fuzzy black and white TV screen, wide-eyed and not a little terrified, as a deep, stentorian voice announced that

---

[**] The original X-certificate, replacing the H certificate, was issued between 1951 and 1982 by the British Board of Film Censors in the United Kingdom. It was introduced as a result of the Wheare Report on film censorship. From 1951 to 1970, it meant "Suitable for those aged 16 and over", and from 1970 to 1982 it was redefined as meaning "Suitable for those aged 18 and over." The X certificate was replaced in 1982 by the 18 certificate.

'Somewhere…Between science and superstition…There is another world…

A world of darkness.'

On the screen, a woman's face was lit by the flickering glow of a candle as she peered pensively around an otherwise pitch black attic room. Suddenly, the flame flared dramatically causing the woman to utter a startled scream.

And then, the flame was extinguished, leaving only the silent, waiting darkness…

This part of the trailer lasted but a millisecond, but the effect was intensely frightening just the same. Not least because you were instinctively aware that this was a merest hint of the horrors yet to come. The pervasive hush is irreparably broken by the sounds of a young girl screaming for her mother over and over again with a tangible sense of desperation, competing with a series of frenetic banging noises issuing from the same bedroom. It sounds for all the world like the soundtrack to a bad night in Bedlam.

Or else the nether regions of one of *'Hell's Darkest Chambers,'* (to paraphrase the late, lamented lyrical genius that was *Joy Division's* Ian Curtis)

The woman in the attic, who it emerges is the screaming child's mother, charges headlong up a flight of stairs, and just before she wrenches open the bedroom door to confront, God only knows what, there is the briefest, tantalising glimpse of the wooden legs of a large double bed shaking violently as if lifted by countless pairs of invisible hands.

The girl's screams take on a low, guttural quality that have more in common with the sounds made by a wild, feral animal than anything remotely human.

The mother stands framed in the doorway, bathed in a sickly, unnatural glow as the camera zooms in to show her face transformed into a mask of fear and revulsion.

We don't get to see the source of the horror, and perhaps we don't need to.

The screen goes blank, save for two words. They say simply this…

I received William Peter Blatty's excellent novel as a hugely welcome stocking filler for Christmas that year, and devoured it at such a rate I'd polished it off by Boxing Day evening.

I re-read it several times over the course of the holidays, and by the time we returned to school at the start of January, I could quote entire passages virtually word for word, which I did on frequent occasions, much to the eye-rolling dismay of my family and friends.

In the meantime, the tabloids persisted in running major articles about the film and the heady cocktail of myth, half-truth and dark rumour that continued to brew in the wake of its release. And these stories, once spun out, could never be reeled back in.

According to these somewhat less-than reliable tabloid journalists, *(and honestly, do you know of any 'red-top'** reporter who can be considered to be a genuine paragon of truth and integrity?)* almost from the start, the controversial subject matter had caused a fair degree of consternation among the cast and crew.

I remember Jason Miller, who plays Father Damien Karras, summing up the levels of superstitious dread that constantly surrounds the subject of the Devil and all his works, even in the midst of the so-called Age of Scientific Enlightenment.

'When I was filming *The Exorcist*, I would go to this little restaurant which was in the Jesuit quarters, and I'd sit there and study my lines. I was in there one day, and this very, very old priest handed me this medal of the Blessed Virgin Mary, and he said; "Do you know why I am giving you this?"

I said, "No, why?"

He replied, "I am going to tell you something about Intervention. Did you ever hear of the concept of Intervention?"

I said, "No."

He said, "It's a nasty concept...Comes out of the 15th Century. If you do anything on the Devil, anything at all on the Devil, to reveal Him as the Trickster that He is, He will

---

** For those not in the know, `red top` newspapers, such as *The Sun* and *The Daily Mirror* are immensely popular tabloids aimed at a resolutely-downmarket audience.

seek retribution against you. He will even try to stop what you're trying to do, ie; unmask Him."

And he added, "This medal will protect you. You be very careful. Take care of yourself."

And the old priest's ominous warnings appeared to have been well-founded if one was to lend even the slightest degree of credence to half of the stories that sprung up during the making of the film.

Terence Donnelly, the Assistant Director, told reporters at the time that:

"...of course, on any fifteen month schedule, as we had, you certainly expect that the laws of probability would presume that certain things would happen, but in my 32 years of making films, I've never had a set burn down.

We did on *The Exorcist*."

The cause of the devastating conflagration which occurred on a Sunday, of all days, and when, fortunately, there was nobody on the set, destroying the 'possessed girl's house' at the Ceco 54th Street Studios, is certainly something of a genuine mystery. The fire shut down production for about six weeks.

Bill Malley, the production designer, remains perplexed to this day:

"They couldn't find an electrical problem, they couldn't find an arsonist, they couldn't find a substantial reason why the fire had occurred".

And then, of course, there were the wide-reported,

'...unusually high number of deaths involved in the making of the movie'.

The actual total of fatalities seems to vary depending on who it is you believe, but Ellen Burstyn (who played Chris MacNeil, the possessed girl's mother), claimed in the press that

"There were nine deaths associated with the film, which seems an enormous number. Some very directly, like the actor Jack MacGowran (Burke Dennings), who also gets killed in the film. He completed filming, and then died for real."

Mr Blatty, understandably keen to help promote the success of the movie, in one way or another, was quick to voice his belief that Dark Forces had plagued the set.

"It is impossible to put all these things down to mere coincidence - if anyone wanted proof that evil forces do indeed exist, I think the strange and inexplicable occurrences that took place during filming would be enough to convince them."

Also included in Ellen's 'Roll Call Of The Deceased,' were Max Von Sydow's brother, who died in Sweden, and the assistant cameraman's wife's baby, who was born during the shoot, and who died before filming wrapped up. The unnamed man who refrigerated the set passed away suddenly, as did a young, black night-watchman and Linda Blair's grandfather.

There were a series of near fatalities, too....

Jason Miller's son, Jordan, was struck by a speeding motorbike during a trip to the local beach, causing him to spend a brief spell in intensive care, a gaffer's fingers (or was it toes?) were amputated on set, and Ellen Burstyn ricked her back (although the latter may have had something to do with the fact that William Friedkin, the director, insisted upon realism in his movies, and during one scene had requested that one of his assistants push the unfortunate actress to the floor with as much force as possible).

Perhaps the most bizarre claim however, was the report that Blatty's secretary Noni, had mysteriously been taken ill whilst her roommate had gone completely insane and had to be carted off to the nearest lunatic asylum in a straitjacket...

Not even the voice of sanity provided by the aforementioned Max Von Sydow, who points out - rather sensibly you might think - that if you only have a two or three week shooting schedule, the chances are there will be nothing untoward involved, but if you have a production that lasts for a year, or eighteen months, as was the case with this movie, then it's almost inevitable that a lot of incidents are going to happen, including accidents, technical hitches and even deaths.

On the other hand, Friedkin, of course, was only too happy to play up the rumours of a 'Satanic curse' surrounding the film. A few weeks after the film's initial release, he asserted that the finished movie contained:

> "...amazing double images and visions that showed up on the film that were never planned. There are double exposures in the little girl's face at the end of the one reel that are unbelievable!"

At one stage, during production, he even called upon the film's 'spiritual advisor,' Father Bermingham, to 'exorcise' the set. Not surprisingly, the priest declined.

> "I said no, Billy. I don't want to increase anxiety or anything like that."

Also, following the general release of *The Exorcist*, the world's media were fed stories of how Linda Blair had herself been driven crazy by the psychological impact of her starring role, despite her constantly appearing at countless interviews looking perfectly healthy.

Friedkin also attempted to suggest that Linda had consented to appear in every scene in the film, including that extremely disturbing crucifix masturbation shot. It has long since emerged however, that a stand-in by the name of Eileen Dietz acted as Linda's double during several of the more controversial scenes.

Whatever the doubtful merits of the director's motivations in seeking to publicise his masterpiece, the fact is when the film was released on Boxing Day 1973, it generated what the highly-respected movie critic Mark Kermode has since called 'a tidal wave of audience hysteria, the likes of which hadn't been seem since the opening of the 1931 Frankenstein, from which patrons ran screaming, causing cinema managers to lay on smelling salts and ambulance crews for the adversely affected.'

Not too many weeks passed before the film's reputation became such that stories began to circulate that just simply viewing *The Exorcist* could be bad for your health. Some of the tales that sprang up took on an almost modern urban folklore-ish sense of unreality, (incidentally, the finished print of the film, at that stage over 200 hours of unedited footage, had to be submitted to the highly appropriate address; 666, 5th Avenue - how's that for a case of uncomfortable synchronicity?) There were reports of people vomiting, fainting, suffering heart attacks and at least one reported miscarriage.

In Berkeley, USA, an unnamed man sustained superficial injuries after he literally threw himself at the cinema screen in an ultimately doomed attempt to *'get the Demon.'*

To be fair, I've since learned that it wasn't just the sensationalistic tabloids that were anxious to clamber aboard the *The Exorcist* bandwagon with all the subtlety of an inebriated hippo riding a unicycle.....upside down.

While researching an article on the movie, in tandem with its re-release in the autumn of 1998, I came across a clipping from the highly reputable-sounding *Toronto Medical Post*, which included a reference to four unnamed women who, the paper contended, had been *'confined to psychiatric care'* after seeing the film.

They even quoted a Chicago psychiatrist named Dr Louis Schlan, as saying;

> 'There is no way you can sit through that film without receiving some lasting negative or disturbing effects.'

Even more worrying, were the global accounts of a number of cases of criminal and suicidal behaviour attributed to the 'powerful evil of evil' permeating *The Exorcist*.

In the former West Germany, the death of 19-year-old Rainer Hertrampf, who shot himself with an automatic rifle at some unspecified point after viewing the film, led to the predictable calls for it to be banned.

Meanwhile, back here in England, an inquest concerning the death of 16-year-old John Power, who had somehow managed to sneak his way past the assembled nuns, religious groups, ushers (ask yer dads, kids), and eagle-eyed ticket collectors, to see the film, found that the fatal epileptic fit he subsequently suffered was entirely unconnected with the movie.

Nevertheless, his entirely coincidental death didn't do anything to allay the fears of an increasingly credulous public, and just to like, you know, re-dress the balance somewhat, in October 1974, *The Exorcist* was cited as being responsible for the murder of nine-year-old Sandra Simpson by teenager Nicholas Bell, who told York Crown Court;

> 'It wasn't really me that did it. There was something inside. Ever since I saw that film, I felt something take possession of me. It has been inside me ever since.'

Perhaps this sounds a trifle dismissive, but this kind of confession reminds me of an over-enthusiastic caller from my home-town of New Ferry, frantically ringing an episode of *Most Haunted Live*, to tell a bemused Derek Acorah, that the light bulb in his bathroom had winked out the moment the so-called medium was taken over by a particularly bothersome spirit on Pendle Hill!

In company with the unmistakable clunking sound of barrels being scraped, there were yet other examples of alleged supernatural/subliminal phenomena connected with the movie doing the rounds, including a ghostly face appearing in a vaporous cloud of Max Von Sydow's condensed breath (caused by the well-below zero temperatures induced by the refrigeration of the Regan bedroom set), as he sits by the possessed girl's bed. This supposed 'face' was said by witnesses to have been 'consciously invisible' to the film's viewers. Likewise, another subliminal scene, when Jason Miller prays in a local church, a skull-shaped shadow was said to have appeared on the white wall behind him.

I have to say, Dear Reader, that despite diligently scrutinising the celluloid, frame by frame, much to my abject disappointment, neither of these images are discernible on the DVD edition of the movie that I have in my (ahem) possession.

Maybe I need to look with the un-jaundiced eyes of the true believer!

Another 'explanation' for the lack of contemporary evidence of the existence of these images may lie in the persistent rumours amongst conspiracy theorists, that *Warner Brothers* may have withdrawn all copies of the video print and re-cut the film, removing the subliminal clips in case they happened to run into legal difficulties.

That the film continues to retain a fearsome reputation to this day (despite the purported 'numbing of the senses' in the wake of a plethora of so-called 'video nasties'), is perhaps best illustrated by two fairly recent incidents, involving yours truly....

I went along to see the 1998 re-release of *The Exorcist* at the *Odeon* in Bromborough, together with one of my good friends, Matty Weedall. I wanted to see the film on a big screen, with a large audience, and much to my delight the Screen One was packed to the rafters. This was likely due to a couple of factors, not the least of them being that it had its premiere on October 30th, day before Hallowe'en. For the first half of the film, the hour or so of slow-burn build-up where, in truth, not a great deal happens (certainly not as far as the 'gore-hound' generation are concerned, anyway), no-one seemed to be taking a great deal of interest, as evidenced by the hugely irritating hum of murmured conversation and cupped-hand snickering amongst a large section of the audience.

And then, during the now infamous crucifix-masturbation scene, two teenage girls suddenly leapt up and ran screaming and in tears from the cinema yelling:

"You're all sick watching this evil film! You should be ashamed of yourselves!"

I thought at first it was some sort of William Castle-type publicity stunt, (the b-movie film producer of the 1950s and 60s, who was notorious for employing novelty gimmicks in the theatres where his movies were being shown. During the inaugural run of *The Tingler (1959),* for example, he had the arms of the seats in the auditorium wired up with buzzers to administer a mild electrical shock at the precise moment the creature appeared on screen, thereby feeding the entity, which thrived on human screams.

The cynical part of me suspected at first that they been planted by the film's promoters, in an ultimately doomed attempt to engender some modern-day hysteria. But the expressions of outright disgust on the girls' faces certainly appeared to be genuine, and a stunned silence was followed by a ripple of nervous laughter.

Not long after this incident, a female work colleague refused point blank to even consider her borrowing a copy of the film, even though she'd watched the hour-long documentary screened on *BBC2* to celebrate the 25th Anniversary of the initial release of the movie, and found it to be nothing short of fascinating.

When I asked her why she didn't want to see the film in its entirety, she looked at me as though I'd put forward the suggestion that she strip stark naked and walk widdershins (anti-clockwise) around St Andrews Churchyard on the wrong side of midnight, in a Pazuzu mask, shouting; 'Your mother sucks cocks in hell,' over and over, until the first grey light of dawn….

"I'm sorry, Lee,"

…she'd said, looking nervously over her shoulder, lest someone should be eavesdropping on our conversation:

"It may sound soft, but I don't even want to touch the *box* the film's in. It gives me the friggin' creeps just havin' a quick spout at the cover."

And she shivered as though some dark and formless shadow had reached out and caressed the nape of her neck.

The incidents of supposed paranormal phenomena continued unabated, albeit on a much smaller scale, with the release, in 1990, of the original film's first 'proper' sequel (if we conveniently skip over the quite frankly abysmal *Exorcist II: The Heretic), Exorcist III: Legion.*

In an interview just prior to this film's premiere, the redoubtable William Peter Blatty, alluded to his experiments with Electronic Voice Phenomena or EVP.

This highly subjective process is said to involve leaving a tape recorder in a closed room, preferably sealed against all outside noise and stimuli, but with recording levels set at their highest. Alternatively, you can do pretty much the same thing, except you remain in the room to ask any passing discarnate entity whatever questions may happen to take your fancy.

Whichever method is used, the idea is to rewind the tape at the end of the session and listen to what, if anything, has been recorded….

Blatty experimented with his own recording equipment and told reporters at the time:

> 'At the risk of sounding like a complete Whacko, I'll tell you now that it is an authentic phenomenon, these taped voices. I don't know how they get on tape. But they're here alright. All those supposedly fictional voice messages in my novel *Legion*, were based on tapes I have of real 'Demonic' voices'.

Interestingly enough, the enduring legacy of the film continues to echo down the years like an agonised scream reverberating through a series of dark, deserted chambers. Proof of this is provided by a vicar from Liverpool, the Reverend David Gait, who was all too willing to state on record that he is a firm believer in the theory that evils committed in the past can haunt the present-day, like the most remorseless of restless spirits.

For the past 25 years, (at the time of writing), Reverend Gait has been appointed the role of advisor on the so-called Deliverance Ministry, and has sat on a panel set up by Bishop David Shepherd to assist those who are convinced they are being attacked by evil discarnate entities.

At least once a week, the good Reverend is called upon by the Church to visit these victims of the *'Dark Side of the Supernatural'* (as he catchily refers to them), taking with him various members of his parish for support. He then takes the hand of the afflicted person and recites *The Lord's Prayer* along with a special deliverance prayer.

And having gotten the religious formalities out of the way, the Reverend Gait promptly sits down and begins braying with laughter.

He told reporters from *The Liverpool Echo*, that he regards hilarity as being an unorthodox method of exorcism:

> 'Laughing is an important part of the process because the spirit hates to feel it is being laughed at. When we laugh, it helps to send the spirit away!'

Since he was invited to sit on the Pythonesque-sounding, *Bishops Panel for the Ministry of Healing*, Reverend Gait maintains he has done battle with all manner of other-worldly entities and has been involved in investigating alleged cases of Satanic Ritual Abuse. And he remains unshakeable in his conviction that Good always, eventually, triumphs over Evil.

The father-of-four was asked by professional doctors, surgeons and the clergy to join the panel way back in 1974, following a case in Wakefield, when a man who had apparently been exorcised by two well-intentioned clergy, murdered his wife not long after. Originally from the Norris Green district of Liverpool, Rev. Gait has always steadfastly refused to discuss his past experiences when he was a young student studying science at Oxford University, although he readily confesses to having dabbled in the occult.

> 'After I had on several occasions experimented with the powerful effects of the occult, I was in a perfect position to attempt to help those who had been assailed by evil forces,'

…he has been quoted as saying.

> 'Although I don't feel entirely comfortable with it, I messed around with the occult from the age of 18, until one day, towards the end of my time at Oxford, when I was sitting in my research lab in October, 1971. I was eating my butties and thinking about whether or not I should take a job I had been offered lecturing in Boston, America, when I heard a booming voice suddenly shout; *"I want you to be a vicar!"*

I had more than a few friends who were real practical jokers so I started looking under the desks and in all the cupboards, fully expecting to find one of them hiding there. But I couldn't find anyone and I started to get a bit worried, so I went to a Christian that I knew and told him what had happened. I thought he would dismiss me as being totally off me head, but instead, to my pleasant surprise, he advised me to talk directly to God.'

After discussing the matter further with the college chaplain, (with whom, ironically enough, David had argued only months before regarding his atheistic views regarding the existence of a single supreme entity), he went straight to Ridley Hall in Cambridge where he was ordained three years later. Following his indoctrination, David moved back to Liverpool in order to work as curate for St Paul's Parish Church in Litherland.

Three years later he moved to St. John's Church in Widness, where he was subsequently asked to join the panel and later still, became a fully-fledged vicar. His daily duties from then on involved everything from helping those who are worried about apparently unexplained happenings in their homes to exorcising others who claim to have been possessed by evil spirits.

'None of them make me feel scared,'

…the good Reverend has gone on record as stating, perhaps a little ill-advisedly.

'I have only come up against someone who was so overwhelmingly possessed that I had to visit them three times.

For many of the others, a visit from an evil spirit has a similar effect to a piano which has been placed on a carpet – long after the piano has been moved, the imprint is still there – leaving the person believing the spirit is still there when it has moved on.

If people do something they shouldn't do, like mess with an Ouija Board, in all likelihood, an evil spirit will be summonsed to set about plaguing them, but it doesn't, in my experience, ever stay around for long.

There are two ways of telling whether a person is truly possessed by evil forces. These two things are pointed out in the Bible…One is that the person is considerably stronger than usual. And the second is that the person has unaccountably obtained a special knowledge.

When I want a spirit to go, I use the Lord's Prayer together with one of the old Latin prayers translated into English and command it to go.

When I get rid of a spirit, I always take people with me, people from the panel, or from my parish. I have never had any problems because I listen seriously to anyone I see….So even if they have psychological problems, they realise I am taking them seriously. Sometimes, those who claim their house is possessed are often wrong. I find it is often the actual people who have the problems, not the house.

And there are those people who want to get a new council house and they will often tell the council the property is haunted or possessed.

I often find this happens just after programmes or films featuring the paranormal have been on television, so I have to be prepared for whatever stories they come up with, most of which will have come straight off the television.'[*]

*Source: *Liverpool Echo*, 16th January 2002

DEAD OF NIGHT

SOMETHING WICKED THIS WAY COMES'
Clowns, Fairgrounds & Amusement Arcades

Of course, I know I am by no means alone in my inherent, skin-crawling fear of clowns of *all* kinds, and not just the horror movie staple they seem to have become in recent years (Pennywise, the balloon-sharing resident of the sewers below Derry, Maine, those laugh-a-minute *Killer Klowns From Outer Space*, Bobo, *Out Of The Dark's*, mad serial murderer, and the tragic-comic Mr Jelly from *Psychoville,* to name but a few of the more notable examples).

I'll readily admit that these entirely fictional, celluloid nightmares are terrifying enough. At least for the hour and a half or so they get to spend dancing and capering with lunatic glee across our TV and cinema screens.

What I find far more frightening though, precisely because they are *real* and not merely the product of some talented author's feverish imagination, are the "ordinary, workaday" clowns, the ones that inhabit the garishly-coloured tents of a travelling circus, perform complex juggling feats in the middle of city-centre precincts to advertise the arrival of a carnival, or are invited to pay a personal home visit to entertain the guests at some 'lucky' kid's birthday party.

The profound sense of dread these so-called 'funny-men' inspire in a huge cross-section of people is so prevalent these days in fact that sociologists have conjured up a typically fancy-dan* name for it: Coulrophobia.

---

* Flashy, ostentatious

According to these serried ranks of know-it-all 'experts,' those who suffer from this deep-rooted pathological fear of the falsely-smiling, grease-painted denizens of Clown-dom exhibit highly visible symptoms, including shortness of breath, rapid breathing, an irregular heartbeat, bouts of nausea, the cold sweats and a grim, ominous feeling of foreboding. The origins of the phobia, they contend, are recalled childhood memories of encounters with frightening-looking women (and occasionally *men*) caked in heavy make-up, individuals of either sex who have the terrible misfortune to be cursed with an exceptionally bulbous, honk-worthy nose, a set of madly staring eyes or a ravenous grin that reveals a mouth full of hideously pointed, vulpine teeth.

Although little in the way of what could conceivably be termed genuine scientific research has ever been carried out on Coulrophobia, (those responsible for funding these types of studies are apparently far more interested in supplying financial backing for hugely more important, immensely beneficial to the future of mankind-type experiments such as those that involve sewing human ears onto the backs of laboratory mice, seeing how many pins you can pick up using only a humble pomegranate and whether a person can possibly sit through all 238 episodes of *Friends* back to back, without pausing to take a single nap).

Back in 2004, however, one particularly diligent researcher by the name of Joseph Durwin, compiled a review article for Trinity University, in which he postulated that the reasons behind the fear of clowns were twofold; firstly, and one might think, hardly surprisingly, the terrified reaction may well have its roots buried deep in a 'negative personal experience with a clown at a young age.'

His second theory is that:

> '...mass media has created a hype surrounding evil clowns to such an extent that even children who are not personally exposed to clowns are trained to dislike or fear them.'

To give him his due, Mr Durwin is humble enough to accept that neither of these theories are of themselves, entirely satisfactory.

Far more pertinent, he maintains, is the somewhat shady history of the clown and its long-ago former incarnations as The Jester, The Trickster and The Fool.

> 'In ancient times, these costumed entertainers would be given licence to represent the deviant side of human nature, from openly defying the sexual norms of the day, to being allowed to publicly mock the Gods. As time went on, however, The Jester morphed into The Trickster, a much more sinister figure with intentions that were less than honourable.
>
> The modern circus clown is an outgrowth of the tramp clowns of the Depression era. Tramp clowns were largely members of the "unsavoury" underclass who entertained the more privileged with a caricatured look at their daily existence. Although most tramp clowns were harmless, a seedy underbelly did exist among the clown circuit.'

Joseph cites what he believes are a couple of particularly significant examples of coulrophobia-inspiring accounts from the early 1930s and 70s.

The first of these involved one of the more infamous members of the clown fraternity; a man named Emmett Kelly, who was more widely known by his alter-ego of "Weary Willie". The paradoxical situation that exists amongst many comedians certainly applied where Kelly was concerned, however. He might have enjoyed a meteoric rise to fame to the point where his clownish persona became a virtual household name, but his personal life was a complete mess, and, not to put too fine a point on it, was at one stage in dire danger of embarking upon a personal journey up through the echoing chambers of his own arse!

His wife eventually filed for divorce, claiming that, frighteningly enough, the Weary Willie clown character had succeeded in taking over Emmett's personality. Even more bizarre, when their son Emmett Kelly Jr. decided to adopt the role when his father finally chose to retire, the mischievous youth elected to make the character even more strikingly memorable, but ultimately his wife also felt that before too long, the clown had taken over *her* husband's character. And just to add to the fun and frolics, by the 1970s, Paul Kelly, the son of Emmett Kelly Jr, decided to take on the mantle of the new Weary Willie, despite losing his leg in a terrible train accident. He began calling himself Emmett Kelly III, and performing as the now played out character of Weary Willie. His decision to adopt the persona coincided with him sliding into a life of drugs and sexual debauchery, a bit like a modern-day politician, but without the expense fiddling. In 1978, Kelly III was arrested for the murders of two of his many homosexual partners. He was quick enough to accept his part in the killings, but, disturbingly enough he named 'Willie' his alter-ego as an accomplice.

It was hardly a shock when Emmett was diagnosed as suffering from multiple personality disorder. 'Willie' had completely taken over every ounce of his being, his sense of individuality, just as the clown had taken over Kelly's father and grandfather.

A strange tale, indeed, and little wonder that Joseph Durwin was quick to remark that:

> 'Although this sort of case appears of be isolated, and most clowns do not show deviant behaviour, the case was reminiscent of the malevolent trickster archetype of earlier lore.'

He concluded by adding;

> 'Throughout history, clowns have represented the side of us that is not acceptable to society. That side is formed from our most primal urges and is not always neat or pretty. Perhaps the clown both attracts and repels because he or she holds up a mirror to our inner selves.'

And I guess that just about succinctly sums up the paradoxical reactions in people that clowns can elicit, often without any degree of purpose or intent on their part.

Whatever the 'true' origins of the phobia, from an entirely sociological perspective, I can pinpoint with categorical certainty the precise moment when *I* first encountered real live clowns, in the flesh, so to speak....

I recall I was ten-years-old when my Dad took me to sample the 'spectacular, jaw-dropping delights' of *Barnum & Bailey's Circus*, which used to roll into town every year when I was growing up in the mid-1970s. Each September, a large convoy of heavy-goods wagons would snake along New Chester Road, bringing the regular traffic to a standstill and causing adults and children alike to pause in whatever they were doing to gawp in amazement as the vehicles trundled slowly by. And little wonder. The sides of each of the trucks were emblazoned with eye-catching illustrations that served to whet the appetites of even the most cynical and blasé of local residents. Amongst the more memorable of these suitably lurid paintings were scenes of ferociously snarling lions and tigers, fangs bared, mighty claws extended, as the ring-master, dressed in a top hat and a bright red waistcoat, confidently cracked his whip, to keep the big cats at bay. There was a bikini-clad woman tied to a revolving wheel, her eyes bulging in terror as a blind-folded Indian Brave prepared to launch the next in a series of enormous, razor-sharp daggers in her general direction, and a trapeze artist performing an act of impossible agility without a safety net at a height where mere mortals would require a welter of incredibly sophisticated breathing apparatus just to keep from losing consciousness.

The colourful procession would eventually grind to a halt in the centre of New Ferry Park, and the travelling people would quickly set about pitching their tents and caravans and erecting the impressive-looking Big Top, side-show stalls and fairground rides with a speed that quite literally boggled the senses. In just under an hour, the muddy, overgrown playing fields would be magically transformed into an enchanted wonderland of dazzling colours and entrancing sounds, of whirling carousels and stomach-churning rides, the shouts and squeals from the Waltzers and the Bumper Cars, and the loud-mouthed barkers bellowing their promises of the multifarious delights hidden beyond the flapping folds of canvas....

'Roll up! Roll Up! See the dancing freaks!'

…they'd yell, their eyes shining with barely controlled excitement.

'Feast your eyes upon The Lizard Woman, captured by intrepid explorers from the depths of the Amazon Jungle! Gape in astonishment at Adam White & Eve Black, the original half-man, half-woman! Scream in abject terror at the terrible sight of The Thing in the Jar: the Pulsating Foetus-like horror that cries like a new-born baby, but bears no resemblance to anything born of womankind!'

*****

New Ferry Park was only a little way up the road from where we lived at the time and I remember walking there with my Dad on an achingly beautiful Saturday evening. It was the last weekend before the dreaded return to school at the end of the summer holidays, a vacation that began bathed in the long green light of late-July, stretched like a golden blanket across the sultry dog-days of August, and wound up nudging into early September, like an unwelcome and bothersome house-guest at the end of a wonderful party, when the nights started to draw in, the air grew chilly and the leaves began to turn. Needless to say, this completely unexpected trip to the New Ferry Festival had considerably softened the blow of the imminent return to 'normality'.

Anyway, in truth, I actually *smelled* the circus long before I actually first set eyes upon it.

The pungent aromas of sawdust and diesel, of fresh doughnuts and pink cotton candy floss, caged wild animals and crowds of excited people drifted on the bluish twilit air and it had been difficult to resist the urge to race off ahead of my father, such was my eagerness to set foot in this veritable *'Carnival of Delights.'*

We walked through the entrance to the park in the company of a fairly large crowd of people, at a little after six-thirty, and as the main event of the evening wasn't due to start till eight, we had plenty of time to sample the assorted sideshow attractions and various rides, and that was just fine with me. I felt like one of the lucky kids let loose for a while to gorge on the delicious wares in *Willy Wonka's Chocolate Factory,* itching to try anything and everything all at once.

All too soon, it seemed though, a smartly-suited barker equipped with a large bull-horn, appeared at the front of the Big Top and announced that it was time to form an orderly queue – the show was about to begin. We took our seats, in reality little more than a series of wooden benches that stretched around the circus ring, and the air inside the vast tent crackled with barely restrained excitement.

Of course, I was soon to learn that there was a marked and hugely disappointing difference between the actual *quality* of the entertainment on offer and that promised by the fairground wagon's eye-catching artwork. As soul-crushing let-downs went, it was right up there with my constantly being lured into the cinema by the glorious poster art of the latest science-fiction and horror movie releases displayed in the lobby of the *Odeon*, only to find that the films they advertised were invariably nothing more than a typical zero-budget, poverty row schlocker.

So, surprise, surprise, the loin-clothed trapeze artist had a weathered and grizzled face and a beer belly that wobbled like a plate of jelly every time he performed the slightest manoeuvre. The knife thrower was undeniably skilful with a blade but was about as much a Red Indian brave as I was a chest-beating native of Skull Island or an inhabitant of the distant planet of Altair-4, and the big cats had looked bored and moved as sluggishly as if heavily sedated (which of course, they very probably were).

Perversely, I actually found myself immensely enjoying the show, and would doubtless have walked home later that evening with a big beaming smile on my face and my head filled with a kaleidoscope of delightful images.

But then the overhead lights had suddenly dimmed, there had been a dramatic drum-roll, followed by trumpet blasts that sounded like the off-key cries of a herd of drunken elephants, and when the circus ring was fully illuminated once more, it revealed a mini fire truck and a trundling buggy that looked to have emerged from the pages of a kid's comic book. It was coloured an eye-dazzlingly bright shade of yellow, had dark blue tyres and a pair of owlish, rolling eyes in place of headlamps. Oh, and the shape of the radiator grill alternated between an aw-shucks grin, a round 'O' of surprise, and a grimace of despair.

This was all mildly amusing if a little surreal, even to young boy gifted with a keen imagination, but what had immediately caught my attention were the people who were sat in the vehicles: a motley collection of garishly made-up clowns, all false, painted-on smiles, bizarre clothing and too-loud, maniacal laughter.

As they began indulging in a series of supposedly hilarious antics that included 'accidentally' drenching each other with fire hoses and metal buckets filled with water, and tripping over ladders and strategically placed banana skins, most, if not all of the other kids present, were clutching their stomachs with laughter or literally rolling in the aisles at the slapstick antics of *'Mr Giggles,' Bozo,'* and *'Charlie Farley.'* I was busy meanwhile, cowering in fear behind my Dad's back, or desperately trying to worm my way between the gaps in the row's wooden seating to hide face-down amongst the discarded Coke cans, cigarette stubs and greasy hot-dog wrappers.

If anyone had thought to ask me why clowns should inspire such a level of intense fear within me, I would have been hard-pressed to put my finger on the precise cause. Looking back, however, I think it may have been due to the fact that these supposedly 'manna-from-comedy heaven' figures appeared to be constantly sweating white, sickly-looking greasepaint under the hot glare of the overhead lighting, that there was a flicker of evil intent hidden behind the heavy make-up, or even that they were possessed of a rage-fuelled Demonism, the likes of which I later equated with that terrifying scene of Jack Nicholson hacking his way through the toilet door with an axe in Stanley Kubrick's version of *The Shining*, (although of course, I didn't see the film for a good decade or so after my trip to the circus - viewing that iconic celluloid image all those years later, instantly brought to mind my inaugural encounter with clowns).

The upshot of this memorable for-all-the-wrong-reasons experience was that I got to spend the entire walk home peering anxiously over my shoulder at the patches of darkness that pooled beyond the street-light's sodium glare. And later that evening I had to slow descend into fitful slumber plagued with visions of pale white faces looming up out of the shadow-filled corners of my bedroom like colourless balloons un-tethered by a shrieking autumn gale...

*****

Thirty-odd years down the undulating path of my life, I was enjoying a mini-break on the edge of the delightful Cheshire town of Frodsham with my then wife, Paula. The storm-lashed Easter weekend of 2008 had seemed more akin to the grim depths of mid-winter than early spring, and so, on a squally Sunday morning, deterred from embarking on any type of outdoor pursuit, and after scanning the hotel's guidebook of local attractions, we decided to pay a visit to a candle-works situated just outside the village of Burwardsely.

I know what you're thinking, Readers. It doesn't exactly sound like an all-guns blazing odyssey to Thrills-Ville, Arizona, but the weather was so un-remittingly awful, anywhere had seemed a more appealing alternative to sitting in our soulless hotel room, staring mournfully out the window at flat, rain-sodden countryside with a lukewarm cup of instant coffee in one hand and a stale, imitation Bourbon biscuit in the other. And before anyone starts, the imminent arrival of the pesky cleaning maid had ruled out any inclination for me and Paula to spend the day in bed together!

And so, a little before the regular eleven o'clock sweep-a-thon, we prepared a packed lunch, topped up the hip flask with a good malt whisky to ward off the chill, and with faces set with grim determination, we set out to brave the elements.

*****

Located at the top of a small hill surrounded by a patchwork quilt of farmers' fields and thick swathes of leafless woodland, the candle-works and the adjoining craft centres resembled a vast collection of converted stables, which indeed they may originally have been. The place was obviously very popular with tourists, as packed to the rafters as it was with bedraggled parents and their equally drenched offspring. I remember thinking, as they shuffled around the sweetly-scented, gently illuminated showrooms, they resembled hordes of refugees from some deluge-stricken country, desperately seeking warmth and shelter in the company of their fellow man.

And indeed, *candles*.

Hundreds and thousands of them, and of virtually every size and shape imaginable.

Certainly, it was easy to see why people were so attracted to the place, and never mind any cheesy clichés about moths being drawn inexorably to the flickering flames. Even the briefest of glances through the large bay windows provided the starkest of contrasts between the un-seasonal gloom outside, and the cheery, welcoming glow that permeated the buildings, creating an almost Christmassy feel to the place.

After spending the best part of an hour or so marvelling at the intricately-carved, gorgeous-smelling wax designs, we found ourselves in an adjoining section on the ground floor that featured garden ornaments, bird baths and hand-crafted benches, when the air was suddenly filled with wild gales of lunatic laughter.

The sound immediately caused me to break out in a cold sweat, and glancing reluctantly over my shoulder, I saw a painted sign above a door that read '***The Old Time Penny Arcade.***'

> "Hey, Lee, this looks interesting,"

Paula said, tapping me on the arm and almost causing me to scream out loud.

> "Let's go and have a quick look around."

Before I could venture that I would sooner spend the afternoon swimming with a shoal of hungry piranhas dressed in nothing but a three-sizes too small pair of *Speedos,* than seek out the source of that crazy hilarity, she grabbed me by the hand and virtually dragged me into what amounted to an exhibition room, filled with fully working 'mechanical wonders' preserved from the 1920s and 30s - the golden age of seaside amusement arcades. There was a cacophony of noise emanating from these machines, the vast majority of which seemed to employ a horror theme, living proof that whatever the self-appointed guardians of morality might say to the contrary, people of all ages, even the very youngest of children, have an in-built fascination for the supernatural, the uncanny and the bizarre.

A suitably lurid set of posters at the entrance served to pique the interest and enticed you to dip your hands deep into your pockets.

> *'See what the butler saw in the early 1930s!*
> *See the amazing magic machines!*
> *You won't believe your eyes!'*

I hadn't been at all sure about that. I still remembered the equally promising New Ferry Circus adverts of my youth which had in reality delivered all the excitement and spectacle of watching a pair of pensioners pull a cheap Christmas cracker at the end of a Yuletide shindig on a wet Monday evening in Birkenhead town centre.

Still, I couldn't deny that there appeared to be some fascinating items on display, and despite the fact that the arcade inspired in me a bitter-sweet nostalgia, a feeling eerily similar to clearing out the attic and discovering a crumbling picture postcard from a once popular holiday resort, encrusted with sand and marked by the tears of a painful goodbye, I felt compelled to check them out.

To operate the machines you first had to change your money with the middle-aged man sat at the counter near the entrance to the exhibition. You handed over a modern pound coin in exchange for a stack of old copper pennies, inserted them into the requisite slot, stood back, and let the fun begin.

We started with 'The Haunted House,' a mini-representation of a typically Edwardian dressing room, complete with towering bookcases, gas-lighting and an old grandfather clock, chiming midnight every sixty seconds or so, whilst spectres materialised hanging suspended from the ceiling and a piano played all by itself, (and the feelings of melancholy were intensified when I recognised the tune as *When The Harvest Days Are Over,* one of my Nanna Smith's favourite songs, which she had played constantly after her husband, Alfie, died: a soundtrack to the heart-sick emptiness of irretrievable loss).

We next headed over to 'The Cave Of Horror,' a *'ghastly grotto'* containing secret doorways that constantly slid open to reveal tantalising glimpses of clutching claws, slithering, lizard-like tails and Devilish faces floating in the midst of a greenish glow whilst an explorer searched the caverns, blissfully unaware of the terrors slowly creeping up around him.

'The Mummy's Finger,' also caught our attention, a severed, blood-soaked digit swathed in ancient, ragged bandages which we viewed by peering down the lens of a metal scope, as did *'The Gypsy Fortune Teller,'* a swarthy-skinned beauty in a head-scarf and with gold earrings the size of dinner plates, whose predictions turned out to be uniformly dire and pessimistic.

We tried out all of these arcade games, and several more besides, but I quickly discovered that two exhibits completely dominated the room, both on a literal and personal level.

The first of these was an almost life-sized character called *'Jolly Jack',* a rosy-cheeked, sailor-suited individual, whose sole function was to constantly rock back and forth, cackling like an escaped lunatic at absolutely nothing at all. Or at least nothing that I could see.

He was stood before a painted background of towering sea cliffs and cloudless blue skies, whilst a white-sailed yacht bobbed on the choppy waves of the bay. It was easy to imagine the accompanying soundtrack: the mournful cries of seagulls interspersed with the crashing of the surf, the sighing of a gentle, salt-tinged breeze, and the excited yells of children playing on the beach below. This idyllic, summer-holiday vista did nothing to dispel the feelings of unease *'Jolly Jack'* inspired however.

The hypnotic way his eyes slid slowly from side to side as he laughed, like a character in a Terry Gilliam cartoon, and the huge, liver-lipped grin that threatened to split his face clean in two, were more than enough to stir vague recollections of half-forgotten childhood terrors, although I couldn't quite see the precise shape of them at first. That revelation wouldn't occur until I laid eyes upon the large, heavily made-up clown sat in a glass case holding an acoustic guitar in its white-gloved hands, and with plastic balloons and multi-coloured ping pong balls piled up high all around it.

In an instant, I was transported back to that warm, late summer evening thirty years earlier, at The New Ferry Festival, cowering in the Big Top at *'The Arrival of the Terror Clowns.'*

Only this particular specimen was infinitely worse than anything I remember from back then.

Its teeth were bared, the thick, blood-red lips pulled back in a grimace that resembled a vicious snarl of anger or the prelude to a high-pitched, spit-flecked scream. It strummed its guitar with all the finesse of a butcher hacking at a slab of beef and sang a supposedly cheerful ditty in a whining falsetto that grated on my nerves like the screech of an out of tune violin.

When at last it had finished its nonsensical song, the clown threw back its disproportionately large head and brayed uncontrollably, and it seemed to me on that freezing cold Easter Sunday afternoon, it was the mean-spirited laughter of the cruellest of practical jokers, the malevolent Trickster who revels in the terrible misfortunes of others, and who feeds voraciously on all the bitter hurts of the world.

It appeared too, that the figure regarded me with a knowing, mocking expression, as if it could somehow see into the darkest corners of my inner being, the very core of my soul laid bare like a set of sun-bleached bones that had been endlessly picked over by carrion birds and other wild scavengers in the midst of a blighted patch of wasteland.

Here were the true sources of the clown's eternal hilarity: life's lost opportunities, the roads not taken, the unwise choices, the loves that went bad....

It became apparent to me then that this particular clown, (and who knew, maybe *all* clowns/) found such terrible things immensely comical, and this realisation brought with it new meaning to the word 'amusements.'

Before setting foot in *'The Old Time Penny Arcade'*, I had always assumed the games on display were there for *our* amusement.

I'd never dreamed it could be the other way around.

"Come on, I've seen enough,"

I said to Paula, trying to sound casual and off-hand.

"Let's go and get a drink. There must be a pub around here, somewhere."

She just shook her head wearily and gave me one of her famous *'Oh no, what's up with Mr Hypersensitive now?'* looks, and just then *Jolly Jack* and *The Singing Clown* started up again and I almost physically pushed Paula towards the exits, so desperate was I to get the hell out of there.

When we finally stepped outside into the freezing March afternoon, the raw wind stinging our faces and turning our gloveless fingers instantly numb, Paula turned to me and said,

"Honest to God, Lee, sometimes I really worry about you!"

I opened my mouth to reply, but then promptly snapped it shut, knowing there wasn't anything I could possibly say.

Nothing that would make any kind of sense, anyway.

Instead, I hunched my shoulders against the cold and began making my way across the car-park, eager to be sat in the passenger seat of our Renault Megane, with the heater on and the comforting sound of an Indie compilation CD blasting from the stereo.

It was while I was shivering at the car door, waiting impatiently for Paula to find the keys, that I heard the sound a hysterical peal of laughter carrying on the wind, and for one insane moment I was sure that *'Jack' a*nd the *'Clown'* had somehow broken free from their glass cases and had followed us out of the candle-works.

Then I saw that it was just an ordinary, bald-headed man stood a few feet away, trying to frighten his young son with a puppet in the shape of a scrunchy-faced witch. The poor kid did indeed appear to be genuinely terrified, and this only seemed to actively encourage the father, who began yelling,

"She's gonna get yer!' She's gonna get yer, and eat you all up!"

...causing the boy to burst into floods of tears.

The man suddenly saw me looking, grinned and winked in a *'Well, you've got to scare yer lad's young if yer want them to grow up to be men!'* conspiratorial manner, before dragging his son into the back of their station wagon and slamming the door on his fear-filled sobbing.

Less than four months after our visit to Burwardsley, Paula and I had separated and were headed down the rocky, emotional pot-hole-ridden road to divorce, with no hope of reconciliation.

The break up of our marriage was as entirely unexpected as it was devastatingly heart-breaking, and though time has passed and I've tried to put a brave face on things, as you simply have to do, there are still those days when I'm sent reeling by the sheer enormity of all that's been lost.

For a while, I'd wake in the early hours from a bad dream in our old double bed, and stretch across to where my wife used to sleep, anxious to hold her in my arms and take comfort in the warmth of her presence, only to find there's no-one there, just a vast empty space filled with nothing but the hurting chill of absence.

Often on such occasions, just as during the days of childhood, my attention would be drawn to the shadows that gathered in the far corner of the room, a roiling blackness that no slab of moonlight can ever hope to penetrate.

I can imagine a figure concealed there somewhere.

A permanently grinning individual, with a bulbous red nose and grease-painted skin.

The Joker.

The Trickster.

The Clown.

Silently laughing at the horror of my darkest days....

THE STILT-WEARING KILLER CLOWN

One of the most frightening TV programmes I've ever seen was the allegedly true-life documentary screened late one night sometime during the late 1990s.

I was still living at my parent's address at the time, and I remember lying in bed with all the lights off flicking through the channels with the remote control, and I stumbled across a series featuring reconstructions of unusual murders.

Frustratingly, I can't recall what the programme was called now and I've never seen any reference to it since, despite constantly trawling the Internet, and there have been times I have half-suspected I only dreamed that I saw it.

God knows, it was bizarre enough.

The story concerned the highly-unusual case of an axe-wielding serial-killer, whose *modus operandi* was highly unconventional, to say the least. Actually, as understatements go, the above is on a par with saying scoffing a two-and-a-half thousand pound *'Super Scooby Burger'* for dinner every day might not do your arteries or cholesterol levels a whole pile of good.

Filmed in some small, nondescript American town, caught in the frigid grip of deep-mid-winter, (the name of which escapes me because I missed the start of the programme), I tuned in time to catch a scene featuring the local sheriff, complete with a pale brown Stetson and a gleaming silver star, standing in the middle of a deserted, snow-bound street, shaking his head in frustration and bemusement as a TV reporter quizzed him about an unsolved series of local murders.

> 'The townsfolk are badly frightened, sheriff,'

...the correspondent drawled accusingly.

> 'And I think it's fair to say you can hardly blame them. Four brutal murders of young women in this town in as many years and no-one has even been arrested for the crimes, let alone charged!'

He pauses for a second, and then asks pointedly.

> 'The people want answers, Sheriff. Are you able to supply them with any?'

The sheriff doesn't respond straight away. He just stares off into the middle distance, and there's an unmistakably haunted look in his tired, crow's feet-lined eyes. He bears all the hallmarks of a man who's just the teensiest sliver away from his wit's end. Someone who's hunted for the truth down an endless series of twisting corridors, and emerged with nothing more than a whole new set of imponderables for his troubles.

> 'Well, sheriff,'

…the reporter prompts after several long moments of silence.

> 'Can you assist in calming the public's fears, or are you and your men still lost without a single clue right now?'

The sheriff sighs, hitches up his pants, then looks directly into the camera.

> 'Look, I can promise the good people of this town *one* thing at least' he says slowly, his breath puffing to steamy clouds. 'Whilst it's true we may not have any definite leads at this present time, we are doing everything in our power to track this killer down, and I remain convinced we will catch him sooner rather than later.' He jabbed his gloved middle finger at the unseen reporter for added emphasis. 'In the meantime, I would ask members of the public to remain vigilant but to go about the business of their daily lives. And to report to us immediately anything they regard as being remotely suspicious.'

The camera suddenly pulls away from the scene of the interview at breakneck speed at this point, and goes careering along the winding, ice-encrusted roads that lead out of the winter-sleepy town with its softly-lit store fronts and blinking traffic signals imbuing the scene with a perverse festive atmosphere. And when the last of the lonely-looking houses dotted about the outskirts of the town are finally left behind, and the woods begin to close in on either side of the road, the programme's narrator begins describing, in suitably sonorous tones, how a number of apparently unrelated young women, all of whom aged between 18 and 25, had been killed over a four year period, and bodily dismembered by a maniac armed with an axe.

In each case, the dismembered, though fully-clothed, corpses had been found lying face-down in the thick snow-drifts at the edge of the forest. And that wasn't the only strange thing about the apparently motiveless slayings, either. Investigating officers were further mystified to find that at the site of the murders, there only appeared to be *one* set of footprints; that of the *victim's;* a series of wildly zig-zagging scuffed indentations, that marked a frantic and ultimately futile dash across the pristine virgin snow.

There was absolutely no trace of the pursuing psychotic axe-murderer's footprints.

In fact, there was not the slightest sign that anything remotely *human* had chased the women for a fairly lengthy distance, stretching from the edge of the road, across a hundred feet or so of deep snow to the beginnings of the ranks of fir trees. The only 'tracks' of any kind were a series of small, rectangular holes that ran alongside the victim's prints, the origin of which remained a mystery.

Equally perplexing was the question of just what the hell were these four, solitary young women doing out in the proverbial middle of nowhere, in sub-zero temperatures, in the first place?

Our friendly neighbourhood Sheriff, when quizzed on camera about this very point, managed to drum one plausible, if highly disturbing theory:

> 'It's possible that the killer kidnapped each of the victims, placed them in a vehicle, drove to the location on the edge of town, and then released them with nothing more in mind than the thrill of the chase.'

As deductive speculations go, this does make a perverted kind of sense, but it didn't explain the absence of the murderer's footprints or the presence of the mysterious holes in the snow, and of course, it brought the police no nearer to identifying the culprit.

The programme then featured a filmed reconstruction of the latest murder, and as staged sequences go, this proved to be especially chilling.

It opens with a quiet stretch of slushy road. It's late afternoon. The sun has just gone down beyond the distant tree-lined hills, leaving behind cloudless blue skies that contrast sharply with the high banks of freshly fallen snow. The scene has an almost three-dimensional quality. There's not a breath of wind and the very air seems frozen.

Or else is waiting for something terrible to happen…

The literal freeze-frame is a relatively brief one, as the serenity is disturbed by the sudden appearance of a female figure dressed in a bright red hat and coat and a pair of black boots running in a veering, panicky fashion from some unseen assailant towards the supposed sanctuary of the woods. The camera zooms in, and as real time turns to dreamlike slow-motion, we see a fresh-faced young woman, little more than a girl, really, with loose strands of fine blonde hair flying from beneath the woollen bobble hat, as she scampers and peers periodically over her shoulder, her eyes bulging madly in terror. Meanwhile on the soundtrack we can hear the crunchy, pounding of feet mixed with the woman's increasingly laboured breathing and hitching little gasps of terror.

Due to the footage being shot from the camera's point of view, we can't see the source of her fear, but two things *are* abundantly clear. One: the hunter is rapidly gaining on its prey with each passing moment. And two: the woman's constant looking back to seek confirmation of this dreadful fact, is only going to result in an inevitable outcome.

And sure enough, as she glances back for what proves to be the final time, she loses her balance and goes sprawling headlong into the snow….

The camera lens bends over her ominously…

And the scene quickly switches to a large flock of huge black birds, crows most likely, taking flight in a startled, wing-flapping flurry, their raucous cawing mingling with the sound of hysterical human screams.

And these screams carry across the brittle air, and echo through the dead, January fields and along the winding back-roads, with their isolated farms and darkened homesteads, and down along the centre of the main street leading to the centre of town where they merge with the ear-piercing shriek of the factory's whistle, announcing the close of the working day.

The screen fades to black.

And when 'the curtain rises,' once more, it reveals a bright, sun-lit day with our old friend, the Sheriff, standing beside a colourful poster pasted to the wall of a convenience store announcing the imminent arrival of the travelling circus.

He stands before the camera an expression of grim resignation clouding his kind features.

'You know, looking back now,'

...he sighs,

'...I can hardly believe I didn't put two and two together at a far earlier stage of the investigation. Maybe then, we could have saved the life of at least one of those poor young women.'

He shakes his head ruefully, and glances sideways at the lurid poster emblazoned with the words:

'The Extravaganza Of Eternal Excitement Is Coming!'
A Thousand And One Delights, For Young And Old Alike!

'I remember I was walking home from another of those interminable press conferences over at City Hall, which included a heart-breaking appeal issued by the parents of the latest victim, and seeing these posters for the circus plastered all over town, and it struck me as being more than a tad distasteful, disrespectful, even, that the carnival should be rolling into town at this particular low-point in our history. I mean, who really felt like having a good time in the wake of this latest tragedy that touched just about everyone in this closely knit community?

I remembered something else then, too,'

...he adds, wiping the back of his hand across his forehead, a weary gesture that speaks of frustration and bitter regret.

'I'd somehow forgotten, though God only knows how, that I'd felt exactly the same way almost a year to the day. At the time the remains of the previous victim were found. And, come to think of it, I'd felt pretty much the same powerful mixture of guilt and anger the year before that, too.

And hot on the heels of that little revelation came another, far more pertinent one:

All three murders had taken place the very day the circus arrived in our little town!'

(There is a pause here, as a strident burst of calliope music accompanies some grainy, slightly out-of-focus footage of a parade of jugglers and mime artists, horse-drawn painted wagons and capering dwarves)

'And I realised then,'

...says the sheriff in a halting, almost incredulous voice, (*as the cheery hurdy-gurdy melody slides hideously out of tune*),

'...that the killer was a *clown!*'

A killer clown....On *stilts!*'

No sooner has he issued this utterly preposterous-sounding statement than we see a swaying, grinning clown bringing up the rear of that madcap procession balanced precariously on a set of unfeasibly tall stilts, and though at first this image only seems to confirm the absurdity of the assertion that a costumed stilt-walker, no matter how skilful, could possibly be physically capable of committing these terrible acts, somehow, it all makes a crazy, perverted kind of sense. And instinctively you just *know* that the sheriff is one hundred per cent correct in his suppositions. Especially when he goes on to provide some fairly compelling evidence to support his theory.

'I went back to the station and dug out the photographs of the various murder scenes,'

...he says,

'...and I have to say it was kind of like I was truly seeing them for the first time. It became clear to me pretty much straight away that those strange, unidentified marks in the snow we found around the victims, could only have been made by a pair of stilts, and although it's kind of hard to imagine how the hell anyone could have managed to carry out these terrible crimes by chasing down physically fit young women, especially in the ankle deep snow, whilst wielding a big heavy axe, there really was to my mind at least, no other explanation that could readily account for all the known facts about these cases.'

Somewhat frustratingly, the programme ended soon after this 'revelation', with no indication as to whether anyone, clown or otherwise, was ever arrested or charged with the murders, and leaving in its wake about a thousand unanswered questions (amongst them: did the perpetrator don his clown outfit and make-up before or after he, presumably(?), kidnapped the women? Did he drug his victims so that they slept whilst he climbed up onto his stilts, in order that he could then pursue them the moment they regained consciousness? How did he manage to catch and kill his victims whilst on stilts, especially in such treacherous conditions? And of course, most pertinently, why go to such ridiculously difficult lengths to commit a series of murders in the first place, even allowing for the obvious fact that the perpetrator was completely insane?)

The screen faded to black once more, and as the credits rolled, in the absence of answers, the viewer's mind is filled with a truly nightmarish mental image: a demented circus clown on ten-foot high stilts, bounding with unnatural grace across virgin-white expanses in a silence broken only by the hitching breath of the hunted, the rich crunch of snow, and a blood-soaked wood-cutter's axe slicing through the freezing, twilit air…..

A CORNUCOPIA OF CLOWNS

Back when I was the Editor of *Dead Of Night* magazine, during the late-1990s, I was sent the following account all the way from Chicago, USA. The 'article' was in the form of a letter that contained the simple signature C Brown, and there were no further details.

'This is totally true. When I was about six years old, I had to attend a birthday party, and needless to say there was a clown present, supposedly to entertain the kids and allow them to be photographed with it. I want you to be clear that I had absolutely no fear of clowns at this point in my life, and in fact I'd always previously thought they were kind of neat. So when it was my turn to get my picture taken with him I happily jumped up into his lap, smiling like the cat that got the cream.

Until that is, the clown turned to me and said in a deep, quiet whisper, "I like *you* a lot. You smell *good!*"

That was bad enough, but what was even worse was the putrid, obscene smell that came out of his mouth...a mouth that I noticed was coloured an unnaturally bright red inside. Its breath smelled so bad in fact, that I actually gagged, and as strange as it sounds, the whole incident seemed to take place over an inordinate length of time, and no-one present seemed to be aware of my obvious discomfort.

After what seemed like an eternity, I heard someone shout' 'Hey, kiddo, smile for the camera!' but I refused to do so. Instead, I almost peed my pants and ran off to get away from that damned clown. I couldn't just leave the party on my own though, and every time I had occasion to run past the clown, he constantly stared at me and mouthed something unintelligible, and to be honest, I didn't want to know what he was saying. I don't think I'll ever be able to forget that godawful smell or the way the clown looked at me and I'll probably never know if he was some kind of pervert or something even worse than that....

Something purely *evil'*.

- ## AMERICA'S PHANTOM CLOWNS

Fortean author, Loren Coleman, makes reference on his excellent *Mysterious America* web site, to a wave of *'Phantom Clown'* attacks across the USA, back in the early 1980s.

According to contemporary accounts from Boston to Kansas City, wandering gangs of 'Killer Clowns' were rumoured to be driving around in plain, unmarked vans in search of unwary children or preying on unaccompanied kiddies standing at bus-stops.

As Mr Coleman pointed out, these remarkably consistent accounts spread like proverbial wildfire, over a huge area, despite the fact that we are talking here - of course - of the unimaginable dim and distant past; the days before the inexorable rise of *MSN, You Tube* and other information-sharing, rumour-sparking internet sites. Whatever the true origin of the scare, it is worth noting that the newspaper reports of these alleged *'Phantom Clown'* incidents bore striking similarities to each other, despite the periodicals being completely unaware of the widespread nature of these cases.

And if you were labouring under the comforting illusion that this was purely a weird 1980s phenomenon, the decade that spawned *Killer Klowns From Outer Space*, the kid-bothering doll-clown from *Poltergeist* and most significantly of all, Stephen King's wonderfully chilling novel, *It,* then you'll doubtless find it a tad disconcerting that, according to Mr Coleman's site, an almost identical series of incidents began occurring in Chicago, as recently as October 2008.

Reports in the local press described how:

> *'...a man wearing clown make-up and a wig is using balloons to in an attempt to lure children into his vehicle on the South Side of Chicago, Illinois. Police issued an alert about a week after a man with a similar description was spotted on the West Side. The man, who wears a clown mask or white face paint with teardrops on the cheek, has approached children walking to and from school, police have been quoted as saying. Witnesses told officers he was seem driving a white or brown van with the windows broken out.'*

The incident was not an isolated one, either.

Somewhat worryingly, the police also pointed out that the clown sightings were not confined to one specific area, but rather there had been multiple reports of clowns right across the city.

There were a large number of e-mail messages posted in response to Loren's disturbing revelations, and amongst the more interesting of these were the following: an anonymous witness who claimed he was a law enforcement officer, stated that one of his former associates who worked for The Illinois Department of Corrections and The Federal Bureau of Prisons, once told him that while at Menard State Prison, he had met the notorious John Wayne Gacy; the real-life killer-clown, shortly before his execution, and described him as being surrounded by 'an aura of absolute Evil.' [*]

The anonymous poster also raised an intriguing, if somewhat incredible hypothesis concerning the reality of the Phantom Clown Phenomenon:

---

[*]Equally intriguing was another anonymous post in which the author related that he grew up just outside of Chicago during the "Clown Scare," of the early 1990s.

'I don't know if the mysterious sightings of clowns are copycat individuals or simply a personification of pure evil that moves from place to place looking for a host body to use,'

…he posted.

'In my career I have had the misfortune of being around individuals who committed a series of such "Demonic" acts, they could only be diagnosed as being "possessed," in the literal sense of the word.'

'A friend's mother told us all to watch out for a brown raggedy van with a clown in it,' he stated. 'I didn't really believe her until a few days later at my grade school we were issued with a similar warning and told not to accept rides or candy from anyone in clown make-up. Still sceptical, I was in for a shock when that same weekend, I was joshing about with my friends, we did in fact see a man in clown make-up driving a busted up brown van down 15th Street.

As I remember he had black and white face make-up with a single tear (similar to the recent sightings in the Chicagoland area), strange, plushed out red hair and a look in his eyes that was fucking eerie. He slowed his car down to stare at us as he approached. My two friends and I exchanged a single, wordless glance and then bolted, very probably leaving dust outlines of ourselves behind us.

I still can't explain the weirdness of that moment to this day. There has never been any mention of who this person was or what they wanted. To the best of my knowledge, no child was ever taken, no crime was ever committed. But I can say this; the Chicagoland area has always had an interesting relationship with clowns. Back during the locale's earliest history when a gambling house and tavern at the mouth of the Chicago River would occasionally host travelling performers in (what would now be called), clown make-up, to the lake-front being regularly occupied by travelling circuses through the mid to late 1800's, there were a whole series of outlandish circus shows during the Columbian expedition which brought in performers from all over the world.

Even Bozo the Clown got his start in Chicago, and actually remains based there. Since the 1970s though, Chicago's been a bit spooked on the idea of killer clowns. I'm speaking of the serial murders committed by John Wayne Gacy, which may be an impetus behind the rash of clown-related weirdness. It might be the natural psychological reaction of a certain portion of the population living in one of the most corrupt cities in America. The rash of killer or evil clown sightings puts a face on the unaddressed fears we face everyday. The whole phenomenon may be a mass hysteria of sorts giving people an outlet for feeling powerless from their fear. It may also be that a few people feel so afraid they are pushed to commit horrifying acts as a way of coping with feelings of anger or powerlessness. In any case, I often wonder if my clown encounter many years ago was with a lunatic child-snatcher, a hysterical delusion, or just some guy running late to a kid's party.'

And finally, whilst reading Stephen King's excellent *'anatomy of horror'* overview, *Danse Macabre*, I came across the following fascinating circus-related anecdote;

On July 6th, 1944, the *Ringling Brothers* and *Barnum & Bailey* circus was giving a performance in Hartford, Connecticut, before 7,000 paying customers. During the performance, a huge fire broke out, and 168 persons died in the blaze and 487 were injured. One of the dead, a well-dressed, highly-presentable young girl, thought to be about six years old, couldn't be identified by any of the relatives of the victims. Despite the authorities launching an exhaustive, state-wide investigation, no-one came forward to claim her. This was especially mysterious as the girl had died of smoke inhalation and her face was therefore completely unmarred. A series of photographs were taken of her and distributed first locally and then throughout the whole of the United States. The days and weeks quickly turned into months, but still she remained stubbornly unidentified, and her identity remains unknown to this day.

So, the question is, where on earth (or off it) did she come from?

AND SPEAKING OF 'PEOPLE FROM NOWHERE...'

I know there'll doubtless be readers who will find my habit of adding an endless sequence of footnotes, somewhat infuriating, but I feel it necessary to add that the disconcerting phenomenon of involuntary *'teleportation'* is not as uncommon as you might think.

For instance, *'The Lock Haven Pennsylvania Express'*, reported that on June 7th, 1956, a man by the name of Thomas R. Kessell, a brewery worker from Johannesburg, South Africa, suddenly regained consciousness from what he described as a deep, dreamless sleep, to find himself walking along a busy street in the centre of New York City.

He had absolutely no memory of how he had come to be suddenly 'teleported' from a Johannesburg tavern where he was employed the previous April.

Paranormal investigators have frequently speculated that it may be possible for a human being to walk around a 'dimensional bend' to find themselves mysteriously transported to another country.

As veteran investigator has been quoted as saying; 'Perhaps the shortest distance between two points may *not* be a straight line, after all.

'Perhaps an amnesiac reaction would be necessary for survival of the experience for the sake of one's sanity.'

*** On January 6th, 1914, according to contemporary accounts, a naked man suddenly appeared from out of the proverbial blue on High Street, Chatham, in Kent, England. People who were walking along the same street told of how the man 'was just suddenly there, without warning, confused, frightened and without a single stitch of clothing on a freezing cold mid-winter's day.'

Even stranger, between January 14th, 1920 and December 9th, 1923, a total of six people were discovered wandering on the streets near the small town of Romford, Essex, England. Not a single one of these 'mentally distraught individuals' was able to give any explanation as to how they came to be in that particular location.

Even more perplexing is the case of a Mr Thomas R Kessell, who claimed that he suddenly and unaccountably found himself wandering aimlessly along a street in the middle of New York City, seconds after walking out a bar in Johannesburg, South Africa. His admittedly fantastic tale was given a fair degree of credence by the fact that there was absolutely no accounting for how Mr Kessell could have entered the U.S. without the requisite documents, ie a passport, and it would have been very difficult for him to have boarded a ship or a plane without one. There was also the curious fact that Mr Kessell did not recover his memory until he had been treated by a psychiatrist. Only after he had undergone a couple of intensive sessions did he remember who he was and where he was from.

And finally, *Fate Magazine* reported back in 1961, that a 17-year-old girl named Carmen Chaney was involved in a bizarre incident in Fresno, California, one idyllic summer afternoon in 1936.

She was making her way along Tyler Street, in the company of her Aunt Frankie, engaged in everyday carefree conversation as the sun beat down from a flawless sky, when Carmen suddenly noticed what she later described as a 'strange old lady,' crossing the street at the intersection.

'The old woman moved slowly, with difficulty, as if her legs weren't functioning properly,' Ms Chaney later told reporters, and assuming that she must be afflicted with some debilitating illness, the two women immediately ran over to assist her.

The old lady however, didn't appear to want their help or anyone else's. On the contrary, she reacted as though she the mere sight of her two potential benefactors terrified her to the point of total panic.

The author of the article in Fate Magazine, described what happened next;

> 'Only 20 feet from her now, they were fascinated by her large, blazing eyes, set deep in a white-chalk face, the skin of which appeared to be stretched tightly over her skull. She was about four feet, ten inches tall, thin and scrawny: snow-white hair showed in wisps under her large black hat; she wore a high-necked, short-sleeved dress and high button shoes of a decade gone by. The black of her hat, which was pulled down low over her face, as well as that of her dress, was old to the point of decay, as both had turned greenish. She carried no bag or purse. Altogether she was a pathetic figure. 'By now several of the neighbours on the block were watching the strange old woman retreating from the two well-meaning women. The old lady hobbled into an alley, then she looked around helplessly, as she realised that more than thirty people were intensely observing her bizarre behaviour.
>
> 'She stopped for a brief moment... then she vanished. Disappeared in the blink of an eyelash!' 'The many witnesses to the fantastic disappearance excitedly exchanged opinions and speculations. Police officers who were summoned to the scene chose to believe that the old woman had been ill and had simply stumbled out of sight of her observers. But an extensive search of the alley and the houses on either side revealed no such person of that unique description.'

THE SPIRIT OF DARK AND LONELY WATER

A strong candidate for the scariest advert ever, (or Public Information Film, if you want to be Mr Pedantic and give it its 1970's contemporary title), this two minute vignette was responsible for doling out more generous helpings of nightmares than any horror movie I've seen before or since. And yet, despite this, as I sat glued to the regular kid's TV programmes that ran from late afternoon to the reading of the headlines on the Evening News (*Ace Of Wands*, *The Tomorrow People*, *Captain Pugwash*, *The Double-Deckers*, etc), I'd secretly be willing that sinister, hooded apparition to appear on the screen.

Everyone in our society, no matter the size of its membership, were in unanimous agreement that in the Chart of 'Frightening Things' that haunted the halcyon days of our youth, this was the perennial, undisputed chart-topper ....

The opening shots are of stretch of stagnant water in the cheerless grip of mid-winter. Thick with rotted vegetation, the muddy-brown rivulet seeps across the landscape like pus from an oozing sore. The mournful cry of a lost seabird echoes from the nearby woods. The leafless branches drip with a treacly moisture that resembles the fever-sweat of infection...

And then the camera pans to reveal an eerie black-robed figure, The Grim Reaper, the age-old personification of Death, floating on the scummy surface of the mist-shrouded bog like some obscene parody of Christ.

For an impossibly long second or two, an all pervasive silence descends.
An unnatural caught-breath hush.

And even that hopelessly lost seagull knows better than to break it.

When The Spirit eventually speaks, its voice is cold and forbidding, the pitiless tones of absolute evil:

> '*I am the Spirit of Dark And Lonely Water, ready to trap the unwary. The Show-off. The Fool. And this is the kind of place you'd expect to find me.*'

The scene then switches to a patch of barren wasteland riddled with pot holes and gravel pits half-filled with filthy, discoloured water. It's exactly the sort of drab, featureless, battlefield-type setting that acts as a magnet for bored kids during the first half-term break of the year. And here are a whole bunch of pre-teenagers, dressed in the horrendously ugly fashions of the day, playing on the edge of a particularly muddy pool beneath white March skies.

One of the young boys, showing off the impress the girls* by employing the time-honoured method of acting like he's some kind of invincible superhero, (perhaps inspired by the antics of one of his mates, who's running around with the hood of his anorak over his head while the rest of the coat billows behind him like *Batman's* fluttering cape), sliding down the mud-caked banks to poke at the water's surface with a stick. Quite what he's hoping to achieve is anyone's guess, but as the rest of the gang stare in silent fascination, the shrouded figure of Death approaches, unseen, looming behind them, the better to conduct the proceedings.

> 'But nobody expects to find me here,'

The Reaper speaks, in tones of mild disbelief.

> 'It seems too ordinary. But that pool is deep. The boy is showing off. The bank is slippery....'

At this, the boy falls face first into the water with a resounding splash to be sucked down into the murky depths by Death's cold embrace.

The figure turns away, satisfied with a job well done, as the terrified children open their mouths to scream....

The scene switches to another seemingly tranquil location: The sweet breath of a summer breeze teases the surface of a duck pond surrounded by gently swaying reeds. Near to one of the banks, a blonde-haired boy framed in a spill of sunlight is using the branch of an overhanging tree to stretch for something, an errant football perhaps, floating tantalisingly just out of reach.....

Oh, and here's those slyly mocking tones once more, to provide a sinister soundtrack to this seemingly innocuous scene;

> 'The show-offs are easy. But the unwary ones are easier still. This branch is weak, rotten. It'll never take his weight!'

No sooner have these prophetic words been uttered, than the weakened bough breaks there's an almighty splash, and water fowl take to the air in a flapping, squawking panic....

And Death, standing alone amidst the reeds, turns away, in search of its next victim.

The final scene features a municipal dump piled high with accumulated refuse. Surrounded by a chain-link fence rendered obsolete by a series of gaping holes torn by vandals, the entrance gate features a starkly-lettered sign that reads simply;

DANGER! No Swimming

> 'Only a fool would ignore this,'

...points out that dread-inducing voice.

> 'But there's one born every minute. Under the water there are traps. Old cars, bedsteads, weeds, hidden depths. It's the perfect place for an accident?'

This last word is uttered as a question. Confirmation, if such were needed, that the black-garbed entity is not merely an observer, a collector of souls who just happens to be in the right place at the right time. This particular dark spirit is a more than active participant in the deaths of these children.

Something which makes this film all the more terrifying.

In the middle of the junk-infested pool a boy a shirtless boy is clearly floundering, his cries for help all but drowned out as his head bobs beneath the water.

Almost as though he were being dragged beneath the oily surface by some unseen assailant.

But then, just as it seems 'the fool' will be added to the growing list of fatalities, another boy and a girl appear on the scene. The young lad shouts in a thick cockney accent:

'Oy, look. There's someone in the water! Get us that big stick to get him out.'

Startled by this intrusion, the Figure of Death whirls around and bemoans their sudden appearance.

'Sensible children!'

It curses vehemently.

'I have no power over them!'

Incorporating the lore of age-old faerie-tales, the spirit is exorcised by something as simple as a child's refusal to believe in Its reality, and deprived of Its power, It dissolves as rapidly as a Nosferatu-style vampire exposed to morning sunlight.

The kids manage to rescue the *'Fool'* and escort him, dripping wet, across the city dump.

'Oy mate, that's a stupid place to swim,'

…the 'sensible' boy asserts, by way of a reprimand. He then turns to the girl and says:

'Hey, go over there and get that thing to wrap him up in.'

The girl does as she's told and stoops to pick up the Spirit's discarded robe. It's lying, mud-stained and half-soaked in a dirty puddle. She stoops to pick it up, whilst her boyfriend sympathises with the half-drowned, foolish ignorer of warning signs.

'You don't half feel cold, mate. How long was you in there?'

The girl takes hold of the discarded robe, and an expression of sheer disgust suddenly wrinkles her face. She mutters something unintelligible (*'ooh, it's all awfid,'* is the about the closest interpretation I have been able to discern), then immediately throws it into the water.

The children walk away, whilst Death, seemingly defeated, sinks slowly beneath the surface…

But then, like all the truly classic horror movies, from *Don't Look Now* to original Japanese version of *The Grudge*, the most disturbing image of all is reserved for the film's climax. As the mud-caked cloak disappears from sight, the defiant voice of *The Spirit Of Dark And Lonely Water* echoes across the debris strewn-junkyard, issuing a bone-chilling promise that you instinctively know in the darkest corners of your soul, will be well and truly-kept and acted upon:

'I'll be back, back, back, back!'

BOOK TWO
The Last of the True Believers

'The eating of our own words is the greatest sacrifice that truth ever requires of us

Arthur Conan Doyle – 'The Parasite'

Is it just me, or is it getting really difficult of late to find the slightest trace of a genuine, open-minded approach to the study of the paranormal?

I could of course be somewhat mistaken, but it surely seems that in these 'post-cool, truth-seeker's times,' the prevailing attitude amongst the 'experts' in the field is one of - at best - barely concealed derision, and - at worst - outright scepticism, the latter viewpoint adopted by the likes of Blackmore, Wiseman and Persinger[**], frantically pedalling their Temporal Lobe Of The Brain Hypothesis for all their worth, (and gathering up a growing number of converts, by all accounts).

It sometimes seems as though things have gotten so bad during the early part of the 21st Century, that I have recently been plagued by a maddeningly recurring mental image: one that troubles me greatly.

It begins with a bunch of 'fair-minded Fortean investigators' gathered around an honestly befuddled eyewitness to some form of unexplained phenomena. Let's say, for the sake of argument, he's captured some top notch video footage of a daylight UFO. The assembled researchers are nodding sagely, thoughtfully stroking their chins in a professorial manner and taking copious notes whilst making 'umming' and 'aahing' noises in all the right places.

They then retire to the nearest available pub, minus the aforementioned witness, of course, to guffaw heartily over a few pints of 'Oak Wobbly Bob,' at the woeful ignorance of the average man in the street.

[**] Temporal Lobe Epilepsy (or TLE), has been proposed as being responsible for all kinds of paranormal experiences by various cognitive neuroscience researchers, including the aforementioned Michael Persinger. The theorists postulate that stimulating the temporal lobe electromagnetically can cause TLE and trigger hallucinations of UFOs, ghosts, religious manifestations, lake monsters and just about every type of Fortean phenomena imaginable (with the notable exception of fish falls, unexplained ice bombs and er, rabbit-killing goblins). The estimable Mr Persinger has even gone so far as to create what he calls, with typical 'modesty' a 'God Helmet.' This remarkable piece of machinery can, he insists, 'evoke altered states of consciousness through stimulation of the parietal and temporal lobes.' According to Wikipedia, 'Neurotheologians speculate that individuals with TLE, having a natural tendency to experience states of consciousness such as euphoria or samadhi, have functioned in human history as religious figures or shamans.

'Oh, puh-lease, how can he be so gullible...He's so obviously shot nothing but footage of a common or garden weather balloon, Peter!'

'Quite right, Sue. Still, at least the film will suffice as a perfectly fascinating example of the Psychosocial Hypothesis. You know, Mr Average's penchant for mistaking the perfectly mundane and attributing extraterrestrial properties to it at the drop of a hat.'

'Oh, super. I'll be able to hold over that article concerning 'Hypnagogic and Hypnopompic Visions and how they are the ONLY Viable Explanation for EVERY Type of Reported Paranormal experience, EVER!' until the next issue of out esteemed publication.'

'Shall we inform the tabloids now then, Adrian?'

'Oh, no, no no. Let them publish their stills and carry the story for a few days. Give good ol' Joe Public something to natter about over their Cornflakes. We'll look far more superior if we provide the real explanation after everybody else claims to be completely flummoxed.'

'Excellent. Fancy another pint, Michael?'

'No thanks. I'm just off to Sheffield to patronise some poor deluded soul who seems to believe his house is haunted by a poltergeist. What's that? Yeah, I know, noisy ghosts are so passé, Richard. Still, beats working for a living, eh?'

'Haw, haw, haw haw!'

A mite unfair?

Perhaps. But Lordy, even the 'good guys,' those redoubtable stalwarts who provided this particular writer's inspiration for my becoming fascinated with the subject and who, if truth be told, served to instil in me a sense of child-like wonder, even they seem to have grown increasingly incredulous as the years without definitive answers have rolled by.

And yes, I suppose that sceptical attitude is more than a little understandable. Extraordinary claims require extraordinary proof, and all that, and the admittedly perfectly logical, well-reasoned explanations proffered by the increasing number of sceptics in the field are difficult to argue against because, well, they make intrinsically coherent sense, But I would contend that we shouldn't immediately accept they are in possession of all of the answers and fall upon our knees to worship at the altar of the Great And Venerable Union Of Hard-Nosed, Ultra-Dismissive Sceptics.

To dispense altogether with that 'child-like sense of wonder.' Our questing instinct. Our objective, open-minded Fortean search for answers.

To do so, with nary a second thought, would surely have Old Charlie himself, spinning in his grave.

Never mind, though. If the estimable Mr Fort were unable to rest easy in his coffin, I'm sure Peter, Susan, Michael and the gang would be able to drum up a fashionably 'sensible' explanation for this seemingly supernatural Gyrating Body Phenomenon, probably just before last orders....

Am I right, guys?

*****

Despite the above, or perhaps in some perverse way because of it, I decided to go searching for the 'Last True Fortean Boys', on a mild, windless night in the early October of 2001, just as the leaves were beginning to turn and the air held that first faint tinge of wood-smoke.

I'd read about a group calling itself 'Para-Science,' in the pages of the local press back in the previous summer-that-never-was. The clipping in The Birkenhead News had served to grab my attention like a cat's eye marble shining amidst a pile of brown, decaying detritus of autumn.

Okay, so the contents of what amounted to little more than a ten-line advert were hardly encouraging. There were far too many patronising references to 'Ghostbusters,' 'recruitment drives,' and 'people being brave enough to attend,' for my liking.

Still and all, there was a phone number at the conclusion of the snippet, and there didn't seem to be anything to lose in my giving Steve, the leader of the group, a call.

I'm not at all sure what I expected: a fast-talking hustler, keen to sell me a genuine 'Multi-Dimensional Entity Detector,' or an Absolutely-Can't-Fail-Book-Of-Love-Spells. A religious fanatic, who was seeking new members to join his 'Aliens Are Here To Save The Planet' cult. Or the type of eternally sad bloke who stands on street corners, screaming to all and sundry that the Great Beast of Revelations was loose in the land.

By the time I'd finished speaking to him on the phone, however, I'd discovered, (much to my relief), that Steve was about as down to earth as it was possible to get.

He plainly knew his stuff, too.

He talked enthusiastically of allegedly haunted schools, houses, museums and pubs. Of a bunch of American tourists who were convinced that a mist that had descended (in an admittedly spooky fashion), over Marston Moor[*], was in fact the ghostly gathering of the fallen victims of that terrible battle[*] back in July, 1644. And, most interestingly of all, of people who had turned up at the group's meetings complaining that they had alien implants inserted in various parts of their anatomy. Or believed they had stumbled upon the underground entrance to Richard Shaver's Hollow Earth[**]. Or were possessed by the Devil. Or even a heady combination of all four!

The group's inaugural meeting was due be held that coming Monday at one of my favourite (if you'll forgive the pun), 'haunts'; The Civic Centre Library in Bebington Village, at 8pm.

And so, in the company of my then-trusty assistant editor, Jason Dignam, I arrived at the large, 1970s art-deco building just as the St Andrew's Church clock chimed the three-quarter hour.

There was a gang of young lads sitting on the wall that lined the library's car park. I caught sight of one of their faces, bathed in the sodium glare of a street light and I could have been mistaken, but he'd looked to me as though he were weighing us both up, maybe trying to decide whether either of us had anything worth robbing, and I mumbled as much to Jase. Whatever the seriousness of the threat level, however, we still had cause to pause by unspoken agreement at the entrance to the library.

I can't speak for my friend, but suddenly my stomach had begun roiling with that queasy mixture of excitement and anticipation and not a little fear; a powerful recipe familiar to anyone who's ever had to face the dangerously uncertain: the first date; a job interview; an appearance on stage.

Or a ride on the mother of all fairground ghost trains.

"Are you sure you really want to do this?"

---

[*] The Battle of Marston Moor, as well as being the title of a song by Alan Partridge's favourite band ELO, was fought on July 2nd, 1644, during the First English Civil War, of 1642-1646, The combined forces of the Scottish Covenanters and the English Parliamentarians defeated the Royalists at Long Marston, North Yorkshire.

[**] The Hollow Earth Theory was most notably, (in relatively recent times at least) propounded by Richard Shaver, who in the late 1940s, published a series of short stories in science fiction magazines, most famously, Amazing Stories, in which he claimed he had encountered an ancient civilisation that possessed fantastically advanced technology in vast caves beneath the Earth's hollow surface. These stories of a race called the Deros (an abbreviation of 'detrimental robots'), were published as works of fiction, but both Shaver, and the magazine's editor, Ray Palmer, maintained they were based on truth, that the Earth was indeed hollow, and that these evil-intentioned beings actually existed.

I asked, trying to keep the tremor of out of my voice.

> "Well, we've come this far, so we might as well,"

Jase replied, not unreasonably, though in truth he sounded about as enthusiastic as someone who was about to attend a gig by Pol Pot's Death March Orchestra.

> "Okay. But the first sight of anyone resembling David Koresh[**], at his most zealous-looking, and we're getting the hell out of there faster than a cheetah with a firework tied to its tail, right?"

> "Is right."

> "Right!"

We nodded in unison, the automatic doors slid open, and we stepped inside.

I suppose it's fair to say that I felt more than a little embarrassed when we had no option other than to ask the blue-uniformed security guard, stood at the front desk, exactly where the 'Para-Science Group Meeting' was being held.

It's not that I am in any way ashamed of my interest in strange phenomena, far from it. But I always sort of half-expect people, especially authority figures, to take the proverbial whenever I broach the subject. Quite frankly, they usually regard me as though I've just informed them I'm looking to spend a few hours spinning the discs in the Fun Pub at the very Gates of Hell.

This man didn't so much as smirk, however. Instead, he politely advised us to take the stairs up to the third floor.

Unfortunately for us, he neglected to mention which particular room the meeting was being held in.

Not that this appeared to present too much of a problem, at first. Although the landing contained a door-studded corridor, the very first room we came to was brightly-lit and filled with a crowd of old men and women, sitting around drinking coffee or studying the various display boards.

Jase and I exchanged a worried glance. I think I've already made it clear that neither of us had known quite what we were letting ourselves in for. But attending a seminar with an audience who, with all due respect, looked to be so uniformly ancient, it was hard to shake the notion that my friend and I had intruded upon a convention of spirits of the recently departed, had certainly not been high on any list of expectancies...

I shrugged my shoulders and repeated Jase's 'well, we've come this far,' speech of a little earlier. And anyway, it wasn't the audience we'd come to listen to, but a speaker, who, if he proved to be half as interesting as he'd sounded during our telephone conversation a couple of days earlier, would ensure our journey hadn't been entirely in vain.

So we dutifully took a couple of seats near the back of the room. In truth, they were the only ones available. All the others were either occupied or had coats draped across their backs. If nothing else, the meeting was certainly well-attended.

[**] Mr Koresh, a wannabe singer-guitarist, with a neat sideline in prophesying the end of the world and announcing to anyone who'd listen that he was the "son of God," took over leadership of the Branch Davidian religious sect in 1989. He allegedly began preaching polygamy and free sex, (for the cult leader, at least – hey, those are the perks of people fortunate enough to have been specially 'chosen by God' to save the faithful from the coming apocalypse), amongst his followers at Mount Carmel, in Waco, Texas, and was confident that he would become a martyr to his faith at some point. He was accurate in this prediction, at least....He met his death along with 75 of his 'disciples,' in a FBI shooting spree and subsequent raging inferno at the tragic climax of a 51-day siege by the authorities.

I'd barely taken out my trusty Loch Ness souvenir pen and begun scribbling in my notepad, when a bearded, late-middle-aged man, kitted out in what appeared to be a mountaineers outfit, strode purposefully into the room.

He was wearing a thick woolly jumper visible beneath a blood-red Berghaus coat, matching thermal trousers and a sturdy pair of climbing boots. His upper body was criss-crossed with large coils of rope and a pair of opaque goggles completely hid his eyes from view.

Oh, and he was clutching a lethal-looking ice-pick in one gloved hand.

I was so surprised by his unconventional appearance I dropped my favourite pen on the floor, and watched it roll unerringly towards this imposing figure as he continued to stride forward to the very edge of the circle of chairs. He crushed it beneath one of those Frankenstein Monster-style boots, as carelessly as if he'd trod on a particularly bothersome bug. I opened my mouth to say something, but then I remembered he was clutching an ice pick, and I slammed my mouth shut double-quick.

A hush descended then. The sort of eagerly, respectful silence you only ever hear in church or when you're in the presence of a truly great orator and you're mustard keen to catch every word.

The grey-haired, hook-nosed man sitting next to me even stopped slurping from his polystyrene cup as we waited for Mr Mountain Man to speak.

After making a great show of clearing his throat, he duly did.

> "I'd like to start, if I may, by thanking you all for coming,"

…he began.
> "It really gladdens my heart to see so many enthusiasts gathered here for what is assumed by many cynics to be a minority pursuit."

He paused for effect, and I was certain that if I could have seen his eyes at that moment they would have been shining with tears of pride.

> "Well, my dear friends, I would like to proclaim loudly, here and now, that you are living proof that the efforts of those who would pour scorn on our beliefs, are of no consequence and their criticism is as insubstantial as a fine mountain mist burned off by the morning sun. So thank you all, once again".

This last inspired a spontaneous round of applause and Jase and I felt compelled to join in. And why not? The speaker might be dressed in an unconventional manner, but I supposed it was merely an outfit to help him get into character for when he launched into tales of Yeti-hunting in the Himalayas, Almas-tracking across the Russian Steppes, or collecting evidence for the existence of The Big Grey Man from Ben MacDhui in Scotland, and he seemed genuinely sincere in his appreciation of being in the presence of so many 'kindred spirits.'

I began to feel sure we'd made the right decision in coming here. I fished in my pockets for a spare pen, and despite the fact that my Loch Ness memento was still busy leaking all over the linoleum, and I could only come up a plain ol' plastic Biro with a crack down the middle and a chewed-to-bits top, I still managed to conjure up a smile. I wanted to scribble down as much as I possibly could of what I assumed would be a hugely rewarding lecture.

As it turned out, I was right.

Though not here. Not in this room, with its assembly of attentive pensioners, and with Mr Mountain Man as the guest speaker.

Oh no….

It seems hard to believe looking back now, but when our lecturer opened up the talk proper by saying;

> "Right, ladies and gentlemen: The Geology of The Alps…Where to begin?"

I actually wrote down the five words that made up the title of the speech in my notepad, without their actual significance sinking in.

It wasn't until Jase suddenly nudged me, and whispered

> "What's so paranormal about 'Geology of The Alps, Lee?"

…that the words suddenly swam into focus and I began to have my first sneaking doubts that we might just be inadvertently sitting in on the wrong lecture.

These suspicions were confirmed when our speaker began launching into tales of the savage grandeur of the snow-capped peaks and the fabulously varied fauna and flora that thrived amidst these virtually inaccessible cloud-shrouded heights, and I'm sorry, but it was all I could do to keep from braying wild gales of laughter.

> "Juh..juh..juh……eeologee…Juheeologee of The Freakin ALPS!"

I snorted into my cupped hands, as I shook my head in sheer disbelief.

I shot a quick glance at Jase, and just as quickly looked away. His face had gone a beetroot shade of red, his cheeks were puffed out and tiny little fart-like sounds emerged from between the thin line of his lips. He put me in mind of an over-heated boiler getting ready to explode.

One thing was abundantly clear: We had to get the hell out of there before both of us succumbed to a gargantuan fit of the giggles and risked incurring the wrath of Mr Mountain Man and his deadly ice-pick. We could try explaining that we weren't to know that the Merseyside Geology Society held their meetings that same night as The Para-Science people. But something told me he wasn't the kind of guy who would appreciate an interruption from a couple of relatively young 'whipper-snappers' like us, and I silently thanked our lucky stars that we were sat near the back of the room and that our escape route appeared to be free of any obvious obstacles. Without daring to look at him again, I tapped Jase gently on the shoulder and pointed in the general direction of the door. He got the message, somehow managed to struggle to his feet, and bent half-over as though he were afflicted with a terminal case of bellyache, fumbled with the doorknob and threw himself over the threshold.

I wasn't far behind, although for one terrible moment I was sure I wasn't going to make it. I could clearly see and hear Jase cackling so hard, he'd collapsed in a boneless heap in the middle of the corridor.

> "Close the door behind you, sonny Jim,"

…someone croaked behind me.

> 'Yes Sir Edmund Hillary!'

I said, snapping a smart salute prior to pulling it to. Once safely on the other side, I slithered to the polished floor, emitting a laughter that was so intense, it was all but soundless.

A good while passed before I was able to gain some measure of self-control, (my stomach muscles ached like hell the following day, like I'd done about a hundred sit ups, or something), and it took Jase a little longer, despite the fact that he'd had a head start.

In the end, the chiming of the church clock, far-off and somehow dream-like, served to bring us both to our senses.

I hauled myself my feet.

And immediately felt my heart sink

It was 8:15. We'd very likely missed the start of that damned elusive paranormal meeting. We'd both might as well concede defeat and slope off home.

At that very moment, however, a young woman dressed entirely in black, and carrying a sheaf of official-looking papers, appeared at the top of the stairs. She glanced briefly in our direction, before hurrying past and knocking gently at a door five rooms along from Mr Mountain Man's Domain.

> "Maybe we're not too late...We can still..."

Jase and I said at the exact same time. Without another word, we raced up alongside the mysterious Woman in Black, just as a voice from within the room shouted;

> "Okay, you don't have to knock. We haven't even started yet."

> "Excuse me, is this the right place for the Para-Science meeting?"

I asked the lady as she pushed open the door, (hastily confirming that we weren't about to lurch into the Port Sunlight Flower Arranging Class or the *Throbbing Gristle* Industrial Grindcore Appreciation Society, by mistake).

> "Well, I should hope it is,"

...she said smiling radiantly.

> "I'm due to give a talk on the Ghosts of Ellesmere Port Boat Museum, tonight."

Reassured and not a little delighted, I afforded myself a silent cheer as, for the second time in less than half an hour, we stepped into a brightly-lit room filled with people, (this time, of various ages), yattering away merrily or nosing at the assembled display boards.

My eyes were immediately drawn to a newspaper headline posted up on one of the stands that proclaimed; 'Ghost Caught On Camera,' but before I could get close enough to check it out, a stocky, short-haired man wearing a UCLA sweatshirt (but with not the slightest trace of any mountaineering gear, praise the Lord!), called for everyone to please take their seats. Once again, the only chairs available were located right at the very back. Fortunately, that didn't make a whole pile of difference because the room was so small, wherever you sat you were no more than a few feet from the table behind which Steve (for it was he), and the Woman In Black were seated.

As the crowd fifty or so people settled down, Steve rose slowly, surveyed the audience, then pointed directly at me and said;
> "You must be Lee, right?"

I had no way of knowing it then, but the second big shock of the evening was just a mere sentence or two away....

But first, a quick word or two about 'coincidence.'

*****

One of my favourite ever horror movies is the 1957, black and white classic, *Night of the Demon*.

Based on M.R. James's wonderfully atmospheric short story 'Casting the Runes,' the plot revolves around a Black Magician named Julian Karswell, (played with an understated sense of menace by the excellent Niall MacGinnis), who places a curse upon the disbelieving paranormal investigator, (cripes, being closed-mindedly sceptical was fashionable, even back then!) John Holden (Dana Andrews).

The reason for this decidedly unsociable behaviour? Dr Holden threatens to expose Karswell's 'Devil Cult' for the bunch of charlatans he assumes them to be. In response, Karswell summons up an ancient Fire Demon to destroy Holden, unless he drops his investigation in three days. He places the curse by secreting a parchment containing runic symbols amongst Holden's papers, during a visit to the library at the British Museum.

And it's during this impromptu encounter that Karswell, in answer to the good Doctor's question as to how Karswell knew he would find him there at the library, states in a voice dripping with sarcasm:

> 'Oh, isn't it the scientist who tries to dismiss what he can't explain as coincidence? Let's call this coincidence.'

Okey dokey, let's call it that.

'COINCIDENCE.'

The neat little catch-all explanation for a random series of events that, if you didn't know better, seem to be supernaturally linked.

'COINCIDENCE.'

A compelling exhortation to clap your hands firmly over your ears when certain other, well-respected Fortean investigators, whisper darkly about the potential involvement of mischievous sprites and capricious cosmic jokers.

The acceptance of this logic should make me feel a whole lot better about what was soon to take place in that tiny, spartan conference room as a raw October wind suddenly sprang up and began buffeting around the windows.

But it doesn't, you know.

Not a bit.

*****

When Steve identified me at the beginning of the meeting, I didn't immediately feel any embarrassment. He explained that he'd only guessed my name because I was carrying a copy of the then current issue of Dead Of Night, and I'd posted him an old back issue, a few days earlier.

I had to pretend to ignore the people who had craned their necks to gape at me with puzzled expressions on their faces, but that was no big deal.

What certainly did have me squirming in my seat however, was what Steve said next:

> "So, how long have you had an amputee fetish then, Lee?"[*]

---

[*] Oh, dear, it's time for the inclusion of another of those maddeningly intrusive, not to mention blatantly self-indulgent footnotes, people....

Back in the summer of 1986, I experienced a true-life, tragi-comic romance with a gorgeous-looking girl during a week's long holiday in Presthaven Sands, North Wales.

So far, so Mills & Boon. The interesting thing here, though, was that I subsequently discovered, at the most inopportune moment imaginable, that the reason this young lady had been walking with a pronounced limp was not, as I had previously suspected, due to her being drunk, but because she had a prosthetic right leg.

Now, I'm sure I could have overlooked this unfortunate deformity if it hadn't have been for the disconcerting fact that she insisted on taking it off and placing it on the bedside table where it was illuminated in a shaft of moonlight. God knows it wasn't the poor girl's fault, and I honestly felt nothing but sympathy for her, but as a passion killer it was right up there with being forced to dance a cheek-to-jowl slowie with Jo Brand, whilst she bleated on endlessly about cakes.

When Steve, who had very obviously read the confessional piece, made reference to the subject in front of a room full of people, none of whom I'd ever met.. Well, that was pretty bad.

But worse was to follow.

"I have to say,"

Steve said, smiling strangely,

"I can particularly relate to your story."

"Why?"

I asked.

"Have you ever been to North Wales for a spot of holiday romance?"

"Er, not recently, no. My affinity goes a lot deeper than that."

…he replied.

"Aye, aye. You haven't got off with a girl with one leg missing, have yer?"

I said grinning a grin that felt like it had been ironed on. I'd suddenly been aware that I was standing on the brink of some horrible revelation that I really didn't want to have to face.

"Not quite."

He paused, as if considering whether or not he should go on. Then, with a shrug of the shoulders, he said,

"Take a look under the table, Lee".

I looked. And did a double-take, as Steve hitched up the left leg of his jeans to reveal …a shiny metal artificial limb.

I could only state in disbelief, and for a single, endless moment, no-one spoke, and in truth, there didn't really seem like there was a whole lot to say. All I can remember thinking is, what were the odds stacked against this particular set of circumstances?

- My writing 'The Girl with the False Leg' story in the first place (and believe me, it was not an easy decision to set about penning that article).
- Spotting the tiny Para-Science article, tucked away, so you'd hardly notice, in the pages of the local press.
- Sending Steve that particular edition of my magazine when any other back issue, or even the current issue, would have sufficed.
- And Steve being a right-legged amputee.

It was difficult to shake the notion that whole thing had somehow been scripted, though of course, according to accepted scientific reasoning, such things simply cannot be. I was therefore left with no other option than to stare wide-eyed at the complex mechanics of Steve's artificial leg whilst mentally quoting the words of Julian Karswell:

'Isn't it the scientist who tries to dismiss what he can't explain as coincidence…
Let's call this coincidence.'

*****

If Steve had been in any way embarrassed by my reaction to his 'revelation,' to his credit, he never showed it.

Instead, the formalities dispensed with, he immediately launched into a brief description of what ParaScience were all about.

"We are a non-profit-making organisation dedicated to investigating, at first hand, if at all possible, any form of paranormal phenomena,"

…he began.

"We try and adopt scientific methods, hence the computers and various gadgetry you see placed on the table before you.

Now, although we take the subject very seriously, we've found it helps if you're equipped with a very strong sense of humour, on occasion. When we're conducting an investigation of a reputedly haunted site, the vast majority of our time is spent sitting very quiet and very still in total darkness with nothing much to occupy your mind. It's pretty near total sensory deprivation during the forty minutes spells - or "vigils", as we prefer to call them - that take place throughout the night, so let nobody be under any illusions, this definitely is not The X Files.

Neither is it remotely glamorous or thrill-a-minute Hollywood-style entertainment. More often than not, it's boring, backside-numbing, mind-deadening work, and it takes a special kind of person to display that level of dedication. Anyone who doesn't think they can hack it shouldn't bother signing up for the on-site fieldwork. I'm not trying to put anyone off, though. On the contrary, the whole point of us arranging this meeting was to, quite frankly recruit as many fresh victims... Ooops, sorry, I do of course mean new members, as possible. I just want you all to be aware of the downside of investigating haunted houses, schools, factories or whatever."

Steve paused for breath, an expression of wry amusement on his face as though he were thinking:

'Right, that just about rounds off my Negative Aspects speech. Now let's see how many of the prospective victims...Ooops, sorry, **members,** get up and leave.'

Everyone remained seated, however.

And, I'm not sure, but I could have sworn Steve had looked ever-so slightly disappointed. Like the Ghost Train owner surrounded by a bunch of bickering kids, loudly declaring that they hadn't been the slightest bit scared by his ride.

"Okay,"

…he cleared his throat.

"Rather than have you listen to me waffle on endlessly, I'm going to hand you over to one of my esteemed colleagues, who'll recount the details of one our exclusive case histories ..."

So saying, that Mysterious Woman in Black (whose name was disclosed to us, but sad to say, I failed to record it), took the chair, so to speak, and began narrating the following....

"One of the most fascinating cases I've come across during my five years with ParaScience, concerns the apparent sighting of a terrifying entity known as a Doppelganger. For those amongst you who are unfamiliar with the term, Doppelganger is a German word, and roughly translated, it means 'Double-Goer,' a person's exact double, or in other words the apparition of a person who's still very much alive. The reason many people fear encountering a Doppelganger is because they are almost universally regarded as being harbingers of ill fortune and sometimes foretell the death of those unlucky enough to set eyes on them.

What I want to tell you about took place last summer, and concerned a couple named Samantha and Simon, who live in a place called Hopwood in Lancashire.

At the time I'm talking about they had been together for about four years. This is a very important point, because I need to stress they were pretty well acquainted, as you might imagine, with each other's facial features, and were hardly likely to mistake either person as being someone else who merely looked like them...if that makes any kind of sense.

Anyway, Sam told me that sometime between 9:30 and 10pm, during late August, I think it was, Sam's brother, Paul, and a friend of his were stood on the roadside outside the couple's house trying, with a deplorable lack of expertise, to start up Paul's battered old Cortina so that they could drive back to their home town of Liverpool. They had been to visit Sam and her fella, and were huddled over the exposed engine throwing in a series of unvaryingly useless suggestions. Meanwhile, Simon's Capri was parked on the driveway of a place called The Old Vicar's House, a building owned by Paul's father that had acquired a somewhat sinister reputation amongst the local populace, who claimed all kinds of odd occurrences had taken place on and near the premises.

Paul was feeling strange at the time, overcome with an unexplained sense of melancholy and as he'd never been particularly comfortable in the Old Vicar's house, situated in the grounds of Hopwood Hall College, he was anxious to get back on the M62 and head on back to Merseyside.

Samantha, who knows as much about as the inner workings of cars as she knows about back-engineered, alien technology, decided to keep well clear and watch the proceedings from a safe distance.

Simon had just walked past her to go and get something from inside the lounge of the house, and that's when Samantha says the 'strange thing happened.'

"I wasn't quite sure what I was looking at first," she told me. "My attention had wandered for a minute or two, then I suddenly found myself thinking, "that's funny, why is Simon sitting in the back of his own car?" In a moment, my reasoning had returned, when I realised that he simply couldn't be, because he had just passed me and gone inside the house. Whoever or whatever the figure was, it undeniably looked liked Simon – but it was somehow subtly different. It reminded me of one of the Pod People in Jack Finney's Invasion of the Bodysnatchers, what with the blank, vacant expression on its face, and the fact the figure just sat there completely motionless, staring straight ahead as though in a trance, or was waiting for some signal to activate its movements.

I don't know how long it was before I finally found my voice, but when I eventually did, all I could do was scream at the top of my lungs for Simon – that's the real one, I should point out, not the phantom imposter sitting there, calm as you like in the back seat.

'I could see Sam was really distressed about something,' Simon later commented. 'She was almost hysterical as I ran from the lounge to see what was up. She couldn't do anything other than point over at the Capri, and it was only then that I saw it, too. I

> know it sounds quite lily-livered now, but I was immediately struck with a feeling of abject terror, and simply couldn't bring myself to approach the car, either. We took Samantha inside to calm her down, although, I'm not ashamed to say, I wasn't too far behind in the scared-out-of-my-wits stakes. When we finally summoned the courage to go and look again, which to be honest, was a good ten minutes or so, the figure had disappeared.
>
> The following day I told my mum what had happened, and contrary to my expectations, she didn't seem to be overly surprised. Apparently, the evening before the incident she and my sister Michelle had both dreamed identical dreams that I was dying, which, as you can imagine, served to cheer me up no end...."

That part of the meeting over, Steve stood up to declare it was high time for a coffee break, and everyone duly shuffled into the corridor to insert their coins into the vending machine.

I managed to catch up with Steve, intending initially, to apologise for any offence I might have inadvertently caused him by writing and sending him that (fast approaching legendary status), 'amputee' article.

Much to my relief, he merely shrugged his shoulders and told me that he'd thoroughly enjoyed reading the piece and thought my magazine reminded him of *Fortean Times*, back during its pre-hit-the big-time days of the 1970s and 80s, (high praise, indeed!)

We then got talking about many things: the group's fruitless search for Alien Big Cats in the pitch-black depths of a stretch of local woodland, which resulted in nothing more than a farcical series of injuries suffered as a result of various group members colliding with each other in the near impenetrable darkness.

Of clandestine visits to military installations where, according to the more conspiracy-minded of ufologists, top secret experiments were being conducted involving secret meetings with high-ranking officers and EBE's (Extra Biological Entities), back-engineering technology courtesy of recovered alien spacecraft and sinister deals aimed at protecting the Earth from imminent invasion by the planet-conquering Reptoids.

There's hidden floors within that installation, where the top brass hobnob with the friendly aliens on a regular basis one particular ufologist informed Steve, in all seriousness.

When the Group went round to the facility to see what they could find for themselves, fully expecting to be refused admission, they were in fact shown around the entire complex without any restrictions whatsoever. Of course, if you're a full-blown conspiracy theorist, no amount of apparent candour displayed by the authorities is going to persuade you that they've really got nothing sinister to hide by conducting something as innocuous as a guided tour.

Steve also told us of trips to reputedly haunted pubs, only to find, when they arrived at the location, the landlord sent them packing like they were a bunch of religious fundamentalists on a mission to convert the misbegotten sinners of this world (and make a big fat pile of cash in the bargain).

Perhaps saddest of all, however, was the case of an old woman who had contacted the Group as she believed her house was haunted by a Poltergeist that delighted in hiding her money. When the team arrived, and duly began their investigations, they soon discovered the true origin of this 'cash-stealing spirit':

> "It was what we 'experts' refer to in the trade as a 'Scumbag Ghost,' "

Steve announced, a grimace of distaste, like he'd just trodden in something squishy and stomach-churningly foul, clouding his features.

> "In other words, it was an all-too human culprit – the sort who delights in breaking into pensioners' homes and stealing their most valued and sentimental belongings."

He heaved a world-weary sigh and shook his head.

> "The terrible thing was, she was absolutely convinced that a ghost must be responsible for the disappearance of her possessions because she simply refused to accept that anyone would stoop so low as to break into her home. She'd been born and raised in an earlier, more innocent age.
>
> You know, it often seems easier to believe in the existence of angels, ghosts and Ufonauts, than the rose-tinted reminiscences of our grandparents, but they swear there really was a time when you could leave your front door unlocked at night, and trust your neighbours implicitly."

There were about a trillion and one other things that we wanted to discuss, but it was another unfortunate case of so many questions, so swift time's flight...

The adjournment was over. It was time to head back to the conference room.

To be perfectly honest, the second part of the meeting was something of an anti-climax. Several people seemed to have cried off (so perhaps Steve's attempt at culling the audience had been fairly successful, after all), and most of the final hour was taken up with viewing the group's admittedly impressive website on the bank of computers. There was just time however to pick up a couple of press releases featuring further investigations at various places throughout Merseyside. It was all potentially fascinating stuff, but with little of substance to report, (well, the investigations hadn't even started at any of these sites, so the team could do little aside from provide the technical details of the various types of electronic equipment they would be utilising during their proposed vigils).

And so, clutching our ParaScience information packs, we stepped out into the October chill, with another classic quote from *Night of The Demon*'s Julian Karswell, aimed at the serried ranks of sceptics, running around my head:

> *'Where does imagination end and reality begin?*
> *What is this twilight that you profess to know so much about?'*

Hopefully, the search for some definitive answers to those questions was about to begin....

*****

But just before we embark upon our epic journey into the unknown, can I crave your indulgence for just a little while longer while, (to use classic salesman terminology), I issue the briefest caveat emptor?

The following stories are either first-hand accounts related to the author by witnesses who I consider to be essentially honest and completely trustworthy. Or, they are admittedly slightly more dubious, second-hand reports provided to the author by correspondents in response to a request for personal encounters with, for want of a better term, paranormal phenomena.

I accept that many serious-minded Forteans may experience more than a little difficulty in trying to swallow some of the more 'colourful' details contained within this collection of weird tales, true-life 'supernatural' occurrences, urban legends, and local folklore.

I appreciate, too, that I face being arrested by the serried ranks of Authenticity Police, for my use of artistic licence in the re-telling of some of these stories. The truth is though, it was never my intention to promote this book as being some sort of intensely academic, pseudo-scientific treatise on the reality or otherwise of the supernatural. There are plenty of those lining the bookshelves of 'serious-minded' researchers, already. No. I wrote it because there are, it seems to me, far too few publications that attempt to approach the subject with an open-minded sense of wonder, a willingness to suspend disbelief and put aside one's innate scepticism and attitude of refusal to give even the slightest degree of credence to anything that doesn't fit into the accepted order of things for at least as long as it takes to read the contents of this volume....

If I've failed in this entreaty, it is, I would contend, every bit as depressing a vista as catching Peter Pan and the rest of The Lost Boys checking in the mirror for the appearance of crow's feet.

And, not to labour the point or anything, but I am more aware that telling blatant lies, even apparently harmless white ones, can have unforeseen consequences, as the true-life following tale helps to illustrate…

THE LYING GAME

Okay, let's get one thing clear at the outset.

We all of us resort to telling lies at some point in our lives.

You'd be, well, lying, I guess, if you even tried to claim otherwise.

Sometimes these patent untruths, be they lies of the little white variety or the sort of out and out, one hundred per cent, porkies that would make Walter Mitty or Tony Blair turn a deep shade of beetroot red, can actually be good things; telling your best mate that he's so much better off without the woman who's dumped him seeing as how she was an ugly old boiler, with zilch personality and all the fashion sense of a redundant scarecrow, when you know very well that said girl is a total babe, whose ineffable beauty turns heads wherever she goes. Smiling your biggest shit-eating grin when and grunting…

    "Yummy, that was totally deeelicious!"

…when you've manfully struggled through the Sunday roast your beloved has spent a couple of hours cooking, despite the fact that the meal actually has all the gastronomic allure of a rancid pair of sweaty old socks. Or, as I have often had to do in my former capacity as a criminal law legal advisor, reassure a client's heartbroken mother who's just witnessed their son or daughter receive a lengthy custodial sentence, that all of the awful rumours she may have heard concerning the prison regimes at Walton or Styal were nothing more than gross exaggerations.

At other times, of course, lies, well-intentioned or otherwise, can make an already bad situation a thousand times worse.

From a personal perspective, one of the best (or worst, depending on your point of view) examples, in fairly recent times at least, concerns my standing at RMNJ Solicitor's photocopier late one October afternoon.

I think I'd been running off a set of legal depositions for some multi-million pound fraud case (although, if the truth be told, I could just as easily have been copying the black and white pictures from FHM's 'Top 100 Most Beautiful Women'), with one eye on the machine to make sure it was feeding the sheets correctly and the other on the wall clock, trying vainly to wish away the final half hour or so that remained of the working day. I was so preoccupied, that I didn't notice the gorgeous work-experience girl approach the machine until she tapped me on the shoulder and asked me, in a voice so husky it should have been pulling a sleigh,

> "Excuse me, have you nearly finished?"

At that precise moment, two things happened in quick succession. First, I opened my mouth to speak, but found, to my consternation that, faced with such a heavenly vision of jaw-dropping beauty, I'd seemingly forgotten every word in the English language. All that emerged was an unintelligible sort of grunt, which I suppose might have made some kind of sense if by some far-fetched miracle, Ms Work-Experience had been especially fluent in the long-forgotten dialect of pre-Neolithic Apeman.

And second, the horribly embarrassed silence that had descended in the wake of this girl's appearance was suddenly broken by the unmistakable sound of a terminal paper jam.

Normally, I would have cursed loudly at such an annoying malfunction, but on this occasion, I silently gave thanks to the Capricious Gods of Photocopiers that they'd chosen that precise moment to help me out.

Snapped out of my awestruck trance, I found I was now able to say something vaguely comprehensible, even if it proved to be so utterly banal, the cheesiest game show host on the planet would likely balk at its sheer…Well, banality.

> "Paper jam,"

I said, pointing unnecessarily at the banks of flashing lights that indicated the points at which various sheets of paper were busy entangling themselves amidst the complicated series of cogs and gears that made up the hub of the infernal machine.

> "Bloody typical, eh? Ah, well you know me and photocopiers!"

Yeah. I agree with you entirely.

It was a hell of a dumb, throwaway type of thing to say.

And you'll no doubt be glad to learn it provoked a suitably caustic response from Ms Work Experience.

> "No,"

…she said dismissively.

> "I don't know you or the photocopier. But just out of interest, are you saying photocopiers have a habit of breaking down whenever you're around?"

> "Yeah,"

I lied (so far as I could remember, I hadn't had any more problems with the damn things than anyone else).

> "Mad innit?"

She looked at me then, as if truly seeing me for the first time, and then grinned humourlessly.

> "Well, that's strange,"

…she said.

> "Because even if I don't actually know you, I've seen you working on the photocopier lots of times, and I've never seen it break down once."

This was entirely true, and I should have simply agreed with her, there and then. For some unfathomable reason, however, I felt compelled to lie still further.

> "Oh, I don't mean this one, so much. But you wanna see what I'm like with the one I've got at home. Honest to God, I only have to look at it in the wrong way, and it's either churning up paper at an Amazonian Rainforest-threatening rate, or spilling ink in big black, apocalyptic floods."

I shook my head wearily as though even thinking about that terminally fucked up piece of machinery was almost too much to bear.

> "I mean, it really is fiddly beyond all hitherto ideas of fiddliness."

Now, as I'm, sure as you've already guessed, I've no more personally owned a photocopier, hopelessly unreliable or otherwise, than I've been in possession of a high-wire walking hippopotamus or a full-size replica of a camouflaged Challenger Tank. But I'd somehow gotten myself into one of those hideous situations where one lie leads inexorably to another, and I couldn't have stopped myself fibbing at that juncture anymore than I could have stopped the leaves from falling in the autumn.

I'm not at all sure what I expected Ms Work Experience to say in response. I suppose I was hoping she would shrug her shoulders and simply walk away. Instead, she regarded me thoughtfully for a moment and then a mischievous smile slowly spread across her face.

> "Oh, that's great!"

…she said.

> "I wonder perhaps if you could do me a small favour, then?"

> "Yeah,"

I replied, as though in a dream.

> "Just name it."

> "Well, the thing is,"

…she said, shamelessly fluttering her thick, black lashes.

> "I've got a stack of copying I need doing for my college course, and I was going to see if Mr Nicholas (the head partner of the New Ferry branch of the firm), would allow me to copy some of it here. But I didn't like to ask. I mean, he might think I'm being a bit cheeky, seeing as how I'm only here for a little while.
>
> And so I was wondering…"

> "You were wondering whether I could do some for you,"

I interjected.

> "Yeah. No problem. Just bring in whatever it is you need copying, and I'll do it for you el lickety splitto!'

> "Thanks very much,"

...she smiled again, and this time it was a genuine smile that lit up her face like the sun emerging from between a gap in the clouds.

>"I'll bring it in tomorrow, then."

>"Great stuff,"

I said giving her a thumbs up gesture just to show how truly great it really was, and she walked away leaving me standing there silently praying that she would forget all about this bizarre little conversation.

But she didn't, of course. Despite the fact that I spent most of the following day trying my best to avoid her, and actually succeeded, right up to the final seconds before five when I was ambushed by Ms Work Experience just as I was sneaking to the exit with my head down and my face all but obscured by a Liverpool scarf.

>"Alright, mate,"

...she said, tapping me on the shoulder and almost causing me to scream as I reached for the handle to the front door.

>"Haven't forgotten to do these for me, have you?"

I turned around and saw she was clutching a thick stack of paper in her gloved hands.

>"I'd be made up if you could copy this lot. When you get the chance, like. There's no big rush."

She was smiling that damned calm-a-werewolf-out-of-its-bestial-rampage-type smile and fluttering her lashes like a speed-addled Tiny Tears doll, and once again, I fell prey to her considerable charms.

>"Okey dokey, no problem whatsoever,"

I assured her, taking the collection of articles and samples of artwork from her with all the enthusiasm I could muster.

>"I'll do them tonight."

>"Oh, if you could, I'd be ever so grateful,"

...she said, placing her hand on my arm and letting it linger there for a few heavenly seconds. She inclined her face towards mine, and I could smell the sweetness of her breath and for one crazy moment, I felt sure she was going to kiss me. But instead, she simply whispered in my ear,

>"I knew you wouldn't let me down,"

...and turned and walked away with a spring in her step leaving me standing there feeling like I'd been run over by an out of control steamroller....

*****

Looking back now, I suppose I should have just told Ms Work-Experience the following day that upon being confronted with the eighty sheets of A4 paper she'd handed me, (I'd counted them on the way home with the grim fatalism of a chronic drunk counting off his double shots as he careers headlong down the road to oblivion), my photocopier had immediately reverted to type and had promptly conked out the second I placed the first piece of paper on the platen glass.

I should have. After all, the daft assertion that I was in possession of a dodgy photocopier was precisely what had gotten me into this situation in the first place.

But of course, that would mean disappointing a beautiful looking girl, looking like a complete pleb in front of said beautiful girl and most probably never having said beautiful-looking girl smile and flutter her eyelashes at me ever again.

And so I did the only thing I reasonably could do in the circumstances: I walked home, raided my small change money jar, dug out £40 worth of five and ten pence pieces and headed for the Civic Centre Library's Reference Section, and its pay-as-you-go photocopier.

*****

The following morning I walked to work somewhat lighter in the pocket, but filled with the deep sense of satisfaction that comes from having helped someone out when they were so obviously relying upon you.

The fact that the recipient of the favour happened to be blessed with looks that had me drifting towards the stratosphere in a balloon of romantic marvellousness, had nothing to do with it, of course.

I handed over the copied coursework during our late afternoon break and I was rewarded with a hug that was as overwhelming as it was surprising, and I quickly found myself promising I would gladly copy anything for her, anytime.
"Well, that's handy,"

…she said reaching into the large Burberry bag she always seemed to be carrying around with her, and pulling out another large sheaf of paper.

"I was hoping you might be able to copy this for me, as well. It's the rest of my course work. There's about 200 pages here."

I looked at her to see if she was joking, but I felt my stomach lurch as I saw quite clearly she was deadly serious.

Not only that but she was busy weaving her trance-inducing spell, and I could no more have resisted the sweet musical sound of her voice than I could have closed my ears to the deadly seductive song of the Siren….

"And maybe when you've got that little lot sorted, you could run off my best mate, Katie's, art college portfolio, and then after that there's me dad's work's newsletter needs doing, it comes out once a week, so you might have a few late nights on your hands, but I'm sure you can cope. Oh, and you simply must do the entire contents of me Nan's photo albums, there's about twenty volumes in total, all the pictures are black and white, so don't worry, they'll come out okay, and I could do with several copies of me other best mate, Gemma's, massive CD album collection list, and me big stack of love letters I want to keep together in a series of ring binders, oh, and I almost forgot, the series of articles I wrote for my school magazine, and then there's the extremely important pages of that book on White Magic…."

I learned two of life's harshest lessons that afternoon in late October, as the air turned blade-sharp and the first of the season's frosts glittered like a false promise in the sunlight's dying rays.

One: Don't ever tell an innocuous-seeming lie to try and impress a girl.

And two: If you really must tell an innocuous-seeming lie to try and impress a girl, make sure you've got a whole bunch of five and ten pence pieces for the local library's photocopier.

Chances are you're gonna need em!

THE PLACE WHERE EVIL DWELLS

>'Atmosphere, plus a generous helping of fear, can make your brain project the image it expects to see. Now, I am going to take this bloodcurdling conjecture one stage further. Is it not possible that one or more people can create a "fear ghost" that becomes part of the surroundings and is later seen by someone who is – at first – not particularly frightened?'
>
>'Imagine, you may be on the receiving end of someone else's fear.'
>
>R Chetwynd Hayes – From his Introduction to
>The 18th Fontana Book of Ghost Stories

One of the more sinister legends amidst the rich tapestry of ghostly lore that permeates the British Isles (once dubbed by some paranormal 'expert' as 'the most haunted country on Earth'), is that of the 'discarnate evil entity' that is said to either physically push or, at the very least, actively encourage people to leap to their deaths from the roofs of very high buildings, or the tops of steep, sheer-faced cliffs.

Thankfully, this type of report is relatively infrequent when compared with say, the many 'traditional' accounts of spectral ladies frequently seen wandering the winding, deserted corridors after midnight, wringing their hands in despair over some real or imagined crime. Or the restless spirit of a young child who's doomed to inhabit the twilight zone between life and death because it hasn't yet come to terms with the fact that it should have long since passed on to that quasi-mythical 'higher plane of existence.'

But just because stories of wholly malevolent supernatural entities are rare, and don't fall within the cosy, rose-tinted world view of many spiritualists and paranormal 'experts' - namely that ghosts are incapable of inflicting serious physical pain on any living human being - I would contend that it does not follow we should simply choose to ignore these accounts or dismiss them as being nought but the morbid fantasies of people who've watched Poltergeist, or The Legend Of Hell House, one time too many.

The motif of the inherently evil spirit that appears to delight in the destruction of its intended victim is one that is firmly rooted in folklore both ancient and modern….

And who but the most insensitive amongst us can honestly say that they have never awoken in the wee hours before dawn in the sweaty, shaking aftermath of a bad dream, feeling suddenly sure, irrationally certain, that there is some purely evil presence sharing the bedroom with them?

Something standing in the dark with a long white face that's not quite human.

It might be a demented mime artist, with a couple of dead-man's pennies covering its eyes and a blood-red gash for a mouth.

It might be a formless, capering horror that sits and gibbers on the edge of your bed.

Or it might be a black-cowled monk that creeps silently up to your bedside and whispers seductively in your ear about how easy it would be to walk on over to the window, gaze longingly at the distant drop below, and clamber onto the ledge to take a jump…..

*****

Listen….

Back in the winter of 1976, my dad was working as a foreman for the British Leather Company, right next door to the vast, sprawling complex of Cammell Laird's shipyard in the very heart of Birkenhead.

The factory, along with the hundreds of people who laboured and sweated long hours there, has long since stood redundant. In fact, the bulk of what was known amongst the workforce as 'The Tan Yard,' was completely gutted by an intense fire several years ago. Nothing but an empty shell remains now. A secret place of charred timbers and collapsed floors. And even those final crumbling remnants are facing complete demolition. Judging from the way the ex-employees, my father amongst them, were treated by the firm that ran the place during its declining years in the early 1980s, I guess it's fair to say that no-one paused to shed any tears for its inglorious passing.

Unless they were the tears born of bitter satisfaction.

I only went there on one occasion, when I was barely a week shy of becoming a fully-fledged teenager, and it's no exaggeration to say, once was definitely more than enough.

Three days before my thirteenth birthday, my Dad had promised to take me to the match as a special birthday treat. Liverpool were at home to Ipswich Town, he had two tickets for The Kop, and all I had to do was accompany him to 'The Tan Yard' early that Saturday whilst he worked the morning shift.

> "It makes more sense than me having to come back home to get you,"

…he'd told me the night before.

> "And besides, it's only gonna be for a couple of hours. You can pack some sarnies and bring along one of them books you've always got your head buried in. The time will fly by, you'll see."

I remember telling him I was so excited about going the match, I would have quite happily ran all the way to hell and back if he'd have asked me.

And as things turned out, and at the risk of sounding overly melodramatic, perhaps that wasn't so very far from the truth.

*****

When the artist and poet William Blake, wrote of England's 'dark, Satanic mills,' it's easy to believe he'd composed that wonderfully evocative phrase after having set eyes on The Tan Yard and its relentlessly grim environs, if not in reality, then in one of his more vividly recalled nightmares.

I remember as my Dad and I walked through the front gates, with the dawn barely touching the sky and my eyelids still gummy from lack of sleep, I was almost overwhelmed by a desperate kind of sadness. Part of it stemmed from my stepping over the threshold and being confronted with a less-than-cheery vista: two rows of high-roofed buildings, their walls caked with a filth that gleamed wetly in the blinding glare of an arc lamp, stretched ahead for as far as the eye could see. As regular work stations went, they left a lot to be desired, being little more than glorified cattle sheds. And maybe that was entirely appropriate because 'British Leather' were in the business of refining cattle hides for commercial use. From within came the incessant hammering of heavy machinery that shook the very earth beneath my feet, and jets of steam hissed from the underground vents in great billowing clouds.

So yeah, part of it was that. But mostly I think, it was the dreadful realisation, hidden from me until that moment, that my Dad, who I looked up to with the reverence usually afforded to a fictional super-hero, had to spend so much of his precious time here. This awful place was where he worked five, sometimes, six days week, 50-odd weeks of the year. I honestly couldn't see how he could stand it. Being compelled to breathe in lungfuls of that foul-smelling air, breaking his back for a boss he probably never set eyes on, and where the only relief from the leaden monotony was the pitifully short ten-minute tea-break and the quick half hour pint in The Castle at dinnertime, and the chance to swap the same old jokes with the same old faces over a crumpled copy of The Daily Mirror, and a quick drag on a shabbily assembled rollie.[**]

The question weighed heavily on my mind as my Dad ushered me into the nearest of the buildings, and I almost went and asked him his opinion out loud, but just then, several of his workmates sidled up and he made a big show of introducing me to them and I had to stand there with a big stupid grin on my face, pummelling their grimy hands until it felt like my right shoulder would come away at the socket.

And after I'd made the acquaintance of just about every single member of staff on the morning shift, the moment had gone. Afterwards, it had felt a little too imprudent to ask, especially when my Dad showed me, with no small measure of pride, his foreman's desk, which I saw contained several family photographs, (including one of me taken the previous summer, standing on the edge of a makeshift football pitch at Butlin's Holiday Camp, with a seven-a-side tournament winner's medal dangling from my skinny neck). I noticed, too, that the wall directly behind the battered, graffiti-strewn desk was covered with yet more pictures, both snapshots and a large collection of drawings that my younger brothers and sister and I had produced during art class at school. The sight of those instantly familiar, downright homely images was enough to bring the first genuine smile to my face since I'd set foot in 'The Tan Yard.'

It was only later, lying in my bed that night replaying the day's events over in my mind that a terrible thought crossed my mind: what if the main motivation for my Dad keeping that varied assortment of photographs and sketches close to his work desk was due to the fact that he'd found spending more than a few short hours in that damnable place, where no blade of sunlight pierced the all-pervading gloom, you simply had to have those images within constant eyeshot simply to remind you of the reason you were labouring here in the first place? What if, being forcibly shut up all day within those dreary, soul-destroying surroundings, it would be all too easy to forget many things, even the faces of those you loved unconditionally, and who loved you right back…?

*****

By mid-morning, having fortified myself with a steaming mug of coffee and the tuna sandwiches my mum had thoughtfully packed in a plastic lunch box for me, my spirits had risen sufficiently for me to put down my dog-eared copy of *The Hobbit*, and whilst my father was stood talking to some workmate whose name had already slipped my mind, I wandered off to explore the rest of the site.

[**] hand-rolled cigarette.

Of course, I hadn't expected to find anything remotely interesting. I mean, when you've seen one dingy factory floor you've seen them all. Twenty minutes or so of poking my nose into those dark crannies of undiluted misery was more than enough to quell any initial enthusiasm, and I was about to return to my Dad's office when my attention was suddenly drawn to the sound of raised voices at the entrance to a large warehouse situated right at the end of what I'd already mentally coined Skid Row.

Curiosity renewed, I wandered over to where two men were arguing fiercely about whose turn it was to 'run the hides through Big Bertha,' whatever the hell that meant. Both parties seemed equally determined not to back down and it was clear there was a likely to be a fight if someone didn't intervene pretty soon. That someone wasn't going to be me, though. With their mean-looking, scrunched up faces criss-crossed with a variety of scars, they looked for all the world like extras from some 1950s gangster movie, who'd swapped their smart black designer suits for a pair of multi-stained overalls. Trying to appear as inconspicuous as possible, I'd hunched my shoulders and slunk right past them whilst they were busy turning the cold air blue with a string of expletives.

I quickly dodged into yet another of those non-descript buildings. A sign above the half-open door announced that I was setting foot into The Salt House. That didn't make an awful lot of sense to me, either. Not at first. The room appeared to be empty save for several stacks of soaking cow hides and a huge circular vat with a metal outer rim and a wooden wheel that revolved very slowly like the spokes of some great paddle steamer. There was a steel ladder running up one side that led on to a thin platform, and in a moment, I was scrambling up those rungs, eager for a closer look. I was completely awe-struck by the impressive size of the machine, its sheer magnitude. It nearly touched the ceiling, which must have been forty feet high at least, and the sound of that immensely powerful wheel rumbling as it turned like summer thunder, bade me pause half-way, transfixed, remembering one late July afternoon when I was a young child...

*****

...It was my grandfather's 75th birthday party, and my family's friends and relations were hastily packing away the charred remnants of a barbecue as the storm that had been bubbling up since mid-morning finally threatened to break. The wind had dropped. The humidity level had grown to levels that were all but unbearable, and the light had taken on a surreal cast and you could smell the ozone on the air. The first crack of thunder had been so ear-jarringly loud, that everyone, my parents included, had instinctively ducked, and I'd promptly burst into tears, thinking with a child's logic, that if the adults were so obviously terrified, maybe something truly awful was about to happen; like maybe the very sky itself was going to cave in and fall upon us.

My black mood hadn't been helped any by the mad dash rush for the shelter of the house, and as the thunder roared and the lightning cracked and the rain pelted the windows with an unrelenting fury, I went into virtual hysterics. No-one could calm me. Not my parents. Not my aunts and uncles. Not even my best friend, Stevie Gee, who'd been invited at my request.

Ordinarily, my screaming fit would have been the cue for my mum and dad to have called a taxi and shunted me the hell out of there to save any further embarrassment, but on this occasion it must have been pretty obvious to them that my fear was genuine and that I wasn't just selfishly seeking attention.

And so, the booming thunder and I continued our unofficial; Let's See Who Can Hit The Loudest Decibel Competition, (popular opinion later had it down as an honourable draw), until eventually, my Grandad took me to one side and sat me down on his bony old knee. He'd reached out both arms in an effort to keep me from squirming away before regarding me with an expression of such overwhelming kindness and understanding that I'd ceased struggling immediately.

'Come on, son, there's no need to be afraid.' he'd assured me. 'The storm can't harm us in here. You're safe. Safe amongst your family and friends.'

I nodded my agreement, but my body was still racked with dry, heaving sobs.

'You know, I used to be terrified of the thunder and lightning,' he continued. 'About a million light years ago it seems to me now. My own dad, though, he used to tell me that the rumble of thunder was nothing but the sound of God's engines of creation hammering away in Heaven. He also said he was sure that lightning was merely Jesus taking pictures of the angels...and I believed him. I really did.'

'Of course,' he added with a chuckle,' my old man also used to tell me the reason he drank so much beer was because the sawdust at the timber yard where he used to work was forever getting caught in the back of his throat, and that he was only acting on doctor's orders....But I believed him about the thunder and lightning. And, maybe I still kind of do. I mean, here I am, 70-plus years on, and I've never been harmed by either of them, yet. So, like I said, you're as safe as houses here with me, son. Now come on and give your old Grandad a hug!'

Just listening to that gently lilting voice was enough to gradually banish my fears, and I'd reached out to throw my arms around his neck and bury my head in his old tweed jacket, breathing in the reassuringly familiar aromas of 'Old Spice' and 'Brylcreem', and in later years, long after my grandfather had passed away, whenever there was a storm brewing, I'd close my eyes and I would clearly 'see' flashbulbs illuminating the bruised-looking clouds and great contraptions slowly revolving, whilst a being, all dressed in white with the kindest face, my grandad's face, stood at the head of a long flight of stairs, turning a handle on one of the machines ('The Engines Of Creation').

He'd smile, and beckon me to come on up and join him and give him a big hug, and it was the least I could do to thank him for helping banish my fears, and I'd eagerly climb the stairs to be with him, as the cameras flashed and the engines rumbled ...and I felt loved and safe as I reached out my hand to touch...to touch....

*****

...to touch the smooth, metallic surface of the side of the machine in The Salt House...To reach out and run my fingers absent-mindedly across the outline of the closed gate above which someone had chalked **'BIG BERTHA'** in block capital letters.

As if in a dream, I began climbing further up the ladder, filled with a sudden desire to see what was contained inside, as if there could be anything remotely exciting about that cumbersome-looking mechanism. I made my way onto the platform keen to open the gate, and peer in, and quell my burning curiosity. I'd just about managed to get it about half-way open and had caught a brief whiff of some bitter fragrance that stung my nostrils and caused my eyes to water, when someone suddenly shouted from below:

"Oi, what the hell do yer think you're doing? Get down from there. Right now!"

I jumped out of my skin, and for a second there I'd very nearly lost my balance and tumbled backwards over the low railings onto the concrete floor, forty feet or so below me.

I hastily attempted to recover my composure, but still my knees were knocking together like a manic pair of castanets. I looked down and saw one of the men who had been arguing earlier standing at the foot of the ladder. His scowling expression and the clenching of his fists carried with them the promise of extreme violence, and you can be sure I descended those rungs as fast as I possibly could.

When I was finally on solid ground once more, I half-expected to find myself being dragged into some dark corner of the room (and let's be honest, he would have been spoilt for choice in trying to select just one – The Salt House was a real haven for shadow-filled corners), and kick ten kinds of multi-coloured crap out of me. As it turned out, however, although he did actually lay his hand on me, causing my entire body to begin shaking in tandem with my knees, it was only to usher me away from 'BIG BERTHA,' and lead me back out into the frigid February air.

The man's sidekick from before was stood just outside the entrance, his hands cupped around a flaming match as he tried in vain to light a cigarette. He raised his eyebrows quizzically at the sight of this terrified-looking kid being gently but firmly marched off the premises by a hulking great extra from Angels With Dirty Faces.

> "I found him sniffing round that damned old machine,"

…he said in answer to the unspoken question.

> "I reckon she had him in her spell there for a little while. It would have been more than long enough, though, if I hadn't come along when I did."
>
> "He climbed the ladder?"

Shady Sidekick's thick, bushy eyebrows arched in surprise.

> "All the way to the very top?"
>
> "He had the friggin' gate half-way open, if you please."
>
> "Christ Almighty. Have you got an honest-to-God death wish, son?"

I tried to form a reply, but my tongue suddenly seemed glued to the roof of my mouth and all that emerged was a kind of strangled 'Ugggg.' My mind was busy trying to conjure up less-than-enchanting visions of my being beaten to an unrecognisable pulp by both 'Hitman' and his trusty 'Sidekick' (two beatings for the price of one, you might say).

But when 'Hitman' spoke again, his voice was considerably lowered – his tone slightly less aggressive.

> "Hang on a minute, you're Charlie Walker's son, aren't yer?' Good God, lad, yer must have at least a little bit of yer owld fella's good sense. This place isn't a playground. It can be very dangerous. Certain parts of it more so than others."

He cast a furtive glance back in the direction of 'The Salt House,' brooding under a white, late winter sky.

> "My advice to you is to get on back to yer Dad's office. He'll likely be knockin' off soon, and he'll be wonderin' where you've got to. Get goin' now, and I won't say nuthin' about what you've been up to.' He stuck out his calloused, grease-stained hand. 'Have we got ourselves a deal?"

Still unable to find my voice, I shook his hand limply, and trying not to break into a run, I made my way back to the foreman's quarters, just as the factory's noontime whistle sounded. Every single step of the way I was trying to decide which was the more frightening: the threat of a beating from the two hardcases I'd just encountered, or the fevered stench of their own fear, coming off of them in waves so thick it had almost made me want to vomit….

I had absolutely no idea of what they were so obviously afraid of at that moment.

And as things turned out, I didn't discover at least part of the reason until one balmy summer evening, six months or so later….

*****

I remember I was watching Scooby Doo on the TV, with a wet paper towel clutched to my forehead and a glass of chilled lemonade close to hand, when news first broke of the tragedy at The Tan Yard.

I'd been left in charge of my two younger brothers and sister whilst my Mum had gone to work at the nearby Viota confectionary plant, and I'd been unable to keep one eye from straying over to the thermometer over in the far corner of the living room wall. The temperature hadn't dropped below 85° Fahrenheit for the best part of a week, and the entire country had felt like it was slowly melting out of existence.

I was just mentally debating whether I could be bothered summoning up the energy to traipse into the kitchen to fetch a couple more ice cubes from the freezer, when my brother, Grant, came dashing in from the back garden babbling about how there'd been something on the radio about an accident at Dad's works. I didn't pay him much heed at first. I was sure he was either playing some crappy practical joke or else had simply misheard the broadcast. I waved him away as though he were one of those maddeningly whirring ladybirds, sky-darkening swarms of which had plagued Britain that summer, and went right on watching Thelma and Daphne and the rest of those 'pesky kids' set about solving yet another spooky haunted mansion mystery, until somehow, the time had gotten round to 6 o' clock, and a vague sense of disquiet began to manifest itself, despite my best efforts to ignore it. The realisation dawned that my Dad still hadn't returned from his stint on the day shift, and that was decidedly unusual. He normally knocked off at bang on the stroke of five, and he was always home within a quarter of an hour, even if he stopped to call in at 'The Top Shop' on pay day to buy us all a bar of chocolate or an ice lolly (depending on the season), as a treat.

He was now, by even the most generous of allowances for delays, a good forty-five minutes late.

I jumped up from my seat and quickly tuned in to Radio City News, and heard the announcer confirm, three or four stories in, that which our Grant had already told me.

The exact nature of the accident and the identity of the person involved were withheld, but even if they had blared the details full blast through a pair of giant 10,000 watt speakers, I wouldn't have heard them. I was far too busy paying attention to the panicky, whispering voice that had crept uninvited into my mind….

> 'Someone's suffered a terrible accident at 'The Tan Yard,'

…it said with grave solemnity.

> 'Your brother told you so, but you didn't believe him. You refused to listen. And while you were sitting there glued to the goggle box, someone's been very badly injured. Maybe they've had one or more of their limbs amputated by a piece of machinery, their precious life-blood spraying the walls like a gushing scarlet geyser. Maybe they've broken their neck after falling from atop a pile of assembled cattle hides. Maybe they've been permanently blinded by the scalding steam when one of those endlessly twisting pipes burst open….
>
> Or maybe, only maybe, mind, maybe they are as dead as the proverbial doornail. Lying there with their eyes wide open, staring sightlessly at the cool, white ceiling of the ambulance as it pulls into the hospital car park, thirty seconds too late….And while you're busy considering that, wonder about this: Why the hell isn't your Dad home yet?'

With a growing sense of dread, hauntingly familiar to anyone who has ever awaited the return of a loved one on a storm-lashed evening on the wrong side of midnight, I stared out the front window, trying to desperately to will my Dad home. I prayed too that the phone would remain silent. In the movies and the TV soaps, its shrill, insistent ringing could mean only one thing: a cold, emotionless tone at the other end of the line relating a message that invariably began with the awful words:

> 'I'm afraid I have some bad news…'

Time seemed to stretch out interminably, although I couldn't have been stood there for more than a few minutes, lost in an imaginary argument with myself as I watched a couple of love-birds holding hands as they walked up Eccleshall Road, a ten-year-old kid trying (and failing) to do a single wheelie on his ten-times-too-big Chopper bike, and several neighbours washing their cars or sweeping their driveways as the shadows began to inexorably lengthen.

And then, incredibly, here came my father, turning the corner, a little sombre-looking, maybe, but otherwise as right as rain, and hardly daring to believe my eyes, I'd ran to the door to greet him with a neck-enveloping hug (something I hadn't done since the days of early childhood).

"Aye, aye, what's all this?"

…he'd exclaimed as Kearry, Grant and Dale had gathered round, eager to express their relief, too.

"Do you mind if we leave the big welcome home's till I get inside the house. I've had a hell of a day."

He'd spoken gruffly, but I could see in his eyes he'd been moved by the reception. We'd had about a thousand burning questions to ask our Dad, but we let him pass without another word. He was plainly shattered and in no mood for conversation.

It was only later that night, when my Mum returned from her part-time job, and my younger brothers and sisters had been sent to bed, that I managed to find out what had happened. As the eldest son, my Dad decreed that it was perfectly alright for me to hear the gory details, and after being ushered into the unusually silent living room, (the TV and radio were both switched off – wonder of wonders!), we sat, mopping our brows in the midst of the un-yielding humidity, as my father related what had taken place….

It seems that a young lad by the name of Andy Thompson, who'd been assigned to The Salt House work party just a few weeks earlier, had disappeared without trace sometime after he'd returned from the pub at the end of his lunch hour. The last anybody could recall seeing him was when he'd been busy feeding untreated cow hides into that enormous wheel-like machine, '**Big Bertha**'.

No-one had missed him until the shriek of the Five o' Clock Whistle had signalled down tools and Andy had failed to appear to punch his card. Even then, no-one had been unduly concerned. It was widely assumed he'd turn up soon enough, wearing a sheepish grin and with cheeks the colour of fresh beetroot.

By five thirty, though, when he still hadn't shown, Head Office had ordered a full-scale search of the premises, and the entire workforce had been mobilised, several of them muttering under their breath about how they had to get home and what they wouldn't do to that 'lazy dickhead' when they got their hands on him. The workers, my Dad included, had split up into several groups and they'd dutifully searched the site from top to bottom without success. As time had wore on, so the threats and curses had gradually died away as the realisation that something a good deal more serious than a mere spot of skiving had been going on here.

And eventually, there had been only one place left to look.

The inside of the very machine Andy had been toiling on earlier that day.

'Big Bertha'

I'd detected a slight tremor in my father's voice as he'd described how it had seemed that every single member of the day shift had somehow crammed under the high-beamed roof of The Salt House. And in my mind's eye, I'd pictured the workers gathered like disciples come to worship some vast mechanical demi-god, their faces lit with the twin expressions of fear and anticipation….

No-one had quite dared to step forward and press the release lever, and when one of the foremen had asked for a volunteer, the crowd had begun shuffling nervously and there'd been much staring at multi-scuffed, steel-capped work boots, as if studying the creases could somehow reveal their missing colleague's whereabouts.

Eventually, one of the charge-hands, his jaw set in grim determination, walked over and pulled the lever. He quickly jumped out of the way as a deluge of soaking wet hides, drenched in the acid that was used for burning off the fine cattle hairs, went sloshing into a twelve foot deep gutter, the hides swept along like so much flotsam until the drains did their work and the level slowly subsided.

When finally the last of the acid had leaked away, all that had remained were the cow skins, glistening, ironically enough, like a bunch of new-born baby calves lying in the middle of a sun-bright farmer's field.

And there, half-hidden amongst the piles of newly-slick leather, had lain the bloated, hairless body of Andy Thompson, neither skiving, nor sleeping on the job, but dead to the world and forever beyond the muttered threats (empty or otherwise), of mortal men.

The memory of that undeniably powerful image has remained with me all my life and I suppose that's hardly surprising given the gruesome nature of Mr Thompson's demise. But what has remained especially vivid was the final thing my father said, just before he changed the subject to something much more mundane:

> "If I'm lucky enough to live to be a hundred, I don't think I'll ever be able to get that poor man's face out of my mind. Both of his eyes had completely gone and the acid had burned his lips clean off. All you could see was this perfect set of teeth and I know it sounds stupid, but it looked for all the world as though he was staring up at us from out of those black-holed empty eye-sockets. Staring up and grinning. Slyly. Like he'd just played some mean, small-minded practical joke on us all."

My dad sighed wearily, and I was shocked at how tired and old he looked at that moment, sitting in his favourite armchair, from where he frequently held court like the lord of all he surveyed, he appeared momentarily, to have diminished in stature, to have shrunken somehow.

> "I tell yer, both,"

…he said in a voice that was little more than a half-whisper;

> "…that frightening impression, as totally nonsensical as it was, gave me the creeps more than anything."

*****

Did I say earlier that it took me six months to learn the reason for 'Hitman' and 'Sidekick's' all-too apparent fear of The Salt House? I did? Well, you'll pardon me, I'm sure, if I ask you to strike that error from the record and rectify it by saying it actually took a good while longer than that to arrive at the real truth.

Ten whole years longer, to be precise.

And, as with most revealing discoveries, I stumbled upon it quite by accident, when 'The Tan Yard' and Andy Thompson's tragic death were the furthest things from my mind.

Two days before Christmas, 1986, I was standing at the bar of a pub with the cosily evocative name of *The Garrick Snug*, getting the ale in for Grant and Stevie Gee. We wouldn't normally have set foot in the place, it being something of an 'owld man's' watering hole, but we'd been seeking refuge from the massed ranks of last-minute Christmas shoppers, pushing and shoving with a fervour that bordered on the maniacal. Knowing that this particular pub would be comparatively quiet, even on the very brink of the holiday season, we'd popped in for a quick pint and the chance to unwind. I'd drawn the short straw, hence my standing at the bar whilst my two companions, snickering at their good fortune, went and sat themselves at a table over in the far corner of the lounge.

Whilst I was waiting to be served, I became aware of a man staring at me intently, and casting a sidelong glance, I saw a bearded, grizzled individual whom I was sure I'd never seen before in my life. He plainly believed he had business with me, however, and worried that he was about to either try to bum a drink off me or else pick a fight, I began whistling tunelessly, in a decidedly unconvincing attempt at showing I wasn't intimidated. It was so ineffective, in fact, that a few seconds later, he staggered over to me and breathing a heady combination of whisky fumes and acute halitosis into my face, he said;

> "I know you, don't I?"

I was about to beg to differ, but before I could open my mouth, he was nodding in agreement with himself.

> "Yeah, that's right. You're Charlie Walker's son. I remember you, even though you've sprouted up a little bit since I last clapped eyes on you. Now, how long ago was that, I wonder?' He stroked his unkempt beard thoughtfully. 'Jesus, I reckon that must have been way back in the winter of 1976. Not long before I left that godforsaken, shitheap of a Tan Yard for the last time."

At the mention of my Dad's former workplace, (my father had suddenly been made redundant after more than a decade's loyal service, three years earlier), there was an instant flash of recognition, and I realised I was talking to 'Sidekick' – the B-movie heavy, from that freezing February morning, looking like he'd aged by about thirty years. His hair was thin and snow-white, and what you could see of his bearded face was deeply lined and careworn. A quick mental calculation assured me he couldn't have been a day over fifty, but he could easily have passed for one of the assembled old timers; the sort of men who were sitting at the domino-strewn tables, sipping pints of 'Guinness,' or small bottles of 'Mackie's,' and who always looked as though they'd seen too much, and carried far too great a grief all their lives.

The fact that I realised I knew him didn't fill me with any great enthusiasm to begin chatting with him, though, and after exchanging a few standard pleasantries, I made as if to walk away. Before I could do so, however, he'd shaken my hand and introduced himself as Stuart Mckinley (Stewie, to his friends). Despite my protests, he insisted on paying for the round of drinks, and I knew better than to rebuff his generosity. I didn't want to offend him. He may have looked old, but he was thin and wiry, and he looked well capable of handling himself in a bar-room scrap.

And so, we'd started up a mostly one-sided conversation, a constant stream of anecdotes centred upon his time at British Leather, interrupted only briefly when Steve had wandered over to find out where the hell I'd gotten to with the drinks.

The longer he went on, the more desperate I became to escape this wearisome bore, and I'd been on the very brink of risking all to declare I simply had to get back to my friends, when Stuart ('Stewie' to his friends), had said something that had immediately gained my undivided attention.

> "But of course you know, mate, the lowest point, the final nail in the coffin, you might say, was the death of that poor bastard, Andy Thompson. It might sound soft, but I couldn't bring myself to set foot in the place after that. Some of the lads on my shift took the piss, of course. They joked that I was scared that Andy's ghost had taken to haunting the premises. That kind of talk might have got to me once, and I'd have kicked off big time, but the truth is I was scared, though not of some lonely spirit stalking that miserable owld building. Those smart-arse wind-up merchants: they like to think they know it all, but when you get right down to it, kidder, none of them have got a jar of glue!"
>
> "So what was it you were afraid of?"

I asked, honestly interested in what he had to say for the first time since I'd re-made his acquaintance.

> "Don't you know?"

...he smiled incredulously.

> "You, of all people, should do. I remember me good mate, John, rescued you from Her clutches all those years ago. I've gotta say, lad, that's not something I'd easily forget!"
>
> "Yeah, I remember the incident you're talking about,"

I assured him.

> "But I still don't understand what it was your mate was supposed to have saved me from."
>
> "Christ, I thought John did a very good job of explaining it to yer that afternoon outside The Salt House. Maybe you weren't listening. Maybe you didn't want to listen. Whatever. The plain and simple facts of the matter are, you were very likely caught under Her spell, and if John hadn't have come along when he did…"
>
> "Hang on a minute. What are you talking about, spell? You mean a curse or something. Cast by whom, exactly?"
>
> "Her. The thing that tried to lure you to your death. The same thing that killed young Andy Thompson. That damned machine in The Salt House…Big Bertha!"
>
> "Oh come on,"

I shook my head in disbelief.

> "That was just an accident, surely Tragedies like that happen from time to time. And as for me climbing up that ladder when I was a kid: I was just being nosey. I was curious to see what was inside the machine, that's all."

Stuart favoured me with an expression of ill-disguised contempt, leaned a little closer so that the stench of his breath was almost overpowering, and spoke in a hoarse whisper:

> "Alright. I'm gonna tell you something now, lad. Something I've never told anyone before, and I'll leave it up to you to decide whether to believe it or not."
>
> "God, who do you think you are, Mr Robert Ripley?"

I snorted, and made to move away, but before I could do so, Stuart placed a calloused hand on my shoulder, and said:

> "Please, son, just hear me out. I need to get this off my chest."

Something in his voice, bade me pause for a second (always fatal when in the company of a drunk who is dead set upon telling you his life story), and completely against my better judgement, I sighed and told him to get on with it,

> "…but make it quick, I'm supposed to be out with me mates for a few pre-Christmas bevy's!"
>
> "I will,"

…he said, and to be fair, he was.

"John and I were both made up when Andy was assigned to our shift.

He seemed like a good lad, even if he was a little bit full of himself. We were willing to forgive him for that. I mean, God, he'd only just turned eighteen, and who's head isn't full of dreams at that age? Besides, Andy was an excellent worker. He more than did his fair share, even when it came to mucking in with the horrible jobs, like feeding the skins into Big Bertha. No-one liked doing that. It was such bloody back-breaking work. It was always unbearably hot, too, even in the depths of mid-winter. You had to feed the hides through by hand as fast as you could and even though they gave you a face mask and a pair of plastic goggles, that didn't stop the fumes from stinging your eyes and somehow seeping down your throat. And when you got home at night, you wouldn't be able to sleep for coughing your guts up.

All of that was motive enough, you might think, for avoiding that particular detail for as long as you possibly could. But the real reason I dreaded being sent up those ladders was not so easily explainable. I can only tell you what I personally felt nearly every time I stood before the open gate at the side of that drum-machine. I'd be lifting the first of the hides, and I'd instantly get the impression that I was being watched. I could feel this pair of burning eyes glaring at me, and I'd whirl around and find there was absolutely no-one there. I'd curse myself for a fool, and go back to work, and sometimes that would be the end of it, but on several occasions, there'd be something else; a sensation like a soft breathing on the back of my neck and the smell of cheap perfume, a sickly sweet odour like rotting violets…

And one afternoon, a week or so before Andy joined the shift, I'd been busy hauling in those heavy cattle-skins, when I suddenly felt a gentle little push from behind. There really wasn't a lot of strength in that shove, but combined with the weight of the hide, it was enough to force me to go cart-wheeling to keep my balance. It was a near thing. I almost went flying over the edge of the platform, and only the safety railing prevented me from doing so. It really doesn't matter whether I imagined that sneaky little push or not. I got out of that place just as fast as I possibly could.

Aside from John, did anyone else on our crew ever encounter anything unusual when they were working in and around Big Bertha? I can't say for certain, because I never dared discuss any of my experiences with them. I was too afraid of being laughed at by my work-mates. They were mostly a good-hearted bunch, but a bigger gang of piss-takers you're never likely to meet. Besides, once I'd clocked off, I tried to rationalise the incident, and it was easy to convince myself I'd imagined the whole thing when I was sat at home with the wife and kids or propping up the bar with my friends.

So when Andy Thompson came up to me one lunch hour, a couple of weeks later, and suddenly started babbling excitedly about how he'd heard voices whispering in his ear during his fourth of fifth stint on Big Bertha, I'd merely clapped him on the back and in a reassuring voice told him it was just his mind playing tricks, or the sound of the wind rustling in the eaves.

Either way, I'd keep what you've just told me to yourself though, Andy." I'd said feeling like the world's biggest shit-bag. "You don't want people round here thinking you've got a bad case of the horrors,"

A few days or so after that, I was sitting in the work's canteen reading the paper, when in had walked Andy, head down, muttering to himself, and looking as though he were carrying the weight of the world on his shoulders. That struck me as more than a little strange because normally he was such a bubbly, happy-go-lucky individual. From the expression on his face, it was immediately obvious that this was no mere sponsored-teenaged sulk. I went over to him to ask what was wrong, but he refused to answer. He simply told me to go away, that there was nothing I, or anybody else, could do to help him and I noticed there were dark circles under his eyes and his face was as pale as candle wax, and to be honest, the thought crossed my mind that he might be on drugs or something. I told him to cheer up and snap out of it. God, how cold-bloodedly heartless that sounds now.

And that was the last time I ever saw Andy alive.

I did clap eyes on him later, of course. Or rather what was left of him. By then, though, he really was beyond the help of anybody.

I didn't find the note Andy had left me until the morning after we found his body, floating on the river of acid that came gurgling out of Big Bertha.

Actually, maybe the word 'note,' is a bit misleading. A crumpled piece of lined paper upon which he'd scrawled a disjointed sequence of words might be more accurate.

'Stewie,

Those voices I mentioned to you

Those tricks in my mind.

That wind rustling in the eaves.

They all keep telling me there's an easy way to make all my dreams come true.

They say all I've got to do is take a little jump.

And I think maybe they're right.

I suppose there's only one way to find out for sure....

Andy'

I never showed that note to anyone. I never told a soul about it, either. I simply tore it up and threw it in the nearest available bin, and I think that's the only reason the coroner was able to record a verdict of accidental death at the subsequent inquest."

*****

"So it wasn't an accident. It was suicide,"

I muttered with a mixture of awe and profound sympathy whilst taking an almighty chug on my pint. "Jesus."

"Jesus hasn't got anything to do with it,"

Stewart retorted.

"I haven't quite finished this cheery little Christmas tale yet. Perhaps when I have, you'll see exactly what I mean by that.

I couldn't face going back to work immediately after they found Andy's body, so I threw a few blag sickies in. I'll be honest, I spent most of my time stood in here, drinking myself stupid, trying to drown the feelings of guilt that otherwise kept me awake most nights. It was only a temporary form of escape, of course. In the end I had to go back. I mean, I've got a family to support and bills to pay.

And although I didn't think I'd ever be able to face it, eventually, it came around to my turn to work on Big Bertha again.

I remember I was filled with feelings of stomach-churning dread the day that I stood on the platform for, as it turned out, the very last time. My entire body seemed to be sheened in beads of cold sweat as I tried to mentally prepare myself for any of the things that had I'd sensed had happened before; the chilled breath on the back of my neck, the unmistakable certainty that I was being watched, the pungent aroma of dead flowers. But right up until the very end of the shift, nothing remotely strange occurred. And when it got to the stage where I'd only had a couple more cattle skins left to deal with, I began to dare to hope that my fears would prove unfounded.

But then, just as I was feeding in the last of the hides, I distinctly heard someone whisper my name; 'Stewwwwiiieeeeee.'

I spun round quickly, half-expecting to see one of my workmates lurking in the shadows, playing a sick, but typically 'Tan Yard' crew-type joke. But the building was empty. There was not a single soul in sight.

And then it came again, stronger and louder this time; a croaky, burned out voice that brought to mind terrible memories of visiting my late Uncle Steven, as he lay on his death bed, trying desperately to speak my name though his throat, like the rest of his body, was riddled with cancer;

'I'm in here, Stewwwwiieee.'

I instantly slung the untreated cow-skin aside as I finally realised precisely where that disembodied voice was coming from.

The dark depths of that infernal machine.

As mad as it sounds now, my first thought was that somehow, somebody had got themselves trapped inside Big Bertha, and I stuck my head through the open gate, squinting into the darkness, unable to see a thing until my eyes gradually adjusted to the gloom.

Eventually, I was able to make out the mass of cattle skins slowly revolving on the spokes of that gigantic wheel, and as I watched, it suddenly juddered to a violent halt as though something had jammed its inner workings.

A human body spun into view, lying on its side, stark naked and very obviously dead. It was entirely hairless and every inch of its skin was covered with a series of open, running sores. I started to scream for help, but then it slowly raised its ruin of a head, and I saw with very little surprise, that it was poor Andy Thompson.

And even though he was as lifeless as an obsolete store-front mannequin or a theatre puppet that's had its strings unceremoniously snapped, Andy laughed, a deep slow chuckle that sounded like some thick, viscous fluid being slowly washed down a grid.

And then he fell silent for a moment, seemingly regarding me with his hollow, eyeless sockets.

"Why don't you jump, Stewwwiee?"' he said. "Please jump. You know you want to. I did. And I've never looked back. Come and kiss goodbye to all your cares and woes. All you've got to do is take one tiiiiiny little jump…"

I shook my head frantically, and tried to tell myself that I was simply hallucinating. That there really couldn't be a body splayed across that metal wheel like the bloated carcass of some pale-white sea creature washed up on a heavily polluted shore. And even if there was, it couldn't possibly be speaking to me.

My attempts at denying Andy's corpse's existence made not the slightest bit of difference, however. It went right on beseeching me to join it deep down in the rotten black heart of Big Bertha.

'Come on Stewwwwieee," he said, raising his arms up towards me imploringly.

"PLEASE JUMP!...PLEASE JUMP! PLEASE JUMP! …PLEASE JUMP…PLEASE JU…."

On and on it went, like an endless tape loop, and if all that I've said so far sounds like the wild ramblings of a middle-aged madman, you'll doubtless think it borders on total lunacy if I tell you that the longer I listened to that rasping, acid-scorched voice, the more I began to see the sense, the inarguable logic, in what it was proposing. It was indeed sorely tempting to have the opportunity to leave behind this world with all its attendant fears and petty hatreds, all its empty promises and cheap, worthless, victories…lying down there in the secret dark with Andy, would be a little like being a child once more. We could make big mad plans and have endless fun and games without a care in the world, for all eternity.

I'd actually climbed half-way through the gate and was preparing to take "Andy's" advice and jump, when out of the corner of my eye, I saw something flash and go spinning into the blackness. It was the gold-plated bracelet my wife, Denise, had bought me the previous Christmas. The one with the faulty clasp that was forever coming undone every time I bent down, and which I had been meaning to take to the jewellers to get fixed for weeks. I made a desperate lunge for it, and very nearly lost my balance, and suddenly the spell was broken. I realised where I was and what I was contemplating doing, and the shock gave me all the strength I needed to throw myself backwards onto the safety of the platform. I quickly scrambled to my feet and raced down the ladder, several rungs at a time, my screams echoing round the old Tan Yard like the shrieking wail of some demented banshee.

I didn't stop to speak to anybody. I didn't stop to clock out. I simply charged through the main gates and careered down Old Chester Road, as though the hounds of Hell were nipping at me heels, and I never once paused to catch my breath or to glance back over my shoulder, till I'd run the four miles or so it took for me to reach the safety of my home on the outskirts of Bromborough Village.

And that's pretty much all there is to tell.

I handed in me notice by phone the very next day. That didn't exactly go down very well with me wife, and went down a whole lot worse with the scumbags at the New Ferry Job Centre. But I didn't much care, to tell you the truth. They hadn't seen what I believed I'd seen, grinning up at me out of the darkness of a huge, acid-filled drum, arms stretched wide, ready to receive another "willing" victim in its cold embrace...

I never set foot in The Tan Yard again. And I never heard tell of any further fatal "accidents" taking place there.

But I'll tell you this: The day they demolish that Godforsaken shit-house, is the day that I'll personally throw the mother of all street parties...."

In September, 1994, following the blazing inferno that completely engulfed the premises, Stewie 'The Sidekick,' finally got his wish.

I sincerely hope, wherever he is, he's boogieing till dawn....

*****

What are we to make of this story, Dear Reader?

Do we simply dismiss it as being nothing more than the drunken ramblings of a bitter, guilt-ridden man?

Would it make sense to submerge it in the murky depths of Modern Urban Folklore, along with the equally spurious tales of exploding poodles in microwaves, crocodiles thriving in the sewers and hosts of 'Grey', bug-eyed extraterrestrials engaged in the mass abduction of human beings?

Or do we dare to afford it the merest hint of credence? A tacit confirmation of the deep-rooted suspicion some of us have that certain places, (and in some cases, entire areas), are just not right?

It's hard to deny that even the most insensitive amongst us can sometimes discern the way in which in certain locations, the air hangs heavy with some indefinable burden of grief, the quality of light always seems to be a sickly ghost shroud of grey, and the atmosphere seems permanently tainted, filled with the embodiment of a hundred not quite-realised fears and disquiets.

Locations, not to put to fine a point on it, where 'Evil', in all its various forms and guises, chooses to dwell...

In the cold light of day, that particular contention may seem dangerously paranoid, but oh, in the black watches of the night....

Consider this....

Just across the road from where The Tan Yard used to stand, there used to be a pub called *The Britannia Inn*.

Standing on the corner of Green Lane, near to a railway station in one of Tranmere's decidedly less-than-salubrious locales, there was nothing remotely special about it. You'd scarcely have afforded it a second glance if you'd have happened to pass it by, and it came as no great surprise that it closed its doors for good in the mid-1990s, not long after the fire at The Tan Yard, and the sad demise of Cammell Laird, the once-thriving shipbuilding company.

Before 'The Britannia' was finally demolished a few years ago, the sight of its façade was as depressing as it was symptomatic of the area's rapid fall from economic grace. The few windows that weren't boarded up were so opaque with grime, they were the colour of slate and simply reflected the over-riding drabness of the surroundings. A broken 'Tetley Bitter' sign swayed drunkenly at the slightest breeze. The fly-posters glued to the welded-shut doorway advertising some long-ago circus (and featuring a particularly sadistic looking clown), were washed out and faded.

It was always hard to shake the impression that the building was part of some lazy artist's unfinished landscape. That they had drawn the preliminary sketch in grey, leaded pencil, but ran out of colours before they ever got a chance to properly paint it.

It was a depressing enough vista from the outside, but it provided little clue as to the horrors that have reportedly been encountered within.

The history of the pub is mundane and uneventful, although just like The Tan Yard, it might be of some relevance to note that it was built on former consecrated ground. In fact, Birkenhead Priory, (featured elsewhere in this book), is less than half a mile distant, as is Holborn Square, the site of various reports of 'evil dwarf-type entities' (also see elsewhere in this book).

The focus for the recent stories surrounding the inn appear to be centred upon a single solitary room situated on the third floor. One particular witness, known only as 'John', told of how, many years earlier, when he was twelve-years-old, he was plagued by what he can only describe as 'Demonic manifestations.'

The experiences were said to have begun with the sudden appearance of archetypal phantom monks in John's bedroom when darkness fell. Initially, these apparitions didn't do an awful lot. They simply partially materialised, to the point where they were barely discernible, and kept a discreet distance lurking amongst the shadows in the darkest corner of the room.

With each succeeding night, however, their outlines grew ever more defined, and the young boy's ears were filled with a monotonous low chanting, as the monkish shapes emerged from out of the pervasive gloom.

And worse, John, had to deal with the disconcerting fact that on each occasion they appeared, the black-cowled figures began to creep ever closer to his bed.

Eventually, they gathered around John's prostrate form to recite their endless litany, and although these forms were essentially human-like, they were joined by what John described as 'other beings, shapeless forms that seemed to be content to merely observe the "rituals" from the periphery'.

The witness was naturally terrified by these nightly visitations, and tried to tell his parents who - at that time - were the landlords of the pub, what was taking place in his room after sundown. They refused to believe him, of course, and dismissed the whole thing as being nothing more than a series of vivid nightmares or the product of an overactive imagination. Ultimately then, he was left with little option other than to learn to accept these frightening intrusions into his childhood world.

His mother and father did eventually become concerned enough about John's behaviour to perform what they assumed to be a perfectly logical form of 'exorcism'. They set about giving their son's bedroom a thorough renovation.

There were apparently layers upon layers of dirty, discoloured paper that had to be stripped from the walls like sheets of ancient parchment or the long-dead skin of a mummified corpse. After an eternity of peeling, they finally revealed the bare plaster beneath, only to find that the cold, mildewed surface was completely covered with

'...bizarre symbols and diagrams, painted largely in some sort of off-red substance.'

The parents very quickly painted over the strange inscriptions, to prevent John from seeing them, but if they expected the dramatic transformation of the room's décor to assist in eradicating their son's bout of 'Night Terrors,' they were to be sorely disappointed.

The robed figures were back that very night, and whilst John was in what he described as being 'a state of consciousness somewhere between sleep and wakefulness,' he sensed himself being 'initiated into something. I distinctly felt something alien enter into me.'

The percipient later went on to tell a paranormal investigator by the name of Mike McKeown, (former editor of the now sadly defunct *Ghost Watch* magazine), that he remained convinced long into adulthood that whatever it was, the entity continued to co-exist with him even after he'd left the pub for the very last time.

Now, you might be thinking at this point, this is all very interesting , but what, if any relevance does it have to the story of Big Bertha, 'The Haunted Machine' of The Tanyard's Salt House?'

Well, the answer is simply this. Also resident at *The Britannia Inn*, (according to contemporary accounts), was a 'Whispering Demon,' which reportedly delighted in seeking to encourage guests and tenants alike to 'take a run and jump out of the pub's third floor window!'

If this latter account is to be believed, (and of course, as I've sought to make clear throughout this book, that's an important caveat), there are at least two suicide-inducing entities (or maybe, given the close proximity, the same one), active in an area no wider than a couple of football pitches placed back to back.

That's some kind of coincidence, wouldn't you say?

And there are plenty of other, disconcertingly similar stories doing the rounds, from locations far beyond the borders of Merseyside.

Consider this…

Back in 1924, on the island of Skellig Michael, just off the coast of Kerry, Ireland, Tom Lethbridge, the famous psychic investigator, was climbing a hill on a sunny but cold, early spring day, in order to view the ruins of an 8th Century monastery. When he reached the summit and looked about him, he could clearly see, directly below, the remains of a rubbish dump. Intrigued, he began making his way down the hill to see if there was anything worth salvaging from the tip. As he did so, an awful sensation suddenly came over him, and he was filled with a dreadful certainty that something was going to push him off the edge of the cliff.

Quickly, he climbed back up and walked down a low hill past the nearby monastery. He then described what he termed as being some type of 'presence' that bade him turn around quickly, and as he did so, he was suddenly knocked over by a pair of powerful hands. As he scrambled to his feet, he saw to his astonishment that the hillside was completely deserted, with not the slightest trace of an assailant, human or otherwise, anywhere in sight.

There was only the mournful keening of the wind and the sun sliding from behind a patch of cloud.

Consider this…

Ebury Lodge was built in 1883, on the crest of a hill, (the archetypal Hill House, one might say), overlooking Ealing, West London.

The site was originally an orchard, and, as with *The Britannia Inn*, there appears to have been little trace of anything untoward occurring in its past that may have acted as an obvious catalyst for what was to later transpire.

The unpalatable facts are though, that over a fifty-year period starting in 1883, a total of twenty people have killed themselves (another was apparently murdered), within the confines of this one building.

And, mark this, if you will. Every single one of the deaths were caused by people jumping or 'accidentally' falling from the top of the 70-foot tower situated at the front of the house.

The 'suicides' culminated in 1934, with the 'murder' of a baby thrown from the parapet by a nurse who then 'elected' to take the same route to the unforgiving earth below, killing herself instantly. Not surprisingly, following this latest tragedy, the building stood empty and fell into a state of abject disrepair. People refused to live there, despite it being an outwardly desirable location, and it soon acquired an evil reputation.

Andrew Green, the well-known author and 'Ghost Hunter,' had cause to visit the house, now renamed '16, Montpelier Place', sometime during the Second World War. Andrew, then aged 15, went along to accompany his father who was then the chief re-housing officer for the area. At the time, all derelict property had to be inspected to see if it could be of any use for storing 'goods and chattels.' Part of Mr Green Sr.'s job was to make sure that the structure wasn't damp or could cause any possible damage to the goods that may potentially be stored there. Being more than aware of the building's notoriety, he asked his son if he would care to see his first haunted house. Andrew, like most teenagers faced with the prospect of adventure, was only too glad to accept the invitation. His chief interest at the time was photography and he thought it might well present an ideal opportunity to get in some practice with his camera.

Apart from a mysterious smell of sulphur (traditionally, an odour associated with Demonic manifestations), Mr Green Sr., passed the building as being suitable for the council's purposes, although, ominously enough, one of the foremen of the removal men 'blacked' the location because of the number of apparently 'supernatural' incidents, such as unexplained footsteps in empty rooms, and various tools going unaccountably missing. Andrew, although intrigued by these events, did not it seems, set any great store by their occurrence, and it wasn't until he made his way up the ill-reputed tower that he encountered a truly strange phenomenon.

When he reached the top, he saw the parapet wall was level with his waist and from his excellent vantage point, he could see right across London. The day was idyllic. The weather perfect. And after the oppressive, almost claustrophobic atmosphere of the old house, the air seemed especially fresh and invigorating.

Suddenly, he was filled with an all-consuming desire to walk in the large, luxuriant garden of the house, and rationally enough, it seemed to him, the quickest and easiest way to get there would be to simply step over the surrounding wall and land feet first on the grass below, which suddenly appeared to be no more than a mere foot or so beneath his feet. Eager to stroll across the lush, immaculately tended lawns, and sample the heady fragrance of the roses in the flower garden, Andrew had already cocked one leg over the parapet, when he was grabbed by the neck and spun round to safety by his frantic father.

Still unconcerned, Andrew explained that he was only going to take a little walk in the garden below, and it was only when his dad asked him to take another look down that a wave of vertigo-induced dizziness washed over him.

And he was shocked to see that there was not a single blade of grass in the garden, never mind an aromatic bloom.

Only a wide expanse of solid concrete crazy paving.

Consider this...

In a letter to the excellent, though sadly erstwhile, occult magazine, *Man, Myth and Magic*, published in the early 1970s, (and one of my all-time favourite periodicals), a Mr G. G. C. (real name withheld), of Deal, Kent, had the following story to tell...

> 'Where I live now is only a few minutes walk from the sea and a narrow beach backed by chalk cliffs from 100 to 300 feet high.
>
> Several years back I decided to go night fishing for bass beneath these cliffs and borrowing my son's motorcycle, I set out about 9pm, along the narrow road which passes beneath the cliffs, and which led to the spot where I intended to fish.
>
> When I arrived there the night was fine and warm with the occasional cloud drifting gently across the moon.
>
> I cast out my line and sat waiting for a bite. As I sat there, the warm night suddenly grew cold. An icy wind, tainted with an indescribable foulness, was blowing towards me from the face of the cliff directly behind me.
>
> I had a terrifying sensation of being attacked by some supernatural force. My whole mind was dissolving into chaos and my physical strength seemed to be draining away. I felt myself to be the direct focus for an emanation which was unendurably Evil and unbelievably powerful.

Somehow, like one groping in a nightmare, I managed to dismantle my rod and stumble to where the motorcycle was propped at the foot of the cliffs.

I made a number of discreet enquiries about the place amongst the villagers, but apart from being told that in the past the place had been called "Dead Man's Bay," I discovered nothing.

A year or two later, I met a parish councillor who had been born and bred locally. I quietly asked him about the place and, looking at me a bit strangely, he warned me solemnly to keep away from the spot. To my utter astonishment, he told me that he had been subjected to an ordeal which sounded identical to mine. The only difference was that he hadn't even stopped to dismantle his fishing tackle, but had left it there and collected it the following day. He was profoundly impressed when I told him of my experience and we compared notes, but could come to no conclusion whatsoever.

This psychic assault on two people – and there may well be others who have endured it – still remains an absolute mystery.'

And finally consider….

The 600 foot coastline of Beachy Head, near Eastbourne, in Sussex, has earned (if that's quite the right word), a dreadful reputation as being a veritable magnet for many would-be suicides.

Figures as to the actual number of people who have hurled themselves off the edge of the sheer, white-faced cliffs vary according to various sources, but the esteemed researcher Michael Goss, quoted an unnamed journalist who, writing in 1976, stated that Beachy Head averaged ten deaths a year,

'...of which six would be clear cases of suicide, accidental falls being rare,'

…therefore making the former figure a cautious underestimate[*].

This extraordinarily high number has been interpreted, by some paranormal investigators, as being due to the actions of some unspecified 'dark force,' said to manifest in itself in various forms. In 1976, for example, a woman was walking her corgi across the nearby Downs, when she suddenly encountered a ghostly woman in grey. Curiously, it was the dog who was the most adversely affected of the percipients, (animals, like very young children, are of course, often believed to be extremely sensitive to the presence of supernatural entities). The badly frightened corgi began to growl and cowered as the phantom slowly approached, and it eventually ran off howling when the ghost attempted to reach down and stroke it.

The spirit disappeared simultaneously.

The most popular incarnation however, (and certainly the most recent), seems to be that of a black-cowled monk, which, as we have already seen, is a constantly recurring image in the annals of paranormal phenomena.

The legend of Beachy Head first shot to prominence back in February 1952, with publication of the sensationalistic stories of exorcism carried out during a midnight séance held by the medium, Ray de Vekey. But we'll return to this in just a little while.

The locale certainly looks the part, and is not without its historical antecedents. Folklorists, researchers and authors who write about the unexplained, such as Eric Maple, in his *Supernatural England*, (Hale, 1977), are quick to remind us that places like Beachy Head are often associated with

---

[*] **Source:** *Magonia* Issue 55.

> '...horrors of all kinds from time immemorial. In pre-Christian ages, human sacrifices were carried out in similar places, and later, in the days of the Anglo-Saxons, it was customary to hurl criminals from high cliffs into the sea. One theory that has been advanced to account for the Beachy Head phenomena is the presence there of the earthbound spirit of someone who committed suicide or was executed on this spot many centuries ago.'

The grandly-named author, Arthur R. Thurston Hopkins makes the first reference that I've come across, concerning the alleged 'evil presence' haunting Beachy Head, in his book *The World's Strangest Ghost Stories* (World's Work, 1955).

In its pages, he relates how he remembers that in

> '1938, a young girl almost toppled over the edge of "The Head," and was escorted from the spot by a mounted policeman. The following gives some idea of her unpleasant experience. 'She had set out for a day's rambling on the Downs, feeling fit and happy, but after reaching Beachy Head, she stretched on the grass for a rest. It was then that the exhilaration which had been with her for the best part of the walk, gradually faded...
>
> She began to feel vaguely tired and agitated. A dark shadow seemed suddenly to descend on her. She looked round. A mounted policeman was slowly riding towards her – possibly a quarter of a mile away. No-one else was in sight. The sun was shining brightly, and a lark was singing in the skies high above. Everything around should have given her a feeling of happiness and excitement. Yet a feeling of suspended misfortune seemed to cast a blight over the scene. She said she felt herself in an atmosphere she had never breathed before. For the few moments that it lasted she was surrounded by evil influences which overpowered and staggered her. A huge menacing form seemed to catch her up in its immensity, rather than touch her. She prayed and shrieked for help, and began to run – run madly away from the cliffs and after a while stumbled on the side of a down, fell and rolled over and over down the hillside until she sat up before a policeman mounted on a horse.'

And the redoubtable Mr Thurston doesn't leave it there. He further claims to have met several scramblers who had done a little chalk-climbing on Beachy Head.

> 'One or two of them agree that the cliff exudes a sense of ancient ferocity and ill-natured life.
>
> "The soft, deceptive chalk is always waiting to hurl you headlong downwards, with a horrible suggestion of intelligence, and there is a menacing feeling all around," is how one of the climbers put it.
>
> There can be little doubt that few people can stand near the edge of Beachy Head without feeling that some almost hypnotic power lurks in its towering cliff.'

Strong and convincing words, but it really wasn't until that aforementioned exorcism that took place back in February, 1952, that the legend became more than just some entirely local superstition and instead became national Sunday newspaper-headline-making news.

The true facts of the matter have understandably become more than a little hazy in the telling and re-telling, but what seems to have happened is that a group of spiritualists held a midnight séance in a bid to rid the location of the 'evil entity.' Ray de Vekey claimed afterwards that a spirit had materialised and promptly seized him. He described it as being the ghost of an elderly, bearded man dressed in an ankle-length robe like a monk's habit, with a black marking on the back.

> "It was in chains,"

…he said.

> "Not handcuffs, but ancient, wrought-iron shackles. I don't think anyone could have jumped from the cliff in chains like that. I imagine it was the spirit of somebody who had been bound and thrown from the cliff-top centuries ago."

The real object of the service though was to use it as an attempt to try to establish contact with some of the spirits of the people who had committed 'suicide' at Beachy Head.

And Mr Thurston made the following comment, back in 1955:

> '…remember, over a hundred people have hurled themselves to perdition from this cliff during the last twenty years!'

Witnesses apparently heard De Vekey shout:

> "There is a voice calling "Oh, Helen. There is a George Foster being called. Peggy Jordan destroyed herself here. She was to give birth to a child. She is full of tears. There is a bearded man. He is wearing a long, flowing robe with a cowl like a monk. It is going back a long, long time. This is evil. He is calling us a lot of fools, "blaspheming fools, I will sweep you all over."
>
> Everyone happy shall be thrown over. He has lain in wait for years."

The medium's movements became more frantic and violent.

After the séance he said;

> "This is the strongest influence I have ever had. It came on almost at once. I seemed impelled towards the cliff edge when it came through to me. It was someone who was bound himself, perhaps a sacrifice, and who has hated and wished ill to all, ever since. Later, after prayers had been said there, I could contact nothing. I believe that this unquiet spirit has been laid to rest forever."

I think it's fair to say though that Mr De Vekey's confidence was more than a little misplaced.

The 'evil' influence of Beachy Head still sings its deadly siren tune, from time to time, it seems.

On 26th June, 1997, an accountant named John Chetwynd, viciously attacked his Vietnamese wife Thi Le, at their home, leaving her for dead. He then drove his two sons, aged three years and nine months, out to the Head where his car was later found abandoned at seven in the morning. Once Mr Chetwynd arrived at the cliff-top, it's thought he forcibly pushed the children over the edge, before hurling himself onto the rocks 600ft below. The bodies were later recovered in a five-hour operation.

A police source was quoted as saying;

> 'We are treating the incident as a double murder and suicide. We don't know what sparked it off, but it's an appalling tragedy.'

It's only a matter of pure speculation of course, but I can't help but wonder…

Is it possible something actively encouraged John Chetwynd to take that one-way trip to Beachy Head? Something like a hideous, grinning Demon or a vengeful black cowled monk, constantly whispering in his ear about how good it would be…How easy it would be to take a run and jump into the next life…?

THE HORROR OF HOLBORN SQUARE

Interestingly enough, just up the road from *The Britannia Inn*, is Holborn Square, a former quarry that's relatively recently been transformed into an industrial estate, and is another area reputedly haunted by an evil, dwarf-like entity.

A friend of mine by the name of Thomas Brown, related the following account, which he said occurred on the early evening of November 4th, 1996.

> "At the time I was employed by a company involved in the renovation of the Tranmere area. We were based in a series of porta-cabins huddled in the looming shadow of the former quarry near to the steep flights of stone steps that the locals had always called, for reasons never fully explained: "The Monkey Steps."
>
> I had volunteered to work a couple of hours overtime along with an older guy, who I knew only as Jock. We were working on a temporary unit that had been loaned so we could carry on extra building work after darkness fell. As there was no electricity in the building we had to use petrol-powered lighting. As we were finally finishing up, at around about 7pm, I set about locking up the unit, whilst Jock took the lighting equipment back to the main office. A few seconds later, he came back babbling about the place being haunted.
>
> He was so terrified that I couldn't get any sense out of him at first, and he refused point blank to discuss it until we left the area altogether. I agreed to accompany him to a nearby pub, The Crooked Billet, and after he'd threw down a double malt whisky and half a pint of Guinness, he calmed down sufficiently to tell me what he'd seen.
>
> As he'd walked around to the back of the unit, he'd glimpsed the dark, shadowy figure of a small man whose attention was apparently focused on the reconstruction work we'd been carrying out. As he approached the figure intent upon asking him what he was doing there, it suddenly disappeared. That was more than enough for Jock, who had turned tail and ran as fast as his legs would carry him away from the area. He refused to further discuss what he'd seen during the rest of the time that I worked there."

The strange thing is, his reference to ghosts in the area immediately struck a chord with me because it ignited a half-forgotten childhood memory…

Back in 1973, and on November 4th, coincidentally enough (?) I'd been out collecting wood for a bonfire along with a group of friends, in and around Holborn Square, which was then little more than an unofficial town dump. As we were rummaging through the assembled piles of junk for combustible material, one of my friends suddenly screamed hysterically claiming that he had seen the figure of a small, grotesque old man leering at him from the edge of the pile of refuse, before promptly vanishing into thin air. The figure had apparently appeared in pretty much the same spot as that in which Jock experienced his encounter 23 years later.

There is a local legend about how a man threw himself and his dog over the edge of the quarry that dominates the landscape around Holborn Square, and there have been rumours of at least three other similar suicides in the area. The locale is also associated with the Birkenhead Priory monks who used to have accommodation in the vicinity, speaking of which...

NEVER AN ABSOLUTION

THE HAUNTING OF BIRKENHEAD PRIORY

According to that font of all knowledge, *Wikipedia,* Birkenhead Priory is the oldest standing building in the county of Merseyside, founded, as it was, around about 1150AD, by Hamon de Masci, 3rd Baron of Dunham Massey, for the Benedictine Order. The monks who resided there for over 400 years, organised the first regulated Ferry across the Mersey, and provided shelter for weary travellers on the occasions when the weather dictated that the River was far too rough to safely traverse by boat.

(Above): The ruins of the Priory's cloisters, the monk's sleeping quarters, and the setting for many a merry meal for dog-tired travellers who would be made more than welcome by the Brotherhood

Legend has it that during the time of Henry VIII's infamous Dissolution, the Abbots had decreed that all the treasures of The Priory should be hidden away in the network of caves and tunnels that ran beneath the edifice. These underground chambers were said to run below the acres of green fields and woodland, themselves long since destroyed and covered by the once thriving shipyard at *Cammell Laird*.

The gold and silver was duly stashed away for safe-keeping, but unfortunately several of the monks couldn't resist the temptation to attempt to steal the treasure for themselves, and set out to line their cassocks with as much booty as they could possibly carry. Divine retribution was close at hand however, and no sooner had they laid their greedy hands upon the loot than a large slab of rock, which had stood for countless years as a natural supporting pillar, suddenly collapsed with catastrophic consequences for the men caught in the tunnels.

They were all killed, either instantly by the resultant cave-in, or with agonising slowness due to starvation or lack of air.

No sign of either the tunnels, caves or fabulous riches have ever been uncovered, but the legend endures thanks to the sightings of the tortured spirits of the dead monks, which are said to wander the grounds of the Priory, most frequently on the anniversary of the underground disaster; seeking in vain for an absolution for their sins.

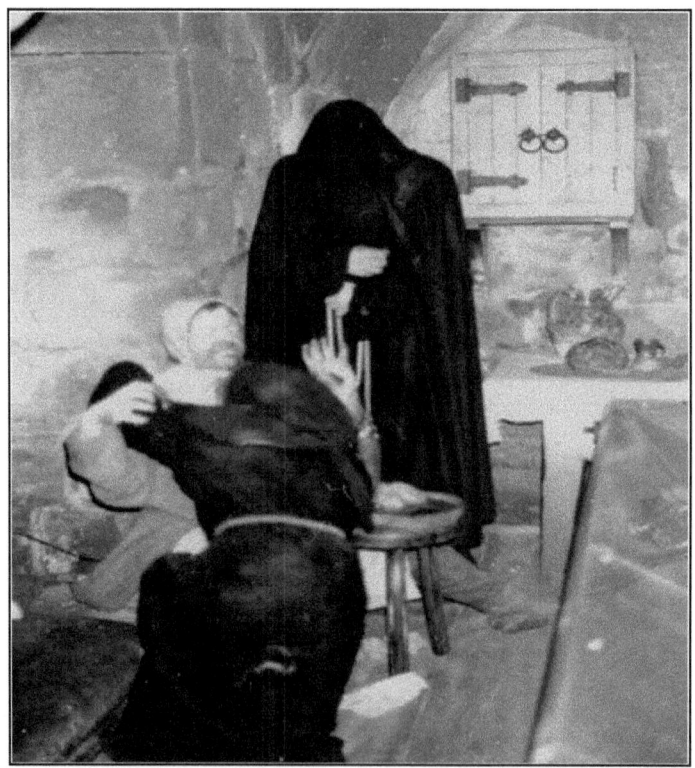

(Above): The Priory is also the reputed location of several sightings of ghostly, black-cloaked figures, chanting as they walk, heads bowed, cowls covering their faces...

St Mary's Tower, was a later addition to the original building and was part of Birkenhead's first parish church opened in 1821, and was later dedicated to the 99 victims of the tragic HMS *Thetis* disaster on June 1st, 1939. (The *Thetis* was a submarine built at *Cammell Laird*, which sank during sea trials in Liverpool Bay, with the loss of all but four of its crew, due to the fact that the Admiralty decided that the men were expendable so long as the bulk of the submarine could be salvaged, although this only emerged after decades of official cover-up, lies and bare-faced denials – now, doesn't *that* sound mightily familiar!).

And it was St Mary's Tower, following a series of extensive renovations at the Priory during the summer of 1990, that various witnesses reported encountering a mysterious Woman in Black, whilst they were visiting the site.
The old church tower, (the top of which rewards those willing and able to ascend the steep, spiral stone staircase with a wonderful panoramic view of the Liverpool waterfront on one side and the snow-capped mountains on the other), was given a £350,000 face-lift after being re-opened to the public.

One of the unforeseen consequences though were persistent reports from various, unconnected individuals of an old woman dressed entirely in black, walking alongside the base of the tower. Amongst those willing to recount their sightings to the local press, was the Priory's then-custodian, Geoff Halewood. He told the reporters that he saw an old woman's face peering in through the window of his office one afternoon. Assuming at first that she was a perfectly ordinary, flesh-and-blood visitor, he went outside to invite her in, only to have her run off for some unspecified reason. Puzzled, he followed her into a passage, which he knew led only to a dead end. There was no way out save for the old woman to turn around and head back towards him. However, to Geoff's amazement, when he reached the mossy, moisture-soaked wall at the end of the passage, there was no sign of the old woman. Not long after this sighting, site construction workers, including foremen, claimed that they had seen a shadowy figure which promptly vanished into thin air the moment the labourers attempted to give chase.

David *Hillhouse* (now there's an appropriately evocative Shirley Jacksonian surname!), as being the curator of the nearby Williamson Art Gallery, was supervising the restoration work at the time and was quoted as saying in the pages of *The Liverpool Echo:*

> "There have been lots of stories about the site which to be frank, aren't very credible.
> But the people who reported these two sightings are not ones to fantasize.
> We don't know who the ghost is, but during the restoration work, a driveway collapsed and revealed a Victorian family vault containing a total of five coffins inscribed with the name, Bailes.
>
> Perhaps we released a spirit at the same time?"

THE MONK'S FERRY POLTERGEIST

The area around Monk's Ferry Brow, situated near to the banks of The River Mersey, and not a million miles from the monk-haunted Birkenhead Priory, was the focal point of a letter penned by Mr Alan Moss, who hails from Noctorum in Birkenhead. This is his story....

I used to be employed as a plant fitter at Weston Ship Repairs, at Monk's Ferry Brow, on the night shift. I was invariably working on my own, and it fell to me to ensure that both the docks and the plant itself were kept running efficiently. There were other electricians working in the same engine shop but they were usually to be found on the other side of the building. They slept in an office which they always kept securely locked, whilst I had to find somewhere within the large building that made up the engine shop, to sleep after the work was finally completed.

We would go out for refreshments at what passed for "lunch-time" i.e. 9.30-10.30pm. It was during one of those typically surreal lunch-hours (my body clock having been subjected to some pretty serious tampering about with. To be honest, it often felt like I'd been teleported to some distant foreign country with its own completely different time zone), that I discovered a conveniently-abandoned van to sleep in. The vehicle had been brought in for repairs. I had a camp bed in my car and I didn't waste any time transferring it into the van.

After locking the workshop doors, I tried to get my head down, intending to sleep away the remainder of my shift. At about 2am, however, I was rudely awoken by the sound of the van doors rattling. My first thought was that the foreman had decided to pay a visit to the site to check if anyone was skiving, and was about to catch me red-handed, sleeping on the job. Warily, and with a growing sense of dread, I got up to wrench open the van doors.

They were rather difficult to open, the hinges hadn't been oiled in God only knew how long, but it didn't matter much anyway, because when I finally managed to open the doors, I found, much to my initial relief, that there was no-one there.

Then the thought struck me that one of the politicians had come looking for me, but when I confronted them they denied having done any such thing.

The incident had unnerved me sufficiently for me to decline the use of the van the following night. I removed my camp bed once more, and secured it to a nearby bench. I fell asleep at roughly the same time as the previous night, but again, at bang on 2am, I was once more rudely awakened from my slumber.

This time it was a terrible shaking that had me staring wildly around for a second or two, before I was suddenly and unceremoniously thrown to the workshop floor. Luckily for me, my head didn't make contact with the solid concrete, but I was still understandably shocked and extremely shaken.

I was more than aware that I simply could not have turned over and fallen from the bench in my sleep, perhaps troubled by a nightmare, because there was very large vice beside the bench that would have prevented me from doing so.

The very next night, I decided, you might not be too surprised to learn, not to go to sleep, but to stay awake for the duration of the entire shift in the workshop on my own. The electricians went to sleep in the blessed sanctuary of their office, as usual, and thoughtlessly locked the door.

All was quiet until the dreaded time of 2am, when a radio that had previously been switched off, suddenly blared into life of its own accord. I got up and switched it off.

Two hours later, it switched itself on again, and after having wearily turned it off once more, I swallowed my pride and went to see the electricians to wake them up. I tried to explain what had happened, but they weren't remotely interested in what they deemed to be my "imaginary troubles."

To be honest, they were mightily pissed off, and they warned me in no uncertain terms, not to bother them again.

I kept my counsel until the next morning, when I told the electrician whose radio it was about what had happened. He was due on the day shift, so I asked him if the radio had a timer on it. He merely looked at me in astonishment and shook his head.

Round about then, my foreman approached me and inquired as to whether I had thrown the contents of a gearbox, which a fitter had been repairing, all over the shop. I told him no, of course I hadn't and he replied that it must have been one of the electricians, then.

I was of the opinion that not even one of those selfish 'sparks' would have stooped so low as to carry out such a spiteful act, but I kept that view pretty much to myself.

Apparently though, there had been several other occasions when similar incidents had occurred – and it hadn't just been gearboxes that had been thrown around.

As for my own experiences, well, I guess I chose to keep them to myself for fear of inviting ridicule.

For the remainder of that week's shift, I locked the main workshop up, and went and slept in the comparative safety of my car, situated as it was, out in the car park.

Later, when I went back to the blessed relief of the day shift, I spoke to some of the day-shift fitters who had, on occasion, worked the night-shift and it soon transpired that they too had undergone similar experiences.

Most curious of all, however, was the account of an employee who had worked the over night on and off for years at Monk's Ferry. He told me that he had on several occasions seem a whole parade of ghostly monks 'walking' through the dock gates with lighted lanterns, and he stated it was well-known locally that the area was a "haunted spot."

DEFINED BY EMOTIONAL DARKNESS:
Dibbinsdale's Phantom Hitchhiker

*'In the dead sound,
A single note drones on and on and on....'*

All Cats Are Grey – The Cure

An old grey stone bridge that crosses a small river, roughly halfway along the winding stretch of road that runs between the suburbs of Spital and Bromborough, has long been rumoured to be haunted by the lonesome spirit of what has been variously described as a White Lady, Ghostly Nun, or Phantom Hitchhiker (all of whom, of course, are the type of apparitions that are right up there with Black-Cowled Monks, Glowing Orbs and The Spirits of Well-Known Historical Characters at the top end of the Most Frequently Reported Supernatural Entity Chart).

According to the most oft-repeated local legend, the spirit is that of a girl who had set out from nearby Poulton Hall, many years ago to make her way to the local nunnery. As she was crossing the bridge however, she was violently attacked by a homicidal rapist who sexually assaulted her and then murdered her, before callously throwing her body into the muddy waters below.

Whatever the truth of this story, what is for certain is that over the last hundred years or so, the place has become synonymous with the appearance (and rapid disappearance) of some sort of female apparition, even if the descriptions of the entity have varied somewhat according to the testimony of the various witnesses.

Numerous people have reported encountering the phantom lady as they have driven towards the bridge that fords the River Dibbin, and not all of the accounts occurred at some time in the dim and distant past, diluting their believability to the point where they take on the dubious quality of an oft-repeated folk tale, either.

One autumn evening, back in the late 1990s, a former taxi driver, originally from the Tuebrook district of Liverpool, told me how he was 'willing to swear on a giant stack of bibles' that he'd encountered something that if it wasn't the ghostly White Lady, 'was near enough so as not to make a spit worth of difference.'

'Spud,' (I'm ashamed to say I never got around to asking him his real name, despite the frequent occasions I'd jumped a cab with him at the wheel) told me this tale when he was driving me home from a night out with friends in Eastham Village.

> "It was mid-October, and I remember it was raining hard. The windscreen wipers were sweeping furiously back and forth, whilst on the radio Michael Stipe was bemoaning the fact that he was stuck in some corner, in dire danger of 'losing his religion'. Through heavy lidded eyes, I'd viewed the road ahead, glistening in the street-lights' sodium glare, and to tell you the truth, I hadn't been in the mood for any kind of conversation, least of all the sort of homespun, barrel-cracker wisdom that appears to be exclusive to Barbers, Bartenders, and Cab drivers, (or the 'Unofficial **B.B.C** World Service,' as I've come to regard them). If you're foolish or desperate enough to afford them the courtesy of lending them your ears for a short while, in return they'll gladly offer you the 'benefit' of their advice on just about any subject you care to name."
>
> Wanna know the real reason behind the Hick's and Gillett's stubborn refusal to relinquish their 'ownership' of Liverpool FC? Concerned about those pesky Iranians and their nuclear ambitions, or The Coalition's dire predictions of an imminent terrorist attack? Curious about just how many other members of Boyzone, might be light in the loafers?
>
> Well, kiss those frustratingly sleepless nights spent tossing and turning as you ponder the imponderable a hugely welcome goodbye. The boys and girls from the **'B.B.C'** will happily fill you in with the true stories behind the headlines and the very latest breaking news as they clip your hair, pour you a pint, or take you home at the fag end of yet another miserable night peering into the murky depths of your umpteenth pint of 'Cain's Raisin Ale.'
>
> And what's more, bargain fans, (pause for a suitably dramatic drum roll), all of this inestimably wise counsel is available at absolutely no extra cost to the standard fare!"
>
> 'Nuthin' ain't worth nuthin,' but it's free,'

…as some country and western singer once opined.

On that rain-lashed autumn evening, the best part of a decade ago, speeding along a road that stretched away like the business end of an amusement park water slide, I couldn't have cared a fig if 'Spud's' previous fare had been Jesus Christ Himself, in the company of assorted Cherubim and Seraphim, en route to Westminster to announce the dawning of A New Age of Peace and Prosperity for All.

I hadn't wanted to talk.

I hadn't even wanted to listen.

I'd simply wanted to get home, greet my so-called 'lucky' Garfield teddy that my ex-girlfriend had bought me for Christmas, the previous year, with a healthy, rugby-style drop-kick and climb into bed, draping the covers firmly over my head to block out the world in time-honoured fashion.

As the more observant amongst you may already have surmised, the evening's festivities hadn't exactly filled me with good cheer and an amiable disposition towards my fellow man (or indeed, woman).

I won't bore you with the details. Suffice to say that what had started out as being a potentially promising prospect, had in the event proven to be about as much fun as bathing naked in a bath filled with bleach.

So when 'Spud' had suddenly looked at me out of the corner of his eye and said:

> "Do you mind very much if we don't take the short-cut route back to The Ferry?"

I simply shrugged my shoulders in an 'I-honestly-couldn't-care-less' gesture.

> "I know it's a bit quicker, like, going down the back roads,"

…he continued.

> "But I prefer to stick to the A41 dual carriageway, if that's alright with you."

Without waiting for a reply, he quickly assured me that this wasn't just some kind of less-than subtle ruse aimed at increasing the taxi fare. He said he simply didn't like driving along the Spital to Bromborough road, and although I thought that was a little bit strange, it didn't particularly bother me, and I told him the A41 was fine with me.

> "Thanks, mate,"

…he said with a sigh, and I was a little shocked to see the expression of relief etched plainly on his face. He looked for all the world like a condemned prisoner who had just received a last-minute reprieve.

And then he glanced sideways at me again.

> "It's decent of you not to think to ask me why, lad,"

…he said.
> "But I think it's only fair that I give you an explanation."

I wanted to tell him that he didn't have to worry. Whatever his reasons, he could keep them to himself, but quite frankly, by that point, I really didn't have the energy. I guess he must have mistaken my brain-numbed silence for unspoken consent, and 'Spud' therefore happily began rambling away and I'd had to grit my teeth to stifle a scream.

I'd been sure I'd be subjected to some great big pile of meaningless hot air, and it was more than stiflingly toasty enough inside the cab as it was.

But to be fair to him, what he did have to say couldn't have taken me more by surprise than if he'd have suddenly announced he kept finding a couple of stray zebras wandering into in his kitchen every Wednesday morning…

> "I suppose the easiest thing to do would be to tell you I hate driving along those back roads, convenient short cuts though they may well be, simply because they're fairly poorly-lit and chock full of winding bends and blind corners. The route can be even more of a king-size pain in the arse when it's slick with ice, or sheets of teeming rain, or filled with giant dirty-brown puddles, each roughly the depth of the Marianas Trench.

Any single one of those things would make most drivers think twice before taking those roads.

The truth is though, I could quite easily put up with all of that. I've been a cab driver for more years than I care to remember, and it takes more than a few adverse weather conditions to put me off taking a short cut or two whenever the opportunity arises.

But then something happened to me a couple of years back. An incident that still gives me the chills, just thinking about it. But I promised I'd fill you in, and I'm a man of me word, so here goes….

During the pre-dawn hours of a freezing, January morning I was driving back to my base in Higher Bebington. I'd just dropped off a fare in nearby Bromborough, and I was really looking forwards to a piping hot cup of coffee and maybe a bite to eat; one of those Sayer's Cornish Pasties, warmed up in the microwave. Oh, aye, you can't beat them lad. They are absolutely boss!'

Anyway, it was chilly in the car, colder than a witch's tit, not to put too fine a point on it, even with the heating turned up full blast, and the harsh frost that sugared the landscape and rendered the darkened back roads treacherous with black ice, meant that I was taking extra special care as I drove. The gritters had been out in force the previous evening, but they'd done little to make conditions any less hazardous. The ragged remnants of a low-lying mist clung stubbornly in the dips and hollows like a bunch of barfly's hanging on for just one more shot, long after closing time.

The road was completely clear of other traffic, and I hadn't seen a single pedestrian since I'd left Eastham, but just as I was approaching Dibbinsdale Bridge, I saw, illuminated in the glare of my headlights, a female figure clad in a white, hooded cloak standing on the left-hand side of the road. I was startled to see anyone, least of all a woman, out at this time of night and in this weather. She had her head bowed, almost as though she was lost in silent prayer and being the chivalrous type, I instantly felt sorry for her.

'Christ, she must be bloody freezing!' I thought as I drew close enough to her to see the pitifully thin garments she was wearing were hopelessly inadequate for such bone-freezing temperatures.

"Alright, love, can I offer you a lift?" I called as I wound down the window on the passenger side, admitting a blast of frigid winter air as I did so.

She didn't reply, just simply stood there with her shoulders hunched and her head slumped, the body language of someone bereft of all hope, like she'd just been dumped by the man of her dreams, and she gave no indication that she was even aware of my presence,

"Don't worry," I said, in what I hoped was my most charming and reassuring voice. "I'm not gonna charge yer any money or anything. There's no strings, honestly. I just wanna see yer get safely home.' I shivered and pulled me coat and scarf more tightly around me. "You shouldn't be stuck all the way out here on your own. Not on a night like this."

I expected her to swallow her pride, or bury her fears then, and plonk herself down on the back seat, eager to get in out of the cold, but she didn't. She simply continued to stand there, refusing to meet my gaze, and after a few long seconds had trickled by with the cab door wide open and the taxi's exhaust fumes combining with the mist to obscure both the immediate surroundings and the road up ahead, I'd just about decided that the woman was either simple-minded, or off her head on ale or drugs or both. I shook my head and moved across to pull the cab door shut when the cowled figure suddenly raised its face to mine, and I saw with heart-stopping clarity she was as beautiful as an angel. The kind the great artists, the likes of Michelangelo, depicted on the ceilings of the world's most magnificent cathedrals. She smiled sadly at me, and it was an expression of such unimaginable sorrow and loss, I suddenly felt close to tears myself.

And her eyes...

Her eyes were filled with the horror of a thousand nightmares, of hurts endured and heartbreaks suffered, and it's not very often I'm lost for words, as I'm sure you've probably noticed, but at that particular moment the path between my brain and any kind of meaningful speech was suddenly hit by a series of terminal road-works.

As it turned out, I didn't need to say anything, anyway.

With a barely perceptible nod of her head, she gracefully manoeuvred her way into the front passenger seat of me cab, and sat herself down without saying so much as a mumbled 'thank you.' She pulled the cab door closed, and stared straight ahead through the windscreen as though in a trance. I asked her where she wanted dropping off and she simply raised her right hand and pointed at the fog-shrouded road before us. Yeah, of course, I thought that was more than a little strange, but I held me tongue and gently put me foot down, assuming I was heading in the right direction and that she'd tell me her destination when she was good and ready.

We travelled for a few minutes without speaking, and although I didn't realise it till later, the volume on the cab radio; the late night tunes on Magic FM, and the familiar crackling of the calls from the base, had all but faded to a sleepy background drone. There was no way I was going to fall asleep at the wheel though, not with an especially gorgeous damsel-in-distress sat right beside me, and I continued to drive carefully towards the outskirts of Bromborough, seeing as how that was the direction the strange young woman had indicated she wanted to go. I tried several times to engage her in conversation, but I may as well have been talking to myself for all the good it did, and I soon gave it up and lapsed into a reluctant silence.

Again, it was only much later, back at the taxi base, that I suddenly became aware of another strange thing about that already weird, Twilight-Zoney night...The back road from Dibbinsdale to Bromborough can't be any more than two or three miles long, at the very most, and it should have taken no longer than ten minutes or so to travel along, even in such hazardous driving conditions. The fact is though, I had soon lost track of time and it had seemed, somehow, like we'd been driving for hours...I know that sounds ridiculous, but I honestly felt like I was in a kind of dream state, somehow floating in a timeless vacuum, and although it didn't occur to me at the time, the image that has since sprung to mind is of one of some lurid illustration featured in a magazine I once read about Great Unsolved Mysteries. It was a piece about the tragedy that befell Flight 19; a squadron of five Navy Avenger fighter planes that went unaccountably missing on a routine training mission somewhere in the midst of the so-called Bermuda Triangle, and the vivid mental picture that has stayed with me ever since was of the flight leader, Captain Charles Taylor, repeatedly radioing his base at

Fort Lauderdale, Florida, in a voice laced with scarcely concealed hysteria; "It looks like we are entering white water…We are completely lost!"

For a few moments there, I think I had an inkling of the type of blind panic that Captain Taylor must have endured, because due to my own personal 'white-out,' I couldn't for the life of me differentiate where the hell the road ended and the sky began, and I had to shove me left hand in me mouth to keep meself from screaming.

To be honest, I don't think even that would have prevented it from erupting like some blaring sonic geyser if the mist hadn't have suddenly begun to thin and split apart just then, like the tattered remnants of a bad dream upon waking.

"Thank Christ, for that!' I said, sighing with relief, as I turned to my companion. 'At least now I can see where we're goi…"

Gooseflesh spread up my arms, and the words froze on my lips as I saw the woman was no longer there.

She'd disappeared without a trace, and there was no way on God's earth she could have gotten out of me taxi without me being aware of it.

This inexplicable vanishing was the final, crowning absurdity, and here at last came that long held-back scream, and had anyone been around to hear, it would doubtless have conjured up images of a wild November gale, shrieking through a pile of old animal bones, or a keening wail drawn deep from within a well of scarcely-remembered childhood fears….

Many is the time that I've since considered the possibility that I imagined the whole thing. That it was a nothing more than an especially vivid dream brought on by a combination of tiredness and the undeniably creepy atmosphere of Dibbinsdale Bridge, when the sun dips over the horizon….

But the truth is, however logical that might seem, I'm convinced that I really did pick up a passenger who somehow slipped through a dimensional gap in time and space, and stepped into our world, for a little while at least.

And that's why I don't go driving along that particular stretch of road after dark, any more.

To be perfectly honest, I try and avoid taking that road during the daylight hours, too. It doesn't hurt to be extra cautious. The other cabbies might take the Mick, but quite frankly, I don't mind that too much. I console myself with the knowledge that they really don't know any better.

They don't believe in the existence of ghosts or spirits or whatever you want to call them…

And they didn't see what I saw that night".

THE HAUNTERS OF THE DARK

I think it's fair to say that for as long as I can remember, I've been mortally afraid of the dark.

Blame it on an admittedly over-active imagination, my parents' liberal-minded attitude in allowing me to stay up and watch late-night horror movies, or my devouring of the works of M.R. James, Clive Barker, Edgar Allen Poe et al, not to mention the 'true-life' ghost stories my half-Irish Auntie Anne used to regale us with every Boxing Night; William MacKenzie, the gambler who sold his soul to the Devil, the bogeyman who lurked in the shadow-filled depths of our school's boiler room, the shambling monstrosity that haunted the treacherous mud-flats of the Mersey Estuary.

All of these horrors and a thousand more doubtless contributed to the sense of dread I'd feel creeping into my bones when I came to climb the stairs long after my brother had gone to bed, and I was forbidden from turning on any of the lights in case I woke him. Quietly closing the door behind me I'd step into the near total darkness. The

thick, heavy curtains were nearly always pulled firmly together, even at the height of summer, admitting nought but the tiniest sliver of moonlight. It was like entering a black, featureless void where anyone or anything could be lying in wait, ready to grab at the slightest hint of exposed flesh with wormy fingers, or tear with razor-sharp claws.

I'm not ashamed to say that I frequently ran (on tip-toes) for the sanctuary of my bed and would leap onto the mattress with all the grace of a shot albatross before throwing the covers over my head and reaching under the pillow for my cheap plastic torch. It's a little strange, but I don't remember ever actually switching the torch on, though. I only used it as a sort of psychological last resort. Just knowing I had the option of a light source within easy reach proved to be a great comfort and helped me to sleep most nights.

As we've already seen, however, there were occasions when no amount of 'protection' could provide an effective barrier against 'The Terror That Comes By Night.'

Things were bad during the long golden space between late March and September.

It got even worse when the summer slipped away for another year.

I've always dreaded what I came to call (with a barely suppressed shudder); 'The Gloom-Laden March of The Dark Nights'

I found their coming always begged the most pertinent of questions:

Why on Earth do those in authority consciously choose to inflict an extra sixty minutes of gloom (in every sense of the word) upon a populace already beset with the frightening prospects of further terrorist attacks, inner city rioting, senseless gun crime, and the potential for a full-blown bird flu epidemic?

World-weary cynics might well suggest that the government are more than happy to see this country's citizens skulking around wearing expressions so grim they look as though they've just been informed they've won front row tickets for an S Club 7 reunion tour, with a Celine Dion tribute act as support, as it's all part of some fiendishly clever plot to ensure the electorate are to busy being maniacally depressed to question the wisdom (or otherwise) of their policies.

What is for certain is from the onset of the very second that the hands of the clock are dragged back an hour at the tail end of October, until the onset of an impossibly distant-seeming spring, that additional spell of darkness is doled out like a double helping dreariness scooped from the dregs of the Misery Bowl.

And never mind whether we choose to feast on this foul concoction or not.

But I digress.

The fact is that an estimated 500,000 people suffer from Seasonal Affective Disorder (appropriately enough given the acronym SAD), so is it any wonder the working day mornings are almost exclusively populated by sour-faced individuals with their noses pushed up against a rainy bus window?

Honestly, it's enough to inspire you to make like Ray Winstone in the excellent movie The Proposition who, when gazing with narrowed eyes at the less-than-promising vista of the sun-bleached, arid wasteland of the Australian outback, mutters disconsolately:

'What fresh hell is this?'

For many years, I thought I was the only person to suffer from the 'Night Terrors.' I mean, I was well aware that most people have bad dreams from time to time, usually as a consequence of eating too much rich food prior to going to bed, or when excessively stressed, or caught in the wretched throes of depression.

But this was markedly different. I often felt that the source of my terror was undeniably real. I was convinced that I was wide awake when what I referred to as 'The Mur Mur Man' chose to pay a decidedly unwelcome nocturnal visit.

What was even more disconcerting was the regularity of these dreams. They would occur at least once a month, and it got so bad at one point that I was too scared to go to bed, sneaking back downstairs to sleep on the living room sofa with all the lights switched on, until I was somewhat embarrassingly caught out by my parents.

They were fairly sympathetic to my plight, but their suggestion that I should perhaps refrain from watching so many scary movies and lay off the spooky novels for a while didn't appeal to me one iota.

(...and besides, there was the troubling fact that on a couple of occasions, I'd dreamed that I'd awoken from a quite terrible nightmare, and my Mum and Dad had come into my bedroom, switched on the light, and asked me what was wrong.

'There are Things in here!' I screamed into their bemused faces. 'They've come to get me!'

And to my dismay, far from reassuring me that I was alright, 'You've had a bad dream, that's all,' they simply grinned and whispered, 'We know. We let them in!')

Okay. I know at first glance that my endless bleating may ring hollow, and that like the hangover victim who can't stop hitting the bottle, my suffering was entirely self-inflicted, but there was, I would contend, a logic to my stubborn refusal to kick the 'horror bug', and it had nothing to do with selfish addiction. I strongly believed that, in some strange way, the posters of the likes of King Kong, The Wolf-Man and the Frankenstein Monster that adorned my walls, the shelves that literally groaned under the combined weight of the works of Stoker, Bloch and Herbert, and the phosphorescent models of Mr Hyde, The Mummy, and The Old Witch, acted as a kind of magical protection. They were verification of the ancient edict that states Evil cannot bear to look upon itself, and of course, the reasoning behind the creation of the incredibly ugly and intricately detailed gargoyles that adorn the roofs and ceilings of countless Christian churches and cathedrals.

And so, I was left with little option other than to (quite literally) sweat it out in my bedroom. The dreams continue with varying degrees of regularity to this very day. I still wake up some nights sure that something is waiting in the black.

Waiting to brush its cold lips on the back of my neck and rasp my stomach with its jagged fingernails.

SCREAMING ON A BLADE OF DREAMS

It was only in comparatively recent times that I became aware that far from being the only one to be plagued by this type of experience, there were literally thousands (and quite likely hundreds of thousands) of people who had been afflicted with similar nightmares.

In fact, it's so common psychologists even have a typically fancy name for it. As nonsensical-sounding tongue-twisters go, how about trying this one for size; 'Sleep Paralysis with Hypnagogic and Hypnopompic Hallucinations.'

You may never have heard of it spoken of in those precise terms before, but the phenomenon apparently has a long and venerable history too.

The main features of the typical sleep paralysis experience are as follows: at the onset there will likely be an impression of wide-awakefulness combined with total immobility.

This inability to move a single muscle may be exacerbated by a very real fear of moving, as if by revealing your awareness of 'The Entity's' presence in the room, you may inspire it to act. This refusal to let It know you are even awake may even result in you refusing to open your eyes so that you won't have to be confronted by the true shape of the awful apparition. After all, seeing as how 'The Entity' is almost always inherently evil and extremely threatening, acknowledging its presence by gazing upon its awful visage is probably not the best of ideas. It may be human, animal, or some formless, capering horror that gibbers amidst the darkest shadows of the room. It may content Itself with simply watching the petrified sleeper. Or it may, in some instances, choose to openly interact with the percipient by speaking to, or even physically assaulting, its victim. These attacks usually take the form of a feeling of intense pressure on the witness' chest, but it can also involve pushing, choking or smothering.

Sometimes, these 'Entities' are totally silent, but on the rare occasions when they do make a noise, the most commonly reported sound is that of footsteps or a soft shuffling in the room's inky blackness. Heavy breathing has also been described by certain witnesses.

As previously stated, 'The Entity' can take many shapes, but their appearance tends to conform to some or all of these five categories; (as defined by J.A. Cheyne of the Department of Psychology, based at the University of Waterloo).

    1: Ghostly humanoid form in featureless silhouette

    2: Dark and grey in colour

    3: Often, only a disembodied face or 'Demonic mask' is discerned.

    4: The eyes of The Entity are often the only distinctive feature later recalled by the percipients.

    5: The basically humanoid Entity may undergo a sudden and unexpected transformation

On rare occasions, the percipient may also undergo an apparent Out-of-the-Body-Experience, a feeling of being lifted up towards the ceiling, an occurrence often accompanied by a strange tingling or vibrating sensation.

In terms of frequency, these Night Terrors most commonly occur either once in a person's lifetime or with large intervals in between the repeated experiences. Sometimes however, just to complicate things, these intervals can be punctuated by a 'run' of attacks that occur during the majority of nights that encompass a one to two week period. There are, thankfully, very few instances where attacks are experienced on a very frequent, or even nightly basis.

Not surprisingly, sleep paralysis and its attendant hallucinatory properties have been held responsible for everything from Demonic manifestations to ghostly phenomena to the modern-day Alien Abduction controversy.

Now pay attention, readers.

Here comes the science bit.

J.A. Cheyne has described the symptoms of sleep paralysis in the following terms:

> 'It is a condition in which someone, most often lying in a supine position (that's on their back, for the laymen amongst us) about to drop off to sleep, or just waking from sleep, realises that they are unable to move or speak or even cry out. This may last a few seconds or several moments, occasionally longer. People frequently report feeling a 'presence' that is often described as malevolent, threatening or Evil. An intense

> sense of dread and terror is very common. The presence is likely to be vaguely felt or sensed just out of sight, but thought to be watching and monitoring, often with intense interest, sometimes standing by, or actually sitting on the bed.'

He goes on to state that on some occasions, the presence may attack, strangling and exerting crushing pressure on the chest. People also report auditory, visual, and tactile hallucinations, as well as floating sensations and OOBEs. These various sensory experiences have been referred to collectively as stated earlier, as Hypnagogic and Hypnopompic experiences, or 'HEEs', amusingly enough.

After a varying duration of fleeting seconds or the passing of entire minutes, (or longer, if you're really unlucky), one feels suddenly released from the paralysis, but is likely to be left with feelings of grim melancholy and lingering anxiety.

> 'People may also report severe pain in their limbs while trying to move them,'

…he adds.

> 'Several recent surveys suggest that between 25-30% of people say that they have experienced at least a mild form of sleep paralysis at least once, and about 20-30% have had the experience on several occasions.'

He winds up by issuing a statement filled with a perverse kind of optimism,

> 'Aside from the very disturbing features of the experience itself, the phenomenon is quite benign.'

Right. So that's all sorted then. We can all sleep soundly in our beds, tonight.

Interestingly, it seems that Sleep Paralysis often begins in the years of adolescence, although in truth, it can start up at any age. It is unusual though for it to kick in after one reaches their 30s. So if you're advancing into middle-age, or have passed life's roughly half-way stage, and you haven't yet had the 'pleasure' of an attack of the 'Night Terrors', it's unlikely (though by no means impossible) that you'll ever be subjected to the sickening fear it can inspire during the slow silent hours before first light.

The nightmare, as a form of nocturnal attack has of course been closely linked to Demonology and stories of ghostly visitations since time immemorial. One of the most common Entity descriptions is that of 'The Night Hag', the wizened, cackling crone familiar from the pages of countless Fairy stories and the Witchcraft pamphlets of medieval Europe.

The Sumerian Demon Ardat lili or Lilitu, the prototype for the later Hebrew Lilith, and the Roman Lamia, was one of the earliest Hag Demons. She was capable of flying at night and took great delight in attacking unsuspecting men in their sleep. There are it seems, a number of related spirits described in both Middle Eastern and European folklore who also exhibited a penchant for sitting on men's chests and attempting to choke them while they slept on obliviously. Some of the better known spirits of this sort are Greek Ephialtes ('one who leaps upon'), and Mora (the night 'mare' or monster, ogre, etc), the Roman Incubus and Succubus ('one who presses or crushes'), the German Mar/Mare nachtmar, and the Old English Maere, (Mab, Mair, Mare-Hag). Other countries such as Norway, Spain and Poland also had their remarkably similar Night-Mares, and the interested reader might want to check out the works of the likes of D.J.Hufford for a thorough overview of the history of the Old Hag phenomenon.

As well as attacking helpless humans in the dead of night, these creatures were notorious shape-shifters, able to take on various forms when carrying out their attacks.

These Demons were often identified with the spirits of the forest, such as the Great God Pan, as well as Satyrs, Sirens, and Sylvani, and even with the Goddess Diana. Many of these creatures were depicted as having the upper body of a human being, and the lower half of a goat or faun, (but please extinguish all mental images of that cricket-jumper wearing balloon-head from the mobile phone advert, if you would!)

Pan, of course, was the originator of the word 'panic,' and he was frequently described as being the 'instigator of dreams and visions, especially those that produced sudden, violent terror.'

There was also certain classes of Angels called Watchers (not to mention the Fallen Angels) who were said to be associated with the Incubus. According to Christian belief, some of these Watchers were sent to observe human affairs and wound up getting sexually involved with mortal women. As you do. The progeny of such illicit encounters were, predictably enough, inhuman monsters and Demons who thought it a great sport to assault humans lying in bed at night.

But such lore is not exclusive to Western culture.

- In St Lucia, in the West Indies, the attack of the Kokma comes at a time when the victim is just falling asleep or in the throes of waking up. The sensations should by now be familiar: the pressure on the chest, the inability to move, the fear and dread of the perceived presence, etc. In this part of the world, however, 'The Entity' is the spirit of a dead baby that haunts the area. They apparently enjoy jumping on the chest of their victims and clutching at their throat. The victim is therefore unable to cry out for help. The Kokma cannot be controlled. They grab people's throats for the sheer hell of it.
- Interestingly, the idea that the Terror is the spirit of an un-baptised baby (or a whole squadron of un-christened infants) is also prevalent in Ireland.
- In Thailand, the phenomenon is known as the Phi um (Ghost possessed) and involves pressure, immobility, and something black covering the body. In Japan, Kanashibara ('to tie with an iron rope') is a common and widely known experience. In Korea, people are said to be afflicted by the ka wi nulita ('scissors possessed'), inspired by an overwhelming sense of fear.
- Meanwhile in Laos, da chor is described as follows: 'You want to speak, you are dumb. You want to call out, you cannot. You feel you are dying, dying, you want to run away. You piss with fear in your sleep.'

Charming.

As David Hufford wrote, back in 1976, the Sleep Paralysis Nightmare is widespread,

> '...at least in Western culture. It has been regularly reported for more than 2,000 years and has been attached to a variety of narrative frameworks....But regardless of the framework, the experimental features have remained basically the same. This consistency of detail, apparently rather independent of tradition, is the most surprising and difficult to account for.'

In simple English, the striking similarity of the entities encountered and the experiences shared between the widely different cultures, is more than a little strange.

And then there is something else worth mentioning at this juncture. Although there are literally hundreds of folk remedies available to help ward off these nocturnal attacks, the most common preventative measure is something as deceptively simple as taking care not to sleep on your back. I'm sure there's a rational explanation for why this should be, but the fact remains that the vast majority of reported attacks have taken place whilst the sufferer has been sleeping in that position.

Apparently, there are two recognised types of sleep paralysis. One is called, imaginatively enough, **'Common Sleep Paralysis'**, a state where a person wakes up to find their body 'frozen.' This temporary paralysis affects the body's motor functions and macro muscle groups. This state can last for anywhere between 15 seconds to a minute, although there are rare cases where it has reportedly lasted for far longer.

In fairly recent times, researchers have discovered that hormones released during the R.E.M./dream state paralyse the body and prevent it from acting out the complicated plots of your dreams or nightmares. During most regular sleep cycles, the hormones begin to wear off even before the dream is completed, and thus people wake up with a fully functioning body. On rare occasions, the hormones are still actively suppressing the gross motor functions of the body and thus upon waking, the individual finds his or her body temporarily paralysed.

Though waking to this state of helplessness can be frightening, it is, by definition, fairly common and perfectly harmless.

According to the 'experts', anyway.

However, the second form of Sleep Paralysis, the one which we've been referring to throughout this chapter, known as the Hypnagogic (the state between sleep and wakefulness), or the 'Hag Phenomenon', is a far more terrifying experience.

There is evidence that this can simultaneously afflict an entire locale, for example, a whole village, in much the same way as an epidemic. A region that had previously had no reported cases of the 'Hag Phenomenon' can quite literally, overnight, be inundated with stories of sleepers being attacked by so-called 'Bedroom Invaders'. And it seems, these newly-afflicted areas can remain 'infected' with the 'Night Terrors' for up to three years, according to the 'experts' who have studied these exotic sleep disorders.

One frequently asked question is why are the victims of the phenomenon only ever confronted by visions of categorically 'Evil' Entities and not faith in the-triumph-of-light-affirming Angels?

Our old friend Dr Al Cheyne has a theory that may well provide the answer; 'Recent evidence from neuro-imaging studies during REM, shows that (and here's where the language gets a trifle academic), amygdala and several related limbic structures in the brain – the centre of our emotional being – are active during REM sleep. These strictures are associated with instinctual responses, including fear, and what is called the 'threat-activated-vigilance system.' This is thought to be activated by subtle clues for threat, which the system then attempts to corroborate by searching for further cues for danger. Such cues are especially active during anxiety dreams and nightmares and probably stimulate unpleasant memories, including culturally conventional images of threat, such as ghosts and aliens.

> 'The fear of undetected threat is exacerbated because the person is awake, paralysed and usually in a helpless, supine position. These are hardly circumstances to generate pleasant hallucinations. This throws up ghostly images; the confrontational Grim Reaper and other hooded figures are popular ... some people have even seen Darth Vader.'

'WHAT DO YOU SEE AT NIGHT, WHEN THE DEMONS COME?'
A Brief Sample of Night Terror Case Histories

What if, though, the "experts" are completely wrong in their confident assertion that these malignant Night Terrors, be they Demons, Goblins, Aliens, Ultraterrestrials, whatever, really exist? Not just as disconcertingly vivid figments of the sweaty aftermath of a nightmare, but as some kind of otherworldly visitant, a multi-dimensional entity capable of interacting with humans on occasions of their own choosing?

And before you reject my theorising with a dismissive wave of the hand, perhaps you'll at least afford me the courtesy of considering the following account, and give pause to wonder.

Certainly, the relatives of seven residents of Canyon County, Idaho, USA, who died in their sleep during a five-month period in 1997, may have had cause to pose a question similar to that of my own.

Area doctors were forced to call in state and federal health officials to attempt to explain the mysterious deaths. These enigmatic demises were widely reported in the American press, including 'USA Today'. No official explanation was ever forthcoming.

'There were some unusual findings in the cases that suggest they might be tied together,' Mercy Medical Centre pathologist Thomas Donnelinger stated at the time, without, frustratingly, choosing to elaborate on any more of the details.

Back in 1995, David Musson, a 29-year-old architect from Croydon, England, experienced a classic 'Night Hag' visitation.

In Mr Musson's words:

> 'I'm not sure what it was that woke me up, but right away I had this horrible feeling that someone else was in the room. It was a few seconds after that I realised I couldn't move at all. By then I was panicking, and at the same time I felt there was someone leaning right over me, not touching me at that point, but really close, looming.
>
> And then I saw this face coming quickly out of the dark, just for a second, really horrible, ugly and old. And I realised I couldn't breathe properly. It felt like someone was pushing down really hard on my chest.
>
> I thought I was going to die. I'm not sure if the pushing on my chest stopped before or after I found I could move again.' **

During the April of that same year, two women reported to the admittedly less-than-reliable Sunday press, of how an 'icy-fingered spirit-Demon' climbed into their respective beds, and had sexual relations with them. Mrs Pamela Day and Ms Kathleen Dallaway, made the bizarre claim that they suffered sleep paralysis as the 'Invisible Assailant' had its wicked way with them, whilst they were residing in a block of flats in the Walsall district of England.

Mrs Day, 47, told reporters of how she felt she needed 'professional help' to exorcise the amorous spirit.

> 'Three weeks ago, I was in bed with my boyfriend. He had his back to me. I suddenly felt a cold presence next to me and two icy fingers caressed my spine. Then, a week later, the spirit got into bed with me again and the bed began to move up and down. It was a ghost having sex with me!
>
> I later mentioned my experience to another tenant, and she said she had exactly the same thing happen to her.'

The 'Invisible Assailant', whose actions are eerily reminiscent of those employed by the legendary Incubus, made no sexual advances when it first made its presence known, a whole two years earlier. Pamela Day stated that the spirit used to merely 'play about, messing up the bedclothes and sitting on my daughter's leg as I lay on the couch.'

> 'But one night I became aware of a presence bending over me in bed. In certain lights you can just make out the outline of a male figure.'

Meanwhile, Kathleen Dallaway, a 26-year-old single mother, who lived on the seventh floor of Victoria House, described how, two weeks prior to Pamela's experience, 'I could feel a spirit climbing into bed beside me. There was no sexual thing, I could just feel his cold presence on my back. I was paralysed with fear.'

Source: *Daily Mirror*, 23rd January 1995

DEAD OF NIGHT

There were, so far as I am aware, no follow-ups to this story, which originally appeared in The Sunday People, in April 1995, providing ammunition to those who suspect the account has all the veracity of a politician's smile. I know from my incessant trawling through the newspapers and other periodicals that such encounters are not as uncommon as you might think.*

Another percipient, Matthew Jones-Chesters, 30, is a neuro-psychologist who works for North Exeter Mental Health. He described how, back in November, 2001, he would often awake 'rooted in bed, watching as a black shape gathered in the corner of the room, as if from nothing.'

> 'I can see it, like a huge bat, massive and caped. It fills the room and comes closer, and eventually it's around me, cloudy and dark. I feel its pressure and it's holding me, and then, under its weight and power, I feel I'm sinking and being dragged down.
>
> I fight to bring myself around, but I can't - and this is the truly awful part - I can't because I'm totally paralysed. The best I can do is make a noise in my throat in the hope that I'll bring myself round. It's horrible.' **

One of the regular correspondents to 'DON' is a diligent Fortean researcher named Neil Arnold. He sent me the following article on the subject of 'Night Terrors'. It makes for interesting, thought-provoking reading...

NIGHT BRINGS THE HAG

The following tale is a true account. I believe that it may well be rather unique with regards to the phenomenon known as the 'Old Hag', or what science and psychology likes to call Sleep Paralysis.

I have read countless books on the paranormal and many articles and papers on 'the terror that comes in the night'.

I have also experienced such an apparition, too, and now I find I'm filled with the need to write about the encounter, not least because I have never read or heard of any other quite like it. My friends and family have also undergone a bout of the 'Night Terrors', and have their own stories to tell, but again they bear little similarity to my own.

I am unable to recall the specific dates of the events I am about to relate, although I can confirm they occurred within the last couple of years. After reading a book called *The Terror That Comes in the Night* by David Hufford, I was intrigued but not satisfied with the explanations put forward for the experiences recounted within its pages.

Okay, so the Sleep Paralysis effect, not yet fully explained by conventional science, may well be the catalyst for many of the reported encounters with (quite literally) nightmarish phantoms, but why should witnesses from widely differing countries and cultural backgrounds all describe eerily similar entities? And is the modern-day Alien Abduction phenomenon a natural progression of the ancient Night Hag experience? I am not convinced that we fully understand the workings of the mind. Is it possible that it

---

* **Source:** April, 1995 *'The Sunday People'*
** **Source:** *The Guardian*

may in itself be a separate entity, holding the keys to the 'super unknown'? Perhaps apparitions and ghosts truly do exist, but only within the field of our own mental perception.

I am not saying that everything peculiar we see is simply 'all in the mind' but when people say, 'Oh, the mind is just playing tricks,' maybe they're closer to some weird immutable truth than they think.

The so-called 'Hag Attack' can occur at any time. Whilst the hours of darkness seem to be more suited to such encounters, I know a number of people who have experienced such a presence during daylight hours. Many cases simply describe a strange, forceful pressure on the area of the chest, which gradually eases after a period of time, sometimes minutes, sometimes (worryingly) hours. Witnesses will usually describe how their bodies are overcome with an awful state of paralysis, rendering their entire body immobile. This, it must be stressed, is the common Sleep Paralysis attack, and may well be explainable in purely psychological terms.

However, quite often, there comes the feeling of a dreadful presence entering the room, often taking the shape of an Old Hag, adorned in dark vestments. The bony, ancient-looking crone may move quickly towards the bed, and in the most extreme cases, leap onto your chest. This in fact happened to a good friend of mine, who later told me that he felt as if 'I was fighting to save my soul.'

It is not uncommon for the victims to feel drained mentally and physically by this entity, although eventually they are able to wrestle themselves free of the presence and the accompanying paralysis. One way of securing release, is to focus on a certain mundane object in the room in order to be able to concentrate upon its everyday reality and gradually conquer their fear.

Another of my friends, who has personally investigated the famous Blue Bell Hill Phantom (sometimes described as being a hideous old Witch or a withered-faced hag), has reportedly seen just such an Entity in his bedroom, which although appearing small, actually fought him physically. On one occasion he was forced to grab the apparition by the shoulders in order to save himself from serious harm.

If such encounters are mere sleep-induced hallucinations, then something is very wrong here. Sceptics may argue that such vivid 'dreams' are caused by over-active imaginations and being deluged with media images of the strange and uncanny, even when we appear to be unaware of it. But whilst I readily concede that excessive tiredness, illness and stress can induce nightmares, I do not see why so many people should report being attacked by such an obviously decrepit figure…

Having said that however, my own personal 'attacks' have involved peculiar apparitions totally unlike The Hag, and are more akin to the denizens of the realm of the completely ridiculous.

I enjoy engaging in a little bit of clandestine occult activity, as well as tracking exotic animals in and around Kent, hunting Vampires in Highgate Cemetery, and endlessly writing papers on all manner of things weird and wonderful. This should not be taken to imply that I am more easily susceptible to these nightly visitations. Indeed, a majority of people who have experienced Sleep Paralysis and its attendant phantoms have not any interest whatsoever in the paranormal or the occult, and many have never even heard of 'The Old Hag Phenomenon'.

My first experience came just prior to nodding off one night. Yes, I had a lot of things on my mind, hell, most of us do. Yet the fact that I wasn't fully asleep made the whole thing more bizarre. It must have been around midnight when I caught of something white in colour and about the size of a squirrel scuttle out of my bedroom door. It promptly disappeared. This 'thing' never returned. It never attacked me and I never discerned any great degree of detail, and although I thought the whole situation odd, I soon put it out of my mind.

My next experience was a whole lot weirder.

I awoke one night after I had felt 'something' touching my left hand. I sat up in bed and in the darkness I was just about able to make out a 'blob' sitting on my hand. This thing somehow felt attached to one of my fingers, and although it didn't seem to be biting, it felt as though it was somehow draining me. In shock and horror I jumped up and slammed my hand on the bed over and over in an attempt to dislodge this 'thing' from my finger. Eventually, the presence vanished, and when I summoned up enough courage to get up and switch on the bedroom light, there was no trace of the whatever-it-was.

The next morning however, I discovered a blood blister on the very same finger. I tried to dismiss this as being a direct result of my hammering my hand against the mattress.

The strangest thing of all occurred quite recently, and was completely different to the other manifestations. Again, it took place at night. I had barely been asleep, so it must have been around 12:30am when I felt a presence in my bed. I was lying on my stomach and could feel something on one of my legs and it was moving slowly up my body. The thing moved up my left-hand side and I could feel it faintly. I sat up quickly, wondering what was going on and simply sat there for a short while.

Suddenly, and without warning, 'The Thing' was on my left shoulder and it appeared to be a white, misty mass. Absolutely terrified, I leapt up and began brushing at my shoulder with my right hand. 'The Thing' seemed to disappear after a few well-aimed swipes. I was stood on the floor and I noticed that my left arm was numb and there was a tingling feeling all over it.

'The Thing' was nowhere to be seen.

How could I adequately seek to explain this incident?

The Entity seemed insect-like in appearance, and was roughly the size of a rugby ball. It was oval-shaped and seemed to have weird, stubby appendages protruding from its sides. The only living creature I could possibly compare it to would be a jellyfish.

After this experience I trawled through many books and magazines dealing with the paranormal to see if I could find any cases that were similar to mine. But whilst there were many unique and horrifying encounters, and many occurred during Sleep Paralysis, and a significant amount featured either strange light formations or Hag-like Entities, none involved anything remotely like what I had seen.

Even more peculiar was the fact that about a year later, my father was sitting in the living room around 6pm one evening, reading a newspaper when something caught his eye. Upon looking up he saw a plum-sized form whizz across the floor and vanish before his eyes. He described the manifestation as being a whitish, almost transparent form that was so weird it was surreal.

A relative of mine claimed it could have been ghostly plasma.

After my experience, my cousin also reported a strange encounter with what he described as a 'black blob,' one night. It was about 11.30pm, and he was lying on his back in bed. He was dozing fitfully, but kept waking up. All of a sudden, something dropped onto his foot. This startled him, but he surmised that one of his books had toppled front the top of a stack piled at the end of his bed. But still he looked at the afflicted area and was shocked to see a 'blob' the size of a bird positioned on his foot which was under the blankets at the time. He was horrified by the sight of the 'Thing;' and flicked his foot in a state of panic. Involuntarily, he sat straight up in one movement. The 'Thing' flicked up onto the window ledge. On this particular night, he had left the window open, and now he could see the black object just behind the curtain. Trying to be rational, he thought that maybe it was a bird or even a bat, but then the object, whatever it was, vanished into thin air.

I have often been of the opinion that 'Psychic Vampires' truly exist, at least in the sense of dark forms of energy which float in the atmosphere and are able to somehow draw even more energy from human beings. Those slumbering are, for some reason, more vulnerable to these attacks. I also believe that so-called 'wet dreams' are the work of these Entities which have a lot in common with the old folk tales of the Incubus and Succubus; the male and female Demons which were said to feed off the secretions of the living.

Again, I accept that science will dismiss these views as arrant nonsense, but I haven't seen any evidence yet that would disprove my beliefs.

I am also of the opinion that the state of sleep can somehow enhance our ability to perceive spectres and apparitions. Perhaps this is because our subconscious can enable the rest of the body to connect with the ethereal, which is why everything seems normal when one is in the dream-state.

Perhaps these other presences are able to filter in and out of our dream-induced visions?

ALL THE COLOURS OF DARKNESS

But on the other hand….

If, like me, you've ever experienced the terrifying sensation of suddenly waking up in the early hours to be confronted by a darkness bereft of even the tiniest sliver of illumination and a silence so absolute, it often seems as though time itself had stood still, you'll no doubt appreciate how easy it is to see things lurking in the dark that really aren't there.

I can remember occasions when I lived at my parent's house in New Ferry, when the thick black curtains prevented any source of light seeping into the room and even the sounds of the house settling or the comfortingly familiar ticking of the bedside alarm clock (increasingly obsolete in the digital age), failed to reach my ears.

At such times, starved of any amount of sensory input, the human mind struggles to cope and winds up doing the only thing left for it to do…create its own images from out of the all-pervasive inky blackness.

And all-too frequently, these images are the stuff of man's worst nightmares.

In January, 2008, the BBC's *Horizon* programme conducted an experiment that sought to answer the question of what happens to a person when they are left alone in the dark in solitary confinement for two whole days.

Six volunteers, including the stand-up comedian Alan Bloom, agreed to be shut inside a cell in the hollow centre of a nuclear bunker, and the programme revealed how within a mere half an hour of the metal doors being locked, obliterating even the tiniest sliver of light, all of the subjects elected to lie down and go to sleep. The true ordeal only really began however, when they woke up to find they had absolutely no idea what time it was, or even if it was day or night.

For the duration of the 48 hours they were monitored by CCTV cameras and an on-site psychologist. The footage revealed that as the time passed by with agonising slowness, the subjects, deprived of any sensory input whatsoever, became increasingly disorientated, and Alan Bloom was heard to exclaim:

> 'It's really hard to stimulate your brain with no light. It's blanking me. I can feel my brain just not wanting to do anything.'

There have been similar experiments involving civilian volunteers in the past. Several years ago, a bunch of scientists in the USA, persuaded several students (well, actually, they dangled a crinkly green wad of cash in their faces as a highly tempting bargaining chip) to remain in conditions of sensory deprivation for varying lengths of time. The vast majority of them quit the experiment after 72 hours, and hardly any of them lasted longer than four or five days. The combination of sheer mind-numbing boredom and the dreadful sense of isolation induced by the experiment were too much to bear for any appreciable length of time.

Of course, sensory deprivation is a highly controversial subject, with allegations that the technique has been used as an interrogation strategy at that shining example of the fairness of the American justice system, Guantanamo Bay. And thousands of prisoners around the world are kept in solitary confinement, often with a hugely significant lack of sensory input.

The programme makers, however, were quick to point out that they were not interested in obtaining any hidden truths from their human guinea pigs, they were simply exploring the theory that sensory deprivation makes people much more suggestible.

And it's that last sentence that leapt up and grabbed my attention. You'll doubtless be aware, having read thus far, that your humble author is something of a self-confessed coward when faced with the grim prospect of being cast adrift on the eventide, or swept up and abandoned on 'the night's Plutonian shore'.

Or, if you'd prefer to dispense with the flowery language and replace it with plain-speak; I was shit-scared of the dark.

And sometimes, with good reason.

When I lived at my parents' home, I would often wake up to be confronted by a series of surreal images straight out of a Salvador Dali painting. I used to see ships, huge ocean liners with their portholes and deck windows lit up at night beneath starless skies. These gigantic vessels, the sort that would make The Titanic look like a miniature toy yacht, would sail in flotillas on calm, mirror-like seas, as though they were part of some country-less naval task force, but it wasn't only their sheer size that terrified me. It was the fact that the port-holes and windows would suddenly be transformed into shining silver eyes like the pennies they used to place on the eyes of recently dead men.

Adam, the laff-a-minute comedian, meanwhile, experienced similarly bizarre hallucinations and/or dreams after 30 hours had elapsed in the noiseless, formless void.

> 'I thought I could see a pile of oyster shells, five thousand oyster shells,'

…he said, before adding jokingly,

> 'They were all empty, to represent all the nice food I could have eaten while I was inside here.'

It wasn't long before the other participants were assailed by illusionary images, either. A postman by the name of Mickey, described how he was terrified by the mosquitoes and fighter planes that buzzed around his head in deafening swarms, whilst Claire, a psychology student, made light of the images of little cars, snakes and zebras that she saw in the cell, but she described feeling frightened by the sense that somebody was standing watching her, just a few feet away.

The programme makers were also eager to canvas the opinions of people who had undergone an almost inconceivable amount of time in the silent dark. Brian Keenan, having spent four years as a hostage in civil war-torn Lebanon, related his nightmarish experiences:

> 'I reckon I was in the dark for about six or seven months, although I can't honestly be sure. It's very hard to tell the time in those conditions.
>
> The nothingness, that was extremely hard, because the question in your head is: "How am I going to get through the next ten minutes?" Or, months later, "How am I going to get through the next day? Is there enough left in my head?"
>
> I remember one occasion waking up and having to squeeze my face and chest and thinking to myself; "Am I still alive?"

Mr Keenan also underwent periods when his information-starved brain conjured up a welter of unwelcome images. One particularly unpleasant auditory experience involved musical instruments growing progressively louder and louder in his ears.

> 'I got really afraid and that's when I started banging my head against the wall, just to make this go away,' he recounted.
>
> You would try to engage your mind forcefully on something else…It was not comforting. And it went on for a very, very, long time.'

At the programme's conclusion, Professor Robbins pointed out, somewhat obviously, that, 'In the dark room there is nothing to focus on. In the absence of information, the human brain carries on working and processing information, even if there is no information to process, and after a while it starts to create that information itself.'

All of which begs the question, are at least some accounts of Night Terror visitations entirely illusory, brought upon by the mind's wonderful capacity for creating vivid mental images in the absence of any external sensory input?[*]

---

[*] **Source:** BBC Horizon: Total Isolation BBC 2 22nd January, 2008

THE ENTITY

One of the most unnerving, disturbing and downright terrifying TV programmes I've ever seen was screened on Channel 4, during November 2001.

It's partly my own fault, of course.

I guess I should have known what I was letting myself in for when the announcer at the outset of the programme issued a warning that the contents might alarm certain viewers...

No sooner had this caveat been issued, (and summarily dismissed with a contemptuous, seen-it-all-before grin curling the corners of my lips), than the screen went black and the lilting tones of a Scottish narrator informs the viewer that:

> 'There is a nightmare more terrifying than any other. A nightmare that has haunted thousands of people from all over the world.
>
> A presence comes into the room, paralyses its victim, then leaps on their body and assaults them.
>
> 'Sometimes it's a shadowy figure. Sometimes an Old Hag. Sometimes a Demon. But whatever shape it takes, The Entity, as it is often called, has concrete effects, leaving its victims battered and exhausted, their lives in pieces. Sufferers are sure that when they see it they are awake and it is real. Science, psychology and religion have all grappled with this phenomenon.
>
> Can any explain the mystery of The Entity?'

And then we're off and running with the eye-witness accounts.

The first comes a from a suburb of Houston, Texas, where it seems, one 32-year-old woman has been suffering Night Terror attacks for most of her life. They began when she was just five years old, in fact.

During an interview, (shot by a cameraman who appears to have a *Blair Witch Project* fixation, with lots of shots of the witness' bulging left eye filling the screen), Jamie Jackson relates her personal history of 'Entity' visitations.

> 'The first thing I remember as a child was one night when my mother had just put me to bed, and I could see the lights on in the living room. I just lay down, and I could hear my parents and I could hear the television. And I looked up, and to my right I saw a couple, very shadowy, very dark, in my bedroom.
>
> It was a man and a woman and they started walking towards me. It was very frightening. I couldn't speak. I wanted to call out to my mother but I couldn't call out to her. I was just terrified. And around about that time my mother walked into the room and it appeared she walked directly through the two people who were standing to my right, and I began asking her, "Who are these people in my room? What's going on?"
>
> She kept telling me that it was just a dream and to go back to sleep. I told her that it wasn't a dream and that I hadn't been asleep. I could hear the television in the other room.'

As Jamie grew older, the entities that stalked her grew more vivid and more violent.

In a truly spine-chilling reconstruction that begins with a woman lying alone in her bed at night, Jamie narrates

> 'As soon as I become aware that there's someone in the room, I'll go into immediate paralysis. I can't move...

(she grips the thin white sheet covering the mattress)

> ...and I can't shout out. I'm unable to call for help and I'm unable to ward off any attack ...

(her rolling eyes frantically scan the depths of the darkness for signs of movement)

> 'It feels like I've been drugged somehow.'

On the screen, a slightly out of focus, stickman-like figure appears, slowly unwinding itself in the far corner of the room. When it rises to its full height, it towers over the terrified victim.

Jamie christens this undoubtedly masculine silhouette, *Shadow Man*.

In a sudden blur of movement, this sinister Entity races over to the side of the bed and begins throttling Jamie as she lies helplessly on the bed.

> 'He's very violent. He doesn't use any caution whatsoever. He couldn't care less if my neck is broken.'

The Shadow Man is then joined by his equally frightening accomplice, The Old Hag. At first she merely stands at the edge of the bed, draped in many layers of raggedy clothing, and with dirty unkempt hair poking out from beneath an ill-fitting bonnet. After a few seconds she slowly crawls onto the bed and sits astride the woman's chest, her hideously wizened face mere inches from Jamie's.

> 'She's not extremely heavy but she's heavy enough that it's very hard to breathe. I can't get my lungs to expand. And the attack becomes twofold. The Shadow Man will have hold of the base of my neck and the Old Woman will be choking me near the top part so violently that I think that my voice box is going to collapse. I can't move. The Shadow Man's got my arms down, and the Old Lady's sitting on my chest. And there's nothing I can do.'

As stated earlier, Jamie is convinced that she is awake during these attacks.

> 'The fear is extremely real. You are looking around the room. You're looking for any way out. I can see my clock. I can see my curtains. I can see everything in the room, and that tells me that this is real. That this is happening to me. And I'm wondering why my husband can't hear them. Why he can't hear the struggle. Why he can't hear the fight. And beyond that, I'm wondering what's going happen to me after they kill me. Who's next?
>
> Your mind and your body thinks that you've been through it. But to everyone you associate with, your workmates, your friends, your family, your doctors; they say it's just a dream. Just get over it.'

The narrator then announces that during research for the programme, there were literally hundreds of phone calls from people who claimed to have encountered similar 'Entities' and undergone remarkably similar experiences.

A series of audio-taped recorded commentaries of Night Hag experiences is then played, courtesy of Matt Watkins, 25, who hails from Wiltshire, England.

In the recordings, Matt, who is a psychology student at the University of the West of England, describes in suitably terrified tones, how the 'Old Hag' appeared in his bedroom.

During another, equally creepy reconstruction, Matt's bedroom door opens agonisingly slowly. Unholy white light floods the threshold from the centre of which a bent and crooked female figure gradually emerges.

> 'I just remember she was old,'

a still-noticeably shaken Matt recounts to camera.

> 'She looked me in the eyes. And she ran right up to my face.'

At this, the ominous 'Old Hag' runs on her tip-toes towards the bed where Matt lies immobile with fear, with distinctly unnerving, spider-like speed.

> 'She stopped right in front of my face and literally two inches away from my nose, looked me right in the eyes, and she had what could be described as black eye-liner running down her face in rivulets.'

The hideous apparition, straggly white hair blowing in some decidedly unnatural breeze, leans towards him, her dead eyes bleeding blood the colour of thick molasses, her pale, cracked lips parted in a mirthless grin.

Not surprisingly, these 'visitations' and their associated phenomena have had a profound effect upon Matt.

> 'It's made me question the nature of reality. It's made me look into many different areas; psychiatry, parapsychology, all these different areas. I realise that there could be other explanations for this, and I started looking into it a bit more. I decided to make The Entity the focus of my degree.
>
> Searching through ancient texts, I was surprised to find evidence of the Entity Experience dating back over 2,000 years.'

At this point, a sinister whispering voice intones the following quotation.

> 'When doomed to death I will attend you as a nocturnal fury: I will attack your faces, and brooding upon your restless breasts, I will deprive you of repose by terror.'**

But it wasn't only classical literature that made reference to The Night Terror.

During the Middle Ages, The Entity was often represented as a horned beast that prayed on sleeping women, and was sometimes thought to rape them (Incubi and Succubi).

At this point the narrator asks a couple of very pertinent questions. Why were there so many depictions of the Entity Experience? And why were they so similar?

Before seeking to answer these queries, the programme returns to the case of the Entity-plagued Jamie Jackson:

> 'Every time I'm attacked like this, I don't really tell anyone about it, and I try to forget all about it.
>
> But, I've woken up with cuts in my hands from my fingernails clenching my fist. I've cracked teeth in my sleep, just from the intensity of everything. Clenching my jaws.

** Horace – 1st Century B.C.

I did think a few times about taking my own life. You just don't see any way out of it. What happens is, you get to the point where you are so tired. And every night you go to bed you know it's going to be another fight, a struggle, you become afraid to fall asleep.'

In the search for a logical, scientific explanation, we get to put a face to the aforementioned 'expert' Dr J Allan Cheyne (you'll remember him from earlier in this chapter. Or you will if you've been paying attention). He's a heavily-bearded professor of psychology from the University of Waterloo in Canada (and, somewhat fittingly, he bears an uncanny resemblance to the horror author, Stephen King).

'When we are dreaming,' he asserts,

> '...a mechanism in the brain paralyses us to prevent us acting out our dreams. Some people get trapped in the state between wakefulness and dreaming called Sleep Paralysis.
>
> I have studied over 9,000 cases, and I believe it (Sleep Paralysis) may have been experienced in mild form, by up to 30% of the world's population.
>
> Sleep Paralysis, as I view it, is a type of dream. A waking dream. Or perhaps more accurately, a waking nightmare.
>
> Imagine, if you will, there are two mechanisms deep in the brain stem. One of these mechanisms we'll call "The Wake Up Mechanism," and the other we'll call "The Dream-On Mechanism"
>
> So, when this one is turned on, you're awake, alert, conscious of your surroundings, able to respond to your surroundings. Imagine that as your wake up system turns down, if there's a problem, particularly with neuro-transmitters, it may not be inhibiting the other system, so this one may turn on, before this one turns off, so you have two systems on now, so you're awake and you're dreaming.'

Sounds logical enough, to me, if a little bit on the *'Oh God, here comes the incomprehensible science bit'* to this writer.

But we still have to look for an explanation as to why sometimes, there is a shared scenario in the attacks.

And, huzzah, the good doctor reckons he's got the answer to that, too.

> 'A way in which the hallucination may build might be where you imagine that there is something on your chest. Perhaps it's simply the fact that you can't take a deep breath, because you are paralysed after all. One interpretation is that there really is something on your chest preventing you from taking a deep breath.
>
> If you've also had a visual hallucination, it's easy to conclude that whatever that thing was, it is now on your chest. Initially, it's just a feeling that there is something there, and you're searching for it, and if your eyes are closed, you'll be thinking if you could just open your eyes it would be there.
>
> If your eyes are open, it might be just out of sight. Perhaps you will see it. Perhaps you will see some form, some vague shape. Maybe you'll hear something. Footsteps. Movement in the room. You may actually feel something touching you. And you can see, as each of these things happen, the hallucination gets fleshed out, so this vague sense of a presence can become a concrete entity in the room.'

But can mere Sleep Paralysis adequately explain cases when the Entity attacks reportedly go much further?

We travel next to Glasgow, Scotland, and the horrifying story related by Mark Dillon, 33.

Despite a normal childhood, Mark has been the alleged victim of a particularly vicious series of nocturnal attacks, since entering his late teenage years.

> 'I was only about 17 when this first happened to me. I went to bed as normal. Fell asleep, enjoying a good sleep, when, during the middle of the night, I was awakened by the feeling that someone was in the room.
>
> I couldn't explain what it was. I didn't know who it was. I then felt totally paralysed. I could not move. It was as if the power that was there, the energy, was able to control my body.
>
> I was being held face down on my back. I could feel his hands on me. I could feel that it was a man. I could feel the size of him. It was a fully grown man.
>
> What happened next was a purely sexual act (and here we see disturbing images of him being pushed up and down on the bed, as if violent anal intercourse were taking place). It was as if I could feel him pushing himself on top of me.
>
> I thought I was going to die.
>
> I thought the Demon was going to kill me.'
>
> When the paralysis eventually went away, I felt as if the presence had withdrawn into a corner of the room. There was a creaking as though there was something there.'

Mark's attacks have been so unspeakably real to him that his relationship with his fiancée has suffered badly as a result.

But everything's going to be just fine, 'cos here comes our old chum Dr Cheyne to drum up another healthy dose of logical explanations.

> 'Sexual assaults are not common, but they certainly occur. Our dreams have sexual content because our sexual organs, and sexual areas of the brain are still being activated. So it's not surprising that the combination of fear and sex leads to the sexual assault scenario.'

But how does this account for the fact that Mark's bedroom, where the assaults allegedly took place, once belonged to his older brother, and he apparently underwent similar experiences, unbeknownst to Mark?

> 'A couple of years before the attacks on me,'

Mark says,

> '...my brother was staying in that same bedroom. I started to tell him what had happened to me in that room and he said to me that he had very similar experiences, such as being strangled, and a feeling of someone being there. Is it just a coincidence that that it was the same bedroom?'

And here comes another familiar face of the dreamily surreal world of Night Terror studies. Step forward, Mr David Hufford.

He begins by telling us of his own encounter, years before he became interested in studying the subject.

> 'I once had a Sleep Paralysis attack of my own. I'd never heard of anything like it. It had all the details that I later found in traditions all over the world. I heard footsteps, I sensed a terrifying presence. I saw it climb up on the bed. I couldn't move. I thought I was being killed. It was terrifying. I never told anybody about it, because I didn't want anyone to think I was crazy.
>
> And then, years later, when I got to Newfoundland, and I came across the 'Old Hag Experience', I thought "What's going on here? How can these people have a tradition about what happened to me in a completely different country?"

To deal with attacks, not just on individuals, but on whole communities, we travel next to the exotic climes of Pemba Island (one of the two main islands of Zanzibar, since 1964 a part of Tanzania) off the East Coast of Africa.

Residents here claim they have been plagued by a mysterious Entity they call the Popabowa, for more than a decade. They look to pages culled from the Koran, for protection.

One witness, an old man in his seventies, recollects:

> 'I was asleep, but I felt something in the room with me. All the doors in my house were locked. I don't know how it got into my house. It wanted to rape me. When I woke up...I found semen on my back.
>
> I think it was a Shaatan. A bad spirit. A Devil.'

Meanwhile, another much younger man relates how

> '...the shadow came through the wall. It was walking towards me. It was threatening.'

And a third witness, a nearly toothless individual in his mid-50's, says:

> 'The Entity came into my house. It came to me...I was paralysed. It tried to squeeze my throat. I could not breathe.
>
> The villagers began to complain. We went to catch the Entity. We could not find it anywhere.'

Perhaps it has taken refuge in the East Village area of New York City?

For it's here that Ted Fillpone, 25, has been repeatedly attacked by a particularly vicious Night Terror, a series of assaults that have apparently been witnessed by independent observers.

Ted has been so badly affected by these attacks that he is unable to hold down a regular job and as the visitations occur on a nightly basis, he's unable to sleep most of the time, terrified of what he might see emerging from the darkness at the foot of his bed.

With no-one else to turn to, Ted decided to go to the Catholic Church, and seek refuge in the hostel run by Father Pat Maloney, who claims to have witnessed the phenomena for himself.

> 'There was one particular time…Ted seemed to be very upset. Not so much agitated, as fearful. He said, "Look, it's at me again. It's bothering me." I said "What's bothering you?"
>
> I sat in the corner of the room, about a foot away, then I got just a little bit closer, and I felt an immediate type of vibration. A physical presence of some kind. And yet, I did not feel that whatever was bothering Ted was malevolent. It was as if he were attracting some force. Something outside our dimension.'

Ted's girlfriend, the very lovely Ines Changanaqui, relates the following:

> 'I was sitting on a couch, watching TV, and I was facing the bedroom door, and the bathroom door was open and I saw some type of greyish silhouette walking out of the bathroom. You couldn't really define a shape, male or female. It was just a silhouette, but very tall, cloudy greyish, and it was walking towards Ted's bedroom.'

David Hufford concurs that this case at least, has some truly remarkable connotations.

> 'In a way, every case is sort of remarkable, and some are highly strange. The ones though that really amaze me are the ones where more than one person is involved: where one person is having the Sleep Paralysis, and somebody else in the house sees or hears the same thing at the same time, even though they are not having Sleep Paralysis.
>
> 'How do you account for that? I'm just baffled.'

Equally perplexed is Father Maloney, who is at his wits end (and in all likelihood is probably more concerned with making sure his Bobby Charlton-style comb-over looks the part on screen) calls in, with the help of the programme-makers, a 'professional Demonologist' named Lou Gentille. A practising Catholic, Gentille claims to have helped many people in Ted's situation.

> 'Demonology is the study of Fallen Angels. It's the study of things that are Evil,'

Lou informs us helpfully.

> 'I come across cases that are Evil, malevolent, Demonic, or diabolical on a monthly basis.
>
> In a month, I might get five or six cases that truly have activity that can only be described as Evil.'

Lou and his assistant meet Ted at the hostel and interview him extensively in a bid to determine whether the attacks have a psychological or supernatural origin.

Lou asks Ted whether he's ever taken drugs of any kind, including hallucinogens (eg, acid), and whether he's ever suffered from Tourette's Syndrome, personality disorders, or narcolepsy. To all of these questions, Ted answers in the negative, to which the cynical might respond, 'Well, he was hardly likely to admit any illegal drug-taking on camera now was he?'

Courtesy of some pretty snazzy speed-frame photography, night falls swiftly, like a black curtain over the façade of the hostel.

Lou is convinced, after a gruelling two-hour interview, that Ted's case warrants further investigation. Along with his colleague, they set up fairly sophisticated video and audio recording equipment in an upstairs bedroom and also in Ted's room, the plan being to record any discernible activity should Ted suffer an attack.

Nothing happens for what seems like the longest time, and to be fair, the makers of the programme do a good job of creating an atmosphere of barely repressed tension with some suitably eerie music on the soundtrack and lots of POV shots of Lou and his assistant, and of Ted lying on the bed.

And then, Ted's feet start kicking out an invisible something, and he appears to wake up, raising his head from the pillow and although we don't actually hear him say it, Lou informs us that Ted said something grabbed his leg.

Lou immediately springs into action, taking with him portable Dictaphones in order to record any EVP (Electronic Voice Phenomena), present in the room.

Lou speaks directly to the infra-red camera; 'Since Ted's claiming that something touched him and actually pulled his leg, I'm going to sit by him. I'm going to be asking some questions on the recorder, and see what we get.'

While we wait for any such revelations, the scene is inter-cut with footage of an earlier interview with Ted conducted in broad daylight. 'I've tried communicating with It,' he says. 'And not only did I not receive a reply, the assaults got more intensified within ten minutes of asking.'

I guess somebody should have told Lou, because back in the darkness of the hostel, he's busy firing away queries like there's no tomorrow.

> 'Beginning of EVP, July 30th, 2001, at precisely 2:45am.
> If there is a spirit around us now, please tell me your name on the record.
> Are you a spirit that is of the light of God?
> Please release whatever has been performed on Ted.
> I ask this in the name of Jesus Christ, our Lord and Saviour.'

There is no audible response to any of these questions, but this doesn't really surprise Lou. It's only when the tape recording is played back that we hear something unusual and not a little chilling. In the wake of each of Lou's questions, the tape seems to emit a series of weird noises.

In response to the query:

> 'Is there a spirit around us now?'

...we can discern what sounds like scratching or worse, the grunting of some sort of wild animal. This increases in volume with the question,

> 'Are you a spirit of the light of God?'

...and with repeated viewing, it surely seems that a voice is speaking. I'm sure I can hear the words 'Read' (or is it 'leave') the tape!' on the recording, followed by a burst of diabolical laughter, whilst another whispered voice insists faintly 'Read the tape!'

And finally, when Gentille intones the name of Jesus, he's all but drowned out by what can only be described as the strangled, ear-splitting roar of the completely insane.

Lou is remarkably calm about the quite frankly, bowel-loosening recording, claiming that the sound that we've just heard 'in some people's minds, could be portrayed as static discharge. To me, that's ridiculous because I've heard the things scream blasphemies in people's houses, and they've called people's names, people who aren't even a part of the case.

'What you heard is as real as it gets!'

The programme makers decided to have the tape analysed by forensic 'experts.' They suggested that the only way similar sounds could be created would be from rubbing the microphone or through a remote receiver, neither of which were apparent during Lou's investigation.

With the coming of the dawn, Lou tells Ted his opinion about what he thinks is going on here.

It transpires that Mr Gentille believes that the Entity is engaged upon a mission to try to drive a wedge between Ted and his faith in God.

>'You need to reaffirm your faith,'

Lou assures him.

>'These are nothing but scare tactics. They're going to poke you. They're going to prod you. They're going to hit you. But they are not going to get completely violent because somewhere in your heart you do have faith.'

>'So, let me just get this straight. If I lose more faith, they're gonna get more violent'?

Ted asks anxiously, although you suspect he may well know the answer already.

>'Yes,'

…comes the unequivocal reply.

>'Oh, great!'

Ted turns to face the wall in a gesture of fearful desperation.

>'All I want is to sleep peacefully, without always sleeping with one eye open, looking out the corner of my eye, opening, closing, opening, closing, just to see if there's an Entity in the room. I question myself; *'Why is this happening? Why can't it just stop?'*

Lou believes that only a return to the church can put an end to the Demonic manifestations and physical harassment.

The programme's final segment, deals with perhaps the most bizarre case of all. It concerns a man who hails from Monticello, Arkansas, USA, who believes he is actually possessed by an otherworldly Entity.

The man's long-suffering partner, Monica Forrest, begins the account by stating that she thinks her boyfriend, Cody McKee, is possessed because when he is awake he's not violent,

>'…and he just doesn't even look like himself when he's having a Night Terror. And he doesn't sound like himself.

>He has a terrifying holler. His eyes have a glazed look. They just don't look like his.'

There follows a deeply disturbing sequence of footage secretly filmed by a hidden camera during one of this man's attacks. Lying apparently asleep on the living room couch, he suddenly throws aside the single blanket and leaps to his feet, emitting an animalistic roar as he heads for the living room door, clearly intent on committing an act of violence.

We then switch to broad daylight, and Cody, 26, is seen pushing one of his two children on the back garden swing, looking every bit the doting father, with not a care in the world. He accepts that, as a child, he had a less-than-stable upbringing, but explains that over the years, he has managed to put his past firmly behind him. Cody's only problem now, is quite sadly, the ever-present threat of the Night Terrors.

He cannot recall the morning after the night before, what it was he had seen, or in fact, any precise detail of what the experience entailed.

His family, however, have had seven years of sleepless nights, worrying about what Cody might do while he is in his 'possessed' state.

Cody tells the programme's presenter,

> 'I really can't recall any of it. It's like I go to sleep, I wake up, and I don't know what I did, or what made me do what I've done. I just feel like something jumped in my body and made me go crazy.'

Monica shows the camera some of the damage Cody has caused to the doors of one of the bedrooms, a sequence of holes that appear to be the result of powerful punches by a man consumed by an intense and burning rage. Cody's also knocked holes through walls, stuck his hands in electric fans and lost the tip of his toe when violently kicking at a wainscot.

Cody has one somewhat vague memory of one of these Night Terror incidents:

> 'The only night that I can actually say it felt like something jumped inside of me and took over my body, was the night that I jumped out of the window. When I came to, behind my daddy's car, I heard someone say, "I'll see you later Cody."

> 'Then I started walking back up towards the trailer, and that's when I realised that I'd done something to myself and saw I was cut head to toe. I had sixty or seventy stitches.'

Not surprisingly, Monica can recall these particular events with a lot more clarity:

> 'It looked to me like someone threw him out the window because he did it from a dead stand. He just went out. He hollered and went out the window.'

And it's not just Cody who has been hospitalised by these night attacks. Monica once had her nose broken when she tried to prevent her boyfriend from going towards her child whilst he was in a 'possessed state.' She attempted to grab hold of him to wake him up and was struck fully in the face by Cody's arm. The injury was so bad, a bone protruded from the top of her nose. In the aftermath of that incident, Monica wisely decided not to sleep in the same room as Cody and began locking her bedroom at night. Not only that, but she's been forced to place items in front of the door, such as a heavy bed and a bulky dressing table, in order to keep him out.

Her loyalty may surprise many readers, but Monica has chosen to stand by her boyfriend, for better or for worse. They were unable to afford medical assistance, but the programme-makers arranged for Cody to attend a sleep clinic to see whether they could explain his nocturnal awakenings. The couple travel to the Baptist Health Medical Centre, where they are introduced to Dr David Davila, who offers his services to take on the case. He tells the cameras: 'This is the most extreme case of sleep-walking and Night Terrors that I have ever seen. This is the first one that we've had here at our centre of this magnitude.'

Other doctors assemble to study Cody's brain activity and muscle tone as well as recording him sleeping using infra-red cameras and sound monitoring equipment. With a whole collection of gadgets and wires stuck to his heavily-bandaged head, Cody attempts to get a restful night's sleep while the cameras roll.

During the first night of monitoring, Cody wakes up, apparently scared out of his wits. Eyes bulging, mouth wide-open in a soundless scream, his face is contorted into such an ugly mask of terror, he truly doesn't look like himself.

The EEG machine tells the watching doctors that Cody is still in deep sleep and not dreaming. Which kind of begs the question, what is provoking the all-too apparent fear transforming Cody's features?

The next morning, Dr Devila asks Cody whether he remembers anything from the night before, and he replies in the negative.

All he can say, as he views the video footage in hushed tones of awe, is 'It just looks wicked to see my eyes open like that. I mean, it just doesn't look like me…Really!'

Before you get too far along the road that leads towards a potential supernatural explanation for the attacks, however, here comes sensible Old Dr Davila, to throw a goodly-sized helping of 'logic' on the proceedings.

> 'With his eyes darting around it's kind of hard to know whether he's actually seeing anything or not. He doesn't have any recall of opening his eyes. He doesn't have any recall of seeing anything frightening, although he does look undeniably frightened.
>
> In Cody's case, we cannot find a specific trigger. So he is a mystery at least in that sense. And we cannot determine what is going on in his mind.
>
> For some reason, he is fighting to get into wakefulness and alertness and literally fighting his way into that.
>
> I believe Cody is suffering from an extreme form of sleepwalking that occurs during the deepest stages of his sleep. But what Cody actually sees, or why he is driven to such violence, still remains a mystery.'

Cody, needless to say, is somewhat less than impressed with the doctor's diagnosis.

> 'They haven't given me a reason why I do it or what causes it. All they know is that they can put me on medication and that maybe that'll stop it. And you know, I hope to God it does. I hope I can rest at night and sleep and not hurt anybody or myself.'

At the time the programme was due to be aired, Cody had been taking the prescribed medication for about three months. Although the Night Terror attacks have noticeably reduced in number, they still occur and are as unpredictable and violent as ever.

At the programme's conclusion, the narrator sums up by saying:

> 'For many, who suffer from nocturnal assaults, their testimony is evidence of an experience that is still not fully understood.'

David Hufford adds his voice:

> 'I've seen lots of different explanations offered as being THE scientific explanation of this phenomenon. In general, in fact all of them that I know of, do not fit the data of the experience well. Now maybe some day, people will be able to get to the point where they really do fit well. But I do think that it's not fair to people's experience and people's understanding of this sort of thing, to take a loose, sloppy, hypothetical scientific explanation, and to hear, "Oh well, at least it's scientific. We ought to accept it."
>
> No, I don't think that's right. It ought to really account for what needs to be accounted for. None of them do yet. Good luck, everybody, keep working on it. But let's not claim that it's been done.'

Whether or not science will one day be in a position to offer an acceptable to all parties-type explanation for these nocturnal attacks is unclear.

But as the narrator points out, just before the final credits roll:

> 'What is clear is that those that suffer will continue to live in fear of what lurks on the other side of sleep.'

THE CROOKED PATH THAT WINDS THROUGH THE REALM OF UNREASON

'She said, "There's something in the woodshed,
"And I can hear it breathing...
"It's such an eerie feeling..."

The Divine Comedy - Something for the Weekend

I guess it's fair to say that the vast majority of people, even the most outwardly sceptical amongst us, have experienced something during our all-too brief time on the planet that, for a single moment at least, we deem to lie beyond the pale of what passes for everyday reality.

True, we may well later, with the benefit of hindsight, and a chance to re-consider the validity of our 'inexplicable experience' (over a whisky and soda in the company of friends, cheered by the rich benediction of summer sunlight or sat before a roaring log fire) casually dismiss the whatever-it-was as being either a clever hoax, sheer coincidence, or the product of a vivid imagination.

Comparatively few people, however, though they may be patently truthful about most other things that occur in their lives, will subsequently admit to themselves or in public, that anything remotely anomalous took place. Not even on those rare occasions, when the welter of rational explanations and arguments proffered by the ranks of so-called 'experts', proves to stand up about as well as Lady Gaga, balanced on the edge of a piano whilst wearing a pair of eight-inch high stilettos.

Perhaps this is because, all but buried in some superstition-riddled corner of our minds, we are scared. Frightened, not so much by 'the event' itself, (though that may well provide us a decidedly unhealthy dose of night sweats and a large amount of inner soul-searching), as the disconcerting fact that its very occurrence provided a direct challenge to all we've come to accept as being the 'normal scheme of things.' Our entire belief system, built up over a period of many years, is suddenly shattered in the time it takes to gaze in open-mouthed astonishment as some 'weird, unearthly aerial phenomenon' traverses the cloudless skies, 'a serpentine, thirty-foot creature rises slowly to the surface of some dark Scottish Loch,' or a long-dead, much-loved relative appears standing at the foot of your bed in the wee hours before dawn....

Fear of the unknown's eternal power is one thing.

Fear of what other, 'right-thinking people' (be they regular golfing partners, long-term lovers, family members or the boss at work), may think if such encounters with the 'otherworldly' be made public knowledge, is far, far greater.

Little wonder then that most people clam up when confronted with 'the inexplicable.'

It's an understandable reaction, and certainly, I think the above applies to my younger sister, Kearry, after she came face to face with something she couldn't rationally explain, back in the early 1980s.

What she saw, or thought she saw, that long-ago spring evening, was every bit as real to her then, as it has since become vague and half-remembered in the three decades or so that have since slipped by with somewhat alarming ease. And its recollection, and my writing of it now, reminds me of how wonderfully uncomplicated it was to be young, and have one's mind open to all sorts of outlandish possibilities, before good old, sensible-headed adulthood kicks in, dons it steel-capped Doctor Martens and gleefully sets about stomping anything 'beyond the pale of the easily explicable' into seven shades of irrelevance.

Or at least it tries to.

The following account is, I firmly believe, more than just an annoying inconvenience to the 'We've Got All The Answers Brigade,' but is rather a testament to the fact that sometimes incredibly strange things occur which require intelligent debate and a genuine search for answers, and can't be simply wellied into the void of pig-ignorant oblivion with all the finesse of an alehouse Sunday League footballer clearing his lines.

Ever since I can remember, my Dad used to keep pet rabbits in the large, do-it-yourself hutch he built at the bottom of our back garden, when we lived at Bolton Road East, New Ferry.

It was an extremely well-fortified affair, with a solid timber frame, and strong, wire-mesh fencing containing gaps so small, nothing bigger than a bulimic mouse could possibly have squirmed its way through.

The hutch, was actually made up of two parts; the animals main sleeping quarters, which constituted a wooden box stacked with layers of straw, and a six-foot long 'play/exercise' area, invariably piled high (despite our best efforts to take turns to keep the run clean), with raisin-like rabbit droppings. The only possible way of gaining entry to the structure was to remove the couple of house-bricks that lay on top of the roof, pull back the covering of musty-smelling lino, and lift up the two thick planks of wood that served as a lid.

Little wonder my father used to joke: 'It would be easier to break into Fort Knox guarded by the Welsh Regiment from Rorke's Drift than it would to get inside that hutch I've built!'

This virtual obsession with security may well surprise some people, but I'll wager they are the sort who've never kept pet rabbits out in the open. The fact is, we sometimes forget, with an insensibility that borders on arrogance, that whether we live in the midst of leafy green suburbia, or the neglected corner of some run-down backstreet, there are an abundance of wild predators lurking in the shadows or prowling the neighbourhood after dark.

Foxes, weasels, stoats, rats, even that fat old ginger tomcat curled up in a furry ball in the middle of next door's shed roof: each one is more than a potential threat to a species not exactly renowned (aside from Fiver, Hazel, Bigwig and the other fictional heroes of Watership Down), for their fighting prowess.

(Above): The heavily-fortified, 'predator proof' rabbit hutch my Dad built back at the dawn of the 1980s

And so, my Dad wisely ensured that our pets were well-protected against their would-be enemies, and never grew complacent or allowed the defences to slacken. Especially when, in the early spring of 1982 (a few weeks before a jack-boot dictator inadvertently saved an ailing Tory harridan from waning popularity by invading those useless chunks of near-barren rock in the middle of the South Atlantic), our family were amazed to discover that the pair of Dutch dwarf rabbits that we'd acquired a few weeks earlier, were not - in fact - just a couple of hyper frisky bucks.

The nine tiny, skinless bundles my brother, Grant and I, came across whilst cleaning out the 'sleeping quarters' one morning, were testament to that hopeless misconception.

My parents, who were not particularly ecstatic about the prospect of being over-run with bunnies, immediately separated the pair, and having 'passed the buck,' so to speak, to a close friend, they arranged to find homes for the babies as soon as they were old enough to fend for themselves.

We were all advised by a local rabbit expert not to make too much of a fuss over the offspring, when finally they emerged from their hay-lined nest, or else we'd likely incur their mother's jealousy, but in all honesty, I suppose it's fair to say that we didn't pay a great deal of heed to that advice. They were just too irresistibly cute to admire from the wrong side of the wire-meshed fence.

Over the course of the next six weeks, we watched in wide-eyed wonderment as the nine minuscule balls of fluff stumbled clumsily around the confines of the hutch or cavorted on the newly-mown lawn in a carefree celebration of new life.

I've often wondered why it is life often seems to choose the seemingly most inconsequential of moments to spring its darkest surprises.

One minute, things are rolling along just nicely and entirely on beam. The next, you're lying in bed on a cold, grey April morning, checking your pillow for defects, when the post-dawn tranquillity is suddenly shattered by the blood-curdling sound of your kid sister emitting a piercing scream from out in the back garden. And you taste ice in your throat and your stomach churns with dread as you throw back the bedclothes and race to the window.

It took a few precious seconds for my eyes to adjust to the light. At first, all I could make out was our tumbledown garden fence, the dark red bricks of the house directly opposite, the top-most branches of a couple of poplar trees and a narrow ribbon of plain white sky.

My attention was finally drawn to my sister, Kearry, standing in the centre of the concrete path that runs down the middle of the lawn, her head in her hands, her screams mercifully quietening to sobs.

I didn't hang around or stand on ceremony. Half-dressed, I charged down the stairs two or three at a time with not the slightest clue as to what to expect, but with all sorts of grim possibilities clamouring in my mind.

I ran barefoot across the dew-soaked grass to where my sister remained standing, but when I asked her what was wrong, all she could do was point towards the rabbit hutch, and burst into tears once more.

I had no option but to look for myself.

And as bad as it undeniably was, I have to admit breathing an audible sigh of relief that none of my very darkest fears had been realised. Far from it, in fact.

Two of the baby rabbits (we hadn't bothered giving any of them individual names, they all looked so similar in appearance it was near-impossible to tell them apart), were lying, atop a large mound of semi-frozen droppings. The fur of their tiny lifeless bodies rippled in the chilly air, and I stood staring transfixed for a while as I silently pondered the question: How had the animals met their death?'

In retrospect, the very fact that I'd even paused to consider the matter now seems to me to be one of the most puzzling aspects of the whole welter of absurdities that were to overtake my family that spring.

I mean, how the hell could I have ever saw fit to mentally debate the issue? Even for a second?

The answer was so obvious, it defied belief.

Even though the rabbit's bodies were completely unmarked, with not the slightest trace of any injury, and although there was very little in the way of blood, and few signs that any kind of struggle had taken place, still the baby rabbit's heads had been crushed as flat as the proverbial pancake.

It was only later, recovering from the shock, with a couple of mugs of steaming tea, in company with Kearry, (both of my parents and younger brothers had gone out for the day), that I suddenly realised that I had experienced a classic case of my brain refusing to accept that which my eyes had plainly been telling me.

And as the cold light of reason began clearing the fog that had shrouded my mind, I realised something else, too. I'd been asking myself the wrong question, gazing insensibly at those impossibly flat heads.

I should have been asking not *how* the creatures had died, but *who* or *what* had killed them and *why?*

buried the pitiful remains at the edge of the barren rose garden in the misted twilight of early evening, whilst Kearry stared forlornly from the kitchen window.

It occurred to me to tell the rest of the family what had happened the moment they stepped through the door, long after dark, and my sister had gone to bed, but they seemed to be in such high spirits that I was loathe to blacken their good humour. I decided instead to tell them the following morning.

As things turned out, I didn't need to.

Next day, there was another dead baby rabbit lying roughly in the same area of the hutch as the previous corpses.

Its body was untouched, but its head was flattened in exactly the same bizarre fashion as before.

My Dad took these losses especially badly. He had little doubt as to what had killed them.

> "It was definitely a weasel!"

…he declared in a voice that brooked no argument.

> "A dirty, vicious, shit-house weasel! I should have known better. They can smell a new-born litter a mile away."

I think it's fair to say he felt guilty for having failed to provide sufficient security for the baby rabbits, no matter how much we all tried to assure him to the contrary, and he spent the remainder of that day searching in vain for the predator's point of entry. He checked and re-checked, but when my Mum called him in for his supper, he walked into the kitchen wearily shaking his head. In a voice laced with bitter resignation, he announced that he'd been unable to find a single weak spot in the hutch's defences.

Even at this early stage, I began to harbour some grave doubts about my Dad's unshakeable conviction that any kind of *animal* had been responsible for these senseless killings.

For me, there were several factors that just didn't tally with an attack by a creature relying purely on instinct, no matter how cunning and resourceful a predator it might be.

Aside from the fact that there seemed to be no way in which even an animal as lithe and supple as a weasel could have gotten into that hutch, there were the further mysteries of why, after somehow gaining access, the 'weasel' had only killed a grand total of three of the ten (including the mother), rabbits, and why in such a peculiarly calculating, systematic way. I mean what were we dealing with here, a methodically sadistic, serial-killing creature?

And how on earth had it managed to completely crush the victim's heads so that they were nothing short of paper thin?

Strangely, no-one else seemed to keen on asking such admittedly awkward, if highly relevant questions at that point. Everyone simply chose to accept my Dad's explanation, and when you got right down to it, who was I to argue?

Besides, what we all agreed was of more immediate importance was to try to ensure that the six surviving members of the litter didn't suffer the same fate.

*****

Regrettably however, all our efforts proved to be entirely in vain. And when, two days later, the fourth victim was discovered, killed in an identical fashion to the others, my Dad underwent a radical change of heart. He began to share my suspicions that the killings were not the work of any animal, and could only be attributed to a human being, and a dangerously sick and twisted one at that.

Contingency plans were therefore drawn up within the Walker household as we embarked upon what amounted to a round the clock security operation in a bid to protect the remaining rabbits.

Admittedly, this was a decidedly low-tech exercise, and basically involved Grant and I taking turns to sit at our bedroom window with the lights turned off, all night long, armed with torches and a couple of broom handles for protection against what we assumed to be a psychotic individual who had a penchant for slaughtering defenceless pets.

The college I was attending back then was in recess for the Easter holidays by this time and so I was able to maintain this nocturnal vigil for the best part of a fortnight, but aside from one occasion when I thought I spotted a vague shadowy form lurking in the thick bushes that lined the very foot of the garden, that was very likely nothing more than a combination of over-tiredness and a trick of the moonlight, the 'stake out' proved to be fruitless.

The only consolation, and it was a big one, was that there were no further attacks on the surviving baby rabbits and by the time the green-tinged days of early April had given way to the verdant fulfilment of its latter stages, we began to dare to believe that whoever (or whatever) had been responsible for the killings, had since moved on or else had elected to get their sick kicks in some other way (and privately, I nurtured the sincere hope that the perpetrator had suffered some really horrendous accident involving a pack of rabid Rottweillers that had developed a ravenous, all-consuming appetite for fresh human testicles. No matter how small a meal they might prove to be).

But any notions that the attacks had ended were well and truly scattered to the four winds the night after we gave up our sentry duty.

'We awoke that morning to find that there were three more dead baby rabbits lying in the 'play area' of the hutch, their bodies completely untouched. Their heads entirely flattened.

I averted my gaze from the by-now depressingly familiar, but nonetheless nauseating sight, only to find myself staring unthinkingly at the concrete base of the washing line post a few short feet away, or more specifically, at the jagged, scrawly writing that was engraved there: the barely discernible signature of my father, a somewhat crude attempt at a five-pointed star and, dominating all, the three numerical figures my Dad had etched there for a spur of the moment 'joke' after finishing laying the garden path, two or three years earlier....

Just three figures that went to make up a single number.

A number afforded enormous religious and cultural significance courtesy of The Book of Revelations and the never-ending series of *Omen* movies.

666

I continued to stare, as if hypnotised at the fruits of my father's dark and quirky sense of humour, and even though I'd seen the engraving countless times before, of course, it freaked me out at that moment, and although you'll doubtless accuse me of possessing an over-active imagination, I could have sworn I heard what sounded like far-away laughter, and as fleeting and ethereal as a snatch of discordant melody, carried on a chill November wind.

*****

I remember it was around about this point, during breakfast, that Kearry made the sensible, if somewhat belated suggestion that we bring the three remaining babies into the house before darkness fell. She argued, not unreasonably, that since all other avenues had been thoroughly explored without any success, this was the only way we could be sure that they would be safe.

Most of the family agreed, she certainly got my vote, but my Dad chose that precise moment to pose a question that had, up until then, failed to occur to any of us.

> "But what if it's the *mother* that's killing them?"

Now, I didn't believe that to be the case for a single second. And yet, paradoxically, at the same time, the possibility that there might be such a down-to-earth explanation was more than a little appealing. In fact, considering the alternatives, it seemed to be plausibly seductive.

Almost before I knew what was happening, I was happily throwing in my lot with the babble of assenting voices that suddenly filled the air in response to this new avenue of potentialities.

> "Yeah, I remember that rabbit behaviour expert warning us that it's dangerous to make a fuss of the litter in front of the mother.

> "She must have got jealous and killed them by crushing their heads with her powerful back legs, out of spite."

> "That's right. That would explain why there was no sign of forced entry. I can't believe we never thought of that at the outset."

> "Something can easily be done about that, then. All we've got to do is separate the mother from the babies after dark."

On and on it went, a ceaseless litany around the breakfast table, and who could honestly blame us? It felt as though we'd been offered a perfectly logical way out of a distinctly abnormal situation. And we gratefully charged headlong towards that escape route at full pelt.

We acted quickly. It was decided, rather than bring the remaining babies inside our house, each and every night, it would serve just as well to place some sort of 'dividing wall' between the mother and the surviving litter, within the 'sleeping quarters.'

In the end, my Dad used a thin, but sturdy strip of metal shelving from our refrigerator, and it certainly seemed to do the job. We could now keep a close eye on the rabbits during the day, and there was no possible way the mother could make any degree of physical contact once the barrier had been inserted just before sundown.

Perhaps now, we thought, we could sleep a little easier in our beds, secure in the knowledge that surely nothing could harm the remaining babies....

But we were only kidding ourselves.

The following morning, there was only one baby rabbit left alive.

The other two were dead.

I surely don't need to describe to you how they had been killed.

The only notable difference from these two corpses and those of its brothers and sisters was that they were lying within the 'sleeping quarters.' And that's hardly surprising, seeing how there was no way out for the brood through the dividing section of metal the previous evening. The mother was blameless, unless she could somehow morph herself through the bars to get at her offspring.

There could be no more debate.

No further attempts to conjure half-baked 'rational' explanations.

There was only one baby rabbit left from a litter of nine. We had no option but to bring it inside.

The general consensus was that we should place the animal in a suitable container and bring it into the kitchen that very night. My Dad, overruled that idea, however, arguing instead that the secure confines of the woodshed situated at the top end of the garden, alongside our extension, would suffice just as well.

So it was, immediately after the sun slowly sank over the roofs of the surrounding houses, Kearry gently lifted the tiny bundle of black and white fur out of the hutch and placed it in her old hamster cage (the hamster had thankfully died a perfectly natural death, a year or so earlier, in case you're wondering). She made sure it was lined with fresh straw and well-stocked with food and water. With due solemnity, she carried the baby in its new home, up to the shed, and placed it carefully on a table that had been previously cleared of its usual array of tools. After weighing down the transparent, plastic lid with a couple of house-bricks, and satisfying herself that there was no way anything, human or animal, could gain entry, unless it happened to be equipped with a ready-made burglary kit, she bolted and locked the only door.

It was April 30th - May Eve. Walpurgis Nacht *

It must have been sometime around 8:30pm, (certainly I recall it was virtually pitch-black outside), that I noticed my sister began to grow increasingly anxious about the welfare of the last remaining baby rabbit.

We were all seated around the flickering TV set watching the brilliant Irish comic Dave Allen, when I caught sight of our Kearry nervously fidgeting and wringing her hands, an expression of intense concern clouding her features, I was just about to ask if she was feeling alright, when she suddenly jumped up and announced in a shaky voice:

"I'm just going to check on the rabbit. Pass me the key, please Dad."

My father rolled his eyes and heaved a world-weary sigh as he threw the keys over to her. '

A BRIEF FOOTNOTE REGARDING WALPURGIS NACHT:

The evening of April 30th has long been associated with Witchcraft and The Occult right across Europe, but chiefly in Germany, Scandinavia and the Low Countries.

The name of the spring festival, which is the night before Beltane, one of the eight Great Sabbats, comes originally from the Catholic Saint Walburga, who died in the year 777 AD.

It's connections with 'Witch revelry' may have s something to do with the ancient festival of fertility and re-birth that surrounds May Day, and the fact that the date is the exact polar opposite in the calendar year of that other 'opening of the gateways between this world and the realm of the dead,' October 31st, Hallowe'en (or Samhain, if you want to be pernickety!).

Walpurgis Nacht is celebrated by the lighting of bonfires, dancing, drinking, orgiastic revels and other forms of what was considered to be decidedly (back in the Middle Ages, anyway) un-Christian method of merrymaking.

In many parts of the countries who continue to celebrate the occasion, people dress up as Witches, Ghosts \and Goblins, and wander the city streets, and it is also looked upon as a form of prank-playing type of 'Mischief Night'. The traditional tricks engaged in by the capricious included throwing that age-old symbol of fertility - the egg - hiding possessions, and, perhaps, tellingly; *tampering with people's gardens* (and, one wonders, the creatures both wild and domestic, that reside therein?)

Perhaps, though, the great Bram Stoker, summed up the occasion perfectly in his short story: *'Dracula's Guest,'* when he wrote: *'Walpurgis Night was when, according to the belief of millions of people, the Devil was abroad - when the graves were opened and the dead came forth and walked. When all evil things of earth and air and water held revel.'*

> "Ok Kegs, be my guest,"

…he smiled, shaking his head.

> "You're wasting your time, though. No-one's gonna break into that shed just to get at a baby rabbit."

But his words, reasonable though they may have been, were completely lost on my sister. I'm not sure she even heard them, in truth, she was out the back door of the extension so quick.

I went back to watching the telly, affecting an air of cool indifference that I didn't truly feel. To be honest, I was trying my best to ignore the sudden tension that permeated the room, a sense of something holding back....and for all of two minutes, I think I succeeded.

Then, for the second time in a few short weeks, the air was filled with the bone-chilling sound of my sister's screaming. And although I all but jumped out of my skin at the Banshee-like screech, I found that I had somehow been more than half-expecting it.

Before any of us had a chance to run to her aid, Kearry came charging through the doorway, her eyes bulging madly, and with flecks of spittle shining on her upper lip illuminated by the glow of the TV screen, and it's my belief she would very likely have kept right on sprinting through the living room and out the front door (perhaps without actually pausing to actually open it), and race along the streets of New Ferry, wailing like a police car siren. At least if my Dad hadn't have leaped up and grabbed her by the arms and forced her to sit down in the nearest available chair.

It took us some time to find out even the bare details of what had happened. Kearry is one of the most articulate persons I know, even back then when she was barely out of her teens, but for a while there, she could no more string a coherent sentence together than she could ride backwards to the North Pole on a unicycle with a slow puncture.

What was immediately obvious however, was that the source of my sister's fear lay somewhere within the confines of the woodshed.

We hastily fished out the torches, and leaving my mother to comfort Kearry, we stepped out into the waiting dark.

A raw, out-of-season wind whipped across the garden and buffeted the brightly-lit windows, and though it blurred our eyes with misted tears, we could clearly make out that the shed door was banging open and shut in the semi-gale and it was obvious Kearry had been too frightened to stop to lock it. It was therefore with a great sense of foreboding that I approached the entrance, but when we shone our torchlight beams into the darkness that filled the interior, we could find nothing amiss or out of place. There was no sign of any structural damage. No indication that there was anything missing. No tell-tale trace of intrusion. And best of all, the baby rabbit was still very much alive. We watched it hopping merrily around, without a care in the world, and we shrugged out shoulders at Kearry's jumping at shadows. I turned back into the house, but as I did so I was halted by a cry of surprise from Grant, as he suddenly exclaimed:

> "Hold on a minute, look at this!"

I followed his gaze, and for a moment I didn't have a clue what he was talking about. And then I saw what he was referring to.

It was nothing overly dramatic.

But it was at least an indication that perhaps Kearry's mind hadn't been entirely playing tricks, after all. It was simply this: the two house-bricks that had been placed atop the plastic cage cover were no longer there. They were both on the floor, a couple of feet from the cage. They couldn't possibly have fallen off by themselves. So unless Kearry had upset them accidentally, or had been moved for some unknown purpose..?

After having placed the bricks in their original position, we firmly locked the door and went back inside to see my sister had recovered sufficiently to be able to tell us what had happened.

It turned out that indeed she had.

But when she'd finished telling us what she firmly believed she'd glimpsed in the darkness of the woodshed, I found myself wishing to God she's stayed silent....

*****

The second Kearry had unlocked the door to the shed and stepped inside, she had instinctively known something was very wrong.

There was a kind of thick, heavy atmosphere about the place that had nothing to do with the dank odours of old paint and sodden carpet rolls that assailed her nostrils. Nor the fact that her torch batteries were so low that the light it gave off barely penetrated the pervasive gloom. It was if she'd somehow stepped into a dreamscape world of waking nightmare.

For some reason, Kearry didn't simply turn and head back into the warmth and comforting reassurance of the house, though. Instead, she remained exactly where she was, playing the thin pencil-beam of watery light across the walls and shelf stacks, heavy with the combined weight of tins of emulsion and creosote, tool kits and piles of dirty oil cloth, bottles of turpentine and ancient home brew. What she was looking for exactly, she couldn't say, either now nor then.

What she did state for certain however, is that it was the curious scraping sound emanating from the direction of the table upon which the converted hamster cage was perched that drew her attention back to the whole point of her being here in the first place.

A kind of shuffling...

Soft, but insistent...

In the dark...

Her initial thought was that the thing crouched between the two house bricks was an exceptionally large rat.

It was only when a sudden shaft of moonlight, peering through a gap in the ragged clouds, boosting the increasingly weak illumination provided by the pocket torch, that its true nature was revealed.

She saw it was actually a two-foot-high creature, crooked and bent, and draped in an all-enveloping cloak that served to obscure most of its features.

She could make out the contours of its face, just fine though.

It was the face of an ancient crone or an impossibly old man. The skin was so heavily wrinkled it resembled weather-worn leather, but its eyes, set either side of a huge bulbous nose, warty and lined with an intricate network of black veins, were bright and filled with a malignant intelligence.

It stared, favouring her with a hideous, lop-sided grin, revealing a set of teeth, both jagged and decayed...

And with chunks of undigested, mushy meat dangling between the many gaps.

But what finally had my sister running from the shed in uncontrollable fear was the sight of that which it held in one gnarled, bony hand...

A lump hammer.

Thick and powerful-looking. Its mallet darkly stained and splattered with strips of monochrome fur, mixed with tiny pieces of shining white bone.

Of course, none of us seriously believed Kearry had seen any such thing.

My guess was that she had been correct in her original assumption. That she'd encountered nothing more exotic than an excessively large, if otherwise perfectly ordinary rat, in admittedly, rather unusual circumstances. Imagination and the poor quality of light had done the rest. The rather sticky problem of how the rodent had got into the predator-proof shed was 'solved' by my supposition that it may in fact have already been hiding somewhere inside before the door had initially been locked, or whilst it had been blowing to and fro in the wind.

I think it's fair to say we were all of us convinced beyond doubting of this, or some similar theory.

And yet...

When it was unanimously decided it might very well be advisable to bring the baby rabbit indoors to absolutely ensure its protection from marauding rats, or any other predators, and we hurried back outside to collect the cage, we found to our horror, that the two house-bricks were back lying on the shed floor, the perspex lid had been pushed ajar, the exercise wheel was gently spinning on its side, looking for all the world like some bizarre instrument of medieval torture....

And the last surviving baby rabbit was lying dead with not a mark upon it, save for the fact that its head was crushed.

Flattened impossibly thin, as though it had been stuck a single blow with some type of blunt, heavy object.

A lump hammer, for example...

*****

We never did find out the truth of what really happened to that innocent, completely defenceless, litter.

That didn't stop the various theories abounding like free-falling confetti, however. Despite the fact that each and every hypothesis proffered only served to throw up more questions than answers.

The most preposterous theory of all was, of course, was that promoted in the wake of what my sister may or may not have seen lurking in the shed , on the last day of April, 1982.

Such things simply don't exist this side of a horror author's more outlandish slices of fiction or some half-heard Faerie Tale from the days of far-off childhood.

Demons. Goblins. Trolls. They have all long since been consigned to the dustbin of discredited superstition and folk belief.

If you really choose, for some obscure reasons, to put your ears to that door, you'll only hear the gales of insanity shrieking maniacally on the other side.

And a total and utter fool would volunteer to do that.

AND YET...in January, 1905, at Binbrook Farm, near Market Rasen in Lincolnshire, *something* killed 225 chickens in a particularly horrible way. Despite a constant watch on the hen-house, whenever the interior came to be examined, four or five of the birds would be found dead. And they were all killed in the same way: the skin around the neck, from the head to the breast, had been pulled off, and the windpipe drawn from its place and snapped.

Neither the culprits, nor their motive were ever discovered.

AND YET...During 1919, in Llanelly, Wales, *something* managed to enter a row of rabbit hutches, and break the backs of an entire litter of rabbits.

AND YET...In the late 1940s, at Alphamstone, Sussex, a family living at Sycamore Farm, bred chickens which were kept in a paddock, surrounded by strong wire, buried several feet under the earth and the doors were firmly padlocked.

But when the family were awakened one night by the noise of the badly-frightened poultry, the farmer thought he saw a 'greyhound' moving through the chicken huts in the centre of the paddock. He raised his gun and fired but the creature simply disappeared through the netting and into a nearby hedgerow. A meticulous search failed to find any point of entry. The farmer was positive the entire enclosure was completely predator-proof.

AND YET...In 1954, in Caracas, Venezuela, a man named Gustavo Gonzalez, swore blind he was attacked by what he described as "a hairy dwarf" with glowing eyes. He stabbed it, but the knife had no effect.

AND YET...In the Orkney Isles, the headless corpses of over thirty seals were found on various beaches. To add to the mystery, the heads had been removed with what seemed to be surgical precision.

AND YET...In the winter of 1977, a series of extremely weird mutilations reportedly occurred near Bay Springs, Mississippi, USA. According to contemporary reports collated by paranormal researchers Janet and Colin Bord, in their excellent book, *Alien Animals (1980)*, several pigs were found in their pens with their ears, and *only* their ears, removed.

The attacks started in early January, when a man by the name of Joseph Dixon, found his sow lying dead with its ears missing, and the very next day, two more animals suffered the exact same fate. On January 9th of that same year, Dixon claimed to have witnessed the predator responsible for the mutilations. He told investigators that it was an animal, and that the creature was some kind of big cat 'bigger than any German Shepherd, and was longer than any dog, and it was jumping further than any dog could ever jump.'

Even more bizarrely, the day after his sighting, Joseph found another of his pigs with half an ear missing, only this particular pig survived He noted that in all of these cases, as well as the amputation of the pig's ears, there was also a 2-3 inch cut in the back of the animal's neck. Joseph was so perturbed by this additional incision, that he was moved to comment:

> 'It's not a tear...It's a smooth cut...As smooth as if you would cut it with a pair of scissors.'

The attacks continued in the area throughout February and March, before suddenly petering out as quickly as they had begun.

No satisfactory explanation for the mysterious mutilations was ever forthcoming.

AND YET...I've saved the best two for last...

Firstly, during the month of July, 2001, in the formerly peaceful community of Guanica, Puerto Rico, a series of mysterious animal deaths occurred across the southern reaches of the island, including the killing of 60 pregnant sheep by what their owner presumed to be a pack of stray dogs, (many of which roam the area).

More disturbingly, at least as far as this writer is concerned, is that which allegedly took place the following month - August 2nd, to be precise, when a man by the name of Carmelo Sepulveda, claimed that his two pet rabbits, a buck and a doe, were attacked at three in the morning (the Devil's Hour). The female was decapitated, while *(and get this)*, the cage was firmly locked.

Its head, along with its entrails, were still within the hutch, whilst the rest of its body, minus its limbs (of which there were absolutely no trace), was outside.

The male, meanwhile, only received fairly superficial injuries to its extremities, but, perhaps not surprisingly, given what we've heard about these type of weird mutilations, it showed no obvious signs of terror.

If you think that this maybe provides at least a smidgeon of potential corroborative evidence for my own family's own incredibly strange experience, *(and even if you don't)*, please take some time to consider this...

One of Carmelo's neighbours later reported that he had been awoken a little after three in the morning *(There's that Devil's Hour, again!)*, by the sound of Mr Sepulveda's rabbits squealing, and quickly stumbled out of bed to switch on the outside light that illuminated Carmelo's backyard. He was unable to discern much of what was happening from his vantage point, so he bravely decided to go out and take a closer look. Carefully tip-toeing across the pre-dawn, soaking wet grass, he saw what he later described as being *(and Dear God, this is a chillingly compelling image to me, for obvious reasons)*:

> 'Something resembling a child standing near to one of the rabbit cages.'

Unfortunately, the poor quality of light prevented the witness from making out any precise details.

Whatever it was (and yes, it may well have been an ordinary *human* child, albeit a ruthlessly cruel one, cursed with such an uncontrollably sadistic streak, that they felt compelled to wander about in the early hours of the morning in search of pet rabbits to mutilate and bodily dismember for no other reason than to satiate their blood-lust, which is arguably even more terrifying a prospect than any of the alternative paranormal possibilities), it surely must, if you have an even partially open mind, give you pause to wonder.

Interestingly, four days after these attacks, there were several more rabbit mutilations in the La Joya sector of Guanica. Mrs Roses Flores, discovered two dead rabbits, one of which had an open chest cavity, completely empty of any internal organs save for the animal's heart. Its legs, fur and eyes had all been carefully removed.

The other rabbit had its skin flayed and its legs amputated. Its chest cavity was perfectly intact, but its body had been completely drained of blood.

Some of Mrs Flores' neighbours reported that they heard dogs barking incessantly at around about 3am, (I'm saying nothing), on the morning of the attacks. There were also the sounds of a frantic commotion emanating from a nearby chicken coop.

When paranormal investigators duly appeared on the scene, they apparently discovered a series of strange claw marks on several of the cages containing the restless poultry. Three and four-fingered claw marks were also found in the lower section of these cages. It was the investigators' opinion that there may actually have been two creatures responsible for these marks because footprints both large and small were found throughout the area.

A week later, there was a secondary incident at Carmelo Sepulveda's home. On this occasion, the rabbit that had survived the initial attack on August 2nd, was killed by an unknown assailant. Its body lay crumpled in the far corner of a cage that had been firmly secured the night before. And, once again, there was no sign that the cage had in anyway been interfered with.

Mr Sepulveda also discovered that another of his female rabbits had disappeared from its hutch, and no trace of its remains was ever found.

Once again, several of Carmelo's neighbours had heard the local dogs barking excitedly on the night of the attack, and even more intriguingly, one unnamed individual reported that she and her husband were getting into their van because they were driving to the local bakery where they worked, when they suddenly noticed a red light that was reflecting off their vehicle. The woman was unable to ascertain its source, and looking towards a leafy tree loaded with edible fruit called a *quenepa*, she saw a 'shadowy figure staring at her with red eyes,' (a reportedly common feature of all forms of multi-dimensional entities).

Upon sighting this being, the woman immediately put her foot down and drove away as fast as she could. She didn't initially tell her husband what it was she thought she'd seen, but when he dared to ask why the hell it was they were speeding down the highway as though the very Devil was hot on their heels, she told him that maybe that wasn't so very far from the truth.

AND FINALLY: During the spring of 2008, in Dortmund, Germany, over 40 rabbits were beheaded and bled dry by some mystery assailant, and despite the setting up of a police task force to try and apprehend the assumed, human culprit(s), no-one was ever caught, and no motive was therefore discovered for the bizarre series of killings.

As the local populace demanded action however, somewhat predictably, the authorities blamed a cult of Satanists as being the chief suspects, due to the fact that the blood had been drained from the rabbit corpses.

AND YET...

AND YET...The truth is, I still am not at all sure as to what exactly killed our brood of baby rabbits all those years ago. I only know that there is a distinct *possibility* that whatever *was r*esponsible for the methodical slaughter, may lie outside the normal boundaries of human experience.

Aside from the very real difficulties that would be faced by anything trying to break into the well-protected hutch, in the first place, there is the added problem of motive. Or to be more precise, the lack of one.

Only my sister, Kearry, can shed (absolutely no pun intended), any further light on the matter.

Except she *can't*.

Remember what I wrote earlier about how people who are suddenly confronted with 'the inexplicable.' can often find it very difficult to adjust and come to terms with what they may have experienced?

So much so, that they choose to clam up, rather than admit to themselves or anyone else that they've jut been a hugely reluctant witness to something that definitely doesn't fit in with their patterns of belief.

Well, it seems we are dealing with just such an instance here, because Kearry, perhaps feeling threatened by her own blades of belief and memory, nowadays refuses point blank to accept that she may have encountered a Goblin, a Dark Faerie, some Multidimensional Entity, call it what you will, armed with a lump hammer, clearly intent on wreaking havoc upon the defenceless little victim that night in the woodshed.

She denies all knowledge of ever having seen anything strange whatsoever.

And it's like getting blood out of a stone persuading her to even discuss the subject.

But *I* remember enough for both of us. I remember the expression of sheer terror on her face. The genuine honesty reflected in my sister's eyes as she described what she *then* believed she had seen, and I often wonder if like me, she still suffers from occasional bad dreams in which a hideous grinning Demonic entity dances madly upon a mound of concrete inscribed with the number 666?

A blood-stained hammer in one, claw-like hand.

A cluster of crushed baby rabbit skulls in the other.

BY THE BALEFUL GLARE OF A DEMON MOON
The Secret Dungeon of Leasowe Castle

Before we get to the meat of this fascinating story, here's an essentially brief (by which I mean, despite some fairly extensive digging around on the internet, and amongst the pages of dusty, leather-bound volumes and crinkly old pamphlets, I really wasn't able to recover much of historical interest) history lesson.

Leasowe Castle was originally built in 1593, for the fifth Earl of Derby, for use as a summer home, the said Earl being, at that time, second in line to the English throne.

After a century or so, the Earls decided to relinquish their residency of the castle and it was sadly left to fall into a gradual state of ruin and neglect, not long after which it became known by the accurate, if slightly less than flattering nickname of 'Mockbeggar Hall.'

During the English Civil War, the newly-christened building passed into the hands of Cromwellian supporters, and rumours of the sadistic torture and imprisonment of their enemies, the Cavaliers, soon became widespread amongst the local populace. It's doubtful whether anyone other than 'Mockbeggar's' residents, and various members of staff would have been able to verify these stories however, seeing as how the stone walls of the building were exceptionally strong, solid and thoroughly scream-proof. Over three inches thick in places, they were designed to keep both would-be invaders out and the tormented yells of unspeakable agony firmly within[*].

Over the course of several decades, the hall served as a temporary home for shipwrecked sailors, until it became the private residence of several, fairly well-to-do families, none of whom seem to have achieved any great notoriety, even in local circles.

Until 1802, at least.

That was the year when it was purchased by a woman by the name of Mrs Boode, whose daughter married one Edward Cust, in 1821. Edward, a former army colonel, rose to prominence across the county for two reasons. Firstly, he tried to turn the former castle into a hotel, without it has to be said, any great degree of success. And secondly, and rather more bizarrely, he had a hand-crafted wooden chair permanently placed in the hotel's back garden, facing the Irish Sea, which he called, with a quite startling display of originality, 'Canute's Chair.' On the arms of the said chair he inscribed the hopelessly optimistic words; 'Sea come nor hither, nor wet the soul of my foot,' and to this day, there are apparently many people who remain convinced that the original King Canute once visited and sat on that particular seat.

Whatever the truth of the matter, sadly there is no trace of 'Canute's Chair' today, although near to where it was formerly supposed to have been situated, stand 'The Mermaid Stones'. These are a series of boulders thought by

---

[*] Another enemy was the tidal waters. The original door was around 6 feet above sea level.

geologists to have been deposited at the location by a glacier during the last Ice Age, and legend has it that the Mermaid of the Black Rock used to love to sit on these rocks, combing her hair and pouting into a sea-shell looking glass, the epitome of female vanity. According to local folklore, this seductively beautiful creature was often seen at midnight, in the silvery glow of a summer moon and at full tide, sitting on the boulders singing to the stars. Like many of her kind, the Mermaid was said to be irresistibly beautiful, and effortlessly succeeded in enchanting a man by the name of John Robinson. One oft-repeated tale tells of how he found her sitting on Black Rock, just off the Leasowe coastline, as he sailed by in his boat. Disregarding all the warnings his mother had given him to steer well clear of the Mermaid, John fell prey to her enticing charms. He invited her aboard his vessel where they engaged in lengthy conversation, before she returned to her home on the sea-bed. She did however give him a ring as a keepsake, but it provided scant consolation, as such mementoes often do, and five days later, John died of that most devastating of maladies, an irreparably broken heart. It is said that many other men have fallen victim to the Mermaid's romantic allure, or have been swept to their dooms by her siren-like singing over the years. In 1974, the former castle became a fully-fledged, splendidly picturesque hotel, with forty-five rooms, fabulous function suites and acres of immaculate golf courses.

The building is reputed to be haunted by at least three different ghosts. According to verbal accounts that have since made their way into the pages of several books dealing with the supernatural, various guests have been rudely awoken in the middle of the night by the appearance of a sullen-looking man and boy stood at the end of their beds. These reported manifestations seem to follow an identical pattern: the apparitions materialise at the bedside. The percipient, still groggy from having barely awoken, stares back at them. The figures make no sound and barely move. There is no reported interaction between the ghosts and the human witnesses.

(Above): The splendour of Leasowe Castle, as it stands today. Set back from the main road at the end of a suitably grand driveway, the building is one of the most splendid in the county of Merseyside. But does its decorative facade mask some dark and terrible secrets, hidden from view of the guests and staff?

Not all of the reported phenomena adhere so rigidly to this type of 'recording ghost'-type manifestation, however. Other people who have stayed there over the years claim to have heard inexplicable noises including the sound of footsteps treading softly behind them on one of the impressively ornate staircases, but when they've spun round to confront whoever they assume to be stealthily creeping up on them, there is never anyone there.

Another local legend tells of how sometime in the dim and distant past, the castle was at the centre of a particularly bitter family quarrel. A father and son were apparently taken prisoner as being the leaders of one side of this acrimonious feud, and were promptly locked up in one of the building's guest rooms.

It's a matter for conjecture, of course, but it would come as no great surprise to learn that they were incarcerated in the very same room where visitors have been roused from their slumber by the restless spirits of a man and younger boy.

As things turned out, the twin medieval delights of hideous torture followed by a lifetime of cruel captivity, (always assuming you survived the initial ordeal, of course), that awaited them proved tpo depressing a prospect to bear, and rather than subject themselves to such horrors, the father decided to kill his son before committing suicide himself, by bashing his head repeatedly against a wall.

I'm not an expert on euthanasia or anything, but I'm pretty sure there are about a million easier and less painful ways of shaking off this mortal coil, but there you go.

Speaking of the castle's less-than-savoury history, I received the following, thought-provoking account from an anonymous woman, back in the early 1990s.

*****

'On October 31st, 1986, I think it was, I went with a group of friends to The Leasowe Castle Hotel, to attend a Hallowe'en Ball.

The event turned out to be something of an acute disappointment, however. I mean, I hadn't quite known quite what to expect, but I certainly hadn't bargained for the usual, boring fancy dress, *'Spooky Disco'* type affair that it anti-climatically proved to be. (By the way, I'm not all sure what qualifies as a *'Spooky Disco,'* as opposed to an *un*-spooky one, but this so-called *'Titan of Terror Road-Show'* consisted of a big fat man in a loud Hawaiian shirt and cheap and nasty werewolf mask, who spoke in an unintelligible faux-American accent, and Michael Jackson's *'Thriller,'* Ray Parker Junior's *'Ghostbusters'* and Bobby Pickett's *Monster Mash,* over and over again in an endless loop. Oh, and he had a melting pumpkin on top of one of the flash-four lights whose Jack o' Lantern features looked to have been carved by a blind leper).

My friends and I had more than had enough well before the 1am call for last orders, and so we were stood at the very edge of the all-but deserted dance-floor trying (and failing) to stifle our yawns and glancing at our wristwatches every few seconds. I'd just about decided to drain the dregs of my last drink and call it a night when we were approached by a young, good-looking hotel porter. I thought at first he was going to hit on one of us, and to be perfectly honest, I was so utterly disenchanted at that point, it probably wouldn't have taken much of an effort on his part to get me interested.

It turned out though that nothing could have been further from the truth.

Without any sort of preamble, or indeed without even introducing himself, (and he wasn't wearing any name tag, although this never stuck me as being remotely unusual, strange to say) he came right out and asked us if we'd care to see a part of the hotel that had long since been closed off to visiting guests, residents and even the staff who worked there.

'Believe me, ladies,' he said 'I can show you something that will definitely make your Hallowe'en. And give you a good scare into the bargain.' He grinned, revealing a set of perfect white teeth; a toothpaste advertiser's dream, and I remember thinking; 'Boy, with a smile like that you could melt to the heart of an ice maiden, never mind a bunch of decidedly tipsy female twenty-somethings!'

We were so taken aback by his boldly coming over to speak to our group that none of us gave an immediate reply, but he must have taken our collective silence as unspoken assent, because he promptly turned and gestured in the direction of the plush-carpeted staircase, and without once looking back over his shoulder, murmured, 'Please, follow me.'

And so it was, not five minutes later, my friends and I found ourselves being led along a series of endlessly winding, oak-panelled corridors, where the only sources of illumination were the flickering torches in their sconces of the walls and the silvery slabs of autumn moonlight that slanted through the latticed windows like the eerie afterglow of the day gone by.

Even accounting for the poor quality of light, however, I could clearly see the passageways were extremely dusty and full of old, wispy cobwebs, and certainly it looked as though nobody had walked here for years beyond counting. The floors were thick with accumulated grime and I could see the outline of our footprints as we walked along in single file, and I was reminded of an illustration I'd once seen as a child in English Class from *Robinson Crusoe*, the sun-burned, wild-haired castaway treading the white virgin sand of what he mistakenly assumed to be an uninhabited island.

The porter chatted away amiably enough all the while, but I can't now recall a single word he said. I was far too busy trying to take in the surroundings, and finding it increasingly difficult with each step that I took, almost as though I were in the midst of a waking dream, the kind where the scenery and the very floor beneath your feet shift and change ceaselessly, and I found it to be a highly disconcerting sensation that left me feeling disoriented and a little nauseous.

Anyway, finally, at the end of one particularly ancient-looking corridor, we came upon a large wooden door with a brass handle in the shape of some hideous Demonic character. Our guide stopped and turned to face us, the dancing shadows and the orange glare of the torchlight distorting his handsome features so that for a moment he was transformed into a real-life Jack o' Lantern Hobgoblin.

Well, here we are!' he announced with a theatrical flourish. 'Please allow me, if I may, to present to you the highlight of our unofficial tour. The door you see before you is usually kept locked and I have the only key. Ordinarily, as I believe I told you earlier, this whole area is completely out of bounds to the general public. And, as I believe I also stated, very few members of staff who work here, even know of its existence.'

He grinned once more, and his perfect set of pearly white teeth suddenly looked to be stained and yellowed and to have somehow grown longer and more pointed and well...wolfish is the word I'm looking for, I suppose, and for the first time, I questioned the wisdom of our agreeing to accompany him on this mysterious midnight jaunt.

Before I could give voice to my concerns though, the porter reached into his pockets and produced a set of jangling keys.

Now, are you quite sure you lovely young ladies definitely want to step inside?' he asked (and I half-expected him to add something suitably portentous, like, 'But if you agree to do so, I feel it is my duty as a gentleman to warn you, you will need all your self-command!')

There was a mischievous glint in his eye as he spoke, but if he was banking on any of us losing our nerve, he was to be sorely disappointed. 'Any reluctance I'd felt for stepping through that door rapidly dissipated to be replaced by a steely determination that I wasn't about to come all this way just to turn back now. One quick glance at my friends was enough to convince me that they all felt exactly the same way. And so, with admittedly some degree of trepidation, we bade him open the door.

It swung open slowly on its rusted hinges making an unnerving, horror movie-style crreeeeakk as it did so.

'Very well,' the porter said, still smiling that unnerving smile. 'Ladies, be my guest.'

After a moment's hesitation, we stepped inside, and the second we did so, our collective jaws didn't so much drop as crash in a thousand shattered fragments around out feet.

'You see before you the legendary castle dungeons, where, hundreds of years ago, prisoners were incarcerated and tortured in various, unspeakable ways,' the porter shouted, his voice echoing around the large, high-ceilinged room. This pronouncement was entirely unnecessary, of course, because one brief glance at the collection of implements gathered in this dank-smelling dungeon, not to mention the pervasive atmosphere of dread and centuries-old suffering, was more than enough to reveal the former purpose of this terrible place. There were numerous sets of manacles and metal cages hanging from various points on the dripping walls, benches lined with sets of thumbscrews, hacksaws, and limb-crushing vices, whilst braziers filled with flaky cinders were standing alongside them.

As I gazed around the room, struggling to take it all in, I saw there was an Iron Maiden over in the far corner, its lid slightly ajar, revealing a set of lethal-looking shiny-silver spikes, and I was struck with another image from long-ago childhood: the toothsome jaws of an enormous prehistoric monster, a Megalosaurus, I think it was called, whose skeleton used to be on display in the foyer of Liverpool Museum.

The object that dominated this real-life chamber of horrors though, was a large rectangular table situated in the dead centre of the dungeon. It too had chains and manacles attached to each of its four corners, and hanging suspended, just a few feet above it, was a semi-circular blade connected to a pendulum and a set of cogs and pulleys. Although it was inactive at the time, it was all too easy to imagine it in full working order, the gradually lowering blade swishing through the air like the instrument of revenge in that classic Edgar Allen Poe story.

'A real beauty, isn't she?' the porter said with a mixture of pride and admiration. 'Come on and take a closer look.'

'Nah, you're alright,' I said, smiling weakly. 'I can see it perfectly well from over here, thanks.'

I could, too. And what I saw made me feel extremely uneasy, although I was damned if I was going to allow our guide the satisfaction of seeing I was troubled in any way. From my vantage point I'd noticed that though the pendulum mechanism must have been somewhere in the region of 300 years old, the blade looked to be razor-sharp and stained with something that was very probably rust, but could just as easily have been blood.

There was also something vaguely disturbing about how deathly quiet the dungeon was. The only noise, aside from the ceaseless dripping of water, was the sound of our own breathing, disconcertingly loud in the absence of the tortured yells and desperate pleas for mercy that, centuries before, had doubtless rent the stale air and pierced the rough, uncaring darkness.

The almost-silence stretched out before us as we girls stood in a semi-circle, almost as though we were in a hypnotic trance, a state from which we were only shaken by my friend, Nadine, who voiced the question that I'd been wanting to ask the moment I'd stepped inside the room:

'Is it just me, or does anyone else think it's a little bit strange that all of these torture implements look to be fairly new?'

'Well, we like to keep them in full, spick 'n' span, working order, just in case any of our guests prove troublesome or refuse to pay their final bill,' the porter replied, and we all chuckled, if a little nervously.

'No, seriously,' he added, when the laughter had subsided, "the truth is, these items are of enormous historical importance, and it would be a shame to allow them to fall into a state of neglect and disrepair, don't you think?'

'Then how come no-one's ever allowed down here to see it?' I inquired. 'Surely it would make sense to permit members of the public access to the 'The Dungeon'?

'Because the boss man doesn't want to scare away custom,' he replied. 'The last thing anyone in the hotel business wants is for their building to acquire an unsavoury reputation. I mean, claiming you've got a resident spook or two is one thing, Chances are the local newspapers will soon get wind of the story and before you know it, you're quite literally turning ghost-busters, spiritualists, religious cranks and the just plain curious away in droves. Torture chambers on the other hand,' he grimaced as though something unpleasant had just crawled into his mouth. 'They only ever seem to attract the kind of seedy, bloodthirsty individuals who get their kicks from revelling in other people's suffering. And we don't want that sort residing here.'

'Present company excepted, of course!' he added quickly as he caught sight of our disapproving glances.

'Well, that's very noble of you,' I said, 'but even so, I simply can't believe any manager worth his salt would turn his nose up at an opportunity to boost the hotel's popularity, purely on moral grounds.'

"You know what, you might just be right,' the porter replied with an exaggerated sigh. 'But hey, I don't make the rules. I only work here.' He shrugged his shoulders and then gestured towards the exit.

"Speaking of which, we'd best be heading back now. If my boss finds out I've brought you lot down here, he'll have me tied to that bench and sliced in two faster than you can say '*Pit And The Pendulum!*'

We didn't raise any objections. We'd seen enough, quite frankly, and besides, it was freezing cold down there and time was getting on. We allowed ourselves to be ushered gently but firmly out the door and the porter turned and locked it behind him. The second the door clanged shut, I cursed myself for not having brought so much as a cheap, disposable Instamatic camera to snap some photographic mementoes of our visit to the dungeons (this incident took place during the technological 'Dark Ages', when mobile phones still resembled house-bricks, and home recording equipment required a Hollywood blockbuster-sized film crew to operate and haul around), we wearily traipsed along the those same endlessly winding corridors to emerge, blinking, back in the well-lit foyer. It took us a while to adjust our eyesight to the bright electric lights and crystal chandeliers. It all seemed so unreal after the dank and musty-smelling darkness of the dungeon.

Eventually, we recovered enough to say 'thank you' to the porter, and in return, he bid us good night and said we were all very welcome. He then walked behind the counter at the reception desk, and with a final wave, closed the door behind him.

We shook our heads, as if to clear them of the dreamy, brain-fuddling fallout of our Midnight Expedition, and smiling uneasily at each other, we looked in our purses to scrape enough loose change for the pay phone, and then walked over to the counter to ask out friendly neighbourhood porter if he knew of any reliable taxi firms in the area. I rang the bell on the desk and almost immediately, a man in his late fifties emerged from the staff room, much to our collective disappointment. Nadine, ever the cocky one, asked him where his younger colleague was, the one with jet-black hair and pearly-white smile was, and the middle-aged porter who, according to the shiny brass tag pinned to his waistcoat, was named Frank, looked at us quizzically and said there was no-one working on the night shift who remotely fitted that description.

Well, we naturally thought it was all some kind of decidedly late-in-the-day Hallowe'en prank, and Nadine laughed sarcastically and insisted that he stop messing about and go and fetch him. Frank looked at her like she was either hard of hearing or so thick she couldn't understand plain English.

'Now look, I'm telling you, young lady, the only other member of staff on duty tonight is my colleague, Jimmy Mullin; a top-notch individual and a close personal friend of mine who, I'm sure won't mind me saying, is completely bald and a bit on the fat side, and just a couple of years younger than my good self! But don't just take my word for it...Jim, mate, can you come out here for a minute?'

The estimable Mr Mullin, who was indeed overweight, hairless and wrinkly of face, emerged blinking from the back room looking like a raggedy-arse, close-shaven dormouse, that had just been awoken from a particularly heavy period of hibernation.

'Jim, me old mucker,' Frank announced brightly. 'I've got some good news for yer! These girls here reckon you're only about twenty-odd! Now, if yer ask me, they must be drunker than a pack of skunks on a three-day absinthe bender, but then maybe you just look ridiculously old for yer age. What do you think?'

They both laughed loud and long, like Frank had just cracked the funniest gag in the history of comedy.

We were most definitely not amused, though, and we made no big secret of the fact. Of course, we didn't want to get the young porter, or anyone else, into trouble, but we were annoyed at having been made the butt of what we still perceived to be some puerile practical joke.

'Excuse me,' I said with a world-weary sigh. 'But when you two chuckleheads have quite finished wetting yourselves, perhaps you'd be so good as to call us a taxi?'

'Certainly, Miss,' Jim replied, struggling to keep the grin from his face. 'Unless you'd prefer "The Phantom Porter" to phone one for you.'

'For God's sake, grow up will you!' I snapped. 'He wasn't a ghost or a figment of our imagination. If you must know, he took us on a tour of the Torture Chamber, The Hidden Dungeon, or whatever it is you want to call it, over in the closed-off-to-the-public part of the Castle. And we certainly didn't dream any of that up!'

I'm not sure what reaction I expected to provoke from this outburst, but I was amazed when all they did was to turn to each other and erupt into fresh gales of maniacal laughter.

'What dungeons?' Jimmy asked breathlessly when he'd recovered enough of his composure to speak words of half-way intelligible English. 'What the hell have you girls been drinking? I've been working here for 25 years, and I've never heard of any dungeons or torture chambers, closed off to the public, or otherwise. What about you, Frank?'

'Well, I've heard all the local legends, of course, but I've walked every inch of this building over the last couple of decades or so, and if any such place ever truly existed, it's long since been demolished or permanently walled up.'

'But that's impossible!' Cynthia, another of my friends, exclaimed loudly. 'We've just spent the best part of the last hour in the middle of that dreadful chamber in the cold and dark and with all those hellish instruments of torture surrounding us on all sides. We were so close we could have reached out and touched them...' She grimaced and was unable to suppress a shiver. 'If we'd wanted to."

'Yeah, that's right,' I added. 'And if you don't believe us, just follow us and we'll show you.'

Frank considered this for a moment and then nodded once, his mind made up. "Okay, this I've simply got to see,' he said. 'You'd best stay here, Jim. Hold the fort, and all that.'

'Yeah, just watch out for the Creepy Dungeon Master and Gi-normous Rack!' Jim, the comedic genius replied slapping his colleague on the back, before holding on to his sides with mirth once more.

Smarting with righteous anger, we motioned for Frank to accompany us as we retraced our steps back down the lengthy flight of carpeted stairs and along the well-lit passageways, but though we walked for what seemed like hours, we couldn't find a single trace of either the stone-walled, dust-laden corridors or that huge wooden door with its gargoyle-faced handle.

Every time we turned a corner, we'd fully expect to come upon the beginning of the old part of the castle, but everything remained frustratingly late 20th Century. The floors were spotlessly clean, the passageways illuminated by fully functional, if rather bland electric lighting, and the windows, through which the pale, silvery-moonlight continued to beam, were double-glazed. Time and time again we came up against dead ends and doors adorned with thoroughly modern fire exit signs and hose-pipes coiled up like sleeping anacondas.

After wandering aimlessly and finally realising we were walking around in circles and getting nowhere fast, we were eventually forced to admit defeat.

'I just don't understand it,' I groaned, the effects of the alcohol I'd drank earlier wearing off at a rate of knots and replaced by the beginnings of a headache. 'The old part of the castle was here somewhere. I know it was.'

Frank merely chuckled to himself, shook his head at our perceived foolishness, and began walking back in the direction of the reception area.

As we traipsed tired and glum-faced in his wake, like a bunch of errant school-kids, who'd been caught on some mischievous, post-curfew wander, none of us said a word. I can't speak for the others, but I felt utterly exhausted and not a little depressed at the scale of the absurdity of the situation, and I honestly didn't have the strength to even attempt to rationalise our increasingly surreal experience.

Instead, all that was left to do was concentrate on placing one foot in front of the other with all the dogged determination of Frodo and Sam, making their way across the Blasted Lands of Mordor, towards Mount Doom.

It was either that, or risk insanity by trying to deal with the unpalatable fact that the seemingly endless medieval corridors that led to The Hidden Dungeon, had disappeared every bit as mysteriously as the anonymous, good-looking porter, who had taken us on our impromptu guided tour in the first place.

And that was plainly something that none of us were prepared to do.

Not then, anyway.

Later, with the benefit of hindsight, and after learning to my very great surprise (and not a little relief) that there are actually hundreds of similar occurrences on record, reported by equally bemused but apparently reliable individuals from all over the world, I was able to mentally debate the reality or otherwise of our experience.

Of course, the possibility did cross my mind that my friends and I had undergone a particularly vivid form of shared hallucination, and I don't suppose it was entirely out of the question that we had been duped somehow by the hotel staff. Sceptics would be quick to point out that any supernatural hypothesis would have to account for the fact that our 'phantom guide' had been dressed in modern-day attire, which was totally at odds with the medieval setting of The Dungeon and the surrounding corridors. The theory that we had encountered a 20th Century ghost equipped with the ability to temporarily transport us back in time, was stretching things just a little too far, it seemed.

On the other hand, having considered all of the logical down-to-earth explanations, it has still been increasingly difficult to shake the notion that on that strange, dream-like

Hallowe'en evening, at the dawn of the 1980s, I learned an incredible but nonetheless compelling truth. Sometimes, on the wrong side of midnight, the thin, wispy veil that separates the past from the present can disperse like a morning mist burned off by the heat of the summer sun.

And when it does, it can provide the insatiably curious (or carelessly foolish, take your pick), the opportunity to step across the threshold and enter a shadowy realm where the past and present seemingly co-exist....

THE PHANTOM STEAM TRAIN OF NEW FERRY

Back in the early summer of 2002, various people in and around New Ferry were rudely awoken from their hard-earned slumber in the early hours of the morning, by what sounded like an old-fashioned steam train, puffing importantly, as though it were pounding along the tracks on some hugely significant journey, just a few hundred feet from their bedroom windows.

This might not appear remotely strange to anyone not familiar with the area. After all, Port Sunlight Station, is less than a mile and a half distant from the town, and I know from experience it's not at all unusual for one to hear the insistent clickety-clack of the *Merseyrail* trains on clear, windless nights. Not even long after the final official public passenger service has terminated at just after midnight. The phenomenon may well have been, you may think, nothing more mysterious than some acoustic anomaly similar to the way sound is muffled by a thick blanket of November fog or can sound ear-piercingly shrill and blade-sharp on a frosty, mid-winter afternoon.

The thing is though, having heard the noise myself on more than one occasion - back when I used to live at my parents' address in New Ferry - I can confirm that there was something undeniably uncanny about the sound.

For one thing, there are not, as far as I am aware, any active *steam* trains still running as part of the local *Merseyrail* service. I suppose it's possible that the people who run The Port Sunlight Heritage Society might have requisitioned an old-style, shunting locomotive as part of their increasingly ambitious plans to attract tourism to the area. But then, if such were the case, why on earth would they be running these trains deep in the cold dead of night when, one presumes, all the "good people of the world" are safely tucked up in their beds?

And, equally pertinent, how was it there were no advertisements in the local press or an eye-catching series of posters in the shop windows or even, and I would contend that this is the biggest absurdity of all, at Port Sunlight Station itself, alerting people to this quaint, alternative method of traversing the scenic splendours of Merseyside?

Wirral Borough Council may have been regarded by many as being stingy in the extreme as regards to its funding for any project that didn't involve them lining their own pockets.

"God Almighty, they're tighter than a pair of boil-washed skinny jeans!"

as one angry correspondent declared indignantly in the letters page of *The Liverpool Echo*, but you would have thought that even their notoriously limited, streamlined budget would at least stretch to printing off a couple of notices announcing the re-introduction of this highly desirable retro form of transport for the benefit of attracting visitors to the area?

Even supposing for a moment though, that you accepted the existence of this super-secret line of antique steam trains transporting some imagined(?) vampiric/zombiesque clientèle and for what nefarious purpose at the literally ungodly hour of 3am, there was still the disconcerting matter of the impossible *closeness* of the 'locomotive's' percussive pounding and the sibilant hissing of steam and vapour, almost as though a latter-day *Flying Scotsman* were shunting along some railway track at the bottom of their garden.

On the occasions that I was awoken by the noises, I would lie there for a while, my brain still foggy with sleep, sure at first that I was still dreaming. And by the time it eventually registered that there really did appear to be a train directly outside my bedroom window, before I could throw the blankets to one side and gaze out into the bright, moonlit night, silence suddenly would fall like someone flicked a volume switch, and there was never anything visible to my eye that could have accounted for the sounds.

This extremely puzzling enigma persisted on a sporadic basis for much of the early part of the summer of 2002, but by the late-July of that year, and so far as I am aware, in all the years that have since slipped by, there has been no reported re-occurrence of the phenomenon.

But during the peak period of this strange acoustic anomaly, someone, whose name and address were withheld, wrote to *The Wirral Globe* to voice his concerns about, quite frankly, his sanity:

> 'I wonder if anyone has had the same strange experience as my wife and I have had in the New Ferry Area?
>
> Some mornings, at about 3:00am...' *

(And there are certain paranormal researchers out there, of varying levels of competence it must be said, who would consider that that particular time; 3am. could well have some significance in respect of all manner of apparent Fortean occurrences...See the footnote below concerning the so-called 'Devil' or 'Witching Hour')

> ...'we have been awoken by a strange noise outside. It may sound mad but the noise sounds like the "chug-chug" of a steam train travelling slowly. My wife first told me about this noise, but I didn't believe her, until I actually heard it for myself, actually being woken up by the loudness of it one morning.
>
> Could somebody shed some light as to what it might be? Has anyone else heard it? Or is it us going mad?'

So far as I can assist (and I've got to be honest, it isn't a whole lot) the answers to those questions are as follows:

To this day, no-one ever did come up with any half-way rational explanation for the enigmatic locomotive sounds, I know for a fact many people in the area heard the same thing or something very similar, and I certainly don't think that the anonymous letter writer need worry too much about the status of his, or his wife's, mental well-being.

Unless that is, the entire population of New Ferry had suddenly fallen victim to a bout of outright insanity that summer...

---

* According to Christian theology (or at least the modern-day popular interpretation) Jesus Christ is said to have died on The Cross at 3pm. Therefore, 3 am is said to be a Devilish inversion of this Holy event, and to be the true 'Witching Hour,' when Demons and Spirits are at their strongest.

World time zones and seasonal variances are not applicable in determining 3am, though the belief seems to be exclusive only to the Christian religion. There does seem to be, though, some anecdotal evidence that odd experiences or sensations occur during the hours of 3 and 4 am, though this may well be attributable to the percipients being in one of those classic hypnopompic/hypnogogic states beloved of the Temporal Lobe Thesis adherents.

AS THE DAY BLEEDS SLOWLY INTO NIGHT

At Hallowe'en, such simple things make me afraid.

It's not the flickering, saw-toothed grins of hollowed-out pumpkins.

It's not the plastic skeleton masks, or ebony silhouettes of cackling Witches on broomsticks.

It's not the Vampires, Goblins and sheeted Ghosts masquerading as 'Trick or Treat' children.

It's not even the way the October air feels somehow dangerously brittle, like thin ice on the surface of a pond, the leafless branches that claw at the starless sky, or the dark shadows that seem to dance beyond the streetlight's sodium glare.

It's none of those things.

At Hallowe'en, the things that scare me most are these...

A bunch of withered flowers.

Steam rising from a half-empty teacup.

A half-eaten slice of fairy cake.

And a pale-faced young girl in a flimsy white dress.

Simple things.

Frightening things.

At Hallowe'en.

Dead of Night

I first learned of the following chilling experience courtesy of a friend I used to work with during my time as a landscape gardener, at St Saviour's Churchyard in Oxton.

For the best part of two years, I was employed on one of those crappy, government-sponsored schemes which I've always thought are nothing more than a convenient way of keeping the jobless figures down to an 'acceptable level,' and a bottomless source of cheap labour. We had to work our proverbial socks off for three days a week, in all weathers, straightening drunkenly-leaning gravestones, erecting wooden fences around the Garden of Remembrance, and digging holes twenty feet deep to remove the embedded roots of dying trees, and all for a lousy £57 per week. And if you didn't agree to a potential placement on one of these schemes, you could wind up getting your benefits stopped completely.

That was some choice. Cheers for that, Maggie.

I started work at St Saviour's in the late autumn of 1986, and whilst I may have been against the scheme in principle, I found I actually enjoyed my time there. The tasks could be arduous, but it ensured you soon got physically fit, burned off any excess fat and labouring outdoors all day helped you acquire a healthy-looking, Mediterranean-style tan.

My fellow workmates were a pretty sound bunch, too.

They all mucked in, there were no shirkers, and it didn't take long for us to realise that the quicker we got the job done, the sooner we could down tools and set up a game of football, or sit off listening to our favourite music (there was a pretty eclectic mix, but 'Steve McQueen' by *Prefab Sprout*, New Order's 'Lowlife' and 'The Queen Is Dead' by *The Smiths*, all but dominated the soundtrack for the next twelve months).

During our hour-long dinner break, or when it rained and we didn't have to work (something to do with health & safety regulations, which you can be sure we had absolutely no problem complying with) we'd take our seats in the canteen and drink endless cups of tea, complete the *Daily Mirror* crossword or read aloud the Readers' Experiences pages of some tacky porno magazine. There'd be heated arguments and lively debates concerning everything from American foreign policy to Liverpool and Everton's chances of winning the league (in the days before Sly Sports took over the game and sold it back to us, repackaged, as the shiny brand new 'Premiership'), and sometimes, we'd swap stories to while away the time while the rain beat urgently at the windows.

More often than not these tales would be nothing but a bawdy resume of the previous weekend's alleged sexual conquests or drinking marathons.

But on occasion, especially when October came around, with the cold, dead heart of winter lurking not too far behind, the talk would switch to darker subject matter - the supernatural.

Probably the scariest tale I heard during those story-telling sessions was related by Dave Taylor, a one-time punk rocker, who had long since 'settled down' and was married with three kids but who still professed to have retained his 'anarchic attitude.' As he was often fond of pointing out to those who claimed he'd sold out:

> 'When I heard Joe Strummer of *The Clash*, singing about how he wanted a 'riot of his own,' I realised he didn't mean that he necessarily wanted to go out into the middle of the street and start chucking bricks at passing police cars or setting fire to his neighbour's houses. He meant he wanted to rebel against the system in any way he could, even if it was only on a very limited basis, to be yourself, and never lose your identity amidst the career ladder-climbing hordes that populate the nine to five rat race...I've always tried to be true to that ideal, no matter what I've done in life.'

Anyway, hardcore punk, or plazzy punk, he certainly had a story to tell, and the following is as near as I can remember it...

'This time last year, I don't mind admitting I was officially unemployed, but working on the side, doing odd jobs, mostly gardening, in and around my home-town of New Ferry.

I wanted to get that confession out of the way, not because I'm riddled with guilt, but because I want you to know that I'm being entirely truthful here, and as I'm going to be asking you to believe some pretty incredible things in a little while, I thought it best to be entirely honest right from the start.

I'm sure there will be those who deeply resent the fact that I was once a 'social security scrounger' and by the end of this account they'll likely be yelling 'Just desserts!' at the top of their voices like preachers whipping up fire and brimstone at a Revivalists' meeting.

The truth of the matter is though, I'd found that trying to raise a family on the pittance doled out every fortnight by the Welfare State proved to be as difficult a task as any of Hercules' Twelve Labours. And of course, there was also the small matter of pride. If you can't find honest work because there's no work to be had, just what the hell are you supposed to do? I learned a hard and terrible truth the day they made me redundant from Cammell Laird Shipyard; You either sink or swim. Sink into a pit of maudlin obscurity so that all that's left to remember you by is a gravestone engraved with the epitaph; "He Failed So Softly You Can Still Hear the Sigh'. Or else, you swim against the tide. Doggy-paddle if you have to. Just keep your head above the water any which way you can.

There. I've recited my sermon. Here endeth today's reading from the Gospel According To David Taylor. My guess is I won't have won over enough converts to make much of a difference, but what the hell? God loves a tryer, right?

Anyway, what I really want to tell you about occurred on a cold Hallowe'en morning, three years ago....

****

Mrs Anna Roberts was 83 years old when I first made her acquaintance and she was pushing 90 at the time the events I'm about to relate took place. She was by far and away my oldest 'client' (I tended her large, sprawling back garden two or three times a week in the summer, twice a month at most in the winter) but in all honesty she could easily have passed for someone twenty-five years younger. She was as bright as the proverbial button – all her faculties were intact – and she could hold a perfectly lucid conversation without even the slightest hint of the scatter-brained senility that plagues so many people her age.

She also bathed regularly, changed her clothing nearly every day and had all her own teeth. Even the multiple wrinkles that creased her face didn't serve to harden her countenance. On the contrary, they gave her a care-worn, grandmotherly appearance that put me in mind of my own beloved Nan, who'd passed away many years before, when I was still at school. I suppose the fact that I still missed her so bad was one of the main reasons I took to Mrs Roberts so readily.

One of the other reasons, equally important to me anyway, was the fact that she was an endless mine of fascinating anecdotes and tales that had as their focal point what she constantly referred to as 'The Slightly Less Than Good Old Days.' She remembered so much about Merseyside's illustrious past, I used to lie awake some nights wondering how anyone could store so much information in their heads without causing their skull to bulge visibly at the seams. It really was a rare pleasure to sit and chat with her for a while, when my chores were completed. Without fail, the minute I came in from the garden, she'd tell me to wash my hands, take off my muddy work boots and make myself comfortable on the living room sofa. There'd be a silver tray of wonderfully refreshing tea (piping hot in the winter, ice-cold when summer came round), and biscuits set upon the table, and Mrs Roberts would lean back in her favourite armchair directly opposite me.

Once seated, I'd invariably catch myself staring at the living room walls adorned with a mixture of black and white photographs, beautifully detailed lined drawings and colour portraits.

Mrs Roberts would follow my gaze and wait patiently until I'd fixed my eyes upon a particular picture. Then, as if reading my mind, she'd smile, nod her head sagely, and launch into an explanatory tale as though I'd asked her about it out loud.

She'd tell me stories diffused with an indefinable magic that bade me share her personal nostalgia for times long past.

How she'd lost her brother on the opening day of the Battle of The Somme during the First World War. How her parents' home had been flattened by a German doodlebug during the Blitzkreig. Her late husband, Billy's many travels to far-off lands during his time as a merchant seaman (sadly, he'd died of a heart attack twenty years earlier). Stories of Spring Heeled Jack terrorising the residents of William Henry Street in Everton. Of Cammell Lairds Shipyard in its heyday, and the Port of Liverpool clogged with vessels from every corner of the globe. Of The Spion Kop at Anfield and how she used to bunk off school to go and watch Billy Liddell and Dixie Dean in action for their respective clubs. Of gas-lit alleyways (or 'jiggers,' as Scousers refer them) snaking their way in between closed concrete courts that formed self-sufficient communities. The cobbled roads, criss-crossed with tram-lines and the overhead railway ('The Docker's Umbrella') that ran above the river front filled with day-trippers on a summer exodus to the Pier Head, where they'd board the Ferry to take them across to the bustling seaside resorts of West Kirkby or New Brighton.

It's fair to say that the recounting of these tales filled me with a powerful kind of longing for the hopelessly unattainable, a feeling similar to being in love with someone forever beyond your reach.

This vast kaleidoscope of someone else's memories would go spinning round my head like a series of video images from the 'Bygone Age of Lost Innocence'. When Mrs Roberts talked, I could clearly see in my mind's eye, yesterday's children gathered around the bandstand in Sefton Park on a sun-bright August afternoon. The largely unpolluted waters of the Mersey lit by golden lances and white-caps prancing like sea-horses. Men in cloth caps and identical grey tweed suits milling around the army enlisting offices, eager to swap one uniform for another.

Mrs Roberts was also a very perceptive person. Once, on a wet April afternoon, she asked me a question, the answer to which she clearly already knew.

'You're a bit of a dreamer aren't you, David?'

I remember I'd looked at her quizzically, and before I'd had a chance to reply, she'd nodded to herself in that worldly-wise way of hers.

'That's okay. I can see that you are'

Then she'd smiled and regarded me with eyes like twinkling starlight. 'And I am also willing to wager you are blessed with the acquaintance of many good friends?'

Again, she never gave me an opportunity to answer and in truth I don't think I was meant to. They were less enquiries and more like sure-fire remarks that were slightly unnerving in their accuracy.

'Let me tell you something, David,' she continued. 'Something that you may or may not be aware of already. People who retain their capacity to dream, when all seems lost, often attract friends who are in a less fortunate position, or are at a low ebb in their lives. Who knows, perhaps these unhappy souls instinctively feel that by being close to someone like you...Well, maybe some of that irrepressible hope will in time, rub off on them.'

'It's a gift, David, The strength to dream!'

Not knowing what else to say, I'd merely shrugged my shoulders self-consciously and hastily tried to change the subject. But by the look on her face I could see she knew I had understood the import of all she's said, and I left her house later that day feeling like I was floating on air.

'The strength to dream'

Yes, I think perhaps I have indeed been blessed.

But in the dreadful days since Hallowe'en, 1983, that pool of vivid dreams has evolved into a lake of rancid nightmares.

And the 'gift' has become nothing short of a curse.

****

Hallowe'en dawned with leaden, cheerless skies and a roiling mist that clung to the frames of the houses like a silken shroud. The first real frost of the season sugared the hedges and lawns, and the cries of children and of car doors slamming seemed to carry a hundred miles on the blade-sharp air. My breath puffed to clouds as I made my way up Eccleshall Road, and I was forced to stick my hands deep into the pockets of my leather bomber jacket in a vain attempt to keep my fingers from going numb.

The truth is, I really hadn't felt much like working that day. For the first time in God knew how many years, I'd wanted nothing better than to while away the hours curled up on the settee with my head buried in a good book, or maybe help Cheryl, my wife, with the Hallowe'en decorations for the party later that night. I wasn't usually given to sudden bouts of laziness, but for some reason, I'd awoken that morning feeling unaccountably depressed and with a knot of Gordian proportions coiling in the pit of my stomach. I remember thinking as Cheryl handed me my packed lunch and I stepped outside the front door, that my mood had been soured by the sight of the red and gold leaves piled high in the gutter: their fall a sad reminder that summer had long since bid another year farewell, and that the grim promise of another endless winter lay just around the corner.

Looking back, however, I think perhaps the true origin of those bleak, pessimistic feelings had their roots in some vague premonition, a dark foreboding, the precise nature of which had been hidden from view, obscured like that morning's sun behind a thick veil of grey cloud...

*****

Mrs Roberts opened her front door in answer to my glove-muffled knock, and on seeing my face had turned a decidedly unhealthy shade of blue, she all but dragged me inside.

'Oh, you poor dear!' she exclaimed. 'You look half-frozen. Quick, go and thaw yourself out by the fire, and I'll make us both a warm drink.'

I opened my mouth to say thanks, but my teeth were busy chattering away like a pair of manic castanets, so I simply allowed myself to be led across to the roaring hearth.

'You're bright and early this morning, David' she said as I toasted my hands before the fire. 'Though you're not as early as some.'

She winked and inclined her head toward the kitchen door, which was standing slightly ajar. She called over her shoulder,' Have you finished your tea and slice of cake, dear?' There's someone here I'd like you to meet. Come and say hello.'

I wondered who she could be speaking to. The only people I had ever seen inside the house were Mrs Robert's younger sister, Annabel, (who, the last I heard had emigrated to Australia, and only came to visit at Christmas and New Year), and her next-door neighbour, Phyliss Baker, another client of mine, a hugely overweight spinster who had no family save for her pet Doberman, 'Maximilian'.

But it turned out to be neither of them.

After a few seconds had passed and Mrs Roberts had received no reply, she'd left me to go into the kitchen, only to emerge almost immediately, wearing a puzzled expression.

'Well, that's strange,' she mumbled, as if talking to herself. 'I always try to give them the benefit of the doubt, but I suppose the youths of today were just born ungrateful and ill-mannered!'

I asked her what she meant, and she looked at me for a moment as though she no longer recognised me or else had completely forgotten I was even there. I could see that it took an effort of will for her to shake herself out of the almost trance-like state into which she'd entered.

An age seemed to pass before she spoke again. Finally, she asked me to accompany her into the kitchen, and with some degree of reluctance, I left my place at the crackling fireside. The minute I stepped into the room, I was struck by the intense chill that pervaded the room, and I soon saw the reason for this. The door leading out to the back garden was standing wide open and the icy October air came eagerly rushing in like an uninvited guest gate-crashing a party.

I started to shiver again, but Mrs Roberts didn't even seem to notice the cold. She was far more preoccupied with what was on the dining table. She raised a single bony finger and I looked in the direction in which she was pointing and I could see on the hand-knitted table cloth was a plain white china plate sprinkled with cake crumbs, steam rising from a half-empty tea cup and a posy of reddish-pink flowers tied with a bow of bright green ribbon.

'She seemed such a nice little girl, too,' Mrs Roberts said breaking the silence. 'I can't believe she'd just leave without even saying "thank you."

Intrigued, I asked her who she was talking about.

'The little girl who called just before you this morning, of course,' Mrs Roberts answered indignantly. 'Abigail, she said her name was. Such a pretty child. Couldn't have been any older than twelve. She called to ask me whether I had any junk for the Church Drive Autumn Jumble Sale. She was only wearing a flimsy white dress – it looked to me like some sort of Hallowe'en costume, and I thought, God, she must be freezing, so I invited her in to wait while I rummaged around for some odds and ends I was sure I wouldn't be needing any more.' She paused and sighed wistfully. 'Oh, I suppose if you're lucky enough to get to be my age, odds and ends tend to start making up a good ninety per cent of the things you own...'

She cast a quick reflective glance at that assembled collection of keepsakes, the tiny little snapshots of memory that doubtless provided some degree of comfort in the dark and lonely hours, before continuing.

'Anyway, I asked her to take a seat in the kitchen, and the kettle was already boiling, so I poured her a cup of tea and gave her a big slice of my home-made lemon-fairy cake. She smiled up at me and handed me these flowers. "These are for you," she said, and I noticed then her face was so very pale...Her lips so very red....I left her wolfing down the cake like she hadn't eaten in weeks, whilst I went to fill up a vase with some water for the flowers. You called round, David, before I had a chance to fetch it. I went to answer the door and now she's gone and left without so much as a thank you or a goodbye.'

'Look!' Mrs Roberts said, pointing to a pile of clothing, old books and various ornaments stacked against the far wall. 'She didn't even take any of the jumble with her.'

On seeing this, my heart suddenly filled with a mixture of sympathy and innate sadness. It was all I could do not to voice that which was immediately obvious to me. She had been made the butt of a bad Hallowe'en joke, and I was sure that the moment I stepped out into the back garden to start work, I would hear a child's laughter floating on the cold October air.

Nevertheless, I was suddenly anxious to brave the freezing temperatures, finish the job and get on home. I'd never felt uncomfortable before in Mrs Roberts' presence. Not even on the day I'd first made her acquaintance. But standing there in her kitchen doorway, casting alternate glances at the dining table and the untidy heap of discarded worldly goods, I felt something had changed between us. A subtle shifting, as imperceptible as the movement of a clock hand, but every bit as irrevocable as the passing of time.

And I realised in that moment, although I couldn't say precisely why, that things would never be the same between us ever again...

My deflated spirits weren't lifted any as I prepared to set to work.

There are few more depressing prospects than a garden bereft of its colour at the business end of The Dying Season.

Endings and beginnings hovered regretfully in the air. The brown earth looked to be as hard and unforgiving as a lead gangster in a Martin Scorcese movie. The grass was wiry and a sickly shade of green. Even the few hardy perennials still in bloom appeared dull and lifeless, like a closed down amusement arcade or a deserted, off-season beach resort.

I stood for a while, my gloved hands clasping the rake I'd cadged from Mrs Roberts' tool shed, and if anyone had been around to ask what I was doing, I would have told them I was mentally debating where to make a start. That would have been a barefaced lie, however, because all I was really doing was trying to think up ways I could get the hell out of there as quickly and as discretely as possible.

I eventually decided I'd set about clearing the lawn of the fallen leaves that had taken on the appearance of soggy, wet Cornflakes, and have a go at mending the panel of fencing that had blown down during the previous week's gales.

It took me the best part of half an hour to rake the leaves into a bonfire-sized pile ready for burning when they'd dried out completely, and I'd just about succeeded in repairing the fence, (I was in fact hammering in the final row of nails that would secure the damaged panel), when the mid-morning quiet was suddenly shattered by a scream so shrill and piercing, it cut right through my body and sent my numb nerve-endings on fire.

I looked wildly about me, unsure at first where that terrible cry had come from, and it was only when it sounded again that my attention was drawn to Mrs Roberts' half-open kitchen window, and I saw the old lady standing there, frantically waving her arms above her head like she was drowning or caught in a pool of deadly quicksand.

Even from where I was stood, a hundred feet or so away, I could clearly see that her kind, gentle features had transformed into a twisted into a hideous mask of fear, and I'd like to say that I acted with all the noble chivalry of a knight in shining armour. That I'd raced to her aid, ready and willing to fend off the source of her terror, be it burglars, rapists, an escaped psychopath or a big fat hairy spider that had crawled up out of the plug-hole in the bathroom sink.

I'd like to say that.

I truly would.

But it's to my eternal shame that my initial reaction was to do just the opposite. To turn tail and run.

Indeed, it was only when she screamed once more (an incredibly powerful sound that I would scarcely have believed capable of being produced by a near-90-year-old woman), that I sent those cowardly thoughts packing and, still holding the hammer with which I'd been busily banging in nails, I charged across the lawn and attempted to prepare myself for whatever awaited me within the confines of that suddenly ominous-looking house.

Mrs Roberts turned towards me as I yanked open the back door and I was immediately stopped dead in my tracks by the sight of her standing by the windowsill, her body bathed in a slab of dead grey October-light. She was shaking like an alcoholic with a bad case of the DTs. All of the colour had been drained from her face, and her lips, thin and bloodless, were stretched in a frozen, rictus-like grin. But it was her eyes, bulging with such force it was a wonder they didn't pop right out of their sockets that affected me most.

With a sudden, lunatic clarity, I found myself recalling an incident that had occurred when I was ten-years-old. My dad had taken me on a pigeon-shooting trip around Brotherton Park Woods, and my father's gun dog, a highly intelligent, black Labrador named Hank (who was run over and killed by a heavy goods wagon from 'Lever Brother's Soap Factory,' just two years later), had sniffed out a rabbit with both of its hind legs caught in the jaws of a steel trap. I'd endured several weeks of nightmares, haunted by the images of the creature's blood-soaked pelt, its pitiful cries, the white bone that glistened obscenely in the spring sunshine. And the panic-stricken eyes that had fixed on me for an eternal second.

'Help me!' those eyes had pleaded. 'Please help me, I'm caught!'

Of course, I had been unable to do anything save burst into floods of sympathetic tears whilst my father had ushered me away deeper into the woods. He'd told me not to worry. To wait right there. He knew a way to set the rabbit free. A few moments later I'd jumped at the sound of a gunshot and my father had returned smiling what he doubtless hoped was a reassuring smile, and although I'd stopped my snuffling, I'd lain awake in bed that night, thinking the whole thing through with a child's cognitive logic. I realised that it wasn't so much the death of a wild animal that had upset me so badly, but the fact that I'd failed to lift a finger to help save a living creature that had looked to me as its last desperate hope.

And here, twenty five years later, here were those selfsame eyes, beseeching me. Imploring me with that horribly familiar expression of utter helplessness.

I was filled with a grim determination not to be found wanting this time around.

I reached out a tentative hand, gently touched her heaving shoulder and asked her what was wrong. She couldn't answer me at first. I could see she was trying hard to work mouth muscles, but they remained locked in that humourless, skull-like leer for what seemed like the longest time. It was clear she was suffering from acute shock, and it was only after I gently shook her that she was able to find her voice...After a fashion.

'She never left, David!' she managed, and the words had seemed like they were stuck somehow in the back of her throat so that they came out sounding like the death rattle of a woman riddled with some terminal disease.

'Who never left?' I asked bemusedly. 'What are you talking about?'

'The little girl...Abigail. She was hiding in the living room. I was hoovering the carpet. I had my back to the sofa and I felt a tiny hand grab hold of my ankle. I turned around and...and...' she began to sob convulsively. I touched her shoulder again in a gesture of mute reassurance.

'I turned around and she was smiling,' Mrs Roberts went on. 'And when she drew back her lips, I could see her teeth...They looked hideously sharp...like two sets of jagged razors.'

'What?' I exclaimed, involuntarily stepping back a few paces.

'It's true. I know how it sounds, David, but I swear it's all true.' She paused in an effort to try and regain some composure.

'And the worse thing of all is, she's still here. Still in the house. When I ran out of the living room, she climbed out from beneath the sofa, grinning at me all the while. At first I thought she was going to chase after me, but when I turned to look back, she was running in the opposite direction. I could hear her climbing the stairs. She's probably up there now. Hiding. Waiting.'

Mrs Roberts shivered and rolled her eyes towards the ceiling.

'Please would you go and check for me, and if she is still here, please get her out. As a friend, will you do that for me, David?'

Faced with such desperate, heartfelt pleas, how could I possibly refuse her? And it really didn't matter if I believed her or not. I felt I owed it to Mrs Roberts to at least seek to dispel her fears before I left for the day.

I went and checked, and though I searched high and low, of course, there was no-one there.

Later, I managed to get Mrs Roberts to sit down at the kitchen table whilst I poured her a cold glass of water.

'Okay, love' I said, hating the patronising tone in my voice, 'I've had a good look in all the rooms upstairs, and there's defo no-one there. She most probably sneaked out while we were chatting.'

'Are you sure?' the old woman stared at me imploringly, and my heart went out to her then even though I was telling the God's honest truth, (I'd even checked the bathroom, the wardrobes and under the bed) and that beseeching expression turned out to be one of two things that served to keep me awake later that night as my wife slept soundly beside me. Of all the myriad fears that line up before you in life like a row of ancient tombstones in some wind-blown, desecrated churchyard, the fear of being alone – like being cast hopelessly adrift in the middle of an ocean with nothing for company save the grim realisation that help will not be coming, not now, not ever, is the one that troubles me greatest.

I'm not ashamed to tell you I cried out at one point during the long hours before dawn, a frighteningly primal sound, the sort that might have been made by our earliest ancestors on occasions when they were sat all alone, gazing into the rough, uncaring darkness beyond the firelight's bright orange glow.

I reached out and pulled Cheryl extra close, all the while counting my blessings, till I finally fell asleep, just as the first rays of sunlight peeked through the gaps in the curtains.

The second of the two things that kept me awake that night was something I honestly thought I'd already forgotten, casually dismissed as being nothing more than a trick of the light or the product of an over-active imagination.

But due no doubt to my melancholy state, the memory came back to haunt me in the wee hours, just the same...

I see myself walking down Mrs Robert's front garden path, towards the rickety wooden gate. I lift the latch and hear it creak slowly open. I'm about to pull it closed behind me when the back of my neck suddenly prickles, and something, I can't for the life of me say what, makes me look up at Mrs Robert's bedroom window.

At first, I can't see anything, and I shake my head at my foolishness. It's cold, and likely to get a lot colder, and Cheryl will be waiting with the kids, and there's a Hallowe'en party to organise and...

Then I see, or think I see, just for a second, the thin, white lace curtain move the tiniest fraction and the suggestion of a young girl's face, unnaturally pale, but with blood red-lips and shining silver eyes, peering out the window at me...

And is there a smile curling the corner of her mouth? A hideously knowing smile? I think maybe there is, and I quickly look away unable to accept the reality of the apparition gazing down at me, and when I finally summon the courage to look again, there is nothing unusual...

Just an empty, half-open window and a thin lace curtain billowing in the chill autumn breeze.....

I didn't find out that Mrs Roberts had died that very night, until a day or so after her body was found by her neighbour, Phyliss Baker.

That's not unusual. She may have been my favourite client, but as far as most people were concerned, that's all she was to me: someone who's garden I tidied every couple of weeks or so, and whilst bad news travels fast in small communities, I suppose I must have been walking round with me eyes and ears closed, because I never heard a murmur until I happened to (quite literally) bump into Phyliss, whilst picking up a few odds and sods in the Kwik Save Store in the middle of New Ferry shopping centre.

I was drifting in a world of my own and for a while I didn't see the mountain of womanly flesh coming towards me, so I only just avoided smacking the front end of my trolley directly into the midst of her not inconsiderable frame, (I've never been able to steer those pain-in-the-arse things – much to Cheryl's constant amusement).

I started to say I was sorry for the near-collision, but she waved away my apologies with a smile and a shrug of the shoulders.

'No harm done,' she said, looking herself up and down, just to make sure there really wasn't anything she could potentially sue me for. 'You might want to start taking lessons in learning how to drive those things properly, though. If you ask me, people should have to pass a test before they're let loose with a trolley in a busy store like this one.'

'Yeah,' I said, smiling sweetly. 'And while they're at it they should build wider shopping aisles for people who are horizontally challenged.'

'Hmmm,' she concurred, plainly not having the slightest clue what I was talking about. I put my hand over my mouth to stifle a smile, and Phyliss made a great business of clearing her throat before blurting out the very last thing I expected to hear;

'Isn't it terrible about poor Mrs Roberts?'

I dropped my hand and peered at her sharply. 'I'm sorry, I don't...' I began.

'Oh, you haven't heard!' she exclaimed, and I saw something then that truly turned my stomach: Her mock-solemn expression was suddenly replaced by a scarcely concealed glee. Sometimes, it seems, the bearers of bad tidings delight in conveying misery. And here was just such a moment.

I wanted to walk away in disgust, but of course, I didn't. I had to hear what had happened. And Phyliss knew this. She had herself a captive audience, and it was clear she was going to enjoy every second of it.

'Well, now David,' she began in affected prim and proper tones, 'seeing as how you regularly used to do her garden, I was once the old woman's unofficial carer. She trusted me enough to cut me my own key, and I had to go and check on her every morning. This could bit of a chore at times. Some days, granted, she was bright as a button, but on others she could be more than a little bit foggy in the head, if you know what I mean, and I had to make sure she'd managed to get herself up out of bed and wasn't just lying there in a pool of her own piss or a stinky pile of warm macaroni...'

Phyliss grinned, revealing a set of nicotine-discoloured dentures, as she leaned towards me. 'To tell you the truth, Mrs Roberts didn't even recognise me at times. I lost count of the times she called me "Bill", if you can imagine that! Me, Phyliss Baker, 18-stone of pure womanly charm being mistaken for her old man, dead these past twenty years!'

She cackled madly and it took a massive effort of will for me not to smash her in the face and send those hideous brown-stained dentures flying like a guided cruise missile straight into the centre of the multi-stacks of Heinz Baked Beans piled halfway down the aisle.

'Anyway,' Phyliss continued, wiping white flecks of foam from the corners of her mouth, 'yesterday, or was it the day before? I can't quite remember, Mrs Roberts didn't answer when I called her name as I stepped through the back door. "Uh oh," I thought to myself, "Maybe she's had a double accident; a "Pissy Shitty Double Whammy," as I like to call it. It wouldn't have been the first time and perhaps she's just too embarrassed to respond." I even went so far as to go to the cupboard to fetch the rubber gloves, a bottle of disinfectant, the mop bucket and a big wooden peg for me nose...'

She cackled again, and this time I clenched both fists and actually saw myself gleefully pummelling her doughy-jowled features smack into the middle of the display rack of 'Special Offer! This Week Only! Half-Price Spaghetti Hoops!' only stopping when I was forcibly dragged away by teams of the 'Kwik Save' security team and mildly concerned members of the public.

But then she was prattling again, and I stayed my hand, and with hindsight, that was probably a just as well for both us.

'Imagine my shock then, when I saw Mrs Roberts lying in the hallway, at the foot of the stairs, very obviously as dead as a doornail. No, before you ask, I didn't have to get a doctor's opinion on that. I've seen more than me my fair share dead bodies before. I used to work in an old people's home in Wallasey, till I got the sack for allegedly stealing items of jewellery from some of the elderly residents. One arl biddy, Elsie Goodman, I'll never forget that name, dropped me right in it when she told me boss I'd tried to nick one of the gold rings she'd left on her bedside table...Just as if! I mean I was skint at the time, and they were a bunch of ungrateful arl, coffin-dodgers, who never mumbled so much as a single word of thanks for anything you did for them, but can you honestly see me doing something as low as that....?

Phyliss didn't pause to wait for an answer, and that was probably just as well for both of us, too.

'Anyhow, like I say, I knew Mrs Roberts was dead straight away. Probably suffered a massive heart attack, just like her husband, hey, how's that for irony? Well, at least it was sudden. That's how I'd like to go given a choice.' (I dearly wanted to tell her I could think of several more fitting demises – death by half-price tins ('for one week only'!) of Spaghetti Hoops being one of them, but I held my tongue).

'Poor Mrs Roberts' I sighed, instead. 'Well, at least now she's reunited with her husband. She was only talking about him the other afternoon...'

'Yeah, if you believe in all that religious crap,' Phyliss sniggered, and before I could react, added quickly, 'Saying that, though, David, I don't normally place much faith in anything I can't see or touch for myself, and if I can't do either of those things, then, as me dear departed Dad used to say, it's probably so full of shit, it squeaks when it walks.'

She paused then, and for a miraculous millisecond, the dry cynicism dropped like a shutter from her face, and she suddenly looked twenty years younger.

'You know what, Dave,' Phyliss said, staring high above the stacks of tinned tomato-flavoured goods. 'There were a couple of really strange things that struck me about that morning. Things I didn't understand then, and that don't make a lot of sense to me even now.'

'Like what?' I said through gritted teeth.

'Well, for a start, Mrs Roberts had died clutching a bunch of withered flowers. Bluebells, I think they were, though it was hard to tell for certain, because they were so withered and dry and wasted looking. The stalks and leaves weren't though. They were as fresh as though they'd just been picked from the garden.

God knows why she'd been clinging to them so tightly, or how she managed to keep hold of them even as she'd dropped stone dead on the floor. Maybe she was on her way to throw them out, who can say, and does it really matter? I probably wouldn't have thought anything of it myself if it hadn't have been for the other weird thing that happened when I picked up the phone in the living room to call for an ambulance. I mean, there was nothing anyone could do for her. Not even with all those fancy new gadgets they've got up at Arrowe Park these days. Mrs Roberts wasn't coming back, and it was a pain in the arse hanging round there when I had so many other things I'd much rather be doing, but I couldn't just leave her lying there in the hallway with her eyes and her mouth hanging wide open, issuing a come and get me invitation to all the fat hairy flies in the area – and Christ knows there's billions of them since they started work on the shit-stinking sewers over at the back of Mayfields.

Anyway, while I was stood there like one of 'Lewis`s', holding the line, waiting for the paramedics to get their act together, that I thought I heard the sound of someone treading softly on the upstairs landing, like someone was sneakily creeping up on me...

I tried to tell myself I was only hearing things, but I felt the tiny hairs on the back of my neck prick up and I broke out in goosebumps, just the same, and I had to go back into the hallway to see who it was making the noises...but there was absolutely no one there. Well of course there wasn't. I told myself I was being stupid, me a fully-grown woman, with a lifetime of experience, getting all spooked-out, just because I'd stumbled upon Mrs Roberts' dead body.

I went back to the phone, and would you believe it, the receptionist, who'd sounded like she was about twelve years old, still had me on hold? I was intending to give her a piece of my mind the minute she came back on the line, but I never got chance, 'cos I suddenly heard the sound of those footsteps again, this time, slowly coming down the stairs all stealthy-like...and there was something else, too. I realise this is going to sound friggin' ridiculous, and I was too scared to go back into the hallway to check for sure, but I was certain I could hear the sound of a little girl, an infant...no more than 10 years old, with her hand over her mouth, trying and failing to stifle a mean-spirited giggle.

Isn't that just the most ridiculous thing?

Well, I slammed down the phone, and legged it out of there. I was absolutely terrified, I don't mind telling you. It seems kind of pathetic now, but if you'd been there you would have....

David, what's the matter? Are you alright? You've gone deathly pale....

David..?

David...'

***

At Hallowe'en, the things that scare me most are a bunch of withered flowers
Steam rising from a half-empty teacup.
A half-eaten slice of fairy cake
And a pale-faced young girl in a flimsy white dress.
Simple things.
Frightening things.
At Hallowe'en.....

BIDSTON HILL – BIRKENHEAD'S WINDOW AREA

Bidston Hill, overlooking the predominantly flat Wirral Peninsula, affords a truly panoramic view of the diverse mixture of green rolling countryside and urban city-scape, the sadly derelict dockyards and the heart of Liverpool's industrial heartland, the majestic peaks of the Welsh mountains and the endlessly shifting seas.

That the Hill itself is ancient, and steeped in local history is irrefutable. Neolithic Man has left his mark in the shape of various Prehistoric carvings and etchings engraved on the damp sandstone, all but concealed these days by overhanging trees and thick clumps of bushes, but in common with other purported 'Window Areas' (locations that seem to be a focal point for all kinds of paranormal phenomena), the place has long been venerated by the worshippers of various pagan deities.

When I visited the site on a dull, overcast winter's afternoon, it was impossible not to be struck by the ominous atmosphere that permeates the place and it was hard too, to shake the vague feeling that you were being watched by someone or something that preferred to remain unseen, hidden from view.

It's certainly easy to see why Bidston Hill has acquired such a sinister reputation over the passage of the years. Especially amongst the local population, who on wild, windswept evenings, whisper in hushed tones, tales of phantoms, strange aerial phenomena and dark deeds of Witchcraft. An astronomer on Bidston Hill, reportedly encountered a number of strange, inexplicable slivers of light that illuminated the night sky and the tops of the surrounding trees, and apparently had a diverse effect upon the delicate instruments within the Hill's resident observatory, by causing them to inexplicably vibrate.

Coincidental to the appearance of the mysterious lights, the unnamed astronomer also told of how he'd frequently heard unusual sounds in the air all around him. He described these noises as sounding like 'low murmurs,' and further stated that he noticed a series of mirage-like effects manifesting on the plain below the old windmill (pictured above), and the research site.

'They caused the air to be teeming with ghostly shapes superimposed on the slopes of the Hill and appearing like thousands of glow-worms.'

The witness suggested that the phenomena might well have some sort of electrical origin, due to the fact that throughout the experiences,

'It was as though some electric current, throbbing, palpitating, were at play.'

Jenny Randles, in her excellent Mysteries of the Mersey Valley, makes reference to a:

'...curious Guardian that seems to have stood by the Hill as if nocturnally protecting the M53 and the housing estates around the nearby town of Upton.'

To illustrate this curious assertion, Jenny recounts the testimony of Gareth Hughes, who, on the 1st May, 1980, was travelling home in the early hours of the morning, when the usually busy motorway was exceptionally quiet. He was driving towards the overhead bridge that leads across the railway station on the opposite side of the carriageway. He had a clear view of Bidston Hill over to his right, and as he passed Junction 3, his attention was suddenly drawn to a 'dark, foreboding object,' silhouetted against the contours of the Hill, in a position south of the research complex. He was astounded by its incredible size and the fact that it seemed to sit aside the closed down railway station. As he passed under the bridge, he wound down his window to afford himself a better look at the object, and reduced his speed to little more than a crawl. He was able to see that the object was, to all intents and purposes, studying him with an equal degree of intensity!

The black mass (no pun intended!) was hanging so low in the sky that it all but obscured the diamond-chip stars in the heavens. It was, the witness said, reminiscent of:

> '...two artillery shells placed side by side but angled downwards so that the front part pointed into the ground, and the curved ends pointed skyward. The overall effect was not unlike a giant pair of binoculars trained onto the motorway. From the front, two beams of light, like headlamps, were shining towards the earth. They were strong, but cut off sharply in mid-air before reaching the hillside. Two small red or pink flames were also visible at the back of the tubes, flickering slightly into the sky.'

There was no sign of any other traffic on the road, but he was determined to acquire another witness to this awe-inspiring sight, and so he drove to his mother's house as quickly as he could. Although she lived less than five minute's drive away, the object, whatever it was, had disappeared by the time he and his mother had returned to the location.

Similar objects have, it seems, been sighted both before and since this account was made public.

Most notably, on December 27th, 1985, Jack and Nicola Limb were returning to Wallasey, on the same stretch of the M53, as Gareth Hughes, five year's earlier. Again, both witnesses expressed great surprise at the total lack of traffic on the normally heavily busy motorway. They suddenly noticed 'a triangle of lights, with two bright white ones at the front and a blob of red at the rear and top.' It was hovering over the same stretch of railway line as in the previous account, directly at the foot of Bidston Hill. The object was ominously silent. They kept it in view

until they passed Junction 2. The object was still hovering beneath the Hill when they lost sight of it as the motorway curved away to the west…

And finally, yet another taxi driver friend of yours truly, penned a rather lengthy letter to Dead Of Night Magazine, a condensed version of which appears below:

According to his account, he'd been returning home on foot on a freezing cold winter's evening in the company of several of his friends Although the writer readily admitted that they'd all been drinking, the chilly temperatures soon served to sober them up and it was just as well, because they had to be careful as they made their way along Boundary Road, (a fairly busy lane that runs along one side of Bidston Hill), due to the fact that there'd been a pretty substantial blizzard earlier that evening, making the roads and pavements extremely hazardous. As they trudged through the snow, they all commented on the unusual absence of street lighting.

Fortunately, there was a full moon that bathed the surrounding woodland in silvery lances, so it wasn't so pitch-dark they couldn't make out where they were headed. As they approached Taylor's Wood, just off to their left, with the sadly obsolete, Flaybrick Cemetery to their right, the taxi-driver was suddenly filled with a feeling of unutterable dread, and he was just about to suggest that they should turn back, when one of his friends shouted; 'What the hell's that?'

He looked in the direction in which his friend was pointing, and immediately saw a pair of glowing red eyes that 'shone like bright rubies sparkling in summer sunlight,' peering at them from out of the wood. At that precise instant, the air was filled with a strange growling noise, and the bushes on the other side of the road began rustling violently. 'The glowing eyes' suddenly appeared to be much clearer and at a greater height than before, as though whatever was crouching there in the trees had raised itself up to its full height…And was slowly creeping in their direction…

The cabbie quickly decided that there was something undeniably evil lurking in those woods, and he began beating a hasty retreat. His friends, who up to that point had been intent on investigating further, followed reluctantly in his wake.

As they walked (with an extra spring or two in their step), they all simultaneously recalled a fire-side horror story that had been related to them by some mutual friend over a few beers; a story about a Demon that was rumoured to haunt the area around Bidston Hill: a creature that was half-animal/half-human, with cloven hoofs, a pair of goat-like horns and red, glowing eyes.

They had understandably scoffed at the tail earlier, when sat before a roaring fireside in The Black Horse, but as they tried desperately to force themselves not to break into a panic-stricken run on a bone-chilling night in the dead heart of winter, the power of the story-teller's words carried a weight that would crush the most valiant of spirits, as easily as an autumn leaf grabbed in a pair of rough, uncaring hands.

And when they heard the unmistakable sound of twigs snapping in the moon-lit woods beside them, and a low-guttural growling, edging closer, ever closer, they did run.

They ran slipping and sliding through the treacherous combination of ice and snow, and never mind the consequences.

They ran and didn't once look back, terrified that they might see the face of something from a waking nightmare staring right back at them.

Something that had emerged from the stinking depths of Hell.

Something irrefutably Evil.

IN THE DEEP NIGHT SILENCE
The Haunting of Liverpool Airport

A few years back, a former security guard at Birkenhead Magistrate's Court, named 'Billy Hynes,' related the following story to help pass the time one dreary November afternoon.

Before I worked here, back in the late 1990s, I used to do a similar job at Liverpool Airport. I was only there for a few months, the money wasn't bad but the hours were an absolute pain in the arse. Working the night shift can really mess your body clock up, big time.

Working for *Easyjet*.

I was waiting for the last flight due to land at 2am. There really wasn't much to do other than hang around in the departure lounge near to Gate 1. The cleaners were in and out making sure the place was spick and span for the following day's mad rush of passengers. As I watched them working, the sensor lights automatically switched on casting pools of dark shadows beyond their glare. At around about 1am, I found myself alone in the lounge. The only thing keeping me company was the odd voice coming over my radio from Air Traffic Control. Suddenly, out of the corner of my eye, I thought I saw something moving, but when I turned to look full on, there was absolutely nothing there. But that didn't stop black shadows scuttling every time I went to walk along the corridor. I tried to ignore what I considered to be a strange trick of the light whilst I nipped to the toilet for a pee, and after I'd finished I was washing my hands when I noticed there were two small handprints in the centre of the steamy surface of the mirror above the sink. I assumed the cleaners whose job it was to polish the mirrors in the toilets, had somehow missed this particular one so I went to go and see if any of them were still about. I caught one of them just as she was about to knock off, and though she wasn't best pleased, she agreed to go and clean the mirror. I went back to Gate 1, to continue to wait for the final in-bound flight. I saw the woman cleaner head back upstairs in a hurry, doubtless desperate to catch up with her mates now that her shift was done.

There was no one else around now. I felt lonely and I remember thinking it was a lot like standing on a hillside and overlooking the evening's city lights and being filled with an overwhelming sense of longing. I'd been absent-mindedly chewing the top of my pen all this time, and I suddenly tasted ink on my tongue and realised that my pen was leaking. Trying not to gag, I raced to the toilets once more to wash my mouth out and clean my face. I spent a good few minutes scrubbing the side of my mouth which was quite literally covered with dark blue ink, and it was only when I'd cleaned the majority of it that I realised I had returned to the same steamy mirror that I'd had to get the cleaner to sort out a little earlier.

And the two small handprints were back, in exactly the same position as before. Not wanting to get the cleaner into trouble, I decided to clean the glass myself, and I set about wiping the surface with a bit of wet toilet paper. It only took a few seconds to remove all trace of the prints, and I shook my head at the perceived laziness of the cleaner in her half-arsed efforts to clean the mirror.

I threw the soggy paper towel in the nearest waste bin and went to wash my hands again in the sink, and as I did so I could clearly see that there was no trace of the handprints whatsoever. I looked away for a few seconds, and when I looked up again at my reflection there they were, those same tiny hand-prints, clearly visible at the very edge of the pane of steamed-up glass.

And there'd been no one round to make them.

I'd heard of the phrase, 'a cold shiver ran up and down his spine,' from a million and one horror stories, but I can honestly say I'd never actually *experienced t*he sensation until that moment, standing in an all but deserted building in the midst of the deep night silence…Faced with the plainly impossible.

I backed away from the mirror, with slow deliberate steps, not daring to tear my eyes away from the sight of those ghostly handprints, until at last I felt the metal door handle prodding into my back. I turned and threw open door and ran back to the entrance to the Departure Lounge. I was suddenly eager for human companionship and I quickly sought out the crew who worked for Air Traffic Control. I made sure I was never on my own again that night, and for the few months that I remained working there, I was seldom alone. And I never wandered into those toilets again, now matter how desperate my need to relieve myself. I found I'd much rather suffer from acute constipation than run the risk of being confronted by the chilling sight of those ghostly hand-prints suddenly appearing without any visible agency, on the cloudy surface of the mirror.

Interestingly enough, not long after leaving my employment at the airport, I learned from a friend who had once worked there several years earlier there was an urban legend prevalent amongst the staff concerning sightings of a small child, boy or girl it was difficult to tell, running around the Departure Lounge in the early hours, unaccompanied, who when approached would slide into the nearest gents or ladies toilets, and despite a thorough and meticulous search being mounted, no trace of the child was ever found.

A NIGHTMARE ON SEEL STREET

'It is in the dying hours of the day, in the last dim moments before darkness overcomes and envelopes day in a dark shroud that imagination runs wild. Then, the unreal becomes real. Fancy becomes fact. Shadow becomes substance.

'In Twilight Time, nothing is impossible.'

Dan Gilbert – Publicist for *The Twilight Zone* **TV series.**

The following account was submitted to me a few years back, by a man named Jeff Davies, a former employee at an old printer's works called 'Swift Print,' located on Seel Street, deep in the very in the heart of Liverpool city centre. The premises are a combination of several 18th Century converted warehouses, and have long been rumoured to be haunted.

One freezing January afternoon back in 1979, during that seemingly endless winter, when it seemed like the whole country was beset with strikes, blackouts and heaps of stinking rubbish piled high on the rain-soaked pavements, I was sat in the staff canteen on the building's third floor whiling away a dinner hour with several of my colleagues. At some point, the conversation turned to the subject of local history, of Liverpool in general, and of Seel Street in particular.

And yes, before anyone starts, I'm well aware that probably sounds as mind-numbingly boring as being forced to sit and watch endless re-runs of Jim 'nick nick' Davidson acting the complete twat on the canteen's black and white, maddeningly flickering TV set, but we were all on a bit of a downer, our spirits still laid low by a debilitating dose of the post-Christmas blues.

And this hangover-style comedown dictated that the usual debates concerning the 'burning issues of the day,' (which included: who was the better live band, *The Jam* or *The Clash*? Who was the fittest: Debbie Harry or that blonde judy from *Abba*? And where was the best venue for our next big massive Lad's Night Out On The Ale?) had been rendered somewhat obsolete. It was hard to drum up any enthusiasm for anything other than sitting off quietly in the corner with your head in your hands, emitting the odd world-weary groan at regular five minute intervals, having a half-hearted go at *The Daily Mirror* crossword or ogling the Page Three Girl in some other shitty rag I can't even bring myself to name these days. Well, not without first washing me mouth out with a bar or two of Imperial Leather, anyway.

I'm not sure now who it was who kicked off this completely out of character historical discussion. It could have been any of us. But I do remember that it was Jimmy Boggs, who soon took over as self-appointed chairman. And no one dared to raise any objections, even though we were bang in the middle of a heated debate about how old the buildings we worked in actually were.

> "If youse load really wanna learn some culture,'

Jimmy had suddenly announced, spreading his hands that looked like a pair of industrial-strength shovels,

> "...pin back yer lug-holes, and listen while I fill yiz in with what I know."

The room immediately fell silent like someone had suddenly taped our mouths shut with thick strips of gaffer tape.

Jimmy was six foot seven, had hands like shovels and had a temper as volatile and unstable as the Three-Mile Island nuclear reactor, so no one present fancied telling him to pipe it in, least of all me. At the time this story takes place, (and after what seemed like the passing of entire centuries), I'd finally managed to get myself a girlfriend who didn't have a face that resembled a mossy boulder that had been kept in a pickling jar for three months. She was a classy bird, (sorry, Lady), from 'over the water,' who lived in a massive big house in the leafy green suburbs of Heswall. I was totally infatuated with her, spent countless hours fantasising that she might be 'The (semi-mythical) One,' and was anxious as hell to make a good impression on her. It therefore didn't take a brain surgeon to work out that raising the ire of Jimmy B, was likely to result in me winding up in Walton Hospital, swathed in so many bandages I'd resemble Christopher Lee stumbling from the forbidden tomb in some old Hammer movie. To say that would hardly have put me in her good books, is a little like saying you'd burn your tongue a little if you licked the sun.

So we plugged our pie holes and listened, and it turned out Jimmy was extremely knowledgeable about the area.

He began by telling us all about the shame of Liverpool's long-ago association with the slave trade, and more cheerily about William Roscoe, a highly-principled individual who fought tirelessly for its eventual abolition, and was buried just over the way on Mount Pleasant, clearly visible from our building's fourth floor window.

He described how the thoroughfare upon which Swift Print was located, was first laid in 1790, and had been named after Thomas Seel, a famous Liverpool merchant and landowner, of how the building in which we worked was erected 120 years further down the line, and had originally been used as a sail-making factory.

And, of particular interest to a wannabe muso like me, how Seel Street had long been at the heart of the city's rich and varied music scene, especially the famous *Blue Angel* night club with its *Beatles* connections and The Alhambra Club at the far end of the street, long renowned as being one of the city's foremost jazz and blues venues.

As fascinated as I was by Jimmy's anecdotes, though, at one point I found myself gazing absent-mindedly at the service lift - which had long since fallen into disuse - at the far end of the canteen. The sight of it often served to catch my attention, although I couldn't for the life of me have said why. It certainly appeared to be perfectly ordinary enough, but nevertheless there was something vaguely hypnotic about the pair of pale green doors and the rusted metal grille that stretched across them. On many occasions I had been struck by the undeniably creepy notion that at any minute, the doors and grille were suddenly going to crash open from the inside, and out onto our floor would stumble, I don't know, something…

"Eh, soft lad!"

Jimmy B's booming voice shook me from my none-too pleasant daydream like I'd been stood too close to one of the Mersey Ferry boat's ear-blasting fog horns.

"Are you listenin' to me, or wha?"

"Suh-sorry, Juh-Jimmy,"

I stammered.

"…think I lost me happy thoughts there, for a while."

Jimmy regarded me thoughtfully, and then much to my surprise, lowered his voice to a virtual whisper:

"You keep starin' at that friggin' elevator, lad,'

…he said,

…"and yer'll likely never get them back."

"Why, what's wrong with it?"

I asked, my curiosity aroused

"Plenty."

"Like what?"

"Well, it's haunted by the ghost of a suicide, fer a start!"

"Honestly? What's the story behind that then, Jimmy?"

"Well, if yer'll do me the onour of shuttin' yer grid fer a few minutes I'll tell yiz….."

Now, you probably don't need me to confirm that if anyone else had started talking about resident phantoms or earth-bound apparitions he'd have been laughed right out of the room and would have been made the butt of the cruellest practical jokes for the rest of his working life.

As I stated earlier, however, you didn't want to get on the wrong side of Jimmy B. So nobody emitted so much as a sneaky little, cupped-hand snigger.

And Jimmy told his story to an 'enraptured' audience.

'I won't keep yer long,' he began, glancing at the clock on the canteen wall. 'There really isn't that much to tell.

The details have gotten a little hazy with the passing of the years, but the basic facts as I heard 'em are these: about a hundred years or so ago, when this place was still making these massive big billowing sails for clipper ships and merchant traders, a young employee named William Boyd made the terrible mistake of falling in love with the bosses' youngest daughter, Katherine, after meeting her at the firm's annual Christmas party.

William's boss was a typically keen advocate of contemporary Dickensian values and despite Mr Boyd's well-earned reputation as being one of the factory's most hard-working employees, the head of the firm wouldn't hear of any romantic liaison between his daughter and a 'common labourer.' Local rumour had it that he was determined to fix her up with his brother - a barrister - 25 years her senior.

As is often the way with young love, though, the couple simply set about defying the wishes of their peers and continued to meet in secret in various locations throughout the city. It wasn't too long, though, before they began to run out of places where they believed they could safely meet without arousing suspicion or risk being spotted by those who wished them ill.

In the end, employing a little bit of reverse psychology, they decided their only option was to meet up in the one place they assumed no one would look: our work's canteen, which was a store room, back then, on the fourth floor of this very building. Right under Mr Boss Man's nose, yer might say.

Katherine had her own key to the premises, and every evening, as St Nicholas' Church clock down on the riverfront, struck ten, she would let herself in and take the lift up to meet her fella, long after everyone else, aside from Bill, of course, had knocked off for the night. He would wait in barely suppressed excitement, after laying down the couple of blankets they kept hidden in one of the utility cupboards, impatiently counting off the seconds until he could be back in his girl's arms again.

This went on for the best part a couple of months, and they must have began thinking they could carry on getting away with their secret meetings indefinitely. It wasn't the best of situations, but at least it meant they could spend some precious time together.

Then one evening, Katherine failed to show long after the Church clock had chimed ten-thirty, Bill grew extremely anxious, as she was always punctual to the point of obsessiveness, and he'd just been about to put on his hat and coat to go looking for her when he was relieved to finally hear the sound of the lift coming up to his floor. With a wide smile cracking his face, he prepared to greet Katherine with a hug, and a shower of kisses, but when the doors slid open he saw with horror that it wasn't his girlfriend at all, but the last person in the world Bill wanted to see at that moment - his boss. And he looked extremely angry, to say the least, like he had a gob-full of wasps!

Bill tried to stammer some half-arsed excuse about how he was working late and had decided to spend the night at the factory, so involved was he in his work, but he was cut short in mid-blabber.

> "Please don't insult my intelligence with your lily-livered excuses, Boyd!"

…he shouted, removing his top hat and tapping his silver-tipped walking stick on the palm of his hand.

> "Be a man about this, and face the consequences of your actions. You've been caught red-handed, sir, and if you have a single shred of honour or dignity about you, you'll remain silent while I inform you of how the path of your immediate future has been mapped out, and how I fully expect you to dutifully take that path."

He sniggered, smugly, to himself.

> "Because as I'm sure you'll soon conclude, Mr Boyd, you really don't have any other option."

His boss was right, of course. There was nothing Bill could do other than sit and listen miserably as he learned the incredible lengths to which Katherine's father had gone in order to ensure his life was thoroughly and irreparably ruined.

> "It gives me great pleasure to inform you that you'll never set eyes on my daughter again,"

…his boss began.

> "I've packed young Katherine off to live with one of my many relatives who live in various far-flung corners of the globe. Now, as I pay your wages, I am sure you haven't the means to travel to this particular exotic location, but just to err on the side of caution I'm not even going to tell you which continent I have sent her too, let alone which country. Suffice to say, it is somewhere on the other side of the world. The ship has already long left port with my daughter safely on board. And even if by some extremely fortuitous quirk of fate you were able to correctly guess her eventual whereabouts, I have left strict instructions with those who I trust implicitly, and whose sworn duty it is to ensure my daughter's well-being, that should they encounter a man fitting your description....well, let's just say, they are to regard you as being a manically dangerous obsessive, with heinous designs on young Katherine…"

He smiled, a dangerous, crocodilian smile.

> "And please, do not assume I am being overly melodramatic, Mr Boyd, when I tell you they have orders to shoot you on sight."

So saying, he turned smartly on his heels, and re-entered the lift, chuckling to himself all the while. And then, just as the doors were about to close, he jammed his cane between them and forced them open once more,

> "Oh, and I suppose it goes without saying, but you're finished here,"

…he said, almost kindly.

> "So you may as well pack up your things and leave. And if you ever set foot in these premises again, I'll have you arrested for trespassing.
>
> Have a nice evening, Mr Boyd."

*****

And those soul-crushing blows, were, as you can probably imagine, more than enough to send poor Bill spiralling into the dark depths of abject despair.

In the space of a couple of minutes, five at most, he had lost everything that he held dear in this life, and the frightening ease with which this had occurred only added to the sense of utter hopelessness, and perhaps it should come as no surprise to learn that he decided on impulse that there was only one realistic option left open to him.

He went and got himself a thick, sturdy length of rope, tied it to one of the metal rafters in the empty lift shaft, and launched himself kicking and reeling into the hereafter. When Bill's body was discovered the following morning, dangling like some rigged up scare on a ghost train ride, it was found that he had pinned a hand-written note to his chest that said simply:

> **'I know my actions are cowardly beyond words,
> but I simply can't face living with only half a heart.'**

Of course, ever since the tragedy, people working the night shift have reported from time to time that they've seen William's ghost on occasions when the service lift doors mysteriously opened of their own accord, or walking the shop floor, his face a mask of grief, wringing his hands in despair at the knowledge that he's lost the love of his life.

So, let that be a warning…If you're ever asked if you'd like to earn a few extra bob doing a spot of overtime, you might wanna think twice before accepting…You might risk encountering the restless spirit of Old William Boyd, so desperate for human contact, he loves nothing better than to touch you with a cold, clammy hand from out of the darkness.…'

It must have been no more than a couple of weeks after Jimmy B's impromptu history lesson, that Eddie Mason, Swift-Print's head honcho, called me into his office to tell me he was very impressed with my work and wanted to offer me a promotion. I jumped at the chance with barely a second thought, especially when he explained that my 'climbing up the ladder,' as he put it, would involve a substantial pay rise.

I remember I couldn't wait to tell my girlfriend the good news. It might mean we'd be able to put down a deposit on a flat or even on one of those smart new council houses that were being built on the outskirts of town, and though it would likely be a bit of a struggle at first, we were both looking forwards to the prospect of making a new life for ourselves.

(Above): The grim, grey facade of 'Swift Print's' former premises on Seel Street, Liverpool city centre. The haunt of a restless suicide or something infinitely more Evil?

The only downside to the deal was that my boss made it clear that if I accepted the position, I would be expected to work late some nights, often (especially if a big order came in) without any pre-warning whatsoever. I would therefore have to be extremely flexible as regard to my availability. I knew my girlfriend would be more than a little annoyed about this proviso, but I told her over dinner that night that we'd just have to consider it a wholly necessary evil. Actually, I tried to make light of the situation by stating:

> "You know, love, I suppose, when you get right down to it, it's just another big slice of proof that we are all of us, ruled by the droopy danglies of "The Man," and the way they swing!"

As sparklingly profound witticisms went, I didn't think it would be causing Spike Milligan any amount of sleepless nights, but it brought a smile to my partner's face, and that helped make it a little easier between us.

For the first couple of weeks after securing my promotion, things went on pretty much as they had before, and I clocked off at the stroke of five along with most of the other lads. The only difference I noticed was the considerably heavier pay packet I received on Friday afternoons, and that was just fine with me.

Late one morning though, just before we broke for dinner in fact, my boss came up to me and, with a big cheesy grin on his face, put his arm around my shoulder and told me he'd just heard that a company from London had placed an order they needed delivering early the following day, so he needed me to stay behind and 'get the job done, no matter how long it takes!'

My heart sank, but I stubbornly refused to let the disappointment show on my face.

> "Nil problemo!"

I said, grinning my own big grin and giving it the thumbs up just to prove what a massive giant 'nil problemo' it really was.

He slapped me on the back hard enough to make me wince.

> "Good man, I knew I could rely on you,"

…he said, and he walked off, whistling cheerfully.

I called my girlfriend during my lunch hour and she was predictably less than thrilled, especially seeing as how we'd planned to go to our favourite pub for a drink and a bite to eat. I tried to reassure her that I'd make it up to her, but she slammed the phone down mid-sentence and I spent the remainder of the day in a foul mood, something that certainly wasn't lost on any of my workmates.

They wound me up something rotten about me having to work the night shift all on my lonesome and soon the air was filled with a series of predictable, if slightly less than convincing, Boris Karloff-style choruses of:

> "Watch out for the hanging lift ghost, Jeff!"

and

> "We wouldn't want be in your shoes, my good friend. Old Billy Boyd's coming to get you, toniiiiight!"

I refused to rise to the bait, of course. That would have been fatal. And anyway, I was honestly more pissed off about having to work late and miss out on a few bevvies and a nice bit of scran, to give much of a flyin' one about spooks and such, but still, I can't deny that as the rest of my workmates made for the exits at the chiming of The Five o' Clock Bell, I couldn't help feeling a little nervous, although I dismissed the feeling as being entirely due to being in an all but empty factory, a prospect that was every bit as appealing right then, as attending a gig by *The Pol Pot Death March Orchestra*.

There was something unquestionably eerie about being on my own in an otherwise deserted building as darkness drew down. Part of it was the sudden solitude, and the prospect of the endless hours that stretched out before me like a bitter promise. But mostly, it was the relative silence that descended with the last fading echo of my colleagues shouting 'see yer tomorrer!' as they trundled down Seel Street with a spring in their step, eager to be home after the rigours of the working day.

Less than five minutes after the last of my work-mates had departed, the only sounds reaching my ears where the whirr of the printing presses, the relentless ticking of the clock on the far wall, and a constantly ringing telephone behind the locked doors of the Head Office, destined never to be answered until the morning shift punched in at 8am.

It reminded me a little of when I was a kid, being kept behind after school on detention, for some minor misdemeanour or other. The empty classroom, redolent with the smell of chalk dust, stale sweat and ancient-looking text books, had always been filled with a similar kind of melancholy almost-hush…

Normally, faced with such a grim prospect I would have immediately switched the office radio back on and whacked the volume all the way up to provide me with a slightly more cheery soundtrack to my seven hour-long exile from the outside world.

Unfortunately, this was way before the days of digital radio, and the old, beaten-up transistor that sat on a shelf atop a pile of old newspapers, resembled an original Marconi prototype, one that could only just about pick up the two local stations: Radio City and Merseyside. I was therefore faced with the "agony" of having to choose whether to listen to some insufferable bore, waffling inanely about local politics and how Britain was going to hell in a handcart or be forced to endure the soporific sounds of 'The Peaceful Hour,' a compilation of sickly love songs and romantic vignettes from heartbroken listeners so sentimentally slushy, it would make Simon Bates go racing off in a mad dash search for a sick bucket.

I decided instead to totally immerse myself in my work, and try and get the job done as quickly as possible, so I could get the hell out of there as soon as I could, and almost before I knew it, I'd virtually completed the task, and when I glanced at the clock, I was amazed to see it was only a little after eleven. I wiped the sweat from my brow, stretched my aching limbs, and allowed myself a smile of satisfaction, before heading for the canteen to put the kettle on. I reckoned I'd earned myself a good strong cup of coffee, and my spirits had been lifted immeasurably by the prospects of me being home within half an hour, and just as importantly, ensuring I stayed well in my bosses' good books.

The kettle was coming to the boil, and I'd just lobbed a couple of spoonfuls of sugar into my Sex Pistols mug when I heard the unmistakable sound of the front door of the premises, down on the ground floor, slowly opening.

It was instantly recognisable because the hinges on that huge iron door hadn't been oiled in years, and as a result it gave out a nerve-grating screech that sounded like a thousand jagged fingernails scratching down the surface of a blackboard. It drove everyone in the firm crazy, causing them to visibly wince as a shiver went skittering down their spine and set their teeth on edge like they'd been chewing on tin foil, but despite much talk of how someone really needed to get their act together and "sort that friggin' door out," no one ever actually took the initiative and set about dousing those corroded hinges with a giant-sized can of 'Free It'

I wasn't remotely frightened at this point. The first thought to cross my mind was that it was very likely to be Eddie, my boss, checking up to see whether I'd finished the job or not, and I all but ran out onto the landing, eager to call down to him that I'd only be another half an hour or so. I was sure he'd be pleased that I'd completed the task, so it surprised me a little when I didn't receive an immediate answer. I was also more than a little unnerved by how loud my voice sounded in the ominous silence, and the way it echoed back along the empty stairwells and deserted corridors. I opened my mouth to call out again, but the words died on my lips and despite my trying to tell myself I was just being stupid, I found I was too scared to shout Eddie's name a second time, though I couldn't have said precisely why (the image that sprang into my mind, unbidden and uninvited however, was of the sound of my voice disturbing someone or something it would doubtless have been far wiser to leave well alone).

I was reluctant to go and investigate, but I knew I really had no choice but to go and check out who was down on the ground floor, and why they hadn't responded to my shouts.

Warily, I began making my way down the first flight of winding stairs, straining my ears for approaching footfalls as I descended. There weren't any, though, and when I finally reached the landing directly above the ground floor, I was halted in my tracks when I discovered that the entire hallway was in complete darkness and the light switch wouldn't work, no matter how much I flicked it on and off.

It was impossible to make out anything in the midst of the thick, opaque blackness. The wire-meshed, metal-shuttered windows admitted not even the tiniest sliver of street light, transforming the hallway into a formless void or the inky depths of a limitless ocean covering the surface of some long-dead planet.

I noticed it was ice-cold down there, too, ("As cold as the graaayyyyve," I imagined one of my colleagues whispering in a now eerily accurate Boris Karloff voice), and that was a little strange, but what was even weirder was the fact that somehow, from over where I roughly calculated the front door to be, there lurked a still darker shadow, an amorphous mass that seemed to constantly shift and pulsate like it was struggling to take on some vaguely recognisable outline.

I was struck by the inarguable certainty that if I hung around for long enough, what would gradually emerge from the Stygian murk would be something that had assumed the shape of one William Boyd Esq; a lumbering, broken figure with a slack face, drool dripping from the corner of its mouth, and a pair of staring eyes that were every bit as flat and lifeless as those of a dead fish on a slab.

With agonising slowness, I began backing up when in truth I wanted nothing more than to sprint for the sanctuary of the lighted floors above. At the same time however, I refused to turn my back on that creeping darkness, sure that if I did so for even the briefest moment, I would feel a cold, clammy hand gently caressing the nape of my neck.

I made it all the way up to the third flight in this decidedly awkward fashion, before I finally cracked, spun round quickly and dashed up the remaining stairs to the printing shop, slamming the door shut firmly behind me. I honestly considered dragging a chair over and wedging it below the handle, but of course, that wasn't going to keep any truly phantasmal figure from materialising through the cracks and fissures, so instead I just stood there for I'm not sure how long, my heart pounding in my chest like an out-of-control jack-hammer, staring at the door, expecting at any moment it would either burst open with frightening force, or that some vaporous horror would begin to seep beneath the tiny gaps to envelope me in its foetid embrace.

I remember feeling angry, too, at the patent unfairness of the situation I'd suddenly found myself in. I mean, here I was doing my first ever stint on the night shift, possibly on the brink of coming face to face with some inescapable nocturnal menace, whilst just a few feet away, on the other side of the factory walls, the world was turning serenely, blissfully ignorant of my predicament.

It was enough to make you fighting mad, but I welcomed the anger simply because it was infinitely better than feeling afraid, and I actually took a couple of steps towards the door intent on wrenching it open to scream at the whatever-the-hell-it-was to leave me alone, but I was stopped dead in my tracks once more when I heard another sound that froze the blood in my veins:

The juddering progress of the service lift as it made its way up from the ground floor.

The righteous fury disappeared in an instant, and here came my old friend, Abject Fear, gleefully slithering into the dark hollows left by wrath's absence, as the elevator slowly ascended, and once more I stood, as if hypnotised, no more able to move a muscle than the proverbial rabbit, caught in the glare of approaching car headlights.

I knew, with soul-crushing inevitability, that the lift was only going to stop when it reached my floor, of course, and I found myself recalling a scene from a horror film I'd seen at the The Rialto over on Upper Parly Street, a couple of years earlier called Burnt Offerings. I'd taken my then girlfriend, a five-foot-nothin' motor-mouth named Helen Jones, who'd fidgeted and munched on monster-sized buckets of lightly salted popcorn all the way through the movie, spoiling my enjoyment, and everybody else's, to the point where I'd been mightily tempted to shove the friggin' popcorn, cardboard buckets and all, right down the back of her cavernous pie-hole.

But not even the maddening sound of my date's relentless chomping had been able to detract from the frighteningly effective sequence, mid-way through the film when an old-fashioned, uniformly black hearse went chugging along the long, gravel-lined driveway leading to some magnificent stately home (even though the building was so obviously haunted it may as well as have had a fifty foot sign posted at the main gates announcing 'HERE BE BOO-HAGS!' in scary Halloween font). Behind the wheel of the vehicle sat a sinister, grey-suited chauffeur with a pallid face and sunglasses, and a nasty yellow-toothed grin, his appearance presaged by the sound of the hearse's engine, comfortably distant at first, but drawing ever nearer with each passing second whilst the film's chief protagonist, (played by the ever-excellent Oliver Reed), breaks into a sweat, his face contorted into a skull-like rictus of anticipatory terror.

I now found myself in a disconcertingly similar situation, waiting for the service lift to reach my floor, and I knew, if there had been a mirror around in which to have viewed myself, at that moment, I would have been horrified by the fearful expression distorting my features, making me appear dead-beat, shrunken and old before my time...

But still I was unable move a muscle, as the elevator continued to rise up from the basement like some nightmarish sea creature ascending from the abyssal depths, until, with a final grinding lurch, it came to a halt and that pregnant silence draped the building again like a shroud, cloaking everything in a sense of dreamy unreality...

The quiet held for a few seconds more.

And then the doors slid open with a whispered sigh.

To reveal...

To reveal...

Nothing.

Nothing, but a bundle of rags lying in an untidy heap in the far corner of the lift

A badly scuffed shoe. A tattered trouser leg. A suit jacket with one its sleeves hanging by a single thread

A pile of discarded clothing that had obviously seen better days...

And that was all.

I opened my mouth to laugh out loud at my own stupidity then just as quickly snapped it shut when I saw something moving within the folds of that falling-to-bits jacket.

Something that writhed repulsively like a colony of pale-white worms suddenly exposed to sunlight by the turn of a gardener's spade. It took me a moment or two to realise they were fingers, human fingers, scrabbling blindly for purchase at the end of a scrawny, though powerful-looking hand, despite the fact that there was no discernible forearm to which it could possibly be attached. Just the flattened creasy tunnel of an empty sleeve. There was part of a torso, too, struggling to upright itself and turn in my direction, as thoroughly crazy as that sounds.

And did I really see a single cyclopean eye, glazed and milky but still somehow filled with a mixture of spiteful intelligence and undiluted hatred, glaring from the centre of that essentially formless pile...?

Dear God help me, I think I did.

Certainly, that crowning absurdity was enough to snap me out of my fear-induced paralysis and I turned and ran towards the fire escape doors that I suddenly remembered were located directly behind me (how I'd forgotten, Christ only knows!). Without pausing to glance back at the lift and its progressively forming horror, I pushed down on the bar beneath the green and white exit signs, and raced down the metal staircase, my piercing screams renting the air and forming a cacophonous duet with the security alarm that began shrieking the second the double doors were opened.

I sprinted across the factory yard at the back of the building, and out along the deserted, rain-spattered pavements, and I kept running until I felt my lungs would burst, and my legs had turned to jelly. Finally, exhausted to the point of near collapse, I stood shaking under the dull glow of the street-lights, whilst the St Nicholas Church clock chimed midnight…

*****

There's really nothing else to add.

Save to say, I never worked the night shift again.

But I guess you figured that out for yourselves already.

The extra money I could earn was important…but then so was the retention of my sanity.

'THERE IS WAKING AFTER DREAMING'
A Final Message from the After-Life

Contrary to popular belief, not all reportedly 'true-life' ghost stories need necessarily result in the involuntary raising of the tiny hairs on the back of your neck or cause a cold slimy worm of fear to go wriggling up and down the length of your spine.

Sometimes, these first-hand witness accounts, made by reliable people who proffer no convenient explanations to suit their own personal agenda or bellow the details of their experience to the eternally gullible to drum up support for some crackpot belief system (that may or may not involve setting up a commune in some remote rural location, donning a uniform of glorified sack-cloths tied with cheap plastic belts, and 'willingly' acceding to a mass invitation to glug on a glass of lip-smackin', thirst-quenching Kool Aid), are narratives brimming with unbridled optimism to the point where they could be considered life-affirming (if that's not a blatant contradiction in terms).

The following story, narrated to me by a wonderfully caring woman named Rachel Dee a week or so before Christmas, 2007, is - I would contend - a perfect example of how sometimes a gleaming beacon of hope can pierce the shadows of "Death's Dark Vale."

*****

I remember it was during the dreadfully disappointingly washed-out summer of 1980, that I managed to get myself a job working as a care assistant at Manor House Nursing Home; a large, white, converted mansion, situated in one of the more prosperous areas of Upton, Wirral.

Set amidst acres of the most sumptuous gardens I'd ever seen, at the end of a winding tree-lined drive, the imposing-looking building with its pristine white walls, huge bay windows and ornate colonnades must surely once have been the home of a local shipping line magnate, a successful factory owner or some bigwig lawyer. It was certainly a suitably grand location for elderly people to live out the remainder of their 'twilight years,' with a fair degree of dignity and comfort.

It wasn't my first experience of caring for the aged and infirm, but it was, by some considerable distance, my most rewarding. Perhaps that isn't saying much when you consider the dreadful state of some of the places where I'd

previously been employed. Although I was only in my early twenties at the time, I was more than old enough to have experienced more than my fair share of filthy, run-down establishments that permanently reeked of the combined odours of urine, stale sweat and food that was long past its sell-by date, and where the staff were so keen on maintaining a strict degree of order, their disciplinary measures bordered on outright sadism.

On the other hand, there were also those equally bloody awful places where the residents seemed to take a perverse delight in making their carer's life a total misery. I'd heard, of course, of how the older people get the greater the likelihood they'll lose a fair portion of their mental faculties, sometimes to the point where they revert to the days of their early childhood. But it's all very well people *describing* (in whiny, high-pitched voices, and a series of sighs aimed at alerting the world to the birth of a new martyr), how they have to bathe and dress and feed the parents who had once done the same for them (though with a damn sight less '*oh-woe-is-me*' caterwauling, one suspects) when *they* were infants. It's quite another to actually *experience* this bizarre role reversal at first-hand. Having to sit at the bedside of someone who could easily be your own Nan or Grandad, spoon-feeding them food that's been mashed and whisked to the point where it resembles the sloppy gloop that oozed out of the meteorites that fell to Earth in all those 1950s sci-fi films they sometimes show late on Friday nights, is more than a little disconcerting. But I suppose it's something many of us have to learn to deal with sooner or later.

I'm afraid to say though that this patiently philosophical outlook did little to shield me from some of the more memorably troublesome individuals it was my misfortune to encounter over the years: I remember one old man in particular, named Sammy Atkinson, a cantankerous old bastard, whose thick, bushy brown beard contrasted starkly with the pure-white hair on his head.

Old Sammy was the kind of unlovable pain in the arse who loved nothing better than playing mean-spirited practical jokes on his fellow residents, such as loosening the screws on the chairs in the canteen, so that people often collapsed in an undignified heap whenever they sat to eat their lunch, or cadging the primitive remote control so that he could constantly switch the channels over on the communal TV in the recreation room, flicking between *The Persuaders* and *The Good Life* or a *World In Action* documentary on war-torn Afghanistan, not because he couldn't decide which channel to tune into, (and there were only three, back then) but simply because he wanted to piss everybody off. *Thoroughly.*

And when he couldn't get hold of the remote, he'd make a point of arriving at the common room five minutes before everyone else, just so he could park his not inconsiderable backside in what he knew full well to be one of the resident's favourite chairs. Many was the time when I'd find him sat there with his feet up, refusing point blank to move, while some poor old dear would stand there looking hopelessly bewildered, as though someone had suddenly pulled the plug on the internal circuitry of their brain.

There was another perpetual charmer, whose name escapes me, who delighted in winding up the staff by telling them that he most definitely did not need to use the toilet as they peered quizzically at his empty brass bed pan. The minute their backs were turned, however, he'd promptly let rip an almighty fart and proceed to crap all over the bedclothes.

"I'm awfully sorry,"

…he'd say, a sly smile curling the corner of his lips.

> "I certainly didn't see **that** one coming!"

Then there was Amelia Whittington, an insufferable snob from the middle class suburb of Heswall, who was beset with delusions of grandeur. She demanded every single member of staff to be permanently at her beck and call, to cater for her every whim, no matter how trivial, and at one point she actually succeeded in obtaining her own personal whistle from an equally toffee-nosed member of her family, which she kept upon a silver chain around her neck. Whenever she required assistance, she would summon one of the carers by blowing loudly on this whistle, its shrill *pheeeeeeps!* piercing everyone's eardrums something rotten, whenever she wanted a vitally important task performing, like acquiring an extra lump of sugar for her coffee, or having her pillows fluffed up and smoothed of any creases, or spraying the room with choking clouds of fly-killer every time some luckless insect flew in through the window, and I'm sure I wasn't the only one who was tempted to sneak into her room sometime after midnight, to throttle her with that bleedin whistle-on-a-chain set whilst she was sound sleep.

So yes, there were more than a few occasions when I had cause to consider my chosen career path to be a little like embarking on a dark journey into worlds peopled by the lost and damaged, but thankfully, there were also plenty of individuals who either worked or resided there who made the job worthwhile, and there were many people whose company I actively sought out.

All of which, is an admittedly rather long-winded way of introducing you to my favourite resident during the time that I was at Manor House: an extremely popular 84 year-old widow named Elsie Goodman. I used to love speaking to her whenever it was my turn to take her meals to her room or to generally check on her well-being, I loved her dreamy reminiscences and her unquenchable zest for life, and we quickly became good friends.

Despite her years, and the fact that she'd lost her husband to cancer back in 1960, and had never re-married, she spoke in the clear, sweet tones of someone less than half her age. Annie Davies, one of my more poetically-inclined colleagues on the night-shift, had once remarked:

> "Honestly, that Elsie reminds me at times of my dear departed Nan. I mean, just like her, she's got one of those voices that conjures up images of liquid honey being poured through a piece of torn silk,"

…and I'd nodded readily in agreement, (whilst cursing my luck that I wasn't born with her natural gift for poetic eloquence).

Considering Elsie's pleasant manner and mental lucidity, it came as something of a shock to learn that her family had only ever taken the trouble to visit her on a couple of occasions, and that had been directly after she'd first been placed into our care. It seemed that once they'd satisfied themselves that she was *'settled in, all nice and snug and comfy,'* they hadn't bothered returning, and had simply left her to get on with it.

I can only imagine how much it must have hurt Elsie to know that her relatives had, to all intents and purposes, abandoned her, but she bore the pain with the stiff-upper-lipped stoicism of a previous generation. She only let her mask slip on special occasions like her birthday or at Christmas. At such times, I'd watch her eyes light up expectantly when the post was given out in the common room, and my heart would go out to her as that light slowly flickered and died as the realisation dawned that there was no mail for her again this time. She would withdraw into herself then, and politely ask that she be left alone in her room for a little while.

Elsie once told me she often felt like a faithful pack horse that had suddenly gone lame, had outlived its usefulness and been put out to pasture. She had also once remarked, with just the faintest trace of bitterness:

> "I suppose all those I've lovingly raised to adulthood can now, with a relatively clear conscience, leave me to my own devices…After all, they are no longer responsible for my well-being."

I remember I took her hand, wrinkled and liver-spotted with age, but with long, graceful fingers, still bearing her wedding and engagement rings, her nails immaculately manicured and painted a soft-pink sheen, and tried to reassure her that her family wouldn't *forever* abandon her, and would surely come to visit any day now. But I didn't tell her what I suspected she'd already considered - perhaps they simply couldn't face travelling to the home because it would remind them too much of the unpalatable fact that one day, they too would be old.

Fortunately, Elsie found some degree of solace by immersing herself in her huge collection of books. Don't get me wrong, she enjoyed talking and craved human companionship as much as anyone, but give her a spare couple of minutes on her own, and you'd invariably find her with her head buried deep in a novel, or a collection of short stories, a wistful expression on her face,

> "Books now, Miss Dee,"

(she always called me that, even though she knew perfectly well what my Christian name was).

> "Books provide the easiest escape route you could ever possibly take to free yourself from a place of confinement, whether it's a cold, dark prison cell, or the humdrum routine of daily existence. You can travel far and wide in your mind's eye, you see. The author's words can, if you allow them, transport you to distant realms, far beyond the confines of your room."

She smiled as she cast a glance at the series of impeccably clean, mahogany shelving filled to bursting point with paperbacks and hardbacks, encompassing everything from slim, pocket-sized *Mills & Boons* romances and current bestsellers, to the timeless classics of Faulkner, Dickens and James.

Her favourite novel though was *Swallows & Amazons*. Elsie said she must have read it a hundred times, at least.

> "It reminds me of my youth, Miss Dee, when my friends and I used to go boating on Raby Mere at the birth of the 20th Century. Oh, that seems such an *impossibly* long time ago to me now."

She'd go on to describe how it was to be eleven years old during "the glorious days of Empire." Of how it felt to be filled with patriotic fervour, unbridled optimism, and an unshakable faith in the wonders of technology, a year or so before the sinking of the *Titanic* and when the cold glower of the First World War was still nothing but a distant, if undeniably ominous, thunder-head looming on the otherwise cloudless horizon.

> "The Mere, as you probably know, if you've ever been there, is actually an artificial mill-pool about a quarter of a mile long, surrounded by a couple of miles of thick woodland which has an abundance of wildlife and offers blessedly cool shade in high summer. I suppose it still gets busy, even now, but in those days, people used to come in droves from Liverpool and Birkenhead and the surrounding areas.
>
> I suppose it all sounds a trifle hackneyed now, but back then we loved to indulge in the sort of simple pleasures most people nowadays would gladly forsake for the alternative of plonking themselves down on the grassy banks (after securing the most advantageous place for topping up their suntan, naturally) and snapping the ring-pulls on cans of lukewarm lager, or uncorking a cheap bottle of rosé wine, to drink oneself insensible as quickly as possible.
>
> We, that is my friends and I, used to enjoy feeding the ducks, taking a stroll along the country lanes in our summer finery, or else hand over our pocket money to hire one of the rowing boats lined up alongside the wooden quayside. There were tea rooms and beautiful gardens with swings and roundabouts and moving picture machines and you could buy a *Fry's Chocolate Bar* for as little as a penny. There would be regular

Sunday School picnics, and the girls would be wearing smart white flouncey dresses that were tied in the middle with a sash of silken ribbon, whilst the boys were all done up in sailor suit uniforms, with knickerbocker trousers and straw boaters perched jauntily on their heads.

I remember one gorgeous late-July afternoon the Mere was all but overrun by a platoon of the *Royal Engineers*. We sat and watched, fascinated, as they skilfully erected a temporary bridge across from one side of the pool to the other. My dad took a black and white photograph of the soldiers as they posed for the crowds of spectators gathered on all sides, and I later placed it in the old album I'd received as a stocking-filler the previous Christmas. When I was growing up, I'd often find myself staring at the beaming faces of the proud young men, as handsome as silent movie stars in their monochrome uniforms, some of them standing in the shallows with their jackets off and their trousers rolled up to their knees, others standing on the bridge, hands on hips, visibly glowing with the satisfaction of a job well done.

And I'd find myself morbidly wondering how many of these boys, for that's what they were (I mean, the oldest amongst them was barely out of his teens), who doubtless thought they had their whole lives ahead of them, gathered amidst the golden haze of that summer afternoon, as the sun danced on the water's surface in bright golden lances, were in fact already doomed, set for the senseless slaughter of the killing fields of France, just a few short years later.

"Not that I believe that death is the end," she'd stated vehemently at this point. "Not for one moment. I don't believe, as someone once said, that time simply flows like running water until we drift into eternal sleep. I have faith we go on, Miss Dee, in some form or other."

She caught me glancing at her sharply.

"Oh, there's no need to look so worried,"

she said quickly.

"I don't plan on dying any time soon. I intend to stick around for as long as humanly possible. But I certainly don't *fear* death and I so look forwards to being reunited with my darling Eddie, after all these years. We'll have so much catching up to do…"

I hastily sought to change the subject. Dealing with death and its messy aftermath was an occupational hazard at Manor House, but it wasn't exactly something people liked to talk about if it could at all be avoided.

"I was just wondering, Elsie,"

I said.

"What do you think of Steinbeck's *Grapes Of Wrath*? A friend of mine recommended it to me…."

And that was all it took to get her off and running again….

*****

I wasn't there the night Mrs Goodman died, a good two years or so on from this conversation.

The last time I saw her alive was on the Friday evening before the August Bank Holiday. I'd booked a long weekend away in Blackpool with my fiancé, Kevin, and Elsie was delighted for me. She'd said she'd miss my company, but had a stack of books she'd been itching to get stuck into and my absence would provide her with the perfect opportunity to do so.'

> "You go right ahead and have a great time. Just make sure you bring me back a big stick of rock. I haven't had one of those in years, and I'd love the chance to chew some candy while I've still got enough of my own teeth left to do so."

> "No problem,"

I told her.

> "I'll make sure I get you one that's so gi-normously massive you'll be chomping on it all the way through to next Christmas."

> "Oh, and just one more thing,"

…she'd said, as I made my way to the door.

> "If you should happen to pay a visit to the Fairground, *Blackpool Pleasure Land*, I think it's called these days, kindly indulge a foolish old lady and do me one more favour, will you?"

> "Anything for you, my dear,"

I said, with a mock curtsey.

She waved her hand in a *pshaw* gesture before regarding me more seriously.

> "Just watch out for that greasy-faced, Laughing Clown, Miss Dee. The one that sits in a big glass box near to the entrance. Oh, I'm sure it's supposed to be hilariously funny, a big-grinned welcome to The House of Never-Ending Fun. But to be honest, it gives me a serious case of the chills. It rocks back and forth like a lunatic in a straitjacket and I swear it cackles like the Spirit of Death itself….and, well… it looks like it'd sneak up on you given half a chance."

She paused to peer over the rim of her horn-rimmed glasses, like a school teacher about to impart some worldly advice to the sort of pupil who thinks they know it all, already.

> "The truth is, Miss Dee. I don't trust it. I don't trust it one little bit!"

I'd thought she was obviously joking, winding me up in that half-annoying, half-endearing way of hers, and indeed as I made to leave, I saw she was smiling broadly.'

> "I'll see you on Monday,"

I said shaking my head at her foolishness.'

> "Goodbye, Miss Dee,"

…she'd replied.'

****

It was only much later, after I'd finished unpacking in my seafront hotel room, whilst the typically British Bank Holiday downpour hammered relentlessly at the window panes, that I was struck by a sudden realisation; a less-than-joyful epiphany that chilled me to the bone.

Mrs Goodman had not returned my cheery; "I'll see you on Monday." She'd simply said "*Goodbye"* with what I now discerned to be an awful, unalterable finality.

And the smile she'd flashed me as I'd left her room…?

It had never touched her *eyes.'*

****

There's really not that much to tell about our weekend break.

In the days and weeks leading up to the trip, Kevin and I had made all these epically grandiose plans about where we were going to go, and what we were going to do, but the deluge of near-Biblical proportions all but swept them clean away, and the truth is we spent most of our time splashing through dirty grey puddles of rainwater or racing along the wave-blasted promenade for the welcome shelter of the various local pubs and restaurants, whilst sea-gulls swooped and screamed directly over our heads.

> "Well, we might as well give our *insides* a good soaking, seeing as how we're totally and utterly drenched on the *out!*"

Kevin had joked as we darted towards an Irish theme bar, and I'd playfully punched him in the arm, and the *'positively-last-one-in-the-shop'* souvenir umbrella with its *'Kiss Me Quick!'* exhortation and a big smiley yellow sun clutching a bucket and spade, adorning its panels, was torn from my grip by a freak gust of wind, and went skittering along the road that led to the pier, like a flimsy piece of tumbleweed. We both gave chase, but it proved ultimately fruitless as the metal spokes of the brolly caught for a few maddening seconds in the wire-mesh fence at the far end of the prom and then, just as we reached out to grab its rubber handle, it chose to vault over the partition into the raging sea below and we stood there for a while, watching forlornly as our cheap memento was borne on mountainous, white-flecked waves in the general direction of The Isle of Man.

I wasn't about to allow the awful weather to completely ruin our trip, though. Kevin may have constantly sighed and shook his head whilst muttering such miserably gloomy one-liners as:

> "Jesus, Rachel, this place sucks like a black hole doing the hoovering,"

…but we were young and in love and I was determined to have a good time, no matter what, and who cared if the resort had 'all the welcoming charisma of a two-week-old, vinegar-soggy battered cod?' (*and yes, that* was *another of Kev's charming little witticisms*).

Our hotel room was cosy and snug and blissfully, wonderfully, *dry.* Not only that, but the lavish four-poster bed was luxuriously comfortable, the sheets sweet-smelling and freshly pressed, and there was a single red rose in the centre of the pillow and a bottle of champagne in an ice-bucket on the dressing table.

And hey, there are infinitely worse ways of spending a holiday than lying in the arms of the person you instinctively know you are destined to spend the rest of your life with.

I treasured the aftermath of our mini-John and Yoko-style love-in, as well. With Kevin snoring softly beside me, I'd lie there feeling safe and loved, replaying the day's events in my head, pondering the heady excitement of the present and the blank-slate promise of the future, or simply listen to the myriad sounds of Blackpool after dark; the cheesy melody of an end-of-the-pier organ, the heavy pounding of drums and thudding bass from a local nightclub, the wild roar of the sea as giant waves crashed repeatedly against the concrete shoreline defences.

And at some point I'd drift into a sleep filled with dreams of ocean-deep puddles, Irish theme bars and pitifully fragile, sea-faring brollies.

It was only on the final night of our mini-break that I suddenly became aware of the shrieking peals of maniacal laughter floating up towards me on the gale force wind. Somehow, up until that point, it had lurked unnoticed and unheralded like some subliminal-trigger phrase whispered into your ear by a gold lamé suited stage-hypnotist. Now it drifted in and out of earshot, the way a distant foreign radio station sometimes swells and fades in volume late at night.

It was The Clown, sitting in its glass cage at the entrance to *Pleasure Land*, of course.

The one Mrs Goodman had 'jokingly' warned me about the last time I'd spoken to her, and it sounded for all the world as though I was the sole focus of its deranged hilarity, although that was plainly crazy, and more than a little paranoid.

I squeezed my eyes tightly shut, and after what seemed like an eternity, I eventually drifted off to sleep with the sound of that dreadful, mirthless cackling echoing along the dark, twisty corridors of my dreams.

And I awoke early the next morning, feeling a little like *death*.

****

I was really looking forwards to seeing Mrs Goodman on my return to work. God knows, I'd needed some cheering up after that (mostly), damp squib of a weekend, and the thought of seeing her eyes light up at the sight of the huge stick of rock I'd bought her lifted my sodden spirits still further. I'd picked up one of those bright pink and white, sickly-sweet confections with **'I Luv Blackpool'** printed right the way through it, the sort that would give any self-respecting dentist a week's worth of nightmares. It gave me a severe bout of toothache just looking at it sealed in its cheap, cellophane wrapper, but I knew Mrs Goodman would be delighted with it, just the same.

I'd also tell her I'd heeded her advice and steered well clear of the funfair, too, though I wouldn't add that the weather had played a large part in my avoidance of *The Realm Of The Laughing Clown*, or the fact that I'd found it all but impossible to get any sleep the night before.

My milk-white pale complexion and the dark circles under my eyes might very likely give me away, of course, but I was already feeling better for having eaten a hearty lunch followed by a quick forty winks on the settee prior to getting dressed for the evening shift. And when I left the house, the sun was shining for the first time in what seemed like weeks, the air was sweet with the smell of apple blossom and freshly-cut grass, and I remember I was whistling an early *Beatles* tune, as I walked (and very nearly skipped like an over-grown school kid, if I'm being completely honest) to the bus stop to catch the number 42 to Manor House.

*****

The minute I walked though the big double doors at the entrance to the Home, I instinctively knew something was dreadfully wrong. None of my colleagues actually came out and announced anything was amiss. Not at first, anyway. On the contrary, it was all "welcome backs", and "did you have a nice break?" and other assorted pleasantries. But there was an unmistakably subdued atmosphere pervading the place, and even more disconcerting was the fact that none of them, not even Theresa, the hard as nails staff sister, would look me in the eye when they spoke to me.

Eventually, one of my best friends, Sally Lewis, took me to one side and spoke in hushed, sympathetic tones.

"You'd better sit down, Rachel. I'm afraid I have some bad news."

"I think I'd just as soon hear whatever it is you've got to tell me standing up,"

I replied.

> "Fair enough,"

…she said, though from her expression, it was clear she was uncomfortable with my display of stiff-upper-lipped stubbornness.

> "Well, I hate to be the one to tell you, but Elsie Goodman died last night. I know you two were really close. I'm so sorry."

Struggling to fight back the tears, I asked Sally to fill me in with the details which were mercifully brief and to the point: Elsie had died peacefully in her sleep, and it was Sally herself who had found her when she'd been carrying out her morning rounds.

> "I honestly thought she was dozing. She looked so peaceful like she was lost in some beautiful dream. It was only when I shook her gently to wake her that I realised she wasn't breathing, and, God Rachel, are you alright….?"

I lost track of what Sally was saying right then, because I heard the sound of hysterical cackling echoing along the corridor. For a single, horrible moment, I was reminded of The Blackpool Clown, rocking back and forth in its glass case with lunatic glee, and a cold knot of dread formed in the pit of my stomach. I very nearly screamed, but then the familiar sound of Terry Scott's voice, raised in righteous indignation at some perceived injustice, filled the air and I realised with relief it was only canned laughter spilling from the TV in the common room.

I managed to summon up the shakiest of smiles, but it did little to reassure Sally that I was going to be able to deal with the situation and she asked me if I wanted someone else to work my evening shift. I told her thanks, but I would just a soon get on with my work. Sally nodded sympathetically. "Well, if you're *sure*."

I told her that I was and went to change into my uniform.

*****

I'm not ashamed to say I cried when, during my first coffee break, I went to Elsie Goodman's room. It took me a few moments to summon up the courage to enter. Finally, with a sigh, I opened the door and went in. The staff hadn't yet had time to clear out her possessions. They had, though, packed most of her books and other personal belongings into a stack of large cardboard boxes, and I was struck by an overwhelming sadness by the bleak thought that this, in the end, was what our lives came down to: a series of accumulated bric-a-brac…all that's left to remind the world that you had once existed.

As I was about to leave, I noticed there was a book lying open on her bedside table. I walked over and saw it was a leather-bound volume that gave off the faintly fabulous aroma of dust and age and secrets. I closed it for a second to glance at the title:

'Three Lines of Old French.'

It had been written by an author I'd never heard of before, by the name of Abraham Merritt, (I later learned he was a wonderful writer who had enjoyed a fairly wide popularity back in the early part of the 20th Century, and had published, amongst other things, many stories containing supernatural elements, which may or not be of any great significance to my story. I'm certainly not going to preach to you on this one way or the other – "The Good Lord gave you a mind of your own for a reason," as my dear old mum used to say when I was a child), and I quickly scanned the page at which Elsie had left it open, only half taking in the words, and saw she had underlined the following lines in red ink.

> *"Nor grieve, dear heart,*
> *Nor fear the seeming,*
> *Here is waking,*
> *After dreaming..."*

I stood there for what seemed like the longest time, reading those lines over and over until they merged into one blurry mass of indecipherable nonsense, and I felt a tear come to rest on my cheek like a salty glass globe....

"I've come to tell you goodbye, Elsie,"

I whispered.

"I'm glad you've gone to a better place, but I want you to know I'm going to miss you more than words can say..."

I was going to add some more, but I suddenly felt a little foolish muttering banalities in the cold, indifferent silence of that empty room. It wasn't as though Mrs Goodman could hear me, after all. Even supposing there was such a thing as an afterlife, and my Catholic faith assured me that such was most definitely the case, if she had been given any choice in the matter, her spirit would have long since "blown this pop-stand," (to use yet another of Kevin's favourite phrases). I could easily picture her soul joyously escaping the confines of Manor House, the way her vivid imagination and the books she'd loved so much, had combined to transport her to realms and kingdoms fair, though in reality, she hadn't physically set foot outside the building for the best part of fifteen years.

And though my heart was gladdened by my unshakeable belief that she had travelled to some infinitely 'better place,' still I was left to face the fact that I wouldn't be seeing her anytime soon.

But, as it turned out, I was completely wrong about that.

*****

I somehow managed to get through the next few hours immersing myself completely in the humdrum of routine. I've often found hard work to be cathartic, even in the wake of bad news, and I had a lot of paperwork to do which was boring as hell, but it helped kill the time. I was writing the reports for the night shift at about 11pm, seated at the far end of the corridor on the second floor. My head was buried deep in the daily log-book and the mountainous stack of reports and resident's case files, my fingers stained with smudges of blue ink. I was writing so furiously, I half-expected to see smoke trails rising from the pages, but as a means of purging my grief, I guess it beat heading home and drowning my sorrows in a bottle of one of Kevin's ten year old malts.

I'm not at all sure what it was that made me look up from my work, though I think perhaps it was the gradual realisation; a seeping into my consciousness like wisps of smoke emerging from under a door, that it had grown so deathly quiet I could hear the ticking of the clock on the opposite wall.

I want to make it clear, before we go any further, that I didn't have much of an interest in the supernatural back then. I mean, I'd read about alleged ghostly manifestations and such in the *'True Life Experiences'* section of the women's magazines I'd casually glanced through on occasion, and had subconsciously stored away in some dim corner of my mind, all of the supposed indicative signs of 'spectral visitation'. Aside from that odd, pervasive silence, however, all of those so-called "tell-tale signs", (a sudden and dramatic drop in room temperature, a series of anomalous sounds, like unseen hands rapping on the walls, or a vague, but undeniable sense of some kind of spiritual presence looming over your shoulder), were conspicuous by their absence.

But nevertheless, when I looked up, there, just a few feet in front of me, was kindly old Mrs Goodman, a smile of blissful serenity lighting up her face.

I wasn't the slightest bit afraid, despite the fact that I could clearly see that my recently deceased friend was only visible from the waist up, her legless body floating in the centre of the corridor like a child's kite bobbing on a length of invisible string, and incredibly, my first reaction was to wonder what the hell she was doing out of bed at such a late hour.

It was on the tip of my tongue to ask her out loud, when she spoke to me in that wonderfully melodious *('like honey poured through torn silk')* voice of hers.

> "I just want to tell you that I'm fine, Miss Dee"

…she said, and did her lips move when she spoke or did I just hear her voice inside my head? I couldn't honestly say for sure. Either way, I received her message loud and clear, and just in case I hadn't, she repeated it for my benefit;

> "You really don't need to worry about me, Miss Dee. I am absolutely fine."

I didn't say anything in response. Actually, *couldn't*, would be a whole lot more accurate. Weirdly, though, my being temporarily dumb-struck wasn't, as you might expect, due to my thinking there was anything remotely strange or unusual in Mrs Goodman suddenly appearing before me, even though I was more than aware that she had passed away the previous evening, and that her earthly remains had been shipped out to the mortuary several hours earlier.

Before I'd even reported for duty, in fact.

No. My silence was more to do with the deep sense of inner calm I felt at that moment, an almost trance-like state of serenity that served to numb my sense of grief and gladden my heart that Mrs Goodman had stopped off from the journey we all must take some day, to pay me this final visit.

And so I continued to simply sit there in awe-filled silence, staring at her watchamacallit….*spirit?* (Well, I suppose that's as good a word as any, even if it does conjure up penny dreadful images of headless horsemen or wailing banshees or chain-rattling entities doomed to walk the midnight corridors for all eternity as penance for some terrible wrong that could never be put right) until eventually, after smiling benignly, Mrs Goodman just sort of winked out of existence. Not with a slow, gradual dissolve. More like the way the screens of those old TV sets used to do when they were switched off after the *BBC* globe began spinning towards the darkness of the overnight close down.

And then I was all alone again in the corridor.

Except I wasn't.

Not really.

I cold still feel the residue of Elsie Goodman's presence, lingering in the air like an expensive perfume, and I knew then the true import of her parting gift to me: those blessed lines of faith-renewing poetry…The words that I've had cause to recollect on many occasions both happy and sad, during the years that have since slipped by with sometimes frightening ease.

"Here is waking after dreaming" indeed.

NOW THERE COMES A DARKER DAY

Death, when it came to the cities of America, chose to visit on a bright Tuesday morning in mid-September.

There was no awful, ear-blasting fanfare to herald *Its* impending arrival. No blazing comets or eerie sequence of blood-red moons. No ominous build-up of thunder-heads gathering on the distant horizon.

Instead, it crept from out of the dark shadows to plunge without warning from the flawless beauty of an Indian summer sky.

Later, many of the inhabitants of Washington, Pittsburgh, and New York, would agree that the obscenity of encountering Death beneath clear blue skies and with blades of autumn sunlight lancing between the trees, only served to intensify the horror of its calling.

That, and the mind-numbing shock that came with the realisation that the World had irrevocably changed for the worse....and that no one could ever truly feel safe, anywhere, again.

Even now, ten years on, with the benefit of (dreadful) insight, it seems hard to believe that anything as remotely terrible as the events that were to overtake us all (to some extent), in due course, could possibly have occurred in the midst of such bustling normality.

Not that anyone should ever pretend bad things never happen in America, you understand.

'The Land Of The Free' has more than its fair share of skeletons: some hanging suspended in musty-smelling closets, others lying in shallow graves, buried just beneath the semi-respectable surface.

And sometimes (and perhaps not quite so rarely as its citizens may like to think) these rattling bones will shuffle out of the imitation-oak wardrobes, or else rend the earth with claw-like fingers to emerge kicking and screaming into plain view.

Nevertheless, the supposition that mainland America would always continue to be blessedly free from any of the monumentally destructive horrors stalking the world beyond its shores had remained constant. If anything, this assumption had strengthened as the sun rose over the Eastern Seaboard on the morning of September 11th, 2001. Spirits were buoyed by the spell of glorious weather and people, whatever their age or social status, were doubtless determined to make the very best of it.

Even those who, as a rule, dreaded every second spent on the nine to five treadmill very likely walked to work with a spring in their step as they drew up plans to spend their lunch break sat around the old bandstand in Madison Square Gardens, while the boys from *The NYPD Choir* performed more than passable renditions of *Danny Boy* and *Sally MacLennane*.

Perhaps they'd simply lounge in their favourite shady retreat, losing themselves in the pages of a good book or else perch on the city's dockside, letting their feet dangle at the water's edge, as the merchant ships and ferry boats drifted down the misted river hush.

At the very least, they'd maybe told themselves that here was a golden opportunity to spend a few precious moments stuffing the cares of the everyday into some heavy-duty trunk, hidden away in the darkest recesses of their minds.

There they'd lie forgotten.

For the space of that stolen hour or two, anyway.

Who knows, maybe they'd whistled a merry tune as they entered the towering office blocks that dominate the Manhattan sky-line.

Maybe they shared a corny joke or an amusing anecdote with their colleagues as they took the lift up to the 82nd floor.

Maybe they sat at their desks, dreamy smiles lighting up their faces as they considered God was in his Blue Heaven, and all was right with the world…

Maybe.

But then Death chose to pay a visit on a bright Tuesday morning in mid-September….

*****

I guess in the years that *(hopefully)* lie ahead, just about everyone will be able to recall precisely where they were when they first heard the news of the terrible tragedy that befell the United States on September 11th, 2001.

For me, the horror began while I was round at my brother's house, having taken the afternoon off work to get into town early for the Liverpool vs Boavista Champions League tie at Anfield. It was our first game proper in the European Cup since the dreadful events at Heysel in 1985, and we were hoping to meet up with some Portuguese fans in the area around Mathew Street, to swap scarves, have a few drinks, and engage in a bit of banter (God, how incredibly trite that all sounds now).

Just before we left our Grant's house, he decided to dig out a video of *The Foo Fighters* appearance at that year's *Reading Music Festival*, and he accidentally pressed *BBC 1* on the remote.

And I trembled at the impossibility of the image that suddenly filled the screen. The Twin Towers of the World Trade Centre, instantly recognisable from countless movies and TV programmes, were aflame, smoke billowing like a cloud of blowflies, totally obscuring the sun.

The newscaster was babbling too excitedly, it was difficult to make sense of what he was trying to say. But if the live commentary was difficult to understand, the text running across the bottom of the screen made it all too clear what had happened:

'Two passenger planes have crashed into both towers of the World Trade Centre. The FBI have confirmed that this is the result of a terrorist attack. It is feared that there will be many casualties.'

The words began to blur as I felt the hot, slithery sting of tears under my eyelids, and I hoarsely begged my brother to turn the TV off.

It seems strange, looking back now, but I was suddenly anxious to get out of the house, to step into the fresh air, to set off for the match as we'd arranged. It was almost as if by refusing to acknowledge something awful beyond words had occurred, I could somehow deprive it of its reality.

This tactic proved so effective, that by the time we'd gotten off the train at James Street, I'd all but managed to convince myself that maybe things weren't quite as bad as they'd first seemed.

A few seconds after stepping into *The White Star,* a pub famous for quality of its guest cask ales, I found I was one hundred per cent correct. Things weren't quite as bad. They were a thousand times worse.

I suppose I should have realised as much the moment Grant and I stepped into the bar and were immediately hit by a heavy cloak of silence. The pub was fairly packed with men and women of all ages, and ordinarily the air would have been thick with bar-room conversation.

But not here.

Not on *this* afternoon.

Instead, the only sounds were the squeak of the hand-pumps, the re-filling of empty glasses and the sombre voice of the *CNN* anchorman as he confirmed that a third passenger plane had hit the Pentagon, causing extensive damage and serious loss of life, and that several other aircraft were unaccounted for.

"Jesus Christ, is this really happening, or is it some kind of wind-up?"

…a middle-aged man murmured incredulously as I half-whispered a couple of drinks in. I didn't bother answering. We both knew, despite the surreality of the pictures being beamed live from across the Atlantic, this was not the trailer from some big budget Hollywood blockbuster.

This was not an attack led by 15-mile-wide alien spaceships, or deadly shards of an ELE meteorite. It wasn't the destructive rampage of a 50-foot tall ape, or a 400-foot high, fire-breathing lizard. It wasn't even an ex-cop yelling *'Yippee ki-yay, motherfucker!'* as he dodges the spectacular explosions and single-handedly defeats the merciless gangsters.

And if we needed proof that this was no celluloid fantasy, it was provided in spades when first one, then the other tower of the World Trade Centre came crashing to the ground in a thick, choking cloud of dust and I was struck by the impression of a sickly, grey shadow falling across the surface of some bright and shining dream.

"Yer know what, Eddie, I'm not one for making predictions, like,"

…an old fella in a cloth cap shouted across to his mate, and I sighed wearily, knowing full well that this was the prelude to him making a prediction.

"But I wouldn't put it past that Texan balloon in the White House, to declare World War Three after this."

"Well yer'd better get the ale in quick, then,"

Eddie replied, sparking a ripple of nervous laughter.

I had to chuckle, too, but it caught fast in my throat when I found myself staring at the row of paintings that hung on the walls of the bar. Each one featured a huge ocean liner ploughing a path across turbulent seas, the *White Star* banner (after which, of course, the pub was named), fluttering proudly from every masthead.

Foremost among them, was the most famous ship of all, *The Titanic*, and the sight of that magnificent, but ultimately doomed vessel sailing unawares towards its date with destiny, caused a whole slew of nasty coincidences/correlations to go swirling through my mind at sickening speed.

We could have been standing in any pub in Liverpool city centre, but for some reason we'd chosen *The White Star*.

There was the picture on the wall of *Titanic* leaving Southampton dock, bound, for all places, New York (and incidentally, almost colliding with another liner, *The New York*, as she did so).

The date disaster struck *Titanic* was April 15th, eerily, the exact same date as another TV-relayed tragedy; Hillsborough (a nightmare experience from which my brother and I had emerged as very lucky survivors), occurred.

The fact that now, as then, we'd set out on a gloriously sunny day with the intention of supporting Liverpool FC in an 'important' football match, but had wound up instead being confronted with scenes of unimaginable horror.

And perhaps most poignantly of all, a line of dialogue that director James Cameron decided to cut from the script of his 1998 movie, *Titanic*, just before shooting began...

At the film's conclusion, Old Rose was to have admonished the entrepreneurial Brock:

> 'There's another iceberg out there, Mr Lovett.
>
> I don't know what it is...
>
> But I do know the force driving us towards it.'

On September 11th, in the space of a single Godforsaken afternoon, I guess we finally got to see both the shape of that 'iceberg' and the fanatical 'driving force' behind it, too.

****

We left *The White Star* a little after 3.30pm, just as news began to filter through that another hijacked plane was rumoured to be heading for Camp David, the US Air Force had been given orders to shoot down any suspicious aircraft and in the tinderbox that is the Middle East, Israel had put its forces on the highest possible state of alert.

We'd been sure we'd find at least some degree of respite from the ongoing atrocities in *Flanagan's Irish Bar*, at the far end of Mathew Street, but we were to be sorely mistaken.

Once again, the pub was packed, but not with the usual noisy, colourful array of both local and out-of-town Liverpool fans, mixed with a healthy smattering of foreign supporters. There were some people present who were obviously going to the match, but they stood mutely amidst the crowds of shoppers, office workers and members of the general public, staring at the huge screen that illuminated the dingy, wooden-floorboarded bar-room.

The systematic destruction of the Twin Towers was replayed over and over again for the benefit of those who hadn't yet witnessed the shocking sequence of events.

The surround sound speakers, which normally blasted out Irish folk music, instead amplified the voices of the newscasters, the discordant screaming of emergency vehicles and the wracked sobs of those desperately searching for their missing loved ones.

The only time the speakers were drowned out was during the awed mass chorus of *'Aaaaaahhhs'* (a sound reminiscent of children gazing up at the Firework Display in Mayer Park, on November 5th), every time *Sky News* showed the second plane crashing into the side of the South Tower.

I'd like to think that the murmured anti-American comments I heard from certain individuals stood nearby, were 'inspired' by a few too many pints of *Guinness* and the less-than-comforting performance of George Dubya, when giving his initial reaction to the attacks, ('We're gonna track down the *folks* responsible,' indeed!)

There's no doubt that the US President – the leader of the most powerful nation on Earth, faced with its gravest crisis since Pearl Harbour, displayed all the charisma of a rusty shoe cast up on the wind-swept New Ferry Shoreline, but I'm not at all sure if that can excuse the spiteful words issued by a couple of boneheads in their early thirties, who were stood with earshot of me and our Kid.

>'I reckon the Yanks deserve it. It's payback for Belgrade and Grenada!'

>'Yeah, and for what they're still doin' to Iraq!'

>'Oh aye. Maybe *now* they won't be so quite so 'andy backin' the IRA.'

>'Is right, lad!'

So saying, they raised their glasses as though they were toasting the unveiling of some great immutable truth, and whilst I can never claim to be any great supporter of American foreign policy, (to use one of their own beloved phrases, it more often than not, *'sucks the big one'*), to voice such sentiments at that particular moment, when thousands of innocent men, women and children had met their deaths, displayed a lack of compassion that does not exactly bode well for the future of humanity.

Sickened, we downed our pints and made our way over to quite probably the only pub in Town that didn't have a TV set. *The Grapes* is one of those classic arl Liverpool alehouses that hasn't changed a great deal in a hundred years or more. Aside from the barmaid's insistence that

>'yer can only come in if yer haven't gorrany bombs on yer!'

…there was no further references to what was unfolding in America.

It was some kind of bliss to be able to sit beneath the gaudy portrait of *Spring Heeled Jack* (cackling wildly as he leapt across the rooftops of the tiny, terraced houses on William Henry Street, where me Grandad used to live) and listening to the hits of *The Beatles* playing over and over on the news-free speakers.

I think it's fair to say I would have quite happily sat there till closing time, gotten rotten drunk, staggered home, and phoned in sick for work the following morning.

It was only the thought of not letting me other brother, Dale, and good mate, Graham, down that prevented me from doing just that. They'd forked out for the match tickets, and we'd arranged to meet them in *The Albert,* just outside the ground. Loyalty dictated that we couldn't just not turn up.

Nevertheless, it took a supreme effort of will to force ourselves out into the street to hail a cab to take us to Anfield. The conversation in the taxi was virtually non-existent. The radio was playing nothing but sad, mournful songs. The mood was as sombre as if we were heading for a funeral.

And that was precisely how it should have been.

I remember as we drove along the top of Everton Brow, I happened to glance across at the Liverpool waterfront, so eerily reminiscent of Manhattan.

It was just coming down dusk and the sunset was that achingly beautiful balance or stillness in which the sun appeared to hover like a bright orange balloon...

And, as it finally disappeared from sight behind a block of flats, I was reminded of the impermanence of things.

The way *nothing* lasts.

Even that which we value most and hold closest and dearest to our hearts.....

*****

You may not be surprised to hear that the match itself bore all the relevance of a half-arsed cabaret show at the fag-end of a seemingly endless day.

The minute's silence was, of course, perfectly observed, but both the atmosphere and the team's performance were understandably flat. For the record, the game ended in a 1:1 draw, but to be honest, the commentator on the *ITV* highlights programme summed up the mood perfectly when he said at the conclusion of the minute's silence, 'On a frightening day for the world, there follows a football match.'

I had earlier tried to convince myself that attending the game might have proven to be slightly cathartic, but in the event, I left the ground feeling as though all the bright lights in the world had been dimmed.

And it was going to take more than a mere game of footy to re-ignite them.

****

In the immediate aftermath of September 11th, amidst all the predictable cries for bloodthirsty revenge and massive retaliation, the economic meltdown, the racist attacks on innocent Muslims living in Western cities, and the obvious reluctance of anyone to board a plane, people resorted to peeking through the gap in the curtain that separates accepted reality from that which is ordinarily dismissed as being groundless superstition.

Proof, once again, that in dangerously uncertain times, even the most level-headed of persons can find themselves seeking answers to why a particular event has occurred and guidance as to what it might portend for the future, in the realms of shadowy conspiracy and the outright paranormal.

We were told, by the serried ranks of 'experts' that there may be a sharp increase in reported instances of religious phenomena, for example, the stories of the appearance of the Angels of Mons during the British Expeditionary Force's chaotic retreat in 1914, the aforementioned *Christ-in-the-Clouds* photograph shot over Korea during the 1950-53 War, and the visions of the Blessed Virgin Mary in the early '80s at Medugorje, in the former Yugoslavia, a decade or so prior to the disastrous disintegration of that country.

There may be much talk of New World Order/Illuminati conspiracies, like those proposed in the wake of the assassination of JFK and the death of Diana, Princess of Wales.

There may be much poring over passages in The Bible (especially the oft-quoted Book of Revelations), fuelling talk of Armageddon and Second Comings, Anti Christs and false prophets. Signs and portents and the ominous conjunctions of distant planets.

The media will be filled with rumours and counter-rumours and urban legends will spring up from out of nowhere (though you can bet a friend of a friend may be able to reveal to you the source).

Those who are perceived as being our enemies will be, quite literally, demonised, to the point where they become less a flesh and blood human being, more a larger than life Bogeyman, one that's more than capable of scaring the hell out of grown ups, just as well as children.

Most wars and rumours or war provide plentiful examples of most of the above.

The terrorist atrocities in the USA, however, provided plentiful examples of just about all of them.

A mere two days after the attacks, the words of that semi-redundant prophet of doom, Nostradamus, were suddenly back in fashion (the accuracy of his Quatrains had been called into question big time, after one of his few specifically dated predictions concerning July, 1999, and the appearance in the skies of *'The Great King Of Terror,'* failed miserably to come to pass – unless he was merely two years and a couple of months out in his calculations, of course.

The press were quick to make reference to a Quatrain which featured the following vision:

> *'At forty five degrees, the sky will burn.*
> *Fire approaches the new city.*
> *Garden of the world near the new city.*
> *In the path of the hollow mountains.*
> *It will be seized and plunged in the vat.'*

An academic by the name of John Hogue, who had, it seems, spent the last twenty years translating the works of Nostradamus, decided not to reveal which of the prophet's works contains this particular Quatrains, but somewhat predictably, he was more than keen to share his interpretation as to its 'true' meaning.

> 'I've always taken "hollow mountains" to mean skyscrapers. The reference to 45 degrees may well refer to New York, as it is close to the 45 degree parallel.

> 'The Garden State of the World could refer to New Jersey, known as the Garden State.'

But if you think this prediction is more than a little vague (no change there, then) you can always plump for the too-good-to-be-true outright fakes that were littering the internet, a day or so after the attacks.

> *'In the city of York, there will be a great collapse.*
> *Two twin brothers torn apart by chaos.*
> *While the fortress falls the great leader will succumb.*
> *Third big war will begin when the big city is burning.'*

Needless to say, you'd have a job trying to locate anything resembling this Quatrain in any of the books featuring the works of Nostradamus.

Nevertheless, many of the nation's bookshops soon sold out of the French seer's works, (after first digging them out of the bargain basement bins where they'd been languishing since July 1999), many people began believing that his prediction of a third Anti-Christ may well be a reference to Osama Bin Laden (the previous two being Napoleon and Adolf Hitler, one presumes).

Strangely, no one seems to be in the slightest bit interested in the fact that even if Nostradamus really could see the future, his prophecies stated that the world wouldn't actually end until 3797, so we've got the best part of another two millenniums to go before we have to worry about having our ears assaulted by the ear-blasting sounds of the Final Trumpet.

JENNY GREENTEETH
A Modern Urban Legend

The fact that I was brought up on a peninsular, surrounded as it is, on three sides by substantial bodies of water, (The Dee, The Mersey and The Irish Sea), it's perhaps no surprise that there is a high-scare factor regarding anything to do with aqueous horrors, both real and imagined.

If there was ever any danger of the central message of that infamous P.O.I. (*'Lonely Water"*), getting lost amidst the welter of nightmarish imagery, you can be sure our parents and the teachers at school drummed it in to us with all the percussive force of Animal from *'The Muppet Show'*, pounding the skins like a psychopathic octopus on PCP, from a very early age.

And the beat went something like this...

**'Children Should Be Extra Careful When Playing Near Any Stretch Of Water!
Be They Rivers, Lakes, Rock Pools, Sink Holes Or Gravel Pits!'**

Unfortunately, the message may as well have been transmitted via bush telegraph in the Yoruba language of the Niger-Congolese for all the effect it had on us danger-seeking adolescents.

Looking back, it often seems as though my friends and I spent a good three-quarters of our spare time if not actually playing *in* some potentially treacherous stretch of water, then at the very least mucking about on the only slightly less hazardous surface.

To be honest, it wasn't really like we had much of a choice in the matter, seeing as how our local childhood haunts consisted of many water-saturated sites, from the two-mile stretch of the New Ferry shoreline, the

gurgling stream that wound its way through Bromborough Woods, to the docks at the bottom end of Bolton Road East.

And most popular of all, was the large, man-made pond that had been created back in the 1940s, on the other side of the equally artificial Big Hill, directly opposite my home. This was the perfect place to relax, whether lying in the leafy shade afforded by the overhanging branches of the trees that lined the banks, skinny-dipping to cool off during the unbearably hot, strength-sapping days of high summer, or for casting out your line into the deepest part of the pool, in the hope of landing one of the monster eels that were rumoured by many to dwell hidden amidst the dark green fronds of pond weed.

And after sundown, especially on humid August evenings, when it seemed the entire world was bathed in purple twilight, gangs of bored teenagers would sometimes clamber aboard a makeshift raft (in reality little more than several planks of wood tied to a collection of rusty oil barrels), to get drunk or get high, or to screw or most likely a heady combination of all three, or sometimes, simply to indulge in the incredibly cruel pastime of inserting drinking straws into the mouths of captured frogs and toads and inflating the amphibians' bodies 'for a laugh' (that this was a hugely fashionable activity in those days was evidenced by the number of times I found several of the unfortunate creatures, floating belly-up amidst the reeds close to the banks like a bunch of mottled green balloons that had been partially inflated by a chronic asthmatic).

The water may have been heavily polluted with petroleum spills and chemical effluence and God only knew what else, but still the place held a strange and magical fascination for us kids, just the same. It was a sanctuary from the cares and woes of the everyday, a constant source of high adventure, and yes, on occasion, it was undoubtedly possessed of a rare and exquisite splendour, like when the sunlight danced across the pond's surface in bars of shimmering gold, turning the gloopy oil slicks into something hypnotically beautiful: the swirling colours of a rainbow floating on the wavelets in a gentle breeze.

Perhaps you couldn't really blame us then for paying little heed to our parents' well-intentioned advice that we steer well clear of the pond, because, as they frequently pointed out, 'The waters are deceptively deep and plagued with 'tricksy' undercurrents, as well as being filled with all manner of limb-snagging debris.'

They may as well have tried to convince us that the Loch Ness Monster was nothing more than a giant sturgeon, a weather balloon was to blame for the Roswell furore or that Bigfoot was in reality just some overweight fella in a moth-eaten ape man suit, lumbering through the backwoods of British Colombia, to scare the bejesus out of the eternally gullible, for all the effect their dire warnings had on me and my circle of friends.

It may seem more than a little weird with the considerable benefit of hindsight, but their frequent admonitions had actually carried a great deal more weight when they had resorted to the age-old method of invoking fantastical childhood monsters to get us to give The Pond a wide berth.

I remember my parents used to swear till they were blue in the face that it was well-known there was an evil spirit called Jenny Greenteeth living just below the surface of those murky depths. They took great pains to describe her as being a sinewy, fish-eyed monstrosity, with two rows of serrated teeth like a man-eating shark's, a set of jagged claws and straggly duck-weed for hair, and was an entity that constantly lay in wait, close to the banks, intent on dragging the unwary - especially young children - into the water to drown them. The Demon wouldn't physically harm them, any more than it had to in its attempts to restrain them, but would instead feast greedily upon their mortal souls by indulging in an obscene parody of a kiss.

Although I was unable to say precisely why, even before my Mum and Dad first made reference to her, Jenny Greenteeth was a name that had already seemed vaguely familiar to me. It was something that hovered on the brink of recall like the shadowy villain of some half-remembered fairy tale. I was sure I'd heard it mentioned at least once by my Grandmother, who used to love sitting in the rocking chair opposite my bed telling me stories, usually on warm spring evenings, with the heady scent of hawthorn and lavender and freshly-cut grass wafting in through the bedroom window and the sound of children's laughter merging with a blackbird's song (*'a serenade for the dying of the day,'* my Nan used to call it), making it difficult to concentrate on much of anything.

Least of all, the gentle, lullaby tones of a much-loved relative.

So when my parents began dishing out dire warnings of the underwater horror that was Jenny Greenteeth, I suppressed a shudder and immediately began making plans to find out as much as I could about the reality or otherwise, of this terrifying creature.

As it turned out, though, I didn't need to visit the Civic Centre Library or trawl through my Dad's extensive collection of books on Merseyside folklore.

I soon uncovered all the information I could handle (and a great deal more that I quite honestly couldn't), courtesy of a teller of tales so tall they floated on the edge of one's credulity like wispy clouds gathered at the peaks of snow-capped mountains.....

ONE

From the 'magical ages' of ten to thirteen, another of my friends' favourite 'hang-outs' were the couple of miles or so of dockland that once stretched across the borders of the villages of Bromborough and Port Sunlight.

Though they have long since fallen into disuse these days, back in the late 1970s, the docks were still in full working order, and were frequently filled to capacity with oil tankers and merchant ships, Royal Navy frigates and ocean liners, their sterns emblazoned with unfamiliar flags and the painted names of impossibly exotic ports of origin. There was a row of large warehouses lining the far side of the harbour and a fenced off scrap yard where various items of rusted equipment had been dumped over the course of many years. There were literally hundreds of old hollow pipes and abandoned goods containers, with clusters of white barnacles still attached to them, giant wooden wheels that brought to mind pictures I'd seen in history books of the huge battering rams used in the epic sieges of magnificent walled cities, and anchors and pulleys and lengths of metal coil that smelled of ocean fog and long-dead fish and bitter, salty brine. These discarded nautical objects were surrounded by swathes of high grass, the stalks of which closely resembled bamboo, and provided ideal cover for secret dens and club-houses, or private places where you could sit off when you needed a couple of hours in order to set your world to rights.

It was the perfect location for cultivating your more outlandish dreams, too. I used to while away many a summer afternoon fantasising about stowing away on one of the ships and sailing to far-off lands – the kind I'd only ever read about in *National Geographic* or seen in TV documentaries.

These imaginings would be further coloured by the sound of swarthy-looking crew members speaking in harsh foreign languages that were frighteningly alien, but at the same time, strangely alluring - their voices carrying on the ever-present river breeze. People of widely different nationalities were constantly working on the dockside, too, unloading the goods that had been imported from across Europe, the Americas and Equatorial Africa, or repairing damage to the hulls of ships tied to the quayside with lengths of rope twice the length of an elephant's thigh.

On occasion, long after sundown, we'd see scantily-clad, middle-aged women with thick Scouse accents staggering down a ship's gangplanks in ridiculously high heels and mini-skirts with hard-looking faces caked in make-up that looked like it had been applied with a trowel by a short-sighted brickie. We'd sometimes ask the security guards who patrolled the dock-side what the women had been up to, and they'd exchange knowing glances and smile slyly, before telling us half-heartedly to get home to our parents, it was way past our bedtime.

As a rule though, both the smartly-uniformed guards and the various people who worked at the docks were fairly tolerant of our trespassing, even if they never actively engaged us in conversation.

There was however one particular worker, who was to prove something of a *big* exception to the rule.

'Panama Jack,' (we never found out his *real* name, or indeed, ever thought to ask – it just didn't seem important back then), was an arc welder in his late thirties, who was supposed to be applying his skills to the various vessels that came into the docks for repairs. In truth though, he seemed to spend most of his time with his arse cheeks parked either side of one of the bollards at the quayside, smoking a sailor's pipe, with a hip flask close to hand and a far-away look in his eyes. If you sought to engage him in conversation however, he'd gab away merrily to anyone willing to listen, as my friends and I quickly discovered not long after we first made his acquaintance a year or so before the recounting of this urban legend takes place. The spring of 1977, that would have been. The year of the Queen's Silver Jubilee, the wonderful *Sex Pistols* rise to nationwide notoriety and Liverpool FC's bid for a then unprecedented treble.

We could tell straight away that Jack was something of a unique character. He constantly wore a thick black overcoat, even on the very hottest of days, and a battered sailor's cap with a semi-transparent plastic peak that turned his face lime green when the sun slanted through it at certain angles and was so cheap and tacky-looking he could well have bought it at any fancy dress store or one of those seaside resort souvenir stalls. He had a tanned and prematurely grizzled face lined with grey stubble, but there was a noticeable twinkle in his eyes when he launched into one of his extraordinary sagas. He had the gift of telling tales with the intimate grace of a confidant, ensuring that each one resonated with the enduring power of an ancient fable.

He told us he'd sailed the seven seas many times over during the course of his life and had experienced many adventures, some more believable than others. He claimed to have spent his early twenties working on whaling ships off the coast of Newfoundland, and on one memorable occasion had fought a cetacean of such leviathan-like proportions, it would have given Captain Ahab second thoughts about spending a lifetime hunting it down, and never mind if that particular whale had succeeded in chomping off *both* of his legs.

He'd also been shipwrecked on an impossibly sun-drenched tropical island in the midst of the freezing wastes of the Antarctic, had once sighted a long-necked sea monster off the Cape of Good Hope, and had his merchant navy vessel attacked by a giant squid, (*'a descendant of the famous Kraken, I tell yer! And may God strike me down if I tell a lie!)* as well as narrowly escaping a tribe of head-hunters while sailing down The Amazon and being besieged by the death-dealing tendrils of intelligent seaweed in the midst of the Sargasso Sea.

To say these fantastic stories had a decidedly flimsy foundation in hard fact is like saying finding blood in your urine is one of the least amusing discoveries you can make whilst paying a visit to the bathroom.

One of my friends, Philly Bennet, made no secret of the fact that he strongly suspected *'Panama Jack'* hadn't been any further abroad than the Isle of Man (and even *that* he declared, was highly debatable). He used to be fond of saying with a level of derisory cynicism that belied his tender years:

> 'I'm surprised he's never been pulled over by the friggin' Authenticity Police'

But none of us, not even Philly, could deny he told great stories….The kind that held you enraptured no matter what level of credence you chose to afford them.

And one of the most memorable of these yarns concerned the supposedly mythical creature that our parents had warned us about since time immemorial.

Jenny Greenteeth.

TWO

Many years ago, when I was in my mid-teens, (this would be back in the late 1950s, if you really want to know), my best friend was a tall, gawky lad named Michael Kavanagh. He used to live in one of those massive big posh houses over in Rock Park, the large Victorian villas that were once owned by shipping magnates and the like, and have since all been converted into luxury communal flats.

Mikey's dad was a managing director at *Lever Brother's* Soap Factory in Port Sunlight at the time, and the family lived at number 26, the former address of the great American author, Nathaniel Hawthorne. Any of you kids ever heard of him? He lived here on Merseyside for four years between 1853 to 1857, and was the American consul to Liverpool. He genuinely loved the area and wrote extensively about The City and its environs. You really should check out some of Hawthorne's novels, though. *The Scarlet Letter* is good. *The House Of The Seven Gables* is even better.

Anyway, I suppose it's fair to say Mikey and I were pretty much inseparable, back then, (not that we didn't fancy girls, or anything. I mean, we might not have been as wildly successful with the ladies as we sometimes liked to brag, but no one could accuse us of being camper than Oscar Wilde standing in the middle of a tent shop, either), and we seemed to spend all of our days acting out the time-worn rituals of boys our age: playing football, getting into various scrapes with the law and gangs of local street urchins, or skulking in the shadow-filled nooks of *The Admiral Hotel,* down by the old Rock Ferry Pier, chugging on the dregs of abandoned pints and half-empty bottles of lukewarm *Higson's Bitter,* seeing as how it would be another couple of years before we'd be able to legally purchase alcohol.

Things may have changed behind the doors of our old local over the years, and God knows, not all of those changes have been for the better, but *The Admiral* was just about the closest thing to paradise we knew, back then. It was full of local characters who would invariably wind up beating the crap out of each other (for no reason that anyone half-way sober could discern), mid-way through the night, only to shake hands, embrace each other, and raise their voices in joyful song an hour or two before closing time, before the whole rigmarole would be repeated the following evening.

Mikey and I used to love nothing better than hanging out there, especially on warm, summer nights when we'd eye up the fit, but hard as nails, barmaids and play endless games of pool or darts whilst Buddy Holly and Jerry Lee Lewis blasted from the boss-sounding jukebox. There'd be outdoor barbecues held in the beer garden on public holidays, and a massive bonfire and firework display every November 5th, and whatever the season, or time of day, you could gaze out across the Mersey at the Liverpool waterfront with a drink in your hand and a dream in your heart and, for the space of a few hours at least, not a single care in the world.

Aye, they were magical times, alright. And you prayed they'd last forever, even though you knew they were always doomed to pass you by in what seemed like the single blink of an eyelid.

And in this case, the catalyst for change was the tragic death of Mikey's brother, Joe.

He drowned in the artificial pond on the other side of The Big Hill. The one down by the entrance to the sewerage plant. You know it, surely? Of course you do. You've probably played there more times than I've had hot dinners. Well anyway, it seems that one freezing winter's afternoon, Mikey and his 12-year-old brother had been messing around, skating on the surface of The Pond, when suddenly the ice had cracked and Joe fell in the water and either froze to death or drowned, depending on which version of the story you happen to hear, and who's doing the talking.

Mikey's family were heartbroken, of course, and it was really no surprise when my friend came to tell me his parents simply couldn't handle living in Rock Ferry anymore. The welter of bad memories haunted both their dreams and a large portion of their waking hours, and two months after Joe's fatal accident, Mikey and his parents moved down south to live with some relatives in far-off Cornwall.

We lost touch, despite the usual promises to stay in touch. We wrote to each other religiously at first, but once I was old enough to join the merchant navy, I found myself engaged in month-long sailing trips to the likes of Puerto Rico, the Florida Keys, Rio de Janeiro, you name it. I'd send him postcards and I'd get the odd phone call in return whenever I got shore leave. But gradually, it reached the point where we didn't even bother to send each other Christmas cards. It's kind of soul-destroying when that happens, but I suppose that even the very closest of relationships can be shattered irreparably by the gulf of distance and the cruel passing of time.

I got on with my life, and I didn't expect I'd ever see Mikey again.

But it turned out I was wrong about that.

Which brings me rather neatly to that which I *really* want to tell you kids about.

An unexpected encounter that took place twenty odd years farther down the line from those halcyon days of youth....

THREE

One drizzly, wind-swept Saturday evening, last September, I was busy propping up the bar at *The Admiral*, staring into my beer glass like I could somehow discern the answer to life's great mysteries by reading the dreamily rising gas bubbles.

I'd not long returned from a three-month stint working as part of the North Sea fishing fleet, one of the hardest jobs I've ever had, and Lord knows that's saying something. It used to put the fear of God into me every time I stumbled aboard that flimsy-looking trawler, knowing that just a few short moments after sailing from the blessed safety of the harbour, I'd be cast upon seas so awe-inspiringly mountainous, they made those described in Poe's novella *Maelstrom* look like tiny breeze-blown ripples on the surface of a puddle.

Anyway, there I was, gazing at my drink like it was a source of great wonderment, when suddenly, the bar room door had slammed open with a fair degree of violence, and what could only be described as a huge 'meathead' sauntered in like he just about owned the place. As he made his way across the un-carpeted floor, I saw he had the obligatory *'Love'* and *'Hate'* tattooed on his knuckles, and for extra added hardness, the letters looked as though they had been carved with the point of an ink-soaked compass. His short, buzz-haircut was literally dripping with 'Vitalis.' There was a virtual roadmap of jagged scars criss-crossing his scowling face and his nose looked to have been broken in several places, and though he might have been in possession of a wobbling beer gut that hung over the belt of his too-tight jeans like a water-filled party balloon, his arms were bulging with muscles the size of bowling balls and to say he looked like the sort of hard-case you really wouldn't want to mess with would be the biggest understatement since Robert Shaw's character in *Jaws* announced mid-way through the film, 'I think we're gonna need a bigger boat!'

And 'Mr Meathead' certainly didn't do anything to dispel this unsavoury impression.

When he was roughly half-way across the room, he suddenly bellowed at the bar-man:

> "Eh, lad. It's half past eight! I've only just got up! I'm spitting feathers! Pour me a fuckin' bevvy or I'll rip yer fuckin' head off!"

He jabbed a finger in the general direction of the hand pump emblazoned with the name of that week's guest ale, and the pub went so deathly quiet you could have heard a pint drop. It was like a scene from one of those Saturday afternoon Westerns they used to show on BBC 2, for all those people who weren't remotely interested in sport, and I watched this mini-drama unfold with a mixture of bemusement and aching nostalgia.

The bar-man, Johnny Oates, a sixty-seven-year-old, with a face more wrinkled than an ancient bloodhound, and who was no more of a 'lad' than I was related to the Dalai Llama, put his hands up in a calming gesture and said, reasonably enough,

> "Alright, mate, there's no need for that!"

Somewhat predictably though, such placatory measures were wasted on this particular revolutionary throwback.

> "Just pour me a fuckin' bevvy!"

…he snarled, actually baring his teeth like a viciously rabid dog, and I noticed Johnny's hands were visibly shaking as he poured him a pint of *'Castle Eden.'*

Mr Meathead threw it down in a three massive gulps without spilling a drop.

> "Now pour me another fuckin' bevvy!"

…he roared slamming the empty glass down on the bar, and this time Johnny complied without comment.

He snatched the drink in his right hand the second Johnny had finished pouring it, but Mr Meathead only sipped at his drink this time, leaving behind a frothy white moustache in the process, before stomping over to the darkest corner of the bar, where he sat himself down at a glass-less table glowering at the regulars as if daring them to say anything remotely out of line.

No one present dared too, of course.

Something had very obviously served to put Mr M in a foul, stinking mood, and no one had any desire to risk incurring his wrath further by gawping at him like he was some dangerous zoological exhibit (even though some suicidal part of me kept wanting to stare, just the same).

Once it became apparent that the excitement had, for the moment at least, died down, the ordinary hub of bar-room conversation gradually filled the room once more, and I'd been just about to return to my scientific studies of the contents of my glass, when the front door suddenly burst open for the second time in the last five minutes.

And in stepped a ghost from my distant past.

To my great surprise, I saw it was my old friend Michael Kavanagh, who I hadn't seen in over twenty years or more, and who as I said earlier, I quite honestly never expected to encounter again during my lifetime.

In truth though, I had to do a triple take as Mikey trudged towards me looking dog-tired and terribly dishevelled, because I barely recognised him. His face was deeply lined, his shoulders stooped as though they were bowed with the weight of some impossible burden, and what little hair he had left was a blinding shade of pure snow-white. But I suppose when you've grown up with someone and spent most of your formative years in that person's company, you can quickly put a name to their face, no matter how dramatic the changes in their physical appearance.

Mikey didn't acknowledge my presence, or anyone else's for that matter, until he'd pulled up a rickety-looking barstool and plonked himself upon it with all the grace of a shot albatross. Then, in a voice that was a barely audible mumble, he ordered a neat double whisky and threw it down like Dr Jekyll frantically gulping one of his bubbling potions, eager to unleash the evil alter-ego within.

> "That's no way to treat a fine single malt!"

I muttered in Kit-Carson-esque tones of admonishment.

> "Drinkin' it that way is considered to be damn near sacrilegious in the dese here parts!"

Mikey swivelled towards me, the scowl on his face gradually softening as the light of recognition dawned in his eyes.

> "My God, Jack!"

…he cried, clapping me on the shoulder.

> "Panama Jack, as I live and breathe!"

He stuck out his hand, which I couldn't help noticing was shaking like a man with a bad case of the DTs although his grip was firm enough.

"How the hell are you?"

"All the better for seeing you,"

I told him, surprised to suddenly find myself on the brink of tears.

"I can't believe you're actually here in our old stomping ground. Not after all these years."

I quickly called Johnny Oates over and ordered us a couple more *Laphoraig's,* and drank to our health and the good fortune that had brought two old and trusted companions together against all the odds and the capricious whims of fate.

"Of all the bars in all the world, it had to be *The Admiral!*"

Mike declared in a rough approximation of Bogey's famous line from *Casablanca,* raising his glass again as he did so.

"It's just like old times, eh, Jack,"

…he said and I heartily agreed, even though I think we both knew that this rainy, late September evening was about as far removed from the golden, blue-skied summers of our youth as it was possible to get.

It was hugely rewarding though to engage in bouts of carefree conversation and, if you'll kindly pardon the rather glib analogy, cast ourselves adrift on a sea of reminiscences for the space of a few precious hours. And who knows, we may well have waffled away merrily like that until Johnny rang the bell at closing time, if I hadn't finally given voice to the question I'd been burning to ask Mikey the moment he'd entered the bar.

"So me old mucker, what brings you back to Rock Ferry, then?"

For an endless moment I didn't think he was going to answer. There was a noticeable souring of the atmosphere. A darkening of the mood, and I silently wished I'd kept my big trap shut.

Eventually though, Mikey leaned back and withdrew his wallet emptying its contents onto the beer-stained bar top. Ignoring the wad of bank notes and loose change, the credit cards and the old ticket stubs, he held up a crumpled black and white photograph of a gawky, nine-year-old boy sporting wire-rimmed glasses and a Teddy Boy's quiff. The boy was grinning as he hugged a Border collie that was nearly twice as big as he was; the carefree joy of the moment caught in eternal freeze-frame.

I could see immediately it was a picture of Mikey's kid brother, Joe, snapped at a Christmas party the year before he'd died.

Joe…

Who I knew from what Mike had once told me (his face flustered with rage and exasperation) had drawn a big, black moustache on his favourite Dixie Dean poster, laced his tea with half a dozen laxatives and cut up his precious collection of *Eagle* comics for a laugh.

Joe…

Who'd also, on one 'memorable' occasion, used Mike's Rock'n'Roll records as impromptu Frisbees *('they couldn't half fly! Especially them Elvis ones!'*') and swore blind to Karen Smedley, she of the buck-teeth and terminal acne that his older brother fancied her like mad.

Joe...

Who'd selflessly piled in to help his older brother, when the Harvey Gang had jumped him on the way home from school, had emptied his savings jar after he's accidentally spilled black paint all over Mike's blue suede shoes to pay to get them repaired, and had placed a Kop ticket for a Liverpool v Everton Derby match inside a *Get-Well Soon* card when Mike had been ill in bed suffering from a mild case of glandular fever.

Joe...

Now lying in a coffin beneath the iron-hard, sugar-frosted earth of Landican Cemetery, dead these past twenty years.

There would be no more tricks or practical jokes.

No more heart-warming examples of brotherly love.

Only a tiny plot of land, riddled with hopelessness and broken dreams, beneath the cold, black emptiness of a starless winter sky.

Joe...

*****

> "For the last two decades, I'd somehow managed to convince myself that I wouldn't ever have to return to Rock Ferry,"

Mikey stated, shaking his head wearily.

> "...and I would've laughed long and loud in the face of anyone who'd even suggested it as a possibility. Wild horses couldn't drag me back my birthplace,"

I remember telling a bunch of half-carted business associates at the fag end of a dinner party. "Here's to a future of glorious potentialities!" And everybody cheered, and raised their glasses, and even though I was totally smashed, I'd certainly *meant* what I'd said.

But in the end, herds of horses, wild or otherwise, hadn't been required.

> "Oh God, Jack",

...he said, as a wet tear rolled down to rest on his cheek like a tiny glass globe.

> "I miss him so much. Even after all this time."

He turned to face me and my heart went out to him at that moment. There was nothing I could say or do, though, except mumble a few standard banalities about how he had my deepest sympathies and that at least his brother was in a better place now...

> "Is that right?"

...he snapped bitterly.

"You *really* think so, do yer?'

He wiped his eyes on his sleeve.

"Oh aye, that's what everyone tells me, from the do-gooder counsellors and the parish priest, to my know-it-all workmates down south, but you know what, Jack? none of them have got a friggin' clue!"

"Alright Mike",

I said taken aback by this.

"I don't blame you for being a bit cynical, but…."

"Just take a really good look at that,"

…he said sliding the photograph along the bar.

"Tell me what you think."

I picked it up and saw that attached to the back of the Polaroid with a paper clip was a small newspaper article that had been cut from a three-month-old edition of *The Guardian*. It bore the stark and simple headline:

'Youngster Tragically Drowns In Gravel Pit '

'The grieving parents of nine-year-old Richard Williams, spoke yesterday of their loss after their son tragically drowned in a gravel pit, less than half a mile from their home..

'The couple, from Tranmere, Merseyside, spoke of how their son was out playing with a group of his friends on a patch of of derelict wasteland when he apparently slipped and fell into the water whilst trying to retrieve a frisbee that had been caught in a freak gust of wind.

His body was recovered by labourers who were working on a nearby building site, but despite their best efforts, they were unable to resuscitate him.

"We always warned Richie to stay away from the pool," his mother, Mrs Anne Williams, told reporters, 'It looks harmlessly shallow, but it's actually very deep and the water's freezing, even at this time of year, and is nothing short of a potential death trap, especially for young children."

"I can only hope other parents learn from our awful experience" she added. "Please make sure your kids stay away from ponds and gravel pits, unless they are accompanied by an adult. I wouldn't want anyone else to be subjected to what we've had to go through. Honestly, it's been a living hell!"

The tragedy has increased calls for the waste-ground to be properly cordoned off to prevent children from playing in the area.

Of course, I'd heard about this terrible incident. It was featured on the radio news and there was a fair-sized piece in *The Liverpool Echo*, and as it only occurred a couple of miles or so away, you kids probably know of at least one person who knew the dead boy or members of his family.' I still didn't understand why Mikey had the clipping pinned to the back of his brother's Christmas photo, though. That didn't make sense to me at all, and I said as much.

"Why are you carrying that round with you, Mike?"

I asked shaking my head,

"It's a bit morbid, isn't it? I mean, after what happened to Joe and all...."

"Oh, the answer's quite simple really, Jack,"

...he responded.

"When I first came across this story, last July, it knocked me for six, and not just because of the obvious similarities between Joe, and this latest kid's death." He shrugged his shoulders. "Children drown in accidents all the time, sad to say, and if it was something that straight forward, I would have been commuting between Cornwall and Rock Ferry as often as I could, these past 20 years."

"'Then what the hell was it?"

"The triggering of a memory,"

...he replied.

"A long-forgotten something I'd buried away deep inside the shadowy realm of my subconscious."

Mikey paused to take a more considered sip of his malt before continuing.

"It might seem hard to believe, but that tiny article, tucked away at the bottom of the newspaper page like an afterthought, was all it took to release those suppressed memories like a Biblical flood or the Aswan Dam suddenly bursting."

"I still don't know what you're talking about,"

I said, honestly bemused, and not a little frightened by the fanatical expression that had suddenly appeared on my friend's face.

"Let me spell it out for you, then. I'd all but blocked out the images of that awful day when Joe died, probably due to the level of shock I'd suffered. My mind's defensive mechanisms had kicked in during the immediate aftermath, to shield me from the horrors. But now I find I can recall *everything* that happened with total clarity. Although I wish to God that it wasn't so."

I opened my mouth to speak again, to tell him to please shut up, most likely, because I didn't really care for the way the conversation was going.

But before I could say a word, he leaned forward, stared at me intently with his haunted, bloodshot eyes, and described what had really happened to his brother on that freezing February afternoon....

FOUR

" A Sunday afternoon in the bleak heart of winter...

The trees were leafless and claw-like against a roseate sky. A thin layer of frost hardened the ground and sugared the lawns and fields. The very air felt brittle, ready to shatter into a million pieces at the snap of a branch in the stillness of a wildwood, a bird tapping its beak against thick, sheeted ice, or braying laughter that sounds uncomfortably close to a scream.

Stillness...

Sheeted ice...

Laughter...

And the old weed-choked pond behind the abandoned army storage depot not five minutes walk from our home.

It was the one place our parents officially listed as being off-limits as Joe and I left the house around noon, burdened by their time-worn admonishments and the sheer bulk of our thick winter clothing.

'I want you both in before dark. And I don't want either of youse even toying with the idea of going skating on that pond,' Dad told us in his familiar 'I Will-Brook-No-Argument' voice. 'The ice might not be anywhere near as firm as it looks, and it might not take yer weight if you wander out onto it, so steer well clear, alright!'

Of course, we both of us promised we wouldn't go within a mile of the old pond, and who knows, maybe we even meant it. We were good kids, and we didn't much hold with breaking promises, if we could at all help it. But the fact of the matter is we were just that: kids (well, actually, I'd just turned seventeen, but I was still a child at heart, and if I wasn't hanging round with you, Jack, I always enjoyed spending some quality time with my younger brother, especially on a bitterly cold, mid-winter's day, when it seemed like everyone else in the world was safely indoors, curled up on their sofas before a roaring coal fire, with their heads buried in a book or glued to their tiny black and white TV sets). And though the two of us spent most of the day trying to scrape together enough of the thinly scattered snow to build something half-way resembling a snowman, or taking turns to sledge down Eccleshall Road (nearly colliding with old Mrs Fosdyke, as she stepped outside her front garden gate), somehow or other, whether by accident or design, here we were standing on the banks of the forbidden pond, with scarcely an hour of daylight left in the pink-hued sky.

We stood in silence for a single endless moment.

Neither of us spoke.

Neither of us moved.

We merely stared in wonderment at the expanse of frozen water, and it's almost as if we both knew exactly what the other was thinking, Our Dad's warnings seemed like a groundless over-reaction. Okay, so we were, technically speaking, trespassing on private property. We had clambered through a hole in the wire mesh perimeter fence, cut by the infamous Harvey Gang the previous summer, but every kid in the area knew about it and no one, not even the local council, had bothered their arses to repair the damage, so surely we weren't doing any real harm by being here. And if that was the case, then it couldn't hurt if we were to take a quick, flittering skate over the smooth, solid-seeming surface of the pond below them.

There was nothing to fear here.

Just the opposite, in fact.

In the end, the temptation proved too great.

We stepped on to the ice with a guileless innocence that would perhaps have been touching in other circumstances.

Time quickly ceased to have any meaning once the pair of us began slipping and sliding across the glass-like surface, our whoops of excitement ringing through the trees and bouncing off the virgin ice. We were lost to the simple pleasures of what amounted to child's play, when the concerns and worries that go hand-in-hand with the painful day-to-day business of growing up are cast aside, like an unwanted item of clothing. We failed, therefore, to notice the ever-lengthening shadows, the pools of darkness that quickly surrounded us like a seeping, pitch-black tide.

It was only when the gloom became so apparent that we realised we couldn't see any further than the white edges of the pond, and the topmost branches of the winter-naked trees, and we suddenly paused for a second.

And, it seemed, everything else paused right along with us.

The air was preternaturally still. There was not the slightest breath of wind, and all was silent save for the call of a marsh bird somewhere deep within the midst of the reeds – an achingly haunting sound that carried on the brittle air.

I felt struck by a strange sense of lonesome melancholy, and it took a real effort to shake it off.

'Okay, Joe, I suppose we'd better start heading home,' I said, struggling to keep my voice light. I didn't want to alarm my brother, but I felt like a weary driver who's fallen asleep at the wheel and had awoken just in time to prevent a devastating accident.

I could not identify the precise cause of the coiled knot of dread that formed in the pit of my stomach, but I strongly suspected that it might have at least something to do with the fact that our parents would likely throw a king-size dicky-fit and kick our arses all the way to West Kirkby and back, the minute we set foot through the front door. We were late, and neither of us could lie to save our lives.

I was sure that Joe, despite his tender years, was more than aware of the sorry fate that awaited us, but all he could say out loud was, 'Yeah, Mum and Dad will be getting worried, won't they?'

He shuffled towards me, but I'd already turned my back, as anxious to be away from this place as I'd earlier been excited by the prospect of messing around here.

Suddenly, and without warning, there was a loud crack that echoed like a pistol shot, shattering the heavy silence, and I swivelled round to see my brother lying sprawled face-down on the ice.

Joe cried out more in surprise than any real degree of pain and then, incredibly, he was laughing at his own clumsiness and for a moment, relief swept over me, and I began to giggle myself.

But then, the ice split apart, and a gaping rent, like the hungry mouth of some giant Arctic beast, opened up directly beneath Joe's legs. Almost immediately, another fissure snaked a jagged path a few inches in front of him, the ice floe upon which he lay broke away and then began tipping slightly. 'Before he had time to react, my brother began to slide backwards at a frightening speed. He tried vainly to grab some purchase on the too-slick ice, and his fingernails rasped and raked, a sound like something equipped with razor-sharp talons scratching at a frosted window in the dead of night

'Help meeeeee, Mikey!' he screamed, and I shook off the shock-induced paralysis and began to skate the 30 feet or so distance between us as fast as I could.

I realised straight away, I wasn't going to make it. Even as I flung myself full length across the ice in a desperate attempt to grab hold of Joe's hand, I knew it was too late, and as the force of my own momentum carried me forwards to the very lip of the fissure, I saw Joe slip into the bitterly cold water and begin thrashing wildly.

My brother wasn't a particularly strong swimmer, but he could still swim (we'd both had compulsory lessons at school and had been the local open-air baths in New Ferry, on many occasions the previous summer). I tried to keep the rapidly rising panic out of my voice as I shouted for Joe to stop struggling and to try and swim for it. I knew that he wouldn't likely survive for long in those sub-zero temperatures, but I remained hopeful that if Joe could somehow manage to regain his composure sufficiently enough to doggy-paddle just a few short feet in my direction, I'd be able to haul him to safety.

But Joe appeared to be gripped by blind terror and before too long I knew I had no choice but to jump in myself.

I was preparing to do just that when he was suddenly swallowed up whole by the inky-black waters, and disappeared from view.

He didn't resurface.

I didn't waste another second.

I dove straight in.

The shock of the biting cold immediately seeped into my bones, first stinging, then turning my entire body numb. It took a supreme effort of will to for me to submerge and begin searching for Joe. But after gasping in a great lungful of air, I ducked my head under and started frantically looking this way and that.

Although the pond was entirely artificial in its construction, it was choked with tangled weeds and a variety of cloying algae. It was also heavily polluted with foul-tasting effluents and a thick, black viscous substance, most likely a chemical spill from one of the local factories, lines the bottom.

Visibility then, is not good at the best of times, but with the dusk coming down fast it was all but impossible to see your hand in front your face. Despite the level of contamination, the pond remains fairly well-stocked with several species of fish, and crazily, I found myself remembering how one of my friends at school, a keen angler named Andy Boyce, had told me that he'd once caught an eel in here that was fully 12 feet long. He'd described its wormy body as being a sickly pale-white colour, and it had blind albino eyes and a set of barbed teeth that looked like they could easily tear a grown man to pieces.

I hadn't been sure I'd truly believed Andy, back then. But at that moment, immersed in the icy waters of the pond, it was far too easy to imagine all kinds of unnameable horrors lurking in the gloom of those seemingly bottomless depths.

And when, at that precise moment, something touched my leg, I almost screamed my way to the surface. Only the grim determination to find my brother kept me from doing so.

Eventually, however, I was forced up to breathe.

By now I was so cold I was barely conscious, and a feeling of detachment, of dreamlike unreality, began to wash over me.

This feeling was further enhanced by the sight that confronted me, immediately that I broke the surface.

Over by the reeds, on the far side of the pond, forty odd feet away, I saw there was another hole in the ice. And in its centre, Joe's body lay floating on its back. Even accounting for the rapidly fading half-light, I could see that his face was a pallid shade of blue and that his eyes were staring sightlessly up at a sky laced with the first smattering of stars.

I could also plainly see that Joe was dead.

Faced for the first time in my fifteen years with the awful, irrevocable finality of death, I was totally unable to accept that which I was seeing. Instead, I simply stared, uncomprehending, the way a jungle native might regard his first sight of an aeroplane. My mind retreated within itself when faced with such an apparent absurdity.

And in less time than it took to muster up a scream, the world tilted further into surreality and I entered the realm of the completely insane.

There was a sudden, violent commotion, and something from a nightmare surfaced alongside Joe.

It appeared so fast that I didn't even have time to notice its presence. All that I could do was watch as a hideous, vaguely female form slowly reared itself up out of the water, clutching at my brother's body as if it were a piece of flotsam. It remained in that position for a while, then it turned and glanced in my direction, regarding me with eyes that were cold and unfeeling, and though I knew that I simply must be suffering from a trauma-induced hallucination, that the thing before me couldn't possibly be real, I found I could nevertheless see, with a ghastly clarity, every detail of it just the same: the mottled skin glowing with a soft green, phosphorescence, like a poisonous fungus in the wild-wood after dark. The white bone that peered through an ugly gash in its forehead, the straggly hair, matted with pondweed, draped across a pair of sinewy shoulders.

The blade-like claws.

The wormy lips.

And when the thing opened its mouth, revealing three rows of serrated teeth, the awful stench of its breath wafted across the distance between us. It smelled of mud and decay and of things that dwell in sunless places.

It was this last that got me moving. A sort of dreamy terror had floated into the hollows of my body, paralysing me up until that moment. Mewling and gasping, as the thing grinned at me from beside Joe's lifeless body, I began furiously scrabbling at the ice at the edge of the fissure, in a desperate bid to haul myself out of the water.

My efforts proved to be every bit as futile as those of my brother, however. The surface was as smooth as polished glass and my fingers were so numbed with cold, they no longer felt a part of me. Still, I redoubled my efforts and emitted a thin, high scream when I heard the sound of wet, slapping feet squelching slowly across the ice towards me. The smell became almost over-powering, and now it reeked of spoiled meat, flyblown and rancid and though I flatly refused to glance behind me, still I knew it was almost within touching distance. This was confirmed when I felt its hot breath on the back of my neck. And the sound of those lethal-looking jaws snapping shut like a hunter's trap.

I shrieked loudly for my mother in hopeless desperation, the way we do when the bones of our deepest fears are laid bare, free to be picked over by the gibbering horrors that lie waiting, secret in the dark. And though I knew my mum was likely to be sitting at home at that moment, alternately casting worried glances at the clock on the mantelpiece and my increasingly anxious father, I went right on yelling for her anyway, and as I did so, something happened that later, I honestly struggled to explain, even to myself.

My arms were thrashing wildly about, no longer seeking to gain a purchase, but still somehow, I manage to find one regardless, almost as if it had been there all along. Not only that, but the feeling quickly returned to my frozen hands. I could actually sense the blood rushing in an unstoppable torrent from my veins to my fingertips with not the slightest hint of pins and needles, and after securing a grip on the ice and employing a new-found strength, I heaved myself clear of the water.

Half-expecting at any moment that a pair of hooked and twisted claws would reach out and drag me back into the freezing waters, I managed to struggle to my feet, skate crazily across the ice and scramble up the snow-covered slope that led down to the pond.

I didn't stop when I reached the top. Nor did I once look back to check and see if the thing was following. I simply ran in a blind panic, scarcely aware of the direction I was taking, my feet pounding the frosted earth like pistons, as if they had a mechanical will of their own, and maybe it was instinct, maybe it was sheer luck, maybe it was the worldly-wise voice of "Jiminy Cricket" singing in my ear, whatever, something guided me to the hole in the fence; a magical portal that led me to Land Of The Righteous And Sane. I virtually threw myself through the opening, and charged headlong across the empty playing fields, and didn't stop until I reached the brightly-lit car park at the top of Corniche Road.

It's doubtful whether I would have stopped running, even at that point, if it hadn't have been for the unwitting intervention of Steven Horton. The old man had his head buried beneath the hood of his battered car, fiddling around with the engine, when I came hurtling around the corner and, choosing that precise moment to dare to sneak a glance behind me (just in case that unholy Thing had followed me across the footy pitches), slammed into Mr Horton's back, very nearly knocking the unfortunate man face-first into the tangled mass of gears and wires.

'What the hell?' Mr Horton yelled, swivelling round with a speed that was quite surprising for a man his age. I think he was about to give me a right mouthful, maybe launch into a lecture about the impetuosity of youth, and of how children had respect for their elders in his day, but the words died on his lips when he caught the look of sheer terror I imagined was etched on my face. He later told his wife he had only ever been confronted with such a sense of panic-stricken helplessness once before in his life, and that he'd long prayed he would never see it again. It was exactly the same expression as that worn by his best friend, a second or so before their commanding officer had raised his whistle to his lips to signal they were about to go over the top on the first day of the Battle of the Somme. The same best friend who had been blown to pieces by a German artillery shell before he'd taken more than a couple of paces into the blasted hell of No-Man's Land.

'What's wrong, lad?' he shouted, his voice heavy with concern. 'What's happened? Are you alright?'

I could only whimper softly and cover my face with my hands. And when the old man reached out to place a comforting hand on my shoulder, I screamed and screamed, and the sound of it echoed in the February air like a note of long-lost hope…

FIVE

I've got to be honest, and say that in normal circumstances, I would have readily dismissed Mikey's story as being nothing more than the wild-eyed ravings of someone driven to the brink of lunacy by grief and irretrievable loss. His tale was so fantastic that certainly no one could have blamed me if I'd done so.

But there was something about the way he narrated the events which proved to me that he plainly believed it all to be completely true, to the extent where it bade me pause in my scepticism, at least until I'd heard everything he had to say.

Even if "everything he had to say", sounded like the ravings of a complete and utter madman.

> "You look more than a little shocked and disbelieving,"

Mikey said with a rueful smile.

"Christ, Jack, I can hardly claim I expected to you to react any differently. If things were the other way around, I daresay I'd be heading straight for the wall phone and dialling up the men in the white coats to come and take you away to the psychiatric ward at Clatterbridge.

But I believe you asked me a question, and as my friend you deserve a truthful answer, no matter how unpalatable that 'truth' might prove to be.

I actually returned to Rock Ferry, over two months ago,"

...he continued, and now the smile was gone, replaced by a look of steely determination.

"Luckily for me, I've got an understanding boss, and he allowed me to take an extended period of leave from my job whilst I attended to a couple of intensely private personal matters.

I didn't elaborate as to what these matters were, of course. But having undergone the hugely unnerving experience having had a long-buried memory suddenly shamble into view like a rotting, fly-blown zombie from some late-night horror movie, I felt compelled to return to my home-town for two good reasons: the first of these was to learn all I could about the evil spirit I firmly believe exists beneath the surface of that damned pond. To do this properly, I had to keep a low profile. I didn't want to look up any of my old friends, not even you, Jack. Please don't take offence. I had too much to do to allow myself to be distracted. I knew I had to at least try and get to the bottom of what happened to my brother that day out on the ice, or I really would go insane.

I booked myself into *The Bridge Inn,* that quaint mock-Tudor hotel in the middle of Port Sunlight Village, and used it as the base for my investigations. To begin with, this involved nothing more than spending hours leafing through hundreds of old and obscure volumes in the Reference Sections of Birkenhead and Bebington Libraries, and to my not very great surprise, I quickly learned there existed a long and colourful tradition of malignant water-dwelling entities that, according to folklore, inhabited various rivers and stagnant pools up and down the length of the British Isles, and beyond. In every single account I came across, these Dark Faeries, for want of a better term, were described as being essentially female in origin, which may or may not say a great deal about man's inherent fear of women, but I'll dispense with the pseudo-Jungian psychology analysis, if it's all the same to you.

I discovered that she has a name, too. Actually, strike that, *She* has a whole *variety* of names. She's called Peg Powler up in the north east of England, Grindylow in Yorkshire, the bucca-boo in Cornwall, Black Annis across Leicestershire, and Peg O' Nell and Nellie Longarms in the depths of the Cheshire and Shropshire countryside.

And the stories of her predations aren't limited to this country, either. She's known as Bean-Fionn in Ireland, Kappa in Japanese mythology, the Slavic people call her Rusalka, and she is referred to as La Lorona in parts of South America.

Personally however, I prefer the name she's known by right here on Merseyside...Jenny Greenteeth.

Whatever name she goes by, though, the descriptions of what she's meant to look like remain virtually identical across the board: 'a horrifyingly grotesque green-skinned woman, with duck weed for hair, a set of razor-sharp teeth (also coloured a sickly mucus shade of emerald, hence the name), that look as easily capable of ripping through sheet metal as tissue paper'.

The stories people tell about her, too, are remarkably consistent, no matter what part of the world they originate from. People tell of how she can lie hidden out of sight below the water's surface, to enchant passers-by with her captivating siren song, seducing her victims to the extent that they will quite happily drown themselves just to be by her side. Others believe the entity is the vengeful spirit of a murdered pregnant woman, who delights in meting out justice by drowning any of the local children foolish enough not to heed their parents' warnings and steer clear of her domain.

By far the most oft-repeated stories however, and this is what virtually leapt off the musty-smelling pages of some ancient treatise on Lancashire folklore, the moment I first read it, refer to how Jenny Greenteeth is a member of a particularly nasty species of Dark Faerie – one that takes up residence in ponds covered with layers of green scum and thick mats of algae. According to legend, once she's firmly established in her habitation of choice, she immediately finds herself filled with an insatiable hunger to attack and devour humans who stray a little too close to the water's edge.

Now, it appears our very own pond-dwelling entity contents itself with feeding on its victim's souls, as opposed to their physical bodies, but otherwise, that *modus operandi* sounds uncomfortably familiar, don't you think?

Oh, and listen to this, Jack. Several authors have been at pains to point out that she prefers to prey on children who play on or near a stretch of faerie-haunted water on The Sabbath Day...

Sundays, in other words.

Remember what day it was that me and Joe stepped out onto the ice?

Of course, you do. How could you forget?

Anyway, when I'd learned all I could from studying books and old pamphlets, I began speaking to local people about The Pond, and whether they'd had any unusual experiences there. It didn't take me long to realise there's plenty of evidence to be gathered if you persevere for long enough and ask the right type of questions.

Normally of course, people don't like to talk about this type of stuff. Mention anything that carries the remotest whiff of the supernatural and they'll give you a queer look and quickly mumble their excuses before dashing off on some vitally important errand, or else hastily seek to change the subject. But if you can persuade them that you're not taking the piss, and succeed in earning their trust, you'll find there are some people who are willing to talk to you. More often than not, (though not always), they are the archetypal old-fogeys, those vaguely bewildered looking individuals who are long-retired from work and have nothing but too much spare time on their hands and a desperate need to fill their empty hours with some meaningful conversation. Or maybe, seeing as how they've discovered they're drawing uncomfortably close to being on first name speaking terms with the tall, black-robed fella with the hour-glass and the lethal-looking scythe, they're not quite as afraid to discuss the type of stuff those young whippersnappers who honestly think they're gonna live forever, prefer to dismiss as being patently ridiculous and therefore not worthy of serious consideration.

Okay, I'll grant you, no one came right out and admitted to my face they'd ever encountered a sinewy-armed, water-dwelling creature with green, mottled skin whose only objective was to drown as many young children as is *in*-humanly possible. But I heard more than enough anecdotal evidence to convince me that I didn't simply imagine the thing I saw dragging my brother beneath the surface of the pond on that terrible day, all those years ago.

You know, Jack, if I was planning on writing a book about the subject, which I'm not by the way, I would probably sub-head this chapter,

Tenuous Traces Of Corroborating Evidence That Fell From The Mouths Of Strangers....If You Only Had The Time And Ears To Listen...

...And if that didn't send the readers running and screaming when confronted with such artily pretentious flowery-prose, they could learn, as I did, of:

Tantalising Little Hints:

'I was messing around with a couple of friends, on a makeshift raft when I was a kid, and I remember when we were out in the middle of the pond, the deepest part, something fairly substantial struck the underside of the raft with such force it nearly knocked us all into the water. We laughed about it later and we reckoned it was probably a pike or some other large type of fish, and I suppose it was, but sometimes, I can't help but wonder...'

Half-whispered rumours:

'I've never told anyone this, and I'll deny it till I'm blue in the face if you ever repeat it to anyone, but one afternoon a few years ago, I was doing a spot of fishing over at the pond at the back of The Big Hill. By early evening, I hadn't had a single bite, and I was about to give up and go home, when, just as the light began to fail, something finally took the bait, It struggled like a bastard, and I thought I'd hooked a *bona fide* whopper! Something worth bragging about to me mates for the rest of my days down at *The Railway*, - who knows, I remember dreaming that they might even put a photo of me and my prize catch up on the pub walls – and wouldn't that make me drinking buddies green with envy? 'After one helluva battle, with my arms aching like they used to do after a work out during me old sparring days at The Triangle Boxing Club, I was daring to hope I'd gotten the better of whatever it was that was churning the water to a frothy foam out there in the middle of the pond, with the rod bending like a flimsy tree branch in the midst of a full-blown gale when the line suddenly snapped as though something with incredible strength had chewed through the wire....and my prize catch disappeared back into the depths.'

Almost Proof:

'I remember one long hot summer, forty-odd years ago, my parents bought me a cheap plastic snorkel and flippers set as a reward for getting a good school report. I was supposed to be saving it for exploring the deep rock pools at Presthaven Sands in North Wales, later that summer, but that wouldn't be until late August, and it was only early June, and you know how kids are at that age...I simply couldn't wait that long to try them out so I went down to nearest stretch of water to my house, which happened to be The Old Artificial Pond, the one opposite the Sewage Plant, and dived straight in. I was a strong swimmer, even back then, and I was out in the middle of the water in double-quick time searching for anything remotely interesting down the on the pond bed. I spotted something silvery glinting amidst the weeds, and I thought for a minute it might be an item of jewellery or a collection of old coins, and I swam closer to take a better look. As I did so however, I saw something else, something that, as mad as it sounds, looked a lot like a large pair of bulbous eyes, giving off a greenish glow amidst the silt-filled gloom.

I remember my first thought was that I'd stumbled upon some sort of genetic mutation. The waters of The Pond were heavily polluted even during the 1940s, with God only knew what kind of chemicals, and I didn't particularly want to encounter anything that might be dangerously contaminated, so I scrambled to the surface and got the hell out of there as quick as I possibly could...'

So yeah, Jack, there were several other people who had strange stories to tell, and to me that seems to suggest there is something out of the ordinary inhabiting The Pond but I sincerely doubt you'd ever get any of them to testify as such on a pile of *Whizzer'n'Chips* comic books, never mind a stack of Holy Bibles.

All of which got me thinking, what if, on some occasions at least, the warnings our Mums' and Dads' gave us when we were kids weren't simply latter day folk tales designed to scare us away from any treacherous stretch of water.

What if they *really* do exist.

What if Jenny Greenteeth *really* exists?

And what if she's still living beneath the surface of The Old Pond at the back of the Big Hill, lying in wait for fresh victims.......?'

SIX

Of course, I didn't really afford any degree of credence to his outlandish theories.

The idea that a creature from a particularly foul and rancid nightmare could possibly exist in the real world, let alone be responsible for the death of a child was plainly, as I believe I told my friend at the time, 'crazier than a shit-house rat caught in a U-bend!'

And you can be sure I tried my level best to convince him he was hopelessly deluded, and that he needed to get his head together and stop blaming himself for what had happened to his brother, which was naturally what I assumed was really going on here: a struggle to come to terms with his loss that had resulted in him taking a bizarre detour into the realms of some deeply disturbing fantasy.

Trying to talk any kind of sense into Mikey, however, proved to be more than a little difficult because by the time he'd finished his charming story, he was clearly more than three sheets to the wind, which was hardly surprising given the amount of whisky he'd knocked back. I knew from bitter experience, trying to reason with an inebriated man intent on drawing deep from his own bottomless well of grief is a lot like screaming for your own salvation into an endless, empty void.

Not that *I* was entirely sober, of course.

I only wish I had been.

Things might have turned out differently, then.

Certainly, I'm sure I would never have left Mikey on his own, not even for a single minute whilst he was in such an obviously drunken and emotionally vulnerable state.

The fact was though, my bladder had been full by this point in the festivities, and I'd simply had to nip to the toilets or risk soiling myself big-time.

> "I've come back to kill her, yer know!"

Mikey slurred, as I unsteadily got down from my bar-stool. 'I know exactly how I'm gonna do it, too!'

I remember he grinned at me, and it chilled me to see the lack of humour present in that grin. It reminded me of an awful picture I'd once seen of some nameless SS Commandant standing at the head of a line of emaciated prisoners queuing for 'the showers' at a Nazi death camp. It had the same, maniacal, pitiless quality, and it caused me to hesitate for a second or two. Long enough anyway for me to catch the words he mumbled under his breath, almost as if he were speaking to himself.

> "I am not gonna let her drown any more kids. Tomorrer's a Sunday. The Sabbath.
>
> Tomorrer, *she's* the one whose gonna die!"

I was going to try and reason with him some more, desperate for the bog or not, but before I could say a word, our old friend Mr Meathead chose that moment to wander back over to the bar and began loudly demanding another drink, in his own inimitable style:

> "A pint of the same, and do us a favour , pull yer finger out this time, soft lad!"

The words died on my lips then, not least because trying to talk logical sense over the Mersey Ferry fog-horn sound of Mr M's eloquent homilies was as thankless and pointless a task as cooking up a great big stack of veggie sausages at a Texan barbecue.

I was only in the loo for a short while. The time it took me to do my business, wash my hands and dry them on the cheap and nasty paper towels that fell to soggy bits the minute I dragged them from the dispenser, but when I pushed the door open and stepped back into the bar, Mikey had disappeared.

I immediately asked Johnny Oates if he'd seen my friend leave and he told me that if I meant the old guy who looked like he was carrying the troubles of the world on his scrawny shoulders, then he'd just watched him staggering out *The Admiral*, clutching what looked like a photograph before him like a priest armed with a crucifix in anticipation of a vampiric assault.

I swore under my breath and ran out after him, but the incessant rain had become a full-on deluge, and the moonless night was so pitch dark you could hardly see the flooded road ahead. I tried calling Mikey's name, but the wind was so strong it was difficult enough to draw breath, never mind make yourself heard.

I consoled myself with the thought that Mikey wouldn't do anything stupid tonight, in these awful conditions. Hadn't he said himself that he was going to confront his 'Demon' the following day, and I'd still had no reason to disbelieve him. After all, tomorrow was, as he'd pointed out, a Sunday, and according to Mikey's twisted sense of logic, the most propitious day of the week for killing 'soul-stealing monstrosities.' He'd likely headed straight back to the inn where he was staying to sleep off the alcohol, so I made plans to set my alarm, and grab some breakfast with him at *The Bridge* early the next morning.

Maybe when Mikey had sobered up, and had gotten some good strong coffee inside him, he might wind his neck in and stop all this lunatic talk of evil, water-dwelling entities, along with whatever mad, hare-brained scheme he'd drawn up to combat 'the creature.'

It had been an evening crammed to the rafters with outright absurdity.

Better to put it to bed and let things lie till daylight (and, hopefully, a shining shaft of sanity), dawned.

SEVEN

The next morning, despite my king-size hangover, I managed to resist the urge to hurl my alarm clock against the wall and haul myself out of bed, at bang on 6:30am. I showered and shaved, and was out of the house half an hour later. It was a beautiful autumn day with not a single cloud in the sky, the only trace of the previous night's storm were a couple of fallen branches in some of the tree-lined gardens along Water Street, and the dirty brown puddles that had collected in the leaf-clogged gutters at the bottom end of Bolton Road. I felt uplifted by the change in the weather, and already the memories of the night before had begun to quickly fade like some half-remembered dream upon waking. I was looking forwards to meeting Mikey, and I was whistling cheerfully as I entered the reception area of *The Bridge Inn,* and the mouth-watering aroma of bacon and eggs and fried tomatoes caused my stomach to rumble loudly.

I walked up to the front desk, rang the bell for attention, and asked the pretty blonde-haired receptionist who appeared, if she could call the room number where Mr Michael Kavanagh was staying. She smiled and asked me to wait a moment while she scanned the register.

She ran her perfectly manicured fingernails along the list of names a couple of times, before she eventually looked up and shook her head.

"I'm awfully sorry, sir"

…she said, still smiling sweetly.

"But Mr Kavanagh checked out very early this morning".

"Are you sure?"

I asked, my heart sinking, desperately hoping she'd made a mistake.

"Yes, I'm quite sure. Just after 5am, it says here."

She suddenly slapped her forehead in an *'oh-aren't -I-the-dozy-one!'* gesture.

"Actually, I really should have remembered the name the minute you mentioned it. Mr Kavanagh had originally booked to stay for another fortnight, but yesterday, at breakfast, he told us he had to cut short his holiday and get back to Cornwall at the earliest opportunity."

"Did he say why?"

"No, and I didn't think it was my place to ask him...Are you a close friend?"

"We're like brothers. We grew up together."

"Well, I'm not really sure I should be telling you this, but just before he left, I happened to overhear him talking on the pay phone over in the *Hesketh Lounge*. He was telling the person on the other end of the line that he would definitely be back by Monday afternoon at the latest. There was something important he had to do first, though. He had a very important meeting with a woman named Jenny...I don't think he mentioned her surname, I didn't catch it if he did and then he......"

She stopped mid-sentence, her bright blue eyes wide with sudden concern.

"Excuse me for saying so, but are you alright, sir? You've gone awfully pale..."

EIGHT

I ran the mile or so to The Big Hill and the artificial Pond - where Mikey's brother Joe had drowned three decades earlier - like a man possessed, a feeling of unutterable dread increasing with every step. When I finally reached the chain-link fence that surrounded the abandoned oil storage depot, my entire body was dripping with sweat and a rancid, stinking odour that had more to do with abject fear than the unseasonably warm temperatures or my physical exertions, seeped from every pore.

I had to frantically search for a few minutes before I found a jagged hole mid-way along the fence, and I was forced to get on my hands and knees to crawl my way through. The last time I'd gone walking in the area not twelve months earlier, there had been a path of sorts winding its way around the side of the woods that led down to The Pond, trampled by the feet of local kids and optimistic fishermen. This summer had obviously seen a dramatic decline in the number of visitors, however, because the trail was barely discernible, obscured by thick clumps of rank-smelling undergrowth and swathes of knee-high rye grass growing wildly, even this late in the year.

It seemed to take an eternity to negotiate my way along to the muddy banks, plagued every step of the way by swarms of end-of-season horse flies, blood-hungry 'mozzies' and other biting insects, but eventually there I was, staring across the surface of the water, half-expecting to be confronted by the sight of a wild-eyed obsessive, standing somewhere in the shallows, a harpoon clutched in his hands like a latter-day Captain Ahab.

There was absolutely no sign of my friend, however.

From my vantage point I could see right across the length and width of The Pond, and it was clear that somewhat unusually, even this early in the morning, there was no one else around. If Mikey had ever been here, I thought, he'd either long since left or had maybe come to his senses and boarded the first train back to Cornwall.

Either way, I felt a great tide of relief wash over me, and I decided to sit for a while at the water's edge, to catch my breath and take in the scenery. There may have been no people around, but The Pond was teeming with various forms of wildlife. Teals and mallards were bobbing along on the rippled surface, I spotted a curlew flitting in and out of the gently swaying reeds, and brightly-coloured dragonflies were darting around an empty plastic bottle of *Lilt* (*"with de Totally Tropical Taste!"*), that had washed up against a half-submerged tree branch.

Everything seemed to be idyllically peaceful and in its place like a scene from a *Walt Disney* nature documentary, and I'm not sure whether it was the blissful serenity, the warm autumn sunshine or the fact that I hadn't slept too well the previous night, but one minute I was watching a water vole scrabbling its way onto the far bank before disappearing into its den, the next my head had dropped onto my knees and I'd drifted into a deep and dreamless sleep.

*****

I was awoken by the sounds of a frantic splashing from the shallows on the opposite side of The Pond, and I looked up in time to see a massive heron dipping its long beak into the water, attempting to catch a large fish, and I rubbed the sleep from my eyes to watch fascinated as the creatures engaged in the eternal struggle between predator and prey, hunter and hunted.

Suddenly, the heron took to the air, its beak entirely empty, as if it had been startled by something in the water. Although it was a good distance away, I felt sure I could almost hear the powerful whooshing of its wings and feel the abrupt displacement of air as this prehistoric-looking giant ascended into the September skies.

I shivered, and was surprised to find goose-pimples erupting on my bare arms as I followed the bird's progress, and I soon saw why. A thick bank of bruised-coloured clouds had bubbled up from out of nowhere and in a matter of seconds, had all but obscured the sun. This rapid bleeding away of the light was reflected on the surface of The Pond, the water turning jet-black, giving the impression that it was impossibly deep, and it was suddenly easy to believe that all manner of monstrosities might exist, hidden in those abyssal depths. Gigantic eels. Razor-toothed fish. Bug-eyed mutations. Hideously grinning female Goblins....

All lurking in the dark.

I shivered again, and ineffectually rubbed my arms in a bid to keep warm. A chill wind had sprung up, and I no longer felt remotely sleepy or enchanted by the view before me, and I decided to head for home.

I was just about to turn away when I happened to catch sight of something floating, bright white in the pitch-black water. There was nothing outwardly remarkable about it. To be honest, I almost dismissed it as being nothing but discarded litter. For some unfathomable reason though, I was transfixed by what I soon saw was a plain square piece of paper speeding towards me like a flimsy raft desperately seeking the shelter of a sheltered harbour. The wind, which was gathering strength by the second, meant that it only took a minute or so for it to cross The Pond, and soon it was pushing up against the bank beneath my feet, looking for all the world as though it were trying to clamber up out of The Pond. Like it had a life of its own.

Despite myself, I was fairly anxious to see what, if anything, was printed on the reverse, but I really didn't want to put my hand in the water to fish it out. I was suddenly convinced that if I did so, a claw-like set of mottled green fingers would suddenly reach out and grab my wrist to drag me down into the middle of those black, swirling depths.

I decided instead to use a fallen branch that was lying amidst a nearby clump of weeds.

I scooped it up and flipped it over, and held it for a second in my shaking hand.

It was the faded colour photograph of a smiling ten-year-old Joe Kavanagh.

The exact same one Mikey had shown me in *The Admiral* the night before.

As I looked, the picture's emulsion started to run, Joe's beaming smile slowly distorted into a silent scream of agony, whilst the rest of his features slowly slid like melted wax into an obscene parody of a human being.

I stood there for a while, holding the picture in horrified fascination, as the day slowly darkened, and I heard a marsh bird calling from the centre of the wildly-blowing reeds.

And to my ears at that moment, it sounded uncomfortably like cold, slyly mocking laughter....

(Above): The Old Artificial Pond and the recently erected Water Treatment Plant, resembling a building that's been transported wholesale from some otherworldly, futuristic landscape, presides over what local folklore rumours to be the ancient lair of a timeless, childhood horror...

NINE

I never saw Mikey again after that drunken night in our former local.

In the days and weeks after he'd checked out of *The Bridge Inn*, I tried to make some enquiries as to his whereabouts, but it was a pretty hopeless task seeing as how I didn't have so much as forwarding address or any idea what company he worked for. He hadn't told me whether or not he was married, had any family, or even whether his parents were still alive. If he was reported as being missing to the authorities, I never heard any news of it, which is a good thing, I suppose, because most of the time I have absolutely no trouble imagining Mikey sat at home with his wife, happily watching their favourite TV programmes with a mug of tea and a box of chocolate biscuits close to hand and the sound of his children's carefree conversation filling the air.

There are occasions, however, more often than not on dark, moonless nights, when rain rattles at the windows and a late-September wind howls its mournful lament for another summer's passing, when I find it equally easy to imagine a far different scene...

Mikey is sat at the bottom of the artificial Pond, all alone, save for the swimming, squirming things that live in darkness and shun the light, the red empty holes where his eyes should be, staring sightlessly at the unspeakable thing that cavorts before him, flicking its tongue across its pale green lips in anticipation of the feast to come...

And the only sound...

Is the sound of an endless, silent scream...

HAUNTED BY AIGBURTH'S INVISIBLE 'MR NOBODY'

Cathie O' Donnell, who currently resides in Dorset, but who is originally from Merseyside, wrote to me several years ago with the following account of an Invisible Entity....

Between the ages of one and twenty two, I lived in the Aigburth Vale area of Liverpool, quite close to Sefton Park and Otterspool Promenade. Me and my mum, (she was sadly divorced from my father by the time I was just two years old) resided in a large, typically rambling Victorian terraced house that teetered on a slope in a quite posh area of the city. As I grew older, I became aware of several strange things happening around our home. Doors would open and close of their own accord, floorboards would creak mysteriously, and there were a series of unaccountable "cold spots."

Of course, all of this "phenomena" can be quite easily explained by our living in such an old house, but it was harder to be so dismissive when dealing with other incidents such as objects being moved about by themselves, items going missing without a trace only to turn up in some decidedly odd locations, ie: a pair of mislaid shoes appearing in, of all places, a fridge.

By the time I'd turned fourteen, the "spook", for want of a better word, really began to get into the swing of things. For a start, there would often be an overwhelming sense of an invisible, but unmistakably male presence standing close behind me, looking over my shoulder. The sensation was so strong that I was convinced that if I could only spin round fast enough, I would get to see it "in the flesh," so to speak, but I never did.

And it wasn't just me that was experiencing this overbearing "feeling." Many of our guests and friends who came to stay would tell of experiencing a similar sensation on occasion, too. At least three of these people flatly refused to sit in the dining room after encountering 'Mr Nobody,' as we came to call the unseen presence. The entity seemed to display a great gift for mimicry. On countless occasions, I would be outside a room or going down the stairs, when I would glimpse Mum disappearing along the hall, outside a particular room, or heading down the stairs, when in fact, she was in the lounge or chatting to a friend in the kitchen.

She would also apparently see me going somewhere when I was in a completely different room. Our names would also be called from points around the house. I'd often hear my name "Catherine," being shouted, in a voice that sounded identical to my mother's, only to later discover that my Mum hadn't called me at all. Perhaps more disturbing were the times that my Mum would hear "me" crying and would come running to my aid, to find that I was perfectly fine and not at all moved to tears. This behaviour would often be annoying, but mostly we were quite impressed with Mr Nobody's talents for uncannily accurate impersonation.
However, in 1996, things took a decidedly more sinister turn.

My Mum made the decision to re-mortgage the house during that year, intent upon giving the old building a thorough renovation. The house was re-wired, re-plastered and damp-proofed.

A new kitchen was fitted, new windows and central heating were installed. I'd just turned sixteen, and was positively awash with raging hormones and boundless energy. It was kind of hard then to shake the notion that Mr Nobody appeared at this point to be setting about absorbing some of this youthful vigour…Or maybe "he" simply didn't like the home improvements.

Whatever the case, on the occasions "he" now chose to stand behind me, "he" was constantly sulky. Not only that, but electrical plugs were yanked out of their sockets when my Mum and I were watching the TV or playing records, and the doors would suddenly slam loudly.

One balmy July evening, everything seemed to come to a head.

Me and me mum and me boyfriend were sitting in the lounge. I'd been undemocratically voted to make a steaming pot of tea. It was 9:15pm. I walked along the hall into the morning room, heading towards the kitchen. As I was about half-way across the morning room, I felt "Mr Nobody" directly behind me. And it was all so different this time. He felt "totally pissed off". I could actually hear the sound of carpet slippers slowly shuffling, coupled with heavy, asthmatic breathing. And, oh, he was so very close. So close that I most certainly didn't want to have to turn around and face him.

I felt the hairs on the back of my neck and head actually crackle and bristle, and an air of electrification pervaded the room. I was absolutely terrified and let out an ear-splitting scream. As I did so, I was able to break out of my trance-like state and hurtle into the kitchen, hiding behind the sanctuary of the freezer. My mum and my boyfriend came running and they both later confirmed that they too had felt a large patch of icy-coldness in the centre of the morning room.

When I told my mum that "Mr Nobody" had sneaked up on me and scared me half to death, she completely lost her rag. She promptly stormed into the morning room and began yelling at the invisible entity.

> "Don't you dare scare my daughter again!"

…she roared, and no sooner had the words dropped from her lips than the door between the hall and the morning room slammed shut with such force that the whole house seemed to shake with the impact.

And that was that.

"Mr Nobody" didn't really bother us again after that. There would still be the odd shout, the occasional cold-spot, but nothing like as bad as it had been during the previous years.

My ghost-busting mum moved out of the house in 1994, and a young couple moved in. And who knows, maybe they are right now enduring their own experiences of "Mr Nobody?"

**** As an interesting footnote to this story, contained within the same letter, was the following story that Cathie also wanted to share with me, and whilst it didn't occur anywhere near Merseyside, is sufficiently terrifying, to bear repeating if only for that reason....

'A good friend of mine, named Debbie, used to live with her parents at a place called Billington, in Dorset, right next to a Hed Hill, with has a host of ancient rings and Neolithic burial mounds. When her parents booked a holiday in Cyprus, one year, she jumped at the chance to house-sit. The house is situated completely off the beaten track, the nearest neighbours are half a mile away. Along with Debbie and another friend named Fiona, I agreed to pile round for a girl's night at the address. It had been a roasting hot day, and we'd made ourselves a curry (though we'd drunk far too much to really appreciate it), when Fiona suggested we attempt to walk off the food by traipsing to the nearest pub; *The Ox*.

It was now fully dark and we ambled along the single lane, often tripping in the near ebon blackness bereft of even the slightest hint of moonlight. Perhaps unwisely, given the circumstances, we started talking about ghosts and by the time we finally reached the pub, we were all giggling nervously. Fiona spotted a fella she knew and pointed at him saying; "Now, he's got a good scary story to tell!"

She called him over, and after much cajoling, he eventually told us of an experience that had left him terrified. In the summer of 1996, Steve, the name of the chap concerned, had been in *The Ox*, enjoying a few bevvies. His brother's wife was in hospital at the time, and he'd agreed to stay at his brother's place to keep him company. He'd borrowed his bike in order to get to *The Ox*, leaving the car at his brother's address.

After last orders, he helped the landlord and his wife tidy up, and left at some time around 12:15am. To get to his brother's house he had to cycle between two large hills. The road, incidentally, is known as the Old Roman Road, and is very seldom used, particularly at that time of night. As Steve cycled along, he was pleasantly surprised at how well-illuminated the area was thanks to a silvery bright full moon. After a while, he became aware of a strange rustling and crashing in the hedgerow to his left. Initially, he wasn't especially frightened. He just assumed it to be some fairly large countryside animal, a badger for instance.

Whatever it was, though, it clattered about for a while, and finally emerged behind him onto the black tarmac. The "Something" then struck Steve, and he could discern immediately that it was actually very large in size. He could hear it breathing, along with the unmistakable sound of claws raking across the road surface-like a dog. It was only then that he was struck with an almost overpowering wave of fear. He slowed down and risked a look behind him. Inside of seeing the huge black dog that he'd half-expected to encounter, he was instead confronted by a man with very long hair, running on all fours!

Steve, not surprisingly, screamed aloud in terror, and the "Man-Thing" scampered off into the undergrowth on the other side of the road. Steve later told us that he'd never pedalled so fast in his life. He found that people had a great deal of difficulty in believing his story, so after a while, he decided to keep quiet about it.

However, when he related the tale to me, I found him to be a solid, down-to-earth country bloke, who had seemed genuinely scared out of his wits. Two years on, and he still refuses to drive down that same stretch of road, let alone cycle along it. Interestingly enough, there have been a number of 'Black Beast' sightings throughout the locale during the late 1990s.'

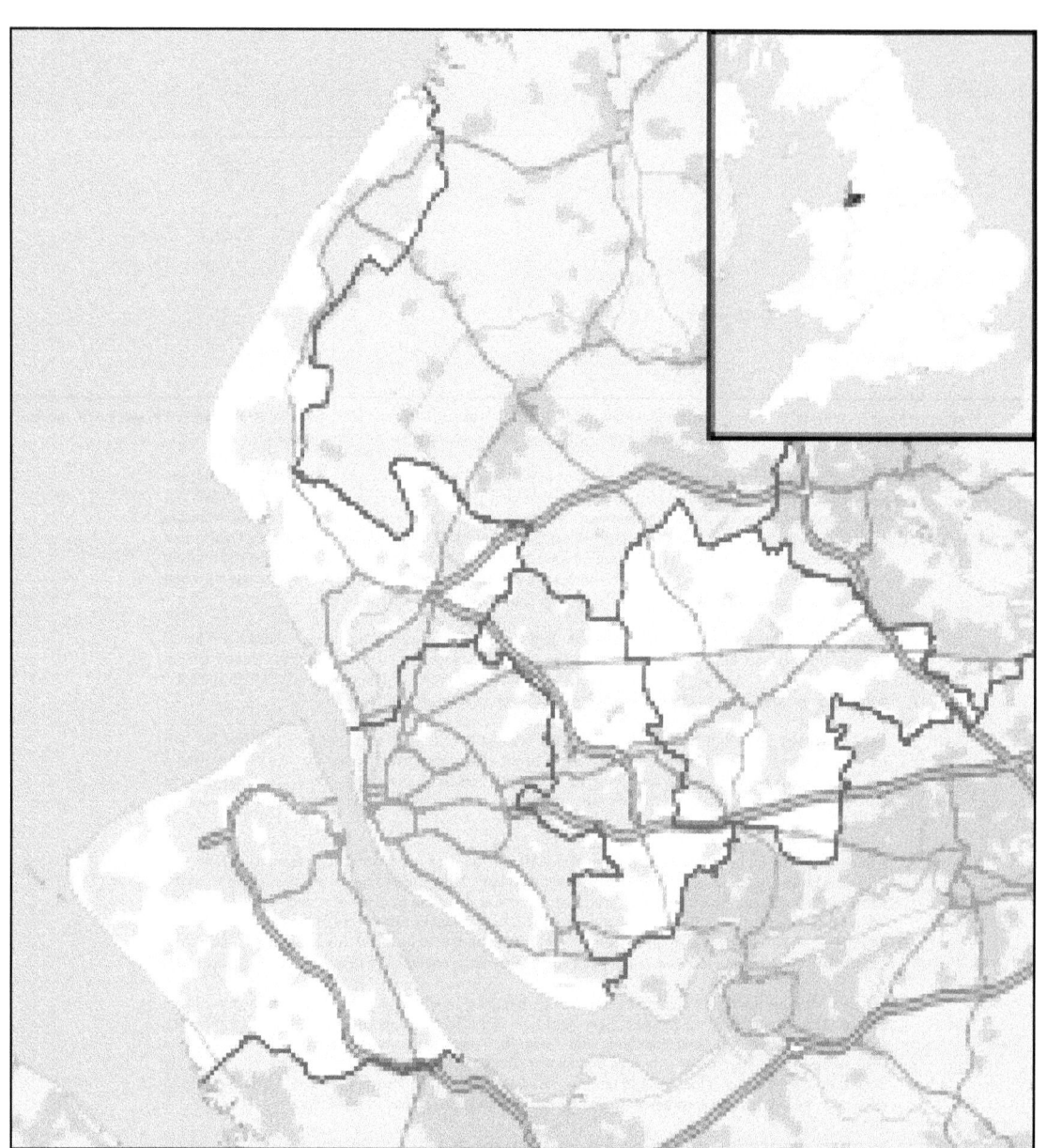

WEST KIRBY WEIRDNESS

The town of West Kirby, stands on the north-west corner of the coast of the Wirral Peninsula, directly opposite the River Dee and the green-swathed hills and snow-peaked mountains of North Wales.

According to the smart-arse know-it-all, though undeniably invaluable Wikipedia, the town's name is derived from the Viking Kirkjubyr, meaning 'village with a church'. It goes on to specify that the 'West' was later added (the earliest recorded reference dates from 1285), in order to distinguish it from 'the other town of the same name in Wirral, Kirby-in-Walea (now the modern town of Wallasey).

Like several of the coastal resorts located throughout the Peninsula, its popularity with tourists, at least those from outside the area, has waned a little in recent times, but the river-front still boasts a fine Victorian promenade which includes the large Marine Lake, where sailing boats of various sizes emerge from the nearby Yacht Club, and can be seen traversing the large expanse of water most Sunday afternoons. There are miles of golden sand that stretch away towards Hilbre Island and a lonely-looking lighthouse, and at low tide, during the summer months (assuming it ever stops raining, of course) you can spend a pleasant couple of hours traipsing across the dunes to check out the thriving seal colony, or sit off and have a picnic - whatever, if you'll excuse the cheesy maritime pun, floats your boat. The only down side is you can't indulge in that rarest of luxuries - squeezing cool wet sand between your toes as you walk, especially when the air is thick with the steamy heat of an August afternoon. Going barefoot, you see, isn't really an option. Not unless you choose to ignore the numerous signs warning of the presence of weaver fish, highly poisonous little blighters that hide just below the surface of the sand, ready to plunge their nasty, venom-filled barbs into any area of exposed flesh, usually, the tender soles of someone's feet. The stings are not fatal, but I have it on good authority that they hurt like hell.

But I digress. Jo Wood, a former resident of West Kirby, (who, as far as I know has never trod on any species of fish, poison-barbed or otherwise) used to live with her family in Island Court, near the centre of town. There used to be an empty plot of land next door, and although it was something of a local eyesore, there was nothing outwardly remarkable about it. However, almost from the moment they moved in, Jo's family had been acutely aware that there was something indefinably wrong with the neglected mixture of churned earth and weed-infested ground. The impression they got was that the very soil itself had been blighted somehow. Poisoned. Rendered sour.

After a while, they managed to learn to live with this depressing vista 'greeting' them each time they looked out of their upstairs window, averting their gaze on such a regular basis that they were pretty soon blanking the sight from their minds without even being aware that they were doing it.

But then, one exceptionally warm evening during the high summer of 1997, Jo's nine year-old daughter suddenly burst into her mother's bedroom, screaming that she'd seen 'a strange man, wearing funny clothes,' standing in the middle of the 'rubbish tip next door.'

Jo was shocked into wakefulness when her daughter informed her that as she'd gazed down wonderingly at the figure, it had suddenly pointed up at her in a distinctly threatening fashion. He had then lowered his finger and gestured at the ground beneath his feet, before simply vanishing without a trace.

Jo went to look for herself, and of course, there was nobody there, but any initial degree of scepticism on her part was somewhat lessened when she asked her daughter for a more detailed description of the ominously pointing figure. The girl sat down and produced a remarkably detailed picture of what appeared to be a 16th Century cavalier replete with a jet black hat, feather, pantaloons and a pair of shiny leather boots. What made the picture even more extraordinary was the fact that the nine-year-old had never studied that particular period of history at school up to that time, and there was therefore no obvious point of reference for her to have focused on for inspiration.

Jo later told reporters from The Wirral News,

> 'I honestly tried to laugh it off and calm my daughter down but she will never go into that room in the dark again, and I will never stare out of that window into that plot of land next door for too long.'

And in fact, not long after, they moved to a new address, although it's not at all clear whether the families upping of sticks was due to further unwelcome visits from ghostly Cavaliers with a penchant for materialising in the middle of rubbish tips....

BE CAREFUL WHAT YOU WISH FOR

The following cautionary tale was related to me during one of those depressingly cold, dark January lunch-breaks at the criminal solicitor's firm where I used to work, when it seems like spring is nothing but an impossibly distant dream, and there's really nothing else to do but huddle around the office radiators, putting the world to rights or swapping increasingly outlandish stories with one another. As with many of the accounts contained within this book, I have absolutely no way of verifying its authenticity, especially seeing as how it was narrated by one of my more imaginative colleagues; a tall, skinny, mop-haired individual named Ben Thompson. Widely known for his quirky sense of humour, and the fact that he couldn't have been any more bohemian if he'd have permanently dressed himself in a crushed purple smoking jacket made from the wings of exotic species of moths, I wouldn't blame you for dismissing Ben's 'friend-of-a-friend' tale as being similar to the type of supposedly 'true-life- experience recounted by the likes of Elliot O' Donnell, (a very good writer, of Irish origin, whose ghost story books are well worth checking out, as long as you strictly adhere to the caveat that Mr O' Donnell loved employing a degree of 'artistic licence,' to say the very least).

Whatever the precise element of truth here though, one thing remains certain:

As a means of discouraging a person from resorting to dabbling in 'magic' of the black or white (or indeed, grey) variety, in order to achieve their goals, I would contend that this is a highly effective deterrent.

*****

It's one of life's great truisms that we are, all of us, even those who consider themselves to be hard-headed realists and one hundred per cent rational in their dealings with the trials and tribulations life throws our way, prone to various forms of superstition, to a greater or lesser degree.

Oh, I'm sure there those will throw their hands up in despair and regale me with some suitably charming homily like, "Ben, you're so full of shite, you squeak like a mouse on helium when you walk!"

And that's okay.

I think I can understand that in this age of so-called scientific enlightenment, there's not a lot of room for belief in the efficacy of four-leaved clovers, lucky horseshoes, or twirling silver coins in the glare of a full moon.

But ask yourselves this: Would you really not take steps to avoid encountering a black cat that's about to run across your path, or deliberately walk under a ladder on the way to a vital appointment, a first date with the woman or man of your dreams, or a plum job interview?

Would you dare to walk counter-clockwise (Widdershins: an ancient method of calling up Evil spirits, fact fans), around a reputedly haunted cemetery, on the wrong side of midnight?

And would you risk bringing a supposedly accursed object into your house the night you were hoping to clinch that all-important business deal, or awaiting a phone call from the hospital concerning the welfare of a loved one?

And if, your answer to any of the above is yes, then you're a damn sight braver than me.

Not that I'm excessively superstitious myself, you understand. I'm more a pupil of the school of thought that errs on the side of caution. 'If there's nothing in it, then what's lost? And why take a chance when the shape of your destiny hangs in the balance? At worst, it might cost you a brief moment of red-faced embarrassment if someone catches you touching wood or throwing salt over your shoulder, when you accidentally spill a bit at the dining table.

Assuming you're open-minded enough to accept that there's the merest chance that you can influence fate to your advantage by doing something as simple as crossing your fingers or spitting three times whenever a magpie flies in from the left, then you may at least not think my friend, Tom, as being *totally* off his cake when I tell you that prior to asking a gorgeous girl out on a date late last year, he first invested in a single strip of parchment, a pink candle or two, and a packet of 'magic almonds'.

Tom reckoned he first set eyes on the girl of his dreams one cold September morning, when he was walking to work, head bowed as much by the dreary prospect of another day spent stuck in Birkenhead Magistrate's Court Cells, taking bail instructions from the usual array of depressingly familiar criminal clients, as by the near-horizontal slats of icy rain that stung his face.

He'd been splashing across the puddle-strewn precinct alongside the imposing facade of the Town Hall building, staring gloomily at the collection of dirty leaves, cigarette stubs and empty crisp packets caught in the swirling current that went roiling along the gutters, when he'd very nearly bumped into a young woman walking directly toward him.

"Oops, sorry,"

Tom mumbled, only narrowly avoiding a collision, and he would have carried right on walking without once raising his eyes, had it not been for the sweet waft of perfume that carried on the autumn breeze, stinging his heart and bringing to mind the stack of old love letters he'd kept in a shoebox as 'consolation' in the wake of a stack of previous failed relationships.

The effect was so potent, Tom had stopped dead in his tracks and stared in wonder at the most beautiful girl he had ever seen in his life. And although he assured me later that he had never regarded himself as being the sort of hopeless romantic who believed in love at first sight, I think it's fair to say that from that fateful moment, he fell prey to instant infatuation: the kind that knocks you for six and conjures up images of Butch The Bulldog, from the old *Tom And Jerry* cartoons, smitten by the sight of an attractive female, his heart beating so fast, it threatens to burst its way right out of his chest, as defying the laws of gravity, he floats skywards, before drifting back to earth in a gentle falling leaf motion.

It's also the kind of burning obsession that can have you spending countless nights lying awake as you frantically search your love-befuddled brain for ways that you can break the ice with the object of your affections, whilst still retaining at least a tiny shred of dignity.

Of course, I'm well aware that's impossible. There are no easy, risk-free methods available, and never mind what all those know-it-all agony aunt newspaper columnists may tell you to the contrary. And so, never having been blessed with recourse to an endless supply of potent chat up lines, Tom was unable to do anything but blush furiously, and mumble another apology. As romantic gestures went, it was about as seductive as some hairy-arsed builder ordering up a packet of pork scratchings, and Tom, who put his head back down and began trudging over to the courts, without another glance, assumed that would very much be that, and he'd likely never see her again.

As luck would have it however, that very afternoon, Tom decided to try out the new butty shop that had opened half-way down Market Street, and he told me that when he stepped inside, who was there but the very same girl he'd bumped into a few hours earlier, stood behind the service counter, wearing an identity badge that announced her name was Nikki. There were two older women working alongside her, busy inserting various sandwich fillings, but they may as well have been invisible for all the attention he paid them. Tom said he immediately felt his face turn a bright, glowing shade of crimson when he saw Nikki staring at him questioningly. In fact, he was so nervous he hastily garbled his order and wound up being served with a hugely unappetising combination of cheddar cheese, hummus, mayonnaise and chopped green pepper slapped into the middle of a whole-grain baguette.

"Yum, that looks absolutely delicious!"

...he'd said, as he left, grinning at her like he'd just been handed a three-course gourmet meal cooked up by some celebrity chef.

In the days and weeks that followed, Tom became a regular visitor to what he soon began referring to as '*Nikki's Sarnie Bar,*' even though it took him the best part of a month to sail close enough to the shores of coherent speech for him to actually acquire a butty that at least resembled that which he'd had in mind upon entering the shop.

Sadly, Nikki must have been totally unaware of my friend's hopelessly smitten state, even if she had been blessed with a finely attuned sense of female intuition. This was largely due to the fact that Tom outwardly showed about as much interest in her as he would a rain-sodden council tax reminder.

The reason for this air of affected indifference?

Tom was so paranoid, he was afraid that if Nikki had even the slightest notion that he was head-over-heels besotted with her, she would immediately resign from her job, pack her cases, and book the earliest possible flight to some far-flung foreign country, Outer Mongolia, say, in a desperate bid to escape his advances.

And so things might very well have carried on in that hopeless, *Kaw-Liga – The Lovelorn Wooden Indian* vein, until two things happened in fairly quick succession, a week or two before Hallowe'en.

Firstly, Tom finally managed to acquire funding from his firm in order to take his police accreditation exams, which meant most of his evenings would be spent performing probationary police station call-outs and studying for all he was worth to ensure he passed the three difficult tests that now lay before him.

And this need to bury his head in expensive academic tomes led directly to the second thing.

For the first time since leaving school, twelve years earlier, my old mate Tom, found himself filling in an application form to re-join Picton Library in Liverpool City Centre.

*****

It was mid-way through the third consecutive evening of intense studying in the Library's silent-as-the-grave reference section that Tom had suddenly been struck with an overwhelming desire to sweep the dusty law books to one side and go and read something a damn sight more interesting instead. Unable to resist the temptation, he strode across to the Sports and Entertainment Section and began checking out the array of titles. He wasn't looking for anything in particular. After hours spent poring through *The Magistrate Court's Sentencing Guidelines* even the likes of *'Laugh Along With the Taliban'* or *'The Philosophical Musings Of Katie Price'* would have seemed like fascinating works of literary genius. He eventually settled for a *Guns 'n' Roses* biography and a couple of football encyclopaedias, and it was as he was pulling out the latter of these from the middle of the tightly-packed upper shelf, that a large heavy volume wedged alongside it, slid out and almost landed on his foot. With a grunt, Tom reached down to pick it up and gazed briefly at the cover, and was confronted with a plain, leather-bound jacket embossed with gold-leafed lettering:

'A Guide To Modern Witchcraft,'

…it read.

'By Diana Fortunata.'

Tom almost shoved the book straight back onto the shelf. It had obviously been mis-shelved, but it wasn't his job to try and find the section where it properly belonged, and as he didn't believe in any of that 'new age crap,' he wanted to be rid of it as quickly as possible. Something written on the back cover caught his eye before he could do so, however, and he paused for a moment to scan the blurb. The olde-English-style text highlighted the book's contents, which included, amongst other things:

'Curses & Counter Curses, Conversing With Nature Spirits, and *'The Great & Lesser Sabbats'*

But it was the penultimate sentence that had grabbed Tom's attention and held it like he'd spotted some bright shining jewel amidst a pile of dirty fallen leaves.

'Also Includes A Selection Of Highly Efficacious Love Spells.'

Silently berating himself for his sudden recourse to superstitious gullibility, Tom nevertheless felt compelled to read this chapter, at least, and casting anxious glances around him to make sure there was no one around to catch him reading this tripe, he placed the book between the ones he'd previously chosen, and made his way back to his desk. Even when he'd surrounded himself with the door-step thick law volumes, leaving just enough gaps so that he could see anyone approaching, still he felt strangely guilty, like when he was in the local newsagent's and he was trying his best not to look up at the magazines that lined the top shelf.

The library was filled with the usual array of sixth-formers, college students and old men reliving their past in the black and white photographs contained in books with titles like *The Light Of Other Days,* and none of them seemed to paying Tom the slightest attention. But still he half-expected someone to sneak up on him unawares, see the content of the book now open before him and snigger whilst making slow twirly motions with their forefinger in the general direction of their temporal lobe.

No one did come over, though, and as time was getting on (the clock over on the far wall, plastered with autumnal-themed decorations, was ticking towards seven o' clock, and the Library closed at eight sharp.

And so, with the only sounds the soft rustle of turning pages and the hum of the over-head globe lights, Tom began to read....

He merely leafed through the majority of the book, anxious to get to the chapter dealing with 'Love Spells,' and once he'd located the section, he devoured the information with a fanatical gleam in his eye.

Tom's enthusiasm waned a little however, when he realised that many of the invocations involved either the purchasing of hugely expensive items such as jewel-encrusted daggers, solid gold amulets and intricately hand-carved ceremonial wands, or acquiring impossible to obtain objects such as *genuine* Dragon's teeth, the horn of a Unicorn or the blood-soaked tip of The Spear of Longinus.

There was one spell, though, roughly two thirds of the way through the chapter that seemed ridiculously simple by comparison, and Tom, almost without thinking, reached for his pen to copy down the details in his legal note-pad.

'One of the most effective and straightforward ways of attracting a special lover,'

Ms. Fortunata assured the reader,

> *'...is to carry out this basic spell on a moon-lit Friday evening, the day sacred to the Goddesses Freya and Venus.*
>
> *All you will need is a sturdy branch from a Willow Tree, a pink candle, a collection of red, green and white ribbons, a cocktail stick, a packet of plain almonds and a piece of virgin parchment.*
>
> *You then simply have to visualise his or her physical and spiritual being in your mind's eye, and attach a magical name to him or her, before inscribing this name on the side of the candle using the cocktail stick.*
>
> *On the virgin parchment, otherwise known, in more mundane terms, as a sheet of blank paper, write your own name down then braid the ribbons around the paper, after tying nine knots to secure the nine almonds in a line, all the while keeping the object of your affections in your mind's eye.*

> *Take the braided ribbons, candle and Willow out into the silver moonlight, and ask the Goddesses to bless them. Set the candle down and light it.*
>
> *Concentrate on its flickering glow and picture yourself walking hand-in-hand in some idyllic location with your new love.*
>
> *Wind the braided ribbons around the Willow in a clockwise direction as you watch the candle melt your lover's name. Seal each end of the ribbon to the Willow with melted wax.*
>
> *Keep the charm close when you go to bed.*
>
> *Then un-braid the ribbons the following day to free the spell and bring your new love to your side.'*
>
> *So mote it be!'*

No sooner had Tom finished scribbling this down than he was struck by a fresh wave of scepticism.

'What the hell am I thinking?' he said under his breath. 'This kind of stuff might work in cheesy horror films, but in real life there's more chance of me getting a date with Rose MaGowan or Sarah Michelle Geller, than there is of this spell actually working.'

He moved to slam the book shut, but then hesitated, as one of the concluding lines of the chapter seemed to leap out at him and cause him to pause. Something the 'White Witch' had written about how these sort of enchantments only work due to the confidence they inspire in those who even *half*-believe in them. And if you imbued the spell with the requisite amount of faith, she claimed, it was one hundred per cent effective.

> *'I have never known this charm to fail,'*

...she stated with irrefutable confidence.

> *'Rest assured, Dear Reader, the magic lies in the strength of will and the level of faith of the Spell-Caster.'*

Tom felt he was lurching from one extreme to another, as though he were on the deck of a rickety sailing ship cast upon turbulent, storm-tossed seas, but the unquestioning levels of conviction exhibited by Ms Fortunata, parted the clouds of uncertainty once more, and with a mental shrug of the shoulders, he gently tore off the page containing the spell from his notebook, folded it carefully and placed it in his pocket. He then stood up, and with a loud sigh, walked out into the mist-shrouded October evening...

*****

As luck or fate would have it, the following day was a Friday (sacred to the Goddesses Freya and Venus, you'll remember), as well as being the night before Hallowe'en, and Tom took this a sign that what he was planning on doing was right and it justified his decision to go along with this 'well-what-have-I-got-to-lose' scheme.

He was also further encouraged by the fact that he had very little trouble acquiring all of the items he needed to cast the spell from the stalls of Birkenhead Market, and the shelves of the local *Asda* store, during his lunch hour.

Tom later told me he'd found himself counting down the hours till 5 o' clock with a barely suppressed sense of anticipation, and he'd all but ran from the office, eager to set about preparing for the 'magical rite.'

When he finally arrived at his home address, however, he was faced with the first real obstacle since he'd stumbled across Diana Fortunata's book (although perhaps it would be more accurate to say *it* had stumbled across *him*). Tom lives in one of those posh flats down by Monk's Ferry, overlooking the Mersey. I'm sure you know the ones I mean. The thing is though, they may be big, top-notch penthouse suites that are hideously expensive to rent, but they have at least one major downside: there are no gardens whatsoever. Not even communal ones. Just tiny strips of wiry grass that are somewhat euphemistically called by people with extremely vivid imaginations, 'lawns.' They didn't afford any degree of privacy, either, and it was clear from the Witch's instructions that the ceremony had to be performed out-doors, (preferably beneath *'ebony skies sprayed sprayed with shining jewels, lighting up the Vaults of Heaven')*. Tom therefore had no option other than to carefully place the 'occult paraphernalia' in a backpack and head for the patch of over-grown waste-ground just across the road from the flats. All but hidden behind a series of high hawthorn hedges and a rusted metal fence, the couple of acres that had once served as the unofficial town dump, were seldom frequented by anyone other than the occasional tramp or homeless druggie. It was so plain, featureless and devoid of points of interest, even the local kids seemed keen to avoid it. The site was therefore ideal for carrying out intensely private operations like...well, like performing various types of 'white magic' to boost your chances of a getting a date, and it was little wonder that my friend made a bee-line for the place.

It wasn't difficult for him to find a suitable spot, out of sight of prying eyes beneath the branches of a single, lonely fir tree that had somehow sprouted up amidst the masses of poison ivy, nettles, thistles and other assorted species of weeds. That was something else that had contributed to the waste-ground's lack of popularity amongst young and old alike. It seemed just about every type of stinging, prickly, foul-smelling plant indigenous to these Isles, and quite a few whose seeds looked as though they must have been blown in on winds from distant, exotic climes, had taken root here, and thrived in wild and unnatural profusion. Treading carefully through the tangled undergrowth, Tom had made his way across to the fir tree, and when he was safely concealed beneath its over-hanging branches, placed his backpack on the ground and took out its contents. Kneeling, he re-arranged the items in sequence exactly as outlined in the instructions he'd copied so carefully from that arcane library book, and prepared to cast the spell.

Surprisingly, Tom felt at peace with himself. Any remaining trace of scepticism had quickly drained away like a Death Valley puddle, and he found himself filled with supreme confidence that not only was he doing the right thing, but that he would be completely successful in his endeavours.

Although he was scarcely aware of it at the time, he had begun chanting rhythmically as he performed the enchantment, a sort of rudimentary, though nonetheless powerful incantation, the source of which he later told me, seemed to have originated from somewhere deep within his inner-most being, dredged up like thick, oozing liquid from some newly-tapped oil well. And if that was a little weird, even stranger was the fact that, just a few seconds after casting the spell, he claimed that he couldn't for the life of him recall a single word of that endlessly repetitive mantra, other than a couple of vague references to those twin ancient Goddesses of Love.

And as Tom chanted, he passionately wound the braided ribbons around the branch he'd cut from a willow tree in nearby Birkenhead Park, (after first asking for the tree's consent – Ms Fortunata had warned in her book against taking anything from nature without asking permission, as this was seen as a lack of respect for the spirit of the tree and could greatly reduce the efficacy of the charm). He then visualised himself being with Nikki, walking hand in hand across a stretch of golden sand, the scene so vivid in his mind that he could almost smell the salty tang of the ocean and feel the sun's rays warming his face, and he was filled with intense elation.

Tom later described the sensation as being similar to the 'chilled out, trance-like state' he'd experienced after smoking his first joint back when he was a student at John Moore's University. He'd completely lost track of time and was unable to even hazard a guess as to how long he'd remained beneath the single, lonely fir tree, lost in sweet, blissful imaginings.

He finally came to his senses when a couple of the spare, 'non-magic' candles he'd brought along for illumination (ordinary torchlight had seemed too garishly modern and inappropriate for spell-casting), had burned so low, their flames were guttering fitfully, and he became aware the air had turned colder and the idyllic images quickly faded from view like the dissolve between movie scenes. Suddenly Tom was filled with dreadful realisation that he must look (if there had been anyone around to see), kneeling in the middle of a patch of long-neglected waste-ground, surrounded by burned-out candles, and other items like a poor man's version of some great and mighty magician, Merlin, say, or Dr John Dee (actually, by his own admission, Tom thought that by that stage in the proceedings, he felt so bone-tired and drained, he must have made Paul Daniel's look like the Grand Wizard of China, in all his pomp and splendour!).

He stood up and groaned as he was all but overcome by an attack of pins and needles so severe he was forced to lean against the rough bark of the tree trunk in order to retain his balance, and it was only when the sense of balance had returned to his legs that he realised he was still holding the willow twig and its strip of red ribbon, sealed at each end with candle wax. This was the charm, of course. The net result of his nocturnal endeavours. The spell had now been all but cast, and the thought struck him that there was no longer any reason for him to remain standing there in the chilly, late October darkness, so he began making his way back to the perimeter fence.

Tom was roughly two-thirds of the way across the field when he was suddenly struck with an acute feeling of dark foreboding. He glanced around him and saw that a light, wispy mist had formed in the surrounding dips and hollows, and was slowly drifting towards him with an almost spectral-like quality. Tom watched as the tendrils weaved amongst the plants and clumps of over-grown grass, and noticed something that sent a chill running up and down his spine.

"You know those weeds that I told you about before looked merely exotic?"

Tom later told me with a distracted, not-entirely-sane grin on his face.

"Well, they'd *changed* somehow. God, Ben, there were even some that looked as though they'd mutated into some wholly unique species, the kind that could only exist in some madman's nightmare. I didn't dare step any closer to investigate. Instead I tried desperately to keep my eyes fixed on the fence ahead of me, but just then I heard a rustling coming from those plants, and yeah, I'm fairly sure it was nothing but rats foraging for food, or maybe a fox...

But, and this is the *really* mad part, Ben, as I was straining to see if I could make out the source of the noise, I could have sworn I saw the weeds had developed clusters of milky-white, pupil-less eyes dangling from their twisted stalks, like some kind of hideously deformed fruit.

I stood there, staring as if transfixed, or maybe *hypnotised* would be a better word, and who knows, I might very well have remained standing there till sunrise if I hadn't heard what sounded like muffled laughter, as though someone had clamped their hands over their mouth in a bid to stifle a mutinous snigger, coming from the very centre of the clump of mutated plants that were now literally quivering with movement.

That awful sound broke my paralysis, and I all but flew over the spike-topped railings with all the grace of an Olympic pole-vaulter, (although the image that leapt into my mind was a ludicrous vision of me soaring into the air whilst wearing a pair of knee-high boots that had powerful coiled springs attached to their heels. Mad, I know, and don't ask where that mental picture came from, 'cos I haven't got a clue!), and I raced back to the warmth and blessed sanctuary of my flat without once pausing to glance back over my shoulder."

*****

When Tom finally reached his apartment, sweating like a pig, despite the chilly temperatures, he nearly tore the front door of its hinges and locked it firmly behind him. He then went into the living room to pour himself a

Scotch, and threw it back in a single gulp. Then he poured another one, so large some of it spilled over the lip of the glass, and after lighting the gas fire and switching on the TV, he collapsed into an armchair and tried to forget about the evening's events.

Tom said later that the effects of the alcohol soon calmed his nerves, but just before he felt himself dozing off, he was startled to see the wax-sealed 'Love Charm' lying on the coffee table, although he couldn't for the life of him remember putting it there. But as he glanced across at the fruits of his labour with woozy, exhausted eyes, he found the sight oddly comforting and reassuring.

And the last thing he recalled before spiralling down into the dark well of sleep, were the words of Diana Fortunata: The White Witch, reverberating in his mind like a cavernous echo.

> *'Rest assured, Dear Reader, the magic lies in the strength of will and the degree of faith of the spell-caster.*
>
> *So mote it be!'*

Tom awoke the following morning feeling refreshed and thoroughly rested. After a shower and a hearty breakfast, he found he was eager to face the rigours of the day, and not even the prospect of asking Nikki for a date could release the usual squadron of butterflies to go careering round his stomach in a fluttering frenzy.

Instead he was filled with an abundant degree of confidence, a little like the way he imagined a gambler must feel when they're caught in the feverish grip of a hot winning streak, and he was half-way out the front door before he remembered the *'Love Spell,'* still lying on the coffee table where he'd left it the night before. He went over and picked it up, and after weighing it in his hands for a few moments, filled with a sense of giddy anticipation, Tom gently un-braided the ribbons at either end of the willow branch and...

> *'freed the magic to bring your new love to your side.'*

As anyone who encountered Tom on that dank and misty Hallowe'en morning will readily attest, he was walking with a spring in his step and seemed to be permanently whistling a bright and cheerful tune that, if they couldn't quite put a name to, still it spoke to them of fresh beginnings, new roads taken and joy at the end of heart's longing.

It turned out Tom had every reason to deliriously happy, despite the fact that like me, he had to work Saturdays.

He told me he'd virtually floated up to the Sarnie Bar's counter, made straight for Nikki, who fortunately also worked weekends, and after placing his order in a clear, strong voice, (and *there* was a first), he'd boldly asked her if she was doing anything later after she finished work.

> "It was so ridiculously easy, Ben,"

...he announced when he returned to the office after lunch, wearing a great big goofy grin.

> "I mean, it was like it wasn't even me doing the talking, like I was having an out-of-the-body type experience or something.
>
> All that panicking, he continued, shaking his head. 'All those angst-ridden nights lying awake, playing out the scene in my head, and how I'd cope with the inevitable 'Sorry, lad, I'm washing my hair,' grim off, when I asked her for a date....And when I finally did summon the courage to ask her out? She smiles at me and says yes, she'd very much like to go for a drink with me."
>
> "Actually, you're a life-saver,"

Nikki had said, and when I asked her what she meant, she explained that she was supposed to be going to a Hallowe'en house party, and had been looking for a half-way feasible excuse to get out of it.

> "It'll just be the same old boring crowd doing the same old boring things,"

Nikki had added with a world-weary sigh.

> "You know, playing lousy games of Duck Apple, or Truth or Dare, or even worse, dragging out my mate, Jenny's, Ouija Board for a series of 'honestly-I'm-not-pushing-the-glass' attempts at spirit communication."

She'd wrinkled her nose, and pulled a face, and then smiled again and said,

> "I'd much rather spend a nice, relaxing evening watching some of the wall-to-wall horror films on *Sky*, with a bottle or two of red wine and a pepperoni pizza."

Nikki paused then and fluttered her eyelashes, before adding,

> "And some good company, too, of course."

Tom had agreed that this sounded like a top-notch idea and invited her over to his flat, and Nikki had nodded eagerly and after he'd given her his address, she said she'd be there at nine, she had a few things to do first, and Tom said that was just fine with him.

And that was pretty much that.

Date sorted.

*****

And Tom's good luck streak just kept right on going. Normally he'd have to work until five, but he managed to persuade one of the bosses to allow him an early dart, and he clocked off a couple of hours early. After stopping off on the way home to pick up the evening's supplies, Tom used the painfully slow-crawling hours prior to Nikki's arrival to make a heroic attempt to tidy up the flat and decorate the living room to provide it with a little seasonal ambience. He dimmed the lights, lit a few incense sticks, and placed a candle inside the hollowed-out, jagged-toothed pumpkin he'd bought during his shopping trip, before setting it on top of the mantelpiece from where it grinned with a suitable degree of impish glee.

Satisfied with his efforts, Tom rewarded himself with a cold can of lager from the fridge, and wandered over to the large bay window to gaze across at the Liverpool water-front. It was a little before four, and dusk was already swiftly descending. It had been a dank and gloomy day, and now a thick, billowing fog had obliterated the normally spirit-stirring view. He could barely make out anything beyond the line of trees directly outside his apartment, their few remaining leaves dripping with condensation. On impulse, Tom opened the window and poked his head out, and the dead smell of the river, of waters polluted by decades of chemical spills and the careless pumping of all kinds of reeking effluence and poisoned waste immediately assailed his nostrils. Strangely, the pungent aromas didn't cause him to gag reflexively or slam the window shut in disgust. Rather it held him rapt with a powerful sense of nostalgia, as did the only sounds emerging from the midst of the grey blanket: the excited yells of invisible children 'Trick or Treating,' on the streets below and the mournful blare of foghorns from the Mersey, the latter an oddly sinister sound that brought to mind vivid images of his Grandad's tales of Edwardian 'pea-soupers,'[**] smugglers plotting in the shadowy nooks of river-front pubs and mysterious, black-cloaked figures lurking at the dark end of city centre side streets and alleyways.

[**] A particularly unpleasant fog – what these days we would probably call 'smog' where particulate air pollution caused by indiscriminate coal burning, mixed with fog – with unfortunate results.

The sensation wasn't entirely unpleasant. He'd loved his long-departed Grandad, and his seemingly inexhaustible supply of stories of old Merseyside, but after a little while, the chill began to slowly seep into his bones, and with a sigh he closed the window and switched on his expensive sound system. The FM band automatically tuned to *Radio City*, the most popular of the local stations, and as Tom half-listened, the DJ suddenly interrupted the tuneless wailing of some *X-Factor* 'no mark' to announce that they were getting reports of a serious accident involving multiple vehicles on the Wallasey-bound lane of the M53.

'Police and emergency services attending at the scene have confirmed that there have been several fatalities,' the DJ stated in appropriately sonorous tones. 'The authorities have provided an emergency telephone number for anyone concerned about their loved ones,' he added, 'and will release further information in due course.'

The programme's presenter paused for a second or two before swiftly moving on with 'The current UK Number One Single!' and a breathless reminder to his listeners that 'Tonight is the night for all you guys and *ghouls* out there to strap on your good-time rocket boots and *paaarrrty!*'

Shaking his head at the DJ's inane ramblings, Tom hadn't really given the news bulletin, sad as it was, much thought. And really, who could blame him for that?' He felt a passing moment of sympathy for the victims and their families, but he never for one second imagined that anyone he knew personally, had been involved.

Well, we never do, do we?

He switched off the radio and turned on the telly instead, just as the final moments of *The Bride of Frankenstein*, were being played out on the screen. It was one of Tom's favourite films ('It beats the 1931 original all ends up,' he used to state in a voice that brooked no argument, whenever the subject of all-time classic movies was being discussed), and he paused to watch the tragic, explosive finale, even though he'd seen it a thousand times before.

The house phone rang, just as Boris Karloff grabbed his 'betrothed,' (the spectacularly coiffured Elsa Lanchester), by the hand to declare solemnly, *'We belong dead!'* and Tom very nearly jumped out of his skin at the shrill sound of its insistent tones, before chuckling nervously as he considered he was living out a corny, horror film cliché.

He picked up the phone with hands that were still visibly shaking and struggled to regain some composure.

"Hello, Tom, it's me, David,"

…said the voice on the other end of the line, and Tom immediately recognised the clipped, posh, Wirral accent of one of his closest friends, David Thompson.

"Alright, Dave, how's it going?' Tom asked. 'Still looking for the Loch Ness Monster?"

This was an old in-joke between the two of them, centred upon Dave's childhood obsession with the fabled denizen of that famous Scottish lake.

His friend didn't snort derisively or fire back the standard response; 'Well, are you still chasing after the girl of your dreams?'

Instead there was only a yawning silence, so intense that Tom began to assume they'd been disconnected, before his friend finally spoke once more.

"Listen, mate, I'm sorry to have to be the one to tell you this, but I'm afraid I have some bad news …"

Tom half-laughed, convinced he was about to be made subject of some weak Hallowe'en prank, but the barely-suppressed panic evident in Dave's voice caused the smile to freeze on Tom's lips and a cold knot of dread slowly uncoiled in the pit of his stomach.

"I've been involved in a terrible car crash,"

Dave explained.

"You might have heard about it on the news.' I'm alright, just a few scrapes and bruises. Nothing a few plasters won't fix."

There was another pause, and Tom was startled to find his friend appeared to be on the brink of tears.

"But God, Tom,"

…he croaked.

"I saw a couple of the victims who weren't so lucky being stretchered into an ambulance, and from where I was stood, at the side of the motorway, I could tell straight away that six of them at least, were dead. There was far, far too much blood, and some of the bodies had limbs missing or were so horribly burned they looked barely human. And a couple already had the sheets drawn over their heads to afford them a last final shred of dignity...And then...and then..."

Dave's all but choked in the struggle to get the words out.

"Oh Jesus, I'm so sorry, Tom,"

…he finally managed.

"But one of the dead was that pretty young girl who works at 'The Sandwich Bar,' in Birkenhead. The one Ben told me you'd finally had the courage to ask out earlier today.' Nikki, I think you said her name was."

Nikki...

At the mention of her name, the room had begun spinning and Tom felt unreality wash over him. He'd suddenly wanted to hang up, as if by cutting off his friend's voice he could deprive his words of their innate truth. Instead he tried, half-heartedly, to persuade Dave he might possibly have been mistaken, what with the inevitable shock and confusion in the aftermath of the accident, but Dave's response soon served to shatter that fragile hope.

"Mate, honestly, I got a really close up look at her face. Much closer than I wanted to get, to tell you the truth. And it was *definitely* Nikki."

As he said this, for the first time, Tom became aware of the unmistakable sounds of a hospital bustling in the background and he had to fight to suppress a sob of pure anguish. And then Dave was telling him that he was really sorry once again, before mumbling that he had to go, and there was nothing but the soft click of disconnection...

Tom gently replaced the receiver, stood there for a few seconds in the centre of the room, silently regarding the phone, before trudging zombie-like to the fridge in the kitchen, and dragging out a six-pack and a couple of bottles of wine. He then returned to the living room, sat down on the sofa and popped the tab on a can of *'Fosters'*, uncorked the wine, and took turns chugging and swigging from them both in series of huge gulps. The overwhelming sorrow he felt might seem to me and you like a melodramatic, over the top reaction, seeing as how he'd only just broken the ice with Nikki, and could by no stretch of the imagination claim to have been close to her.

To be fair, though, nobody should ever presume to know the true intensity of a person's love, long unrequited, or otherwise, so perhaps we shouldn't be too quick to condemn him.

Anyway, regardless of whatever you or I may think,' Tom was more than successful in his endeavours to seek refuge in the 'blessed waters of oblivion', and well before 11pm, he'd passed out on the couch in a drunken stupor.

*****

The nightmare, when it came, however, ensured his sleep would be far from untroubled....

He dreamed he had awoken sometime before dawn in a room that was pitch-dark save for the glow cast by a single pink candle – a left-over from the Love Spell, no doubt – placed in the centre of the coffee table. As he stared at the hypnotically dancing flame, he heard the sound of bare feet, slapping along the tiled corridor leading to his flat. There was something ominously implacable and dreadful of purpose about the footsteps, and Tom knew with the logic wholly peculiar to dreams, especially bad ones, that they would eventually shuffle to a stop directly outside his apartment.

And of course, they did just that.

There was an agonising pause, as if someone out there was silently debating whether to enter the premises or not, and then the front door, which in 'reality', was always kept firmly locked, creaked open slowly.

Tom was too terrified to crane his neck around the arm of the sofa to see who,(or what), it was that had chosen to call, uninvited, in the empty soulless dead hours that stretch for a seeming eternity between midnight and the first grey-light of dawn.

In the dream, he waited, staring at the candle, perfectly immobile, hardly daring to breathe, as if by refusing to acknowledge the existence of his 'guest,' or at the very least, by tricking it into thinking he was sound asleep, and completely unaware of its presence, it might just go away and leave him alone.

For a few blessed seconds, it seemed these tactics had proved effective. Certainly, he hadn't heard anything actually enter the room. All was quiet, save for the jack-knife hammering of his own heartbeat and the gentle sputtering of the candle flame.

But then he heard a furtive, girlish giggle – eerily similar to the sneaky laughter he'd heard emanating from the clumps of diseased-looking weeds in that disused patch of wasteland, the night he'd cast the Love Spell....

Involuntarily, he turned his head to see who was standing there, and Nikki's horribly disfigured face had suddenly loomed up out of the darkness like some phosphorescent horror propelled to the surface of a deep black lake, and Tom desperately tried to will himself awake.

Despite his best efforts, he was unable to do so, and he was forced to watch helplessly as Nikki leaned ever closer to him, and he was able to see that most of her head had been crushed and that the right hand side of her face had been so badly burned, the only recognisable feature remaining was an empty black eye socket. He saw too, that large clumps of her once lustrous, free-flowing tresses were missing, exposing blood-stained sections of skull and secretions of grey matter oozing from the numerous chips and fractures.

The ultimate obscenity though, was that the other side of Nikki's face was porcelain perfect, completely unblemished and heart-stoppingly beautiful.

And when she hovered, just a few inches above him, and licked her tongue against what was left of her lips...Lips as dry and colourless as a pair of desiccated worms, in obvious preparation of a lover's kiss, Tom struck out blindly, lost his balance on the edge of the sofa and rolled onto the floor, kicking and screaming madly into the 3am darkness...

He awoke for real, drenched in cold sweat and quite literally shaking in abject terror. Fear had, it seemed, seeped into his very marrow, and it was a good while before he was able to scramble clumsily to his feet and in a barely suppressed panic, switch on every single light in the apartment, along with the TV, to add some reassuring background noise.

Tom was determined to quickly exorcise the most frightening nightmare he'd ever had in his life, and he tuned to the *MTV2* channel, sitting on the floor, facing the screen in a lotus position as he watched a host of familiar faces belting out a series of classic *'All Night Indie Anthems.'* The songs provided him with company of sorts, until the first thin fingers of morning-light began to claw their way from between a gap in the curtains.

Only then did Tom begin to feel brave enough to make his way to the bathroom to take a shower, but a couple of minutes spent immersing himself in jets of hot, skin-tingling water, served to revive him to the point where he was mentally cursing himself for having gotten so drunk the night before, even if the reasons for having done so were perfectly understandable.

As he stepped out of the shower and was drying himself off, he felt a little much better, even if the dark clouds of depression inspired by the terrible tidings of the night before were still hovering on the horizon, ready to descend at a moment's notice, the very second his guard was down.

It was a Sunday, his day off, but the last thing Tom wanted was to hang around the flat on his own mulling over the fact that he'd never get to experience that glorious, long-awaited opportunity of meeting up with Nikki, the semi-mythical 'girl of his dreams.' He was intolerably lonely and craved company, so he decided he'd have a quick shave, make himself as presentable as possible and call up several of his closest friends to see who amongst them was available for some highly cathartic conversation over a pint or two at his local, *The Swinging Arm*.

He picked up his razor, liberally smeared his face with shaving cream and looked in the mirror.

Beyond the grim reflection of his haggard, sleep-deprived features, Tom noticed that the door to his bedroom was standing slightly ajar.

He'd left the light switched on in there.

The room was brightly illuminated.

And there was a human adult form lying over on the far side of the bed.

All at once, that familiar, creeping sense of dread began slowly to unwind deep in his guts, and Tom did his best to quell it before he was reduced to a gibbering wreck once more.

> "Come on, lad! Get a grip on yourself!"

…he muttered to his foam-obscured reflection.

> "That shape on the bed is nothing but a bunch of crumpled blankets. I must have forgotten to make the bed the last time I last slept in it, a couple of nights ago, that's all."

He tried on a smile, but it looked blood-red and clown-like and horribly false against the white of the shaving cream and it dropped from his face like a guillotine blade when the bed-clothes rippled with sudden movement and the mattress springs wheezed beneath a shifting weight, and Tom swore he heard a familiar voice, croaky and hoarse, but still recognisable…

> *'Are you coming to bed, darling?'*

…the dead thing that used to be Nikki, rasped seductively.

'It's so cold here lying on my own.'

There was a sly giggle.

'It's as cold as the grave ...'

*****

"Okay, okay, I know what you're thinking, Lee,"

Ben held up his hands in a placatory gesture to ward off the protests that were ready to come spewing forth in a Niagara-sized torrent from my lips at the conclusion of this supposedly true story.

"Of course, I know exactly what you're gonna say. Tom's account sounds suspiciously like the plot-line of that old W.W. Jacob classic *'The Monkey's Paw,'* or an episode of *'Tales From The Crypt.'* To be honest, I must admit I had a great deal of difficulty believing his story, myself, so I can't blame you for being more than a little sceptical".

Ben sighed, and regarded me with a look that said I should at least afford him the opportunity to explain himself further.

"The thing is..."

Ben continued,

"I've known Tom for virtually my entire life. He's a remarkably level-headed individual, or at least he had been up until this incident with the 'love spell' and all that, and I am totally convinced *he* believes in the reality of his experience, and I suppose that's all that matters, in the end.

What *is* undeniable though is the fact that he had a complete mental breakdown not long before Christmas, that year. He was off work for months. So long in fact that he lost his job. He looked awful. He'd lost far too much weight, had dark circles under his eyes and his hair had begun turning grey even though he was only in his early thirties.

I remember him telling me one night over a few drinks, that he'd done a moonlight flit from the flat and was staying at various friend's houses, just so he had somewhere to get his head down.

"But it's no good, Ben," he'd said miserably, his vacant, haunted eyes staring sightlessly over the rim of his beer glass. "I can't escape her. She's with me virtually all the time, now. I know you probably think I've lost it big time, but it's that damned love spell...I've read countless books on Witchcraft and the Occult, but it seems that once cast, this particular type of spell simply can't be broken.

You see, I made a wish that Nikki would love me forever and would always be by my side.

And God help me, it seems I got my wish..."

Tom had laughed then, but there had been nothing remotely mirthful about it.

Rather it was the hollow, humourless laughter of the eternally damned.

I have to say I wasn't all surprised when I heard Tom had been sectioned and was now a permanent in-patient at Clatterbridge Hospital.

Immensely saddened, maybe, but no, not surprised.

I went to visit him one cold, but sun-bright afternoon in mid-January, and was shocked to see that he looked even worse. Clad in a pair of striped pyjamas and plaid dressing gown, and sat in an uncomfortable-looking armchair, he reminded me of the awful pictures of the victims of Serbian ethnic cleansing in the former Yugoslavia. His features were horribly emaciated, his glassy eyes bulging in their sockets. He wasn't raving about Nikki, any more. He just sat there in drug-induced silence, staring at nothing, and in truth, I don't think he was even aware of my presence.

I'm ashamed to say, I couldn't bring myself to stay with him for long. It hurt me far too much, to see my friend reduced to this pitiful state, and I made my excuses and left well before the allotted one-hour visiting time had elapsed.

I did pause to speak to his doctor before leaving the hospital, however. A tall, bespectacled man with steel grey hair and a healthy-looking complexion, he told me what I suppose I already knew. Tom was suffering from severe delusions and hallucinations, and had been diagnosed as a paranoid schizophrenic. He'd been prescribed powerful medication, and was receiving constant supervision and was making slow progress.

'Believe me, your friend is in good hands', the doctor assured me as he took a fountain pen out of his pocket and absent-mindedly twirled it between his fingers. 'The very best. So please try not to worry yourself too much.'

Flashing a brief, sympathetic smile, he turned and walked away, and I stood there speechless as a nurse hurried along the corridor, her white shoes squeaking on the shiny floors, while a voice on the intercom paged a Doctor Campbell to Room 27.

At a loss as to what else I could do, I headed wearily for the exits.

******

"Here at last we reach the end of *my* story, Lee. Or rather my somewhat limited involvement in what is essentially Tom's tale.

And no, I don't expect you to believe me any more than you believe him.

That's alright.

I'm not sure I truly give any credence to what I thought I glimpsed as I stepped outside onto the grounds of the hospital on that eye-wateringly bright winter afternoon.

What is for certain is that as I walked along the white-gravelled path that runs adjacent to the in-patient's wards, I happened to glance back in the direction of what I knew to be Tom's room. And as I did so, I saw through the window, another nurse standing side on to me, facing my friend who was still sat in that tortuous-looking wheelchair. Even from a distance of forty feet or so, I could see Tom's pale white face gazing up at her fearfully, like a child about to be chastised by an especially strict teacher or a cruel parent. I went to turn away, thoroughly depressed by the scene, when something else caught my eye.

It was very likely nothing but a trick of the dazzling January sunlight, shards of which were slanting through the glass like golden lances...but nonetheless, it appeared to me that the right-hand side of the nurse's face was charred and burned by a heat so intense, that at least half of her facial features had been obliterated.

But that didn't stop her from smiling: A crooked grin that seemed to me to speak of arcane secrets, lifetime trysts and unspeakable horrors yet to be....

Then, as Tom appeared to cower even more fearfully in his wheelchair, he opened his mouth to scream.

And the nurse suddenly reached up...

And with hideous finality, firmly drew the blinds........

HOW TO START A PUBLISHING EMPIRE

Unlike most mainstream publishers, we have a non-commercial remit, and our mission statement claims that "we publish books because they deserve to be published, not because we think that we can make money out of them". Our motto is the Latin Tag *Pro bona causa facimus* (we do it for good reason), a slogan taken from a children's book *The Case of the Silver Egg* by the late Desmond Skirrow.

WIKIPEDIA: "The first book published was in 1988. *Take this Brother may it Serve you Well* was a guide to *Beatles* bootlegs by Jonathan Downes. It sold quite well, but was hampered by very poor production values, being photocopied, and held together by a plastic clip binder. In 1988 A5 clip binders were hard to get hold of, so the publishers took A4 binders and cut them in half with a hacksaw. It now reaches surprisingly high prices second hand.

The production quality improved slightly over the years, and after 1999 all the books produced were ringbound with laminated colour covers. In 2004, however, they signed an agreement with Lightning Source, and all books are now produced perfect bound, with full colour covers."

Until 2010 all our books, the majority of which are/were on the subject of mystery animals and allied disciplines, were published by `CFZ Press`, the publishing arm of the Centre for Fortean Zoology (CFZ), and we urged our readers and followers to draw a discreet veil over the books that we published that were completely off topic to the CFZ.

However, in 2010 we decided that enough was enough and launched a second imprint, `Fortean Words` which aims to cover a wide range of non animal-related esoteric subjects. Other imprints will be launched as and when we feel like it, however the basic ethos of the company remains the same: Our job is to publish books and magazines that we feel are worth publishing, whether or not they are going to sell. Money is, after all - as my dear old Mama once told me - a rather vulgar subject, and she would be rolling in her grave if she thought that her eldest son was somehow in `trade`.

Luckily, so far our tastes have turned out not to be that rarified after all, and we have sold far more books than anyone ever thought that we would, so there is a moral in there somewhere...

Jon Downes,
Woolsery, North Devon
July 2010

Other Books in Print

Weird Waters – The Mystery Animals of Scandinavia: Lake and Sea Monsters by Lars Thomas
The Inhumanoids by Barton Nunnelly
Monstrum! A Wizard's Tale by Tony "Doc" Shiels
CFZ Yearbook 2011 edited by Jonathan Downes
Karl Shuker's Alien Zoo by Shuker, Dr Karl P.N
Tetrapod Zoology Book One by Naish, Dr Darren
The Mystery Animals of Ireland by Gary Cunningham and Ronan Coghlan
Monsters of Texas by Gerhard, Ken
The Great Yokai Encyclopaedia by Freeman, Richard
NEW HORIZONS: Animals & Men *issues 16-20 Collected Editions Vol. 4* by Downes, Jonathan
A Daintree Diary -
Tales from Travels to the Daintree Rainforest in tropical north Queensland, Australia by Portman, Carl
Strangely Strange but Oddly Normal by Roberts, Andy
Centre for Fortean Zoology Yearbook 2010 by Downes, Jonathan
Predator Deathmatch by Molloy, Nick
Star Steeds and other Dreams by Shuker, Karl
CHINA: A Yellow Peril? by Muirhead, Richard
Mystery Animals of the British Isles: The Western Isles by Vaudrey, Glen
Giant Snakes - Unravelling the coils of mystery by Newton, Michael
Mystery Animals of the British Isles: Kent by Arnold, Neil
Centre for Fortean Zoology Yearbook 2009 by Downes, Jonathan
CFZ EXPEDITION REPORT: Russia 2008 by Richard Freeman *et al*, Shuker, Karl (fwd)
Dinosaurs and other Prehistoric Animals on Stamps - A Worldwide catalogue by Shuker, Karl P. N
Dr Shuker's Casebook by Shuker, Karl P.N
The Island of Paradise - chupacabra UFO crash retrievals,
and accelerated evolution on the island of Puerto Rico by Downes, Jonathan
The Mystery Animals of the British Isles: Northumberland and Tyneside by Hallowell, Michael J
Centre for Fortean Zoology Yearbook 1997 by Downes, Jonathan (Ed)
Centre for Fortean Zoology Yearbook 2002 by Downes, Jonathan (Ed)
Centre for Fortean Zoology Yearbook 2000/1 by Downes, Jonathan (Ed)
Centre for Fortean Zoology Yearbook 1998 by Downes, Jonathan (Ed)
Centre for Fortean Zoology Yearbook 2003 by Downes, Jonathan (Ed)
In the wake of Bernard Heuvelmans by Woodley, Michael A
CFZ EXPEDITION REPORT: Guyana 2007 by Richard Freeman *et al*, Shuker, Karl (fwd)

Centre for Fortean Zoology Yearbook 1999 by Downes, Jonathan (Ed)
Big Cats in Britain Yearbook 2008 by Fraser, Mark (Ed)
Centre for Fortean Zoology Yearbook 1996 by Downes, Jonathan (Ed)
THE CALL OF THE WILD - Animals & Men issues 11-15
Collected Editions Vol. 3 by Downes, Jonathan (ed)
Ethna's Journal by Downes, C N
Centre for Fortean Zoology Yearbook 2008 by Downes, J (Ed)
DARK DORSET -Calendar Custome by Newland, Robert J
Extraordinary Animals Revisited by Shuker, Karl
MAN-MONKEY - In Search of the British Bigfoot by Redfern, Nick
Dark Dorset Tales of Mystery, Wonder and Terror by Newland, Robert J and Mark North
Big Cats Loose in Britain by Matthews, Marcus
MONSTER! - The A-Z of Zooform Phenomena by Arnold, Neil
The Centre for Fortean Zoology 2004 Yearbook by Downes, Jonathan (Ed)
The Centre for Fortean Zoology 2007 Yearbook by Downes, Jonathan (Ed)
CAT FLAPS! Northern Mystery Cats by Roberts, Andy
Big Cats in Britain Yearbook 2007 by Fraser, Mark (Ed)
BIG BIRD! - Modern sightings of Flying Monsters by Gerhard, Ken
THE NUMBER OF THE BEAST - Animals & Men issues 6-10
Collected Editions Vol. 1 by Downes, Jonathan (Ed)
IN THE BEGINNING - Animals & Men *issues 1-5 Collected Editions Vol. 1* by Downes, Jonathan
STRENGTH THROUGH KOI - They saved Hitler's Koi and other stories by Downes, Jonathan
The Smaller Mystery Carnivores of the Westcountry by Downes, Jonathan
CFZ EXPEDITION REPORT: Gambia 2006 by Richard Freeman *et al*, Shuker, Karl (fwd)
The Owlman and Others by Jonathan Downes
The Blackdown Mystery by Downes, Jonathan
Big Cats in Britain Yearbook 2006 by Fraser, Mark (Ed)
Fragrant Harbours - Distant Rivers by Downes, John T
Only Fools and Goatsuckers by Downes, Jonathan
Monster of the Mere by Jonathan Downes
Dragons:More than a Myth by Freeman, Richard Alan
Granfer's Bible Stories by Downes, John Tweddell
Monster Hunter by Downes, Jonathan

Fortean Words

The Centre for Fortean Zoology has for several years led the field in Fortean publishing. CFZ Press is the only publishing company specialising in books on monsters and mystery animals. CFZ Press has published more books on this subject than any other company in history and has attracted such well known authors as Andy Roberts, Nick Redfern, Michael Newton, Dr Karl Shuker, Neil Arnold, Dr Darren Naish, Jon Downes, Ken Gerhard and Richard Freeman.

Now CFZ Press are launching a new imprint. Fortean Words is a new line of books dealing with Fortean subjects other than cryptozoology, which is - after all - the subject the CFZ are best known for. Fortean Words is being launched with a spectacular multi-volume series called *Haunted Skies* which covers British UFO sightings between 1940 and 2010. Former policeman John Hanson and his long-suffering partner Dawn Holloway have compiled a peerless library of sighting reports, many that have not been made public before.

Other forthcoming books include a look at the Berwyn Mountains UFO case by renowned Fortean Andy Roberts and a series of books by transatlantic researcher Nick Redfern.

CFZ Press are dedicated to maintaining the fine quality of their works with Fortean Words. New authors tackling new subjects will always be encouraged, and we hope that our books will continue to be as ground breaking and popular as ever.

Haunted Skies Volume One 1940-1959 by John Hanson and Dawn Holloway
Haunted Skies Volume Two 1960-1965 by John Hanson and Dawn Holloway
Space Girl Dead on Spaghetti Junction - an anthology by Nick Redfern
I Fort the Lore - an anthology by Paul Screeton
UFO Down - the Berwyn Mountains UFO Crash by Andy Roberts

www.ingramcontent.com/pod-product-compliance
Ingram Content Group UK Ltd.
Pitfield, Milton Keynes, MK11 3LW, UK
UKHW051257180426
11947UKWH00020B/1752